Praise for

Advances in Active Portfolio Management

Grinold & Kahn have been true pioneers in both the development and application of science and quantitative techniques in investing, and their work has been foundational to the tremendous success of many of the investment strategies at Barclays Global Investors and, later, BlackRock. *Advances in Active Portfolio Management* is an outstanding resource of insights and advances that can greatly benefit *any* investor in today's complex and increasingly "efficient" markets.

—**Blake Grossman,** former CEO of Barclays Global Investors and Vice Chairman of BlackRock.

Richard Grinold and Ronald Kahn's *Active Portfolio Management* has become a bible for active quant managers since its publication in 1995. Now, *Advances in Active Portfolio Management* brings readers up to date on critical issues—the estimation of expected return and risk in a dynamic environment, the effective implementation of insights, and accurate assessment of portfolio performance. Along the way, it addresses contemporary developments, including the role of active management in a world of smart beta and factor investing, the increased use of leverage and its effects on portfolio risk, and the importance of assessing crowding. Grinold and Kahn continue to advance the theory and practice of quantitative investing.

—**Bruce I. Jacobs,** Co-chief Investment Officer and Co-director of Research, Jacobs Levy Equity Management

Successful portfolio management requires a framework for understanding the elements that matter the most, how they interact, and how to best make the requisite trade-offs. In this book, the authors build on their prior groundbreaking work to advance our intuition about (1) the dynamic aspects of active portfolio management—where signals, opportunities, and risks evolve over time; (2) the use and misuse of diversification and leverage in portfolio construction—and especially the implications for the management of tail risks; (3) the importance of placing one's own approach in the context of what other market participants are doing; and (4) understanding the nuances of how fees impact portfolio performance. This is an important book for anyone concerned with alpha generation, risk assessment, and portfolio management at a time when practitioner sophistication is considerably advanced, much of it because of the work of Grinold and Kahn.

—**André Perold,** Co-Founder, Managing Partner, and CIO of HighVista Strategies and the George Gund Professor of Finance and Banking, Emeritus at Harvard Business School

If a sequel could ever outshine the original, *Advances in Active Portfolio Management* threatens to do just that. Building on their earlier masterpiece, Grinold and Kahn offer fresh insights into the central problems in investing and provide solutions to many new ones. By taking on fully the dynamic nature of active management with all its real-world complexity, the authors show how their framework can be adapted to meet new needs. Written primarily for asset managers, it is fruitful reading for asset owners too, provided one is willing to navigate through the evolving chain of notation!

—**Cheng Chih Sung,** CEO of Avanda Investment Management and advisor to multiple sovereign investors in Norway, Singapore, and Thailand

Richard Grinold has been a leading authority on quantitative active management for decades. With active management evolving and becoming more systematic, this latest book by renowned authors Grinold and Kahn is an excellent resource for active managers. It provides insight into applications of modern investment techniques and the changing dynamics in the pursuit of alpha.

—**Morry Waked,** Managing Director and Chief Investment Officer, Vinva Investment Management, former Global Chief Investment Officer, Active Equities, Barclays Global Investors (BGI/BlackRock)

Grinold and Kahn's *Advances in Active Portfolio Management* is the Bible for professional investment managers who fight in chaotic markets to squeeze "alpha" out of diverse investment opportunities. Based on research and practice in quantitative asset management over decades by the authors, this book turns art of investing into science, skills into technology, and intuitions into systematic thought process with mathematical reasoning. The essential insights for portfolio managers are neatly organized and presented in this book.

—**Katsunari Yamaguchi,** CFA, Chairman, Ibbotson Associates Japan, Inc.

ADVANCES IN ACTIVE PORTFOLIO MANAGEMENT

New Developments in
Quantitative Investing

RICHARD C. GRINOLD
RONALD N. KAHN

McGraw Hill

New York Chicago San Francisco Athens London Madrid
Mexico City Milan New Delhi Singapore Sydney Toronto

1 2 3 4 5 6 7 8 9 LCR 24 23 22 21 20 19

ISBN: 978-1-260-45371-3
MHID: 1-260-45371-5

e-ISBN: 978-1-260-45372-0
e-MHID: 1-260-45372-3

Library of Congress Cataloging-in-Publication Data

Names: Grinold, Richard C., author. | Kahn, Ronald N., author.
Title: Advances in active portfolio management / Richard Grinold and Ronald Kahn.
Description: New York : McGrawHill, [2019] | Includes bibliographical references and index.
Identifiers: LCCN 2019027001 (print) | LCCN 2019027002 (ebook) | ISBN 9781260453713 (hardcover) | ISBN 9781260453720 (ebook)
Subjects: LCSH: Portfolio management.
Classification: LCC HG4529.5 .G753 2019 (print) | LCC HG4529.5 (ebook) | DDC 332.6—dc23
LC record available at https://lccn.loc.gov/2019027001
LC ebook record available at https://lccn.loc.gov/2019027002

To Leilani

and to Julia

Contents

SECTION 2.2 Portfolio Analysis and Attribution

SECTION 3

Applications of Active Portfolio Management

SECTION 3.1 Expected Return: The Equity Risk Premium and Market Efficiency

SECTION 3.2 Expected Return: Smart Beta

SECTION 3.3 Risk

SECTION 3.4 **Portfolio Construction**

SECTION 4

Extras

SECTION 5

Conclusion

Acknowledgments

We have worked on the material in this book over roughly the past 30 years, though most of the work occurred in the most recent half of that long period. With that in mind, we have benefited from the support of several institutions including BlackRock, Vinva, Barclays Global Investors (BGI), and Barra; and especially key individuals at those institutions: Ken Kroner, Raffaele Savi, and Jeff Shen at BlackRock and BGI; Morry Waked at Vinva and BGI; Blake Grossman at BGI; and Andrew Rudd at Barra.

We have also benefitted from coauthors on many of the articles that form chapters in this book. Those coauthors include Gerry Garvey, Seanna Kim, Ken Kroner, Mike Lemmon, Dean Petrich, Raffaele Savi, Matt Scanlan, Scott Shaffer, Larry Siegel, Dan Stefek, and Mark Taylor. Larry Siegel has the distinction of coauthoring an article separately with each of us. While acknowledging the contributions of all our coauthors, we take full credit for any remaining errors in the book.

Most of our articles have appeared in the *Journal of Portfolio Management*, the *Financial Analysts Journal*, and publications of the CFA Institute Research Foundation. We are strong supporters of these premier practitioner journals and publications, and we thank them for their permission to include our articles in this book.

We thank our editor at McGraw-Hill Education, Noah Schwartzberg, for his support of the project throughout.

This work represents the views of the authors and not necessarily those of our current or former employers.

Preface

At the end of 2017, Richard Grinold suggested that the two of us work on a book collecting all the articles we have written since the second edition of *Active Portfolio Management* came out in 2000. We had written many articles over that time—together and separately—enough to form a coherent body of new material.

The idea of this new book deftly addressed our challenge in trying to advance the framework we developed in *Active Portfolio Management*. The second edition of that book is approaching its twentieth anniversary. It is a long book that addresses the theory of active management in a timeless manner. Its limitations include a focus on active management mainly as a single-period problem (rather than the dynamic problem it is) and a scope limited to problems known as of 2000 or earlier. That said, the material covered by *Active Portfolio Management* remain relevant and important. We didn't need to replace that book but rather to augment it.

As we started to work on the project, we realized that our efforts and articles over the past 20 years or so fell into two broad categories of *advancing* the theory presented in *Active Portfolio Management* and *applying* that theory to issues that have risen to prominence since 2000. The book began to take shape.

When we published *Active Portfolio Management*, we both worked as active managers at Barclays Global Investors (BGI). Nineteen years later, Richard is retired and Ron is working at BlackRock (in the same group as back then, but after BlackRock's acquisition of BGI). Our perspectives on active management remain closely aligned, and modern technology has eliminated most of the challenges of working in different locations. We both remain committed to applying rigorous analysis to investing, and we continue to believe, as we stated in our earlier book, that the art of investing is evolving into the science of investing.

We hope our readers see this book as an invitation to constantly question and improve the status quo, as we have been attempting to do over our careers, including since 2000. For investors interested in this area, much of this work is currently dispersed in time and across sources. Having it in one accessible place will enhance its power and impact.

1

Introduction: Advances in Active Portfolio Management

The quantitative approach to active management has developed over the past 65 years. In 1952, Markowitz framed investing as a trade-off between expected return and risk—which he defined as the variance of return—opening portfolio management to quantitative analysis.[1] Subsequent developments like the capital asset pricing model and the efficient markets hypothesis quickly focused academics on indexing: passive investing. But, starting in the 1970s, a number of separate efforts created a quantitative framework for active investing.

In 1995, and with a second edition in 2000, our book, *Active Portfolio Management*, brought all these threads together into a coherent theory of active management. We described how to develop forecasts of risk, return, and cost and how to combine those elements into active portfolios. We presented the *information ratio*—the ratio of active return to active risk—as the key statistic for active management. All investors seek active managers with high information ratios. The fundamental law of active management (Grinold 1989), a central concept of the book, shows that high information ratios require some winning combination of skill in making investment decisions; breadth of those decisions, for diversification; and efficiency of implementation, so that the portfolio accurately captures the manager's views. The book was very popular when first published, and remains popular to this day, because it is the recognized authority on quantitative active management.

We have not stood still since 2000. The theory and framework of *Active Portfolio Management* were state-of-the-art when written, but we have

1. Harry Markowitz, "Portfolio Selection," *Journal of Finance* 7, no. 1 (1952): 77–91.

advanced the state of the art since then, in particular in viewing active management as a dynamic problem rather than a one-period challenge, and also in advancing portfolio analysis to provide new perspectives.

The world of active management has also not stood still since 2000. Issues, trends, and challenges have appeared since the publication of *Active Portfolio Management*, and we have published many articles on these emerging trends in refereed journals. Those articles applied the *Active Portfolio Management* framework to analyze new problems.

This book, *Advances in Active Portfolio Management*, is a companion and successor book to *Active Portfolio Management*. Articles and essays we have written—together and separately, mainly since the publication of *Active Portfolio Management*—compose the chapters in this book. We have chosen articles mainly along three dimensions: a recap of *Active Portfolio Management*, advancing the *Active Portfolio Management* framework, and applying the *Active Portfolio Management* framework to newer problems. We have used those three dimensions to organize the book. For each article or group of related articles, we have added an introduction reviewing the material with the benefit of time and providing context and background useful for reading the articles.

Section 1 recaps *Active Portfolio Management*. After the introduction to this section comes the chapter "Seven Insights into Active Management," a summary of seven key themes in that original book. "A Retrospective Look at the Fundamental Law of Active Management" reviews how this key idea has impacted the field in the 30 years since its publication. "Breadth, Skill, and Time" then provides significant additional insight and detail into the concept of breadth, the least understood component of the fundamental law.

Section 2 covers advances in active portfolio management. The chapters in this section fall into two general categories: dynamic portfolio management (Section 2.1) and portfolio analysis and attribution (Section 2.2). The introduction to Section 2.1 provides an important overview to a set of articles describing theory that developed over time. This dynamic portfolio management section includes five articles: "Implementation Efficiency," "Dynamic Portfolio Analysis," "Signal Weighting," "Linear Trading Rules for Portfolio Management," and "Nonlinear Trading Rules for Portfolio Management." The "Dynamic Portfolio Analysis" paper won the Bernstein Fabozzi/Jacobs Levy Award for the best article in the *Journal of Portfolio Management* the year it appeared.

Section 2.2 covers portfolio analysis and attribution—in particular, an approach that converts most attributes of interest into portfolios and then provides analytical results through covariances and correlations between those portfolios. The introduction to this subject provides a broad tutorial on the topic, after which the included articles present the ideas in more developed form and show examples. The introduction also discusses two articles not included in the book that delve more deeply into particular points. The two included articles are "Attribution" and "The Description of Portfolios." Both articles won outstanding article awards from the *Journal of Portfolio Management* as part of the Bernstein Fabozzi/Jacobs Levy Awards.

Section 3 covers applications of active portfolio management. This section includes a broader array of topics within four main areas: expected return, smart beta, risk, and portfolio construction.

Section 3.1, "Expected Return: The Equity Risk Premium and Market Efficiency," includes chapters on estimating the equity risk premium ("A Supply Model of the Equity Risk Premium"), the many uses of beta ("Is Beta Dead Again?"), and a useful statistical test of whether benchmark portfolios are efficient ("Are Benchmark Portfolios Efficient?"). Each of these chapters has its own introduction.

Section 3.2, "Expected Return: Smart Beta," is on smart beta/factor investing. It includes an introduction followed by four chapters: "Who Should Buy Smart Beta?," "Smart Beta: The Owner's Manual," "Smart Beta Illustrated," and "The Asset Manager's Dilemma." All these chapters provide insight into this new product area that is disrupting active management.

Section 3.3, "Risk," includes an introduction and a chapter on alternative definitions of risk titled "Heat, Light, and Downside Risk."

Section 3.4, "Portfolio Construction," includes an introduction and five articles. "Optimal Gearing" identifies and analyzes an issue not well understood among investment managers—that one cannot independently specify risk level and gearing. "The Dangers of Diversification" describes challenges associated with multistrategy or multimanager portfolios—overdiversification and too much exposure to some common factors like smart beta—which lead to heightened tail risk. "The Surprisingly Small Impact of Asset Growth on Expected Alpha" describes a model of capacity. While it describes a quantitative approach to investing that in principle maximizes capacity, a key challenge is that all managers following similar (correlated) strategies *share* that capacity. "Mean-Variance and Scenario-Based Approaches to Portfolio Selection" describes some challenges associated with using scenario-based approaches to building portfolios. This chapter relates to the downside risk chapter and includes important guidelines to controlling the scenario-based process. The last chapter in this section, "Five Myths About Fees," is more about fees than portfolio construction, though it includes insights that can help investors compare products with different fee structures. This article also won the Bernstein Fabozzi/Jacobs Levy Best Paper Award the year it appeared in the *Journal of Portfolio Management.*

After covering these three main sections, we end with a few extras in Section 4. "Presentations upon Receiving the James R. Vertin Award" contains the authors' remarks on winning this award, which is "presented periodically by the CFA Institute to recognize individuals who have produced a body of research notable for its relevance and enduring value to investment professionals."[2] "What Investors Can Learn from a *Very* Alternative Market" is an essay on behavioral finance using the example of baseball and Michael Lewis's book *Moneyball.* The "UCLA Master of Financial Engineering Commencement Address," hopefully appropriate for the penultimate chapter in the book, provides some career advice for students just

2. CFA Institute website, https://www.cfainstitute.org/en/research/foundation/vertin-award.

beginning their financial engineering careers. We end the book with a Conclusion that provides some perspective on the record of quantitative investing over the past 65 years.

Before finishing this Introduction, we need to provide readers with some logistical warnings. This book is mainly a collection of previously published articles (and many technical appendices originally only available upon request). These articles did not follow completely consistent notation as the authors have developed and refined their notation over time. We have moved these chapters closer to consistent notation, but they still do not follow completely consistent notation.

Related to that, equation numbers and exhibit numbers begin anew with each chapter. Because the chapters began as independent articles, there is no referencing of equations in one chapter by another chapter.

Finally, we have used the benefit of hindsight to make some improvements to the articles, in addition to commenting on the articles in the introductory chapters. While each chapter is highly correlated with its original published article, the correlation falls a bit below 100%.

With this introduction behind us, let's move on to Section 1.

SECTION 1

Recap of *Active Portfolio Management*

2

Introduction to the Recap of *Active Portfolio Management* Section

Before focusing on advances to and applications of the theory and approach we outlined in *Active Portfolio Management*, this first section of *Advances in Active Portfolio Management* recaps some of the key elements of that predecessor book. We include three articles here:

- "Seven Insights into Active Management" by Ronald N. Kahn
- "A Retrospective Look at the Fundamental Law of Active Management" by Richard C. Grinold and Ronald N. Kahn
- "Breadth, Skill, and Time" by Richard C. Grinold and Ronald N. Kahn

The first article covers seven insights that mostly make up the key themes in *Active Portfolio Management*. The second article looks back on the impact of the fundamental law of active management, 30 years after Richard Grinold's original 1989 paper and 24 years after its appearance as a central theme of *Active Portfolio Management*. The third article provides additional insight into breadth, the least well understood element of the fundamental law.

"Seven Insights into Active Management"

Of these three articles, this first one comes closest to actually recapping the material in *Active Portfolio Management*. After the book first came out, we presented a talk, "Seven Quantitative Insights into Active Management," at a number of investment conferences and later turned that talk into a series published in the *Barra Newsletter* and Barclays Global Investors' *Investment Insights* publication. The second edition of *Active Portfolio Management* mentioned that talk in the Preface.

The version we have included here reflects some editorial changes, plus the adherence of one of us to the "rule of seven" organizing principle. We have dropped two of the original insights and replaced them with two other insights we deemed more central to active management, even if they aren't key elements of our previous book. We now start with Sharpe's "arithmetic of active management,"[1] certainly a key insight into active management even if not mentioned in *Active Portfolio Management*. We also include an insight about allocating risk budgets to investment products in proportion to information ratios, an insight of importance to product allocators even if we never explicitly called it out in *Active Portfolio Management*.[2] At the same time, we dropped the insight that active management is forecasting—a key element of *Active Portfolio Management* but one that came across as having few actionable implications. We also dropped the insight that it's hard to distinguish skill from luck, in part because the insight that data mining is easy covers much of the same ground.

The chapter now includes the following insights:

1. The arithmetic of active management shows that it is worse than a zero-sum game.
2. Information ratios determine value added.
3. Allocate risk budgets in proportion to information ratios.
4. Alphas must control for skill, volatility, and expectations.
5. The fundamental law of active management shows that information ratios depend on skill, breadth, and efficiency.
6. Data mining is easy.
7. Constraints and costs have a surprisingly large impact.

As noted above, these mainly capture the key insights in *Active Portfolio Management*.

"A Retrospective Look at the Fundamental Law of Active Management"

Thirty years after Richard Grinold's 1989 article, it seems worth looking back at the impact of the fundamental law of active management. This chapter discusses the fundamental law and its implications, efforts to improve the fundamental law since its publication, and its impact on the investment world.

Insight 2 above, right after the arithmetic of active management, shows that the information ratio determines value added. All investors should

1. William F. Sharpe, "The Arithmetic of Active Management,." *Financial Analysts Journal* 47, no. 1 (1991): 7–9.
2. The book essentially contains this result, we just never explicitly use it.

prefer high information ratio products to low information ratio products. Differences in risk preferences will lead to different overall capital allocations, even if investors agree on the rank ordering of products. This insight is important in framing the fundamental law: Given the central role of the information ratio, what can we say about the ex ante information ratios of different strategies?

According to the fundamental law, the expected information ratio of an active investment strategy—its ratio of exceptional active return to active risk—is:

$$IR = IC \cdot \sqrt{BR}. \tag{1}$$

The information coefficient, or *IC*, is a measure of skill in each investment decision. It is the correlation of forecasts with subsequent realizations. The breadth, or *BR*, is a measure of diversification. We define it as the number of investment decisions per year.[3] High information ratios follow from high levels of skill and/or high breadth or diversification. The law requires some simplifying assumptions, but its value comes from its simplicity and its use in making strategic decisions: Are we better off investing in our team so as to increase their skill in investment decisions or to expand their coverage universe? How viable is basic tactical asset allocation—shifting between stocks, bonds, and cash on a roughly quarterly basis? As a statement about expected information ratios—where we don't expect three decimal places of accuracy—the fundamental law provides a simple and intuitive relationship in exchange for a few reasonable simplifying assumptions.

While we have seen many attempts to improve the fundamental law, most involve slight improvements in accuracy in exchange for considerable increases in complexity—clear violations of the babies and bathwater tenet. None of those proposed improvements have been widely adopted. There are two developments worth mentioning, however. First is the very useful and elegant improvement due to Clarke, de Silva, and Thorley: the transfer coefficient, or *TC*, to extend the fundamental law to handle real-world portfolios built in the presence of constraints and transactions costs (poor portfolio construction too).[4] The transfer coefficient, which measures efficiency, is the correlation of the actual portfolio held with the optimal paper portfolio built without constraints and costs.

The second development is an elaboration of the notion of breadth that takes into account the flow and aging of information. That is the subject of the third paper in this section. We will withhold discussion of that paper until later in this introduction.

The extended and widely adopted fundamental law is:

$$IR = IC \cdot \sqrt{BR} \cdot TC. \tag{2}$$

3. Per year because we define the information ratio as an annualized number.

4. Roger Clarke, Harindra de Silva, and Steven Thorley, "Portfolio Constraints and the Fundamental Law of Active Management," *Financial Analysts Journal*, September/October 2002, 48–66.

The fundamental law, Equation (2), has a very basic implication for active managers, investors, and consultants. Every active manager, no matter their investment style, must articulate some winning combination of skill, breadth, and efficiency. Quantitative strategies tend to focus on all three of these. Fundamental strategies aim in particular for high *IC*—deep understanding of the relatively few stocks they hold—in combination with lower breadth and efficiency. Both approaches can, in principle, lead to high information ratios, depending on the details of skill, breadth, and efficiency. Tactical asset allocation strategies, which used to be popular in the 1980s and 1990s, are much less popular today in large part due to the fundamental law. Their breadth is sufficiently low so that even reasonably high levels of skill do not suffice to deliver high active return per unit of active risk. These debates, framed through the fundamental law of active management, are now among the daily discussions between managers, investors, and consultants.

"Breadth, Skill, and Time"

Four elements comprise the fundamental law of active management:

- *IR*: the information ratio
- *IC*: the information coefficient
- *BR*: the breadth
- *TC*: the transfer coefficient

Investors understand the information ratio quite well. It is the ratio of two quantities—active return and active risk—central to investing. Investors also understand the information coefficient and the transfer coefficient, as both are correlations, and they generally understand correlations. Breadth is different. We have described it as the number of independent bets per year. It is a rate and not a number. In particular, it's not the number of portfolio holdings. We know from years of experience that many investors are confused about breadth.

This article uses an equilibrium dynamic model—a type of model that will appear in many chapters in this book, and especially in Section 2.1, "Dynamic Portfolio Management"—to provide insight into the concept of breadth, as well as a refined notion of skill. In equilibrium, the arrival rate of new information exactly balances the decay rate of old information. We call that the information turnover rate, g. It is relatively easy to measure for any investment process. If the investment process forecasts returns on N assets, the breadth of the strategy is $g \cdot N$. Skill—the correlation of forecasts and returns—increases with return horizon for small horizons, but then asymptotically decays to zero for very long horizons. Our main result is that the ex ante information ratio (i.e., assuming $TC = 1$) is $IR = \kappa \cdot \sqrt{g \cdot N}$, where κ is a measure of skill.

3

Seven Insights into Active Management[1]

Our book *Active Portfolio Management* brought together a set of ideas, many developed between the 1970s and 1990s, that constituted a systematic approach to active investing. At a time when academic finance was firmly anchored on efficient markets, we asked the question, If you had some information about future asset returns, how would you most effectively use that information?

This chapter provides a rough summary of many of the key ideas contained in *Active Portfolio Management*. It also includes some ideas and examples not in that book but consistent with it in spirit. It overlaps to some extent with the 1999 summary *Seven Quantitative Insights into Active Management*, published by Barra (now MSCI) and Barclays Global Investors (now BlackRock).

Framework

Let's start with the basic framework for active management. We separate asset (and portfolio) returns into a systematic (benchmark) component and a residual component, $\theta_n(t)$:

$$\begin{aligned} r_n(t) &= \beta_n \cdot r_B(t) + \theta_n(t) \\ Cov\{r_B, \theta_n\} &= 0 \end{aligned} \tag{1}$$

1. This is Chapter 4 in Ronald N. Kahn, *The Future of Investment Management*, CFA Institute Research Foundation, 2018. Most of the ideas come directly from *Active Portfolio Management* by Grinold and Kahn.

The capital asset pricing model states that the expected residual return is zero. However, the active manager, having identified some useful information, g, forecasts residual returns not equal to zero:

$$E\{\theta_n\} = 0 \qquad (2)$$
$$E\{\theta_n \mid g\} \equiv \alpha_n$$

Much of the job of an active manager is to forecast residual returns. Active managers can also forecast market returns, and some do. As we show in this chapter, however, it's difficult to deliver consistent performance by implementing such forecasts (timing the market). Note that active managers and investors use the term *alpha* for several different things: forecast or realized residual or active return (where active return is simply the return minus the benchmark return).[2] We consistently use alpha to denote *forecast residual* returns. If we need to discuss any of its other meanings, we explicitly clarify them.

We need to connect forecast residual returns with optimal portfolios. We do this via Markowitz mean-variance optimization. Given our alpha forecasts and risk forecasts for any possible portfolio, we can find the portfolio that achieves the highest expected alpha for any given risk level. In particular, we define utility as follows:

$$\begin{aligned} Utility &= \mathbf{h}^T \cdot \boldsymbol{\alpha} - \lambda \mathbf{h}^T \cdot \mathbf{V} \cdot \mathbf{h} \\ &= \alpha_P - \lambda \omega_P^2 \end{aligned} \qquad (3)$$

In Equation (3), $\mathbf{h}$ is our vector of portfolio holdings, $\mathbf{V}$ is the covariance matrix for the assets, λ is the risk-aversion parameter capturing investor preferences, and ω measures risk.

We choose the portfolio that maximizes utility. To do that, we take the derivative of the utility with respect to each of the holdings and set those equal to zero. For the optimal portfolio, Q,

$$\boldsymbol{\alpha} = 2\lambda \mathbf{V} \cdot \mathbf{h}_Q \qquad (4)$$

Equation (4) directly connects our forecast alphas to portfolio positions. As we vary the risk-aversion parameter, λ, the optimal portfolio will vary. The overweights and underweights (or long positions and short positions) will scale up and down. In this way, the optimal portfolio risk will vary with risk aversion.

2. The difference between active return and residual return may be thought of as follows: Active return is simply the arithmetic difference between the return on an asset or portfolio and that of its benchmark. To calculate the residual return, one *leverages the benchmark* up or down to match the beta risk of the asset or portfolio and then calculates the difference.

Insight 1. Active Management Is Worse Than a Zero-Sum Game

William F. Sharpe published "The Arithmetic of Active Management" in 1991. It is a two-page paper containing no equations whatsoever. In it, he makes a simple argument:

- The sum of all active management and index management positions is the market.
- The sum of all index management positions is the market.
- Hence, the sum of all active management positions is the market.

Based on this simple argument that active management in aggregate sums to the market, Sharpe concluded that the (asset-weighted) *average* active manager matches the market's performance before fees and costs. This is true whether or not the market is efficient. So, after fees and costs, the average active manager must underperform the market. Index funds are above-median performers, once again independent of whether the market is efficient.

Sharpe's argument is quite powerful, though he does make a few assumptions. He assumes that all index management positions sum to the market. This assumption isn't exactly true even for just the broad market index funds, because those funds are often managed to different indexes. In the United States, we have broad market index funds managed against the S&P 500, the Russell 1000 Index, and the MSCI USA Index—not to mention broad market small-cap indexes. There are also sector and other not-broad index funds whose positions wouldn't necessarily sum to the market. On the active management side, professional active managers are trying to outperform market indexes. There are also investors who hold non-market-cap-weight portfolios (which are active because they differ from the market) but who are not professional active managers. These investors hold positions, often with little active trading, either because their holdings might be part of executive compensation, because trading would trigger significant capital gains, or for other reasons.

Still, considerable empirical evidence supports the key implication of Sharpe's arithmetic of active management: that the average active manager underperforms the market. For example, Eugene Fama and Kenneth French (2010) showed that active US equity mutual funds have produced a realized alpha of roughly zero on average before fees over the period from 1984 through 2006. They estimated the average realized alpha after fees to be somewhere between –0.81% and –1.13% per year, with the exact number depending on whether they control for one, three, or four factors. Our definition of alpha controls for only one factor—the market (or a broad market index)—but Fama and French also controlled for size and value factors and, in their four-factor analysis, momentum.

There are at least three important implications of the arithmetic of active management. First, tests of whether successful active management is possible need to look beyond average active performance. We know that the average active manager will underperform every year, even if a few successful active managers outperform year after year. Relatedly, if you want to become an active manager, it's not good enough to be average. You need to believe that you can consistently be a top-quartile active manager.

The second implication is that broad market index funds will be consistent second-quartile (or at least above-median) performers. This performance is independent of the efficiency of the market, and it provides a strong argument in favor of indexing. Unless the investor has the ability to identify successful active managers, he is better off with indexing. Otherwise, he is randomly choosing managers with negative expected alpha.

The third implication is that the burden of proof is on active managers to demonstrate that their expected active returns will more than compensate for added risk and cost.

Insight 2. Information Ratios Determine Added Value

Let's focus on the active manager's job: outperforming a benchmark. Active managers build portfolios by trading off alpha against residual risk (denoted by ω and shortened to simply "risk" in this discussion). As noted previously, the utility, or added value, from active management is given in Equation (3).

Individual preferences enter into the utility only in how individuals trade off residual return against risk. More risk-averse investors will demand more incremental return for each unit of risk.

The information ratio is the manager's (annualized) ratio of residual return to risk:

$$IR_P = \frac{\alpha_P}{\omega_P} \tag{5}$$

We will consider this a fundamental constant defining the manager, assuming it does not vary with time or the level of risk. A manager can deliver more residual return only by taking on more risk:

$$\alpha_P = IR_P \cdot \omega_P \tag{6}$$

This assertion is exactly true in the absence of constraints. For example, if the manager overweights one position by 5% and underweights another by 3%, leading to a given forecast alpha, she can double both the alpha and the risk by increasing the overweight to 10% and the underweight to 6%.

Understanding Information Ratios

We can think of the information ratio as a measure of *consistency* of performance—that is, the probability that the manager will realize positive residual returns every period. Exhibit 1 shows the probability distribution of alphas for three different information ratio distributions.

EXHIBIT 1 Alpha Distributions

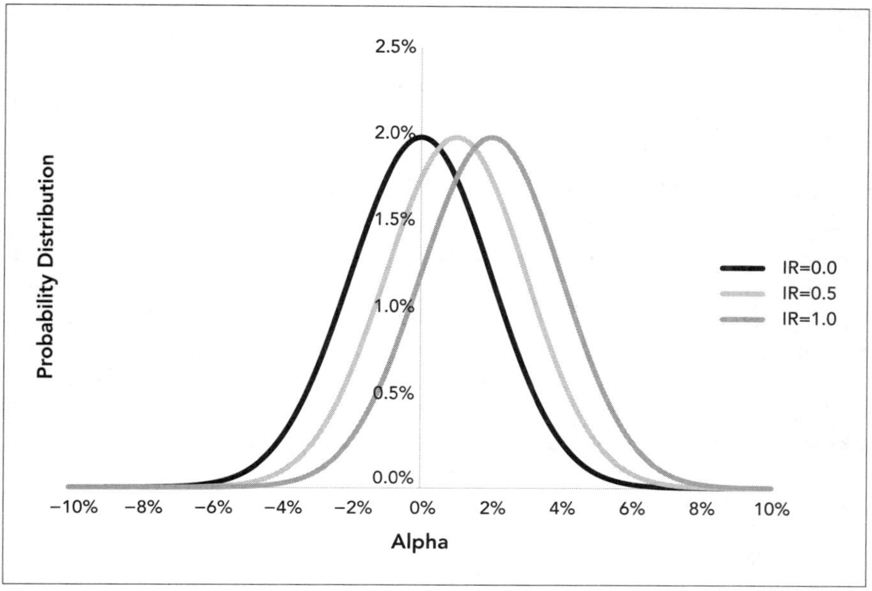

In this simple illustration, all three distributions have a residual risk level of 2% and the residual returns are normally distributed. As the information ratio increases, the distribution simply shifts to the right. The probability of realizing a positive residual return is simply the area under the curve to the right of $\alpha = 0$. This probability strictly increases in this example as the information ratio increases.

Even if we are comparing distributions with differing risk levels, if the residual returns are normally distributed, we find that the probability of realizing a positive residual return is:

$$Pr\{\alpha > 0\} = \Phi\{IR\} \tag{7}$$

where Φ is the cumulative normal distribution function. At least in the normal distribution case, the consistency of performance is a monotonic function of the information ratio: the higher the information ratio, the more likely it is that the manager will realize positive residual return in any period. Although residual returns are not exactly normally distributed, we do generally observe that consistency of performance increases with information ratios.

Utility Analysis

Using Equation (6), we can rewrite the utility (i.e., the added value) as:

$$Utility = IR_P \cdot \omega_P - \lambda\omega_P^2 \tag{8}$$

Exhibit 2 shows graphically how utility depends on risk. The active manager chooses the portfolio corresponding to the maximum point in Exhibit 2. At this point,

$$\omega^* = \frac{IR_P}{2\lambda} \tag{9}$$

$$U^* = \frac{IR_P^2}{4\lambda} \tag{10}$$

Equation (9) describes the optimal level of residual risk, ω^*. Optimal residual risk depends inversely on risk aversion and directly on the information ratio. More risk-averse investors will choose lower levels of residual risk. The higher the information ratio—and as we have seen, the higher the consistency of performance—the more residual risk an investor will tolerate.

EXHIBIT 2 Utility as a Function of Risk

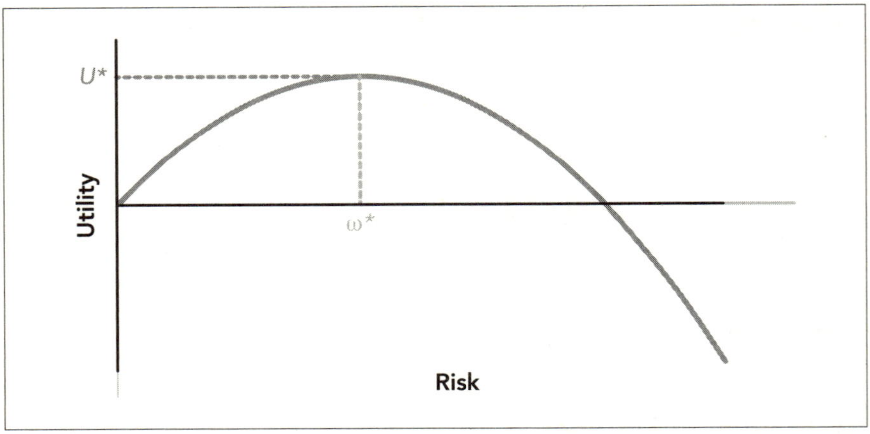

Each investor's maximum added value depends, according to Equation (10), directly on the square of the information ratio and inversely on the risk aversion. This is the critical point. It means that a very risk-averse investor, one with a very high value of λ, will maximize added value by investing with the manager with the highest information ratio. But a risk-tolerant investor, with a low value of λ, will reach exactly the same conclusion. The only difference between the two is how much they will invest with that manager versus an index fund, the zero-residual-risk choice.

All investors, regardless of their preferences, will agree that the highest information ratio can provide the most value. Equation (10) shows that information ratios determine added value.

Typical Values for Information Ratios

Given the central role of information ratios, it is useful to know their typical values. Based on research at Barra and BlackRock, the typical before-expenses distribution of information ratios is shown in Exhibit 3, and specific empirical results are shown in Exhibit 4.

EXHIBIT 3 Typical Distribution of Information Ratios

PERCENTILE	*IR*	PR{$\alpha > 0$}
90	1.0	84%
75	0.5	69%
50	0.0	50%
25	–0.5	31%
10	1.0	16%

EXHIBIT 4 Information Ratio Empirical Results

	EQUITY			FIXED INCOME	
PERCENTILE	MUTUAL FUNDS	LONG-ONLY INST.	LONG-SHORT INST.	INSTITUTIONAL	AVERAGE
90	1.04	0.77	1.17	0.96	0.99
75	0.64	0.42	0.57	0.50	0.53
50	0.20	0.02	0.25	0.01	0.12
25	–0.21	–0.38	–0.22	–0.45	–0.32
10	–0.62	–0.77	–0.58	–0.90	–0.72

Notes: These results are for US data over the five-year period from January 2003 through December 2007. Empirical studies included 338 equity mutual funds, 1,679 equity long-only institutional funds, 56 equity long-short institutional funds, and 537 fixed-income mutual funds.

Source: BlackRock.

Exhibit 3 shows the typical distribution numbers. A top-quartile manager can add 50 bps of realized residual return for every 100 bps of residual risk, before expenses. This finding holds for both equity and fixed-income funds. Exhibit 4 shows results for studies of US equity mutual funds and institutional portfolios, and fixed income institutional portfolios over the five-year period from 2003 through 2007. These studies used Sharpe (1992) style analysis to separate style from selection return for each fund. The style component of the return represents the effective benchmark of each fund. Exhibit 4 shows information ratios of the selection returns. Exact results will vary with the historical period, the asset class under review, and the methodology. These empirical results are roughly consistent with the data in Exhibit 3.

Insight 3. Allocate Risk Budget in Proportion to Information Ratios

Insight 2 showed that investors should choose active managers on the basis of their information ratios. What should an investor do when confronted with many investment choices, with a variety of information ratios? The investor will find the highest-information-ratio manager the most attractive, but should the investor place all his money with that manager?

We can also analyze this situation with mean-variance optimization. Let's say the investor has identified N different managers, each offering a particular expected alpha, α_n, at residual risk ω_n and hence information ratio IR_n. For simplicity, assume that these managers' residual returns are all uncorrelated. We don't need to make this assumption, but it simplifies the analytical results.

The investor places a fraction h_n with each manager. The portfolio alpha and risk are:

$$\alpha_P = \sum_{n=1}^{N} h_n \cdot \alpha_n \tag{11}$$

$$\omega_P^2 = \sum_{n=1}^{N} h_n^2 \cdot \omega_n^2 \tag{12}$$

The investor chooses allocations to maximize her utility. The results are:

$$h_n^* = \frac{\alpha_n}{2\lambda\omega_n^2} \Rightarrow \frac{IR_n}{2\lambda\omega_n} \tag{13}$$

$$h_n^* \cdot \omega_n = \frac{IR_n}{2\lambda} \tag{14}$$

Equation (13) shows that the investor optimally allocates capital in proportion to information ratios divided by risk. But, perhaps more naturally, Equation (14) shows that the investor allocates risk in proportion to information ratios. The quantity $h_n^* \cdot \omega_n$ is the investor's capital allocation times the risk, which is the *risk allocation*. It measures how much risk the investment contributes at the portfolio level. For example, if the investor places 20% of the capital in a fund with 5% risk, that allocation contributes 1% risk at the portfolio level.

The key observation here: Investors allocate risk in proportion to information ratios.[3] The investor does not allocate all the capital, and all the risk, to the best manager—that is, the manager with the highest information

3. For those worried about our assumption that these investment choices are uncorrelated, if we take correlations into account, we find that

$$\mathbf{h} \cdot \boldsymbol{\omega} = \frac{\boldsymbol{\rho}^{-1} \cdot \mathbf{IR}}{2\lambda}$$

where **h** is the vector of capital allocations, **ω** is a diagonal matrix with residual risks on the diagonal, **ρ** is the correlation matrix, and **IR** is a vector of information ratios.

ratio. She allocates the most risk to that manager but still diversifies among other managers because she does not know which manager will have the best performance after the fact; the information ratio is just an expectation, not a guarantee, of performance.

Insight 4. Alphas Must Control for Skill, Volatility, and Expectations

This insight shows how to process raw information into alphas, which are critical inputs for active management.

Raw signals, such as analyst earnings forecasts, broker buy/sell recommendations, and the number of cars in a Walmart parking lot the week before Christmas, hopefully contain information useful in forecasting returns. But these raw data are not alphas (expected residual returns). They are not even necessarily denominated in units of return.

A basic forecasting formula governs the connection between these raw signals and alphas. This formula refines the raw signals into alphas by controlling for expectations, skill, and volatility. In many cases, we can simplify this formula to a particularly intuitive form.

The basic forecasting formula provides the best linear unbiased estimate (BLUE) of the residual return, θ, given the raw signal, g:

$$E\{\theta \mid g\} = E\{\theta\} + Cov\{\theta, g\} \cdot Var^{-1}\{g\} \cdot \left[g - E\{g\}\right] \tag{15}$$

According to Equation (15), the expected residual return conditional on g equals the unconditional expected residual return plus a term that depends on the difference between the observed signal and its unconditional expectation. Reordering terms, we see that:

$$E\{\theta \mid g\} - E\{\theta\} = Cov\{\theta, g\} \cdot Var^{-1}\{g\} \cdot \left[g - E\{g\}\right] \tag{16}$$

As discussed at the beginning of this chapter, the unconditional expected residual return is zero, and alpha is the expected residual return conditional on the manager's information, g.

This formula controls for expectations. Only if g differs from its unconditional expectation will the expected residual return differ from its unconditional expectation. Put another way, only if g differs from its unconditional expectation will the expected alpha differ from zero.

This result is intuitive. If company earnings exactly match expectations, we do not expect the stock to move. That happens only when earnings do not match expectations.

Now let's simplify Equation (16) into a more intuitive form that reveals how alphas include controls for skill and volatility. The definitions of variance and covariance tell us the following:

$$Var\{g\} = \left(StDev\{g\}\right)^2 \tag{17}$$

$$Cov\{\theta, g\} = Corr\{\theta, g\} \cdot StDev\{\theta\} \cdot StDev\{g\} \tag{18}$$

Substituting Equations (17) and (18) into Equation (16) leads to:

$$\alpha = Corr\{\theta, g\} \cdot StDev\{\theta\} \cdot \left[\frac{g - E\{g\}}{StDev\{g\}}\right] \tag{19}$$

We commonly refer to the correlation of the signal and the subsequent realization as the *information coefficient* (IC), and the standard deviation of the residual return is the residual risk (ω). We refer to the standardized raw signal as a z-score, or score for short, because by construction it has a mean of 0 and a standard deviation of 1. If the z-scores are normally distributed or close to normally distributed, then about 95% of the time z will range from –2 to +2. That is usually the case, but we will not assume that it is always true. Putting this together, we get:

$$\alpha = IC \cdot \omega \cdot z \tag{20}$$

We have decomposed alpha into three components: an information coefficient, a volatility, and a score.

Equation (20) clearly shows how alphas control for skill, volatility, and expectations. The information coefficient is a measure of skill. With no skill—that is, no correlation between signal and subsequent return—the information coefficient is zero and Equation (20) sets the alpha to zero, as it should. The greater the skill, the greater the alpha, other things equal.

Understanding Skill

It is useful to provide some context for this important measure of skill. First, Exhibit 5 shows the range of typical information coefficients.

EXHIBIT 5 Typical Information Coefficients

SKILL	*IC*
average	0.00
good	0.05
great	0.10

These correlations are small. Consistent with the arithmetic of active management, the average information coefficient is zero. But even a great information coefficient is only 0.1. We know that, as a correlation, the maximum possible information coefficient is 1. But these numbers are much lower than that. Forecasting residual returns is difficult. To better understand these magnitudes, we can relate the information coefficient to a simpler measure of skill: how often the manager correctly forecasts the sign of the residual return. If the manager gets the sign right only 50% of the time, he doesn't have skill. If we assume that residual returns and forecast errors are normally distributed and that the information coefficient is much less than 1, we find that:

$$fr = \left(\frac{1}{2}\right) + \left(\frac{1}{\pi}\right) \cdot \arctan\left\{\frac{IC}{\sqrt{1 - IC^2}}\right\}$$
$$\approx \left(\frac{1}{2}\right) + \left(\frac{IC}{\pi}\right) \quad \text{for } IC \ll 1 \tag{21}$$

We can see more explicitly that if the information coefficient is zero, the manager correctly forecasts the sign of the residual return 50% of the time. But as the information coefficient increases, the manager correctly forecasts the sign more than 50% of the time. Exhibit 6 expands Exhibit 5 to convert information coefficients into probabilities of forecasting the correct sign.

EXHIBIT 6 Probability of Forecasting the Correct Sign

SKILL	*IC*	*fr*
average	0.00	50.0%
good	0.05	51.6%
great	0.10	53.2%

Exhibit 6 and Equation (21) help us understand how difficult it is to correctly forecast residual returns. An exceptional information coefficient of 0.1 corresponds to correctly forecasting the sign of the residual return about 53% of the time. I soon show that the key to turning that small edge in each investment decision into a high information ratio is diversification.

Volatility serves two purposes in Equation (20). First, it causes the forecast alpha to be expressed in units of return. The information coefficient and the score are dimensionless. Second, it controls the alpha for volatility. For a given skill level, imagine two stocks with equally bullish scores of +1. We believe both stocks will go up. Equation (20) says that the higher-volatility stock will go up more. If both a low-volatility utility stock and a high-volatility technology stock achieve earnings one standard deviation above expectations, the technology stock should rise more. Both stocks will rise, but the technology stock will rise more than the utility stock.

Keep in mind that optimal holdings are roughly proportional to alpha divided by residual variance. Even if we give the more volatile stock the higher alpha, it will receive a smaller position. The amount of risk we take in each position, though, is proportional to the score.

The score implements the control for expectations because it has an expectation of zero. Only when the signal doesn't match expectations does the score differ from zero.

Understanding the three constituent parts of an alpha can inform our intuition. It can also provide structure in unstructured situations, where the connections between raw signals and alphas are unclear.

Examples

The ultimate example of an unstructured situation is a stock tip. Even in this case, Equation (20) can provide structure. Imagine that the stock in question has a residual volatility of 20%. Exhibit 7 shows the range of possible alphas as a function of the information coefficient and score.

EXHIBIT 7 Alpha of a Stock Tip

	VERY POSITIVE	VERY, VERY POSITIVE
IC	*Z* = 1	*Z* = 2
Great: 0.1	2%	4%
Good: 0.05	1%	2%
Average: 0.0	0%	0%

Because stock tips are always presented as very, very positive ("I make only one or two recommendations a year, and you are the first person I called . . ."), converting from the tip to an alpha requires only estimating the tipper's information coefficient. Ask yourself, Is Warren Buffett on the line, or is it someone you have never heard of?

For an institutional money manager, a more relevant example involves converting broker buy/sell recommendations into alphas. This common situation has relatively little structure, but understanding alphas can help. Exhibit 8 shows an example, assuming that the broker has a good information coefficient of 0.05.

EXHIBIT 8 Broker Buy/Sell Alphas: Information Coefficient of 0.05

ω	VIEW	SCORE	ALPHA
15%	BUY	1	0.75%
20%	BUY	1	1.00%
15%	SELL	–1	–0.75%
30%	BUY	1	1.50%
25%	SELL	–1	–1.25%

Our conversion from recommendations to scores is straightforward. Notice that the first two stocks in the list, both recommended, have different alphas. We expect the second stock, with a higher volatility, to go up more than the first stock. Contrast this with simply giving every stock on the buy list an alpha of 1%. If all the buy recommendations have the same expected returns, an optimizer would choose the minimum-risk portfolio of those buy recommendations—loading up on the least volatile stocks.

Insight 5. The Fundamental Law of Active Management: Information Ratios Depend on Skill, Diversification, and Efficiency

Previously, we learned that the information ratio is the key to active management. Given that fact, how can we achieve high information ratios? Let's begin by looking at a relationship Richard Grinold first described in 1989 as the "Fundamental Law of Active Management." This law expresses the information ratio in terms of three other statistics—the information coefficient, a measure of skill; breadth, a measure of diversification; and the transfer coefficient, a measure of efficiency of implementation:[4]

$$IR = IC \cdot \sqrt{BR} \cdot TC \tag{22}$$

We previously examined the information coefficient in detail, and we know that it measures skill. If the information coefficient is zero, no correlation exists between a manager's forecasts and the subsequent realizations and the manager's information ratio is zero.

Understanding Breadth

Breadth—really breadth *of skill*—measures the number of independent bets the manager takes per year at an average skill level of IC. It measures diversification. We define breadth as bets per year because we define the information ratio as an annualized quantity.

According to the fundamental law, to achieve a high information ratio, a manager must demonstrate an edge in making individual investment decisions and then diversify that edge over many separate decisions. But breadth is still a measure of the diversity of decisions to which the manager has skill to apply. The fundamental law does not say that there is any advantage to investing in asset classes about which the manager knows nothing.

Breadth is the part of the fundamental law that is hardest to understand. As the number of independent bets per year, it is a rate, not a number. It's not the number of assets in the portfolio. We expect twice as many bets over two years than one year, so the number of holdings isn't the right concept.

To provide some additional insight into breadth, consider an investment process in equilibrium. Old information decays as new information arrives. In equilibrium, the two are in balance, and so the information turnover rate, γ, captures both the decay rate of old information and the arrival rate of new information. We can capture this situation schematically with Equation (23):

$$\alpha_n(t) = e^{-\gamma \cdot \Delta t} \cdot \alpha_n(t - \Delta t) + \tilde{s}_n(t) \tag{23}$$

Equation (23) shows that old information decays over time and new information, $\tilde{s}_n(t)$, arrives over time. Equation (23) implies that the decay and

4. Grinold (1989) included only the first two terms, effectively assuming perfect implementation. Clarke, de Silva, and Thorley (2002) extended the fundamental law, adding the transfer coefficient to account for imperfect implementation.

arrival of information happen somewhat continuously, which isn't usually true. It does show how old information (last period's alpha forecast) decays over time while new information keeps arriving. Assuming that these two processes are in balance, we can show that the breadth of this forecast is:

$$BR = \gamma \cdot N. \tag{24}$$

Equation (24) shows how the breadth relates to both the number of assets under consideration and the information turnover rate.[5]

This result is useful. Given a signal for N assets over time, we can estimate the coefficient, γ, using Equation (23) and then estimate breadth via Equation (24). For example, if we run a cross-sectional regression of $\alpha(t)$ against $\alpha(t - \Delta t)$, we can estimate $e^{-\gamma \cdot \Delta t}$ as a regression coefficient.

As a particular example, imagine we follow 300 stocks and every week we receive new information on 12 of those stocks. We don't know ahead of time which 12 stocks the new information will cover. Our breadth is 12 × 52 = 624.

But we could also represent this information process as:

$$\alpha_n(t) = \begin{bmatrix} \text{No change,} & p = \left(\dfrac{288}{300}\right) \\ \text{New information,} & p = \left(\dfrac{12}{300}\right) \end{bmatrix} \tag{25}$$

Because we cannot predict the new information, our expected alphas become:

$$E\{\alpha_n(t)\} = \left(\frac{288}{300}\right) \cdot \alpha_n(t - \Delta t) \tag{26}$$

But comparing Equations (26) and (23) leads us to estimate:

$$\begin{aligned} \gamma \cdot \Delta t &\approx \left(\frac{12}{300}\right) \\ \gamma \cdot N &\Rightarrow 12 \cdot 52 = 624 \end{aligned} \tag{27}$$

The mathematical formalism of Equation (23) leads back to the intuitive answer.

Noninvestment Example

Before considering the third term in the fundamental law, the transfer coefficient, let's consider a noninvestment example of the law: the roulette wheel. The American roulette wheel includes the numbers 1 through 36, 0, and 00. Consider players betting that the roulette number will be even. The players win if the number is 2, 4, 6, . . . , 36. The casino wins if the number is 1, 3, 5, . . . , 35. The casino has a small edge because it also wins if the final number is 0 or 00. The roulette wheel can stop at 38 possible numbers. The

5. See Grinold and Kahn (2011) for details. This is Chapter 5 in this book.

player wins if 18 of those numbers come up. The casino wins if 20 of those numbers come up. Now imagine that during the course of the year, players bet a total of \$2.5 million on this roulette wheel. Consider two possible scenarios. In the first scenario, the players all agree to pool resources and bet all \$2.5 million on one spin of the wheel. In the second, that \$2.5 million consists of 100,000 spins of the wheel with a \$25 bet on each spin.

Exhibit 9 shows the first scenario, from the casino's perspective. The casino has a 52.6% chance of winning \$2.5 million and a 47.4% chance of losing \$2.5 million. Let's analyze this situation in a bit more detail. View the forecasts as ±1 and the realized returns as ±100%.

EXHIBIT 9 \$2.5 Million Bet on One Spin of the Wheel

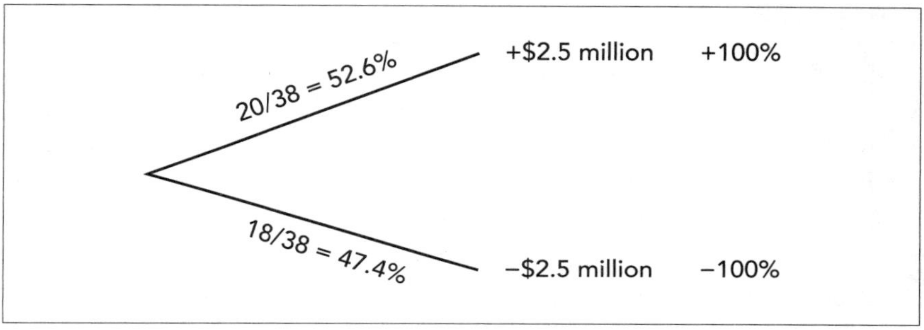

We start with the casino's expected return and variance of return:

$$E\{r\} = 0.526\,(100\%) + 0.474\,(-100\%) = 5.2\% \tag{28}$$

$$\begin{aligned} Var\{r\} &= 0.526\,(100\% - 5.2\%)^2 + 0.474\,(-100\% - 5.2\%)^2 \\ &= (99.9\%)^2 \end{aligned} \tag{29}$$

The casino's expected return is 5.2%, and the standard deviation of the return is 99.9%. In dollar terms, the casino's expected winning is \$130,000, with a standard deviation of almost \$2.5 million. The notably high standard deviation isn't surprising, because the casino faces only two possible outcomes—up 100% or down 100%—with the positive outcome only slightly more likely.

We can also calculate the casino's information coefficient. It is positive because it forecasts winning, and the casino does win 52.6% of the time:

$$\begin{aligned} Cov\{r, g\} &= E\{r \cdot g\} = 0.526\,(+1) + 0.474\,(-1) = 0.052 \\ IC &= 5.2\% \end{aligned} \tag{30}$$

In this simple case, the variances of r and g are almost exactly 1, so the covariance and the correlation are effectively the same.[6]

We can now check out the fundamental law of active management. We can calculate the information ratio directly on the basis of our calculations of the casino's expected return and its standard deviation. We can then compare it to the fundamental law result, with a breadth of 1 for this scenario.

$$IR = \frac{5.2\%}{99.9\%} = 0.052 = IC \cdot \sqrt{BR} \tag{31}$$

The information ratio is quite low, yet the information coefficient looks good from the perspective of active management. The problem is that the breadth is very low. It is not surprising that casinos do not encourage this approach to roulette.

The analysis of the second, more standard scenario is somewhat similar. In this case, though, we play the game 100,000 times over the course of the year and assume each game involves 1/100,000 of the capital. The expected return doesn't change if we do this. The expected return is 5.2% for each game n, so averaging over 100,000 games still gives us an expected return of 5.2%:

$$E\{r\} = \sum_{n=1}^{N} \left(\frac{1}{N}\right) \cdot E\{r_n\} \Rightarrow 5.2\% \tag{32}$$

The variance of return, however, is quite different. Now we calculate it as follows:

$$Var\{r\} = \sum_{n=1}^{N} \left(\frac{1}{N}\right)^2 \cdot Var\{r_n\} = \frac{Var\{r_n\}}{N} = (0.32\%)^2 \tag{33}$$

The casino's expected return is the same in both scenarios. However, the casino clearly much prefers the second scenario from a reward-to-risk ratio. In the first scenario, the casino has a 47.4% chance of losing \$2.5 million. In the second scenario, the casino could only lose that much if it lost 100,000 games in a row, which is enormously unlikely. In fact, Equation (33) shows that the standard deviation of casino outcomes is only 0.32%. The casino is unlikely to win more than 5.9% or win less than 4.5%. It has effectively locked in winnings of around 5%. Exhibit 10 shows how the return distribution has changed from one scenario to the other.[7]

6. To be more precise, we are analyzing a gamble on evens from the casino's perspective. The casino's signal is +1 for odds. But the expected signal is zero, as the gamble could have been on odds, in which case the casino's signal would be –1, i.e., a bet on evens.

7. The graph is a bit misleading due to the very different scales involved in the two distributions. In fact, the area under each distribution is the same: 100%.

EXHIBIT 10 Comparative Roulette Return Distributions

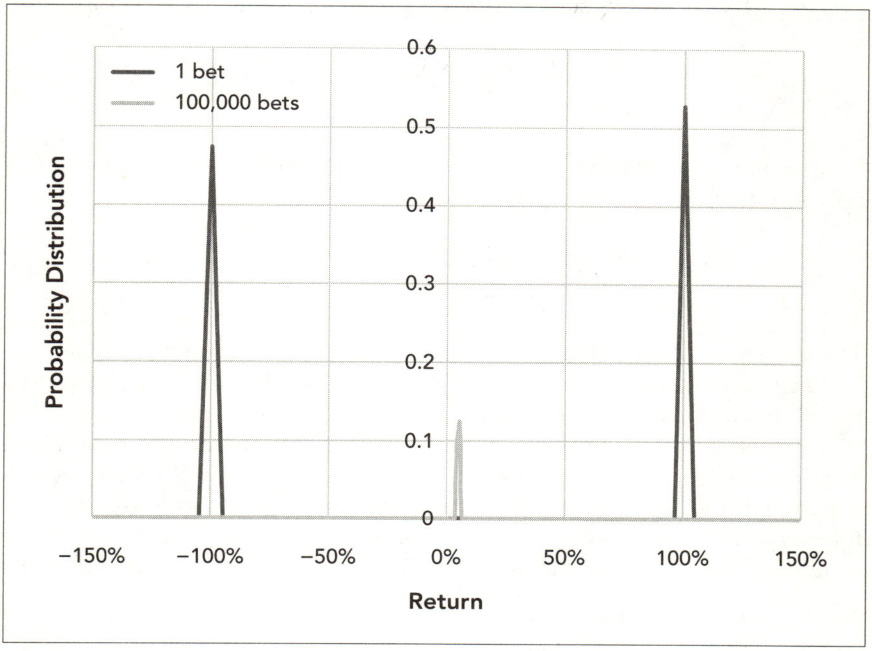

How does the fundamental law do in this case? We can calculate the information ratio directly and compare it to the fundamental law result with a breadth of 100,000:

$$IR = \frac{5.2\%}{0.32\%} = 16 = IC \cdot \sqrt{BR} \tag{34}$$

In this simple example, breadth works to reduce the variance of outcomes—exactly what we expect from diversification. It doesn't alter the expected return. Its impact on the information ratio is through the denominator.

Understanding the Transfer Coefficient

Now back to the third term in the fundamental law, the transfer coefficient. It measures the correlation between the return of a paper portfolio that optimally implements the manager's views without regard to costs or constraints and the actual portfolio the manager is running. The information ratio of the paper portfolio is $IC \cdot \sqrt{BR}$. The information ratio of the actual portfolio—taking into account constraints, costs, and possibly even poor implementation—is typically much lower.

To see where the transfer coefficient arises, go back to Equation (4), which describes the optimal portfolio, Q:

$$\boldsymbol{\alpha} - 2\lambda \mathbf{V} \cdot \mathbf{h}_Q = 0 \tag{35}$$

Portfolio Q is the optimal paper portfolio. Using this relationship, we can calculate the forecast alpha and the information ratio of portfolio Q:

$$\begin{aligned} \alpha_Q &= \mathbf{h}_Q^T \cdot \boldsymbol{\alpha} \Rightarrow 2\lambda \mathbf{h}_Q^T \cdot \mathbf{V} \cdot \mathbf{h}_Q = 2\lambda\omega_Q^2 \\ IR_Q &= 2\lambda\omega_Q \end{aligned} \tag{36}$$

But the manager holds portfolio P, not portfolio Q. We can do a similar calculation, starting again with Equation (35):

$$\begin{aligned} \alpha_P &= \mathbf{h}_P^T \cdot \boldsymbol{\alpha} \Rightarrow 2\lambda \mathbf{h}_P^T \cdot \mathbf{V} \cdot \mathbf{h}_Q = 2\lambda\omega_P \cdot \omega_Q \cdot \rho_{PQ} \\ IR_P &= 2\lambda\omega_Q \cdot \rho_{PQ} = IR_Q \cdot \rho_{PQ} \end{aligned} \tag{37}$$

The information ratio of any portfolio P is the information ratio of portfolio Q times the correlation of P and Q. Clarke, de Silva, and Thorley (2002) called that correlation the *transfer coefficient.*

Here are some examples of transfer coefficients to provide insight into its magnitude. Let's assume for these first two examples that residual returns are uncorrelated (the Sharpe [1963] assumption), residual risks are the same for every asset, and scores are normally distributed. If portfolio P was equal-weighted, with long positions for all the positive alpha stocks and short positions for all the negative alpha stocks, it would have a transfer coefficient of $\sqrt{\frac{2}{\pi}} \approx 0.8$. Roughly speaking, 80% of our information comes from the sign of the alpha. Second, what if portfolio P consists of portfolio Q with, for example, the 25% smallest positions removed. Exhibit 11 shows the general result.

EXHIBIT 11 Transfer Coefficient as We Exclude Small Positions

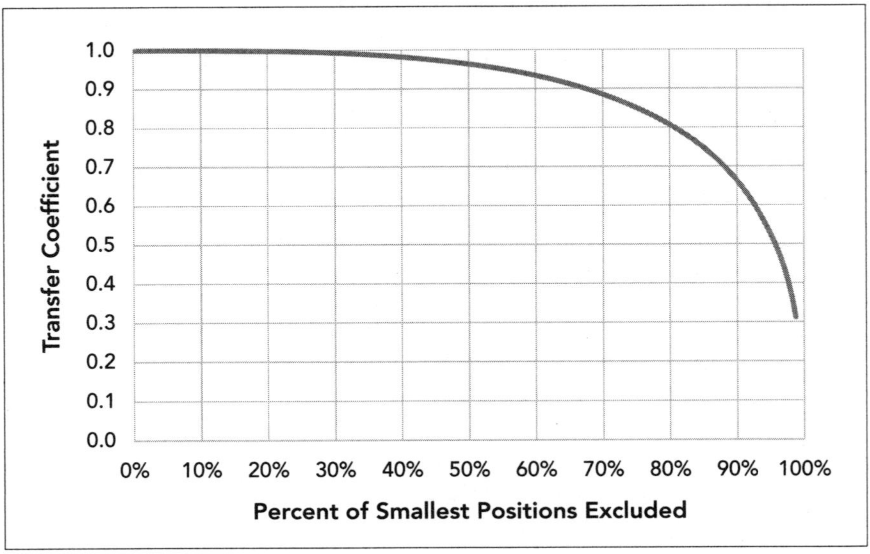

Until you remove about 80% of the smallest positions, the impact on the transfer coefficient is small. Insight 7 will go into much more detail on how the long-only constraint impacts the transfer coefficient. For now, we will just note that the transfer coefficient can vary widely across different approaches to investing. At the high end, long-short portfolios of low-transaction-cost assets (such as futures contracts) can achieve transfer coefficients well above 0.9. But long-only portfolios with additional constraints and high levels of residual risk can experience transfer coefficients well below 0.5.

Investment Examples

Now let's consider four investment examples. First, imagine a stock picker with an information coefficient of 0.05, a small but reasonably impressive level of skill in the active equity management business. This manager follows 500 stocks per quarter, effectively taking 2,000 bets per year. The manager then builds a long-only portfolio with a transfer coefficient of 0.35. The fundamental law implies an information ratio of 0.78 $\left(0.05 \cdot \sqrt{2{,}000} \cdot 0.35\right)$, indicative of a top-quartile manager.

Second, consider a market timer who looks at fundamentals, such as dividend yields and interest rates, and develops skillful new forecasts with an information coefficient of 0.1 roughly once per quarter. This manager runs a long-only portfolio with a transfer coefficient of 0.6. The fundamental law implies an information ratio of 0.12 $\left(0.1 \cdot \sqrt{4} \cdot 0.6\right)$, much lower than our stock picker with half the skill in forecasting returns. It is difficult to deliver consistent performance through market timing. It is, of course, possible to deliver significant performance in one quarter through market timing. That is its appeal. But it's hard to repeat that performance quarter after quarter. That is why I stated at the beginning of the chapter that managers focus (or should focus) more on forecasting residual returns than on the market's return.

For the third example, consider the performance of a tactical asset allocation manager who switches between stocks, bonds, and cash. Assume that this manager has a high level of skill for every bet, with an information coefficient of 0.1. This manager looks at broad macroeconomic trends and develops new views about once per quarter, making 12 independent bets per year (quarterly views on the three asset classes). The manager runs a long-only portfolio with a transfer coefficient of 0.5. In this case, the fundamental law implies an information ratio of 0.17, a bit above the median for active managers. Compared with the stock picker, a higher level of skill per bet does not necessarily translate into a higher information ratio. This is a bit better than market timing, owing to slightly more diversification. Because of the influence of the fundamental law of active management, neither market timing nor tactical asset allocation is a popular strategy anymore.

Finally, let's imagine that our tactical asset allocation manager has made these calculations and determined to improve the information ratio by converting the existing fund into a global macro hedge fund. This fund involves similar analysis, which is now applied to asset classes globally and implemented in an unconstrained long-short portfolio. Let's assume the manager expands from forecasting the behavior of three asset classes quarterly to forecasting 25 asset classes quarterly and, in the process, lowers the average information coefficient to 0.08—still respectably high. By going to a long-short structure and by mainly using futures contracts instead of physical investments, the transfer coefficient rises from 0.5 to 0.9. The resulting information ratio rises to 0.72, which is close to the result for the stock-picking strategy.

The fundamental law of active management has several implications. First, successful strategies require some winning combination of skill, breadth, and efficiency. Skill is the hardest to obtain. Breadth, i.e., diversification, can be the easiest to obtain—for example, by following more stocks—but it works only in combination with skill. We can increase efficiency by eliminating constraints. When hiring managers, investors must understand how they combine skill, breadth, and efficiency. This is one way the fundamental law of active management helps investors choose active managers. In the examples, we saw that market timing and tactical asset allocation strategies had trouble putting together compelling combinations of skill, breadth, and efficiency.

Note that, in spite of its mathematical nature, the fundamental law of active management applies to all active managers, not just quantitative managers.

In summary, information ratios, the key to active management, depend on skill, diversification, and efficiency.

Insight 6. Data Mining Is Easy

Why is it that so many strategies look great in backtests and disappoint on implementation? Backtesters always have 95% confidence in their results, so why are investors disappointed far more than 5% of the time? It turns out to be surprisingly easy to search through historical data and find patterns that have no predictive power for the future.

Investment researchers have long used the term *data mining* pejoratively for the unguided search for patterns in historical data. This approach in general is not effective in finding useful signals for predicting asset returns. Over the past decade or so, however, data mining has become a positive term describing research into extremely large data sets, looking for patterns with higher signal-to-noise ratios than typically observed in investing. Today, for example, parents might be delighted to hear that their son wants to marry his data miner girlfriend. Data mining does have a useful and important role in fields with large amounts of data and reasonable signal-to-noise ratios. The larger the amount of data, the lower the required signal-to-noise ratio. Still, investment research often uses data mining as a derogatory term because many of our data sets are not that big and our signal-to-noise ratios are typically low.

To understand why data mining is easy, we must first understand the statistics of coincidence. Let's begin with some noninvestment examples and then move on to investment research.

Noninvestment Examples

In the mid-1980s, Evelyn Adams won the New Jersey state lottery twice in four months. Newspapers put the odds of that happening at 17 trillion to 1, an incredibly improbable event. Soon afterward, two Purdue University statisticians, Stephen M. Samuels and George P. McCabe Jr., showed that a double win in the lottery is not a particularly improbable event.[8] They estimated the odds against observing a double winner in four months at only 30 to 1. What explains the enormous discrepancy in these two probabilities?

It turns out that the odds of Evelyn Adams (specifically her) winning the lottery twice are in fact 17 trillion to 1. But millions of people play the lottery every day. Thus, the odds of *someone*, somewhere, winning two lotteries in four months are only 30 to 1. If it weren't Evelyn Adams, it would have been someone else. In fact, it has happened again since then.

Coincidences appear improbable only when viewed from a narrow perspective. When viewed from the correct (broad) perspective, coincidences are not so improbable. Let's consider another noninvestment example: Norman Bloom, arguably the world's greatest data miner.[9]

Bloom died a few years ago in the midst of his quest to prove the existence of God through baseball statistics and the Dow Jones Industrial Average. He argued that "both instruments are in effect great laboratory experiments wherein great amounts of recorded data are collected and published." As but one example of thousands of his analyses of baseball, he argued that it was not a coincidence when the Kansas City Royals' third baseman George Brett hit his third home run in the third game of the playoffs to tie the score 3–3. Rather, it proved the existence of God. In the investment arena, he argued that it was not a coincidence that the Dow's 13 crossings of the 1,000-point line in 1976 mirrored the 13 colonies that united in 1776. He also pointed out that the twelfth crossing occurred on his birthday, deftly combining message and messenger. He never took into account the enormous volume of data he searched through—in fact, an entire New York Public Library's worth—to find these coincidences. His focus was narrow, not broad.

The importance of perspective to understanding the statistics of coincidence was perhaps best summarized by, of all people, the novelist Marcel Proust (1982, 178), who often showed keen mathematical intuition:

> The number of pawns on the human chessboard being less than the number of combinations that they are capable of forming, in a theater from which all the people we know and might have expected to find are absent, there turns up one whom we never imagined that we should see again and who appears so opportunely that the

8. Samuels and McCabe (1986), and also Diaconis and Mosteller (1989).
9. For more on Norman Bloom, see Sagan (1977).

coincidence seems to us providential, although, no doubt, some other coincidence would have occurred in its stead had we not been in that place but in some other, where other desires would have been born and another old acquaintance forthcoming to help us satisfy them.

Investment Examples

Investment research involves exactly the same statistics and the same issues of perspective. The typical investment data mining example involves t-statistics gathered from backtesting strategies. The narrow perspective says, "After 19 false starts, this 20th investment strategy finally works. It has a t-statistic of 2."

But the broad perspective on this situation is quite different. In fact, given 20 informationless strategies, the probability of finding at least 1 with a t-statistic of 2 is 64%. The narrow perspective substantially inflates our confidence in the results. When viewed from the proper perspective, confidence in the results falls accordingly.

Given that data mining is easy, how can we safeguard against it? Over time, my team at BlackRock has developed a number of approaches that work effectively for investment research.

To start, one should judge any new investment idea on the basis of whether it is:

- sensible,
- predictive,
- consistent, and
- additive.

The sensibility criterion forces us to consider why an idea might work—and, relatedly, why the market doesn't already understand it—before testing it empirically. This criterion allows an empirical analysis to proceed only if we have a reason to believe it might work. Although sensibility may sound overly restrictive in a world of statistical learning and data-driven understanding, three key issues lie behind its use: the amount of data, the signal-to-noise ratio, and nonstationarity. Where we have plenty of data, high signal-to-noise ratios, and stationary processes, we can rely on statistical learning without ex ante sensibility. There are even areas of investing where we can relax the sensibility criterion: notably, higher-frequency phenomena, such as short-horizon trading signals. But overall, my team at BlackRock has found sensibility to be effective in leading toward valuable research directions.

The other three criteria concern the backtest results themselves. We obviously seek predictive signals—ideas that predict future returns as opposed to those that contemporaneously help explain returns. Backtests probe a signal's ability to predict returns over historical data. Consistency ties directly to high information ratios. We actually care about the consistency of our aggregate forecast rather than the consistency of any one component signal. The additivity criterion judges whether this is a new idea or an old idea disguised as new. Having been in this business for many years, I can say that sometimes what we think of as new ideas are already contained in the existing aggregate forecast.

Beyond these four criteria, ancillary testing of any new idea also helps in determining its potential effectiveness. Our goal is to understand how the idea affects investment returns and, hence, to develop non-return tests. For example, is this an equity idea that predicts earnings surprise (the difference between newly reported earnings and analyst expected earnings) and influences returns through that mechanism? The ancillary test can check whether the signal predicts earnings surprise. This ancillary test provides a second statistical test of the signal's efficacy, increasing our statistical confidence in the result. Going forward, it can provide an early indication if the signal stops working.

We also use the statistical techniques of out-of-sample testing and cross-validation. Out-of-sample testing requires us to hold out part of our historical data. We test and fit the signal on the in-sample data and then run a final test with the out-of-sample data. The held-out sample might be the most recent historical period, but it could also be a subset of the assets.

Cross-validation breaks the data into N periods and then tests and fits the data N times, each time with one of those periods held out. Both approaches limit overfitting to a particular sample of the data.

What Fraction of Positive Backtest Results Are True?

I have attempted to estimate the impact of this overall approach on the ability to successfully identify effective signals, using a methodology proposed by John Ioannidis in his provocative 2005 article on medical research, "Why Most Published Research Results Are False." Ioannidis's analysis is top down. He started by thinking about all the medical studies that have been done and placing each experiment into a 2 × 2 table (see Exhibit 12). To fill out the table, imagine a total of c studies. Ioannidis applied a measure of degree of difficulty, R_{pn}, the ex ante expected ratio of positive results to negative results. This measure shows, ex ante, how many studies are likely to be positive and how many are likely to be negative. Is the research looking for fish in barrels or needles in haystacks? If the researcher is considering 100 different studies and R_{pn} is 1:9, then she expects 10 studies to find a positive result and 90 studies to find a negative result.

Ioannidis then added to his analysis several important considerations:

- f_{fp}, the fraction of false positives caused by statistical noise
- f_{fn}, the fraction of false negatives caused by statistical noise
- b, for bias (Researchers will present some fraction of negative results as positive owing to bias. Statistical noise, bias, or both will lead true negative results to be presented as positive.)
- N, for number of multiple tests (We have discussed this already—testing multiple variants of the signal until we find a variant that works. This increases false positives because the researcher reports a positive result even if only one out of N tests show up positive.)

EXHIBIT 12 Research Findings and True Relationships

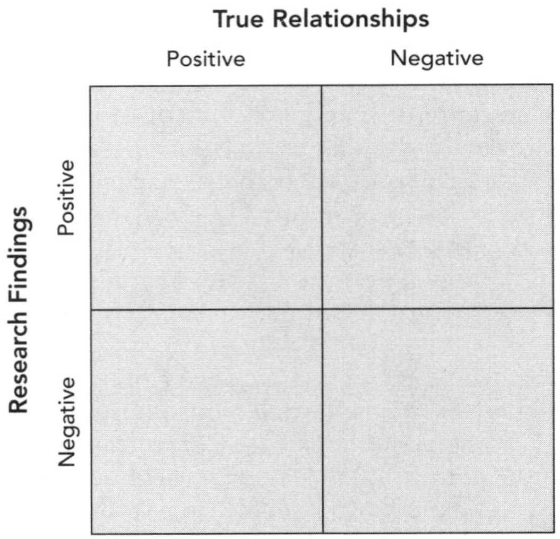

After putting this all together, as shown in Exhibit 12, he then looked at the sum of the top row—all the results that have tested positive—and asked what fraction of those results actually are positive? This measure is the *positive predictive value* (PPV), and it depends on all the variables introduced above. (See the Appendix at the end of this chapter for more details.)

Ioannidis (2005) showed that most published medical research has a PPV of less than 50%—hence, the article's title. He also described the conditions under which research findings are less likely to be true:

- the smaller the study
- the smaller the effect size
- the greater the flexibility in designs, definitions, and analyses
- the greater the financial interest; and
- the hotter the field of study

He stated (page 701) that "finally, . . . before running an experiment, investigators should consider what they believe the chances are that they are testing a true rather than a non-true relationship." That sounds a lot like our criterion of sensibility.

Edward L. Glaeser (2008) covered some of the same ground as Ioannidis, though his work focused on economic research and had less analytical structure. He provided more detail—in particular, on researcher bias caused by incentives faced by assistant professors. He cautioned skepticism of methodological complexity, which offers researchers more degrees of freedom and increases the cost of reproducing results. He also called for skepticism toward analysts who produce and clean their own data, another opportunity for increasing statistical significance.

Financial research isn't the same as medical research. We are looking not for truths of nature but, rather, for relationships we hope will work for some period of time. We live in a nonstationary world and expect that most of our investment ideas will eventually stop working as the market discovers them. Still, we can use a variant of Exhibit 12, where the columns are not about truth but, rather, are about adding value, or not, out of sample. (The Appendix at the end of this chapter provides more details.)

We have used this analysis to estimate the importance of the research criteria and ancillary testing to boosting the positive predictive value—the fraction of signals that pass the tests and work out of sample. Exhibit 13 shows the results, along with specific values we chose for the key variables.

EXHIBIT 13 Research Environment and Positive Predictive Value

RESEARCH ENVIRONMENT	f_{fp}	f_{fn}	*BIAS*	*N*	R_{pn}	*PPV*
Scattershot datamining	0.05	0.01	0.1	20	0.1	**9.5%**
No SPCA* process	0.05	0.05	0.2	10	0.15	**13.8%**
Sensibility	0.05	0.05	0.2	3	0.5	**47.1%**
SPCA, Ancillary Testing	0.01	0.05	0.05	3	0.5	**74.8%**

*SPCA stands for Sensible, Predictive, Consistent, and Additive

We start with scattershot data mining—searching for patterns in data without any prior reason to believe they're there (i.e., no ex ante sensibility)—and run about 20 tests looking for the best results. The PPV is about 10%. In our estimation, adding sensibility boosts the PPV to just under 50%. The full approach described previously—with the four criteria plus ancillary testing—raises the PPV to 75%. Although many of the inputs to the analysis are just rough estimates, it is clear that this approach significantly affects the PPV.

Insight 7. Constraints and Costs Have a Surprisingly Large Impact

The final insight is that constraints and costs can have a surprisingly substantial impact. To illustrate this point, we focus on the long-only constraint, one of the most pervasive and impactful constraints. Most investing is long only. Here, we show the impact of that constraint.

Conveniently, we have a tool to measure the impact of constraints and costs: the transfer coefficient. Constraints and costs affect the efficiency of our implementation, so the transfer coefficient quantifies the impact.

Imagine that we follow a universe of stocks and that our views of them are roughly normally distributed. In the language of stock recommendations, some are strong buys, some are strong sells, and the majority are closer to the middle. Exhibit 14 shows the situation schematically.

EXHIBIT 14 Impact of the Long-Only Constraint

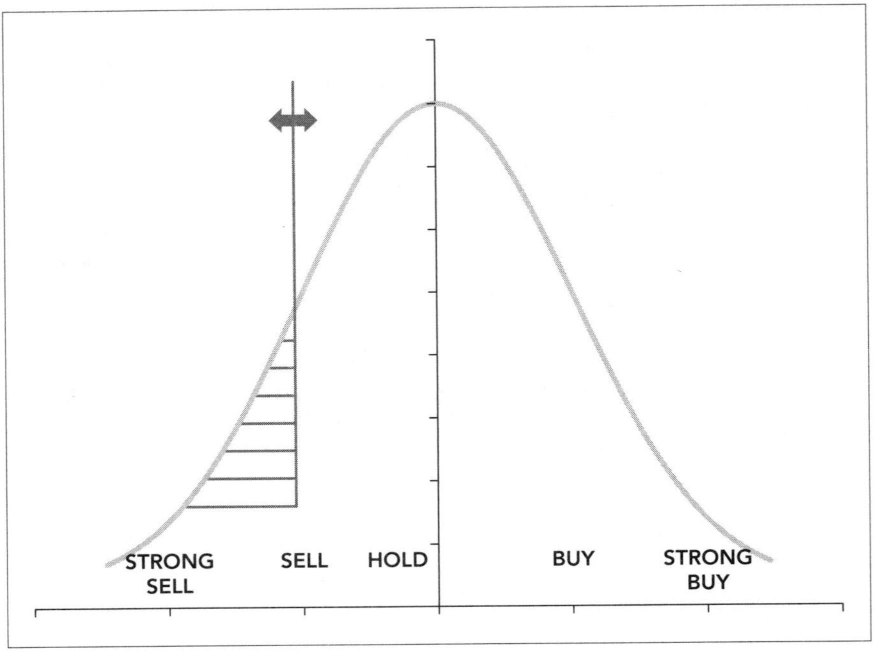

Intuitively, the long-only constraint limits our ability to fully take advantage of the most negative information—that is, those assets to the left of the vertical line to the left of the axis in Exhibit 14. If that line is far to the left, we affect only a few positions. As it moves toward the center, though, it affects more and more assets. What influences the position of that line? A key driver is the residual risk of the fund.

As we increase the fund's residual risk, we take bigger overweights and bigger underweights. As the underweights increase, they increasingly run into the long-only constraint. We expect the impact of the long-only constraint to increase and the transfer coefficient to decrease as the residual risk of the fund increases.

In fact, the impact of the constraint is bigger than this analysis implies. It also affects assets with positive recommendations, because our overweights and underweights need to balance. We can only overweight an asset if we underweight another asset. If we are limited in our ability to underweight, owing to the long-only constraint, we will hence be limited in our ability to overweight.

Simplified Example

Consider this interesting, yet simple, example. We start with an equal-weighted 1,000-stock benchmark. Each stock has a 0.1% weight in the benchmark. Assume that each stock has the same residual risk, that residual returns are uncorrelated (the Sharpe (1963) assumption), and we generate forecast alphas as $IC \cdot \omega \cdot z$, with IC and ω the same for every stock and z generated from a normal distribution. We calculate optimal holdings for a long-short fund as well as for a long-only fund. Exhibit 15 shows the optimal holdings of the two funds, displayed with the stocks sorted from largest forecast alpha to smallest forecast alpha.

EXHIBIT 15 Long-Only and Long-Short Active Positions

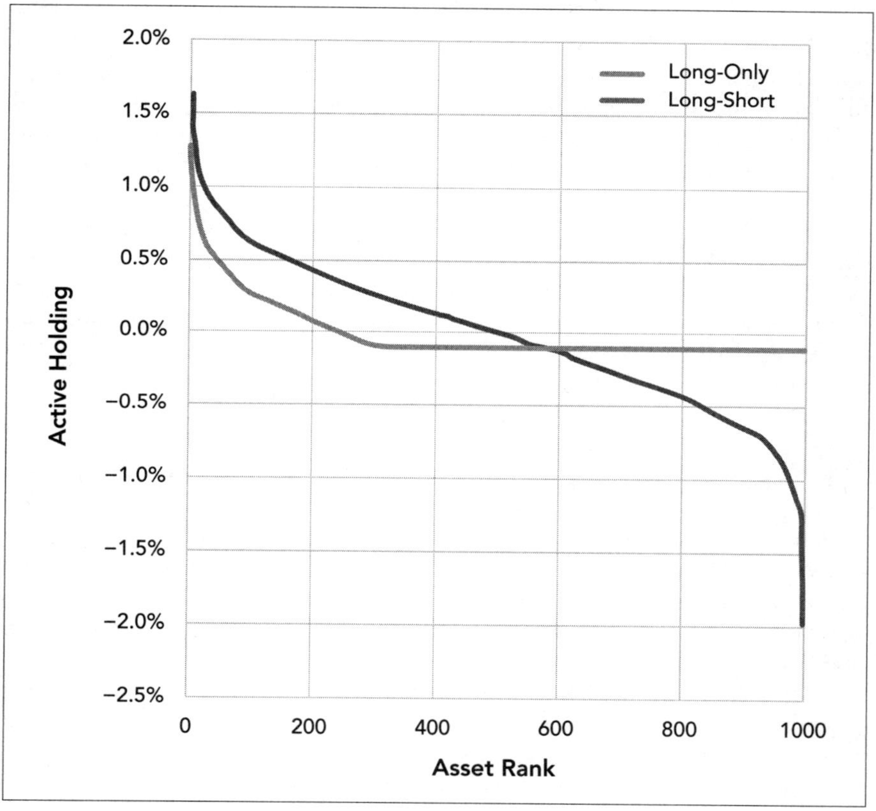

The long-short portfolio holdings look roughly symmetric, with roughly the same amount long and short. The portfolio includes about 500 long positions and 500 short positions. The largest positive positions look similar to the largest negative positions.

The long-only portfolio looks very different. We know the smallest possible position is a 0.1% underweight—that is, a holding of zero in the portfolio—and about 700 stocks have that position. Clearly, the positions of the negative-alpha stocks look quite different for these two portfolios. Exhibit 15 also shows the impact of the long-only constraint on positive positions. Just compare optimal holdings in the two portfolios for the largest positive-alpha stocks. These are notably smaller in the long-only portfolio.

In fact, the long-short portfolio turns out to be 202% long and 202% short, whereas the long-only portfolio is only 73% overweight and 73% underweight.[10] This exhibit provides graphic evidence that the long-only constraint also affects holdings for the most positive alphas because of the constraint that longs and shorts must balance out.

A More Realistic Analysis

To estimate the impact of the long-only constraint in more realistic portfolios, Richard Grinold and I (2000) used a simulation experiment. We started with a benchmark 500-stock portfolio. To use realistic asset weights, we first analyzed several popular cap-weighted equity indexes, including the S&P 500 and the Russell 1000. Although these differ somewhat, their asset weights are not far from lognormally distributed. So, we used a lognormal distribution fit to those typical benchmarks.

With the benchmark set, we generated 900 sets of 500 alpha forecasts. Each set of 500 alphas had an intrinsic information ratio of 1.5. We sampled the alpha forecasts from a distribution uncorrelated with cap-weight. For each set, we built optimal long-short and long-only portfolios of different residual risk levels. We then calculated the forecast alpha and residual risk for each portfolio. After doing that 900 times, we averaged the result for each risk level.

One reason we did multiple simulations is that although the underlying distribution of alphas is uncorrelated with cap-weight, particular samples of alphas might randomly end up correlated with cap-weight. If the alphas were accidentally negatively correlated with cap-weight, such that the larger-cap stocks tended to have more negative alphas, the long-only constraint would be a bit less binding, and vice versa. We generated 900 simulations and then averaged over those accidental correlations, positive and negative. Exhibit 16 displays the resulting efficient frontiers.

The long-short efficient frontier displays an information ratio of 1.5. For example, we have an expected alpha of 6% when our residual risk is 4%, and the efficient frontier is a straight line.

The long-only efficient frontier shows the increasing impact of the constraint with increasing residual risk. It is true that as we increase residual risk, we increase forecast alpha. However, we receive less and less additional forecast alpha for each additional unit of residual risk.

We can also see this effect by looking directly at the transfer coefficient as a function of residual risk, as in Exhibit 17.

The transfer coefficient for each risk level is simply the ratio of the long-only information ratio to the long-short information ratio. The higher the residual risk, the lower the transfer coefficient.

According to this fairly realistic simulation study, at 2% residual risk, the long-only constraint reduces the information ratio by about 30%, and at

10. These numbers were calculated by summing the long positions and the overweights, respectively.

EXHIBIT 16 Efficient Frontier

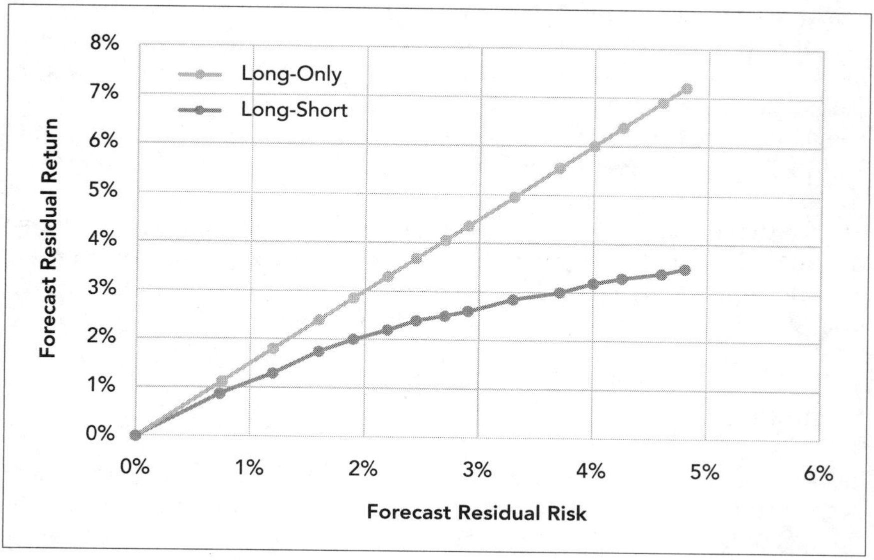

EXHIBIT 17 Transfer Coefficient

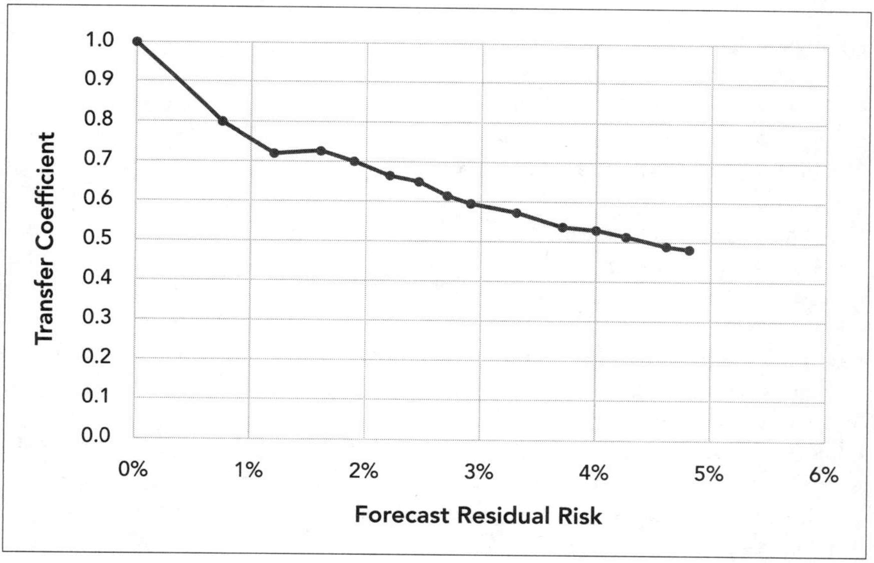

4.5% residual risk, typical for US active equity mutual funds,[11] the long-only constraint reduces the information ratio by about 50%.

Beyond the loss in information ratio, the long-only constraint also induces a small size bias that increases with residual risk. We are more constrained in underweighting small stocks than large stocks in cap-weighted benchmarks. We can start with forecast alphas uncorrelated with size and build a long-only portfolio with a bet on small stocks outperforming large stocks.

Constraints and costs—and the long-only constraint, in particular—can significantly affect expected performance. We are better off running long-only portfolios at low residual risk and using long-short implementations if we wish to run higher-residual-risk portfolios.

Summary

These seven insights into active management, viewed broadly, show that active management isn't easy and that the majority of attempts will fail. The information ratio is the critical statistic for investors and active managers. Successful investors must find winning combinations of skill, breadth, and efficiency.

Bibliography

Clarke, Roger, Harindra de Silva, and Steven Thorley. 2002. "Portfolio Constraints and the Fundamental Law of Active Management." *Financial Analysts Journal* (September/October): 48–66. doi:10.2469/faj.v58.n5.2468.

Diaconis, Persi, and Frederick Mosteller. 1989. "Methods for Studying Coincidences." *Journal of the American Statistical Association* 84 (408, Applications and Case Studies): 853–61. doi:10.1080/01621459.1989.10478847.

Fama, Eugene F., and Kenneth R. French. 2010. "Luck Versus Skill in the Cross-Section of Mutual Fund Returns." *Journal of Finance* 65 (5): 1915–47.

Glaeser, Edward L. 2008. "Researcher Incentives and Empirical Methods," In *The Foundations of Positive and Normative Economics: A Handbook*. Edited by Andrew Caplin and Andrew Schotter. Oxford, UK: Oxford University Press. doi:10.1093/acprof:oso/9780195328318.003.0013.

Grinold, Richard C. 1989. "The Fundamental Law of Active Management." *Journal of Portfolio Management* 15 (3): 30–37. doi:10.3905/jpm.1989.409211.

11. Kahn (2018) discusses data showing that median active risk levels for US large-cap mutual funds was 4.79% over the period from October 1997 through September 2017.

Grinold, Richard C., and Ronald N. Kahn. 2000. *Active Portfolio Management*, 2nd ed. New York: McGraw-Hill.

Grinold, Richard C., and Ronald N. Kahn. 2000. "The Efficiency Gains of Long-Short Investing." *Financial Analysts Journal* 56 (6): 40–53. doi:10.2469/faj.v56.n6.2402.

Grinold, Richard C., and Ronald N. Kahn. 2011. "Breadth, Skill, and Time." *Journal of Portfolio Management* (Fall): 18–28. doi:10.3905/jpm.2011.38.1.018.

Ioannidis, John P. A. 2005. "Why Most Published Research Findings Are False." *PLoS Medicine* 2 (8): e124 696–701. doi:10.1371/journal.pmed.0020124.

Kahn, Ronald N. 1999. "Seven Quantitative Insights into Active Management." *Barra Newsletter* from Barra and *Investment Insights* from Barclays Global Investors.

Kahn, Ronald N. 2018. *The Future of Investment Management*. Charlottesville, VA: Research Foundation of the CFA Institute.

Proust, Marcel. 1982. *Remembrance of Things Past: The Guermantes Way, Cities of the Plain*, Vol. 2. New York: Vintage Books.

Sagan, Carl. 1977. "God and Norman Bloom." *American Scholar* 46 (4): 460–6.

Samuels, Stephen M., and George P. McCabe, Jr. 1986. "More Lottery Repeaters Are on the Way." *New York Times*, letter to the editor (February 17).

Sharpe, William F. 1963. "A Simplified Model for Portfolio Analysis." *Management Science* 9 (2): 277–93. doi:10.1287/mnsc.9.2.277.

Sharpe, William F. 1991. "The Arithmetic of Active Management." *Financial Analysts Journal* 47 (1): 7–9. doi:10.2469/faj.v47.n1.7.

Sharpe, William F. 1992. "Asset Allocation: Management Style and Performance Measurement." *Journal of Portfolio Management* 18 (2): 7–19. doi:10.3905/jpm.1992.409394.

CHAPTER 3
Seven Insights into Active Management

Appendix A

This appendix provides more detailed analysis to estimate positive predictive value.

We start by assuming we test c signals. The number c will drop out of the analysis at the end, but it's clarifying to keep it in for now. The variable R_{pn} measures the ex ante ratio of positive results to negative results out of sample. It measures the degree of difficulty of our research. We, therefore, expect that $\frac{c \cdot R_{pn}}{R_{pn}+1}$ are positive and $\frac{c}{R_{pn}+1}$ are negative out of sample. Of the results that are negative out of sample, f_{fp} of them will test positive and $(1 - f_{fp})$ of them will test negative. We can similarly analyze what happens to the positive out-of-sample results, which lead to Exhibit A1.

EXHIBIT A1 Research Findings and True Relationships

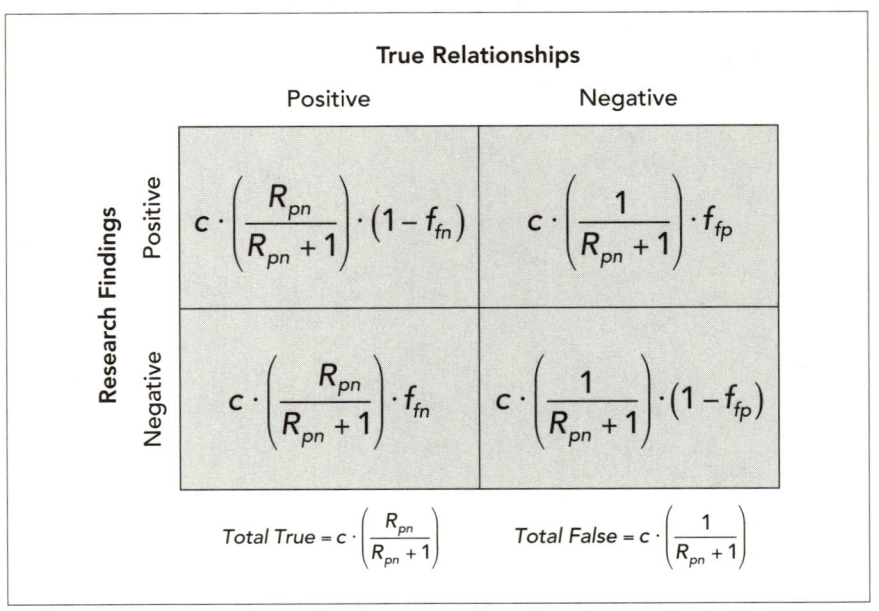

Research Findings	True Relationships: Positive	True Relationships: Negative
Positive	$c \cdot \left(\frac{R_{pn}}{R_{pn}+1}\right) \cdot (1 - f_{fn})$	$c \cdot \left(\frac{1}{R_{pn}+1}\right) \cdot f_{fp}$
Negative	$c \cdot \left(\frac{R_{pn}}{R_{pn}+1}\right) \cdot f_{fn}$	$c \cdot \left(\frac{1}{R_{pn}+1}\right) \cdot (1 - f_{fp})$
	Total True $= c \cdot \left(\frac{R_{pn}}{R_{pn}+1}\right)$	*Total False* $= c \cdot \left(\frac{1}{R_{pn}+1}\right)$

We can see from Exhibit A.1 that the positive predictive value is

$$PPV = \frac{R_{pn} \cdot (1 - f_{fn})}{R_{pn} \cdot (1 - f_{fn}) + f_{fp}} \tag{A1}$$

As the ex ante probability increases and the false positives and negatives decrease, it can approach 1. Of course, it can also fall far below 1.

It turns out that the ex ante ratio of positive results to negative results can have a big impact on the positive predictive value. To see why that happens, imagine that your doctor tests you for a rare disease; only 1 person out of 1,000 has this disease. The test is 99% accurate—that is, the fraction of false positives is 1%—and assume there are no false negatives. The test comes back positive. How likely is it that you have the disease? The answer is not 99% but only about 1 out of 11. Equation (A1) also leads to that answer.

What's going on here? Out of 1,000 people, 1 is a true positive and 999 are true negatives. If we apply the 1% false positive rate to the 999 true negatives, we expect to see about 10 false positives. The group of people who will test positive includes 1 true positive and 10 false positives. The probability of having the disease after testing positive is about 1 out of 11.

We can now see why the ex ante ratio of positive results to negative results can significantly affect our results. If we are testing many signals with low probabilities of being positive out-of-sample, all those negative out-of-sample signals can generate many false positives and even swamp the numbers of true positive out-of-sample signals.

We can also embellish the prior analysis to include two additional effects: bias and multiple testing. For bias, let b represent the fraction of negative out-of-sample signals presented as positive owing to bias. In the details of the analysis, assume that negative out-of-sample results are presented as negative in the absence of bias and statistical noise. In other words, statistical noise, bias, or both will lead to negative results reported as positive.

As for multiple tests, they increase the probability of false positives. Whereas before f_{fp} measured the fraction of false positives, now $1 - (1 - f_{fp})^N$ measures this fraction. If $N = 1$, the outcome is the same as our prior result, but the probability of false positives increases with each additional set of tests.

Putting this all together, we have Exhibit A2.

EXHIBIT A2 Research Findings and True Relationships

Research Findings	True Relationships: Positive	True Relationships: Negative
Positive	$c\cdot\left(\frac{R_{pn}}{R_{pn}+1}\right)\cdot\left[1-\left[(1-b)\cdot f_{fn}\right]^N\right]$	$c\cdot\left(\frac{1}{R_{pn}+1}\right)\cdot\left[1-\left[(1-b)\cdot(1-f_{fp})\right]^N\right]$
Negative	$c\cdot\left(\frac{R_{pn}}{R_{pn}+1}\right)\cdot\left[(1-b)\cdot f_{fn}\right]^N$	$c\cdot\left(\frac{1}{R_{pn}+1}\right)\cdot\left[(1-b)\cdot(1-f_{fp})\right]^N$
	Total True $= c\cdot\left(\frac{R_{pn}}{R_{pn}+1}\right)$	*Total False* $= c\cdot\left(\frac{1}{R_{pn}+1}\right)$

We also update our formula for positive predictive value to account for these embellishments:

$$PPV=\frac{R_{pn}\cdot\left\{1-\left[(1-b)\cdot f_{fn}\right]^N\right\}}{R_{pn}\cdot\left\{1-\left[(1-b)\cdot f_{fn}\right]^N\right\}+1-\left[(1-b)\cdot\left(1-f_{fp}\right)\right]^N} \tag{A2}$$

Note that if we set $b = 0$ and $N = 1$, we end up with Equation (A1).

4

A Retrospective Look at the Fundamental Law of Active Management[1]

Thirty years have passed since the original publication of the paper titled, somewhat presumptuously, *The Fundamental Law of Active Management*.[2] The fundamental law provides a very simple relationship between an investment manager's information ratio (active return per unit of active risk), his forecasting skill, and the breadth over which he applies that skill. The authors of this paper have gained, between them, 36 years and counting of investment experience since the publication, and still believe that the fundamental law can serve as valuable strategic insight and, perhaps more significantly, offers an important perspective for the investment manager.

Our focus on strategic insight is consistent with the fundamental law's mathematical simplicity and dependence on quantities we know only approximately. Its perspective is helpful in the design of new investment strategies and in allocating resources for the maintenance and improvement of existing strategies. We will attempt to demonstrate this point with an example toward the end of this chapter.

Suppose for the moment that we can divide investment managers into two groups: the foxes that know many things, some of which are true, and the hedgehogs that know one big thing that, again, may or may not be true.[3] In this dichotomy, the fundamental law is a paradigm for the foxes and of little use to the hedgehogs. The popular investment literature celebrates

1. The authors thank Barbara Petitt and Stephen Brown for suggesting that we write this piece. We have not published this previously.

2. Grinold (1989).

3. See Berlin (1953) for the original foxes and hedgehogs analogy. Tetlock (2015) and Silver (2012) discuss the analogy applied to forecasters.

those fortunate hedgehogs whose one big thing turned out to be true—for example, in Michael Lewis's *The Big Short*,[4] which describes managers who successfully made large bets during the financial crisis. Little attention is spent on the legions of disappointed hedgehogs unless deceit was involved in their undoing. If you consider yourself a fox, read on. If you are a hedgehog, well, good luck.[5]

Over the past 30 years, the fundamental law has become an increasingly influential concept governing active management. We can measure this several ways. First, as of this writing, Google Scholar lists 300 citations of the original Grinold (1989) paper, as well as an additional 1,245 citations of our book *Active Portfolio Management* (both editions), in which the fundamental law plays a central role. Beyond these citations, the fundamental law is now part of the CFA Level II Curriculum. Generations of CFA charterholders have now studied the fundamental law.

The fundamental law has also directly impacted active management. Tactical asset allocation between domestic stocks, bonds, and cash is less prevalent today than it was in 1989. Investors realize, thanks in part to the fundamental law, that tactical asset allocation will not deliver consistent active returns. On the other hand, quantitative active strategies, designed to exploit the ideas underlying the fundamental law, are much more widespread now than in 1989.

More generally, we can see the impact, anecdotally, of the fundamental law on discussions and interactions between investors, managers, and consultants. The simplicity of the fundamental law has facilitated its impact. Investors increasingly understand that every manager needs some winning combination of skill, breadth, and efficiency to deliver consistent positive performance going forward.

Overall, the fundamental law has had a significant impact on active management. We can say that based on the evidence just mentioned, even though it is a high-level strategic insight, and not, for example, a pricing formula.

We have seen many papers proposing improvements to the fundamental law, and a few suggesting criticisms. With a couple of notable exceptions we will discuss below, most proposed improvements trade improved accuracy for much more mathematical complexity. The improved accuracy, though, often assumes we know various inputs precisely, which we do not, and the increased complexity gives up the trait that has made the fundamental law so impactful—its simplicity.

In this paper we endeavor to describe the fundamental law, state what it is and what it is not. In addition, we describe two valuable enhancements:

- An elaboration of the notion of breadth that takes into accounts the flow and aging of information.

4. Lewis (2011).

5. In a sense we are hedgehogs, and the one big thing we know is that when it comes to investment management it is better to be a fox than a hedgehog.

- The transfer coefficient, introduced by Clarke, de Silva, and Thorley (2002) to measure the information lost in implementation. We will discuss how the rate of information arrival and the rate of trading influence the transfer coefficient.

The fundamental law uncovers the concepts that determine the information ratio. To understand why this is a useful task, we must first describe the vital role the information ratio plays in active management.

The Information Ratio

A prospective purchaser of investment services faces the choice of:

- An index fund with very low fee and almost zero operating cost
- An active fund that invests in roughly the same universe of assets as the index fund, but with aspirations for better performance and the certainty of higher fees, higher operating costs, and additional risk

We call the difference in return between the managed portfolio and the passive index benchmark portfolio the *active return*, the additional risk the *active risk*, and call the entire enterprise *active management*. Some of the jargon we use to describe this enterprise includes:

- Active Return = Return on Managed Portfolio – Return on Index Portfolio
- Alpha = α = Expected Active Return
- Omega = ω = Active Risk = Expected Standard Deviation of Active Return
- Active Portfolio = Managed Portfolio holdings – Index Portfolio holdings[6]

The fundamental law is an ex ante relationship—it's all about expectations. The alpha and omega are what we *expect* to see in the active performance. We anticipate a certain level of active return, and we anticipate a certain variation in that active return. There is another topic, of no small importance, that looks after the fact (ex post) at realized performance and uses statistics to square the promised return (alpha) with the realized return, and the anticipated risk (omega) with the realized risk. In this paper we are dealing with expectations and—mindful of the adage that a hunter who chases two rabbits will not catch either—have left the examination of the realizations, also known as the performance analysis, for another day.

The information ratio is the expected active return divided by the expected standard deviation of the active return expressed on an annual basis.

6. For example, if our managed US equity portfolio includes 3% positions in Apple and Microsoft, and the S&P 500 includes a 3.7% holding in Apple and a 2.6% holding in Microsoft, then our active portfolio includes a –0.7% position in Apple and a 0.4% position in Microsoft. The managed portfolio is underweight Apple and overweight Microsoft.

$$\text{Information Ratio} \equiv IR \equiv \frac{\alpha}{\omega} \tag{1}$$

The information ratio is a particular measure of *consistency*. The higher the information ratio, the higher the probability that the active return over the next period will be positive.[7] Note that delivering a high information ratio is not the same as delivering a high return. Any manager can take on a high level of active risk and deliver high active returns on occasion. The information ratio measures the delivery of consistent positive active returns—the hallmark of long-term successful active managers.

The information ratio is important for three reasons:

- The information ratio describes the size of the active investment *opportunity set*.
- The information ratio, or rather the information ratio squared, is proportional to a measure of the risk-adjusted *value added* by the active manager.
- As noted above, the information ratio measures consistency. The probability that annual active returns will be positive is roughly equal to the probability that a standard normal random variable is less than the information ratio.[8]

Demonstrating these facts will require a bit of algebra that we will try to keep to a minimum. To start with, we introduce some notation:

- *P* and *Q* refer to active portfolios: *Q* is the ideal portfolio and *P* is a portfolio we might hold.
- α_P, ω_P are the alpha and active risk of portfolio *P* expressed as annual percent.
- IR_P is the information ratio for portfolio *P*:

$$IR_P = \frac{\alpha_P}{\omega_P}. \tag{2}$$

- λ is a penalty for active variance, sometimes called the active risk aversion.
- VA_P is the risk-adjusted value added for portfolio *P*:

$$VA_P = \alpha_P - \left(\frac{\lambda}{2}\right) \cdot \omega_P^2. \tag{3}$$

Based on the manager's information ratio, some (alpha, omega) pairs are feasible, and some are not. If the manager's information ratio is an impressive[9] 1.2, she can deliver 6% active return at 5% risk. She cannot deliver 6% active return at 2% risk.

7. As the information ratio increases, more of the active return probability distribution shifts to the right of zero.

8. This is exact if the active returns are normally distributed and a reasonable estimate in more general cases.

9. After the impact of constraints (which we will discuss later), and after fees and costs, a top quartile long-only portfolio will typically exhibit an information ratio of about 0.5.

The value added introduces investor *preferences*: the trade-off between alpha and omega depends on the risk penalty λ, which varies from investor to investor.

Portfolio Q is ideal in two respects:

- It has the highest possible value added.
- It has the highest possible information ratio.

Exhibit 1 illustrates these properties.

EXHIBIT 1 The Opportunity Set and Value Added

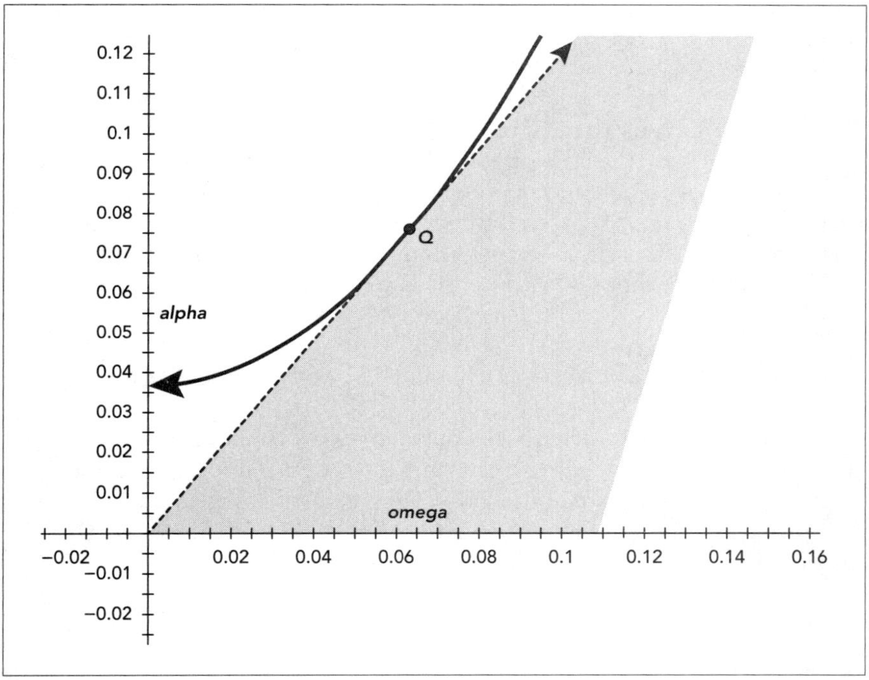

Exhibit 1 displays expected active risk (omega) along the horizontal axis and expected active return (alpha) along the vertical axis. The shaded area is called the *opportunity set*. It consists of the interesting positions that we might choose—all the feasible combinations of alpha and omega. The leading edge of the opportunity set is the dotted line sloping up to the right. The slope of this line is the highest achievable information ratio. For this example, we have selected a very optimistic 1.2 for the information ratio. The index benchmark portfolio sits at the origin in this picture since it, by definition, has no active risk and no alpha.

The curved line moving up and to the right is a line of equal value added. All the alpha and omega choices along this line provide the same value added, in other words, the same alpha with an adjustment for active variance.[10] In particular, on this diagram the risk penalty is $\lambda = 20$, and the value added curve represents a value added of 3.6%. Any investor whose preferences we capture as $\lambda = 20$ will equally value any point along this curve.

This curve touches the opportunity set at the point Q, which means there is a position that provides for that level of value added. If we tried to get more—say, 3.7%—then we would be on a curve parallel to the one in the exhibit but displaced up and to the left. It would not intersect the opportunity set, so while we may desire 3.7%, it is not in the cards.

So we can see that portfolio Q is the unique position with both the highest possible information ratio and the highest value added. In particular,[11]

$$VA_P \leq VA_Q = \frac{IR_Q^2}{2\lambda}. \quad (4)$$

Equation (4) tells us that all investors—from the most to the least risk-averse—are seeking the highest possible information ratio. A very risk-averse investor, given a high λ, will maximize value added by investing in the highest information ratio manager. But that's also true for a risk-tolerant investor, given a low λ. Different investors will differ in how much they invest with that manager, but they will agree on which manager is best.[12]

The Fundamental Law

The information ratio determines our active investment opportunity, and the information ratio squared determines an upper limit in our ability to add value. It seems important to know what determines the size of the information ratio. The answer, provided by the fundamental law, is that the information ratio consists of two ingredients:

- *Skill*, measured by the correlation of our information with returns. We denote this as IC.
- *Breadth*, measured as the annual *rate* at which we obtain uncorrelated information. We denote this as BR.

The fundamental law expresses the information ratio and the potential value added in terms of skill and breadth:

$$IR_Q = IC \cdot \sqrt{BR} \quad (5)$$

$$VA_Q = \frac{IC^2 \cdot BR}{2\lambda} \quad (6)$$

10. The equation for the curve is $\alpha = VA + \left(\frac{\lambda}{2}\right) \cdot \omega^2$.

11. Equation (4) follows from maximizing Equation (3) subject to the constraint that alpha is the information ratio times omega.

12. We are ignoring the fact that different investors may differ in their assessment of the manager's ex ante information ratio.

Note that the relationship between the information ratio and skill and breadth is quite simple.

To see this trade-off between skill and breadth, Exhibit 2 presents various combinations that are all consistent with our ambitious information ratio of 1.2.

EXHIBIT 2 Skill and Breadth Pairs with *IR* = 1.2

SKILL	BREADTH	*IR*
0.03	1600	1.2
0.04	900	1.2
0.05	576	1.2
0.06	400	1.2
0.08	225	1.2
0.10	144	1.2

As we can see, small increases in skill can make up for a large losses in breadth.

It is very important to note that while the fundamental law is an equation, and follows from a mathematical proof, it applies to *all* managers. Quantitative managers may be more aware of the fundamental law, but make no mistake, it applies to every investment manager, regardless of style.

What the Fundamental Law Does Not Say

This section details a few ways in which the results above could be misconstrued. The fundamental law is not a day-to-day management tool. It is a guide to strategic thinking by investment managers, and by potential investors in their products. We can and should use the fundamental law to address the following questions (among others):

- Can this new investment product deliver value to investors?
- How might we improve this existing investment product?
- Will this investment manager deliver strong investment performance going forward?

If the fundamental law were a tool, it would be more earthmoving equipment than diamond cutter. It is useful for some of the heavy lifting but not the precision positioning. The proof of the fundamental law is rife with approximations and assumptions. The most notable of these are complete prior knowledge of the process that generates the information and the covariance of asset returns. The result ignores any enhancement that might arise because our information will reduce the riskiness of the assets. This will be an acceptable approximation at moderate skill levels, say, $IC = 0.10$. As a rough rule, our predictions can decrease forecast risk by a factor of $IC^2 = 0.01$ (e.g., from 5.00% to 4.95%), which we can effectively ignore.

(The proof assumes that $IC^2 << 1$.) We are trying to get a *sense* of the potential information ratio (i.e., looking for a number accurate to within 30%, not three decimal places). We must be mindful that the skill levels we use in its calculation are, at best, guesstimates. Elaborate refinements of crude estimates are delusional.

As mentioned earlier, we are taking an ex ante view. It is possible, indeed worthwhile, to employ this framework for performance analysis. But to make one simple point, to calculate the information ratio ex post requires only the time series of realized active returns. It is easy to calculate their annual mean and standard deviation, and the ratio of those two numbers. We do not need the fundamental law for that.

The fundamental law is not a version of the statistical law of large numbers. This misinterprets both laws. The fundamental law says that more breadth is better if you can maintain the skill level. However, the fundamental law is just as valid with a breadth of 10 as with a breadth of 1,000. The confusion stems from the role of breadth. If you think, incorrectly, of the breadth as the number of assets N and focus on $\sqrt{N}$, then you will be reminded that the standard error in the estimate of a mean by a sample mean decreases with inverse of $\sqrt{N}$.

Last, we need to discuss a bit of semantics. What we have called the information ratio is often called the Sharpe ratio. We like to use the term Sharpe ratio for the ratio of expected total return less risk free return (the *excess return*) to total risk.[13] For example, for the US equity market, if we expect the S&P 500 to return 4.5% for the year, a one-year government bond to return 1%, and the risk of the S&P 500 to be 17.5% annually, then the Sharpe ratio in that case is $(4.5 - 1.0)/17.5 = 0.2$. This determines the feasible expected excess return for each level of total risk.

More on Breadth

When first proposed in 1989, the fundamental law immediately provided useful and valuable strategic insight. However, its dependence on breadth has been a challenge in its interpretation. The information coefficient and the transfer coefficient[14] are both correlations, and hence intuitive to investors and fairly easy to estimate (even if with large error bars). Breadth, originally described as the number of independent forecasts per year, proved to be a more difficult concept to understand or estimate. So, in Grinold and Kahn (2011) (Chapter 5 in this book), we took a closer look at skill and breadth and their dependence on time. In particular, we modeled the flow of information using a simple one-parameter model:

13. If we don't make that distinction we will have two ratios both named the Sharpe ratio, opening the door for confusion.

14. See the next section for more about the transfer coefficient.

$$\begin{Bmatrix}\text{Asset } n\\ \text{alpha at}\\ \text{time } t\end{Bmatrix} = \begin{Bmatrix}\text{Fraction}\\ \text{Retained}\end{Bmatrix} \cdot \begin{Bmatrix}\text{Asset } n\\ \text{alpha at}\\ \text{time } t-\Delta t\end{Bmatrix} + \begin{Bmatrix}\text{New}\\ \text{Information}\\ \text{about asset } n\end{Bmatrix}. \tag{7}$$

$$\alpha_n(t) = e^{-g\cdot\Delta t}\cdot\alpha_n(t-\Delta t) + \tilde{s}_n(t)\cdot\sqrt{\Delta t}$$

We are forecasting active returns for every asset n. The value of old information (our forecast from last period) decreases according to a rate g, as we also receive new information $\tilde{s}_n(t)$. In equilibrium, the arrival rate of new information equals the decay rate of old information. We call g the information arrival rate.[15] If we are applying our skill to N assets, and have an information arrival rate of g, then our breadth is:

$$BR = g \cdot N. \tag{8}$$

Thus, information that helps forecast returns over a short interval will exhibit high breadth. Ideas that play out over several years exhibit low breadth, and we must make up that lower breadth with greater skill in choosing those longer-range positions.

We can also use this model of information flow to estimate the average age of the positions in the ideal portfolio Q. Our forecasts at any time are based on a history of inputs with older inputs gradually (at rate g) losing their relevance. Thus our positions will depend on information that has just arrived, as well as information that arrived yesterday, last week, last month, last quarter, and so forth.[16] It turns out that the average age of information in our forecasts, and hence in portfolio Q is:[17]

$$Age_Q = \frac{1}{g} \tag{9}$$

The Transfer Coefficient

In practice, it is impossible to hold the ideal portfolio Q. That best of all possible portfolios is a moving target. Transactions costs and any constraints on holdings will keep us some distance from that ideal.

15. It is possible to estimate g, although it tends to be noisy. See Grinold (2007) (Chapter 8 in this book) for an example.

16. Starting with Equation (7) and substituting a similar result for $\alpha_n(t-\Delta t)$ as a function of new information at $t-\Delta t$ and the alpha forecast from $t-2\Delta t$, and continuing, we can eventually show that $\alpha_n(t) \Rightarrow \Delta t \cdot \sum_{j=0}^{\infty} e^{-j\cdot g\Delta t}\cdot \tilde{s}(t-j\Delta t)$. So our alphas consist of information that has arrived at various times in the past, decayed based on age.

17. We just saw that our forecasts consist of information of different ages. For example, the information $\tilde{s}(t-j\cdot\Delta t)$ has age $j\cdot\Delta t$. Hence, we can calculate the average age as $Age_Q = \dfrac{\Delta t \cdot \sum_{j=0}^{\infty} e^{-j\cdot g\Delta t}\cdot j\Delta t}{\sum_{j=0}^{\infty} e^{-j\cdot g\Delta t}}$. In the limit as $\Delta t \Rightarrow 0$, we find the result in Equation (9).

Clarke, de Silva, and Thorley (2002) pointed out that the correlation between the active portfolio P and the ideal portfolio Q is an important measure of the quality of implementation. They termed this correlation the *transfer coefficient*. It has three qualities that make it immediately attractive. It is:

- a correlation and thus a familiar concept,
- relatively easily calculated, ex ante with a risk model and ex post using standard statistics,
- a splendid name.

The transfer coefficient, like the information ratio, captures implementation shortfall in two ways. To show this, we need some additional notation:

- $\omega_{P,Q}$ = the forecast covariance between the returns of P and Q.
- $TC_P = \dfrac{\omega_{P,Q}}{\omega_P \cdot \omega_Q}$ = the transfer coefficient, the forecast correlation between the returns of P and Q.

A portfolio's transfer coefficient determines its information ratio, and the transfer coefficient squared puts a limit on a position's ability to add value. For any portfolio P, we have:

$$IR_P = IR_Q \cdot TC_P = IC \cdot \sqrt{BR} \cdot TC_P \quad (10)$$

$$VA_P \leq TC_P^2 \cdot VA_Q \quad (11)$$

The squared term shows the great harm that arises from inefficient implementation. A transfer coefficient of $TC_P = 0.7$ means you have lost more than one half of your ability to add value, and this is *before* subtracting implementation costs and fees from the value added. Exhibit 3 saves about 900 words.

The lower line from the origin shows the leading edge of the opportunity set if we have a transfer coefficient of 0.8. This slices a wedge from the opportunity set. Given that loss of opportunity, the best we can do in terms of value added is to set $\omega_P = TC_P \cdot \omega_Q$, to throttle back our active risk in proportion to the loss of opportunity. In that case the bound on the loss of value added, Equation (11) is tight ($VA_P = TC_P^2 \cdot VA_Q$), so we get 64% of the value added—in this case, 2.3%.

The main sources of drag reducing the transfer coefficient are transactions costs and constraints, most notably the restriction on net-short positions (aka the long-only constraint).[18] Hence we often describe the transfer coefficient as a measure of implementation efficiency—how close our portfolio P is to the ideal portfolio Q.

At the beginning of this essay, we divided the world into just two camps—foxes and hedgehogs—and stated that the fundamental law was for foxes, not hedgehogs. In the real world, with more than just two camps, Equation (10) states that all successful (i.e., high information ratio) active managers need some winning combination of skill, breadth, and efficiency.

18. See Grinold and Kahn (2000), "The Efficiency Gains of Long-Short Investing."

EXHIBIT 3 $TC_P = 0.8, IR_P = 0.96, \omega_P = 4.80\%, \alpha_P = 4.61\%, VA_P = 2.30\%$

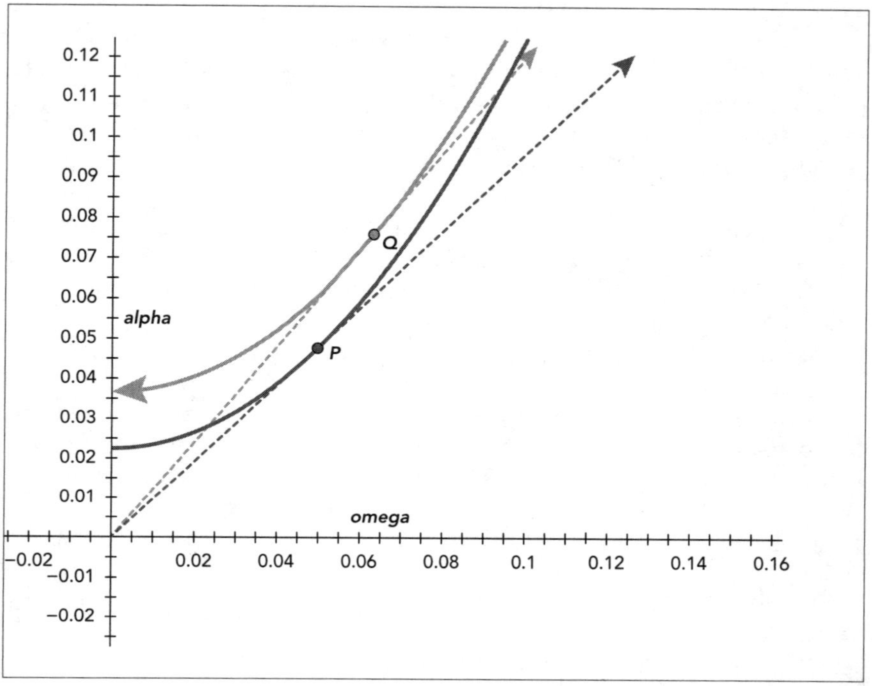

And the more hedgehog-like managers—those with low breadth—need very high levels of skill and efficiency.

In Grinold (2007) (Chapter 8 in this book), the author looks at a special case with no position limits and quadratic transactions costs in order to gain some insight into the effect of cost on the transfer coefficient. That paper proposes a simple trading policy for portfolio *P*. Each period, we compare portfolio *P* to a scaled-back version[19] of portfolio *Q*, and we trade a fraction $d_P \cdot \Delta t$ of the gap. So d_P determines the rate at which we try to close the gap between the scaled-back portfolio *Q* (a moving target) and our less-than-ideal portfolio *P*. As pointed out earlier, $Age_Q = \frac{1}{g}$ is the average age of the information captured by the ideal portfolio *Q*. It turns out that $\frac{1}{d_P}$ measures how far we are behind the curve. In particular:

$$Age_P = \frac{1}{g} + \frac{1}{d_P}. \tag{12}$$

Furthermore, in this simple model, the parameters *g* and d_P determine the transfer coefficient:

19. Because portfolio *Q* is a moving target, the optimal trading strategy aims for a scaled-back (i.e., lower risk, smaller active position) version of portfolio *Q*.

$$TC_P = \sqrt{\frac{Age_Q}{Age_P}} = \sqrt{\frac{d_P}{d_P + g}}. \tag{13}$$

The loss of value added illustrated in Exhibit 3 is all *opportunity cost*. The existence of transactions costs has caused us to slow down trading and be less aggressive. It gets worse when we subtract the cost (direct costs such as bid-ask spread and indirect costs such as market impact) of making the transactions.

Note also that Equation (13) requires d_P to be extremely large, in other words, to trade extremely fast, in order to replicate Q. However, transactions costs will increase with the rate we trade, so we need to balance more efficient implementation against its cost.

Jacobs and Levy (2006, 2007) have looked extensively at the improvements in efficiency gained by easing up on the long-only constraint. A small number of net short positions can provide a large improvement in the transfer coefficient. This is a rough 80-20 rule, where the first 20% of the short positions provide 80% of the improvement. These ideas are behind partial short strategies, sometimes called 120-20 or 130-30 strategies.

Example

As an example, consider how the fundamental law can provide some strategic insight to help invigorate an existing, albeit fairly narrow, multistrategy product. The product currently consists of three separately managed portfolios:

- A long-only portfolio invested in four equity market indices
- A long-only portfolio invested in four bond market indices
- A long-short currency overlay invested in three currencies, from a US dollar perspective

As an existing product, we know its realized information ratio. For this analysis, we are not interested in its historical performance over some particular period, but rather in its expected information ratio on average looking forward.

We can use the fundamental law to understand the expected information ratio of these three portfolios. To apply the fundamental law to the overall multistrategy portfolio, we will assume that the returns to the three portfolios are uncorrelated, and assume that we have optimally allocated capital to those portfolios. In that case, we can calculate the overall information ratio as:

$$IR^2_{Equities} + IR^2_{Bonds} + IR^2_{Currencies} = IR^2_{Total} \tag{14}$$

Exhibit 4 shows a current description of the product. It is our starting point. The numbers are based on history and some preliminary investigation. Some are perfect, like the number of assets. Others are estimates, such as the *IC* based on some research, or the triumph of hope over experience.

EXHIBIT 4 Current Multistrategy Product

	ASSETS	INFORMATION ARRIVAL RATE	BREADTH	SKILL	TRANSFER COEFFICIENT	INFORMATION RATIO	
	N	*g*	*BR*	*IC*	*TC*	*IR*	IR^2
Equities (US, UK, Japan, Europe)	4	1.25	5.0	0.06	0.50	0.07	0.005
Bonds (US, UK, Japan, Europe)	4	0.67	2.7	0.12	0.50	0.10	0.010
Currencies ($, £, ¥, €)	3	1.25	3.8	0.10	0.95	0.18	0.034
Total						**0.22**	**0.05**

We can see from Exhibit 4 that the product's ex ante information ratio is a fairly low 0.22. We are hoping to change the product so that it might achieve an information ratio of 0.5 or higher. How might we do that?

In principle, we have three potential lines of attack:

- We can try to expand breadth by adding new markets. The skill we have developed to forecast four equity markets, for example, should apply to forecasting additional equity markets. The same should be true for our bond market and currency forecasting skill. We may be able to improve breadth by adding some higher turnover information, though we would need to check if this is useful after transactions costs. We can also consider forecasting equity market sector returns and even commodity returns, though we will need to verify that we have forecasting skill in those areas. The difficulty and promise with this approach is that it is new territory that will call for new data sets, a steep learning curve, a new implementation setup, and so on.
- We can improve our implementation efficiency, raising our transfer coefficients, especially for the long-only portfolios. We can switch these to long-short portfolios implemented with futures and forwards, potentially increasing our transfer coefficients quite significantly. This is also new territory, though we already run the currency portfolio long-short.
- We can attempt to improve our level of skill applied to the markets we already forecast. This is often the most difficult line of attack, and in this case, the skill levels already look respectable. Still this is always worth considering, especially as we always need to be researching new ideas, to replace old ideas as their effectiveness decays.

Exhibit 5 shows the potential improvements from these lines of attack.

EXHIBIT 5 Potential Improvements to Current Product

	ASSETS	INFORMATION ARRIVAL RATE	BREADTH	SKILL	TRANSFER COEFFICIENT	INFORMATION RATIO	
	N	*g*	*BR*	*IC*	*TC*	*IR*	IR^2
Equities	14	1.25	17.5	0.06	0.95	0.24	0.057
Sectors	5	1.00	5.0	0.09	0.80	0.16	0.026
Bonds	6	0.67	4.0	0.12	0.95	0.23	0.052
Currencies	10	1.25	12.5	0.10	0.95	0.34	0.113
Commodities	3	2.00	6.0	0.08	0.95	0.17	0.030
Total						**0.53**	**0.28**

It appears that increasing our investment universe of equity, bond, and currency markets, adding equity market sectors and commodities to the mix, and eliminating constraints has the potential to more than double our information ratio, to above our 0.5 target. Of course, we have yet to demonstrate that these changes will actually work. But this example already demonstrates how the fundamental law and its extensions can frame this strategic discussion.

Other Research Directions

We have already described two important fundamental law improvements. Our work defining breadth concretely as the information arrival rate times the number of assets provided a significant improvement in clarity. And the transfer coefficient elegantly extended the fundamental law to handle real portfolios managed with constraints and in the presence of transactions costs.

There are two potential directions for future research on the fundamental law. One is to help investors apply the fundamental law in specific cases. For example, how do we use the fundamental law to help design or reorganize a fundamental investment process?

The second potential direction for future research is to attempt to relax some of the assumptions that underlie the proof of the fundamental law. We are not optimistic about this direction, as in our observation it quickly loses the simplicity of the fundamental law in exchange for only the appearance of increased accuracy. In our view, the fundamental law is sufficiently accurate to provide the strategic insight and perspective for which it was designed.

Conclusion

We have attempted to describe the fundamental law of active management, its importance, and its place in thinking about investment management products. We also highlighted two useful adjuncts: the role of an information arrival rate in calculating breadth, and the transfer coefficient in limiting our opportunities and our ability to add value. Over time, this simple relationship, decomposing the information ratio into three components—skill, breadth, and efficiency—has provided considerable strategic insight into investment strategies.

References

Berlin, Isaiah. 1953. *The Hedgehog and the Fox: An Essay on Tolstoy's View of History.* London: Weidenfeld & Nicholson.

Clarke, Roger, Harindra de Silva, and Steven Thorley. 2002. "Portfolio Constraints and the Fundamental Law of Active Management." *Financial Analysts Journal* 58 (September/October).

Grinold, Richard C. 1989. "The Fundamental Law of Active Management." *Journal of Portfolio Management* 15 (Spring): 30–37; and Chapter 11 in *Managing Institutional Assets*, edited by Frank J. Fabozzi, 225–43. New York: Ballinger, 1990.

Grinold, Richard C. 2007. "Dynamic Portfolio Analysis." *Journal of Portfolio Management* 34 (Fall): 12–26.

Grinold, Richard C., and Ronald N. Kahn. 2000. *Active Portfolio Management: Quantitative Theory and Applications.* 2nd ed. New York: McGraw-Hill.

Grinold, Richard C., and Ronald N. Kahn. 2000. "The Efficiency Gains of Long-Short Investing." *Financial Analysts Journal* 56 (November/December): 40–53.

Grinold, Richard C., and Ronald N. Kahn. 2011. "Breadth, Skill and Time." *Journal of Portfolio Management* 38 (Fall): 18–28.

Jacobs, Bruce I., and Kenneth N. Levy. 2006. "Enhanced Active Equity Strategies." *Journal of Portfolio Management*, Spring, 45–55.

Jacobs, Bruce I., and Kenneth N. Levy. 2007. "20 Myths about Enhanced Active 120-20 Strategies." *Financial Analysts Journal* 63 (July/August): 19–26.

Lewis, Michael. 2011. *The Big Short.* New York: W.W. Norton.

Silver, Nate. 2012. *The Signal and the Noise: Why So Many Predictions Fail—but Some Don't.* New York: Penguin Press.

Tetlock, Philip E., and Dan Gardner. 2015. *Superforecasting.* New York: Broadway Books.

5

Breadth, Skill, and Time[1]

The fundamental law of active management (Grinold 1989) relates managers' level and breadth of skill to their potential to deliver risk-adjusted returns to clients. The drivers of this relationship are:

- The information coefficient, or *IC*, which is the average correlation between forecasts and outcomes,
- The *breadth* of skill, or *BR*, which is the opportunity to diversify across independent investment decisions, over the course of a year.

The relationship between these drivers and the manager's potential information ratio, which is the expected annualized exceptional return per unit of risk, is:

$$IR \approx IC \cdot \sqrt{BR} \tag{1}$$

The symbol ≈ indicates that this is an approximation and strongly suggests that the purpose of the relationship is to provide a strategic link between expected performance and the causes of that ability to add value. The formula provides more of a perspective than a prescription. It tells us how to think about the issue without telling us what to do.

Equation (1) has had considerable impact over the 30 years since Grinold's (1989) work was first published. Although we can measure some of the article's impact in citations, follow-on papers, and proposed embellishments, more generally the relationship between skill, breadth, and information ratio pervades the interactions between investors, managers, and consultants. As investors have focused on this relationship, they have had to confront a disparity between its three terms. Equation (1) describes an ex ante relationship,

1. This article originally appeared as "Breadth, Skill, and Time" by Richard C. Grinold and Ronald N. Kahn in the Fall 2011 edition of the *Journal of Portfolio Management*.

But the realized IR and IC can easily be measured ex post. Hence these are concrete concepts even ex ante.

Breadth is different. The number of independent decisions per year is not the same thing as the number of portfolio holdings. There is a connection, but it can depend on manager style and process. Not all the holdings reflect independent decisions. The "per year" qualifier means that breadth is a rate and grows linearly with time. The number of holdings is not a rate. Without doubt, breadth is the weak link in investor understanding of Equation (1).

The original proof of the relationship doesn't go very far in helping investors understand breadth. Beyond its mathematical sophistication—which limits accessibility for most investors—it uses a framework of single-period analysis that glosses over the dynamics. There is no logical flaw in the proof; it just doesn't provide much help in understanding breadth.

The goal of this paper, then, is to examine the fundamental law of active management in the context of a dynamic model in order to provide much more insight into breadth, as well as a refined notion of skill. This dynamic model makes three reasonable yet simplifying assumptions:

1. The forecasting power of information decays exponentially at one known rate, g. Thus, all information that is t years old retains a fraction e^{-gt} of its original forecasting power.
2. The investment process is in equilibrium so that old information decaying and new information arriving are in balance. Hence information arrives at the same rate g, which we call the *information turnover rate.*
3. The portfolio manager understands the dynamic nature of the information process and uses that knowledge to make optimal asset return forecasts.

In this article, we ignore the impact of constraints and costs on information ratios. Clarke, de Silva, and Thorley (2002) introduced the transfer coefficient, or TC—the correlation between a real portfolio (influenced by constraints and costs) and the idealized paper portfolio (constructed without constraints or costs)—and they amended Equation (1) to account for this as follows:

$$IR_P = TC_P \cdot IR \approx TC_P \cdot IC \cdot \sqrt{BR} \tag{2}$$

Equation (2) is an important real-world improvement, and it allows for the consideration of a research budget in terms of trade-offs among increasing skill, increasing breadth, and improving implementation efficiency. In this article, we ignore the transfer coefficient because its contribution focuses on breadth and skill.[2]

The main result of the article is easy to state. If g is the rate of information turnover, and there are N assets, then the breadth is:

$$BR = g \cdot N. \tag{3}$$

2. A related paper, Grinold (2007) (Chapter 8 in this book), shows how the transfer coefficient is determined by the information turnover rate g and a second parameter that measures the rate of portfolio turnover.

We will show how to measure g for any investment process.

A second result of the analysis is a tighter definition of skill. The correlation between a forecast and the subsequent return depends on the horizon of that return. According to our model, the IC depends on two parameters—the information turnover rate g and an effective skill level, κ—and the dynamic version of the fundamental law states:

$$IR \approx \kappa \cdot \sqrt{g \cdot N}. \tag{4}$$

With these results now stated, we will present the two essential components of our model. The first comes from taking a closer look at the relationship between the IC and the time horizon. The second constructs an equilibrium information process that allows for the arrival of new information to balance decay of old information. These components connect to provide a bottom-up view of the ex ante information ratio. The models behind these results are technical and have partly been relegated to the Appendices.[3]

For the most part, in this article we use the terms *alpha* and *information ratio* loosely. Our forecasts include a benchmark (market) timing component as well as a residual component. In a strict sense, the terms *alpha* and *information ratio* apply only to residuals, however we think the added level of refinement does not merit the extra burden of notation and complexity. For purists, Appendix C describes the procedure for separating the benchmark timing and residual components.

This work has its roots in the fundamental law article by Grinold (1989) and a recent paper on dynamic portfolio analysis (Grinold 2007; Chapter 8 in this book). Other interesting variations on this theme can be found in the work of Clarke, de Silva, and Thorley (2002), Buckle (2004), Qian and Hua (2004), and Ye (2008).

Understanding Information Turnover

Given the central importance of information turnover to our model, we start by defining it, discussing how to estimate it, and providing an example of its connection to breadth.

If we have a history of forecast asset alphas, defined as the annualized forecasts of exceptional return, then it is possible to infer an implied rate of decay in the forecasting power of those alphas. Let's suppose there are N assets in the investment universe and we receive fresh information every Δt years. In our examples in this article, we assume weekly updates, so that $\Delta t = 1/52$.

3. In Appendix A, we construct a model for the correlation of a forecast with return over any time horizon. Appendix A treats one asset and a single forecast. In Appendix B, we consider a general number of assets and sources of information. We go into some detail to build the information flow process (in three layers!) from the bottom up. We employ the information flow in a forecast of exceptional return using the best linear unbiased estimator rule. In Appendix C, we take the forecasts developed in Appendix B and show how they determine the information ratio. Appendix C also derives a portfolio-based interpretation of the results.

We denote the alpha for asset n at time $j \cdot \Delta t$ as $\alpha_n(j)$, and at time $(j-1) \cdot \Delta t$ as $\alpha_n(j-1)$. The information contained in each alpha forecast decays at the information turnover rate g and is replaced by new information. So, we expect:

$$\alpha_n(j) = \gamma \cdot \alpha_n(j-1) + \varepsilon_n(j). \tag{5}$$

The term $\gamma \equiv e^{-g \cdot \Delta t}$ captures the information decay (the one-period-old forecast has less to say about this period's return), and $\varepsilon_n(j)$ represents the new information arriving over period Δt. The new information, by virtue of being new, is uncorrelated with $\alpha_n(j-1)$ and has an expected value of zero.

Note that Equation (5) has the form of a cross-sectional regression we can use to estimate the information turnover rate.[4] The regression coefficient, γ, depends on Δt. In any actual implementation, the estimated γ will vary from period to period; think earnings season. However, one can get a general idea by performing this regression over multiple periods.[5] On average the coefficient gamma will be positive and less than one. We can then estimate the continuous rate of change in the alphas as:

$$g = \frac{-\ln\{\gamma\}}{\Delta t}. \tag{6}$$

We can apply this technique—and estimate g—for any investment process with a history of return forecasts.

It is often intuitive to express this information turnover rate, g, in terms of an information turnover half-life, HL, which is the time in years for the signal to lose one-half of its forecasting power. The link between g and the half-life HL is:

$$e^{-g \cdot \Delta t} \equiv \left(\frac{1}{2}\right)^{\frac{\Delta t}{HL}}, \tag{7}$$

Hence:

$$HL = \frac{\ln\{2\}}{g} \approx \frac{0.693}{g}. \tag{8}$$

In our examples in this article, we will assume an information turnover half-life of three months, $HL=0.25$, equivalent to an information turnover rate, $g = 2.77$. For weekly data, this corresponds to regression coefficient $\gamma = 0.948$.

This method of estimating the information turnover rate is *implicit* in that it depends completely on the change in forecasts over time. There is an important related calculation that can directly determine the relationship between the forecasts and realized returns at various horizons. We first associate the forecasts in each period with an ideal portfolio that has the greatest

4. If V is the N by N predicted covariance of the assets then we calculate the regression coefficient gamma as $\gamma = \frac{\alpha'(j-1) \cdot V^{-1} \cdot \alpha(j)}{\alpha'(j-1) \cdot V^{-1} \cdot \alpha(j-1)}$, guaranteeing $\alpha'(j-1) \cdot V^{-1} \cdot \varepsilon(j) = 0$.

5. This type of study is a valuable diagnostic in a more general sense because it may uncover changes, perhaps unintended and unnoticed, in the alpha-generating process.

forecast return per unit of forecast risk. Then we look at the performance of that portfolio for as many future periods as we have in the data set. For example, with three years of weekly data for both forecasts and returns, we will have 156 ideal portfolios, one for each week. There are 155 ideal portfolio returns in a first week, 154 ideal portfolio returns in a second week, and 104 estimates of ideal portfolio returns after 52 weeks, and so forth. These statistics allow us to calculate a correlation of forecasts and returns at various horizons, and a decay rate in that forecasting power. The results will typically be extremely noisy, so we recommend ocular regression and commonsense priors. The important point is that the actual rate of decay of the forecasting power should be the same (i.e., roughly similar to) the implied rate of information turnover in the forecasts if we are to live up to our assumption that the portfolio manager understands the information process and uses that knowledge to make optimal forecasts of return.[6]

Example

Now let's consider a crude example to provide at least an intuitive link between the information turnover rate and the concept of breadth. More breadth means more insights per year, and more insights per year must mean a greater rate of change in the alphas. Our example includes N assets. In each period, L of the assets—selected randomly—receive a complete refresh of information. The remaining $N - L$ assets have no change in their return forecasts. So:

$$\alpha_n(j) = \begin{Bmatrix} \text{new with probability } \dfrac{L}{N} \\ \\ \text{no change with probability } \dfrac{N-L}{L} \end{Bmatrix} \tag{9}$$

For $N = 300$ and $L = 16$, there is a 5.33% chance of a new alpha and 94.67% chance of no change each week.

We do not know beforehand which assets will receive an information refresh, and we do not know if the new information will be positive or negative. The technical way to say this is that the new information has expected value zero and is uncorrelated with the prior period's alpha. The expected alpha at time $j \cdot \Delta t$ given the alpha at time $(j-1) \cdot \Delta t$ is then:

$$\mathrm{E}\left\langle \alpha_n(j) \middle| \alpha_n(j-1) \right\rangle = \frac{N-L}{N} \cdot \alpha_n(j-1). \tag{10}$$

It is straightforward to calculate breadth in this case. There are $1/\Delta t$ periods per year. We receive L independent information refreshes per period. Thus, the breadth is:

6. More than you may want to know about this can be found in Appendix B.

$$BR = \frac{L}{\Delta t}. \tag{11}$$

For our numerical example, we have $BR = 16 / \{1/52\} = 832$.

It is also clear by looking at Equations (5) and (10) that:

$$\gamma = \frac{N - L}{N} = 1 - \frac{L}{N}. \tag{12}$$

If $g \cdot \Delta t$ is relatively small, we also have:

$$\gamma = e^{-g \cdot \Delta t} \approx 1 - g \cdot \Delta t. \tag{13}$$

For example, if $g = 2.77$ and $\Delta t = 1/52$, we have $\gamma = 0.9481$ and $1 - g \cdot \Delta t = 0.9467$. Combining Equations (12) and (13) with (11), we find the result promised in Equation (3):

$$BR = \frac{L}{\Delta t} \approx g \cdot N. \tag{14}$$

This argument is a proof by example.[7] To get a more general and robust view of breadth we must, somewhat paradoxically, take a deeper look at the *IC*, in particular, the interaction of the *IC* and time.

The Relationship Between the *IC* and Time

We will explore the links between the *IC* and time by looking at the simplest possible situation: we have one asset, and we have a store of information available at time zero that will help forecast future returns. We summarize that store of information in a score, $\tilde{s}$, which is just the alpha rescaled to have a standard deviation of one. The *IC* is the correlation of that score with future exceptional returns.

We would like to know how the correlation of the score with the asset's return varies if we measure the correlation over different time periods (e.g., the next hour, today, this week, next week, this month, or next year). If we let $\theta(\tau, t)$ be the asset's return from time τ to time t, then we are looking for the correlation, $\rho(\tau, t)$, between the return $\theta(\tau, t)$ and the forecast. To develop a theoretical model for this correlation, we make two notable assumptions:

1. Returns are additive.[8] If we have times τ and t, where $0 < \tau < t$, then $\theta(0, t) = \theta(0, \tau) + \theta(\tau, t)$.

7. Grinold and Kahn (2000) provided the example of a stock picker who follows 100 stocks and revises assessments quarterly, for a breadth of 400. If we run cross-sectional regressions (Equation (5)) T times per year, with $T >> 4$), we will find $\gamma = 1$ most of the time, and $\gamma = 0$ for those quarterly revisions, for an average $\gamma = (T - 4)/T$. For large T, we estimate g very close to 4, and hence breadth very close to 400. This information turnover analysis agrees with that prior analysis.

8. This assumption can either be considered an approximation, or one could define the return as the log of the asset's total return over the period less the log of some beta adjusted benchmark return.

2. The forecasting power declines exponentially with time at rate g. So for τ and t, where $0 < \tau < t$, we have $\rho(\tau,t) = e^{-g\cdot\tau} \cdot \rho(0, t-\tau)$.

The returns have zero mean and an annual standard deviation (ω), and are serially uncorrelated:

$$\begin{aligned} &(i.) \quad \mathbb{E}\left\langle\tilde{\theta}(\tau,t)\right\rangle = 0 \quad \text{for all } 0<\tau<t, \\ &(ii.) \quad \mathbb{E}\left\langle\tilde{\theta}^2(\tau,t)\right\rangle = \omega^2 \cdot (t-\tau) \quad \text{for all } 0<\tau<t \text{ and} \\ &(iii.) \quad \mathbb{E}\left\langle\tilde{\theta}(0,\tau)\cdot\tilde{\theta}(\tau,t)\right\rangle = 0 \text{ if } 0<\tau<t. \end{aligned} \tag{15}$$

Now consider a score, $\tilde{s}$, available at time zero, with the following properties:

$$\begin{aligned} &(i.) \quad \mathbb{E}\left\langle\tilde{s}\right\rangle = 0, \\ &(ii.) \quad \mathbb{E}\left\langle\tilde{s}^2\right\rangle = 1, \\ &(iii.) \quad \mathbb{E}\left\langle\theta(\tau,t)\cdot\tilde{s}\right\rangle = \omega\cdot\sqrt{t-\tau}\cdot\rho(\tau,t) \end{aligned} \tag{16}$$

Since $\tilde{\theta}(0,t) = \tilde{\theta}(0,\tau) + \tilde{\theta}(\tau,t)$, we have:

$$\mathbb{COV}\left\langle\tilde{\theta}(0,t),\tilde{s}\right\rangle = \mathbb{COV}\left\langle\tilde{\theta}(0,\tau),\tilde{s}\right\rangle + \mathbb{COV}\left\langle\tilde{\theta}(\tau,t),\tilde{s}\right\rangle \tag{17}$$

But because we know the variances of the returns over different horizons, we can rewrite Equation (17) as:

$$\begin{aligned} &\omega\cdot\sqrt{t}\cdot\rho(0,t) = \omega\cdot\sqrt{\tau}\cdot\rho(0,\tau) + \omega\cdot\sqrt{t-\tau}\cdot\rho(\tau,t) \\ &\rho(0,t) = \sqrt{\frac{\tau}{t}}\cdot\rho(0,\tau) + \sqrt{\frac{t-\tau}{t}}\cdot\rho(\tau,t). \end{aligned} \tag{18}$$

Now, invoking the previously mentioned assumption that the forecasting power decays exponentially, Equation (18) becomes:

$$\rho(0,t) = \sqrt{\frac{\tau}{t}}\cdot\rho(0,\tau) + \sqrt{\frac{t-\tau}{t}}\cdot e^{-g\cdot\tau}\cdot\rho(0,t-\tau). \tag{19}$$

The solution of Equation (19) is:

$$\rho(0,t) = \hat{\kappa}\cdot\left\{\frac{1-e^{-g\cdot t}}{\sqrt{g\cdot t}}\right\}. \tag{20}$$

This is the *IC* as a function of the return horizon. Exhibit 1 displays this graphically. Over the time period from 0 to t, the *IC* depends on two parameters: the information turnover rate, g, and a measure of skill, $\hat{\kappa}$.

The functional form of the *IC* is that measure of skill multiplying a function dependent only on $g\cdot t$. When $g\cdot t$ is small, say, $g\cdot t \le 0.05$, the *IC* is approximately $\hat{\kappa}\cdot\sqrt{g\cdot t}$. It then increases to a maximum of $\hat{\kappa}\cdot 0.638$ when $g\cdot t \approx 1.26$.[9] From there, it decreases asymptotically to zero. When the $g\cdot t$ is large, say, $g\cdot t \ge 4$, the *IC* is approximately $\frac{\hat{\kappa}}{\sqrt{g\cdot t}}$.

9. Another way to say this, the correlation hits its maximum at 1.8 times the signal's half-life, *HL*.

EXHIBIT 1 Correlation (*IC*) of Forecast and Return

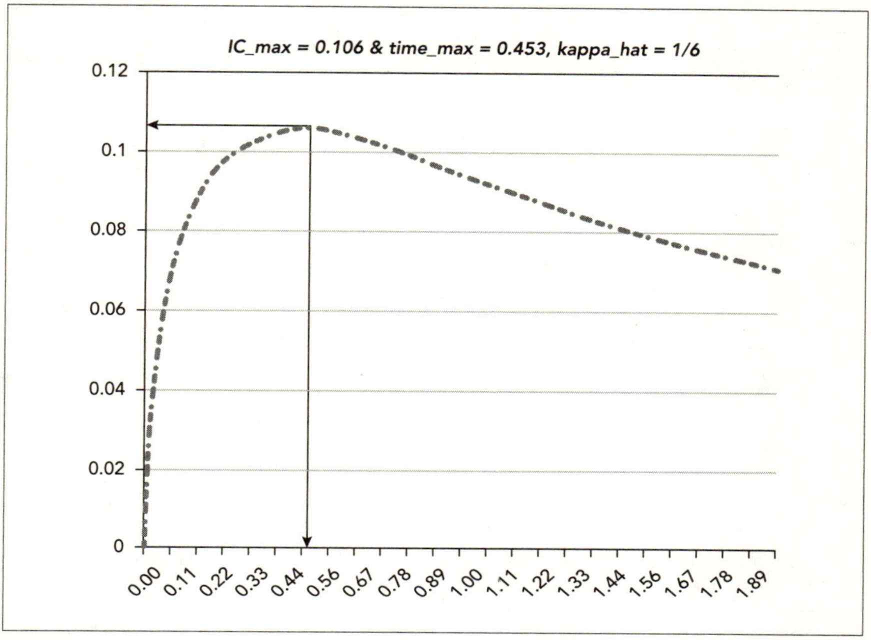

Note: The maximum *IC* of 0.106 and the time the maximum occurs, 0.453 years, are marked by arrows.

The maximum *IC* is directly proportional to the skill level. In other words, more skill means a higher maximum *IC*. The time the maximum *IC* occurs is inversely proportional to the information turnover rate (i.e., rapidly aging information peaks sooner). Higher skill stretches the curve in the vertical dimension, and a higher information turnover rate compresses the curve along the horizontal dimension.

Why does the correlation increase for a while as the return horizon increases, and then decrease after that? The competing influences are the exponential information decay and the increasing volatility of return with horizon. The information decays exponentially over time. Initially, as we increase the horizon, we are adding return that the signal can forecast, and this dominates the increase in return volatility. The correlation eventually decays asymptotically over time, because the score has little to no information about more and more of the return.

Exhibits 2 and 3 show the correlation function $\rho(0,t)$ over a period of two years. Exhibit 2 displays its behavior using a fixed half-life of 0.25 years, thus $g = 2.77$, while varying the skill level, $\hat{\kappa}$. Exhibit 3 fixes the skill level, $\hat{\kappa}$, while varying the half-life from 0.125 years ($g = 5.55$) to 0.5 years ($g = 1.39$).

Consistent with our discussion of its functional form, Exhibit 2 shows how the skill parameter scales the correlation level in the vertical direction, and Exhibit 3 shows how the information turnover rate controls the manner in which the correlation plays out with time.

EXHIBIT 2 Correlation (*IC*) of Forecast and Return

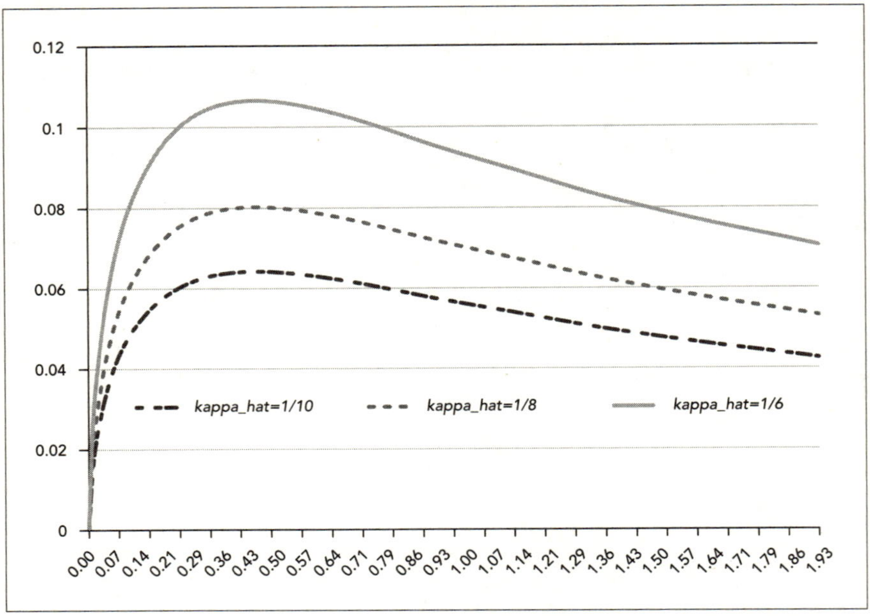

Note: The half-life is fixed at three months ($g = 2.77$) and the various skill levels are 1/6 (high), 1/8 (medium), and 1/10 (low).

EXHIBIT 3 Correlation (*IC*) of Forecast and Return

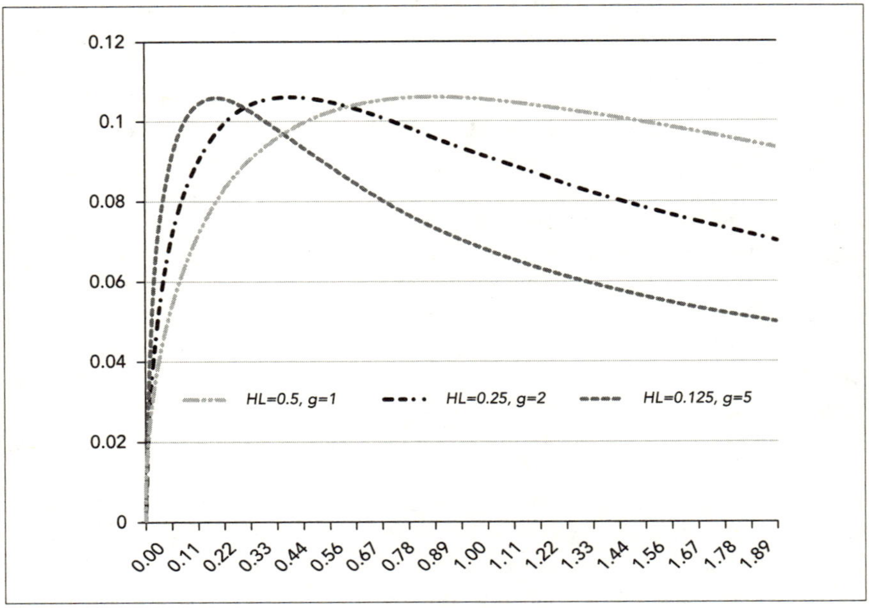

Note: Various half-lives and the same skill level, $\tilde{\kappa}$, fixed at 1/6.

A simulation of the model confirms the results. The simulation varies underlying skill levels and rates of information decay. In each case, we calculated $\rho(0,t)$ for t up to two years. Each simulation includes 10,000 samples, so the standard error for any correlation is still a relatively large ± 0.01.[10] Exhibit 4 displays the results.

EXHIBIT 4 Theoretical and Simulated Results for the Correlations $\rho(0, t)$

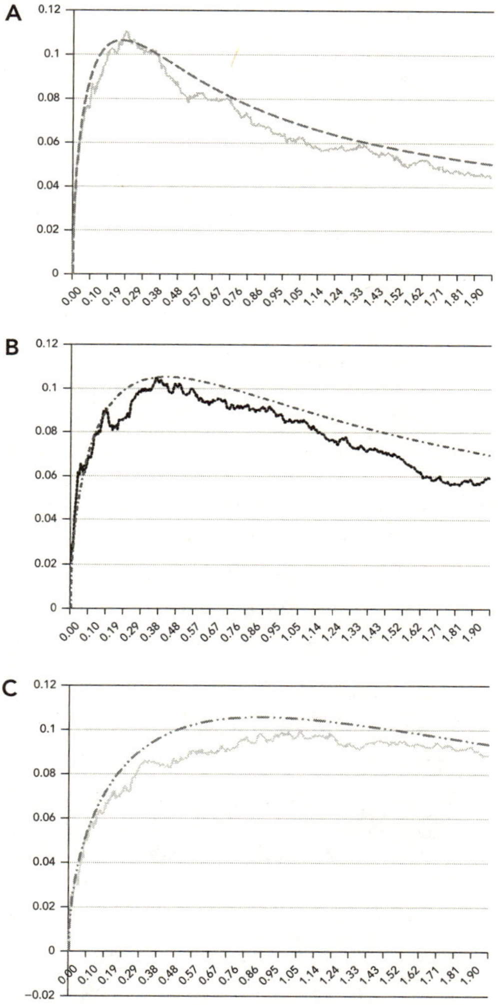

The charts have the same vertical and horizontal scales. All three cases have the same skill levels of 1/6. The chart in Panel A is for a relatively fast signal $HL = 0.125$ years, the chart in Panel B is for the base case, $HL = 0.25$ years, and the chart in Panel C is for a relatively slow signal, $HL = 0.5$. Compare these with the cases illustrated in Exhibit 3.

---

10. The standard error of a correlation with S samples is approximately $1/\sqrt{s}$ for correlations near zero. The errors are correlated by cumulating the returns, so if the estimate of $\rho(0,t)$ is low, then the estimate for $\rho(0,t+\Delta t)$ will most likely be low as well.

The Update Cycle and Effective Skill

The preceding discussion considers a store of information available at time zero that was not refreshed with new information. Now we will examine a model of information flow in which new information arrives continuously. We periodically refresh/update our return forecasts based on the decay of the old information and the arrival of the new. Using Equation (20), the correlation of information available at time zero with the return in the period until the next information update is:

$$\rho(0,\Delta t) = \hat{\kappa} \cdot \left\{ \frac{1 - e^{-g \cdot \Delta t}}{\sqrt{g \cdot \Delta t}} \right\}$$
$$\Rightarrow \rho(0,\Delta t) = \hat{\kappa} \cdot \left\{ \frac{1 - e^{-g \cdot \Delta t}}{g \cdot \Delta t} \right\} \cdot \sqrt{g \cdot \Delta t} \tag{21}$$

Now, we define κ as an *effective skill level*:

$$\kappa \equiv \hat{\kappa} \cdot \left\{ \frac{1 - e^{-g \cdot \Delta t}}{g \cdot \Delta t} \right\} \tag{22}$$

The effective skill depends on the skill $\hat{\kappa}$ and the product $g \cdot \Delta t$. Note that the effective skill κ is less than the skill level $\hat{\kappa}$ and that they are approximately equal when $g \cdot \Delta t$ is small. Think of $\hat{\kappa}$ as the skill level we could achieve with continuous updating and κ as a reduced skill level because we are using periodic updating (i.e., there is a loss in efficiency due to the periodic updates). The effective skill level will be 99% of $\hat{\kappa}$ if $\Delta t \le 0.034 \cdot HL$ and 95% of $\hat{\kappa}$ if $\Delta t \le 0.145 \cdot HL$. In the base case with a weekly update cycle, and a three-month half-life, the effective skill is 97.4% of the potential skill. Thus, the loss in skill is relatively modest if the update cycle is, say, 10% of the half-life of the information. Exhibit 5 displays $\hat{\kappa} / \kappa$ for various half-lives and update cycles.

EXHIBIT 5 Ratio Between the Potential and Effective Skill Levels as a Function of Information Half-Life and Frequency of Updates

HL	*1 DAY*	*1 WEEK*	*1 MONTH*	*1 QUARTER*	*6 MONTHS*	*1 YEAR*
g	174.70	36.0	8.32	2.77	1.39	0.693
Δ*t* 15 minutes	0.988	0.997	0.999	1.000	1.000	1.000
Δ*t* one hour	0.952	0.990	0.998	0.999	1.000	1.000
Δ*t* one day	0.721	0.932	0.984	0.995	0.997	0.999
Δ*t* one week	0.287	0.721	0.924	0.974	0.987	0.993
Δ*t* one month	0.069	0.316	0.721	0.893	0.944	0.972
Δ*t* one quarter	0.023	0.111	0.421	0.721	0.845	0.918

Note: The information's half-life, *HL*, is given in the columns, and the frequency of updates, Δ*t*, is given in the rows. Results are based on 252 trading days per year and seven hours of trading per trading day.

As noted, in equilibrium, the rate at which information decays is also the rate at which it is replenished. If we have rapid information turnover, say the half-life is one week, then an update each week will not be terribly effective. According to Exhibit 5, we will only capture 72.1% of the potential skill. On the one hand, if we update more frequently, say, daily, then we achieve 93.2% efficiency, while hourly updates capture 99% of the skill. On the other hand, consider our base case with $HL = 0.25$ and weekly updates. The efficiency is 97.4%. A move to daily updates will push this to 99.5%. Any further increases in the frequency of updates will have minuscule added benefits.

We combine Equation (21) and Equation (22) to write the correlation as:

$$\rho(0, \Delta t) = \kappa \cdot \sqrt{g} \cdot \sqrt{\Delta t}. \tag{23}$$

We have omitted the dependence of κ on $\hat{\kappa}$, as well as the product of the decay rate of information, g, and length of the update cycle, Δt. This provides a cleaner notation, but bear in mind that ultimately the effective skill κ depends on the product $g \cdot \Delta t$ as per Equation (22).

As a practical matter, the sensitivity of the effective skill to changes in the decay rate is miniscule. For example, in the base case with weekly updates and $g = 2.77$, a 10% increase in g will result in only a one-fourth of 1% decrease in the effective skill κ. This slight decrease in the effective skill is a loss in efficiency caused by a faster flow of information (g increased by 10%) with no compensating shortening of the update cycle (Δt fixed at 1/52).

However, despite the small impact of the 10% increase in the flow rate on the effective skill, the overall effect of that 10% increase in information flow is a sizable 4.6% increase in the correlation $\rho(0, \Delta t)$ over the update cycle.

The Equilibrium Information Process

Now that we have a detailed understanding of the relationship between the *IC* and time, we turn our attention to the equilibrium information process where new information arrives in each update cycle to make up for the decay of the prior information over that update cycle. Exhibit 6 (tracking one source and one asset) attempts to depict the spirit of the process. We relegate the details of the more general analysis (*N* asset returns and *M* sources of information) to Appendix B.

The challenge is to define the elementary building blocks of information, and then assemble them to produce a sequence of signals. As mentioned before, this description will require three layers. Each cell in Exhibit 6 containing an asterisk (*) or an X represents a random morsel of information that is one elementary part of the process. These morsels are the bottom layer.

The following rules govern this process:

1. The information in each cell is uncorrelated with the information in every other cell.

EXHIBIT 6 Schematic for the Information Flow Process

		Period About Which Information Pertains																				
Information Arrival Period	...	j–9	j–8	j–7	j–6	j–5	j–4	j–3	j–2	j–1	j	j+1	j+2	j+3	j+4	j+5	j+6	j+7	j+8	j+9	j+10	j+11	...
	⋮	⋮	⋮	⋮	⋮	⋮	⋮	⋮	⋮	⋮	⋮	⋮	⋮	⋮	⋮	⋮	⋮	⋮	⋮	⋮	⋮	⋮	⋮
	j–9	*	*	*	*	*	*	*	*	*	X	*	*	*	*	*	*	*	*	*	*	*	...
	j–8		*	*	*	*	*	*	*	*	X	*	*	*	*	*	*	*	*	*	*	*	...
	j–7			*	*	*	*	*	*	*	X	*	*	*	*	*	*	*	*	*	*	*	...
	j–6				*	*	*	*	*	*	X	*	*	*	*	*	*	*	*	*	*	*	...
	j–5					*	*	*	*	*	X	*	*	*	*	*	*	*	*	*	*	*	...
	j–4						*	*	*	*	X	*	*	*	*	*	*	*	*	*	*	*	...
	j–3							*	*	*	X	*	*	*	*	*	*	*	*	*	*	*	...
	j–2								*	*	X	*	*	*	*	*	*	*	*	*	*	*	...
	j–1									*	X	*	*	*	*	*	*	*	*	*	*	*	...
	j										X	*	*	*	*	*	*	*	*	*	*	*	...

2. New information arrives every period. Row $j - k$ represents the *new* information that arrives in the update period from time $(j - k - 1) \cdot \Delta t$ to time $(j - k) \cdot \Delta t$.
3. Each period, we receive new information about all subsequent periods. Column $j + i$ represents information about the return in the period starting at time $(j + i) \cdot \Delta t$. All the cells marked with an X pertain to the return in period j.
4. We measure the amount of information in each cell by its standard deviation. Information arriving at time t is more valuable for predicting returns from t to $t + \Delta t$ than returns from $t + \Delta t$ to $t + 2\Delta t$. The standard deviation decreases geometrically at rate γ as we move away from the diagonal. Thus, the information in row $j - 6$ and column j has a standard deviation that is γ^6 times the standard deviation of the information in row j and column j. Both morsels contain information about period j (hence they are both in column j). The information that arrives at the beginning of period j has more value than the information that arrived six periods earlier. Exhibit 6 illustrates this by showing the size of the information morsels shrinking as we move away from the diagonal.
5. The correlation of the information in row k and column i with the return in period j is zero if $i \neq j$ and it is $\kappa \cdot \sqrt{g} \cdot \sqrt{\Delta t}$ (see Equation (23)) if $i = j$.
6. Asset returns in each period are uncorrelated with asset returns in other periods.

All of the nuggets of information pertaining to return in period j are in column j of Exhibit 6 and marked with an X. As explained earlier, they have less forecasting power as they get older (as we move up column j). If life were perfect, we could just add up the bits in column j of the chart and thus isolate all the past information about the return in period j. Alas, there is one more rule in this game. We only observe the sum of the information in each row. In period $j - 8$ we receive the sum of all the cells in row $j - 8$. In period

$j-7$ we receive the sum of all the cells in row $j-7$, and so on. The fact that information only arrives in these sums is the second layer of our information process. So, the information we need to forecast period j's return (i.e., everything in column j) is included in—and obscured by—the row sums. We have to do the best we can, given that limitation. We end up with a best forecast that is *proportional* to:[11]

$$\begin{Bmatrix} \text{Period } j\text{'s} \\ \text{Signal} \end{Bmatrix} = \{\text{New Info } j\} + \gamma \cdot \{\text{New Info } j-1\} + \gamma^2 \cdot \{\text{New Info } j-2\} + \cdots. \quad (24)$$

In Equation (24), the expression New Info j means the jth row sum. Equation (24) shows the third layer of our information process: our forecast for the stock is an exponentially weighted average of the information that has arrived over time.

This rule is consistent with Equation (5), since the rule in Equation (24) also means that:

$$\begin{Bmatrix} \text{Period } j\text{'s} \\ \text{Signal} \end{Bmatrix} = \gamma \cdot \begin{Bmatrix} \text{Period } (j-1)\text{'s} \\ \text{Signal} \end{Bmatrix} + \{\text{New Info } j\}. \quad (25)$$

Finally, we can rearrange Equation (25) to illustrate the notion of information depletion and replenishment:

$$\begin{Bmatrix} \text{Change in Signal} \\ (j-1) \text{ to } j \end{Bmatrix} = \{\text{New Info } j\} - \{1-\gamma\} \cdot \begin{Bmatrix} \text{Period } (j-1)\text{'s} \\ \text{Signal} \end{Bmatrix}. \quad (26)$$

Equation (26) captures the important notion of inflow and outflow. The new information must, on average, be large enough to make up for the erosion of the existing stock of information. Thus, the rate of information turnover is equal to both the rate at which information is being depleted and the rate that information is arriving.

The analysis in Appendix B follows a similar line although it is more detailed and on a larger scale, with multiple assets (N of them) and multiple sources (M of these). The structure is general with the largest restriction being that the forecasting power of each of the M sources of information decays at the same rate g. The result of this analysis is an M dimensional vector of scores, $\mathbf{s}$, one for each source. The resulting forecast of annualized exceptional return on the N assets, $\mathbf{a}(\mathbf{s})$ is a linear function of the scores $\mathbf{s}$.

This represents the best forecast we can make given the quality of the information. With these forecasts in hand we can calculate the desired ex ante information ratio.

11. You actually can do slightly better if you include past returns in the formulation. Because the past returns are correlated with past signals, there is an opportunity to improve. Appendix B shows that the benefits of this complication are miniscule.

The Ex Ante Information Ratio

To calculate the ex ante information ratio, we need the forecasts **a**(s) along with an N by N annualized asset covariance matrix **V** with inverse $\mathbf{V}^{-1}$. For any forecast **a**(s), it is easy to calculate a portfolio, **q**(s), that efficiently captures the forecast:[12]

$$\mathbf{q}(s) \equiv \mathbf{V}^{-1} \cdot \mathbf{a}(s). \tag{27}$$

Portfolio **q**(s) attains the maximum forecasted return per unit of risk.

The information ratio that we obtain using the process that generates the forecasts **a**(s) is defined as:

$$IR \equiv \frac{\text{Expected return of } \mathbf{q}\,(s)}{\text{Square Root of Expected Variance of } \mathbf{q}\,(s)} \tag{28}$$

$$= \frac{E\langle \mathbf{a}'(s) \cdot \mathbf{q}(s) \rangle}{E\langle \mathbf{q}'(s) \cdot \mathbf{V} \cdot \mathbf{q}(s) \rangle}$$

We take the expectations in Equation (28) over all of the possible scores s that might arise. Appendix C establishes a short cut for the calculation in Equation (28), namely:

$$IR = \sqrt{\mathrm{E}\,\langle \mathbf{a}'(s) \cdot \mathrm{V}^{-1} \cdot \mathbf{a}(s) \rangle}. \tag{29}$$

The bridge from Equation (29) to our result, $IR \approx \kappa \cdot \sqrt{g \cdot N}$ (Equation (4)), is constructed in Appendix C.

The following points provide a brief summary:

- Instead of studying the asset returns directly, we repackage them into an equivalent set of uncorrelated returns. We replace the returns on the N assets by the returns on N principal component portfolios whose returns are uncorrelated.
- We assume the M sources are uncorrelated. This is actually not an assumption at all, since we can always repackage any M correlated sources into M equivalent uncorrelated sources in much the same way we repackaged the returns on the assets into uncorrelated principal component returns.
- An N by M effective skill matrix, K, links the principal component returns to the uncorrelated sources. Element $\kappa_{n,m}$ gives the effective skill of source m in predicting the return on principal component portfolio n.

If we use all M sources to predict the return on principal component n, the effective skill for this prediction is:

$$\kappa_n \equiv \sqrt{\sum_{m=1,M} \kappa_{n,m}^2}. \tag{30}$$

12. Portfolio q ignores costs and constraints. We can rescale q to achieve any desired level of risk, however since all such portfolios will have the same ex ante IR, we need not worry about this.

The correlation between the return on the nth principal component portfolio and our forecast of that return in a period of length Δt is, in spirit of Equation (23):

$$\rho_n(0, \Delta t) \Rightarrow \kappa_n \cdot \sqrt{g} \cdot \sqrt{\Delta t} \tag{31}$$

In calculating the information ratio, we can add up the contribution from all of the N principal component portfolios:

$$IR = \sqrt{\kappa_1^2 \cdot g + \kappa_2^2 \cdot g + \kappa_3^2 \cdot g + \cdots + \kappa_N^2 \cdot g}. \tag{32}$$

To make this more comprehensible we introduce the squared average effective skill:

$$\kappa^2 \equiv \frac{1}{N} \cdot \sum_{n=1,N} \kappa_n^2. \tag{33}$$

With this definition the ex ante information ratio, Equation (32), becomes:

$$IR = \kappa \cdot \sqrt{g \cdot N}. \tag{34}$$

Reality

The message of the fundamental law is that skill and breadth are important determinants of our ability to add value. This insight is apt to influence the way we conduct research and manage portfolios.

This article is an attempt to understand skill and breadth in the context of an equilibrium information process, where, as old information becomes stale, new information arrives to replace it. On the whole, this sounds like a reasonable description of active portfolio management. However, our model makes assumptions that ignore the situation faced in day-to-day operations. These compromises are not extremely important, because our goal is to provide a perspective to the investor rather than an operational guideline. Nonetheless we should point out two practical matters we have glossed over.

Most important, information flow is not smooth, it is lumpy. Moreover, the lumps tend to come periodically. Some companies and industries are much more dynamic than others; creative destruction occurs annually rather than over decades. In addition, an investment process may be made up of several sources of information each with its own information turnover rate. If these information turnover rates are similar, then an average or weighted average will approximate the total effect. But if the rates are quite distinct, then it may be wise to separate the processes and analyze each separately.

Lessons

The lessons we take from our analysis are several. First, if the information process is in equilibrium, then the rate that information is depleted must equal the rate that information is replenished. We call that the information turnover rate, and we can measure it for any investment process. Second, in the context of this reasonable equilibrium dynamic model, we have replaced the vague definition of breadth (the number of independent bets per year) with a very specific definition—the number of assets times the information turnover rate. Third, an investment manager can get a direct (and very noisy) estimate by examining the decrease in the correlation of forecast and return with older and older forecasts. A second—implicit—estimate follows from examining the change in forecasts from one period to the next. This estimate requires only a history of forecasts. If the direct and implicit estimates aren't roughly equal, there is an opportunity to improve the forecasts. And last, the correlation of information with return over any horizon depends on the information content (skill) of the forecast and on the rate that the information loses its value. The skill controls the "how much" and the information flow rate the "when."

References

Buckle, David. 2004. "How to Calculate Breadth: An Evolution of the Fundamental Law of Active Management." *Journal of Asset Management* 4 (6): 393–405.

Clarke, Roger, Harindra de Silva, and Steven Thorley.2002. "Portfolio Constraints and the Fundamental Law of Active Management." *Journal of Portfolio Management* 31 (1): 54–63.

Grinold, Richard C. 2007. "Dynamic Portfolio Analysis." *Journal of Portfolio Management* 34: 12–26.

Grinold, Richard C. 1989. "The Fundamental Law of Active Management." *Journal of Portfolio Management* 15 (3): 30–37.

Grinold, Richard C., and Ronald N. Kahn. 2000. *Active Portfolio Management*. New York: McGraw Hill.

Qian, Edward, and Ronald Hua. 2004. "Active Risk and Information Ratio." *Journal of Investment Management* 2 (3): 20–34.

Ye, Jia. 2008. "How Variation in Signal Quality Affects Performance." *Financial Analysts Journal* 64 (4): 48–60.

Appendix A

Modeling Skill over Time: One Asset and One Forecast

This appendix provides some additional analysis (beyond that in the main text) for the case of a single asset and a single forecast. Appendices B and C treat the case of multiple assets and multiple forecasts.

In the main text, we state that:

$$\rho(0,t) = \hat{\kappa} \cdot \left\{ \frac{1 - e^{-g \cdot t}}{\sqrt{g \cdot t}} \right\} \tag{A1}$$

is the solution to the functional equation:

$$\rho(0,t) = \sqrt{\frac{\tau}{t}} \cdot \rho(0,\tau) + \sqrt{\frac{t-\tau}{t}} \cdot e^{-g \cdot \tau} \cdot \rho(0,t-\tau). \tag{A2}$$

In this appendix, we analyze the uniqueness of this solution, as well as its behavior.

Uniqueness

The solution (A1) of Equation (A2) is unique up to a scale factor as long as $g \neq 0$. Suppose we define $m(t) = \sqrt{t} \cdot \rho(0,t)$. Then Equation (A2) says:

$$m(t) = m(\tau) + e^{-g \cdot \tau} \cdot m(t-\tau). \tag{A3}$$

If $\hat{m}(t)$ solves this equation, then $a \cdot \hat{m}(t)$ will also be a solution for any constant a. To adjust for this, let's only consider solutions with $m(1) = \hat{\rho} > 0$. Suppose there are two of these, $m(t)$ and $n(t)$. Consider their difference:

$$d(t) \equiv m(t) - n(t). \tag{A4}$$

Since $d(1) = m(1) - n(1) = 0$, we have for any $0 < \tau < 1$,

$$d(1) = d(\tau) + e^{-g \cdot \tau} \cdot d(1-\tau) = 0. \tag{A5}$$

Therefore,

$$\begin{aligned} &(i.) \quad d(\tau) = -e^{-g\cdot\tau} \cdot d(1-\tau) \text{ and} \\ &(ii.) \quad d(1-\tau) = -e^{-g\cdot(1-\tau)} \cdot d(\tau). \end{aligned} \tag{A6}$$

However, if we substitute item (*ii.*) of (A6) into item (*i.*) we find that:

$$d(\tau) = e^{-g} \cdot d(\tau). \tag{A7}$$

Thus $d(\tau) = 0$ for $0 \leq \tau \leq 1$.

It is easy to show it must hold for all t. Suppose $d(\tau) = 0$, $0 \leq \tau \leq T$. Consider any t in the interval $t \in (T, 2 \cdot T]$, then:

$$d(t) = d\left(\frac{t}{2}\right) + e^{-\frac{g\cdot t}{2}} \cdot d\left(\frac{t}{2}\right). \tag{A8}$$

Since $d\left(\frac{t}{2}\right) = 0$, we have $d(t) = 0$.

The Behavior of Equation (A1)

The generic form of the Equation (A1) is:

$$f(x) = \frac{1 - e^{-x}}{\sqrt{x}}, \quad \text{for } x > 0. \tag{A9}$$

When x is small, say, $x \leq 0.04$, we have $f(x) \approx \sqrt{x}$. The function increases until it hits a maximum value of 0.638173 when $x = 1.256431$. It then declines asymptotically to zero. For large values of x, say, $x \geq 4$, $f(x) \approx 1/\sqrt{x}$.

Appendix B

Modeling Skill over Time: Multiple Assets and Multiple Forecasts

In this appendix we construct an alpha forecasting model from the bottom up based on the flow of information. The relationship between skill and time developed in the main text and Appendix A is a key ingredient in this analysis. These results are used in Appendix C to show how skill and breadth contribute to the information ratio in a dynamic context. The main result of this appendix is Equation (B18) that describes our annualized forecast of return conditional on our "special" information.

1. Introduction

The quick route through this appendix is to examine the structure and notation in section 2 below and then skip straight to Equation (B15). If you believe it is possible to have signals with those properties, then you can proceed from that point. The intervening material (sections 3 and 4) develop a dynamic information process from unobserved building blocks—à la Exhibit 6 in the main text of Chapter 5—that will lead to those signals.

After the derivation of the main result, Equation (B18), four additional sections add some detail and color:

- Section 5 shows how we can generalize the process by adding noise that is uncorrelated with any return.
- Section 6 discusses the calculation of the cross-sectional realized information coefficient.
- Section 7 emphasizes an important point: the decay rate we are using is determined by the predictive power of our information—the link between information and return—and not by the rate of change of the information itself.
- Section 8 shows that a very small improvement in the forecast, Equation (B18), is possible if we use past returns to filter the signals.

We'll start with comments on assumptions, notation, and conventions that are common across all three appendices.

The key assumptions are:

- The covariance of asset returns is the same in all periods.
- We consider a period of length Δt between information refreshes; Δt = 1/252, 1/52, or 1/12, respectively, for a day, a week, or a month.
- The rate of decay in the strength of the information is the same for all signals and all components of return.

2. Structure

We index time by t, length of a period Δt. Therefore index t refers to time $t \cdot \Delta t$ and period t is the time interval $\{t \cdot \Delta t, (t+1) \cdot \Delta t\}$.

Asset Risk and Return

We use a principal components representation.

There are N assets. The returns in period t are:

$$
\begin{aligned}
&(i.) \quad \tilde{\mathbf{r}}(t) = \bar{\mathbf{r}} \cdot \Delta t + \mathbf{F} \cdot \boldsymbol{\Psi} \cdot \tilde{\boldsymbol{\upsilon}}(t), \quad \tilde{\boldsymbol{\upsilon}}(t) \in \mathbb{R}^N \\
&(ii.) \quad \boldsymbol{\Psi} \text{ is a positive diagonal matrix} \\
&(iii.) \quad \mathbf{F}' = \mathbf{F}^{-1}, \mathbf{F} \cdot \mathbf{F}' = \mathbf{I} \qquad \text{(B1)} \\
&(iv.) \quad \mathbb{E}\left\langle \tilde{\boldsymbol{\upsilon}}(t) \right\rangle = 0, \quad \mathbb{E}\left\langle \tilde{\boldsymbol{\upsilon}}(t) \cdot \boldsymbol{\upsilon}'(t) \right\rangle = \mathbf{I} \cdot \Delta t \\
&(i.) \quad \mathbb{E}\left\langle \tilde{\boldsymbol{\upsilon}}(t) \cdot \boldsymbol{\upsilon}'(t+k) \right\rangle = 0 \text{ if } k \neq 0.
\end{aligned}
$$

The annualized covariance matrix for asset return is:

$$
\mathbf{V} \equiv \frac{1}{\Delta t} \cdot \mathbb{E}\left\langle (\tilde{\mathbf{r}} - \bar{\mathbf{r}} \cdot \Delta t) \cdot (\tilde{\mathbf{r}} - \bar{\mathbf{r}} \cdot \Delta t)' \right\rangle = \mathbf{F} \cdot \boldsymbol{\Psi} \cdot \boldsymbol{\Psi} \cdot \mathbf{F}' \qquad \text{(B2)}
$$

The Shelf Life of Information

As in the main text and Appendix A, we assume that information gradually loses its value over time. If we let HL represent the interval of time for the information to decay to one-half its original value, then define rate of loss g by $g \equiv \ln(2)/HL$. The fraction of information remaining after one period is $\gamma = e^{-g \cdot \Delta t}$, and the fraction[13] remaining after j periods is γ^j.

13. We could keep score another way: the fraction of information remaining at time t is $e^{-g \cdot t} = (0.5)^{\left\{\frac{t}{HL}\right\}}$.

3. Unobserved Building Blocks

The substructure of the information model consists of an M dimension vector of building blocks denoted $\tilde{\mathbf{u}}(t,t+k) \in \mathbb{R}^M$. This is information available at time t related to return at time $t+k$ for $k \geq 0$. (In the main text of Chapter 5, the cells of Exhibit 6 contain $\tilde{u}(t,t+k)$, for the case of one asset (N = 1) and one signal (M = 1).) These building blocks are standardized and rotated so that:

$$\begin{aligned} &(i.) && \tilde{\mathbf{u}}(t,t+k) \in \mathbb{R}^M, \quad t = 0, \pm 1, \pm 2, \cdots; k = 0,1,\cdots \\ &(ii.) && \mathbb{E}\langle \tilde{\mathbf{u}}(t,t+k) \rangle = 0, \\ &(iii.) && \mathbb{E}\langle \tilde{\mathbf{u}}(t,t+k) \cdot \tilde{\mathbf{u}}'(t,t+k) \rangle = \gamma^{2\cdot k} \cdot \Delta t \cdot \mathbf{I} \\ &(iv.) && \mathbb{E}\langle \tilde{\mathbf{u}}(t,t+k) \cdot \tilde{\mathbf{u}}'(t \pm i, t+k \pm j) \rangle = 0 \text{ unless } i = j = 0 \end{aligned} \tag{B3}$$

These unobserved building blocks are correlated with the principal component returns:

$$\begin{aligned} &(i.) \quad \mathbb{E}\langle \tilde{\upsilon}_n(t) \cdot \tilde{u}_m(t-j,t) \rangle = \left\{\sqrt{\Delta t}\right\} \cdot \left\{ \hat{\kappa}_{n,m} \cdot \frac{1 - e^{-g \cdot \Delta t}}{\sqrt{g \cdot \Delta t}} \right\} \cdot \left\{\gamma^j \cdot \sqrt{\Delta t}\right\} \\ &(ii.) \quad \mathbb{E}\langle \tilde{\upsilon}(t) \cdot \tilde{\mathbf{u}}'(t-j,t+k) \rangle = 0 \text{ if } k \neq 0 \text{ and } j \geq 0. \end{aligned} \tag{B4}$$

The expression in the curly brackets in item (*i.*) of Equation (B4) is the correlation between this subsignal and the return component. We developed this formula in the main text. We define, again as in the main text:

$$\begin{aligned} &(i.) \quad \kappa_{n,\ell} \equiv \hat{\kappa}_{n,m} \cdot \left\{ \frac{1 - e^{-g \cdot \Delta t}}{g \cdot \Delta t} \right\}, \text{ and therefore} \\ &(ii.) \quad \hat{\kappa}_{n,m} \cdot \left\{ \frac{1 - e^{-g \cdot \Delta t}}{\sqrt{g \cdot \Delta t}} \right\} = \kappa_{n,m} \cdot \sqrt{g} \cdot \sqrt{\Delta t}. \end{aligned} \tag{B5}$$

Note that $|\kappa_{n,m}| < |\hat{\kappa}_{n,m}|$ and item (*i.*) in (B4) becomes:

$$\mathbb{E}\langle \tilde{\upsilon}_n(t) \cdot \tilde{u}_m(t-j,t) \rangle = \left\{\sqrt{\Delta t}\right\} \cdot \left\{\kappa_{n,m} \cdot \sqrt{g} \cdot \sqrt{\Delta t}\right\} \cdot \left\{\gamma^j \cdot \sqrt{\Delta t}\right\}. \tag{B6}$$

As is pointed out in the main text, this treatment makes sense when the update interval is short relative to the half-life. For example, we get $0.95 \cdot |\hat{\kappa}_{n,m}| < |\kappa_{n,m}| < |\hat{\kappa}_{n,m}|$ if $\Delta t \leq 0.14 \cdot HL$.

Let $\mathbf{K}$ be the N by M matrix with coefficients $\kappa_{n,m}$ defined in Equation (B5). Then the matrix version of Equation (B6) is:

$$\mathbb{E}\langle \tilde{\upsilon}(t) \cdot \tilde{\mathbf{u}}'(t-j,t) \rangle = \left\{\sqrt{\Delta t}\right\} \cdot \left\{\mathbf{K} \cdot \sqrt{g} \cdot \sqrt{\Delta t}\right\} \cdot \left\{\gamma^j \cdot \sqrt{\Delta t}\right\}. \tag{B7}$$

Observed New Information Arriving Each Period

In each period we receive new information in the M element vector $\tilde{\mathbf{x}}(t)$. Since $\tilde{\mathbf{x}}(t)$ is new information, it is uncorrelated with past arrivals, $\tilde{\mathbf{x}}(t-j)$, $j \geq 1$. Equation (B8) below defines $\tilde{\mathbf{x}}(t)$ in terms of the building blocks $\tilde{\mathbf{u}}(t, t+k)$ described above, and details several of its properties. (In the main text of Chapter 5, the row sums of Exhibit 6 contain $\tilde{x}$, for the case of one asset ($N = 1$) and one signal ($M = 1$).

$$\begin{aligned}
&(i.) \quad \tilde{\mathbf{x}}(t) \equiv \frac{1-\gamma^2}{\sqrt{\Delta t}} \cdot \sum_{k \geq 0} \tilde{\mathbf{u}}(t, t+k) \\
&(ii.) \quad \mathbb{E}\langle \tilde{\mathbf{x}}(t) \rangle = 0 \\
&(iii.) \quad \mathbb{E}\langle \tilde{\mathbf{x}}(t) \cdot \tilde{\mathbf{x}}'(t) \rangle = \frac{(1-\gamma^2)^2}{\Delta t} \cdot \frac{\mathbf{I} \cdot \Delta t}{1-\gamma^2} = (1-\gamma^2) \cdot \mathbf{I}, \text{ and} \\
&(iv.) \quad \mathbb{E}\langle \tilde{\mathbf{x}}(t) \cdot \tilde{\mathbf{x}}'(t+k) \rangle = 0 \text{ if } k \neq 0.
\end{aligned} \tag{B8}$$

The properties of $\tilde{\mathbf{x}}(t)$ are a consequence of Equation (B3).

The link of these new bundles of information with future return stems from Equation (B8):

$$\mathbb{COV}\langle \tilde{\boldsymbol{\upsilon}}(t), \tilde{\mathbf{x}}(t-j) \rangle = \mathbb{E}\langle \tilde{\boldsymbol{\upsilon}}(t) \cdot \tilde{\mathbf{x}}'(t-j) \rangle = \frac{1-\gamma^2}{\sqrt{\Delta t}} \cdot \mathbb{E}\langle \tilde{\boldsymbol{\upsilon}}(t) \cdot \tilde{\mathbf{u}}'(t-j, t) \rangle. \tag{B9}$$

Therefore, from Equation (B7), for any $j \geq 0$:

$$\begin{aligned}
&\mathbb{COV}\langle \tilde{\boldsymbol{\upsilon}}(t), \tilde{\mathbf{x}}(t-j) \rangle = \frac{1-\gamma^2}{\sqrt{\Delta t}} \cdot \left\{\sqrt{\Delta t}\right\} \cdot \left\{\mathbf{K} \cdot \sqrt{g} \cdot \sqrt{\Delta t}\right\} \cdot \left\{\gamma^j \cdot \sqrt{\Delta t}\right\} \text{ or} \\
&\mathbb{COV}\langle \tilde{\boldsymbol{\upsilon}}(t), \tilde{\mathbf{x}}(t-j) \rangle = \sqrt{g} \cdot (1-\gamma^2) \cdot \gamma^j \cdot \mathbf{K} \cdot \Delta t
\end{aligned} \tag{B10}$$

From Equation (B8) we have:

$$\mathbb{VAR}\langle \tilde{\mathbf{x}}(t-j) \rangle = (1-\gamma^2) \cdot \mathbf{I}, \quad \mathbb{VAR}^{-1}\langle \tilde{\mathbf{x}}(t-j) \rangle = \frac{1}{(1-\gamma^2)} \cdot \mathbf{I}. \tag{B11}$$

Therefore,

$$\mathbb{COV}\langle \tilde{\boldsymbol{\upsilon}}(t) \cdot \tilde{\mathbf{x}}(t-j) \rangle \cdot \mathbb{VAR}^{-1}\langle \tilde{\mathbf{x}}(t-j) \rangle = \sqrt{g} \cdot \gamma^j \cdot \mathbf{K} \cdot \Delta t \tag{B12}$$

Equation (B12) gives us the contribution of the new information at time $t - j$ to predicted return in period t.

4. Forecasts

Apply the forecasting equation[14] using the all of the past (uncorrelated) $\tilde{\mathbf{x}}(t-j)$ to forecast $\tilde{\upsilon}(t)$:

$$\mathbb{E}\left\langle \tilde{\upsilon}(t) \middle| \tilde{\mathbf{x}}(t-j), j \geq 0 \right\rangle = \sum_{j\geq 0} \mathbb{COV}\left\langle \tilde{\upsilon}(t), \tilde{\mathbf{x}}(t-j) \right\rangle \cdot \mathbb{VAR}^{-1}\left\langle \tilde{\mathbf{x}}(t-j) \right\rangle \cdot \tilde{\mathbf{x}}(t-j) \qquad \text{(B13)}$$

In this case, using Equation (B12), we have:

$$\mathbb{E}\left\langle \tilde{\upsilon}(t) \middle| \tilde{\mathbf{x}}(t-j), j \geq 0 \right\rangle = \sqrt{g} \cdot \mathbf{K} \cdot \left\{ \sum_{j\geq 0} \gamma^{j} \cdot \tilde{\mathbf{x}}(t-j) \right\} \cdot \Delta t. \qquad \text{(B14)}$$

Equation (B14) suggests that we can summarize all of the past arrivals of information, $\tilde{\mathbf{x}}(t-j)$ for $j \geq 0$, as a vector of signals $\tilde{\mathbf{s}}(t)$ with the following properties:

$$\begin{aligned}
&(i.) \quad \tilde{\mathbf{s}}(t) \equiv \sum_{j\geq 0} \gamma^{j} \cdot \tilde{\mathbf{x}}(t-j), \\
&(ii.) \quad \mathbb{E}\left\langle \tilde{\mathbf{x}}(t) \right\rangle = 0, \mathbb{E}\left\langle \tilde{\mathbf{s}}(t-1) \cdot \tilde{\mathbf{x}}'(t) \right\rangle = 0, \\
&(iii.) \quad \mathbb{E}\left\langle \mathbf{s}(t) \right\rangle = 0, \quad \mathbb{E}\left\langle \tilde{\mathbf{s}}(t) \cdot \tilde{\mathbf{s}}'(t) \right\rangle = \mathbf{I}, \\
&(iv) \quad \mathbb{E}\left\langle \tilde{\upsilon}(t) \middle| \tilde{\mathbf{s}}(t) \right\rangle = \sqrt{g} \cdot \mathbf{K} \cdot \tilde{\mathbf{s}}(t) \cdot \Delta t \text{ and} \\
&(v.) \quad \tilde{\mathbf{s}}(t) = \gamma \cdot \tilde{\mathbf{s}}(t-1) + \tilde{\mathbf{x}}(t).
\end{aligned} \qquad \text{(B15)}$$

Thus Equation (B14) becomes:

$$\mathbb{E}\left\langle \tilde{\upsilon}(t) \middle| \tilde{\mathbf{x}}(t-j), j \geq 0 \right\rangle = \mathbb{E}\left\langle \tilde{\upsilon}(t) \middle| \tilde{\mathbf{s}}(t) \right\rangle = \sqrt{g} \cdot \mathbf{K} \cdot \tilde{\mathbf{s}}(t) \cdot \Delta t. \qquad \text{(B16)}$$

In terms of conditional expected return forecasts, we have:

$$\mathbb{E}\left\langle \tilde{\mathbf{r}}(t) \middle| \tilde{\mathbf{s}}(t) \right\rangle = \overline{\mathbf{r}} \cdot \Delta t + \sqrt{g} \cdot \mathbf{F} \cdot \boldsymbol{\Psi} \cdot \mathbf{K} \cdot \tilde{\mathbf{s}}(t) \cdot \Delta t. \qquad \text{(B17)}$$

The forecast we are looking for is the annualized exceptional component of Equation (B17):

$$\mathbf{a}(\mathbf{s}) \equiv \frac{\mathbb{E}\left\langle \tilde{\mathbf{r}}(t) \middle| \tilde{\mathbf{s}}(t) = \mathbf{s} \right\rangle}{\Delta t} - \overline{\mathbf{r}} = \sqrt{g} \cdot \mathbf{F} \cdot \boldsymbol{\Psi} \cdot \mathbf{K} \cdot \mathbf{s}. \qquad \text{(B18)}$$

This is the main result of the appendix. The remaining four sections are embellishment and color.

5. Add Noise

Suppose the observed information has a noise component. For example, let:

$$\tilde{\mathbf{x}}^{*}(t) = a \cdot \tilde{\mathbf{x}}(t) + \sqrt{1-a^{2}} \cdot \tilde{\boldsymbol{\eta}}(t) \cdot \sqrt{\Delta t} \qquad \text{(B19)}$$

14. This is the best linear unbiased estimator (BLUE). We are taking liberties using the conditional expectation notation. This is correct in some cases, e.g., the normal distribution. We are using this notation in more general circumstance since it reinforces the motivation.

where $\tilde{\mathbf{x}}(t)$ is defined in Equation (B8), and the noise term, $\tilde{\boldsymbol{\eta}}(t)$, has the following properties:

$$\begin{aligned} &(i.) \quad \mathbb{E}\langle \tilde{\boldsymbol{\eta}}(t) \rangle = \mathbf{0}, \\ &(ii.) \quad \mathbb{E}\langle \tilde{\boldsymbol{\eta}}(t) \cdot \tilde{\boldsymbol{\eta}}'(t) \rangle = \mathbf{I}, \\ &(iii.) \quad \mathbb{E}\langle \tilde{\boldsymbol{\upsilon}}(t+j) \cdot \tilde{\boldsymbol{\eta}}'(t) \rangle = \mathbf{0} \text{ for all } j \text{ and} \\ &(iv.) \quad \mathbb{E}\langle \tilde{\boldsymbol{\eta}}(t+j) \cdot \tilde{\boldsymbol{\eta}}'(t) \rangle = \mathbf{0} \text{ for all } j. \end{aligned} \tag{B20}$$

In this case the skill level becomes:

$$\mathbb{COV}\left\langle \tilde{\boldsymbol{\upsilon}}(t), \tilde{\mathbf{x}}^{*}(t-j) \right\rangle = a \cdot \sqrt{g} \cdot \left(1-\gamma^{2}\right) \cdot \gamma^{j} \cdot \mathbf{K} \cdot \Delta t \tag{B21}$$

Thus, skill levels in the matrix $\mathbf{K}$ are scaled back due to the presence of the noise. However, there is no change in form, we just replace $\mathbf{K}$ with $a \cdot \mathbf{K}$.

6. Cross-Sectional Realized *IC*

With forecast $\mathbf{a}(\tilde{\mathbf{s}})$ given by Equation (B18) and unanticipated returns to the principal components driven by $\tilde{\boldsymbol{\upsilon}}$, we can calculate the realized cross-sectional information coefficient as follows.

Let:

$$\boldsymbol{\theta}(\tilde{\boldsymbol{\upsilon}}) \equiv \mathbf{F} \cdot \boldsymbol{\Psi} \cdot \tilde{\boldsymbol{\upsilon}} \tag{B22}$$

be the component of return that we are trying to predict, and $\mathbf{a}(\tilde{\mathbf{s}})$ from Equation (B18) our forecast of $\boldsymbol{\theta}(\tilde{\boldsymbol{\upsilon}})$. Then the realized *IC* is defined as:

$$IC\{\mathbf{a}(\tilde{\mathbf{s}}), \boldsymbol{\theta}(\tilde{\boldsymbol{\upsilon}})\} \equiv \frac{\boldsymbol{\theta}'(\tilde{\boldsymbol{\upsilon}}) \cdot \mathbf{V}^{-1} \cdot \mathbf{a}(\tilde{\mathbf{s}})}{\sqrt{\boldsymbol{\theta}'(\tilde{\boldsymbol{\upsilon}}) \cdot \mathbf{V}^{-1} \cdot \boldsymbol{\theta}(\tilde{\boldsymbol{\upsilon}})} \cdot \sqrt{\mathbf{a}'(\tilde{\mathbf{s}}) \cdot \mathbf{V}^{-1} \cdot \mathbf{a}(\tilde{\mathbf{s}})}} \tag{B23}$$

We can give a portfolio interpretation to both the forecasts and the returns. Define a prospectively ideal portfolio $\mathbf{q}(\tilde{\mathbf{s}})$ and a retrospectively ideal (aka hindsight) portfolio $\tilde{\mathbf{h}}(\tilde{\boldsymbol{\upsilon}})$ by:

$$\begin{aligned} &(i.) \quad \mathbf{V} \cdot \mathbf{q}(\tilde{\mathbf{s}}) = \mathbf{a}(\tilde{\mathbf{s}}) \Rightarrow \mathbf{q}(\tilde{\mathbf{s}}) = \mathbf{V}^{-1} \cdot \mathbf{a}(\tilde{\mathbf{s}}) \text{ and} \\ &(ii.) \quad \mathbf{V} \cdot \mathbf{h}(\tilde{\boldsymbol{\upsilon}}) = \boldsymbol{\theta}(\tilde{\boldsymbol{\upsilon}}) \Rightarrow \mathbf{h}(\tilde{\boldsymbol{\upsilon}}) = \mathbf{V}^{-1} \cdot \boldsymbol{\theta}(\tilde{\boldsymbol{\upsilon}}). \end{aligned} \tag{B24}$$

The correlation between the returns of portfolios $\mathbf{q}(\tilde{\mathbf{s}})$ and $\mathbf{h}(\tilde{\boldsymbol{\upsilon}})$ is:

$$IC\left\{\mathbf{q}(\tilde{\mathbf{s}}), \tilde{\mathbf{h}}(\tilde{\boldsymbol{\upsilon}})\right\} \equiv \frac{\tilde{\mathbf{h}}'(\tilde{\boldsymbol{\upsilon}}) \cdot \mathbf{V} \cdot \mathbf{q}(\tilde{\mathbf{s}})}{\sqrt{\tilde{\mathbf{h}}'(\tilde{\boldsymbol{\upsilon}}) \cdot \mathbf{V} \cdot \tilde{\mathbf{h}}(\tilde{\boldsymbol{\upsilon}})} \cdot \sqrt{\mathbf{q}'(\tilde{\mathbf{s}}) \cdot \mathbf{V} \cdot \mathbf{q}(\tilde{\mathbf{s}})}} \tag{B25}$$

It is easy to show using Equation (B24) that Equations (B23) and (B25) are equivalent: $IC\{\mathbf{a}(\tilde{\mathbf{s}}), \boldsymbol{\theta}(\tilde{\boldsymbol{\upsilon}})\} = IC\left\{\mathbf{q}(\tilde{\mathbf{s}}), \tilde{\mathbf{h}}(\tilde{\boldsymbol{\upsilon}})\right\}$. From Equation (B25), it is also apparent that the result is a correlation, since it is the predicted covariance between two portfolios divided by each portfolio's standard deviation. This result is general.

We can go one step further and use the model outlined in sections 3 and 4 above to express the realized *IC* in terms of the signals, $\tilde{\mathbf{s}}$, and principal component returns, $\tilde{\upsilon}$. The three components of the calculation specialize as follows:

$$\begin{aligned}
&(i.)\quad \mathbf{q}(\tilde{\mathbf{s}}) = \sqrt{g}\cdot\mathbf{F}\cdot\boldsymbol{\Psi}^{-1}\cdot\mathbf{K}\cdot\tilde{\mathbf{s}} \text{ thus } \mathbf{q}'(\tilde{\mathbf{s}})\cdot\mathbf{V}\cdot\mathbf{q}(\tilde{\mathbf{s}}) = g\cdot\tilde{\mathbf{s}}'\cdot\{\mathbf{K}'\cdot\mathbf{K}\}\cdot\tilde{\mathbf{s}},\\
&(ii.)\quad \tilde{\mathbf{h}}(\tilde{\upsilon}) = \mathbf{F}\cdot\boldsymbol{\Psi}^{-1}\cdot\tilde{\upsilon} \text{ thus } \tilde{\mathbf{h}}'(\tilde{\upsilon})\cdot\mathbf{V}\cdot\tilde{\mathbf{h}}(\tilde{\upsilon}) = \tilde{\upsilon}'\cdot\tilde{\upsilon} \text{ and}\\
&(iii.)\quad \tilde{\mathbf{h}}'(\tilde{\upsilon})\cdot\mathbf{V}\cdot\mathbf{q}(\tilde{\mathbf{s}}) = \sqrt{g}\cdot\tilde{\upsilon}'\cdot\mathbf{K}\cdot\tilde{\mathbf{s}}.
\end{aligned} \tag{B26}$$

With the aid of Equation (B26), we can write the realized *IC* as:

$$IC\{\tilde{\mathbf{s}}\ \tilde{\upsilon}\} = \frac{\tilde{\upsilon}'\cdot\mathbf{K}\cdot\tilde{\mathbf{s}}}{\sqrt{\tilde{\upsilon}'\cdot\tilde{\upsilon}}\cdot\sqrt{\tilde{\mathbf{s}}'\cdot\{\mathbf{K}'\cdot\mathbf{K}\}\cdot\tilde{\mathbf{s}}}} \tag{B27}$$

We will continue this analysis in Appendix C.

7. Processed and Unprocessed Information

This section is a reminder that the rate g is the rate that the predictive power of the information decays. It is not the rate that the raw information decays.

For example, suppose we have vector $\tilde{\mathbf{z}}(t)$ that is a predictor of the principal component surprise $\tilde{\upsilon}(t)$. This predictor is analogous to the scores $\tilde{\mathbf{s}}(t)$ described in equation (B15). To make it relatively simple assume that:

$$\begin{aligned}
&(i.)\quad \mathbb{E}\langle\tilde{\mathbf{z}}(t)\rangle = 0,\\
&(ii.)\quad \mathbb{E}\langle\tilde{\mathbf{z}}(t)\cdot\tilde{\mathbf{z}}'(t)\rangle = \mathbf{I},\\
&(iii.)\quad \tilde{\mathbf{z}}(t) = \phi\cdot\tilde{\mathbf{z}}(t-1) + \tilde{\mathbf{y}}(t),\\
&(iv.)\quad \mathbb{E}\langle\tilde{\mathbf{z}}(t-1)\cdot\tilde{\mathbf{y}}'(t)\rangle = 0,\\
&(v.)\quad \mathbb{E}\langle\tilde{\mathbf{y}}(t)\cdot\tilde{\mathbf{y}}'(t-j)\rangle = 0 \text{ for } j>0 \text{ and}\\
&(vi.)\quad \mathbb{E}\langle\tilde{\mathbf{y}}(t)\cdot\tilde{\mathbf{y}}'(t)\rangle = 1-\phi^2.
\end{aligned} \tag{B28}$$

Note that Equation (B28) implies:

$$\tilde{\mathbf{z}}(t) = \sum_{j\geq 0}\phi^j\cdot\tilde{\mathbf{y}}(t-j). \tag{B29}$$

The parameter ϕ governs the relationship of past values of $\tilde{\mathbf{z}}(t-j)$ with current values $\tilde{\mathbf{z}}(t)$. The parameter, γ, used in earlier parts of this appendix, governs the relationship of current and past values of $\tilde{\mathbf{z}}(t)$ with the principal component returns $\tilde{\upsilon}(t)$. Using the conventions established previously, we have:

$$\mathbb{E}\langle\tilde{\upsilon}(t)\cdot\tilde{\mathbf{z}}'(t-j)\rangle = \gamma^j\cdot\sqrt{g}\cdot\mathbf{K}\cdot\Delta t. \tag{B30}$$

The best predictor of $\tilde{\upsilon}(t)$ given $\tilde{\mathbf{z}}(t)$ is :

$$\mathbb{E}\langle\tilde{\upsilon}(t)|\tilde{\mathbf{z}}(t)=\mathbf{z}\rangle=\mathbb{E}\langle\tilde{\upsilon}(t)\cdot\tilde{\mathbf{z}}'(t)\rangle\cdot\mathbb{VAR}^{-1}\langle\tilde{\mathbf{z}}(t)\rangle\cdot\mathbf{z}=\{\sqrt{g}\cdot\mathbf{K}\cdot\mathbf{z}\}\cdot\Delta t. \quad \text{(B31)}$$

The predictor in Equation (B31) ignores some valuable information contained in the past values, $\tilde{\mathbf{z}}(t-j)$, of the raw signals. To see this, use the uncorrelated past changes in the signals, $\tilde{\mathbf{y}}(t-j)\ j\geq 0$ as the potential sources of information. The best predictor of $\tilde{\upsilon}(t)$ given $\tilde{\mathbf{y}}(t-j)\ j\geq 0$, is:

$$\mathbb{E}\langle\tilde{\upsilon}(t)|\tilde{\mathbf{y}}(t-j)=\mathbf{y}(t-j),\ j\geq 0\rangle=\sum_{j\geq 0}\mathbb{E}\langle\tilde{\upsilon}(t)\cdot\tilde{\mathbf{y}}'(t-j)\rangle\cdot\mathbb{VAR}^{-1}\langle\tilde{\mathbf{y}}(t-j)\rangle\cdot\tilde{\mathbf{y}}(t-j). \quad \text{(B32)}$$

With the aid of Equations (B28) and (B30) we have:

$$\mathbb{E}\langle\tilde{\upsilon}(t)\cdot\tilde{\mathbf{y}}'(t-j)\rangle=\mathbb{E}\left\langle\tilde{\upsilon}(t)\cdot\left[\tilde{\mathbf{z}}(t)-\phi\cdot\tilde{\mathbf{z}}(t-1)\right]'\right\rangle=\gamma^{j}\cdot(1-\phi\cdot\gamma)\cdot\sqrt{g}\cdot\mathbf{K}\cdot\Delta t$$

$$\mathbb{VAR}^{-1}\langle\tilde{\mathbf{y}}(t-j)\rangle=\frac{1}{1-\phi^{2}}\cdot\mathbf{I} \quad \text{(B33)}$$

Therefore Equation (B32) becomes:

$$\mathbb{E}\langle\tilde{\upsilon}(t)|\tilde{\mathbf{y}}(t-j)\ j\geq 0\rangle=\frac{1-\phi\cdot\gamma}{1-\phi^{2}}\cdot\sqrt{g}\cdot\mathbf{K}\cdot\left\{\sum_{j\geq 0}\gamma^{j}\cdot\tilde{\mathbf{y}}(t-j)\right\}\cdot\Delta t \quad \text{(B34)}$$

Now define a refined signal $\tilde{\mathbf{s}}(t)$ as:

$$\tilde{\mathbf{s}}(t)\equiv\sqrt{\frac{1-\gamma^{2}}{1-\phi^{2}}}\cdot\sum_{j\geq 0}\gamma^{j}\cdot\tilde{\mathbf{y}}(t-j) \quad \text{with} \quad \text{(B35)}$$

$$\mathbb{E}\langle\tilde{\mathbf{s}}(t)\rangle=0,\quad \mathbb{E}\langle\tilde{\mathbf{s}}(t)\cdot\tilde{\mathbf{s}}'(t)\rangle=\mathbf{I}.$$

In addition, define:

$$\ell(\phi,\gamma)\equiv\frac{1-\phi\cdot\gamma}{\sqrt{1-\phi^{2}}\cdot\sqrt{1-\gamma^{2}}}. \quad \text{(B36)}$$

Then we can express the best predictor, Equation (B32), as:

$$\mathbb{E}\langle\tilde{\upsilon}(t)|\tilde{\mathbf{s}}(t)=\mathbf{s}\rangle=\ell(\phi,\gamma)\cdot\sqrt{g}\cdot\mathbf{K}\cdot\mathbf{s}\cdot\Delta t \quad \text{(B37)}$$

It is easy to show that $\ell(\phi,\gamma)>1$ if $\phi\neq\gamma$ and $\ell(\phi,\gamma)=1$ when $\phi=\gamma$.

The expression $\ell(\phi,\gamma)$ captures the improvement in the information ratio that one obtains by using the refined signal $\tilde{\mathbf{s}}(t)$ rather than the raw signal $\tilde{\mathbf{z}}(t)$.

After a bit of reshuffling one can show that the signal (B35) is proportional to

$$\tilde{\mathbf{z}}(t)+\{\gamma-\phi\}\cdot\sum_{j\geq 1}\gamma^{j-1}\cdot\tilde{\mathbf{z}}(t-j). \quad \text{(B38)}$$

Thus if $\gamma<\phi$, where the unrefined signal's predictive power dissipates faster than the changes in the unrefined signal, we subtract off earlier values of the unrefined signal in order to compensate.

8. Use Past Returns as Forecasters

In our information structure, past returns on the principal components are uncorrelated with future returns, so they are not of any direct value in forecasting. However, past returns are correlated with past predictors, so it is possible to make a slight improvement in the forecast by adding past returns into the mix. This section will show by example that this is a very small improvement. We will demonstrate the concept and its scope with an example using a single asset.

Let $\tilde{\theta}(j)$ represent the surprise component of return with mean zero and with risk $\omega \cdot \sqrt{\Delta t}$. Let $\tilde{\chi}(j) = \tilde{\theta}(-j)/\omega \cdot \sqrt{\Delta t}$. Using the methods in this appendix, we build up a predictor s and can show that for $j \geq 0$:

$$\begin{aligned} &\mathbb{E}\langle \tilde{\chi}(j) \cdot \tilde{s}(0) \rangle = \gamma^j \cdot \rho, \text{ where} \\ &\rho \equiv \sqrt{g} \cdot \kappa \cdot \sqrt{\Delta t}. \end{aligned} \tag{B39}$$

We want to calculate the expected value of $\tilde{\theta}(0)$ conditional on the predictor $\tilde{s}$ from Equation (B17) and $\tilde{\chi}(j)$, $j \geq 1$. The covariance matrix of these predictors is:

$$\begin{Bmatrix} 1 & \gamma\cdot\rho & \gamma^2\cdot\rho & \cdots & \gamma^j\cdot\rho & \cdots \\ \gamma\cdot\rho & 1 & 0 & \cdots & 0 & \cdots \\ \gamma^2\cdot\rho & 0 & 1 & \cdots & 0 & \cdots \\ \vdots & \vdots & \vdots & \ddots & & \cdots \\ \gamma^j\cdot\rho & 0 & 0 & & 1 & \cdots \\ \vdots & \vdots & \vdots & \vdots & \cdots & \ddots \end{Bmatrix} \tag{B40}$$

If we let a_j, $j \geq 0$ be the first row (and first column) of the inverse of the infinite matrix in Equation (B40), then we have:

$$\begin{aligned} a_0 &= \frac{1}{1-\rho^2 \cdot \sum_{j\geq 1} \gamma^{2\cdot j}} = \frac{1}{1-\rho^2 \cdot \dfrac{\gamma^2}{1-\gamma^2}}. \\ a_j &= -a_0 \cdot \rho \cdot \gamma^j \end{aligned} \tag{B41}$$

The conditional forecast is therefore:

$$\mathbb{E}\langle \tilde{\theta}(0) | s(0), \chi(j)\ j \geq 1 \rangle = \omega \cdot \sqrt{\Delta t} \cdot \rho \cdot a_0 \cdot \left\{ s(0) - \rho \cdot \sum_{j\geq 1} \gamma^j \cdot \chi(j) \right\}. \tag{B42}$$

The variance of the term in the curly brackets is $1/a_0$, so we can rewrite Equation (B42) as:

$$\begin{aligned} &\mathbb{E}\langle \tilde{\theta}(0) | s(0), \chi(j)\ j \geq 1 \rangle = \left\{ \omega \cdot \sqrt{\Delta t} \right\} \cdot \left\{ \rho \cdot \sqrt{a_0} \right\} \cdot s^*, \text{ where} \\ &s^* \equiv \sqrt{a_0} \cdot \left\{ s(0) - \rho \cdot \sum_{j\geq 1} \gamma^j \cdot \chi(j) \right\}. \end{aligned} \tag{B43}$$

The new and improved score, s^*, has expected value zero and standard deviation equal to one. The net effect of this exercise is to increase the skill (per interval of length Δt) from $\rho = \sqrt{g} \cdot \kappa \cdot \sqrt{\Delta t}$ to $\sqrt{g} \cdot \left\{\sqrt{a_0} \cdot \kappa\right\} \cdot \sqrt{\Delta t}$.

Exhibit B1 shows the improvement in skill, $\sqrt{a_0}$, for half-lives in the columns and increasing skill levels (κ). It is based on weekly updates, $\Delta t = 1/52$. The improvements are miniscule.

EXHIBIT B1 Improvement in Skill by Using Realized Return to Filter the Signal

kappa\HL	0.125	0.25	0.50
0.05	1.0006	1.0006	1.0006
0.10	1.0023	1.0024	1.0024
0.15	1.0051	1.0054	1.0055

Appendix C

Calculating the Ex Ante Information Ratio

This appendix uses the results of Appendix A, relating skill and time, and Appendix B, specifying a model of information flow and the resulting forecast of unanticipated returns, in order to calculate the ex ante information ratio. Warning: it is very technical.

The key assumption is that the rate of decay in the strength of the information is the same for all signals and all components of return. We assume that information is available continuously and we update each Δt.

The forecasts developed in Appendix B mix market timing and residual return. In contrast to the main article we will observe this distinction and use the term *generalized information ratio*, *GIR*, for the expected risk return ratio we can obtain with all the information, and reserve the term *information ratio*, *IR*, for the residual component.

1. Introduction

This appendix contains 11 sections. You can get the essentials quickly by reading sections 2, 3, and 6. The other sections supply examples and explanations of the results. The rundown by sections is:

- Section 2 is a review of notation and essential results from Appendices A and B.
- Section 3 defines the calculation of the generalized information ratio, *GIR*, and shows how that calculation specializes for the model considered here.
- Section 4 is an example when each source forecasts the return on one principal component of return and all forecasts have the same effective skill.
- Section 5 is a second example of one source that is equally skillful in the prediction of all principal components.
- Section 6 considers the general case.

- Section 7 shows how the results in the general case can be interpreted as defining effective skill levels, κ_n, for the nth principal components of return.
- Section 8 shows how to split the generalized information ratio into a market and residual component.
- Section 9 shows how we can link each of the M sources to a source portfolio.
- Section 10 continues from section 9 and shows how the general result can be interpreted in terms of an effective skill, c_m, at predicting return on the mth source portfolio.
- Section 11 shows that the realized information coefficient, a concept introduced in Appendix B, should be approximately in line with the effective skill levels defined in this appendix.

2. Building Blocks

Time is indexed by t, length of a period Δt. Therefore index t refers to time $t \cdot \Delta t$ and period t is the time interval $\{t \cdot \Delta t, (t+1) \cdot \Delta t\}$.

There are N assets. We use principal components to separate their returns. The returns in period t are:

$$\begin{aligned} &(i.) \quad \tilde{\mathbf{r}}(t) = \bar{\mathbf{r}} \cdot \Delta t + \mathbf{F} \cdot \boldsymbol{\Psi} \cdot \tilde{\boldsymbol{\upsilon}}(t), \quad \tilde{\boldsymbol{\upsilon}}(t) \in \mathbb{R}^N \\ &(ii.) \quad \boldsymbol{\Psi} \text{ is a positive diagonal matrix} \\ &(iii.) \quad \mathbf{F}' = \mathbf{F}^{-1}, \mathbf{F} \cdot \mathbf{F}' = \mathbf{I} \\ &(iv.) \quad \mathbb{E}\langle \tilde{\boldsymbol{\upsilon}}(t) \rangle = 0, \quad \mathbb{E}\langle \tilde{\boldsymbol{\upsilon}}(t) \cdot \boldsymbol{\upsilon}'(t) \rangle = \Delta t \end{aligned} \tag{C1}$$

The annualized covariance matrix for asset return is:

$$\begin{aligned} &\mathbf{V} \equiv \frac{1}{\Delta t} \cdot \mathbb{E}\left\langle (\tilde{\mathbf{r}} - \bar{\mathbf{r}} \cdot \Delta t) \cdot (\tilde{\mathbf{r}} - \bar{\mathbf{r}} \cdot \Delta t)' \right\rangle = \mathbf{F} \cdot \boldsymbol{\Psi} \cdot \boldsymbol{\Psi} \cdot \mathbf{F}' \text{ and} \\ &\mathbf{V}^{-1} = \mathbf{F} \cdot \boldsymbol{\Psi}^{-1} \cdot \boldsymbol{\Psi}^{-1} \cdot \mathbf{F}' \end{aligned} \tag{C2}$$

The Scores

We base the scores on $M \leq N$ uncorrelated sources of information described in some detail in Appendix B. They are built up from independent and identically distributed bundles of new information, $\tilde{\mathbf{x}}(t)$, that arrive each period. The link between the principal component returns and the information sources is an N by M effective skill matrix $\mathbf{K}$. The resulting score is $\tilde{\mathbf{s}}(t)$ with the following properties:

$$
\begin{aligned}
&(i.) \quad \tilde{\mathbf{s}}(t) \equiv \sum_{j \geq 0} \gamma^j \cdot \tilde{\mathbf{x}}(t-j), \\
&(ii.) \quad \mathbb{E}\langle \tilde{\mathbf{s}}(t) \rangle = 0, \quad \mathbb{E}\langle \tilde{\mathbf{s}}(t) \cdot \tilde{\mathbf{s}}'(t) \rangle = \mathbf{I}, \\
&(iii.) \quad \mathbb{E}\langle \tilde{\mathbf{\upsilon}}(t) \cdot \tilde{\mathbf{s}}'(t) \rangle = \sqrt{g} \cdot \mathbf{K} \cdot \Delta t \text{ and} \\
&(iv.) \quad \tilde{\mathbf{s}}(t) = \gamma^j \cdot \mathbf{s}(t-1) + \tilde{\mathbf{x}}(t)
\end{aligned}
\tag{C3}
$$

The expected return forecasts conditional on $\tilde{\mathbf{s}}(t)$ is:

$$
\mathbb{E}\langle \mathbf{r}(t) | \tilde{\mathbf{s}}(t) \rangle = \bar{\mathbf{r}} \cdot \Delta t + \sqrt{g} \cdot \mathbf{F} \cdot \mathbf{\Psi} \cdot \mathbf{K} \cdot \tilde{\mathbf{s}}(t) \cdot \Delta t. \tag{C4}
$$

If we concentrate on the changes and annualize, we obtain:

$$
\tilde{\mathbf{a}}(\tilde{\mathbf{s}}) \equiv \frac{\mathbb{E}\langle \tilde{\mathbf{r}} | \tilde{\mathbf{s}} \rangle}{\Delta t} - \bar{\mathbf{r}} = \sqrt{g} \cdot \mathbf{F} \cdot \mathbf{\Psi} \cdot \mathbf{K} \cdot \tilde{\mathbf{s}}. \tag{C5}
$$

3. The Generalized Information Ratio

The forecast, Equation (C5), may contain market timing as well as residual return information. For that reason, we employ a more nuanced terminology in this appendix than in the article. We'll use the term generalized information ratio to include a market-timing component and reserve the term information ratio for the residual. Section 8 below shows how to separate the two. In this section we will derive a formula for the generalized information ratio.

Suppose we have a covariance matrix $\mathbf{V}$ as per Equation (C2) and forecasts $\mathbf{a}(\tilde{\mathbf{s}})$ as per Equation (C5) and we wish to elect a portfolio $\mathbf{p}$ to maximize a measure of risk adjusted value added:

$$
\mathbf{a}'(\tilde{\mathbf{s}}) \cdot \mathbf{p} - \frac{\lambda}{2} \cdot \mathbf{p}' \cdot \mathbf{V} \cdot \mathbf{p}, \tag{C6}
$$

where λ is a penalty for active risk.

The optimal solution for Equation (C6) is:

$$
\mathbf{p}(\tilde{\mathbf{s}}) = \frac{1}{\lambda} \cdot \mathbf{V}^{-1} \cdot \mathbf{a}(\tilde{\mathbf{s}}). \tag{C7}
$$

The expected return and variance of this solution are:

$$
\begin{aligned}
&(i.) \quad \mathbf{a}'(\tilde{\mathbf{s}}) \cdot \mathbf{p}(\tilde{\mathbf{s}}) = \frac{1}{\lambda} \cdot \mathbf{a}'(\tilde{\mathbf{s}}) \mathbf{V}^{-1} \cdot \mathbf{a}(\tilde{\mathbf{s}}), \\
&(ii.) \quad \mathbf{p}'(\tilde{\mathbf{s}}) \cdot \mathbf{V} \cdot \mathbf{p}(\tilde{\mathbf{s}}) = \frac{1}{\lambda^2} \cdot \mathbf{a}'(\tilde{\mathbf{s}}) \mathbf{V}^{-1} \cdot \mathbf{a}(\tilde{\mathbf{s}}).
\end{aligned}
\tag{C8}
$$

We define the generalized information ratio as:

$$
GIR \equiv \frac{\mathbb{E}\langle \mathbf{a}'(\tilde{\mathbf{s}}) \cdot \mathbf{p}(\tilde{\mathbf{s}}) \rangle}{\sqrt{\mathbb{E}\langle \mathbf{p}'(\tilde{\mathbf{s}}) \cdot \mathbf{V} \cdot \mathbf{p}(\tilde{\mathbf{s}}) \rangle}} = \sqrt{\mathbb{E}\langle \mathbf{a}'(\tilde{\mathbf{s}}) \cdot \mathbf{V}^{-1} \cdot \mathbf{a}(\tilde{\mathbf{s}}) \rangle}. \tag{C9}
$$

As a bit of motivation, notice in passing that for any $\tilde{s}$ and *any* nonzero portfolio $\mathbf{p} \neq 0$ we have:

$$\frac{\mathbf{a}'(\tilde{\mathbf{s}}) \cdot \mathbf{p}}{\sqrt{\mathbf{p}' \cdot \mathbf{V} \cdot \mathbf{p}}} \leq \sqrt{\mathbf{a}'(\tilde{\mathbf{s}}) \cdot \mathbf{V}^{-1} \cdot \mathbf{a}(\tilde{\mathbf{s}})}. \tag{C10}$$

Using the forecast in Equation (C5) and the covariance matrix in Equation (C2), Equation (C9) leads to:

$$GIR = \sqrt{g} \cdot \sqrt{\mathbb{E}\langle \tilde{\mathbf{s}}' \cdot \mathbf{K}' \cdot \mathbf{K} \cdot \tilde{\mathbf{s}} \rangle}. \tag{C11}$$

In sections 4, 5, and 6 we will examine Equation (C11) in greater detail.

4. Special Case #1

Assume the matrix **K** in Equations (C3) through (C5) is proportional to an identity matrix:

$$\mathbf{K} = \kappa \cdot \mathbf{I} \tag{C12}$$

This means that there are $M = N$ sources. The calculation (C11) is then simple:

$$\mathbb{E}\langle \tilde{\mathbf{s}}' \cdot \mathbf{K}' \cdot \mathbf{K} \cdot \tilde{\mathbf{s}} \rangle = \kappa^2 \cdot \mathbb{E}\langle \tilde{\mathbf{s}}' \cdot \tilde{\mathbf{s}} \rangle = \kappa^2 \cdot N. \tag{C13}$$

Therefore:

$$GIR = \kappa \cdot \sqrt{g \cdot N} \tag{C14}$$

5. Special Case #2

Suppose that there is only one source, $M = 1$, and that the source is equally skillful at predicting every principal component return. In that case:

$$\mathbf{K} = \kappa \cdot \mathbf{e}, \tag{C15}$$

where **e** is an N element column vector of ones. In this case the score is a scalar, $\tilde{s}$:

$$\mathbb{E}\langle \tilde{\mathbf{s}}' \cdot \mathbf{K}' \cdot \mathbf{K} \cdot \tilde{\mathbf{s}} \rangle = \kappa^2 \cdot \mathbb{E}\langle \tilde{s} \cdot \mathbf{e}' \cdot \mathbf{e} \cdot \tilde{s} \rangle = \kappa^2 \cdot N. \tag{C16}$$

Therefore, as in section 4:

$$GIR = \kappa \cdot \sqrt{g \cdot N} \tag{C17}$$

6. The General Case

In the analysis in sections 4 and 5, we assumed either $\mathbf{K} = \kappa \cdot \mathbf{I}$ or $\mathbf{K} = \kappa \cdot \mathbf{e}$. In this section, we consider the general case where **K** is an N by M matrix of effective skill levels linking principal component return drivers and the

M uncorrelated scores. In section 7, we'll present a portfolio-based interpretation of the results.

We are trying (see Equation (C11)) to calculate:

$$\mathbb{E}\left\langle \tilde{s}' \cdot \{K' \cdot K\} \cdot \tilde{s} \right\rangle. \tag{C18}$$

Now we'll show that:

$$\mathbb{E}\left\langle \tilde{s}' \cdot \{K' \cdot K\} \cdot \tilde{s} \right\rangle = trace\left\langle K' \cdot K \right\rangle. \tag{C19}$$

The derivation of Equation (C19) starts with Equation (C9) and then proceeds through a sequence of small steps.

$$\begin{aligned}
&(i.) \quad \mathbb{E}\left\langle \tilde{s}' \cdot \{K' \cdot K\} \cdot \tilde{s} \right\rangle = \mathbb{E}\left\langle trace\left\langle \tilde{s}' \cdot K' \cdot K \cdot \tilde{s} \right\rangle \right\rangle, \\
&(ii.) \quad \mathbb{E}\left\langle trace\left\langle \tilde{s}' \cdot K' \cdot K \cdot \tilde{s} \right\rangle \right\rangle = \mathbb{E}\left\langle trace\left\langle K' \cdot K \cdot \tilde{s} \cdot \tilde{s}' \right\rangle \right\rangle, \\
&(iii.) \quad \mathbb{E}\left\langle trace\left\langle K' \cdot K \cdot \tilde{s} \cdot \tilde{s}' \right\rangle \right\rangle = trace\left\langle K' \cdot K \cdot \mathbb{E}\left\langle \tilde{s} \cdot \tilde{s}' \right\rangle \right\rangle, \\
&(iv.) \quad trace\left\langle K' \cdot K \cdot \mathbb{E}\left\langle \tilde{s} \cdot \tilde{s}' \right\rangle \right\rangle = trace\left\langle K' \cdot K \right\rangle.
\end{aligned} \tag{C20}$$

Thus from Equation (C11):

$$GIR = \sqrt{g} \cdot \sqrt{trace\left\langle K' \cdot K \right\rangle}. \tag{C21}$$

Now we'll attempt to make some investment sense of $trace\left\langle K' \cdot K \right\rangle$. There are two ways we can proceed. The method presented in the main paper is described in section 7, below. Another method using M uncorrelated source portfolios is described in sections 9 and 10.

7. Predicting the Principal Component Returns

In this section we present the investment interpretation of $trace\left\langle K' \cdot K \right\rangle$. It uses the fact that:

$$trace\left\langle K' \cdot K \right\rangle = \sum_{m=1,M} \sum_{n=1,N} \kappa_{n,m}^2 = trace\left\langle K \cdot K' \right\rangle = \sum_{n=1,N} \sum_{m=1,M} \kappa_{n,m}^2. \tag{C22}$$

The generalized information ratio becomes:

$$GIR = \sqrt{g} \cdot \sqrt{\sum_{n=1,N} \left\{ \sum_{m=1,M} \kappa_{n,m}^2 \right\}}. \tag{C23}$$

The remainder of this section shows that we can interpret $\sqrt{\sum_{m=1,M} \kappa_{n,m}^2}$ as an effective skill level, in the spirit of Appendix A, when we use all of the M sources to predict the return on principal component portfolio n.

The unexpected return on principal components portfolio n in any period is $\psi_n \cdot \tilde{\upsilon}_n$ where $\tilde{\upsilon}_n$ has expected value zero and variance equal to Δt. The annualized prediction of this return, using Equations (C2) and (C5) is:

$$apc_n(\tilde{s}) \equiv \mathbf{f}_n' \cdot \mathbf{a}(\tilde{s}) = \sqrt{g} \cdot \psi_n \cdot \sum_{m=1,M} \kappa_{n,m} \cdot \tilde{s}_m \tag{C24}$$

where $\mathbf{f}_n$ is the nth column of the principal component matrix F. The correlation between the return $\psi_n \cdot \tilde{\upsilon}_n$ and prediction $apc_n(\tilde{s})$ depends on the variance of each term along with their covariance. These are easily, if a bit tediously, obtained. It helps that the expected value of $\tilde{\upsilon}_n$ and of $\tilde{s}_m$ is zero. The variance of the principal component return is $\psi_n^2 \cdot \Delta t$. The other terms require an effort. First, the variance of the prediction is:

$$\mathbb{E}\left\langle apc_n^2(\tilde{s})\right\rangle = g \cdot \psi_n^2 \cdot \mathbb{E}\left\langle \left\{ \sum_{m=1,M} \kappa_{n,m} \cdot \tilde{s}_m \right\}^2 \right\rangle = g \cdot \psi_n^2 \cdot \sum_{m=1,M} \kappa_{n,m}^2. \tag{C25}$$

Next, the covariance of the return and prediction is:

$$\mathbb{E}\left\langle \{\psi_n \cdot \tilde{\upsilon}_n\} \cdot apc_n(\tilde{s})\right\rangle = \sqrt{g} \cdot \psi_n^2 \cdot \sum_{m=1,M} \kappa_{n,m} \cdot \mathbb{E}\left\langle \tilde{\upsilon}_n \cdot \tilde{s}_m \right\rangle. \tag{C26}$$

Since $\mathbb{E}\left\langle \tilde{\upsilon}_n \cdot \tilde{s}_m \right\rangle = \sqrt{g} \cdot \kappa_{n,m} \cdot \Delta t$ we have:

$$\mathbb{E}\left\langle \{\psi_n \cdot \tilde{\upsilon}_n\} \cdot apc_n(\tilde{s})\right\rangle = g \cdot \psi_n^2 \cdot \Delta t \cdot \left\{ \sum_{m=1,M} \kappa_{n,m}^2 \right\}. \tag{C27}$$

The correlation between the principal component's return, $\psi_n \cdot \tilde{\upsilon}_n$, and the forecast of return, $apc_n(\tilde{s})$, is defined as:

$$\mathbb{CORR}\left\langle \psi_n \cdot \tilde{\upsilon}_n, apc_n(\tilde{s})\right\rangle \equiv \frac{\mathbb{E}\left\langle \{\psi_n \cdot \tilde{\upsilon}_n\} \cdot apc_n(\tilde{s})\right\rangle}{\sqrt{\mathbb{E}\left\langle \{\psi_n \cdot \tilde{\upsilon}_n\}^2\right\rangle} \cdot \sqrt{\mathbb{E}\left\langle apc_n^2(\tilde{s})\right\rangle}}. \tag{C28}$$

When we substitute Equations (C25) and (C27) into Equation (C28) we obtain:

$$\mathbb{CORR}\left\langle \psi_n \cdot \tilde{\upsilon}_n, apc_n(\tilde{s})\right\rangle \equiv \frac{g \cdot \psi_n^2 \cdot \Delta t \cdot \left\{ \sum_{m=1,M} \kappa_{n,m}^2 \right\}}{\left[\psi_n \cdot \sqrt{\Delta t}\right] \cdot \left\{ \sqrt{g} \cdot \psi_n \cdot \sqrt{\sum_{m=1,M} \kappa_{n,m}^2} \right\}}. \tag{C29}$$

The expression (C29) simplifies to:

$$\mathbb{CORR}\left\langle \psi_n \cdot \tilde{\upsilon}_n, apc_n(\tilde{s})\right\rangle \equiv \sqrt{g} \cdot \sqrt{\sum_{m=1,M} \kappa_{n,m}^2} \cdot \sqrt{\Delta t}. \tag{C30}$$

Let us define:

$$\kappa_n^2 \equiv \sum_{m=1,M} \kappa_{n,m}^2 \quad \text{and} \quad \kappa^2 \equiv \frac{1}{N} \cdot \sum_{n=1,N} \kappa_n^2. \tag{C31}$$

From Equation (C31), we have κ_n as the effective skill in predicting the nth principal component and κ as an average effective skill level over all principal components. With this convention the correlation for the nth principal component forecast with its return becomes:

$$\mathbb{CORR}\left\langle \psi_n \cdot \tilde{\upsilon}_n, apc_n(\tilde{s})\right\rangle \equiv \sqrt{g} \cdot \kappa_n \cdot \sqrt{\Delta t}. \tag{C32}$$

In addition, the entire reward-to-risk ratio becomes:

$$GIR = \sqrt{\mathbb{E}\left\langle \mathbf{a}'(\tilde{s}) \cdot \mathbf{V}^{-1} \cdot \mathbf{a}(\tilde{s})\right\rangle} = \sqrt{\frac{\sum_{n=1,N} \mathbb{CORR}^2\left\langle \psi_n \cdot \tilde{\upsilon}_n, apc_n(\tilde{s})\right\rangle}{\Delta t}} = \kappa \cdot \sqrt{g \cdot N}. \tag{C33}$$

8. Separation of Benchmark and Residual

Suppose there is a reference portfolio W with holdings $\mathbf{w}$, unconditional expected return $\bar{r}_W = \bar{\mathbf{r}}' \cdot \mathbf{w}$ and variance $\sigma_W^2 = \mathbf{w}' \cdot \mathbf{V} \cdot \mathbf{w}$. In order to divide forecasts into benchmark and residual components, we define:

$$\begin{aligned} &(i.) \quad \mathbf{d}' \equiv \frac{\mathbf{w}' \cdot \mathbf{F} \cdot \boldsymbol{\Psi}}{\sigma_W}, \\ &(ii.) \quad \mathbf{L} \equiv \{\mathbf{I} - \mathbf{d} \cdot \mathbf{d}'\} \text{ and} \\ &(iii.) \quad \boldsymbol{\beta} \equiv \frac{\mathbf{V} \cdot \mathbf{w}}{\sigma_W^2}. \end{aligned} \tag{C34}$$

It follows directly that:

$$\begin{aligned} &(i.) \quad \mathbf{d}' \cdot \mathbf{d} = 1, \\ &(ii.) \quad \mathbf{L} = \mathbf{L}', \quad \mathbf{L} \cdot \mathbf{L} = \mathbf{L}, \\ &(iii.) \quad \mathbf{d}' \cdot \mathbf{L} = 0, \\ &(iv.) \quad \tilde{r}_W - \bar{r}_W \cdot \Delta t = \sigma_W \cdot \mathbf{d}' \cdot \tilde{\boldsymbol{\upsilon}} \text{ and} \\ &(v.) \quad \boldsymbol{\beta} = \frac{\mathbf{F} \cdot \boldsymbol{\Psi} \cdot \mathbf{d}}{\sigma_W}. \end{aligned} \tag{C35}$$

We can write the conditional forecast as:

$$\mathbf{a}(\tilde{s}) = \sqrt{g} \cdot \mathbf{F} \cdot \boldsymbol{\Psi} \cdot \mathbf{K} \cdot \tilde{s} = \sqrt{g} \cdot \mathbf{F} \cdot \boldsymbol{\Psi} \cdot \{\mathbf{d} \cdot \mathbf{d}' + \mathbf{L}\} \cdot \mathbf{K} \cdot \tilde{s} \tag{C36}$$

This splits nicely using item $(v.)$ of Equations (C35):

$$\begin{aligned} &\mathbf{a}(\tilde{s}) = a_W(\tilde{s}) \cdot \boldsymbol{\beta} + \boldsymbol{\alpha}(\tilde{s}), \text{ where} \\ &a_W(\tilde{s}) \equiv \sigma_W \cdot \sqrt{g} \cdot \{\mathbf{d}' \cdot \mathbf{K} \cdot \tilde{s}\} \\ &\boldsymbol{\alpha}(\tilde{s}) \equiv \sqrt{g} \cdot \mathbf{F} \cdot \boldsymbol{\Psi} \cdot \mathbf{L} \cdot \mathbf{K} \cdot \tilde{s} \end{aligned} \tag{C37}$$

Note that $\mathbf{w}' \cdot \boldsymbol{\alpha}(\tilde{s}) = 0$, $\boldsymbol{\beta}' \cdot \mathbf{V}^{-1} \cdot \boldsymbol{\alpha}(\tilde{s}) = 0$ and $\boldsymbol{\beta}' \cdot \mathbf{V}^{-1} \cdot \boldsymbol{\beta}' = 1/\sigma_W^2$, so:

$$\mathbf{a}'(\tilde{s}) \cdot \mathbf{V}^{-1} \cdot \mathbf{a}(\tilde{s}) = \frac{a_W^2(\tilde{s})}{\sigma_W^2} + \boldsymbol{\alpha}'(\tilde{s}) \cdot \mathbf{V}^{-1} \cdot \boldsymbol{\alpha}(\tilde{s}) \tag{C38}$$

If we take expectations of Equation (C38), we have:

$$GIR^2 = \mathbb{E}\left\langle \frac{a_W^2(\tilde{s})}{\sigma_W^2} \right\rangle + IR^2, \text{ where}$$
$$IR \equiv \sqrt{\mathbb{E}\left\langle \boldsymbol{\alpha}'(\tilde{s}) \cdot \mathbf{V}^{-1} \cdot \boldsymbol{\alpha}(\tilde{s}) \right\rangle}. \quad \text{(C39)}$$

However:

$$\mathbb{E}\left\langle \frac{a_W^2(\tilde{s})}{\sigma_W^2} \right\rangle = g \cdot \mathbb{E}\left\langle \{\mathbf{d}' \cdot \mathbf{K} \cdot \tilde{s}\}^2 \right\rangle = g \cdot \mathbf{d}' \cdot \mathbf{K} \cdot \mathbf{K}' \cdot \mathbf{d}. \quad \text{(C40)}$$

In the spirit of the analysis in section 7, let us define:

$$\kappa_W \equiv \sqrt{\mathbf{d}' \cdot \mathbf{K} \cdot \mathbf{K}' \cdot \mathbf{d}}. \quad \text{(C41)}$$

Therefore:

$$\mathbb{E}\left\langle \frac{a_W^2(\tilde{s})}{\sigma_W^2} \right\rangle = g \cdot \kappa_W^2. \quad \text{(C42)}$$

The variance of the reference portfolio's return over the next period, and the variance of the forecast, are:

$$(i.) \quad \mathbb{E}\left\langle \{\sigma_W \cdot \mathbf{d}' \cdot \tilde{\upsilon}\}^2 \right\rangle = \sigma_W^2 \cdot \Delta t, \text{ and}$$
$$(ii.) \quad \mathbb{E}\left\langle a_W^2(\tilde{s}) \right\rangle = \sigma_W^2 \cdot g \cdot \kappa_W^2. \quad \text{(C43)}$$

If we recall that $\mathbb{E}\langle \tilde{\upsilon} \cdot \tilde{s}' \rangle = \sqrt{g} \cdot \mathbf{K} \cdot \Delta t$, then we can write the covariance between forecast and return as:

$$\mathbb{E}\left\langle \{\sigma_W \cdot \mathbf{d}' \cdot \tilde{\upsilon}\} \cdot a_W(\tilde{s}) \right\rangle = \sigma_W \cdot \mathbf{d}' \cdot \mathbb{E}\langle \tilde{\upsilon} \cdot \tilde{s}' \rangle \cdot \mathbf{K}' \cdot \mathbf{d} \cdot \sqrt{g} \cdot \sigma_W$$
$$\mathbb{E}\left\langle \{\sigma_W \cdot \mathbf{d}' \cdot \tilde{\upsilon}\} \cdot a_W(\tilde{s}) \right\rangle = \sigma_W^2 \cdot g \cdot \{\mathbf{d}' \cdot \mathbf{K} \cdot \mathbf{K}' \cdot \mathbf{d}\} \cdot \Delta t = \sigma_W^2 \cdot g \cdot \kappa_W^2 \cdot \Delta t. \quad \text{(C44)}$$

Therefore, using Equations (C43) and (C44), the correlation of forecast and return for the reference portfolio is:

$$\mathbb{CORR}\left\langle \sigma_W \cdot \mathbf{d}' \cdot \tilde{\upsilon}, a_W(\tilde{s}) \right\rangle \equiv \frac{\sigma_W^2 \cdot g \cdot \kappa_W^2 \cdot \Delta t}{\{\sigma_W \cdot \sqrt{\Delta t}\} \cdot \{\sigma_W \cdot \sqrt{g} \cdot \kappa_W\}} = \sqrt{g} \cdot \kappa_W \cdot \sqrt{\Delta t}. \quad \text{(C45)}$$

Thus, the information ratio is given by:

$$IR = \kappa \cdot \sqrt{g \cdot N} \cdot \sqrt{1 - \frac{\kappa_W^2}{\kappa^2 \cdot N}}. \quad \text{(C46)}$$

Note that $\kappa_W = \kappa$ implies that $IR = \kappa \cdot \sqrt{g \cdot (N-1)}$; we lose one degree of freedom.

In passing, note that for any nonzero portfolio P with positions $\mathbf{p} \neq 0$ and predicted risk $\sigma_P > 0$ we can define an effective skill, $\kappa_P \geq 0$, in predicting the return on portfolio P through:

$$(i.) \quad \mathbf{y}_P \equiv \frac{\boldsymbol{\Psi} \cdot \mathbf{F}' \cdot \mathbf{p}}{\sigma_P},$$
$$(ii.) \quad \kappa_P \equiv \sqrt{\mathbf{y}_P' \cdot \mathbf{K} \cdot \mathbf{K}' \cdot \mathbf{y}_P}. \quad \text{(C47)}$$

9. Alternative View: Allocating Effective Skill to Prediction of Source Portfolios

In this section, we identify a portfolio with each of the M sources of information and use the resulting analysis to interpret the reward-to-risk ratio in terms of our ability to predict return on these source portfolios.

This analysis will involve another principal components representation. This time we are examining the M by M positive definite[15] symmetric matrix $\mathbf{K}' \cdot \mathbf{K}$. We write:

$$\mathbf{K}' \cdot \mathbf{K} = \mathbf{E} \cdot \mathbf{C}^2 \cdot \mathbf{E}', \quad \mathbf{E} \cdot \mathbf{E}' = \mathbf{I} \tag{C48}$$

where $\mathbf{C}^2$ is an M by M positive diagonal matrix with elements c_m^2 on the diagonal. Therefore:

$$trace\left\langle \mathbf{K}' \cdot \mathbf{K} \right\rangle = trace\left\langle \mathbf{C}^2 \right\rangle = \sum_{m=1,M} c_m^2. \tag{C49}$$

Let c^2 be the average of the c_m^2, i.e., $c^2 = \{1/M\} \cdot \sum_{m=1,M} c_m^2$. Then:

$$GIR = \sqrt{\mathbb{E}\left\langle \mathbf{a}'(\tilde{\mathbf{s}}) \cdot \mathbf{V}^{-1} \cdot \mathbf{a}(\tilde{\mathbf{s}}) \right\rangle} = c \cdot \sqrt{g \cdot M}. \tag{C50}$$

10. Source Portfolios

We can interpret the c_m (see Equation (C48)) as effective skill levels in the spirit of Appendix A, where the correlation over a period of length Δt was $\kappa \cdot \sqrt{g} \cdot \sqrt{\Delta t}$. Consider M portfolios, one for each independent source as columns in the N by M matrix $\mathbf{P}$ where:

$$\mathbf{P} \equiv \sqrt{g} \cdot \mathbf{F} \cdot \boldsymbol{\Psi}^{-1} \cdot \mathbf{K} \cdot \mathbf{E}. \tag{C51}$$

We'll call these the source portfolios. The surprise return on the source portfolios is:

$$\mathbf{P}' \cdot \mathbf{F} \cdot \boldsymbol{\Psi} \cdot \tilde{\boldsymbol{\upsilon}} = \sqrt{g} \cdot \mathbf{E}' \cdot \mathbf{K}' \cdot \tilde{\boldsymbol{\upsilon}} \tag{C52}$$

The variance of the return for the source portfolios using (C51) and (C48) is:

$$\mathbf{P}' \cdot \mathbf{V} \cdot \mathbf{P} = g \cdot \mathbf{C}^2. \tag{C53}$$

Since $\mathbf{C}$ is a diagonal matrix, the returns on the source portfolios are uncorrelated.

The annualized conditional forecast for return on the source portfolios is:

$$\mathbf{a}'(\tilde{\mathbf{s}}) \cdot \mathbf{P} = g \cdot \tilde{\mathbf{s}}' \cdot \mathbf{E} \cdot \mathbf{C}^2. \tag{C54}$$

---

15. $\mathbf{K}' \cdot \mathbf{K}$ is positive semi-definite by construction. If it is not positive definite then one or more of the sources is redundant and could be eliminated.

Recall that the covariance between the return drivers $\tilde{\upsilon}$ and the scores $\tilde{s}$ is $\sqrt{g} \cdot K \cdot \Delta t$ from item (*iii.*) of Equation (C3). With this in hand, the covariance between the source portfolio's return, Equation (C52), and the source portfolio's forecast, Equation (C54), is obtained after grinding through a bit of algebra:

$$\begin{aligned}
&\mathbb{COV}\langle P' \cdot F \cdot \Psi \cdot \tilde{\upsilon}, P' \cdot a(\tilde{s})\rangle = \mathbb{E}\langle P' \cdot F \cdot \Psi \cdot \tilde{\upsilon} \cdot a'(\tilde{s}) \cdot P\rangle, \\
&\mathbb{E}\langle P' \cdot F \cdot \Psi \cdot \tilde{\upsilon} \cdot a'(\tilde{s}) \cdot P\rangle = \sqrt{g} \cdot g \cdot E' \cdot K' \cdot \mathbb{E}\langle \tilde{\upsilon} \cdot s'\rangle \cdot E \cdot C^2, \\
&\sqrt{g} \cdot g \cdot E' \cdot K' \cdot \mathbb{E}\langle \tilde{\upsilon} \cdot s'\rangle \cdot E \cdot C^2 = \sqrt{g} \cdot g \cdot E' \cdot K' \cdot \left\{\sqrt{g} \cdot K \cdot \Delta t\right\} \cdot E \cdot C^2 \\
&\sqrt{g} \cdot g \cdot E' \cdot K' \cdot \left\{\sqrt{g} \cdot K \cdot \Delta t\right\} \cdot E \cdot C^2 = g^2 \cdot \{E \cdot K' \cdot K \cdot E\} \cdot C^2 \cdot \Delta t \text{ so} \\
&\mathbb{COV}\langle P' \cdot F \cdot \Psi \cdot \tilde{\upsilon}, P' \cdot a(\tilde{s})\rangle = g^2 \cdot C^4 \cdot \Delta t.
\end{aligned} \tag{C55}$$

The variance of the forecast on the source portfolios (see Equation (C54)) is:

$$\mathbb{VAR}\langle a'(\tilde{s}) \cdot P\rangle = g^2 \cdot C^2 \cdot E' \cdot \mathbb{E}\langle \tilde{s} \cdot \tilde{s}'\rangle \cdot E \cdot C^2 = g^2 \cdot C^4. \tag{C56}$$

As noted above, the variance of the returns, Equation (C53), is diagonal. In addition, the variance of the forecasts, Equation (C56), is diagonal, and the covariance between the forecasts and the returns, Equation (C55), is also diagonal. Thus, we can examine each source portfolio, or column of **P**, separately. Let $\mathbf{p}_m$ be the *m*th column of **P**. We have:

$$\mathbb{CORR}\langle p_m' \cdot F \cdot \Psi \cdot \tilde{\upsilon}, a'(\tilde{s}) \cdot p_m\rangle = \frac{g^2 \cdot c_m^4 \cdot \Delta t}{\sqrt{g \cdot c_m^2 \cdot \Delta t} \cdot \sqrt{g^2 \cdot c_m^4}} = \sqrt{g} \cdot c_m \cdot \sqrt{\Delta t}. \tag{C57}$$

Therefore:

$$GIR = \sqrt{\sum_{m=1,M} \frac{\mathbb{CORR}^2\langle p_m' \cdot F \cdot \Psi \cdot \tilde{\upsilon}, a'(\tilde{s}) \cdot p_m\rangle}{\Delta t}} = c \cdot \sqrt{g \cdot M}. \tag{C58}$$

11. The Realized *IC*

In Appendix B, we developed an expression for the realized information coefficient in general and a specific result using the model presented in Appendices A, B, and C. The result is:

$$IC\{\tilde{s}, \tilde{\upsilon}\} = \frac{\tilde{\upsilon}' \cdot K \cdot \tilde{s}}{\sqrt{\tilde{\upsilon}' \cdot \tilde{\upsilon}} \cdot \sqrt{\tilde{s}' \cdot \{K' \cdot K\} \cdot \tilde{s}}}. \tag{C59}$$

We can get a rough idea of this value using the following sometimes crude approximations. We are relying on the definition of κ, Equation (C31), to represent $trace\langle K' \cdot K\rangle = \kappa^2 \cdot N$.

$$\mathbb{E}\langle \upsilon' \cdot \upsilon\rangle = N \cdot \Delta t \Rightarrow \sqrt{\upsilon' \cdot \upsilon} \approx \sqrt{N \cdot \Delta t} \text{ and} \tag{C60}$$

$$\begin{aligned}
&\tilde{\upsilon}' \cdot K \cdot \tilde{s} \approx \mathbb{E}\langle \tilde{\upsilon}' \cdot K \cdot \tilde{s}\rangle = \mathbb{E}\langle trace\langle \tilde{s}' \cdot K' \cdot \tilde{\upsilon}\rangle\rangle = \mathbb{E}\langle trace\langle K' \cdot \tilde{\upsilon} \cdot \tilde{s}'\rangle\rangle = \\
&trace\langle K' \cdot \mathbb{E}\langle \tilde{\upsilon} \cdot \tilde{s}'\rangle\rangle = \sqrt{g} \cdot trace\langle K' \cdot K\rangle \cdot \Delta t = \sqrt{g} \cdot \kappa^2 \cdot N \cdot \Delta t.
\end{aligned} \tag{C61}$$

Finally, from Equation (C20) we have:

$$\mathbb{E}\langle \tilde{s}' \cdot \mathbf{K}' \cdot \mathbf{K} \cdot \tilde{s} \rangle = trace\langle \mathbf{K}' \cdot \mathbf{K} \rangle = \kappa^2 \cdot N$$
$$\Rightarrow \sqrt{\tilde{s}' \cdot \mathbf{K}' \cdot \mathbf{K} \cdot \tilde{s}} \approx \kappa \cdot \sqrt{N}. \tag{C62}$$

When we substitute Equations (C60), (C61), and (C62) into Equation (C59), we have:

$$IC\{\tilde{s}, \tilde{\upsilon}\} \approx \frac{\sqrt{g} \cdot \kappa^2 \cdot N \cdot \Delta t}{\sqrt{N \cdot \Delta t} \cdot \kappa \cdot \sqrt{N}} = \kappa \cdot \sqrt{g} \cdot \sqrt{\Delta t}. \tag{C63}$$

SECTION 2

Advances in Active Portfolio Management

SECTION 2.1

Dynamic Portfolio Management

6

Introduction to the Dynamic Portfolio Management Section

This introduction covers the following five articles we have included in Section 2.1:

- Richard C. Grinold. "Implementation Efficiency." *Financial Analysts Journal* 61, no. 5 (September–October 2005): 52–64.
- Richard C. Grinold, "Dynamic Portfolio Analysis," *Journal of Portfolio Management* 34, no. 1 (Fall 2007): 12–26.
- Richard C. Grinold, "Signal Weighting," *Journal of Portfolio Management* 36, no. 4 (Summer 2010): 24–34.
- Richard C. Grinold. "Linear Trading Rules for Portfolio Management," *Journal of Portfolio Management* 44, no. 6, (2018), Special Issue Dedicated to Stephen A. Ross, 109–19.
- Richard C. Grinold, "Nonlinear Trading Rules for Portfolio Management," *Journal of Portfolio Management* 45, no. 1 (Fall 2018): 62–70.

The "Dynamic Portfolio Analysis" paper won the 2009 Bernstein Fabozzi/Jacobs Levy Award for the best article appearing in volume 34 of the *Journal of Portfolio Management.*

This introduction will also summarize results from a related article we haven't included in the book for reasons of space and overlap:

- Richard C. Grinold, "A Dynamic Model of Portfolio Management," *Journal of Investment Management* 4, no. 2 (2006): 5–22.

Transactions costs are the result of motion. Any analysis of the direct and indirect effects of transactions costs on performance must focus on the dynamics of portfolio management. This section is an attempt to understand and control a portfolio as an object in motion.

The first two articles, "Implementation Efficiency" and "Dynamic Portfolio Analysis," strive for strategic understanding—the big picture. They use a simple model that yields analytical expressions for measures of portfolio risk, expected performance, cost, and more. This makes the dynamic model an excellent vehicle for investigating a strategy and asking questions such as: "What is the effect of lowering cost by 10%?" "What is the right rate of trading for this portfolio?" "What happens if I trade too quickly or too slowly?"

The second set of articles, "Signal Weighting," "Linear Trading Rules for Portfolio Management," and "Nonlinear Trading Rules for Portfolio Management," consider operational issues. The five are united by a focus on the dynamic perspective.

Before we start, a warning. Reading the articles is seeing an idea develop and mature. It is not an altogether pretty picture. The notation, terminology, and author evolved along with the ideas.[1] For this reason, the reader would be well advised to go through this introduction before diving into the details. We have included a series of exercises to keep the reader on course and illustrate the richness of the results.

Our initial investigation into the dynamic aspects of portfolio management relies on a tool called linear-quadratic dynamic programming (LQDP). It is also known as linear-quadratic control theory. LQDP evolved roughly around 1960 out of the linear control literature: servomechanisms, feedback control systems, Kalman filters, and the like. In the same era there was a parallel development of dynamic programming, generally associated with Richard Bellman. There is a vast literature on both subjects; see the Internet for generalities and Powell's impressive volume (Powell 2011) for details.

A portfolio optimization problem in its full generality is a large stochastic dynamic programming problem that can't be solved. However, if we make a host of assumptions, many of which we know are rough approximations, then we can pose the problem as a LQDP that can be solved. We must recognize that we are setting ourselves up for a classic trap known as the streetlight effect. In the streetlight story a drunken man searches for his car keys under the streetlight even though he knows he dropped them on the darkened grass some yards away.[2]

The LQDP approach is our streetlight and lets us see very clearly, but we must keep asking if we are looking in the right place and whether we are getting the orders of magnitude and sensitivity right. The results are based on a presumption that LQDP is a large step in the right direction. This means we get the correct order of magnitude of effects and robust insights into the nature of the dynamic portfolio. We will return to the relevance issue after we describe the model and its consequences.

The first three articles in this section use LQDP as a tool. In the linear trading rules article and the nonlinear trading rules article, LQDP supplies

1. We have edited the papers in an effort to get coherent notation. This has been a partial success.

2. There a related aphorism, "For a man with a hammer, everything looks like a nail."

motivation in our search for effective dynamic policies. However, the papers are not about LQDP. Each paper seeks to answer a different investment question. Readers often focus on the technology rather than the product. This is unwise. A cabinetmaker uses a jigsaw to make beds, bureaus, and tables. Look to the beds, bureaus, and tables, not the jigsaw.

Implementation Efficiency and Dynamic Portfolio Analysis

The article "Implementation Efficiency" was the first to use the LQDP framework to get at the direct and opportunity losses associated with trading costs. The paper is in three parts. The first part of "Implementation Efficiency" establishes a number of ways we can express crucial attributes of a portfolio: the risk, the alpha, the transfer coefficient, and the objective value in terms of a covariance or a correlation. The second part of "Implementation Efficiency" uses the optimization's first-order conditions to establish a linear relationship between the optimal position and the ideal no-cost, no-constraint optimal position and positions determined by the constraints and the trading costs. This approach is discussed in Chapter 12, the introductory chapter of the portfolio analysis section.

The dynamic model debuts in the last part of "Implementation Efficiency." The article describes the model and presents closed form solutions of the type related below in a summary that illustrates the main ideas. These notions are carried forward in "Dynamic Portfolio Analysis" and "A Dynamic Model for Portfolio Management."

Inputs

There are four important inputs:[3]

IR_Q	the potential information ratio
λ	a risk penalty
HLY	the half-life of our information, in years
χ	the level of transactions cost

The half-life tells us how long, in years, it will take for our information to lose 1/2 of its forecasting power if it is not refreshed. It easier to think in terms of half-lives but the analytics work better using the decay rate, g, of the information. They are related by:

$$g = \frac{\ln(2)}{HLY} \Rightarrow e^{-g \cdot HLY} = 0.5. \quad (1)$$

3. There is a covariance matrix V in the background. It facilitates calculations and provides scale.

There is one decision (policy) variable:

$$d \equiv \text{the trade rate} \tag{2}$$

The trade rate provides a rebalancing rule and is enough for us to characterize the resulting portfolio we'll call P, with positions $\mathbf{p}(t)$.

Assumptions

The main assumption is that transactions costs are proportional to the variance of the list of assets being traded. This is, at best, a rough approximation although not without some justification. There is a high correlation, say, 0.9, between volatility and transactions cost, and one can make an argument that the price an intermediary will charge to take on a trade list should be proportional to the variance of the list.

The other assumptions are more conventional, concerning stationary system behavior, exact knowledge of volatilities, the forecasting ability of the signals, and the process generating the signals.

Outputs

The outcome is a portfolio, P, that we would hold if we behaved optimally. Results include:

α_P the expected alpha of portfolio P

σ_P the risk of a portfolio P

c_P the expected annual transactions cost of portfolio P

$$O_P \equiv \{\alpha_P - c_P\} - \frac{\lambda}{2} \cdot \sigma_P^2 \text{ the objective value of portfolio } P \tag{3}$$

$$ACIR_P = \frac{\alpha_P - c_P}{\sigma_P} \text{ the after cost information ratio of portfolio } P$$

There are two important ways to use the model:

- Vary the rate of trading, d, and see how key performance parameters change.
- Calculate the optimal level of trading based on the four inputs, see Equation (8) to follow. See how the behavior at the optimum trade rate changes as we vary any of the inputs, λ, χ, g.

Portfolios Q and M

With no transactions cost we would hold a portfolio called Q with holdings $\mathbf{q}(t)$; Q is the *zero-cost* portfolio. Given a trade rate d, the policy is to attempt to track a scaled-back version of Q, which we call the *target* or model portfolio. The target portfolio, denoted M, has position $\mathbf{m}(t)$.

The definition of the model and of the trading rule is:

$$\psi = \frac{d}{d+g} \qquad \text{the scale-back parameter}$$

$$\mathbf{m}(t) = \psi \cdot \mathbf{q}(t) \qquad \text{the target position}$$

$$\dot{\mathbf{p}}(t) = d \cdot \left\{ \mathbf{m}(t) - \mathbf{p}(t) \right\} \qquad \text{the rate of change of the portfolio} \tag{4}$$

where

$$\dot{\mathbf{p}}(t) \equiv \underset{\Delta t \searrow 0}{\text{limit}} \left\{ \frac{\mathbf{p}(t) - \mathbf{p}(t - \Delta t)}{\Delta t} \right\}$$

The trade rate d plays two roles. It defines the target M thorough the scaling parameter, ψ, and it controls the amount of pressure we exert in trying to close the gap between the target and the current position in portfolio P. We'll call the amount we trade per unit time the trading portfolio, $\dot{P}$, which has holdings $\dot{\mathbf{p}}(t)$ defined in Equation (4).

Backlog

The backlog is the difference between the target M and the portfolio P. It represents the trade necessary to get on target. Transactions costs, Equation (7), are proportional to the variance of the backlog. The backlog will continue to play a central role as we make the transition to more complicated dynamic models and trading rules.

Results[4]

All of the key results can be expressed in terms of expected covariances and variances of the portfolios, Q, M, P and $\dot{P}$.

Alpha

$$\alpha_Q = \frac{IR_Q^2}{\lambda} = \lambda \cdot \sigma_{Q,Q} \qquad \text{zero-cost portfolio alpha}$$

$$\alpha_M = \lambda \cdot \sigma_{Q,M} = \psi \cdot IR_Q \cdot \sigma_Q \qquad \text{target portfolio alpha} \tag{5}$$

$$\alpha_P = \lambda \cdot \sigma_{Q,P} = \psi^2 \cdot IR_Q \cdot \sigma_Q \qquad \text{the portfolio alpha}$$

4. These are results for the continuous time case. The analysis is easier in discrete time, but the results are simpler in continuous time, i.e., as the time between trades becomes very small.

Risk

$$\sigma_Q = \frac{IR_Q}{\lambda} \quad \text{zero-cost portfolio risk}$$

$$\sigma_M = \psi \cdot \sigma_Q \quad \text{target portfolio risk}$$

$$\sigma_P = \sqrt{\psi} \cdot \sigma_M = \psi^{3/2} \cdot \sigma_Q \quad \text{portfolio risk} \qquad (6)$$

$$\sigma_{P,M} = \psi \cdot \sigma_M^2 = \sigma_P^2 \quad \text{target-portfolio covariance}$$

$$\sigma_{M-P}^2 = \sigma_M^2 - \sigma_P^2 = \psi^2 \cdot (1-\psi) \cdot \sigma_Q^2 \quad \text{backlog variance}$$

Cost[5]

For the cost we need the variance $\sigma_{\dot{P}}^2$ of the trading portfolio, $\dot{P}$.

$$\sigma_{\dot{P}}^2 = d^2 \cdot \sigma_{M-P}^2 \quad \text{variance of the trade rate, } \frac{\Delta p}{\Delta t}$$

$$c_P = \frac{\chi}{2} \cdot \sigma_{\dot{P}}^2 \quad \text{annual transaction cost} \qquad (7)$$

$$\sigma_{\dot{P}}^2 = d^2 \cdot \psi^2 \cdot (1-\psi) \cdot \sigma_Q^2$$

EXERCISE 1 Given the data in Exhibit 1, calculate the performance of the portfolio, $\alpha_P, \sigma_P, c_P, O_P$, and $ACIR_P$ as the trading rate d varies from 1 to 10 in increments of 0.1. Graph the results.

EXHIBIT 1

IR_Q	lambda	HLY	chi
1.5	20	0.5	1.1

Optimization

The objective is to maximize the value, O_P in Equation (3). The optimal trading rate is:

$$\hat{d} = \sqrt{\frac{\lambda}{\chi}} \text{ which implies}$$

$$\hat{\psi} = \frac{\hat{d}}{\hat{d}+g} = \frac{\lambda}{\lambda + g \cdot \sqrt{\lambda \cdot \chi}}, \text{ and} \qquad (8)$$

$$\chi \cdot \hat{d}^2 = \lambda$$

EXERCISE 2 Using the data in Exhibit 1, vary the cost parameter χ between 0.1 and 10 in steps of 0.1. Select the optimal trade

5. Read this carefully and don't miss the small dot over the P that indicates a time derivative.

rate (Equation (8)) for each level of cost and plot the resulting values of $\hat{d}$, $\hat{\psi}$, α_P, σ_P, c_P, O_P, and $ACIR_P$.

EXERCISE 3 (difficult) Characterize the trade rate, $\breve{d}$ that maximizes the $ACIR$. Is $\breve{d}$ larger than, smaller than, or equal to the trade rate, $\hat{d}$, that maximizes the value, O_P?

Additional Results: The Residual

We can split portfolio P into a component that is correlated with portfolio Q and a residual component, R, with holdings $\mathbf{r}(t)$, that is uncorrelated with Q. The residual constitutes risk with no expected reward; $\alpha_R = 0$. The split is:

$$\mathbf{p}(t) = \psi \cdot \mathbf{m}(t) + \mathbf{r}(t) = \psi^2 \cdot \mathbf{q}(t) + \mathbf{r}(t) \tag{9}$$

Age Profile

We can establish an age profile by decomposing the portfolios into age buckets and calculating portfolios P and Q's exposures to information of different vintages. The average age of the information in the zero-cost portfolio Q and the target portfolio M is $1/g$ years. The average age of the information in portfolio P is $(1/g + 1/d)$ years. With trade rate d we are $1/d$ years behind. The faster we trade, the more we close the age gap.

Opportunity Loss

The structure allows us to allocate the potential risk adjusted gain, $\frac{IR_Q^2}{2 \cdot \lambda} \geq O_P$, to various sources. In Exhibit 2, we set the trade rate at its optimal value so $\psi = \frac{\lambda}{\{\lambda + g \cdot \sqrt{\lambda \cdot \chi}\}}$.

EXHIBIT 2

ITEM	FRACTION
Potential	1
Opportunity Loss	$1 - \psi^2$
Alpha	$2\,\psi^2$
Risk Penalty	$-\,\psi^3$
Transactions Cost	$-\,\psi^2(1 - \psi)$

EXERCISE 4 Using the values for IR_Q, λ, and g from Exhibit 1, vary the cost parameter χ from 0.1 to 10 and plot the fractions of potential value added from Exhibit 2.

Cost Elasticity

As the cost of transacting, χ, increases from zero the optimal trade rate will decrease. Initially the rise in unit cost outpaces the decrease in trading. Costs rise rapidly then start to plateau until:

$$\chi^* = \frac{\lambda}{4 \cdot g^2} \Rightarrow \hat{d} = 2 \cdot g \text{ and } \psi = \frac{2}{3} \tag{10}$$

As the unit cost χ continues to increase there is a greater decrease in trading, so the total cost will gradually decline. A reader who completed Exercise 2 can see this effect. The resulting curve is sending a message. The consequences of underestimating the true cost of trading are far more severe than the consequences of overestimating the level of transactions cost.

EXERCISE 5 Suppose the true level of the cost parameter χ is 2.5 Let a mostly incorrect estimate of cost χ vary from 0.1 to 10 (as in Exercise 2) and the trade rate $d = \sqrt{\lambda / \chi}$ vary as in Equation (8). Plot the expected cost curve (based on the false assumption) and the actual cost curve based on the true level of cost 2.5. In other words, what happens if we choose the trading rate based on the erroneous estimate of the cost parameter equal to, for example 1.3, when it actually is 2.5?

Summary of Implementation Efficiency and Dynamic Portfolio Analysis

This simple model yields a wealth of results. It serves as an excellent starting point for thinking about dynamic portfolio analysis. The results rest on an unencumbered portfolio and transactions cost that are proportional to the variance of the trade list. Are these assumptions too steep a price to pay for the results? A quote from Robert Solow provides a good metric for judging assumptions:[6]

> All theory depends on assumptions which are not quite true. That is what makes it a theory. The art of successful theorizing is to make the inevitable simplifying assumptions in such way that the final results are not very sensitive.

We believe this simplified dynamic model passes that test.

Signal Weighting

Many quantitative investment strategies use multiple sources of information and, in particular, information that acts on different time horizons. There

6. Robert M. Solow, "A Contribution to the Theory of Economic Growth," *Quarterly Journal of Economics* 70, no. 1 (February 1956): 65–94.

may be shorter-term technical information based on returns and data flow. There is very long-dated information based on an analyst's view of competitive forces within a sector and strategic industrial analysis of the prospects of the entire sector. Blending this information is a challenge. The signal weighting article does this based on three inputs: the anticipated strength of the signal as captured by an information ratio, the half-life of the signal, and any correlation between the signals. The approach in the signal weighting article is straightforward. It is a top-down approach; it deals with the signals at the portfolio level not the asset level.

If we assume that transactions costs are proportional to the variance of the portfolio being traded, then the signal weights are a by-product of the LQDP approach. This weighting scheme may not be the ideal solution to the problem, but it establishes a standard and puts the burden of proof on any deviation from that standard.

The notation has to be more complicated since there are multiple sources. In particular portfolios Q and M are now the mixture of J source portfolios.

The signal weighting regime works in two steps.

- **Step 1:** Find the best mix of signals in the case where there are no transactions costs. This is a mean-variance exercise familiar to those who have read *Active Portfolio Management.* The zero-cost weights depend on the strength of the signals, as measured by an information ratio, and any correlation between the signals. The result $\omega_{Q,j}$ is also called a risk allocation, since it has that interpretation as well as the interpretation as a weight.
- **Step 2:** Adjust the weights according to how fast the information decays. This works on a signal to signal basis in exactly the manner we used above in the case of one signal. The adjusted weights are the target weights, $\omega_{M,j}$.

If we trade the aggregate portfolio at rate d and the half-life of signal j in years is $HLYj$, with corresponding decay rate $g_j = \log(2)/HLY_j$, then the target weight for source j is:

$$\omega_{M,j} = \omega_{Q,j} \cdot \frac{d}{d + g_j} \tag{11}$$

The target weights can also be viewed as a risk allocation to the target portfolio. We use the suggestive Greek notation ω to reinforce this interpretation of the weights as an allocation of risk.

More on Step One

The signal weighting article actually involves combining alphas from various sources and skips the task of taking raw information, signals, and turning them into alpha. That task is covered in *Active Portfolio Management*, Chapters 10 and 11. Using those techniques, or the closely related Black-Litterman approach, we produce a collection of return forecasts. Before we weight them, we put them all on the same scale. The standardized alphas are denoted $\{\mathbf{a}_1, \mathbf{a}_2, \cdots, \mathbf{a}_J\}$; each is an N-element vector where N is the number of assets. We use the N by N covariance matrix $\mathbf{V}$ to standardize the forecasts so that $\mathbf{a}'_j \cdot \mathbf{V}^{-1} \cdot \mathbf{a}_j = 1$.

The standardized alphas can also be represented by equally standardized portfolios, $\{\mathbf{q}_1, \mathbf{q}_2, \cdots, \mathbf{q}_J\}$, where $\mathbf{q}_j = \mathbf{V}^{-1} \cdot \mathbf{a}_j$ so that $\mathbf{q}'_j \cdot \mathbf{V} \cdot \mathbf{q}_j = 1$.

By representing each alpha source as a portfolio, we can change the signal weighting problem into a portfolio selection problem. What mix of the portfolios $\{\mathbf{q}_1, \mathbf{q}_2, \cdots, \mathbf{q}_J\}$ do you wish to hold? Since the risk of each portfolio is scaled to 1, 100%, the information ratio of each source portfolio is the same as its alpha. The simple portfolio choice problem is as follows:

$\mathbf{IR} = \left\{IR_j\right\}_{j=1:J}$ The source information ratio

$\mathbf{R}$ Correlation of sources, $R_{i,j} = \mathbf{q}'_i \cdot \mathbf{V} \cdot \mathbf{q}_j$

λ A penalty for risk

$\omega = \left\{\omega_j\right\}_{j=1:J}$ a risk allocation

$$\text{Maximize } \mathbf{IR}' \cdot \omega - \frac{\lambda}{2} \cdot \omega' \cdot \mathbf{R} \cdot \omega$$

$$\text{Solution } \omega_Q = \frac{\mathbf{R}^{-1} \cdot \mathbf{IR}}{\lambda} = \left\{\omega_{Q,j}\right\}_{j=1:J}$$

This is standard operating procedure, straight out of *Active Portfolio Management*. The resulting zero-cost portfolio and the asset alphas are:

$$\mathbf{q} = \sum_{j=1:J} \mathbf{q}_j \cdot \omega_{Q,j}$$
$$\alpha = \lambda \cdot \mathbf{V} \cdot \mathbf{q} \Rightarrow \alpha = \sum_{j=1:J} \mathbf{a}_j \cdot \{\lambda \cdot \omega_{Q,j}\} \qquad (12)$$

More on Step 2

The second step rests on a multisource version of the dynamic portfolio model. Each information source has an information decay rate, g_j. Then, with an *assumed* trading rate d, the modified risk allocations (weights) and resulting target portfolio are:

$$\omega_{M,j} = \omega_{Q,j} \cdot \psi_j \text{ where}$$
$$\psi_j = \frac{d}{d + g_j} \qquad (13)$$
$$\mathbf{m} = \sum_{j=1:J} \mathbf{q}_j \cdot \omega_{M,j} \quad \text{the target portfolio}$$

Much of the signal weighting paper is concerned with the best way to select d, the assumed rate of trading. Inference, trial and error, and common sense are leading contenders. There is also a great deal of material reinforcing the interpretation of $\omega_{Q,j}$ and $\omega_{M,j}$ as risk allocations.

EXERCISE 6: With a risk penalty, $\lambda=20$, a trading rate $d = 3$, and the data on signals in Exhibit 3 below, calculate the risk allocations for the zero-cost portfolio Q and the target portfolio M. Also calculate the resulting alpha, risk, and information ratios of portfolios Q and M.

EXHIBIT 3 Signals Strength (*IR*), Speed (*HLY*) and Correlation *Ri,j*

SIGNAL	IR	HLY	R(:,1)	R(:,2)	R(:,3)
FAST	4	0.008	1	−0.1	0
INT.	1.5	0.333	−0.1	1	0.2
SLOW	1	0.750	0	0.2	1

Implementation: Toward an Optimal Trading Policy

The dynamic perspective is useful in providing strategic insight and top-down signal weighting. Now we'll move toward day-to-day implementation. This starts with abandoning the assumption that transactions costs are proportional to the variance of the portfolio of assets being traded. Instead we'll use more conventional measures of transactions cost such as we find in Equations (15) and (19).

If the goal is complete generality, all signals, all costs, all assets, and all constraints, then we would attack the problem using stochastic dynamic programming. In the linear-quadratic case, it is possible to solve relatively large problems since the optimal policy results from solving a system of linear equations. Once we leave the comfort of the linear-quadratic case we face immense difficulties. Consider a general formulation using dynamic programming with N assets and J signals per asset. The resulting state space is $N^*(J + 1)$ real numbers, **p**, **S** where **p** is an N element vector of current positions and **S** is an N by J matrix of signal values. With 2,000 assets and 29 signals per asset, the state space is 60,000 real numbers. It we discretize these 60,000 states using 10 discrete values along each dimension we end up with $10^{60,000}$ discrete states. MATLAB calls this number *Inf.*

If we lower our sights and choose to analyze a single asset, then the state space would be 30 real numbers. A discretization of these 30, although not quite *Inf*, would be immense. We require a fresh approach.

We have settled on solving single asset problems using the sim/opt algorithm that works by restricting the class of investment policies to a promising and manageable set.

A policy is a function that considers the current situation (the state) and selects an action. In our case the state is the active position in a stock plus the value of J signals that we believe tell us about future returns on that stock: p_0 is the position and $\mathbf{s} = \{s_j\}_{j=1:J}$ are the signals. We call the function a trading rule:

$$\Delta p = f\left(p_0, \mathbf{s}\right) \text{ is a policy/trading rule} \tag{14}$$

There are an infinite number of policies to consider. We will take a page from Voltaire and abandon the search for the best of all possible policies and make an educated guess at a good family of policies. We aim for good, not perfect, solutions.

Our first compromise is to focus on one asset. The second compromise is to reduce the J signals to a single number, the target position, $m(\mathbf{s})$, and then making the driver of our trading rule the backlog, $b\left(\mathbf{s}, p_0\right) = m\left(\mathbf{s}\right) - p_0$, the gap between the desired and actual position.

Linear Trading Rules

The linear trading rule article is an example of this approach. In the one asset linear-quadratic case the optimal policy is linear function of the current state. This is powerful motivation. If a linear trading rule is optimal in a special case, it should be good in a more general case. We call the resulting class of policies linear trading rules, or LTR. This class is based on a discrete (but small) trading interval Δt.

$$\begin{aligned}
&\text{LTR}\left(\delta\right)\\
&m\left(\mathbf{s}\right) = \sum_{j=1:J} s_j \cdot w_{M,j} \text{ the target}\\
&b\left(\mathbf{s}, p_0\right) \equiv m\left(\mathbf{s}\right) - p_0 \text{ the backlog}\\
&\Delta p = \left(1-\delta\right) \cdot b\left(\mathbf{s}, p_0\right) \text{ where } 0 \le \delta \le 1
\end{aligned}$$

The LTR is asset specific. We could have cluttered up the description with notation like $s_{n,j}$, $w_{M(n),j}$, $m_n\left(\mathbf{s}_n\right)$, $b_n\left(\mathbf{s}_n, p_{n,0}\right)$, δ_n, Δp_n. We omit the subscript n to simplify matters to the greatest extent possible. The delta in the LTR is equivalent to what we frequently call the trading rate d. The link is $\delta = \exp\left(-d \cdot \Delta t\right)$.

The model/target $m(\mathbf{s})$ is a weighted sum of the current signals $\mathbf{s}$. In the signal weighting article, we used a top-down approach to establish the weights. Each signal was represented as a portfolio of N assets and the weighting consisted of blending those portfolios. In the case of trading rules, we will work from the bottom up and customize the signal weighting for each asset. Details to follow.

The LTR says you move part of the way from your current position toward the target. The LTR is straightforward. Both the signal weights,

$\omega_{M,j}$, and δ depend on the trading rate d, so it is just a matter of a one-dimensional search to find the best value of δ.

The LTR is the first example of a simple class of policies. We'll consider three more examples and in the process fashion a general framework for defining policies.

The LQDP strongly suggests that the target, $m(\text{s})$, is the best place to be in the presence of transactions costs. Any gap between your current position and the target represents an opportunity loss. Trading incurs a direct loss. Our policy strives for a proper balance between these two sources of loss.

We can illustrate with a case where the transactions costs are linear plus quadratic:

$$c(\Delta p) = c_1 \cdot |\Delta p| + \frac{c_2}{2} \cdot \Delta p^2 \quad \text{Transactions Cost} \tag{15}$$

As before the backlog, $b(\text{s}, p_0) = m(\text{s}) - p_0$, will drive the trading rule.

Suppose we try to balance the opportunity loss against the direct cost of trading with a single parameter, call it τ. For any value of $\tau > 0$, we select the next trade by solving:

$$\text{Minimize:} \quad \left\{ \frac{\lambda \cdot \sigma^2}{2} \cdot \left(b(\text{s}, p_0) - \Delta p\right)^2 + \tau \cdot c(\Delta p) \right\} \tag{16}$$

The first term in Equation (16) is the annual loss in risk-adjusted return we incur post trade if we are a distance $b\left(\text{s}, p_0\right) - \Delta p$ from target. The cost of the trade, $c\left(\Delta p\right)$, is not annual, it is a one-time loss. The parameter τ transforms the transaction cost into a run rate; for example, if we have to incur this cost every four months in order to stay this close to target, then $\tau = 3$ means we pay the cost three times a year. We call it a transactions cost amortization factor, tcaf for short.

For each value of τ, Equation (16) gives rise to a trading rule.

TCAF (τ)

$b \equiv m\left(\text{s}\right) - p_0$ The backlog, current distance from target

$$z\left(\tau\right) \equiv \frac{\tau \cdot c_1}{\lambda \cdot \sigma^2}, \quad k\left(\tau\right) \equiv \frac{\tau \cdot c_2}{\lambda \cdot \sigma^2}$$

$$\Delta p = \left\{ \begin{array}{lll} BUY & \dfrac{b - z\left(\tau\right)}{1 + k\left(\tau\right)} & \text{if } b > z\left(\tau\right) \\ HOLD & 0 & \text{if } -z\left(\tau\right) \le b \le z\left(\tau\right) \\ SELL & \dfrac{b + z\left(\tau\right)}{1 + k\left(\tau\right)} & \text{if } b < -z\left(\tau\right) \end{array} \right\}$$

The motivation comes from the balancing that typically takes place with a single (or multi-) stage optimization. The objective will have three terms: return, risk, and cost. These will be adjusted by selecting the risk penalty λ and also scaling the transactions costs. In the single-stage case, the parameters (λ, τ) are the dials used to tune into a desired level of risk and turnover. That is a top-down version of the TCAF policy. In our bottom-up version, we vary τ for each asset until we find the best performance. Details on the process for selecting τ follow.

EXERCISE 7 Suppose we use a modified alpha, $\tilde{\alpha}(s) = \lambda \cdot \sigma^2 \cdot m(s)$ rather than the true alpha, $\alpha(s) = \lambda \cdot \sigma^2 \cdot q(s)$, and we attempt to maximize:

$$\tilde{\alpha}(s) \cdot \{p_0 + \Delta p\} - \frac{\lambda \cdot \sigma^2}{2} \cdot \{p_0 + \Delta p\}^2 - \tau \cdot c(\Delta p) \tag{17}$$

Describe the resulting trading rule.

Nonlinear Trading Rules

We can go a step further than the single parameter τ and use two parameters (z, k) and select the trade Δp to minimize:

$$\frac{\lambda \cdot \sigma^2}{2} \cdot (b - \Delta p)^2 + \lambda \cdot \sigma^2 \left\{ z \cdot |\Delta p| + \frac{k}{2} \cdot \Delta p^2 \right\} \tag{18}$$

In this case, we get the nonlinear trading rule, NLTR:

$$\text{NLTR}(z, k)$$

$$\Delta p = \left\{ \begin{array}{lcl} BUY & \frac{b - z}{1 + k} & \text{if } b > z \\ HOLD & 0 & \text{if } -z \le b \le z \\ SELL & \frac{b + z}{1 + k} & \text{if } b < -z \end{array} \right\}$$

The NLTR trading rule is similar to the TCAF trading rule except there are two degrees of freedom in the parameter choice.

EXERCISE 8 Show that $LTR(\delta) = NLTR\left(0, \delta/_{1-\delta}\right)$

As a fourth example, suppose our transactions costs use the 3/2 power:

$$c(\Delta p) = c_1 \cdot |\Delta p| + \frac{c_2}{1.5} \cdot |\Delta p|^{3/2} \quad \text{3/2 Power Transactions Cost} \tag{19}$$

We can generate a policy by again selecting parameters (z, k) and then minimizing:

$$\frac{\lambda \cdot \sigma^2}{2} \cdot (b - \Delta p)^2 + \lambda \cdot \sigma^2 \left\{ \cdot z \cdot |\Delta p| + \frac{k}{1.5} \cdot |\Delta p|^{1.5} \right\} \tag{20}$$

The result is called NLTR1.5, the nonlinear trading rule with 3/2 power transactions cost. The resulting trading policy, conditional on (z, k), is:

$$\text{NLTR1.5}(z, k)$$

$$\Delta p = \left\{ \begin{array}{lcc} BUY & y \text{ where } b - z = y + k \cdot \sqrt{y} & \text{if } b > z \\ HOLD & 0 & \text{if } -z \le b \le z \\ SELL & -y \text{ where } -(b + z) = y + k \cdot \sqrt{y} & \text{if } b < -z \end{array} \right\}$$

EXHIBIT 4 The policy as a function of the backlog. The parameter values are $k = 28$ and $z = 0.013$.

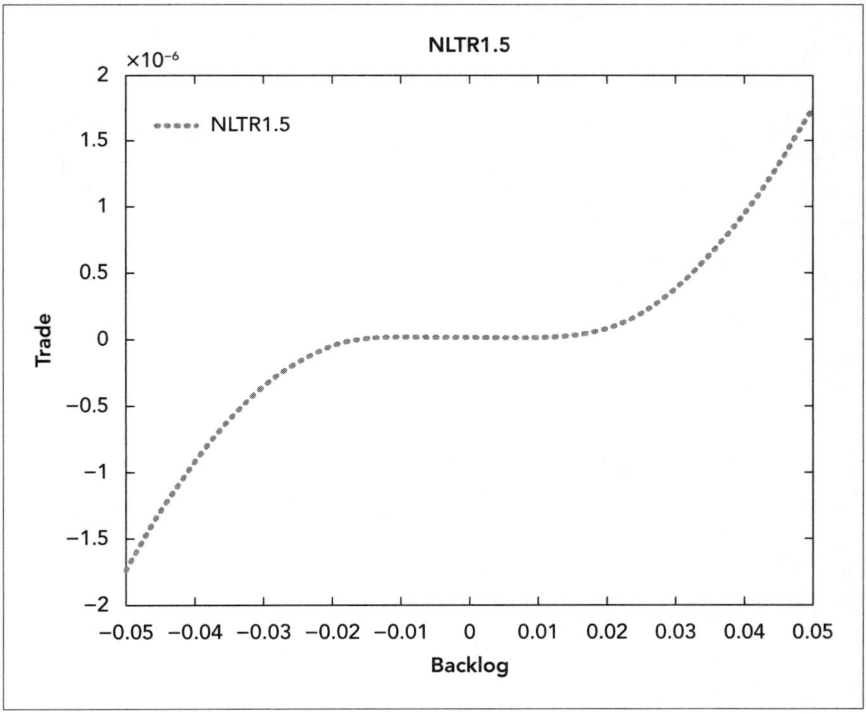

Exhibit 4 shows how the trade size varies when there is a 3/2 power market impact cost and the trading rule, NLTR1.5 is used.

EXERCISE 9 For the trading rule NLTR1.5, suppose $b = 0.02$, $z = 0.01$, and $k = 10$. What is y?

EXERCISE 10 Derive a trading rule, TCAF1.5, when we have the TCAF approach and 3/2 power transactions cost as in Equation (19).

EXERCISE 11 How is TCAF a special case of NLTR?

In all four cases, LTR, TCAF, NLTR, and NLTR1.5, we derive the trading rule by solving a simple one-stage problem with modified transactions cost parameters.

- LTR changes the nonlinear term and ignores the linear term.
- TCAF scales both linear and quadratic terms in the same way.
- NLTR changes the linear and quadratic terms.
- NLTR1.5 changes the linear and 3/2 power terms.

Asset Level Signal Weights

Now we turn to the problem we postponed of selecting the target signal weights at the asset level. What follows is asset specific. We are only considering one asset at a time, so we omit the n notation.

There are J signals. Signals are standardized to have an expected mean of zero and an expected standard deviation of one. Each signal is characterized by a half-life, captured by g_j, and by information coefficients ι_j. The information coefficient is the correlation between the signal and the return we are forecasting. The signals for each asset may be correlated. Let $R_{l,j}$ represent the correlation of the signals i and j. Suppose that θ is the specific return we wish to forecast. Using the results of *Active Portfolio Management*, Chapters 10–11, we can write the best linear unbiased estimator of the return as:

$$\begin{aligned} &\alpha(\mathbf{s}) = Cov\langle\theta, \mathbf{s}\rangle \cdot Var^{-1}\langle\mathbf{s}\rangle \cdot \{\mathbf{s} - E\langle\mathbf{s}\rangle\} \\ &E\langle\mathbf{s}\rangle = 0, \quad Var\langle\mathbf{s}\rangle = \mathbf{R}, \text{ so} \\ &\alpha(\mathbf{s}) = Cov\langle\theta, \mathbf{s}\rangle \cdot \mathbf{R}^{-1} \cdot \mathbf{s} \end{aligned} \tag{21}$$

The volatility of the asset is σ and the correlations of the return and signals are contained in the information coefficient vector $\mathbf{\iota} = \{\iota_j\}_{j=1:J}$. Since the signals have standard deviation equal to one, we have:

$$\begin{aligned} &Cov\langle\theta, \mathbf{s}\rangle = \sigma \cdot \mathbf{\iota}' \Rightarrow \\ &\alpha(\mathbf{s}) = \sigma \cdot \mathbf{\iota}' \cdot \mathbf{R}^{-1} \cdot \mathbf{s} \end{aligned} \tag{22}$$

We prefer to represent the alpha as a position, $q(\mathbf{s})$, where:

$$\alpha(\mathbf{s}) = \lambda \cdot \sigma^2 \cdot q(\mathbf{s}) \tag{23}$$

If we combine Equations (22) and (23), we find the zero-cost signal weights for the asset:

$$\begin{aligned} &\alpha(\mathbf{s}) = \lambda \cdot \sigma^2 \cdot q(\mathbf{s}) = \sigma \cdot \mathbf{\iota}' \cdot \mathbf{R}^{-1} \cdot \mathbf{s} \\ &\Rightarrow q(\mathbf{s}) = \frac{\mathbf{\iota}' \cdot \mathbf{R}^{-1} \cdot \mathbf{s}}{\lambda \cdot \sigma}, \quad \Rightarrow \mathbf{w}_Q = \frac{\mathbf{R}^{-1} \cdot \mathbf{\iota}}{\lambda \cdot \sigma} \end{aligned} \tag{24}$$

We form the target weights and target portfolio in the same manner we used when there was just one signal:

$$\psi_j = \frac{d}{d + g_j}$$
$$w_{M,j} = w_{Q,j} \cdot \psi_j \tag{25}$$
$$m(s) = \sum_{j=1:J} w_{M,j} \cdot s_j$$

The trade rate d is from the optimal delta of the LTR. Thus, we must solve the LTR before proceeding with the other trading rules. Reminder, the link with d and δ is the period length, Δt, $\delta = e^{-d \cdot \Delta t}$.

EXERCISE 12 With the data in Exhibit 5 below, use a spreadsheet to plot the target signal weights as the trade rate, d, moves from 0.1 to 10 in increments of 0.1.

EXHIBIT 5

NAME	HLY	IC	R(:,1)	R(:,2)	R(:,3)
FAST	0.0119	0.25	1	−0.15	−0.05
INT.	0.333	0.1	−0.15	1	0.1
SLOW	0.666	0.085	−0.05	0.1	1

Simulation-Optimization

In Appendix A of the linear trading rules article, we derive analytical expressions that allow us to choose the best value of d or equivalently δ with transactions cost of the type in either Equation (15) or (19). In the case of TCAF, NLTR, or NLTR1.5, we must resort to a less elegant and less exact technique known as simulation/optimization, henceforth sim/opt. Here are the steps in the sim/opt algorithm for one asset.

1. Find the optimal δ for the LTR policy. This produces an optimal linear trade rate d and the signal weights $\omega_{Q,j}$ and $\omega_{M,j}$.
2. Simulate the J signals for each period over a long horizon. In our case, daily (252 trading days per year) for 100 years: the result is

   $$\left\{s_j(t)\right\}_{j=1:J} \quad \text{for } t = 1{:}T.$$

3. The alphas (forecast of annual return) follow from the simulated signals and the zero-cost signal weights

   ω_Q: $\alpha(t) = \lambda \cdot \sigma^2 \cdot \sum_{j=1:J} s_j(t) \cdot w_{Q,j}$.

4. Set the initial position to zero.[7]
5. For any pair (z, k), apply the relevant trading rule. This produces a sequence of positions and trades $\left\{p(t), \Delta p(t)\right\}_{t=1:T}$.
6. Evaluate the performance of the sequence of positions and trades. This involves the following:

$$\text{Value} = \{\text{Alpha} - \text{Cost}\} - \frac{\lambda}{2} \cdot \text{Risk}^2 \tag{26}$$

where:

$$\text{Alpha} = \frac{1}{T} \cdot \sum_{t=1:T} \alpha(t) \cdot p(t)$$

$$\text{Risk}^2 = \frac{\sigma^2}{T} \cdot \sum_{t=1:T} p^2(t)$$

$$\text{Cost} = \frac{c_1 \cdot \sum_{t=1:T} \left|\Delta p(t)\right| + \frac{c_2}{1.5} \cdot \sum_{t=1:T} \left|\Delta p(t)\right|^{3/2}}{T \cdot \Delta t} \tag{27}$$

or

$$\text{Cost} = \frac{c_1 \cdot \sum_{t=1:T} \left|\Delta p(t)\right| + \frac{c_2}{2} \cdot \sum_{t=1:T} \left|\Delta p(t)\right|^2}{T \cdot \Delta t}$$

7. Repeat steps 5 and 6 in a systematic search for the pair (z, k) whose trading rule leads to a sequence $\{p(t), \Delta p(t)\}_{t=1:T}$ with the highest value.

Two Important Points

When we evaluate a policy (z, k), we calculate the transactions cost using the **original** cost parameters (c_1, c_2), **not** the modified t-cost parameters we used to produce the trading rule. Also, the transactions cost used to calculate value is the total cost over the history divided by the number of years thus making it the same annual run rate as the alpha and variance terms.[8]

If we are forecasting uncorrelated specific returns, then the variance terms in Equation (27) add across assets, maximizing each one maximizes the total. The same is true in expectation even with correlated returns as long as the signals that generate the position for one asset are uncorrelated with the signals that generate the position for any other assetas demonstrated by Equation (28).

7. There is an elegant way to choose the initial position discussed in the nonlinear trading rules article. It does not matter. Zero is a good starting point since some assets with low volatility and high transactions cost (somewhat of an anomaly) will *never* trade during the 100-year simulation! Starting at zero helps to spot those outliers.

8. In making these calculations, we suggest that you do not include the first year (or longer) of the simulation to avoid any effects due to the initial conditions.

$$\begin{aligned} &\text{for } n \neq \ell \quad E\langle p_n(t) \cdot \sigma_{n,\ell} \cdot p_\ell(t)\rangle = 0 \\ &\text{if either } \sigma_{n,\ell} = 0 \\ &\text{or } E\langle p_n(t) \cdot p_\ell(t)\rangle = 0 \end{aligned} \tag{28}$$

In aggregate we have:

$$\begin{aligned} \alpha_P &= \sum_{n=1:N} \text{Alpha}_n \\ \sigma_P^2 &= \sum_{n=1:N} \text{Risk}_n^2 \\ c_P &= \sum_{n=1:N} \text{Cost}_n \\ V_P &= \{\alpha_P - c_P\} - \frac{\lambda}{2} \cdot \sigma_P^2 \end{aligned} \tag{29}$$

A by-product of the calculation is another useful performance metric, the after-cost information ratio:

$$\text{ACIR}_P = \frac{\alpha_P - c_P}{\sigma_P} \tag{30}$$

The numerator of $ACIR_P$ is the expected performance and, under an assumption of normal active returns, the probability that a standard normal is less than minus $ACIR_P$ is the probability of a down year.

EXERCISE 13 If $ACIR_P = 0.9$ and $\sigma_P = 4\%$, what is the probability of a down year? What alpha do we expect net of transactions costs?

The Parameter Model

The sim/opt algorithm is a blunt instrument performing a delicate task. Errors will occur. In the nonlinear trading rule article, we propose log-log models to estimate a model of the parameters:

$$\begin{aligned} \log(k_n) &= \phi_1 + \phi_2 \cdot \log(c_{1,n}) + \phi_3 \cdot \log(c_{2,n}) + \phi_4 \cdot \log(\sigma_n) + \zeta_n \\ \log(z_n) &= \beta_1 + \beta_2 \cdot \log(c_{1,n}) + \beta_3 \cdot \log(c_{2,n}) + \beta_4 \cdot \log(\sigma_n) + \xi_n \end{aligned} \tag{31}$$

It turns out that the fitted parameters, call them $\hat{z}_n$, $\hat{k}_n$ have, by design, a smaller cross-sectional standard deviation and, as hoped, perform just as well in terms of Value*P* in an out-of-sample simulation.

Exhibit 6 shows the regression results for a NLTR1.5 model with 3136 assets.[9]

9. There is considerable room for improvement in the parameter model. The regression above accomplishes little save regression to the mean. The model is included to illustrate the concept. In this sample the correlation of $c_{2,n}$ and σ_n was about 0.9 and the other two correlations about 0.7.

EXHIBIT 6 Regression Coefficients for a Parameter Model Using 3,136 US Assets and the Trading Rule NLTR1.5

	IMPACT *k*	ZONE *z*
Constant	–7.86	–8.49
c(1,*n*)	–1.20	–0.15
c(2,*n*)	0.88	–0.27
s(*n*)	–0.66	–0.47
R2	73%	70%

Implementation

Implementation requires a move from the asset to the portfolio level and the use of the n notation to distinguish among the N assets. We strive for the best of both worlds. Our goal is to capture the dynamic policy we have developed at the asset level without losing focus on portfolio level constraints and exposure control. We can do this by minimizing an objective that has two components.

$$\begin{aligned}&\text{Component 1}\\&\frac{\lambda}{2}\cdot\sum_{n=1:N}\sigma_n^2\cdot\left\{\left(b_n-\Delta p_n\right)^2+z_n\cdot\left|\Delta p_n\right|+\frac{k_n}{1.5}\cdot\left|\Delta p_n\right|^{1.5}\right\}\\&\text{Component 2}\\&\frac{\eta}{2}\cdot\left(\mathbf{x}_B-\mathbf{X}\cdot\Delta\mathbf{p}\right)'\cdot\{\mathbf{F}+\mathbf{D}\}\cdot\left(\mathbf{x}_B-\mathbf{X}\cdot\Delta\mathbf{p}\right)\end{aligned}\tag{32}$$

In component 1, $b_n=\sum_{j=1:J}s_{n,j}\cdot w_{M(n),j}-p_n$ is the backlog for asset n. Component 1 has the trading rule—in this case, NLTR1.5—hardwired. If component 2 did not exist and there were no binding constraints, minimizing component 1 would execute the optimal dynamic trading rule NLTR1.5 for every asset.

Component 2 represents tugs in other directions. It presumes desired factor positions based on either risk control or a factor/smart beta tilt. The term $\mathbf{x}_B$ is the factor backlog measuring how far our current position is from a desired exposure. **F** is a factor covariance matrix, and **D** is a nonnegative diagonal matrix that can be used to give extra incentive to stay close to the desired exposures. In addition to this there could be constraints.[10]

10. There is an extended rant on the role of constraints in the linear trading rules article.

Summary

There is a common theme in these six articles, focused on understanding and implementing a dynamic system of portfolio management. This introduction takes the most important ideas from the six articles and presents them in an integrated fashion with a unified notation, an emphasis on the most valuable lessons, and the benefit of hindsight. The articles progress from theory to suggested implementation.

References

Aside from the papers themselves and the results of *Active Portfolio Management*, the key additional reference is:

Powell, Warren B. 2011. *Approximate Dynamic Programming: Solving the Curses of Dimensionality*. 2nd ed. Wiley Series in Probability and Statistics.

7

Implementation Efficiency[1]

1. Introduction

Investment management relies on an ability to understand and manage three forces: return, risk, and cost. The understanding, if not the management, of risk and return is well advanced in the finance field—stemming from Markowitz's notion of mean-variance efficiency and Sharpe's economic explanation of expected return. In that risk-return landscape, any presumed potential for adding investment value can be summarized by the information ratio—that is, the expected exceptional return (alpha) divided by the amount of risk assumed in pursuit of that exceptional return.

Alas, potential is one thing and delivery another. The ability to move the cup of investment potential to the lip of the bottom line is restricted by institutional and economic realities and, in some cases, by a lack of attention to the task. The institutional limitations are constraints either self-imposed or imposed by a principal. The economic realities are costs. These costs take many forms, but the largest costs and the costs most dependent on the investment manager's actions stem from trading. The world of return, risk, and cost is not well understood and is a significant challenge in advancing the theory of portfolio management. This chapter describes a strategic framework for thinking about and analyzing costs or, more broadly, implementation losses. I use the notions of covariance and correlation that are central in the study of risk and return and have been effectively exploited by Clarke, de Silva, and Thorley (2002, 2005) in their study of implementation efficiency.

The information ratio is key to measuring active investment potential. However, analysts should not concentrate on the information ratio to

1. This chapter originally appeared as "Implementation Efficiency" by Richard Grinold in the September/October 2005 issue of the *Financial Analysts Journal*.

the exclusion of our investment objective. As the objective, I use the active management version of mean-variance utility that consists of portfolio alpha minus two penalties—one for active risk and one for implementation costs. This objective is variously called "risk-adjusted alpha" or "certainty-equivalent alpha." I concentrate on the effect of constraints and costs on the objective value. The objective and the information ratio are linked since the strategy that maximizes risk adjusted-alpha in a constraint- and cost-free environment also has a maximum information ratio. When there are costs and constraints, that linkage breaks down, but happily, my work can characterize the impact of costs and constraints on both the objective and the information ratio.

The two barriers to implementation efficiency are opportunity costs and implementation costs. Opportunity costs are the loss in benefits an investor would anticipate if the investor were not limited by constraints or deterred from acting by the presence of trading costs. Implementation losses are associated with the transactions that the investor attempts. These losses include the direct cost of trading, anticipated market impact, and the estimated losses associated with trades attempted but not completed. This article presents a model for the loss of value added with and without the consideration of implementation costs.

Preview

In section 2 we introduce notation and terminology and present the general results before implementation costs. Section 3 offers one method for allocating opportunity loss between the trading costs and constraints and, in general between any number of costs or constraints. Section 4 considers results on an after-implementation cost basis. With the aid of several assumptions, section 4 describes a model that extends the general results of section 2. The exposition tends toward the technical; however, the reader can be assured that most of the theoretical development is left to the Appendix to Chapter 8.[2]

2. General Results: Before Costs

Notation and Terminology

We'll have a brief review of some concepts introduced in prior chapters. We consider a universe of N assets and indicate *active* positions as holdings vectors, $\mathbf{x} = \{x_1, x_2, ..., x_N\}$ and $\mathbf{y} = \{y_1, y_2, ..., y_N\}$ respectively for positions X and Y. These will be called both positions and portfolios. There is *no* requirement that the positions be nonnegative or to sum to either one or zero. Risk is measured with an N by N covariance matrix $\mathbf{V}$. The risk of position

2. Note that this chapter and Chapter 8, "Dynamic Portfolio Analysis," share the Appendix that follows Chapter 8.

X is $\omega_X = \sqrt{\mathbf{x}' \cdot \mathbf{V} \cdot \mathbf{x}}$, and the respective covariance and correlation of positions X and Y are given by by:

$$\omega_{X,Y} = \mathbf{x}' \cdot \mathbf{V} \cdot \mathbf{y} = \omega_X \cdot \rho_{X,Y} \cdot \omega_Y. \tag{1}$$

The forecast of exceptional asset return is $\boldsymbol{\alpha} = \{\alpha_1, \alpha_2, .., \alpha_N\}$. With this we can calculate the alpha of any position P as $\alpha_P = \boldsymbol{\alpha}' \cdot \mathbf{p}$. The information ratio of the position P is $IR_P = \alpha_P / \omega_P$.

Our precost investment criterion is risk adjusted or certainty equivalent alpha. For position P it is:

$$U_P = U(\boldsymbol{\alpha}, \mathbf{p}) \equiv \alpha_P - \frac{\lambda}{2} \cdot \omega_P^2. \tag{2}$$

The second term in Equation (2) is a penalty for active variance. For example, with $\lambda = 20$, and risk levels, ω_P, of 1%, 2%, 3%, and 4%, there would be respective adjustment to the alpha of 0.10%, 0.40%, 0.90%, and 1.60%.

The ideal position attains the maximum of Equation (2). This optimal position is referred to as portfolio Q. The direct link between Q and the forecast $\boldsymbol{\alpha}$ is:

$$\boldsymbol{\alpha} = \lambda \cdot \mathbf{V} \cdot \mathbf{q}. \tag{3}$$

Portfolio Q captures the alphas in portfolio form.

$$\begin{aligned}
&(i.)\quad U_Q = \frac{\lambda}{2} \cdot \omega_Q^2 \\
&(ii.)\quad IR \equiv \sqrt{\boldsymbol{\alpha} \cdot \mathbf{V}^{-1} \cdot \boldsymbol{\alpha}} = IR_Q \ge IR_P \text{ for any } P \\
&(iii.)\quad IR = \lambda \cdot \omega_Q \Rightarrow U_Q = \frac{IR^2}{2 \cdot \lambda}. \\
&(iv.)\quad U_P = U_Q - \frac{\lambda}{2} \cdot \omega_{Q-P}^2
\end{aligned} \tag{4}$$

Important Attributes

Equation (4) describes properties of the ideal position Q. Our task is to determine the properties of a less than optimal position P. For any strategy P there are two measures that help explain the level of implementation efficiency. These measures link position P with the ideal position Q; they compare where we are with where we would like to be.

The first attribute is the *transfer coefficient*. In general, the correlation between any two positions, say, X and Y, is $\rho_{X,Y}$. The transfer coefficient of portfolio X is thus $\rho_{X,Q}$.

The backlog, B, is the difference between a favored position, in this case Q, and the actual implementation P; $\mathbf{b} = \mathbf{q} - \mathbf{p}$ is the trade required to transform P into Q. The second attribute is the variance of the backlog position:

$$\omega_{Q-P}^2 \equiv \omega_Q^2 - 2 \cdot \omega_{P,Q} + \omega_P^2 = \omega_B^2. \tag{5}$$

We will also use the beta of portfolio P with respect to Q:

$$\beta_P = \frac{\omega_{P,Q}}{\omega_Q^2} = \rho_{P,Q} \cdot \frac{\omega_P}{\omega_Q}. \tag{6}$$

Results

The first result links the portfolio's information ratio, IR_P, to the maximal attainable information ratio, IR, introduced in Equation (4). For any position P:

$$IR_P \equiv \frac{\alpha_P}{\omega_P} = \rho_{P,Q} \cdot IR \tag{7}$$

where $\rho_{P,Q}$ is transfer coefficient. Our ability to implement effectively is proportional to our degree of alignment with Q.

We can split position P into two parts, one part that is aimed directly at alpha and a second, residual part, call it R, that has no alpha.

$$\mathbf{p} = \beta_P \cdot \mathbf{q} + \mathbf{r}, \quad \beta_P = \frac{\omega_{Q,P}}{\omega_Q^2}. \tag{8}$$

Position R is by construction uncorrelated with Q, so from Equation (3) the alpha of position R is zero, $\boldsymbol{\alpha}' \cdot \mathbf{r} = 0$. We also see from Equation (8) that the variance of the residual R is is:

$$\omega_R^2 = \left(1 - \rho_{P,Q}^2\right) \cdot \omega_P^2. \tag{9}$$

Thus, a fraction $\rho_{P,Q}^2 \cdot \omega_P^2$ of the variance of P is devoted to the pursuit of alpha while the residual variance ω_R^2 is risk without expected reward.

The difference, $U_Q - U_P$, as the *opportunity loss*, is proportional to the variance of the backlog position.

$$\begin{aligned} L_P &\equiv \frac{\lambda}{2} \cdot \omega_{Q-P}^2 \quad \text{opportunity loss for portfolio } P \\ L_P &= U_Q - U_P. \end{aligned} \tag{10}$$

Note that Equation (10) can be rearranged as:

$$\frac{U_P}{U_Q} = 1 - \frac{\omega_{Q-P}^2}{\omega_Q^2} \leq \rho_{P,Q}^2 \tag{11}$$

The equality follows directly from Equation (10) and item (*i.*) in Equation (4). The inequality follows by fixing the transfer coefficient and then choosing the value of the ratio ω_P/ω_Q that maximizes the right-hand side of Equation (12).

Equation (11) is depressing news. We can think of a transfer coefficient of $\rho_{P,Q} = 0.7$ as operating at 70% efficiency. However, as Equation (11) points out, the consequences of that 70% efficiency for potential added are dire; 70% efficiency limits us to *at most* 49% of the potential value added before dealing with transactions cost. From Equation (9) it means that 51% of the position's variance is not linked to any expected alpha.

Example

Exhibit 1 is based on a comparison between a portfolio *Q* that is optimal without constraints and a portfolio *P* that is optimal with a long-only constraint. The exhibit shows how the transfer coefficient depends on the volatility, ω_P, of an optimal portfolio constrained to be long only. In this case we have done side-by-side comparisons with the average risk of the individual assets increasing from 15% to 35%. Position sizes tend to be inversely related to volatility, thus with the high-volatility assets we bump into the long-only restriction less often.

EXHIBIT 1 Transfer Coefficient Link to Long-Only Investing for Different Asset Volatility Levels and Different Levels of Active Risk

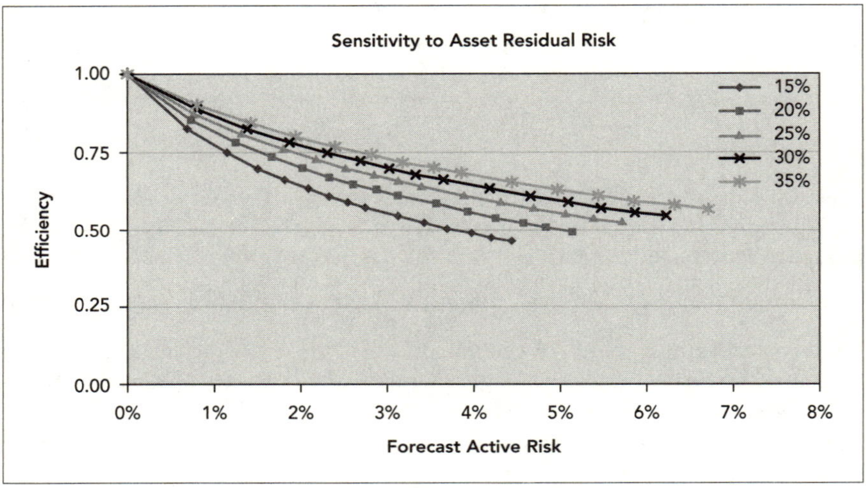

Ex Ante and Ex Post

Our results are expressed in terms of ex ante (forecasted) information ratios and predictions of risk-adjusted returns. One can examine these criteria on an ex post (realized) basis. However, this adds considerable noise to the process and raises a host of questions such as: "Our policy limiting large active positions in growth stocks reduces efficiency on an ex ante basis but actually helps on an ex post basis; does this mean our constraint improves implementation efficiency?" Questions such as this come in infinite variety. If one tries to limit an investment process in *K* ways it will turn out that about *K*/3 or maybe *K*/4 help on an ex post basis. Is this meaningful? Maybe, but this should be considered a backhanded form of data mining until proven innocent.

A more judicious course is to establish a prior hypothesis, something like, "Our most extreme forecasts for growth stocks are more likely to be based on a false premise." Then take steps to dig deeper on extreme forecasts for growth stocks or rein in the alphas in a more formal manner; in other words, identify the problem, verify that it exists, and attack the problem at its source.

3. Allocation of Opportunity Loss to Constraints and Trading Costs

In the previous section we saw how the opportunity loss was equal to the risk penalty applied to the backlog portfolio, Equation (10). That answers the aggregate question. In this section we address a more difficult question. If there are several reasons, say transactions costs and constraints, that cause the opportunity loss, then how do we parcel out the losses to the various sources? There is no totally satisfactory way to do this. We'll present one approach following the notion that it is better to light a candle than to curse the dark.

The approach is general and consistent although a bit on the light side theoretically in that it uses the marginal cost of the constraints and transactions cost to calculate their total impact. In the absence of anything better we can use it while remaining aware of the potential limitations.

We'll turn to a portfolio optimization process that we assume was used to produce the position *P*.

Let's write the optimization problem as:

$$\begin{aligned} &\text{Maximize} \quad \alpha' \cdot \mathrm{p} - \frac{\lambda}{2} \cdot \mathrm{p}' \cdot \mathrm{V} \cdot \mathrm{p} - c\,(\mathrm{p}, \mathrm{z}) \\ &\text{subject to the constraints } \mathrm{A} \cdot \mathrm{p} \le \mathrm{d} \end{aligned} \tag{12}$$

Where:

- Portfolio Z with holdings **z** is the initial position,
- $c\left(\mathbf{p}, \mathbf{z}\right)$ is the cost of moving from **z** to **p**, and
- $\mathbf{A} \cdot \mathbf{p} \le \mathbf{d}$ are the constraints, including upper and lower bounds.
- The objective is called $O_P = U_P - c_P$ for short.

We can write the objective as:

$$\begin{aligned} O_P &= U_Q - \left\{\frac{\lambda}{2} \cdot \omega_{Q-P}^2 + c_{P-Z}\right\} \\ \Delta O_P = O_P - O_Z &= \frac{\lambda}{2} \cdot \omega_{Q-Z}^2 - \left\{\frac{\lambda}{2} \cdot \omega_{Q-P}^2 + c_{P-Z}\right\} \end{aligned} \tag{13}$$

We see from Equation (13) that the optimization is minimizing opportunity loss plus the direct cost c_{P-Z}.

We can with a few reservations split the opportunity loss term into losses caused by constraints and the intimidation of trading cost. If there are several constraints and multiple sources of cost (e.g., spread and market impact), then we can use the concept described below to allocate the opportunity loss among the several sources. The first-order conditions from the portfolio optimization provide the key.

The first-order conditions are a valuable by-product of any optimization. They are a generalization of the rule "set the derivative equal to zero." After some manipulation the first-order conditions will yield an equation for each asset, thus N equations. For problem (12) these may be written as:

$$\alpha = \lambda \cdot V \cdot p + \nabla c\,(p, z) + A' \cdot \upsilon \tag{14}$$

The expression $\nabla c\,(\mathbf{p}, \mathbf{z})$ represents the marginal transactions cost.[3] This is positive if buying and negative if selling. The second expression, $A' \cdot \upsilon$, relates to the constraints, $\mathbf{A} \cdot \mathbf{p} \leq \mathbf{d}$. The vector **d** is a vector of scarce resources. If there are J constraints, then $\upsilon \geq 0$ is a J element vector, called the Lagrange multiplier or dual variable, that captures the marginal value of increasing the scarce resources.[4] The expression $A' \cdot \upsilon$ is a vector, one element for each asset. Note that Equation (3) is the same as Equation (14) when there are no constraints or transactions costs.

Here are three ways to interpret Equation (14):

- If we had started with alpha equal to $\boldsymbol{\alpha} - \{\nabla c\,(\mathbf{p}, \mathbf{z}) + \mathbf{A}' \cdot \boldsymbol{\upsilon}\}$ and ignored both constraints and trading costs, we would find P as our optimal position.
- If we had started with alpha equal to $\boldsymbol{\alpha} - A' \cdot \boldsymbol{\upsilon}$ and ignored constraints, we would find P as our optimal position.
- If we had started with alpha equal to $\boldsymbol{\alpha} - \nabla c(\mathbf{p}, \mathbf{z})$ and ignored trading costs, we would find P as our optimal position.

We can think of Equation (14) as an allocation of alpha. A portion of the alphas, $A' \cdot \boldsymbol{\upsilon}$ is allocated to the constraints and a portion $\nabla c\,(\mathbf{p}, \mathbf{z})$ is allocated to the transactions costs; $\lambda \cdot \Omega \cdot \mathbf{p}$ is left for portfolio P.

We can take a lesson from Equation (3), $\boldsymbol{\alpha} = \lambda \cdot \mathbf{V} \cdot \mathbf{q}$, and express the marginal transactions costs and the marginal cost of the constraints in terms of asset positions:

$$\begin{aligned} \nabla c\,(p, z) &= \lambda \cdot V \cdot k \\ A' \cdot \upsilon &= \lambda \cdot V \cdot f \end{aligned} \tag{15}$$

With the definitions in Equation (15) we can associate a cost position K with holdings **k** and a constraint position F (for force) with holdings **f**.[5] If we combine Equation (15) with Equation (3), then Equation (14) reads as:

$$\begin{aligned} &\mathbf{q} = \mathbf{p} + \mathbf{k} + \mathbf{f} \text{ or} \\ &\mathbf{q} - \mathbf{p} = \mathbf{k} + \mathbf{f} \text{ the backlog.} \end{aligned} \tag{16}$$

The positions K and F have alphas and risks. Indeed, the variances, $\omega_K^2 = \mathbf{k}' \cdot \mathbf{V} \cdot \mathbf{k}$, $\omega_F^2 = \mathbf{f}' \cdot \mathbf{V} \cdot \mathbf{f}$ and the covariance $\omega_{K,F} = \mathbf{f}' \cdot \mathbf{V} \cdot \mathbf{k}$ are the two

3. If the optimization also includes accounting constraints $\mathbf{p}$ – **buys** + **sells** = $\mathbf{z}$, with **buys** and **sells** required to be nonnegative, then the dual variable for the accounting constraints is the $\nabla c\,(\mathbf{p}, \mathbf{z})$ required in Equation (22).

4. Think of υ_j as the partial of the optimal value with respect to changes in the constraint level d_j; $\frac{\partial O_P}{\partial d_j}$.

5. There are too many c-words, cost constraint, etc. Thus, for the transactions cost we use K and for the constraints, F, for force.

parts of the backlog and play a key role in the allocation of opportunity loss. Equation (16) tells us that the backlog, $B = Q - P$ is made up as a cost portion **k** and a constraint portion **f**.

The opportunity loss is:

$$L_P = U_Q - U_P = \frac{\lambda}{2} \cdot \omega_{Q-P}^2 = \frac{\lambda}{2} \cdot \omega_{F+K}^2 = \frac{\lambda}{2} \cdot \left\{\omega_F^2 + 2 \cdot \omega_{K,F} + \omega_K^2\right\} \quad (17)$$

The expression above can be conveniently split, Solomon fashion, as:

$$L_P = \frac{\lambda}{2} \cdot \left\{\omega_F^2 + \omega_{F,K}\right\} + \frac{\lambda}{2} \cdot \left\{\omega_{F,K} + \omega_K^2\right\}. \quad (18)$$

We attribute the opportunity loss $\lambda \cdot \left\{\omega_F^2 + \omega_{F,K}\right\}/2$ to the constraints and the opportunity loss $\lambda \cdot \left\{\omega_{F,K} + \omega_K^2\right\}/2$ to the trading costs.

To look at the value added by rebalancing from the initial portfolio Z to P we have:

$$O_P - U_Z = \{L_Z - L_P\} - c_{P-Z}. \quad (19)$$

The benefit of the move from Z to P is reducing the opportunity loss weighted against the cost, c_{P-Z}, of moving from Z to P.

There is an example of this approach in Chapter 12, the introduction to the section on portfolio analysis. For another example see the article "Attribution of Performance and Holdings" by Grinold and Easton (1998).

4. Specific Model: After-Cost Results

Under special circumstances we can obtain analytic after-cost results for both the information ratio and the objective. This requires a few sacrifices. Since we recall that the hunter who chases two rabbits won't catch either, we'll focus on problems with transactions cost and no constraints. In addition, we'll assume that the costs have a special structure that, although reasonable, is at best an approximation of actual costs. The price we pay for this rough approximation is rewarded by the ability to see the problem completely. It is an illustrative result that shines a beam of light into an otherwise dark space. It does not turn the lights on.

Trading costs influence implementation efficiency in two ways. There is the direct loss in terms of spread and market impact, and indirect opportunity loss due to intimidation. The mere threat of trading costs deters us from trading and opportunities slip by. When costs are extremely high, we don't attempt any trades, and all is lost through intimidation.

To develop after-cost results requires additional notation. Let c_P be the *annual* costs (more on this below) for trading position P. Our goal is to explore the risk-adjusted return after costs discussed above and the after-cost information ratio, $ACIR$.

$$O_P = \alpha_P - \frac{\lambda}{2} \cdot \omega_P^2 - c_P = U_P - c_P = U_Q - \{L_P + c_P\}$$
$$ACIR_P = \frac{\alpha_P - c_P}{\omega_P}. \tag{20}$$

The *ACIR* is handy since it is a good metric for comparing strategies for different risk levels. The numerator is expected performance, and the larger the *ACIR* the smaller the probability of a down year.

In section 2, we compared the zero-cost strategy *Q* that is optimal with no costs or constraints with *any* strategy *P*. In this section, in contrast, we compare *Q* with a strategy *P* that is *optimal* with costs considered. The results, at least with respect to the investment criterion, can be considered as an upper bound on what might be achieved by *any* strategy.

We need four parameters to describe the environment:

IR the strength of the information
λ a penalty for active variance
g the arrival rate of new information
χ a parameter to measure the cost level (21)

We are already familiar with the information ratio and the penalty for active variance. The new characters are the arrival rate of information,g, and the cost parameter, χ.

New information is constantly arriving, and old information is getting stale. We will assume that information flows in at more or less the same rate as it loses its forecasting power. The parameter g measures this rate. Another way to think of it is that $1/g$ is the average age of the information in the system. The half-life of the information, denoted HL, is related to the arrival rate g by $g \cdot HL = \log(2)$.

The Cost Model

If we slice the year up into small periods of length Δt = 1/252 then we can measure the rate of trading at any time through the measure:

$$\dot{\mathbf{p}}(t) = \frac{\mathbf{p}(t) - \mathbf{p}(t - \Delta t)}{\Delta t}. \tag{22}$$

Don't miss the *dot* over the **p** in the left-hand side of Equation (22). This indicates a time derivative. We measure the size of this trading rate using its expected variance that we call $\omega_{\dot{P}}^2$ (again note the dot) where:

$$\omega_{\dot{P}}^2 \equiv E\langle \dot{\mathbf{p}}'(t) \cdot \mathbf{V} \cdot \dot{\mathbf{p}}(t) \rangle. \tag{23}$$

Our assumption is that the annual transactions costs are proportional to the expected variance (i.e., size squared) of the trading rate.

$$c_P = \frac{\chi}{2} \cdot \omega_{\dot{P}}^2. \tag{24}$$

This is a crude and a convenient approximation. It is crude since it is a rough approximation of reality. It is convenient in that it affords an extraordinary harvest of insight into the dynamics of portfolio management. Rough as the assumption, Equation (24), might be, it does capture some basic points about trading costs:

- Costs are superlinear. Double the rate of trading, and you will more than double the cost of trading.
- Riskier assets are generally more expensive to trade than less risky assets.
- A hedged basket of securities, say, balanced by industry, is cheaper to trade than an unhedged basket.
- The measure compares well at the portfolio level with costs calculated with a customized transactions cost model.[6]

What is a range of reasonable values for χ? Is 0.001 or 1000.0 an appropriate value? For reasons that we'll explain below, $\lambda/\{4 \cdot g^2\}$ is a sensible starting point. Thus with $\lambda = 30$ and $g = 2.77$ we have $\chi = 0.978$.

Optimization

The objective in our optimization, O_P, is the value added, U_P, less the annual transactions costs, c_P.

$$O_P = U_P - c_P. \tag{25}$$

The Appendix outlines the development and solution of the model. There are two decisions we have to make:

- How risky do we want the portfolio to be, ω_P?
- How fast do we want to trade the portfolio, $\omega_{\dot{P}}$?

If we choose the risk level and trading rate to maximize the value added net of annual costs, Equation (25), then the strategy is specified and we can examine its properties. It turns out these properties are determined by a parameter we will call psi, ψ. The parameter psi takes on values between zero and one.

In this simple model the transfer coefficient is the square root of psi. Recall from our general discussion—see Equation (9) and the commentary that follows—that the square of the transfer coefficient is the fraction of portfolio P's variance devoted to the pursuit of alpha. In addition, in Equation (11) the square of the transfer coefficient gives us an upper bound on the fraction of value added we can attain with portfolio P.

6. See Keim and Madhavan (1996).

The optimal value of psi is:

$$\psi = \frac{\lambda}{\lambda + g \cdot \sqrt{\lambda \cdot \chi}} = \rho_{P,Q}^2. \tag{26}$$

With this we can determine the basic properties of the optimal solution. Recall that U_Q is the value added for the optimal strategy with no consideration of costs and that $U_Q = IR^2/(2 \cdot \lambda)$. With that in mind the return, risk, and annual cost for the optimal position P are:

$$\begin{aligned} &(i.) \quad \alpha_P = 2 \cdot \psi^2 \cdot U_Q \\ &(i.) \quad \omega_P = \psi^{3/2} \cdot \{IR/\lambda\} \\ &(iii.) \quad c_P = \{1 - \psi\} \cdot \psi^2 \cdot U_Q \end{aligned} \tag{27}$$

Exhibit 2 contains a graph of these basic ingredients as costs, the parameter χ, are increased. For this example we have $IR = 1.75$, $\lambda = 30$, and $g = 2.77$.

EXHIBIT 2 Annual Alpha and Transactions Cost as the Level of Cost is Increased

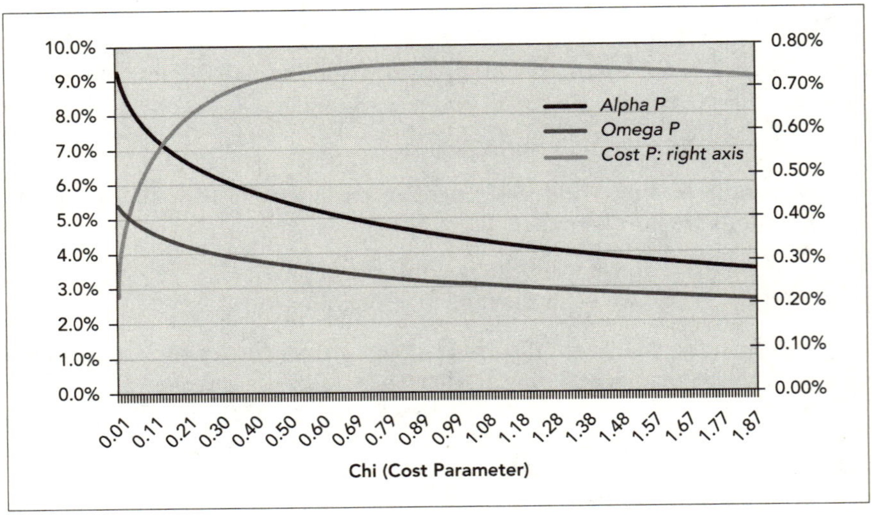

In Exhibit 2 our willingness to commit to the strategy in terms of risk declines monotonically as cost is increased. We start at about 5.5% with very low cost and eventually decreasing to about 2.75%. The projected alpha falls as well from a bit over 9.00% to about 3.5%.

The annual cost of implementing the strategy (plotted on the right axis) increases sharply at first, then peaks at about 0.75% and subsequently declines slowly. The story is a familiar one. At zero or very low cost we trade rapidly. As costs become more significant, we rein in the strategy by reducing risk and slowing down the trading. Eventually the response overwhelms the increase in cost and it leads to a net reduction in cost. The point where cost reaches a maximum is where the cost parameter chi is equal to $\chi = \lambda/4 \cdot g^2$.

At that point the psi, ψ, is equal to 2/3 and the costs max out at 4/27 of the potential value added U_Q. Details are in the appendix.

Exhibit 3 shows the information ratio, before and after cost cost:

EXHIBIT 3 The Effect of an Increasing Level of Transactions Cost on the Precost and Postcost Information Ratio

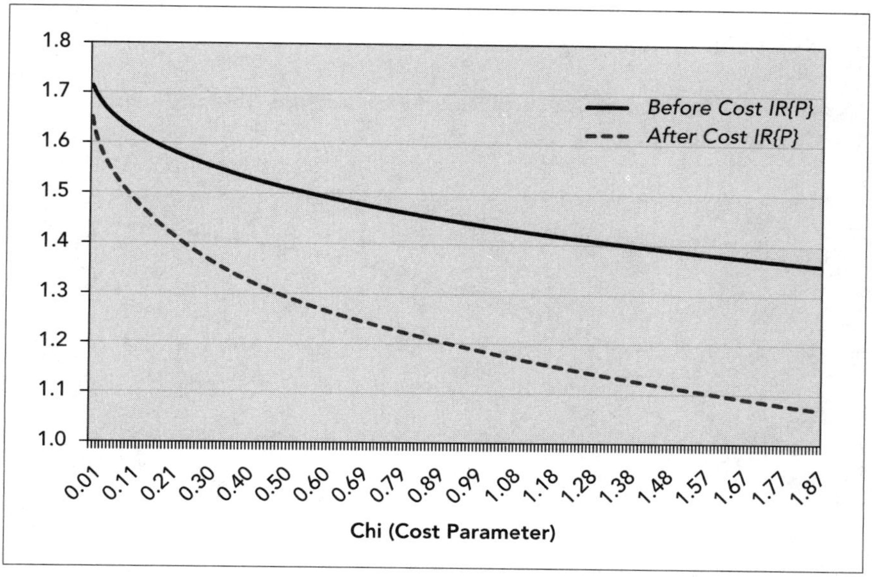

Exhibit 4 shows the policy response to increasing costs: a decreasing level of risk, ω_P, and decreasing turnover. We cannot measure turnover directly in this model, but the trade risk, $\omega_{\dot{P}}$, is an excellent surrogate for turnover.

EXHIBIT 4 The Response of Risk and the Rate of Trading to Increasing Costs

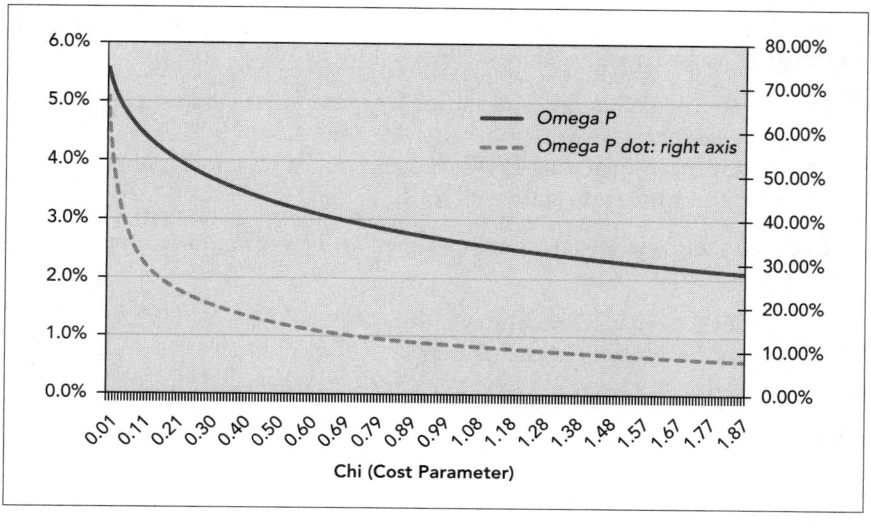

Note in Exhibit 4 that trading decelerates rapidly at first and then decreases in lockstep with the strategy's risk and we get to reasonable levels of cost.

Finally Exhibit 5 examines the response from a loss perspective. The exhibit shows the opportunity loss, dotted line, and the sum of the transactions cost and the opportunity loss, solid line. Although the annual transactions cost incurred by the strategy stay relatively flat as the parameter χ increases, the opportunity loss continues to mount.

EXHIBIT 5 Opportunity Cost and Direct Transactions Costs as a Function of the Cost of Trading, χ

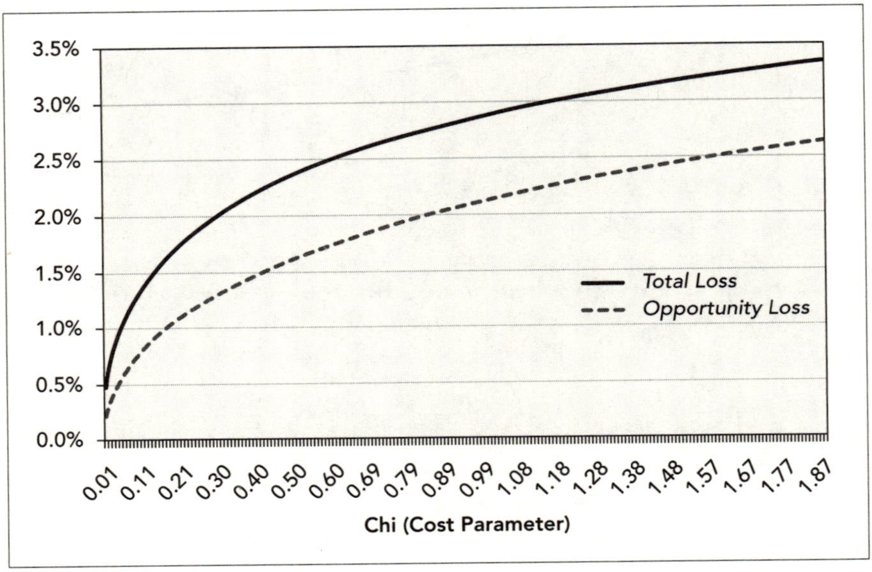

In this section we have presented a simple model of an investment strategy with costs and no constraints. The inputs are:

- the ability to add value measured by the information ratio,
- the risk penalty,
- the rate at information flows into and out of the model, and
- the size of the transactions costs.

With this unadorned structure we can specify the optimal investment strategy in terms of

- the level of risk in the strategy and
- the rate of trading in the strategy.

Finally, with this optimal policy we can analytically describe the characteristics of the optimal policy; see Equations (26) and (27).

The model allows one to explore product design directly and rapidly. It is particularly useful in seeing how policy should adjust to changing circumstances such as a speeding up/slowing down of the information available, a decrease/increase in the information's value-added potential, or an increase/decrease in transactions cost.

5. Summary

This chapter established a framework for the study of implementation efficiency. We explained implementation efficiency within the portfolio analysis framework using constructions such as the backlog risk and the transfer coefficient to capture the essential nature of implementation drag. The framework relies on a comparison between an ideal and actual implementation called, respectively, *Q* and *P*. The standard of comparison is alpha less a penalty for active variance.

The results in section 2 are general. They compare any implementation with an ideal implementation without costs or constraints. The loss in objective value depends upon the risk of the trade needed to move from position *P* to position *Q* called the backlog. In addition, we confirm and generalize the notion of the transfer coefficient as a measure of the fraction of the precost information ratio that is being captured. Indeed, we show that the fraction of objective value that is captured is bounded above by the square of the transfer coefficient.

In section 3 we showed how one could attribute opportunity loss to multiple sources and hopefully provide a clue on how implementation might be improved. The illustration is at the aggregate level but would work down to the level of individual constraints and bounds as well as splitting transactions cost into spread and market impact components.

In section 4 we look at the case where there are costs and no constraints. We assume that transaction costs are proportional to the variance of the trade under consideration. Under this and other less heroic assumptions we are able to obtain simple expressions for implementation efficiency after costs. The model has a property that we have seen in more complicated backtests and simulations. Trading costs rise due to an increase in assets under management. The costs paid however will tend to stay roughly constant over a wide range. The portfolio management process responds by reducing active risk, reducing turnover, and slowing down the trading process. Thus, the bulk of the impact is opportunity loss and not in the costs actually paid.

The efficient management of investment portfolios requires an ability to understand, measure, forecast, and manage risk, return, and costs. If we presume a return forecasting advantage, then implementation becomes a task of balancing that return advantage against the risks and costs incurred. The cost dimension is particularly difficult since cost, by its nature, is a dynamic phenomenon; costs are incurred through changes in positions. Thus, any insights we gain along the cost dimension must be accompanied by a dynamic theory of portfolio management. However, dynamic theories tend to be so highly specialized (a single asset or rebalancing to a fixed position) or so obscure, the classic "black box," that any potential insight is limited.

References

Clarke, Roger, Harindra de Silva, and Steven Thorley. 2002. "Portfolio Constraints and the Fundamental Law of Active Management." *Financial Analysts Journal*, September/October.

Clarke, Roger, Harindra de Silva, and Steven Thorley. 2005. "Performance Attribution and the Fundamental Law." *Financial Analysts Journal* 61 (5): 70–83. doi:10.2469/faj.v61.n5.2758.

Grinold, Richard C. 2006. "A Dynamic Model of Portfolio Management." *Journal of Investment Management* 4 (2): 5–22.

Grinold, Richard C., and Ronald N. Kahn. 1995, 2000. *Active Portfolio Management: Quantitative Theory and Applications*. Probus Press. 2nd ed., McGraw Hill.

Grinold, Richard C., and Ronald N. Kahn. 2000. "The Efficiency Gains of Long-Short Investing." *Financial Analysts Journal* 56 (November/December): 40–53.

Grinold, Richard C., and Kelly Easton. 1998. "Attribution of Performance and Holdings." In *Worldwide Asset and Liability Modeling*, edited by J. Mulvey and W.T. Ziemba, Chapter 5, 87–113. Cambridge University Press.

Keim, Donald B., and Ananth Madhavan. 1996. "The Upstairs Market for Large-Block Transaction: Analysis and Measurement of Price Effects." *Review of Financial Studies* 9: 1–36.

Thorley, Steven. 2003. Private communication.

8

Dynamic Portfolio Analysis[1]

Establishing a Link Between Cause and Effect

1. Introduction

The active long-short investment strategy described here is the simplest system based on three principles:

- Old information becomes stale.
- New information arrives.
- Trading occurs to close the gap between what we hold and what we would like to hold.

There are two parameters. One measures the rate of change of the information driving the strategy, and the other controls the speed of trading in the portfolio. The system can be used in both a descriptive and a normative manner. In the descriptive application, we observe an investment strategy and estimate the values of the parameters. This will let us reconcile our prior views with the estimated values; in other words, we may think we are doing X, but the data suggest that Y is more likely.

The normative application works at two levels. At the strategic level, we evaluate choices that differ according to the speed of the information flow driving the strategy and the perceived strength of the information. At more of a tactical level, given the speed of information flow, its perceived strength, and the level of costs, we can choose the rate of trading in an optimal manner.

1. This article originally appeared as "Dynamic Portfolio Analysis" by Richard C. Grinold in the Fall 2007 issue of *The Journal of Portfolio Management.* It won the 2009 Bernstein Fabozzi/Jacobs Levy Award for the best article in the journal that year (technically in Volume 34 of the journal).

This is called dynamic portfolio analysis. It works at the aggregate level—lots of forest, no trees. We are not trying to capture the detailed nature of the investment strategy, but rather its most salient characteristics. To that end, I do not shy away from simplifying assumptions. Some of these are more open to challenge than the rest, but the true test of them all is the ability of the resulting theory to deliver on its promises. I hope to present a portrait that captures the essence, omits the details, and reveals a constructive perspective.

The section breakdown is as follows. In section 2 of this chapter we introduce two portfolios and the laws of motion (difference equations) that govern their evolution. The first portfolio is called "the model." We would trade to the model if we were given a holiday on transactions costs. The second portfolio is called "the portfolio"; it is the positions we actually hold. The first difference equation describes the information flow via changes in the model. The second difference equation shows how we adjust the portfolio to make it more like the model.

In section 3 we view the strategy from a "stock and flow" perspective. Stock in this case does not mean equity; it refers to the expected absolute size of all positions in the portfolio. Flow is the annual round trip turnover in the portfolio. The relationship between stock and flow is governed by the two parameters that describe the model and the portfolio's laws of motion.

Section 4 shows how our simple structure allows us to characterize the potential efficiency of the strategy in several ways. These include the transfer coefficient and the expected age (vintage) of the information in our portfolio. In addition, we see how the notions of breadth and the transfer coefficient relate to the age of the information in the portfolio.

In section 5 we discuss how we can (roughly) choose an optimal rate of trading to strike an appropriate balance between tracking a model portfolio and trading costs. We provide analytic expressions for the most important characteristics when we are following such a policy.

In section 6 we apply these ideas to a strategy. We estimate the values of the two parameters and use those values and the previously developed theory to explain and predict the portfolio's behavior. Section 7 is a summary. Technical matters are relegated to the appendices to this chapter that serve this article and Chapter 7, "Implementation Efficiency."

2. The Laws of Motion

There are N assets. Time is discrete. We rebalance the portfolio at regular intervals of length Δt years. Think of Δt as a month (1/12), a week (1/52), or a trading day (1/252). The investment strategy is long-short with no constraints. We are concerned with two portfolios. The first is a model, M, with holdings $\mathbf{m}\,(t)$ at time t. It is also known as "the model," or the "target," or simply M. Portfolio M is a portfolio whose holdings have a maximum information ratio. The second is the portfolio we hold (aka "the portfolio" or P), the vector $\mathbf{p}\,(t)$ contains our positions in the N assets at time t. In a world free of transactions cost we would have $\mathbf{p}(t) = \mathbf{m}(t)$; things would be wonderful and less interesting.

Changes in the Model (M)

The change in M, $\Delta\mathbf{m}(t) \equiv \mathbf{m}(t) - \mathbf{m}(t - \Delta t)$, arises from the arrival of new information and the fading of old information. The equation is:

$$\Delta\mathbf{m}(t) = -g \cdot \mathbf{m}(t - \Delta t) \cdot \Delta t + \mathbf{u}(t) \quad (1)$$

The erosion of old information is captured by the term $g \cdot \mathbf{m}(t - \Delta t) \cdot \Delta t$; this is the anticipated change in M. The new information is represented by $\mathbf{u}(t)$, that embodies the unanticipated changes in M. In equilibrium new information flows in at roughly the same rate that it is flowing out. Let ω_M^2 and ω_U^2 be respectively the expected variance[2] of M and the positions implied by the new information. For the system to be in equilibrium we must have:

$$\omega_U^2 = 2 \cdot g \cdot \omega_M^2 \cdot \Delta t \ . \quad (2)$$

The Parameter g

The parameter g plays a leading role in what follows. The parameter g is an annual rate of information loss with $g \cdot \Delta t$ being the expected information loss over one rebalance cycle. We can characterize g in other ways. In section 4 we show that $1/g$ is the average age of the information in the model. We anticipate that the size of any model position will gradually shrink to zero. Let HL be the amount of time until the expected model position is one-half its current size. HL is the half-life of the information and is related to g and the average age of information in the model through $HL = \ln(2)/g$. Since $\ln(2) = 0.693$, the half-life is about 70% of the average age. The term $\gamma = e^{-g \cdot \Delta t}$ is the correlation of $\mathbf{m}(t)$ with $\mathbf{m}(t - \Delta t)$. Exhibit 1 shows various values of g, the corresponding half-lives (in years), the autocorrelation γ (gamma), the fraction of information we lose, $g \cdot \Delta t$ over a daily trading cycle (i.e., $\Delta t = 1/252$), and $1/g$, the average age (in years) of the information.

EXHIBIT 1 The Parameter *g*, Half-Life (in Years), Autocorrelation Gamma, % Loss of Information, and Average Age

g	HALF-LIFE	γ	% LOSS	AVE. AGE
8.00	0.087	0.969	3.17%	0.13
6.00	0.116	0.976	2.38%	0.17
4.00	0.173	0.984	1.59%	0.25
2.00	0.347	0.992	0.79%	0.5
1.00	0.693	0.996	0. 40%	1.00

All based on a daily trading cycle, $\Delta t = 1/252$.

2. At time t with covariance matrix $\mathbf{V}(t)$ the variance is $\omega_M^2(t) = \mathbf{m}'(t) \cdot \mathbf{V}(t) \cdot \mathbf{m}(t)$. The expected variance is $\omega_M^2 = E\langle \omega_M^2(t) \rangle$. In the same way $\omega_U^2 = E\langle \mathbf{u}'(t) \cdot \mathbf{V}(t) \cdot \mathbf{u}(t) \rangle$.

The parameter g is also related to the concept of breadth in the fundamental law of active management (Grinold 1989). That law says that the potential information ratio, IR, of a strategy is equal to the product of forecasting skill (as measured by the correlation of the forecasts with outcomes aka the information coefficient or IC) times the square root of the number of independent forecasts per year (the breadth or BR). In algebraic terms, $IR = IC \cdot \sqrt{BR}$. A reasonable estimate[3] for breadth in an N asset strategy is:

$$BR = g \cdot N. \tag{3}$$

The potential IR is achieved by M so we have for any portfolio P:

$$IR = IR_M = IC \cdot \sqrt{g \cdot N} \geq IR_P. \tag{4}$$

Trading Policy, the Change in P

The change in P, $\Delta\mathbf{p}(t) \equiv \mathbf{p}(t) - \mathbf{p}(t - \Delta t)$, is the amount we trade.[4] The trade is linked to M by a second difference equation:

$$\Delta\mathbf{p}(t) = d \cdot \{\mathbf{m}(t) - \mathbf{p}(t - \Delta t)\} \cdot \Delta t. \tag{5}$$

Unlike Equation (1), there is no uncertainty in Equation (5). We know the pretrade portfolio, $\mathbf{p}(t - \Delta t)$, and the model, $\mathbf{m}(t)$, so the trade size is specified. The uncertainty enters indirectly through Equation (1). Also note that there is no trade if our pretrade portfolio is in the right spot, when $\mathbf{p}(t - \Delta t) = \mathbf{m}(t)$.

The Parameter d

The gap between M and P is called the *backlog*. We close the backlog at an annual rate of d with $d \cdot \Delta t$ being the fraction of the gap closed in any one period. In equilibrium the gap between M and P will stay roughly constant, see Equation (14) below. In section 5 we see that an optimal value of d is linked to trading costs; higher costs call for slower trading and thus a smaller value of d.

As with g, $1/d$ is an interval of time. It is (see Equation (19)) the age gap between portfolios P and M.

We will have occasion to refer to $\delta \equiv e^{-d \cdot \Delta t}$. The term δ is *not* the autocorrelation of the portfolio. The term $1 - \delta \approx d \cdot \Delta t$ is the fraction of holdings that change in any one rebalance.

3. Suppose that in the period Δt we get new information (a complete change) for K of the assets and absolutely no change for the remaining $N - K$ assets. Since there are $1/\Delta t$ periods per year, this implies a breadth of $K/\Delta t$. If we regress $\mathbf{m}(t)$ against $\mathbf{m}(t - \Delta t)$ we get a coefficient $\gamma = \{N - K\}/N$. Thus $K/N = 1 - \gamma \approx g \cdot \Delta t$, or $g \cdot N \approx K/\Delta t$. This is covered in more depth in Chapter 5.

4. We are ignoring changes in relative position size due to price movement. This tends to be a second-order effect.

The Rebalance Interval

The rebalance interval or trade cycle, Δt, should be selected contingent on the values of g and d. If information is flowing rapidly, large g, then Δt should be small. If we are trading quickly, large d, then Δt should be small. A good rule of thumb is that Δt should be small enough so that the approximations $(1-\gamma)=\left(1-e^{-g\cdot\Delta t}\right)\approx g\cdot\Delta t$ and $(1-\delta)=\left(1-e^{-d\cdot\Delta t}\right)\approx d\cdot\Delta t$ are very close.[5] For the remainder of the paper we will treat these approximations as if they were exact and consider the laws of motion, Equation (6), as equivalent to Equations (1) and (5):

$$\begin{aligned}\mathbf{m}(t)&=\gamma\cdot\mathbf{m}(t-\Delta t)+\mathbf{u}(t)\\ \mathbf{p}(t)&=\delta\cdot\mathbf{p}(t-\Delta t)+(1-\delta)\cdot\mathbf{m}(t)\end{aligned}\tag{6}$$

3. Stock and Flow

These results are derived in Appendix B to this chapter.

Stock

The stock is the expected total of the long positions and the short positions.[6] If we let $\tilde{p}_n(t)$ be the uncertain position in asset n at time t then stock is:

$$S\equiv E\left\langle\sum_{n=1,N}\left|\tilde{p}_n(t)\right|\right\rangle.\tag{7}$$

Under special circumstances that are detailed in Appendix B, we can obtain a closed form expression for S. This result, Equation (8) below, is not interesting for the purposes of inference; S is eminently observable. Equation (8) is notable because it reveals the drivers of the value of S. If there are N assets, the strategy's risk is ω_P and the average risk[7] of the assets is $\bar{\sigma}$ then:

$$S=\sqrt{N}\cdot\sqrt{\frac{2}{\pi}}\cdot\frac{\omega_P}{\bar{\sigma}}.\tag{8}$$

Higher strategy risk, ω_P, means larger active positions. If the assets are riskier, more $\bar{\sigma}$, then we can get by with smaller positions and still produce the same risk, ω_P, at the strategy level. As we add more assets, we add more positions. However, these positions are generally smaller because we get the benefit of diversification. The netting of those two effects, more and smaller positions, gives us the result that the total increases as the square root of the number of assets. Thus if we went from 400 assets to 900 assets all with the

5. Another criterion for the choice of the trade interval is making Δt sufficiently large so that any liquidity imbalance caused by a trade made at time $t-\Delta t$ will be resolved by time t.

6. The stock is also the expected leverage or gearing of the portfolio. Some people define those quantities by convention as 50% of the stock.

7. $\bar{\sigma}$ is the harmonic average. If asset n has risk σ_n then $1/\bar{\sigma}\equiv\{1/N\}\cdot\sum_{n=1,N}\{1/\sigma_n\}$.

same average risk, $\bar{\sigma}$, and strategy risk, ω_P, then we could expected that the size of the absolute positions, S ,would increase by 50%. The $\sqrt{2/\pi} \approx 0.8$ arises because the expected absolute value of a standard normal random variable is $\sqrt{2/\pi}$.

Flow

The flow is the expected annual round trip turnover. When the strategy is governed in the fashion of the two difference Equations (1) and (5) then the formula (in fact a rough estimate) for the flow is:

$$F = S \cdot \sqrt{g \cdot d}, \text{ or } S = F \cdot \frac{1}{\sqrt{g \cdot d}}. \tag{9}$$

The intuition appears to be correct. Faster moving information, large g, and faster trading, large d, will add to the flow. Recall that $1/g$ and $1/d$; are measured in years. The square root $1/\sqrt{g \cdot d}$ is the harmonic mean of these two times, also measured in years. We can think of the investment process as setting up F new positions per year each of them expected to last an amount of time $1/\sqrt{g \cdot d}$.

4. Model and Portfolio Characteristics

This section takes the laws of motion and links them to characteristics of M and P. There are three subsections:

- Implementation efficiency deals with the P's ability to capture M's information.
- Age distribution considers the exposure of M and P to information of different ages. That analysis offers a different slant on the notions of breadth and the transfer coefficient.
- Trade flow and trade risk are additional measures of flow that will prove useful in our discussion on optimization.

Implementation Efficiency

Results for this subsection are developed in Appendix A. We start with the transfer coefficient of Clarke, de Silva, and Thorley (2002). The transfer coefficient is the correlation of M and P. We have the surprisingly simple result relating the transfer coefficient of P, denoted $\rho_{P,M}$, to d and g.[8]

$$\rho_{P,M} = \sqrt{\frac{d}{d+g}}. \tag{10}$$

8. A caution. This is only true if portfolio M has maximum IR. We can assume this to be true in the case of one signal. In the case of multiple signals, the model/target portfolio does not have maximum IR.

The intuition is correct. Portfolio P is less efficient if the information moves faster (g increases) and the speed of trading is held fixed. Correspondingly, P becomes more efficient as the speed of trading (d) increases while the speed of information flow is fixed. The transfer coefficient is a precost concept, so it is not sensitive to any adverse effects of increasing the speed of trading.

The transfer coefficient is of interest since the information ratio of P (precost) is equal to the transfer coefficient times the information ratio of M; the relationship is:[9]

$$IR_P = \rho_{P,M} \cdot IR_M \,. \tag{11}$$

Let ω_P be the risk level of P and ω_M the risk level of M. The laws of motion imply that:

$$\omega_P = \sqrt{\frac{d}{d+g}} \cdot \omega_M = \rho_{P,M} \cdot \omega_M \,. \tag{12}$$

There is another way to view Equation (12). We can split P's holdings into a piece that is perfectly correlated with M and a portion called $\mathbf{r}(t)$ for residual that is uncorrelated with M. The partition is:

$$\mathbf{p}(t) = \frac{d}{d+g} \cdot \mathbf{m}(t) + \mathbf{r}(t). \tag{13}$$

Thus $d/(d+g)$ is the beta of P with respect to M. The two parts of the portfolio in Equation (13) are uncorrelated, so we can see, using Equations (10) and (12), that a fraction $d/(d+g)$ of P's variance is compensated risk and, on the glass empty side, a fraction of P's risk budget, $g/(d+g)$, is spent with no compensating expected return.

We get yet another perspective on implementation effectiveness by considering the backlog, $P - M$, mentioned previously. The backlog is the trade we would make if we were given a one-time holiday from transactions costs. The risk of the backlog is the standard deviation of the return difference between M and P, denoted by ω_{M-P} . With our laws of motion, the backlog risk is:

$$\omega_{M-P} = \sqrt{\frac{g}{d}} \cdot \omega_P = \sqrt{\frac{g}{d+g}} \cdot \omega_M \,. \tag{14}$$

Once again, faster-moving information hurts and, at least precost, faster trading helps.

Age Profile

The results in this subsection are derived in Appendix C of this chapter. The idea is to determine the exposure of M and P to information according to its age. Information flows into and out of M. From the perspective of time t, the information that arrived at time $t - j \cdot \Delta t$ that is captured by $\mathbf{u}(t - j \cdot \Delta t)$ is

9. The author first saw this result in some of Barr Rosenberg's notes in the late 1970's. It made its way into the first and second editions of Grinold and Kahn (2000), where it is on pg. 138, Equation (5A.24). Alas, the authors failed to recognize the utility of the relationship.

now $j \cdot \Delta t$ years old. At time t, the model is a mixture of these past bundles of information. If we use $\gamma = e^{-g \cdot \Delta t}$ as per Equation (6) we obtain:

$$\mathbf{m}(t) = \mathbf{u}(t) + \gamma \cdot \mathbf{u}(t - \Delta t) + \gamma^2 \cdot \mathbf{u}(t - 2 \cdot \Delta t) + \cdots + \gamma^j \cdot \mathbf{u}(t - j \cdot \Delta t) + \cdots. \quad (15)$$

The sum of the exposures in Equation (15) is $1/(1-\gamma)$. The fractional exposure at age $j \cdot \Delta t$ is $(1-\gamma) \cdot \gamma^j$. The weighted average age exposure of the information in M is:

$$A_M = \frac{1}{g}. \quad (16)$$

We can apply the same analysis to P. Write P at time t as:

$$\mathbf{p}(t) = a_0 \cdot \mathbf{u}(t) + a_1 \cdot \mathbf{u}(t - \Delta t) + a_2 \cdot \mathbf{u}(t - 2 \cdot \Delta t) + \cdots + a_j \cdot \mathbf{u}(t - j \cdot \Delta t) + \cdots. \quad (17)$$

Equations (6) and (15) can be used to solve for the a_j. The result when $d \neq g$ is:[10]

$$a_j = \frac{1-\delta}{\delta - \gamma} \cdot \left\{\delta^{j+1} - \gamma^{j+1}\right\}. \quad (18)$$

The a_j also sum to $1/(1-\gamma)$ so $(1-\gamma) \cdot a_j$ is the fraction of information in P of age $j \cdot \Delta t$.

Exhibit 2 shows the fraction of information in the model and portfolio at each age.

EXHIBIT 2 The Exposure to Information by Each Age Point for *M* and *P*

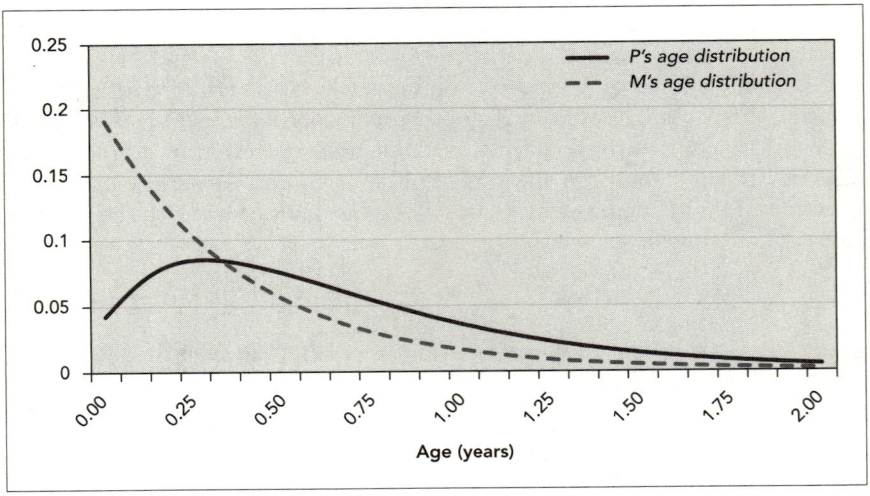

In this example $g = 2.54$ and $d = 2.96$.

In Exhibit 2, M's exposure is also the ability of that information to add value. Recent information is fresh and powerful; old information is stale and weak. This ability to add value declines geometrically in lockstep with M's exposure; M does not waste any effort. P, in contrast, is slow to react to the

10. Appendix C of this chapter has the derivation including the special case $d = g$.

new information, so it is underexposed to the more powerful recent information, in this case up to four months. P is also overexposed to the older information. It is slow in shedding the positions that it built up although they are now largely depleted of any ability to add value.

As with M we can calculate a weighted average age for the information in P. The result is:

$$A_P = \frac{1}{d} + \frac{1}{g} = \frac{1}{d} + A_M = \frac{d+g}{g \cdot d} \tag{19}$$

Thus P is $1/d$ years behind the curve when we use the trading rule, Equation (5). Equation (19), along with Equation (16), sheds light on the prior results, Equations (4) and (20), on the *precost* information ratios of M and P.

If we combine Equations (11), (10), and (4), we get:

$$IR_P = IC \cdot \sqrt{N} \cdot \sqrt{\frac{d \cdot g}{d+g}}. \tag{20}$$

However, from Equations (19) and (4), we see the information ratios can be expressed in terms of the age of the information in the portfolio:

$$IR_M = \frac{IC \cdot \sqrt{N}}{\sqrt{A_M}}, \quad IR_P = \frac{IC \cdot \sqrt{N}}{\sqrt{A_P}}. \tag{21}$$

Equation (21) illustrates the unobserved opportunity loss inherent in transactions costs. The costs slow down our trading and therefore age the information in P. Equation (21) also allows us to connect the transfer coefficient to the relative age of information in M and P:

$$\rho_{P,M} = \sqrt{\frac{A_M}{A_P}}. \tag{22}$$

Trade Flow and Trade Risk

The results in this subsection are derived in Appendices C and A. They are useful in the section on optimization. If $\Delta\mathbf{p}\,(t)$ is the change in P in the period from t to $t + \Delta t$ then the ratio $\Delta\mathbf{p}\,(t)/\Delta t$ is the annual rate of change, what we will call the *trade flow*. The unconditional expected value of the trade flow is zero since at any time we are equally likely to be buying or selling any asset. We will use variance as a norm for trade flow and call the standard deviation of the trade flow the *trade risk*. If $\mathbf{V}$ is the N by N asset covariance matrix then the trade variance is:

$$\omega^2_{\{\Delta P/\Delta t\}} \equiv \omega^2_{\dot{P}} \equiv E\left\langle \frac{\Delta\mathbf{p}'}{\Delta t} \cdot \mathbf{V} \cdot \frac{\Delta\mathbf{p}}{\Delta t} \right\rangle. \tag{23}$$

The trade risk measures both the speed of trading and the risk of the assets that we are trading. The laws of motion link the trade risk to the portfolio risk and backlog risk, Equation (14), as follows:

$$\omega_{\dot{P}} = \sqrt{g \cdot d} \cdot \omega_P = d \cdot \omega_{M-P}. \tag{24}$$

Note the similarity to the stock and flow relationship, Equation (9).

5. Optimality

The analysis above indicated how the laws of motion determine many important characteristics of the portfolio. It is natural to ask if there is an optimal way to select the parameters *d* and *g*. The answers are: "Yes" and "Not really." Yes in the case of *d* as we develop in the remainder of this section and not really in the case of *g*. An optimal choice of *g*, to the extent such a choice is possible, is a strategic exercise involving reweighting sources of information or reengineering the information to have a longer shelf life. The theory, as we demonstrate toward the close of this section, affords a strategic context for that exercise. Technical support for this section can be found in Appendix E of this chapter.

Optimal Trade Rate

In section 4 we showed that a larger value of *d* leads to a higher transfer coefficient, a more effective use of the risk budget, and lower backlog risk. However, there is no free lunch. A higher value of *d* means more trading, Equation (9), and most certainly higher trading cost. The challenge is to find the trade-off between the cost of trading and rewards from being in a high information ratio portfolio.

The objective is the annual risk-adjusted expected returns less annual costs. In algebraic form:

$$O_P \equiv \alpha_P - \frac{\lambda}{2} \cdot \omega_P^2 - c_P \tag{25}$$

where:

α_P	expected annual alpha of portfolio *P*	
ω_P	annual risk of portfolio *P*	
$\frac{\lambda}{2} \cdot \omega_P^2$	penalty (loss in alpha) due to risk	(26)
$\alpha_P - \frac{\lambda}{2} \cdot \omega_P^2$	annual risk adjusted or certainty equivalent expected return	
c_P	annual cost of trading needed to support portfolio *P*	

The criterion is the annual alpha, α_P, adjusted for risk, $\{\lambda/2\} \cdot \omega_P^2$, and the annual transaction cost, c_P. Given the speed of information flow, *g*, we need to choose the speed of trading, *d*, and the level of model risk ω_M to specify an optimal operating policy.[11]

The criterion is completely specified once we have a definition of the annual trading costs, c_P. To make Equation (25) solvable, the annual cost c_P has to have a reasonable and functional form. To this end we assume that

11. It would be more natural and equivalent to use portfolio risk. However, the problem separates nicely when we use model risk. Equation (12) is used to move from one to the other.

the annual cost is proportional to the trade risk that was introduced in section 4. Thus:

$$c_P = \frac{\chi}{2} \cdot \omega_{\dot{P}}^2. \tag{27}$$

This is both crude and convenient. It is crude since it is a rough approximation of reality. It is convenient in that it affords an extraordinary harvest of insight into the dynamics of portfolio management. Rough as the assumption, Equation (27), might be, it does capture a few basic points about trading costs:[12]

- Costs are superlinear. Double the rate of trading and you will more than double the cost of trading.
- Riskier assets are generally more expensive to trade than less risky assets.
- A hedged basket of securities, say, balanced by industry, is cheaper to trade than an un-hedged basket.

What are we to make of this parameter χ? Is 0.001 or 1,000.0 an appropriate value? For the moment we will let χ remain enigmatic. At the close of the section we show how one might infer a reasonable range of values for χ.

From section 4's results, Equation (24), we can express the cost, Equation (27), in terms of the portfolio risk and the parameters g and d:

$$c_P = \frac{\chi}{2} \cdot g \cdot d \cdot \omega_P^2. \tag{28}$$

With the criterion, Equation (25), fully specified we can derive (see Appendix E) an optimal value of d. This optimal value of d (denoted $\hat{d}$) and the consequent value of the crucial ratio $d/(d+g)$ are:

$$\hat{d} = \sqrt{\frac{\lambda}{\chi}}, \quad \frac{\hat{d}}{\hat{d}+g} = \frac{\lambda}{\lambda + g \cdot \sqrt{\lambda \cdot \chi}}. \tag{29}$$

As one would anticipate, large costs imply slower trading. More interesting is that a smaller penalty for risk means faster trading. That is because the theory implies, see Equation (12), that $\omega_P = \rho_{P,M} \cdot \omega_M$, so an increase in $\hat{d}$ will also increase $\rho_{P,M}$ and thus ω_P. It is also notable that $\hat{d}$ is selected independently of g.

The optimal level of M's risk depends upon the choice of $\hat{d}$, Equation (29), the speed of information flow g, the penalty for risk , λ, and the information's potential for adding value as captured by IR_M. That optimal level ω_M is:

$$\omega_M = \frac{IR_M}{\lambda + g \cdot \sqrt{\lambda \cdot \chi}} = \frac{\hat{d}}{\hat{d}+g} \cdot \frac{IR_M}{\lambda}. \tag{30}$$

12. See Grinold (2006) for additional discussion of this cost assumption.

Given g and $\hat{d}$ from Equation (29), the transfer coefficient $\rho_{P,M}$ is known using Equation (10). The remaining components of the optimized strategy are easily calculated:

$$\begin{aligned} \omega_P &= \rho_{P,M} \cdot \omega_M \\ \alpha_P &= \rho_{P,M} \cdot IR_M \cdot \omega_P \\ c_P &= \frac{\chi}{2} \cdot g \cdot \hat{d} \cdot \omega_P^2 \end{aligned} \tag{31}$$

The after-cost information ratio is:

$$ACIR_P = \frac{\alpha_P - c_P}{\omega_P} = \rho_{P,M} \cdot IR \cdot \left\{1 - \frac{1}{2} \cdot \frac{g}{\hat{d} + g}\right\} \tag{32}$$

Finally, we can write the optimal objective value as a function of g and the ability of the information to add value as captured by IR:

$$O_P = \frac{IR^2}{2 \cdot \lambda} \cdot \left\{\frac{\hat{d}}{\hat{d} + g}\right\}^2 = \frac{IR^2}{2 \cdot \lambda} \cdot \rho_{P,M}^4 \tag{33}$$

This analysis, in particular Equation (33), helps us in seeking an improved speed of information flow. If we keep the penalty for risk λ and cost parameter χ constant then we can use Equation (33) to determine the pairs (g, IR) have the same value of O_P as a base case.[13] The situation is illustrated in Exhibit 3.

EXHIBIT 3

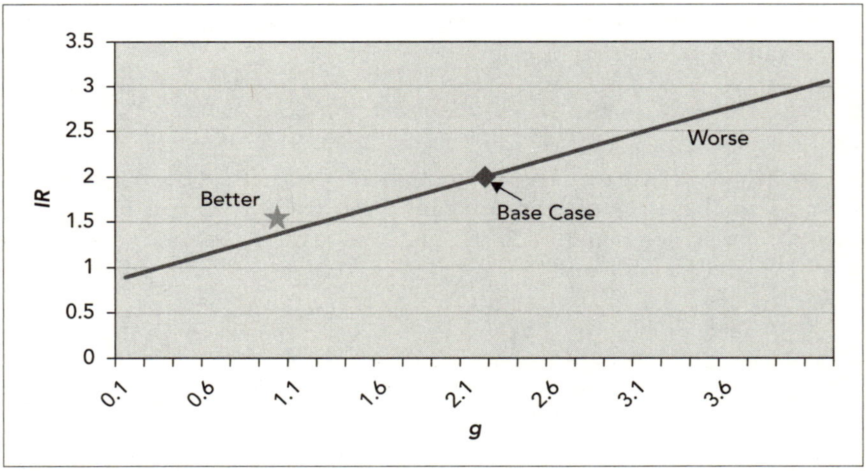

Note: Base case, the diamond, has information ratio of 2.0 and $g = 2.1$. The breakeven curve shows (g, IR) pairs with the same value of O_P as the base case. We are better off above the breakeven curve and worse below. If we slow the model so that $g = 1$ and the IR slips to 1.5 (the star) then we will be better off.

13. We can take this a step further. Recall from Equation (4) that $IR^2 = IC^2 \cdot g \cdot N$. With this substitution we can make it an IC and g trade-off.

We return to the question of a reasonable value for the t-cost parameter χ. Let $c_P^*(\chi, \lambda, g, IR_M)$ be the annual level of costs when we follow the optimal policy determined by Equations (29) and (30). If we consider $c_P^*(\chi, \lambda, g, IR_M)$ as a function of χ, the optimal annual costs will increase (costs are inelastic) until we reach a critical level $\chi = \bar{\chi}$ from that point on further increases in χ will lead to decreases in the annual costs paid (costs are elastic). The tipping point, $\chi = \bar{\chi}$, is easily calculated:

$$\bar{\chi} = \frac{\lambda}{4 \cdot g^2} \tag{34}$$

With this level of the transactions cost parameter the optimal trading rate, from Equation (29), is $\hat{d} = 2 \cdot g$ and the ratio $\hat{d}/(\hat{d} + g)$ is 2/3. Costs are a maximum point in this case:

$$c_P^*(\chi, \lambda, g, IR_M) \le \left\{\frac{4}{9}\right\} \cdot \left\{\frac{IR^2}{2 \cdot \lambda}\right\} \tag{35}$$

Exhibit 4 illustrates the effect.

EXHIBIT 4 Optimal Level of Transactions Cost as a Function of the Parameter χ.

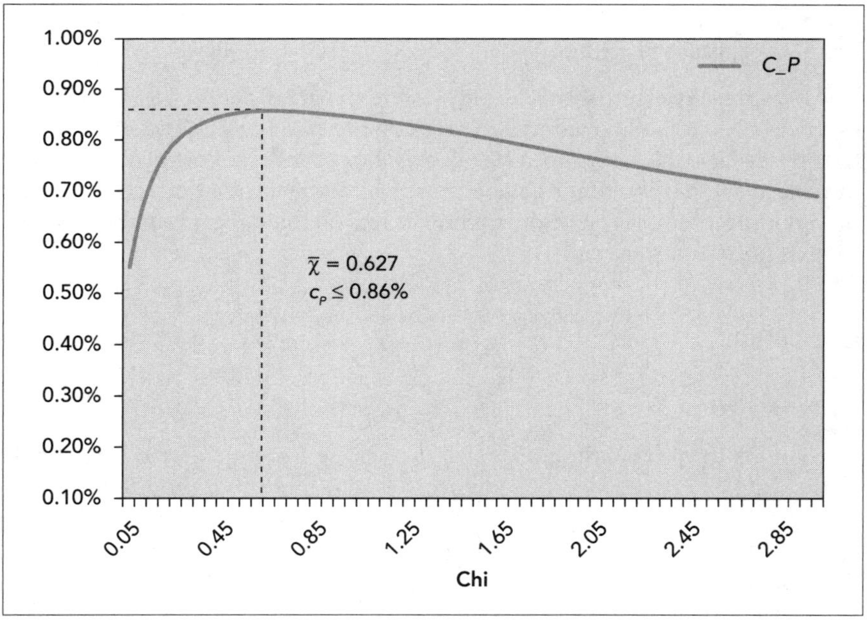

In the next section we demonstrate how the process can be reversed. We start with observed values of g and d plus the strategy's risk level ω_P. Combine these with an assumed value of information, IR_M, and we can infer the value of both χ and λ.

6. Dynamic Portfolio Analysis

We can use the results of sections 4 and 5 to examine the dynamic properties of an investment strategy. This is not performance analysis; we are not trying to relate these ideas to the nature or sources of investment return.[14] Instead, we want to know if we are moving the portfolio about in a sensible and efficient manner. The analysis should lead to a new understanding of the strategy and possibly to improvements in performance. We will, in line with the theory, select a long-short strategy that is relatively unconstrained for an example. This section takes us step by step through an analysis. There are three questions to consider:

- What are the dynamic characteristics (g, d) of the strategy?
- What are the consequences of those characteristics?
- Can we improve matters?

Data

The required data for time t:

- $\mathbf{V}(t)$ is the covariance matrix.
- $\mathbf{m}(t)$ is the model/target portfolio.
- $\mathbf{p}(t)$ is the portfolio.

These represent a set of (preferably) evenly spaced dates. The covariance matrices are available from various vendors. In most cases there will be data that describes the portfolio $\mathbf{p}(t)$. It may be a challenge to reconstruct the model, $\mathbf{m}(t)$.[15] If we don't have a model history but we do have a history of alpha forecasts, $\alpha(t)$, and we know a reasonable target risk level for the model, ω_M, we can use:[16]

$$\mathbf{m}(t) = \omega_M \cdot \frac{\mathbf{V}^{-1}(t) \cdot \alpha(t)}{\sqrt{\alpha'(t) \cdot \mathbf{V}^{-1}(t) \cdot \alpha(t)}}. \tag{36}$$

Time Horizon

The goal is to estimate behavior that is average for most of the assets most of the time. Recall this is the view from 33,000 feet. We should choose an estimation interval that is long relative to the rebalance interval. This will allow time for matters to average out. If we have too short an estimation interval, we will be plagued by microstructure effects such as asynchronous and lumpy arrival of data,[17] liquidity twists and turns, and trading that often focuses on a small subset of the assets at any particular time. To that end we

14. The notions described in this paper could be used in performance analysis.
15. Indeed, one of the objects of this effort is to encourage managers to retain the data that will enable the use of dynamic portfolio analysis.
16. If we think the changes in $\kappa^2(t) = \alpha'(t) \cdot \mathbf{V}^{-1}(t) \cdot \alpha(t)$ from period to period are meaningful, then you could find the average value $\bar{\kappa}^2 = \{1/T\} \cdot \sum_{t=1.T} \kappa^2(t)$ and then set $\mathbf{m}(t) = \{\omega_M / \bar{\kappa}\} \cdot \mathbf{V}^{-1}(t) \cdot \alpha(t)$.
17. There is a fringe benefit of this analysis if we can see how to smooth and rationalize the inflow of information to the strategy.

estimate changes over a lag L that is large compared to the rebalance interval Δt. In the case of our example, the rebalance interval is daily, and we have taken the interval between observations to be one month, $L = 1/12$.

Estimation

We'll start with g. Consider this variation on the law of motion, Equation (6):

$$\mathbf{m}(t) = \gamma(t) \cdot \mathbf{m}(t - L) + \mathbf{u}(t). \tag{37}$$

We select $\gamma(t)$ so that $\mathbf{m}(t - L)$ and $\mathbf{u}(t)$ are uncorrelated; in other words:

$$\mathbf{m}(t - L) \cdot \mathbf{V}(t) \cdot \mathbf{u}(t) = 0. \tag{38}$$

The condition Equation (38) is guaranteed if:

$$\gamma(t) = \frac{\mathbf{m}(t - L) \cdot \mathbf{V}(t) \cdot \mathbf{m}(t)}{\mathbf{m}(t - L) \cdot \mathbf{V}(t) \cdot \mathbf{m}(t - L)}. \tag{39}$$

This value of $\gamma(t)$ produces a point estimate of g through the transform:

$$g(t) = -\ln(\gamma(t))/L. \tag{40}$$

The jagged line in Exhibit 5 shows a time series of point estimates $g(t)$ for a long-short strategy. As mentioned above the portfolios are rebalanced daily and the estimation period, L, was one month. The second line in Exhibit 5 is an exponentially smoothed version of the same data.[18] In the early dot-com years the information was moving rapidly with an average age of 1.5 to 2 months. There is interlude from 1999 through 2004 where the information flow gradually slows. Since 2004 it appears to have stabilized with an average age of 4 to 5 months.

EXHIBIT 5 Point Estimates of the Parameter *g* and an Exponentially Smoothed Version of the Same Data.

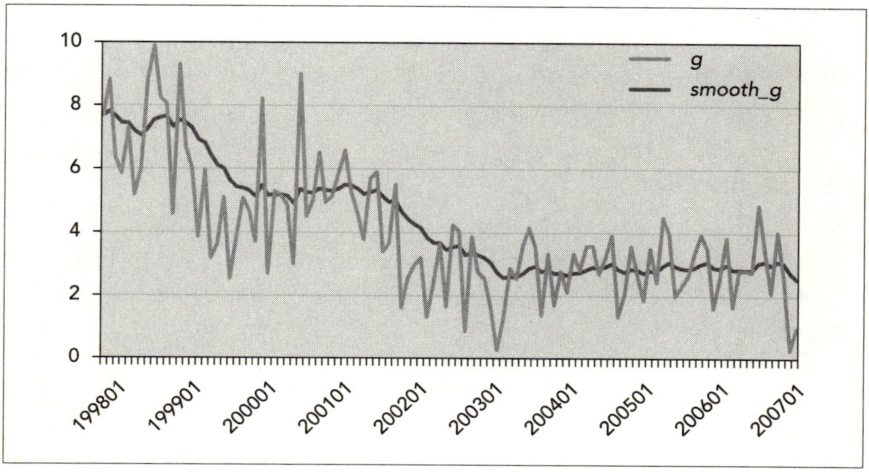

18. These are $g_s(t) = \phi \cdot g_s(t - T) + (1 - \phi) \cdot g(t)$ with $g_s(1) = g(1)$ and $\ln(\phi) = \{T/HL\} \cdot \ln(0.5)$ where HL is the half-life. In our case, $HL = 0.5$ (6 months).

Exhibit 5 illustrates three points:

- Examine the strategy over a reasonable period of time. The cross-sectional estimates are noisy, and the process evolves, so a snapshot is likely to be misleading.
- Don't expect laser-like precision. You will obtain reasonable estimates: 2.5 is different from 3.5 but about the same as 2.7 or 2.3.
- There is value in a long estimation window (large L). In our example we might have gone longer still, say one quarter, $L = 0.25$. The asynchronous arrival of data (think earnings season) causes uneven changes in the model when examined at the monthly level.

We can obtain an estimate of d in a similar but slightly more complicated way. Consider the following system:

$$\mathbf{p}(t) = \delta(t) \cdot \mathbf{p}(t - L) + \theta(t) \cdot \mathbf{m}(t) + \boldsymbol{\varepsilon}(t). \tag{41}$$

We want the residual, $\boldsymbol{\varepsilon}(t)$, in Equation (41) to be uncorrelated with $\mathbf{p}(t - L)$ and $\mathbf{m}(t)$. This requirement is expressed as:

$$\mathbf{m}'(t) \cdot \mathbf{V}(t) \cdot \boldsymbol{\varepsilon}(t) = 0, \quad \mathbf{p}'(t - L) \cdot \mathbf{V}(t) \cdot \boldsymbol{\varepsilon}(t) = 0. \tag{42}$$

If we combine Equation (42) with Equation (41) we get two equations in the two unknowns, $\delta(t), \theta(t)$.

Our interest is centered on the estimate of $\delta(t)$. Since we will most likely not have a model $\mathbf{m}(t)$ that is scaled properly, we cannot expect much from $\theta(t)$. In particular, we should *not* anticipate that $\theta(t) = 1 - \delta(t)$. The point estimate of d is:

$$d(t) = -\ln(\delta(t))/L. \tag{43}$$

Exhibit 6 presents a time series of the point estimates $d(t)$ for the long-short strategy alluded to above. The second line in Exhibit 6 is an exponentially smoothed version of $d(t)$. This indicates that P is somewhere between six months (when $d(t) \approx 2$) to three months (when $d(t) \approx 4$) behind M.

We compared the point estimates $d(t)$ with a history of the strategy's turnover (the flows of section 3) to see if spikes in Exhibit 6 corresponded to periods of rapid trading. They did.

A Sensibility Check

We can check the estimates by comparing the predicted transfer coefficient, Equation (10), with the actual, since the data, $\mathbf{m}(t), \mathbf{V}(t), \mathbf{p}(t)$ allows us to directly calculate the correlation of M and P in any cross section. The directly calculated transfer coefficient is denoted $\rho_{P,M}(t)$, where:

$$\rho_{P,M}(t) = \frac{\mathbf{m}'(t) \cdot \mathbf{V}(t) \cdot \mathbf{p}(t)}{\sqrt{\mathbf{m}'(t) \cdot \mathbf{V}(t) \cdot \mathbf{m}(t)} \cdot \sqrt{\mathbf{p}'(t) \cdot \mathbf{V}(t) \cdot \mathbf{p}(t)}}. \tag{44}$$

Exhibit 7 contains the comparison of the $\rho_{P,M}(t)$ and $\rho_{P,M}$ from Equation (10) using the exponentially smoothed estimates of d and g.

EXHIBIT 6 The Point Estimates of *d* and an Exponentially Smoothed Version of the Estimates.

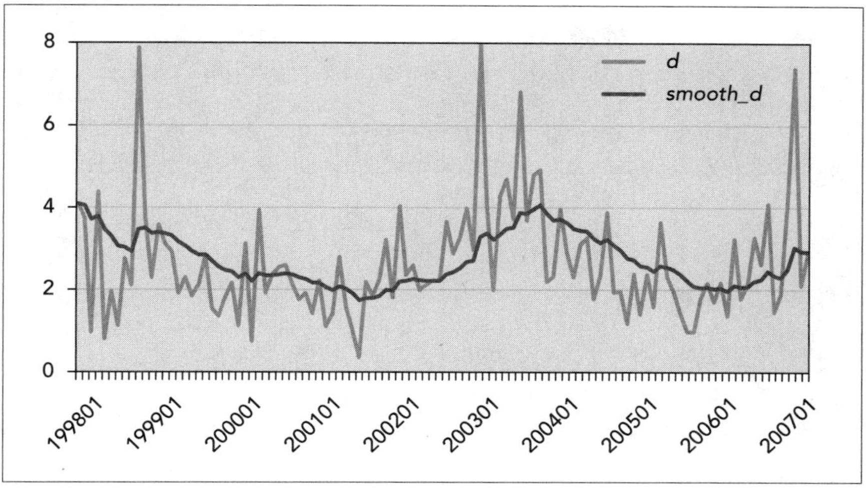

EXHIBIT 7 The Transfer Coefficient as Calculated Directly and Inferred by the Dynamic Theory

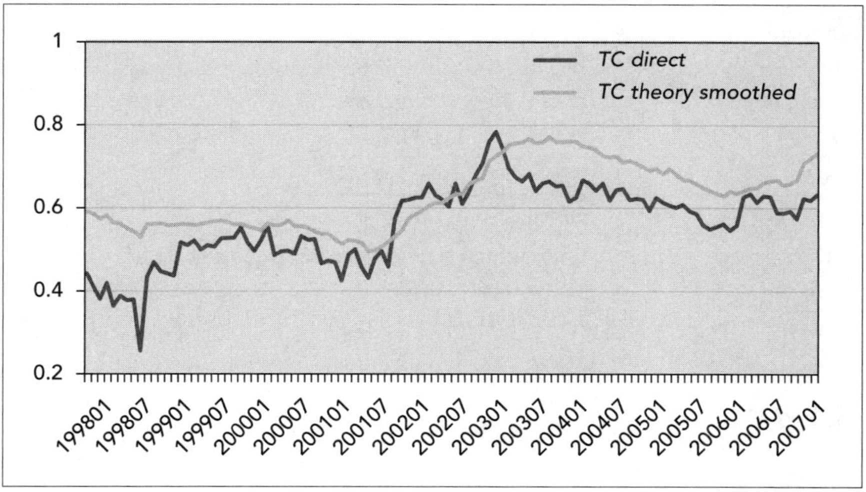

As we can see from Exhibit 7, we get off to a bad start since (see Exhibits 5 and 6) there is a great deal of initial instability in our estimates of d and g. From 2007 onward the results are encouraging. The prediction tracks reality fairly closely. The theoretical results tend to lag the cross sectional estimates because of the natural delay built in by the exponential smoothing of the values of d and g.

An Alternative

There is an indirect direct way to estimate g and d. Suppose that we monitor the rebalancing trades made in the portfolio, $\Delta\mathbf{p}(t)$.[19] Given the covariance matrix $\mathbf{V}(t)$ we can calculate the trade risk as in Equation (23). Let $\omega_{\dot{P}}$ (with a dot over the P) be an average value of trade risk. Then, given the estimate of the transfer coefficient $\rho_{P,M}$ from Equation (44) and P's risk, ω_P, bolstered by Equation (24) linking $\omega_{\dot{P}}$ and ω_P we can estimate g and d as follows:

$$g = \frac{\omega_{\dot{P}}}{\omega_P} \cdot \sqrt{\frac{1-\rho_{P,M}^2}{\rho_{P,M}^2}}, \quad d = \frac{\omega_{\dot{P}}}{\omega_P} \cdot \sqrt{\frac{\rho_{P,M}^2}{1-\rho_{P,M}^2}}. \tag{45}$$

Portfolio Attributes

With the estimated values of d and g and two more items:

- The risk of the portfolio ω_P
- An estimate of the model's information ratio $IR_M = IR$

we can assess other important characteristics of the portfolio based on the results in section 4. The data for our example is in Exhibit 8.

EXHIBIT 8 Predicted Characteristics of the Portfolio Based on the Results in Section 4

ITEM	VALUE	SOURCE
IR	1.75	assume
omega (P)	4.50%	observe
d	3.00	estimate
g	2.50	estimate
rho (P,M)	0.74	theory
IR (P)	1.29	theory
Age (M)	0.40	theory
Age (P)	0.73	theory
omega (P_dot)	12.32%	theory
omega (M-P)	4.11%	theory

The first four rows in the table are the inputs to the analysis. We assume, as noted above, the potential of the information to add value, in our case IR = 1.75. This, of course, should be based on data and rational expectations. We can observe the risk of the strategy (in our case 4.5%) and as discussed above we can make estimates of d and g or we could use "what if" values of d and g to gauge the sensitivity of results to possible changes. The remaining items in the table are calculated respectively as per Equations (10), (11), (16), (19), (24), and (14).

19. To avoid confusion, one should filter out (or prorate) trades motivated by capital inflow or outflow.

Inferred Values of λ and χ.

We can take the analysis a step further and use the results in section 5 to back out the penalty for risk λ and a t-cost level χ that are consistent with the data in Exhibit 8.

If we combine Equations (10), (12), and (30) we see that:

$$\lambda = \frac{d}{d+g} \cdot \frac{IR}{\omega_M} = \left\{\frac{d}{d+g}\right\}^{3/2} \cdot \frac{IR}{\omega_P}. \tag{46}$$

From here is it is easy, using the estimate of d, to infer that:

$$\chi = \frac{\lambda}{d^2}. \tag{47}$$

With these data and the results in section 5 we can predict the outcomes for the portfolio.

These are shown in Exhibit 9.

EXHIBIT 9 Additional Analysis of the Portfolio Based on an Assumption That the Portfolio Risk ω_P and Trading Rate d Are the Result of an Optimal Choice in the Manner Described in Section 5

ITEM	VALUE	SOURCE
lambda	15.67	infer
chi	1.74	infer
alpha	5.82%	theory
risk_pen	1.59%	theory
t_cost	1.32%	theory
O (P)	2.91%	theory
ACIR (P)	1.00	theory

The risk penalty referred to in Exhibit 9 is $\{\lambda/2\} \cdot \omega_P^2$ and the t-cost is $c_P = \{\chi/2\} \cdot \omega_{\dot{P}}^2$. The objective value, O_P, comes from Equation (33) and the after-cost information ratio ($ACIR_P$) from Equation (32).

7. Summary

We have used portfolio analysis to capture the dynamic nature of an unconstrained (long-short) investment management strategy. It is a bare-bones system with only two parameters: the speed that information loses its forecasting power and the speed of trading. These parameters can be inferred from observing the positions and trades of a lightly constrained long-short strategy. The parameters (g, d) are linked to familiar investment concepts. This minimalist setup yields a surprisingly abundant set of results. We can characterize the efficiency of the implementation, analyze and explain many aspects of the strategy, and optimize the rate of trading. More important than the specific results is the change in perception. Looking at the portfolio as a moving object provides a new perspective and opens up other interesting possibilities.

8. References

This paper is related to an earlier work, Grinold (2006) on dynamic portfolio management, and somewhat tangentially to the papers of Qian, Hua, and Tilney (2004) on turnover and Sneddon (2005) on dynamics and active management. The perspective draws on the Grinold and Kahn (2000) paper on the long-only constraint and a paper by Johnson, Kahn, and Petrich (2007) (Chapter 29 in this book) on leverage.

Clarke, Roger, Harindra de Silva, and Steven Thorley. 2002. "Portfolio Constraints and the Fundamental Law of Active Management." *Financial Analysts Journal*, September/October .

Grinold, Richard C. 1989. "The Fundamental Law of Active Management." *Journal of Portfolio Management* 15 (Spring): 30–37.

Grinold, Richard C., and Ronald N. Kahn. 2000. *Active Portfolio Management: Quantitative Theory and Applications*. (Probus Press, 1995.) 2nd ed. McGraw Hill.

Grinold, Richard C. 2006. "A Dynamic Model of Portfolio Management." *Journal of Investment Management* 4 (2nd quarter): 5–22.

Johnson, Seanna, Ronald N. Kahn, and Dean Petrich. 2007. "Optimal Gearing." *Journal of Portfolio Management*, Summer, 10–19.

Qian, E., R., Hua, and J. Tiley. 2004. "Turnover of Quantitatively Managed Equity Portfolios." *Proceedings of the Second IASTED International Conference Financial Engineering and Applications*, November 8–10, Cambridge, MA.

Sneddon, L. 2005. "The Dynamics of Active Portfolios." Westpeak Global Advisors.

Appendix A

The Laws of Motion and Portfolio Characteristics

There is one source of alpha. Portfolio M is *any* portfolio with maximum information ratio, IR. The analysis in this appendix shows the consequences of a policy that attempts to track M. In Appendix E, on optimization, we determine the best choice of M and the trade rate d.

The difference equations driving the analysis are:

$$\begin{aligned}\Delta\mathbf{m}(t) &= -g\cdot\mathbf{m}(t-\Delta t)\cdot\Delta t+\mathbf{u}(t)\\ \Delta\mathbf{p}(t) &= d\cdot\{\mathbf{m}(t)-\mathbf{p}(t-\Delta t)\}\cdot\Delta t\end{aligned}. \quad \text{(A1)}$$

We will treat the representation (A2), below, as roughly equivalent, with $\delta = e^{-d\cdot\Delta t}$, $\gamma = e^{-g\cdot\Delta t}$, since we will eventually make Δt small enough so we can assume $1-\delta = d\cdot\Delta t$ and $1-\gamma = g\cdot\Delta t$.

$$\begin{aligned}\mathbf{m}(t) &= \gamma\cdot\mathbf{m}(t-\Delta t)+\mathbf{u}(t)\\ \mathbf{p}(t) &= \delta\cdot\mathbf{p}(t-\Delta t)+(1-\delta)\cdot\mathbf{m}(t)\end{aligned}. \quad \text{(A2)}$$

The innovations $\mathbf{u}(t)$ have zero expectation, $\mathbb{E}\langle\mathbf{u}(t)\rangle = 0$, and are uncorrelated with $\mathbf{m}(t-\Delta t)$. This implies $\mathbb{E}\langle\mathbf{m}(t)\rangle = 0$. Since we are in a long-short unconstrained mandate, we also should have $\mathbb{E}\langle\mathbf{p}(t)\rangle = 0$. Let $\mathbf{V}$ represent the time-invariant asset covariance matrix. Portfolio Z is the lagged version of portfolio P, with holdings $\mathbf{p}(t-\Delta t)$ at time t. As Δt shrinks to zero, portfolio Z becomes portfolio P. Portfolio ΔP is the same as $P-Z$.

We define the covariance between various pairs as follows:

$$\begin{aligned}\omega_{P,P} &= \omega_P^2 \equiv \mathbb{E}\langle\mathbf{p}'(t)\cdot\mathbf{V}\cdot\mathbf{p}(t)\rangle\\ \omega_{P,Z} &\equiv \mathbb{E}\langle\mathbf{p}'(t)\cdot\mathbf{V}\cdot\mathbf{p}(t-\Delta t)\rangle\\ \omega_{P,M} &\equiv \mathbb{E}\langle\mathbf{p}'(t)\cdot\mathbf{V}\cdot\mathbf{m}(t)\rangle\\ \omega_{M,Z} &\equiv \mathbb{E}\langle\mathbf{m}'(t)\cdot\mathbf{V}\cdot\mathbf{p}(t-\Delta t)\rangle\\ \omega_{M,M} &\equiv \mathbb{E}\langle\mathbf{m}'(t)\cdot\mathbf{V}\cdot\mathbf{m}(t)\rangle\\ \omega_{M,\Delta P} &= \mathbb{E}\langle\mathbf{m}'(t)\cdot\mathbf{V}\cdot\{\mathbf{p}(t)-\mathbf{p}(t-\Delta t)\}\rangle\end{aligned} \quad \text{(A3)}$$

Our first result links the laws of motion, Equation (A2), to the covariance terms in Equation (A3).

Proposition 1

Let $\delta = e^{-d\cdot\Delta t}$, $\gamma = e^{-g\cdot\Delta t}$, and $\psi = \dfrac{1-\delta}{1-\gamma\cdot\delta}$. We assume that the system is in equilibrium. Letting $M(-1)$ be the lagged version of portfolio M, equilibrium means that:

$$\omega_{M,M} = \omega_{M(-1),M(-1)}, \quad \omega_{P,P} = \omega_{Z,Z}, \quad \omega_{M,P} = \omega_{M(-1),Z}. \tag{A4}$$

With those stipulations we have:

(i.) $\omega_{P,M} = \psi \cdot \omega_{M,M}$

(ii.) $\omega_{M,Z} = \psi \cdot \gamma \cdot \omega_{M,M}$

(iii.) $\omega_{M,\Delta P} = (1-\gamma) \cdot \psi \cdot \omega_{M,M}$

(iv.) $\omega_{P,P} = \left\{\dfrac{1+\delta\cdot\gamma}{1+\delta}\right\} \cdot \psi \cdot \omega_{M,M}$

(v.) $\omega_{P,Z} = \left\{\dfrac{\gamma+\delta}{1+\delta}\right\} \cdot \psi \cdot \omega_{M,M}$

(vi.) $\omega_{\Delta P,\Delta P} = 2 \cdot \dfrac{(1-\delta)\cdot(1-\gamma)}{1+\delta} \cdot \psi \cdot \omega_{M,M}$

Proof

Consider Equation (A2) for $\mathbf{p}(t)$. Multiply by $\mathbf{m}'(t)\cdot\mathbf{V}$ and take expectations. This yields:

$$\omega_{M,P} = \delta \cdot \omega_{M,Z} + (1-\delta) \cdot \omega_{M,M}. \tag{A5}$$

Now multiply the equation for $\mathbf{m}(t)$ in Equation (A2) by $\mathbf{p}'(t-\Delta t)\cdot\mathbf{V}$ and take expectations. This yields:

$$\omega_{M,Z} = \gamma \cdot \omega_{M(-1),Z} = \gamma \cdot \omega_{M,P}. \tag{A6}$$

The first equality arises because $\omega_{U,Z} = 0$ and the second because $\omega_{M(-1),Z} = \omega_{M,P}$. Therefore Equation (A5) becomes:

$$\omega_{M,P} = \delta \cdot \gamma \cdot \omega_{M,P} + (1-\delta) \cdot \omega_{M,M}, \tag{A7}$$

or using the definition of ψ:

$$\omega_{M,P} = \frac{1-\delta}{1-\gamma\cdot\delta} \cdot \omega_{M,M} = \psi \cdot \omega_{M,M}. \tag{A8}$$

This establishes (*i.*). Item (*ii.*) follows from Equations (A8) and (A6). Item (*iii.*) is the result of subtracting (*ii.*) from (*i.*).

The calculation of the variance $\omega_{P,P}$ requires slightly more analysis. If we multiply the equation for $\mathbf{p}(t)$ in Equation (A2) by $\mathbf{p}'(t) \cdot \mathbf{V}$ and take expectations, we find:

$$\omega_{P,P} = \delta \cdot \omega_{P,Z} + (1-\delta) \cdot \omega_{P,M}. \tag{A9}$$

If we multiply the equation for $\mathbf{p}(t)$ in Equation (A2) by $\mathbf{p}'(t-\Delta t) \cdot \mathbf{V}$ and take expectations we get:

$$\omega_{P,Z} = \delta \cdot \omega_{Z,Z} + (1-\delta) \cdot \omega_{Z,M}. \tag{A10}$$

However, by the equilibrium assumption $\omega_{Z,Z} = \omega_{P,P}$ and by Equation (A6), $\omega_{M,Z} = \gamma \cdot \omega_{M,P}$. With these changes, Equations (A9) and (A10) become:

$$\left\{ \begin{matrix} 1 & -\delta \\ -\delta & 1 \end{matrix} \right\} \cdot \left\{ \begin{matrix} \omega_{P,P} \\ \omega_{P,Z} \end{matrix} \right\} = \left\{ \begin{matrix} 1 \\ \gamma \end{matrix} \right\} \cdot (1-\delta) \cdot \omega_{P,M}. \tag{A11}$$

Items (*vi.*) and (*vii.*) are the solutions of the equations in (A11). Finally, item (*vii.*) follows since $\omega_{\Delta P,\Delta P} = 2 \cdot \{\omega_{P,P} - \omega_{Z,P}\}$.

Proposition 2 looks at the results of Proposition 1 as Δt becomes small.

We can simplify the notation if we consider ΔP, the change in P, as a rate, thus we define a new portfolio $\dot{P}$ (note the dot on the P):

$$\omega_{M,\dot{P}} \equiv \frac{\omega_{M,\Delta P}}{\Delta t}, \quad \omega_{\dot{P}}^2 \equiv \frac{\omega_{\Delta P,\Delta P}}{\Delta t^2}. \tag{A12}$$

Proposition 2

(i.) $\omega_{P,M} = \dfrac{d}{d+g} \cdot \omega_{M,M}$

(ii.) $\omega_{M,\dot{P}} = \dfrac{d \cdot g}{d+g} \cdot \omega_{M,M}$

(iii.) $\omega_{P,P} = \dfrac{d}{d+g} \cdot \omega_{M,M} = \omega_{P,M}$

(iv.) $\omega_{\dot{P}}^2 = g \cdot d \cdot \left\{ \dfrac{d}{d+g} \right\} \cdot \omega_{M,M} = g \cdot d \cdot \omega_{P,P}$

(v.) $\omega_{M-P,\,M-P} = \left\{ \dfrac{g}{d+g} \right\} \cdot \omega_{M,M} = \dfrac{g}{d} \cdot \omega_{P,P}$

Proof

From (*i.*) in Proposition 1:

$$\omega_{P,M} = \frac{1-e^{-d \cdot \Delta t}}{1-e^{-(d+g) \cdot \Delta t}} \cdot \omega_{M,M} \approx \frac{d \cdot \Delta t}{(d+g) \cdot \Delta t} \cdot \omega_{M,M}. \tag{A13}$$

In addition, we should note $\psi \to d/(d+g)$ as $\Delta t \to 0$.

From (*iii.*) in Proposition 1:

$$\omega_{M,\dot{P}} = \frac{\left(1-e^{-g\cdot\Delta t}\right)}{\Delta t}\cdot\psi\cdot\omega_{M,M} \approx g\cdot\frac{d}{d+g}\cdot\omega_{M,M}. \tag{A14}$$

From (*iv.*) in Proposition 1:

$$\omega_{P,P} = \left\{\frac{1+\delta\cdot\gamma}{1+\delta}\right\}\cdot\psi\cdot\omega_{M,M}. \tag{A15}$$

As $\Delta t \to 0$ we have $\{1+\delta\cdot\gamma\}/\{1+\delta\} \to 1$ and $\psi \to d/(d+g)$. This gives us item (*iii.*) in Proposition 2.

Finally, from item (*vi.*) in Proposition 1:

$$\omega_{\dot{P}}^2 = \left\{\frac{2}{1+\delta}\right\}\cdot\frac{(1-\gamma)}{\Delta t}\cdot\frac{(1-\delta)}{\Delta t}\cdot\psi\cdot\omega_{M,M}. \tag{A16}$$

As $\Delta t \to 0$ we have $2/(1+\delta) \to 1$, $\psi \to d/(d+g)$ and:

$$\frac{(1-\gamma)}{\Delta t}\cdot\frac{(1-\delta)}{\Delta t} \to g\cdot d. \tag{A17}$$

The last result in Proposition 2, (*v.*), is a straightforward calculation using the prior results:

$$\omega_{M-P,M-P} = \omega_{M,M} - 2\cdot\omega_{M,P} + \omega_{P,P} = \left\{1-2\cdot\frac{d}{d+g}+\frac{d}{d+g}\right\}\cdot\omega_{M,M}. \tag{A18}$$

Appendix B

Stock and Flow

This appendix requires four additional assumptions. For that reason, one should treat the results with caution. For example, the assumptions that turnover will roughly grow with the square root of the trading rate and with the square root of the information decay rate will lead to results better interpreted as indicative than as precise. Assume, for this appendix alone, that all the assets are uncorrelated. Let p_n be the (random) position in asset n. The variance of the strategy is given by:

$$\omega_P^2 = \mathbb{E}\left\langle \sum_{n=1,N} \sigma_n^2 \cdot p_n^2 \right\rangle. \tag{B1}$$

In addition, assume that we act to split the risk budget evenly across assets, then:

$$\mathbb{E}\left\langle p_n^2 \right\rangle = \frac{\omega_P^2}{N} \cdot \frac{1}{\sigma_n^2}. \tag{B2}$$

Since the expected holding in any asset is zero, Equation (B2) is the variance of the holding p_n as well. If we assume the holding is normally distributed, then:

$$\mathbb{E}\left\langle |p_n| \right\rangle = \sqrt{\frac{2}{\pi}} \cdot \frac{\omega_P}{\sqrt{N}} \cdot \frac{1}{\sigma_n}. \tag{B3}$$

Thus:

$$S = \sum_{n=1,N} \mathbb{E}\left\langle |p_n| \right\rangle = \sqrt{\frac{2}{\pi}} \cdot \sqrt{N} \cdot \omega_P \cdot \left\{ \frac{1}{N} \cdot \sum_{n=1,N} \frac{1}{\sigma_n} \right\}. \tag{B4}$$

The equation for the flow follows from Equation (B4) and item (*iv.*) in Proposition 2 of Appendix A:

$$\omega_{\Delta P}^2 = \mathbb{E}\left\langle \sum_{n=1,N} \sigma_n^2 \cdot \Delta p_n^2 \right\rangle = g \cdot d \cdot \omega_P^2 \cdot \Delta t^2. \tag{B5}$$

If we assume, as above, that we trade to equalize the expected value of $\sigma_n^2 \cdot \Delta p_n^2$ across assets and that Δp_n is normally distributed, then:

$$\mathbb{E}\left\langle \Delta p_n^2 \right\rangle = \frac{g \cdot d \cdot \omega_P^2 \cdot \Delta t^2}{N \cdot \sigma_n^2} \Rightarrow \mathbb{E}\left\langle \left| \Delta p_n \right| \right\rangle = \sqrt{\frac{2}{\pi}} \cdot \frac{\sqrt{g \cdot d} \cdot \omega_P \cdot \Delta t}{\sqrt{N} \cdot \sigma_n}. \quad \text{(B6)}$$

If we sum Equation (B6) over the N assets and $1/\Delta t$ periods per year we find:

$$F = \frac{1}{\Delta t} \cdot \sum_{n=1,N} \mathbb{E}\left\langle \left| \Delta p_n \right| \right\rangle = \sqrt{g \cdot d} \cdot \sqrt{\frac{2}{\pi}} \cdot \sqrt{N} \cdot \omega_P \cdot \left\{ \frac{1}{N} \cdot \sum_{n=1,N} \frac{1}{\sigma_n} \right\} = \sqrt{g \cdot d} \cdot S. \quad \text{(B7)}$$

Appendix C

Age Distribution

By back substitution in Equation (A2), we can write $\mathbf{m}(t)$ as:

$$\mathbf{m}(t) = \sum_{j=0,\infty} \gamma^j \cdot \mathbf{u}(t - j \cdot \Delta t). \tag{C1}$$

Since we have assumed that the information bundles $\mathbf{u}(t - j \cdot \Delta t)$ are uncorrelated, we can consider $(1-\gamma) \cdot \gamma^j$ as the fraction of information with age $j \cdot \Delta t$. With that interpretation the expected (or weighted average) age of the information is:

$$A_M = \Delta t \cdot (1-\gamma) \cdot \sum_{j=0,\infty} j \cdot \gamma^j = \Delta t \cdot \frac{\gamma}{(1-\gamma)} \tag{C2}$$

As $\Delta t \to 0$, we find:

$$A_M \to \frac{1}{g}. \tag{C3}$$

The portfolio's law of motion is:

$$\mathbf{p}(t) = \delta \cdot \mathbf{p}(t - \Delta t) + (1-\delta) \cdot \mathbf{m}(t). \tag{C4}$$

Suppose we write the portfolio as:

$$\mathbf{p}(t) = \sum_{j=0,\infty} a_j \cdot \mathbf{u}(t - j \cdot \Delta t). \tag{C5}$$

If we substitute Equation (C5) into Equation (C4), and then use Equation (C1), we can solve for the a_j. We find:

$$\begin{aligned} a_0 &= 1 - \delta \\ a_j &= \delta \cdot a_{j-1} + (1-\delta) \cdot \gamma^j \quad \text{for } j > 0 \end{aligned} \tag{C6}$$

The solution to Equation (C6) is:

$$a_j = \left\{ \begin{array}{ll} (1-\delta) \cdot \dfrac{\delta^{j+1} - \gamma^{j+1}}{\delta - \gamma} & \text{if } d \neq g \\ (1-\delta) \cdot (j+1) \cdot \delta^j & \text{if } d = g \end{array} \right\}. \tag{C7}$$

The sum of the coefficients a_j is $1/(1-\gamma)$ so we can say that a fraction $(1-\gamma)\cdot a_j$ of the information in the portfolio is $j\cdot\Delta t$ years old. Then the weighted average age of the information in P is:

$$A_P = \Delta t \cdot (1-\gamma) \cdot \sum_{j=0,\infty} j \cdot a_j \,. \tag{C8}$$

After some manipulation this boils down to:[20]

$$A_P = \Delta t \cdot \left\{ \frac{(1-\delta\cdot\gamma)}{(1-\delta)\cdot(1-\gamma)} \right\} - \Delta t \tag{C9}$$

As $\Delta t \to 0$, this becomes:

$$A_P \to \frac{d+g}{d\cdot g} = \frac{1}{g} + \frac{1}{d}. \tag{C10}$$

20. Hints: $\sum_{j=1,\infty} j\cdot\delta^{j+1} = \delta^2/(1-\delta)^2$ and $\delta+\gamma-2\cdot\gamma\cdot\delta = (1-\delta\cdot\gamma)-(1-\delta)\cdot(1-\gamma)$.

Appendix D

Trading Cost

If the rebalance period is Δt and we make a trade $\Delta \mathbf{p}$, then we *assume* that the cost is:

$$\frac{\chi}{2} \cdot \left\{ \frac{\Delta \mathbf{p}'}{\Delta t} \cdot \mathbf{V} \cdot \frac{\Delta \mathbf{p}}{\Delta t} \right\} \cdot \Delta t, \tag{D1}$$

where:

$$\frac{\chi}{2} \cdot \left\{ \frac{\Delta \mathbf{p}'}{\Delta t} \cdot \mathbf{V} \cdot \frac{\Delta \mathbf{p}}{\Delta t} \right\} \tag{D2}$$

is the annual cost if we trade at the rate $\Delta \mathbf{p} \, / \, \Delta t$ for an entire year.

Suppose there are T periods in the year, $T \cdot \Delta t = 1$, and they are indexed by $t = 1, 2, \cdots, T$. If we trade $\Delta \mathbf{p}\,(t)$ in period t, then the total cost for the year is:

$$c_P = \frac{\chi}{2} \cdot \sum_{t=1,T} \left\{ \frac{\Delta \mathbf{p}'\,(t)}{\Delta t} \cdot \mathbf{V} \cdot \frac{\Delta \mathbf{p}\,(t)}{\Delta t} \right\} \cdot \Delta t = \frac{\chi}{2} \cdot \left\{ \frac{1}{T} \cdot \sum_{t=1,T} \left\{ \frac{\Delta \mathbf{p}'\,(t)}{\Delta t} \cdot \mathbf{V} \cdot \frac{\Delta \mathbf{p}\,(t)}{\Delta t} \right\} \right\}. \tag{D3}$$

However:

$$\frac{1}{T} \cdot \sum_{t=1,T} \left\{ \frac{\Delta \mathbf{p}'\,(t)}{\Delta t} \cdot \mathbf{V} \cdot \frac{\Delta \mathbf{p}\,(t)}{\Delta t} \right\} = \frac{1}{\Delta t^2} \cdot \left\{ \frac{1}{T} \cdot \sum_{t=1,T} \{ \Delta \mathbf{p}'\,(t) \cdot \mathbf{V} \cdot \Delta \mathbf{p}\,(t) \} \right\} \approx \omega^2_{\Delta P/\Delta t}. \tag{D4}$$

By item (*iv.*) of Proposition 2 and Equation (D3), the cost is approximately:

$$c_P \approx \frac{\chi}{2} \cdot \omega^2_{\Delta P/\Delta t} = \frac{\chi}{2} \cdot g \cdot d \cdot \omega_P^2 \,. \tag{D5}$$

Appendix E

Optimization

It is possible to find the optimal policy using dynamic programming. In Appendix A to Chapter 9, "Signal Weighting," we solve the dynamic program with J sources of alpha. In Appendix B of "Signal Weighting" we take an analytic approach similar to the one below for the more general case of J signals.

We'll make a direct stab using the calculus. Going through the dynamic programming analysis and then letting $\Delta t \to 0$ leads to the identical conclusions.

The objective is the annual run rate of alpha minus cost less a penalty for active variance:

$$O_P = \alpha_P - \frac{\lambda}{2} \cdot \omega_P^2 - \frac{\chi}{2} \cdot \omega_{\Delta P/\Delta t}^2 \cdot \tag{E1}$$

We need to specify each of the three components of the objective, $(\alpha_P, \omega_P, c_P)$, in terms of the trade rate d and the model risk ω_M. This is straightforward based on our earlier results.

$$\begin{gathered} IR_P = \frac{\alpha_P}{\omega_P} = \rho_{P,M} \cdot IR, \Rightarrow \alpha_P = \rho_{P,M} \cdot \omega_P \cdot IR, \\ \rho_{P,M} = \sqrt{\frac{d}{d+g}}, \quad \omega_P = \sqrt{\frac{d}{d+g}} \cdot \omega_M \\ \Rightarrow \alpha_P = \frac{d}{d+g} \cdot \omega_M \cdot IR, \end{gathered} \tag{E2}$$

$$\frac{\lambda}{2} \cdot \omega_P^2 = \frac{\lambda}{2} \cdot \frac{d}{d+g} \cdot \omega_M^2, \text{ and} \tag{E3}$$

$$\frac{\chi}{2} \cdot \omega_{\Delta P/\Delta t}^2 = \frac{\chi}{2} \cdot g \cdot d \cdot \omega_P^2 = \frac{\chi}{2} \cdot g \cdot d \cdot \frac{d}{d+g} \cdot \omega_M^2 \cdot \tag{E4}$$

With these results we can express O_P as a function of d and ω_M:

$$O_P\left(d,\omega_M\right)=\frac{d}{d+g}\cdot\left\{IR\cdot\omega_M-\frac{\lambda+\chi\cdot g\cdot d}{2}\cdot\omega_M^2\right\}. \tag{E5}$$

We will find the maximum d and ω_M in two-steps.

Step 1: Hold d fixed and choose the optimal value of ω_M. We obtain:

$$\omega_M\left(d\right)=\frac{IR}{\lambda+\chi\cdot g\cdot d}. \tag{E6}$$

The value using this policy is:

$$O_P\left(d,\omega_M\left(d\right)\right)=\frac{IR^2}{2}\cdot\frac{d}{d+g}\cdot\frac{1}{\lambda+\chi\cdot g\cdot d}. \tag{E7}$$

Step 2: Choose d to maximize (E7). The first order condition is:

$$\left[\frac{g}{(d+g)^2}\cdot\frac{1}{(\lambda+\chi\cdot g\cdot d)}\right]=\left[\frac{d}{d+g}\cdot\frac{\chi\cdot g}{(\lambda+\chi\cdot g\cdot d)^2}\right]. \tag{E8}$$

This simplifies to:

$$\frac{1}{(d+g)}=\frac{\chi\cdot d}{(\lambda+\chi\cdot g\cdot d)}. \tag{E9}$$

If we cross-multiply and cancel terms, we are left with:

$$\lambda=\chi\cdot d^2. \tag{E10}$$

So, the optimal trade rate is given by:

$$\hat{d}=\sqrt{\frac{\lambda}{\chi}}. \tag{E11}$$

Substituting Equation (E11) into Equation (E6), we find the optimal value of model risk:

$$\omega_M=\frac{IR}{\lambda+g\cdot\sqrt{\lambda\cdot\chi}}. \tag{E12}$$

The ratio $d/(d+g)$ at optimality is:

$$\frac{\hat{d}}{\hat{d}+g}=\frac{\lambda}{\lambda+g\cdot\sqrt{\lambda\cdot\chi}}. \tag{E13}$$

Thus, at optimality, we can also write Equation (E12) as:

$$\omega_M=\frac{\hat{d}}{\hat{d}+g}\cdot\frac{IR}{\lambda}. \tag{E14}$$

And the optimal value will be:

$$O_P\left(\hat{d},\omega_M\left(\hat{d}\right)\right)=\frac{IR^2}{2\cdot\lambda}\cdot\left(\frac{\hat{d}}{\hat{d}+g}\right)^2\geq O_P\left(d,\omega_M\right) \tag{E15}$$

The remainder of the results in the text come from substituting Equation (E11) and either Equation (E12) or Equation (E14) into Equations (E2), (E3), (E4), and (E5).

9

Signal Weighting[1]

Introduction

Active strategies face the challenge of combining information from different sources in order to maximize that information's after-cost effectiveness.[2] This challenge is evident for investors who follow a systematic, structured investment process. It is also an issue, although often unrecognized, for more traditional managers who must balance top-down views, the views of in-house analysts, and sell-side analysts. In any case, a decision is made either through default, analysis, or whimsy. We favor analysis, and to that end this article presents a simple and structured approach to the task. This task is commonly called signal weighting, although risk budgeting seems to be a better description. The approach is based on standard methods of portfolio analysis and their extension to dynamic portfolio management.

We can consider an active investment product on three levels: strategic, tactical, and operational. At the strategic level we might target clients, fee structure, level of risk, amount of gearing, level of turnover, marketing channel, decision-making structure, and so forth. At the operational level, we run the product: maintaining and replenishing data, executing trades, tracking positions and performance, informing clients, and so on. At the tactical level, we allocate resources to improve the product and its operations and do some fine tuning on parameters such as risk level and turnover level. The signal-weighting decision belongs at the tactical level. Every strategy has an internal risk budget that shows how the aggregate risk is being allocated among the various sources/themes that we anticipate can add value. We should periodically, say, every six months, reexamine and possibly change that allocation. A similar reconsideration of the internal risk budget should take place if

1. This article originally appeared as "Signal Weighting" by Richard Grinold in the Summer 2010 issue of the *Journal of Portfolio Management*.

2. We'll use the terms *sources*, *themes*, and *signals* as synonyms.

there is a significant change in the signal mix (e.g., adding a new theme) or if there is a major change in the market environment.

The method we present in this article gives substance to the signal-weighting process by isolating the important aspects of the decision and providing a structure that links those features to a decision. The procedure we outline mimics the investment process. Each signal is viewed as a sub, or source, portfolio that is a potential place to allocate risk. We allocate risk to the source portfolios in a manner that makes the most sense at the aggregate level. In this effort we are trying to be comprehensive enough to depict the essentials and simple enough to easily capture the link between inputs and outputs. Thus, we compromise between the desire to be reasonable and robust, on the one hand, and to provide a clear box rather than a black box on the other.

To preserve transparency, we should err on the side of simplicity rather than on excessive elaboration. There is a temptation to more and more closely mimic the actual investment process (e.g., backtesting). Our unadorned approach is to assume the portfolio is run with the straightforward and easy-to-analyze method A, although we realize that we actually use the complex and impossible-to-analyze method B. We have to trade off the benefits of getting sensible, comprehensible answers against the costs of departing from the operational reality. Any effect we want to consider has to argue for a place at the table. The watchword is simplicity, and the burden of proof is against making it complicated. This focus on simplicity also argues against a profusion of sources. In our view, the number of themes should be more than two and certainly less than, say, seven. If you believe there are a larger number of significant alpha drivers of a strategy, you should: (1) look up *significant* and (2) aggregate the signals into broader themes.

One benefit of the proposed approach is that it is based on a theory. There is a logical consistency that lets us track cause and effect. The assumptions are few and transparent. It is not a sequence of ad hoc decisions and jury-rigged improvisations where the often hidden assumptions are many and their implications are obscure. This clarity makes it easy to link cause and effect. In particular, it facilitates the use of sensitivity analysis to study the links between important inputs and outputs.

Signal weighting is a forward-looking exercise. We are planning for the future not overfitting the past. Past performance of signals can, of course, inform us about each signal's presumed future strength, how fast the information dissipates, and how the signals relate to each other. However, we will usually be in a situation with old signals that are part of the implemented strategy and new signals that have only seen hypothetical implementation. In addition, we may feel strongly that some signals will lose strength since they are being arbitraged away. What we see in a backtest is one sample from a nonstationary probability distribution. By all means consider past performance, but add a large pinch of salt.

A caution: the title of the paper contains a twofold misnomer. We are presenting what is generally called signal weighting. However, it's not signals and it's not weighting. What is actually happening is that we are allocating risk to a collection of standardized single source alphas. There is a missing step that involves moving from signals to alphas. That step is covered in Chapters 10–11 of *Active Portfolio Management* and makes a brief appearance in Appendix A of Chapter 10 in this volume. The risk allocations are not a set of numbers that add to one, although we will show how they can be readjusted into a set of weights that do add up to one.

This chapter presents a top-down view of signal weighting. We look at each signal at the aggregate level. Chapters 10 and 11 of this volume employ a bottom-up approach where we adjust the signal weights on an asset-by-asset basis depending on the forecasting power for that signal/asset pair and the rate at which we anticipate trading the asset.

Preview

The paper has the following structure. We initially consider a world free of cost with one signal and then a cost-free world with multiple signals. This exercise allows us to introduce many of the terms and concepts we will use in the more difficult setting with transactions costs.

Transaction costs are difficult to handle in an analytic way. Our approach is traditional: we make an assumption. We assume the portfolio is updated following a simple rebalance rule. The rebalance rule has three parts:

- For each signal we construct a source portfolio that captures that signal in an efficient manner. We aim for the most signal per unit of risk.
- We construct a model/target portfolio that is a mixture of the source portfolios.
- We stipulate a rebalance rule to fix the rate at which the portfolio manager tries to close the gap between the portfolio the manager actually holds and the model portfolio.

In Appendix A, we show that this type of rebalance rule is optimal under certain conditions. We feel that a rule that is optimal under one set of conditions will be good in a much wider group of situations. In Appendix B, we study the consequences of using such a decision rule.

We carry a transparent three signal example through the paper to provide some context to the results.

Other Work

This paper stems from the author's previous work on dynamic portfolio analysis, Grinold (2006) and (2007).[3] The most directly related paper is Sneddon (2008). Similar techniques to those described in Appendix A are used by Garleanu and Pedersen (2009 working paper, subsequently published in 2013 after this paper had appeared).

3. Grinold (2007) is Chapter 8 in this book, "Dynamic Portfolio Analysis."

One Signal and No Transactions Costs

We start with one signal and then expand the analysis to cover multiple signals. There are N assets whose return covariance is described by the N by N covariance matrix $\mathbf{V}$. The basic material in the weighting exercise is an N element vector $\mathbf{a}_1$, called a source alpha. It is scaled to have (on average) an information ratio of one:

$$\mathbf{a}_1' \cdot \mathbf{V}^{-1} \cdot \mathbf{a}_1 = 1. \tag{1}$$

To obtain a weight we need an assessment of the strength of the signal. Let IR be the information ratio of the signal, then:

$$\alpha = IR \cdot \mathbf{a}_1. \tag{2}$$

We are done. With one signal we simply weight the source alpha to have the desired information ratio.

We can get to the same place by a longer route. It approaches the problem from a portfolio perspective. This is worth the extra effort since it generalizes in a natural way when there are multiple signals and transactions costs.

We associate a source portfolio $\mathbf{q}_1$ with our signal.

$$\mathbf{q}_1 = \mathbf{V}^{-1} \cdot \mathbf{a}_1 \Rightarrow \mathbf{q}_1' \cdot \mathbf{V} \cdot \mathbf{q}_1 = 1. \tag{3}$$

The source portfolio is an efficient implementation of the signal; that is, among all positions $\mathbf{x}$ it maximizes the ratio $\mathbf{a}' \cdot \mathbf{x} / \sqrt{\mathbf{x}' \cdot \mathbf{V} \cdot \mathbf{x}}$.

As noted in Equation (3), the source portfolio has an excessive risk level of 100%. Suppose we choose a more realistic risk level ω_Q. This is akin to scaling the source portfolio. If ω_Q is the risk level, then the portfolio is $\mathbf{q} = \omega_Q \cdot \mathbf{q}_1$. This portfolio has an alpha of $IR \cdot \omega_Q$ and variance of ω_Q^2. If we have a risk penalty λ and we do the standard mean-variance optimization we choose the risk level ω_Q to maximize:

$$IR \cdot \omega_Q - \frac{\lambda}{2} \cdot \omega_Q^2. \tag{4}$$

The solution of this is $\omega_Q = IR/\lambda$. If the information ratio is $IR = 0.75$ and we have a risk penalty of $\lambda = 18.75$, the resulting solution is $\omega_Q = 4\%$.

The causality runs from the alpha forecast to portfolio Q. That portfolio is determined by the alphas:

$$\mathbf{q} = \frac{\mathbf{V}^{-1} \cdot \alpha}{\lambda} \Rightarrow \alpha = \lambda \cdot \mathbf{V} \cdot \mathbf{q}_1 \cdot \omega_Q = \{\lambda \cdot \omega_Q\} \cdot \mathbf{a}_1 \tag{5}$$

This gets us to the same place as the straightforward approach, Equation (2), since $\lambda \cdot \omega_Q = IR$.

The reasons for the portfolio optimization approach used in Equation (4) are:

- it generalizes nicely when we have multiple signals,
- it makes things much simpler when we introduce transactions costs.

Now we'll turn to multiple signals and no transactions costs.

J Signals and No Transactions Costs

Suppose we have J signals (substrategies), each with a *raw* alpha $\mathbf{a}_j$ $j = 1, \cdots, J$. Each $\mathbf{a}_j$ is a vector with elements for each of the N assets. We start with a level playing field; each $\mathbf{a}_j$ is standardized so that its information ratio is one.[4]

$$\mathbf{a}_j' \cdot \mathbf{V}^{-1} \cdot \mathbf{a}_j = 1. \tag{6}$$

We can, as above in Equation (3), associate a position with each raw alpha. These positions have, on average, 100% risk. They are the building blocks of the investment strategy.

$$\begin{aligned} \mathbf{a}_j &= \mathbf{V} \cdot \mathbf{q}_j, \quad \mathbf{q}_j = \mathbf{V}^{-1} \cdot \mathbf{a}_j \\ \mathbf{q}_j' &\cdot \mathbf{V} \cdot \mathbf{q}_j = 1 \end{aligned} \tag{7}$$

With one signal the risk allocation to the signal and the resulting portfolio risk are the same. This is not the case with multiple signals. We will continue with the notation ω_{Qj} for the risk allocated to signal j. We will use υ_Q^2 and υ_Q as, respectively, the variance and risk of portfolio Q when we use risk allocation ω_{Qj}.

Since we have multiple signals, we have to take into consideration any correlation between the information sources. We define that correlation in terms of the expected return covariance between any pair of positions.[5]

$$\rho_{i,j} \equiv \mathbf{q}_i' \cdot \mathbf{V} \cdot \mathbf{q}_j. \tag{8}$$

For example, if i is a value signal and j a momentum signal, they will tend to be negatively correlated. Recall that signal weighting is a forward-looking exercise; the correlations $\rho_{i,j}$ are predictions. Nonetheless, a historical analysis of past correlations should be informative.[6] Often there is a fairly stable relationship. In other cases, the relationship appears to depend on the caprice of the market. As a practical matter, if any of these correlations are very large (say above 0.5), then it might be wise to combine the signals. If a correlation is large and negative, then you have either found a very good thing or, more likely, you have uncovered something too good to be true.

We build a strategy by assigning risk levels, ω_j to each of J substrategies. The vector representation is $\{\omega_{Q,j}\}_{j=1,J}$. The result will be a portfolio:

$$\mathbf{q} = \sum_{j=1,J} \mathbf{q}_j \cdot \omega_j. \tag{9}$$

4. It is best practice to have this standardization work in a time average fashion. This allows a natural emphasis on a theme when more information is available and, in particular, avoids trying to make something out of nothing when less information is on hand.

5. Note this also implies that $\rho_{i,j} = \mathbf{a}_i' \cdot \mathbf{V}^{-1} \cdot \mathbf{a}_j = \mathbf{a}_i' \cdot \mathbf{q}_j = \mathbf{a}_j' \cdot \mathbf{q}_i$.

6. If there is a history of the past source portfolios $\mathbf{q}_i(t)$, and dated covariance matrices, $\mathbf{V}(t)$, then $\rho_{i,j}(t) \equiv \mathbf{q}_i'(t) \cdot \mathbf{V}(t) \cdot \mathbf{q}_j(t) / \left\{ \sqrt{\mathbf{q}_i'(t) \cdot \mathbf{V}(t) \cdot \mathbf{q}_i(t)} \cdot \sqrt{\mathbf{q}_j'(t) \cdot \mathbf{V}(t) \cdot \mathbf{q}_j(t)} \right\}$ gives a measure of the correlation at time t.

The information ratios of the J substrategies are given by the J element vector with elements IR_j. The J by J correlation matrix with elements $\rho_{i,j}$ is denoted as **R**.[7]

With this notation the alpha expected by using the weights $\omega_{Q,j}$ is:

$$\alpha_Q = \sum_{j=1,J} IR_j \cdot \omega_{Q,j}. \tag{10}$$

The variance of the portfolio, **q**, with these weights $\omega_{Q,j}$ is:

$$v_Q^2 = \sum_{i=1,J} \omega_{Q,i} \cdot \sum_{j=1,J} \rho_{i,j} \cdot \omega_{Q,j} \tag{11}$$

We choose the ω_{Qj} to maximize:

$$\alpha_Q - \frac{\lambda}{2} \cdot v_Q^2. \tag{12}$$

The solution is obtained by solving the first-order equations:

$$IR_i = \lambda \cdot \sum_{j=1,J} \rho_{i,j} \cdot \omega_{Q,j} \tag{13}$$

We will refer to the solution as the zero-cost portfolio, Q, with positions:

$$\mathrm{q} = \sum_{j=1,J} \mathrm{q}_j \cdot \omega_{Q,j} \tag{14}$$

The information ratio of the zero-cost Q is:

$$IR_Q = \lambda \cdot v_Q$$

$$IR_Q = \frac{\alpha_Q}{v_Q} \geq IR_P \text{ for any portfolio } P. \tag{15}$$

We see from Equation (15) that Q achieves the highest possible information ratio. The potential information ratio from all of the sources, IR, is independent of the risk penalty. We can therefore choose λ to get a desired level of active risk ω_Q in the zero-cost portfolio.

Example

Here is an example with three substrategies. In anticipation of the next section we have classified the signal by the rate of information turnover. The sources are: SLOW, INTERMEDIATE and FAST. The goal is to mix these three sources to get an ideal portfolio with 5% risk.

7. If we let $Y_{i,j}$ be the elements of the inverse of the J by J signal correlation matrix with elements $\rho_{i,j}$, then the information ratio using all the signals is $IR^2 = \sum_{i=1:J} IR_i \cdot \sum_{j=1:J} Y_{i,j} \cdot IR_j$.

EXHIBIT 1 A Three Signal Example

SOURCE	IR	SLOW	INT.	FAST	RISK
SLOW	0.4	1	-0.15	0.1	1.96%
INT.	0.5	–0.15	1	–0.3	3.78%
FAST	0.7	0.1	-0.3	1	4.10%

Note: The input data are the information ratios, *IR*, and the correlations. The optimal risk allocation is in the column called risk.

The data in Exhibit 1 represent our best estimates of what we expect to see over a reasonably long planning horizon, say a year or more. The net effect of this data is an aggregate information ratio of $IR = 1.11$. If we want an overall risk of $v_Q = 5.00\%$ we can set the risk penalty $\lambda = IR/v_Q = 1.11/0.05 = 22.17$ and get the desired result. The final column is the optimal risk allocation solving the first-order equations (13). We can interpret this as running the INTERMEDIATE substrategy at 3.78% risk, the SLOW substrategy at 1.96% risk, and the FAST substrategy at 4.10% risk.

Risk Budgeting

Signal weighting, like portfolio management, is an exercise in risk budgeting. We can express the result in terms of the resulting risk budget. The variance of the ideal portfolio Q is:

$$\begin{aligned}
&(i.) \quad v_Q^2 = \sum_{j=1,J} \omega_{Q,j} \cdot \sum_{k=1,J} \rho_{j,k} \cdot \omega_{Q,k} \text{ or} \\
&(ii.) \quad 1 = \sum_{j=1,J} \left\{ \frac{\omega_{Q,j}}{v_Q} \right\} \cdot \sum_{k=1,J} \rho_{j,k} \cdot \left\{ \frac{\omega_{Q,k}}{v_Q} \right\}
\end{aligned} \tag{16}$$

If we allocate a fraction $\left\{ \frac{\omega_j}{v_Q} \right\} \cdot \sum_{k=1,J} \rho_{j,k} \cdot \left\{ \frac{\omega_k}{v_Q} \right\}$ of the risk to alpha source j we are in effect taking the two covariance terms for sources j and k, $\omega_{Q,j} \cdot \rho_{j,k} \cdot \omega_{Q,k} + \omega_{Q,k} \cdot \rho_{k,j} \cdot \omega_{Q,j}$, and splitting the baby, thus attributing $\omega_{Q,j} \cdot \rho_{j,k} \cdot \omega_{Q,k}$ to signal j and $\omega_{Q,k} \cdot \rho_{k,j} \cdot \omega_{Q,j}$ to signal k.

In our example over 52% of the risk comes from the FAST signal, 34% from INTERMEDIATE, and only 14% from SLOW.

The Alpha Perspective

We can view the result in terms of alphas as well as portfolios. According to Equation (14), the zero-cost portfolio is Q with holdings $\mathbf{q} = \sum_{j=1,J} \mathbf{q}_j \cdot \omega_{Q,j}$.

The alphas that lead to this ideal are:

$$\boldsymbol{\alpha} = \lambda \cdot \mathbf{V} \cdot \mathbf{q} = \sum_{j=1,J} \mathbf{a}_j \cdot \left(\lambda \cdot \omega_{Q,j} \right) \tag{17}$$

Weights

Equation (17) can be interpreted in terms of "weights," that is, numbers that sum to one.

$$\begin{aligned}
&(i.) \quad \alpha = scale \cdot \left\{ \sum_{j=1,J} \mathbf{a}_j \cdot weight_j \right\}, \quad \text{where} \\
&(ii.) \quad scale = \lambda \cdot \sum_{j=1,J} \omega_{Q,j} \\
&(iii.) \quad weight_j = \omega_{Q,j} \Big/ \sum_{i=1,J} \omega_{Q,i}
\end{aligned} \tag{18}$$

The scale factor ensures that the resulting alphas have the correct information ratio, that is:

$$\sqrt{\alpha' \cdot \mathbf{V}^{-1} \cdot \alpha} = IR = 1.11. \tag{19}$$

The resulting weights in our examples are 38% for INTERMEDIATE, 20% for SLOW, and 42% for FAST. These weights are a scaling of the risk allocation. The ratio of Risk Q and Weight Q in Exhibit 2 is similar to but not equal to the risk budgeting numbers mentioned above.

The three ways of presenting the results:

- The risk of each source
- The risk budget
- Weights that sum to one

are illustrated in Exhibit 2.

EXHIBIT 2 Three Views of the Solution to the Signal/Source Weighting Problem When There Are No Transactions Costs

IDEAL PORTFOLIO	RISK Q	RISK BUDGET Q	WEIGHT Q
SLOW	1.96%	14.16%	19.95%
INT.	3.78%	34.10%	38.42%
Fast	4.10%	51.74%	41.64%

Now we turn to the more challenging and realistic situation where we consider transactions costs.

Transactions Costs

The previous analysis showed how to approach the source or signal weighting problem successfully when there are no transactions costs. Transactions costs introduce three new obstacles.

- You pay them either directly through commissions, spread, taxes, etc. or indirectly by demanding liquidity and shelling out too much for purchases and getting too little for sales, aka market impact.
- Costs are intimidating. They keep you from fully exploiting your information. There is an opportunity loss.
- Costs are levied on changes in positions, so the initial position is a crucial part of the analysis.

The last point implies a multiperiod perspective is required. Our approach will be to look for strategies or decision rules that can, in some sense, be considered optimal in a multiperiod setting. To do this we make assumptions that allow us to abstract from the reality of the day-to-day portfolio management environment and still capture something of its essence.

The Portfolio's Law of Motion

An active portfolio is an object in motion. Call it portfolio P. If we look at portfolio P periodically, say, every Δt years, then we see a sequence of positions $\cdots, \mathbf{p}(t-\Delta t), \mathbf{p}(t), \mathbf{p}(t+\Delta t), \cdots$. The changes in these positions, defined as:

$$\Delta\mathbf{p}(t) \equiv \mathbf{p}(t) - \mathbf{p}(t-\Delta t), \tag{20}$$

determine the cost.

The challenge is to capture these changes in a useful way. To do this we will specify a rule, called the law of motion, to show how the portfolio P changes in response to changes in the source portfolios. We'll do this in two steps:

- First, combine the source portfolios into a *model* portfolio M.
- Second, show how the portfolio P attempts to track the model portfolio.

The Model Portfolio

The model portfolio is a mixture of the source portfolios. Its holdings at time t are:

$$\mathbf{m}(t) \equiv \sum_{j=1,J} \mathbf{q}_j(t) \cdot \omega_{M,j}, \quad \text{where } \omega_{M,j} = \omega_{Q,j} \cdot \psi_j \,. \tag{21}$$

The risk levels $\omega_{Q,j}$ are the same ones we used to define the zero-cost portfolio. See Equations (13) and (14). The parameters ψ_j where $0 < \psi_j < 1$ are explained in detail below.

The Tracking Rule

The changes in portfolio P are governed by a linear decision rule of the form:

$$(i.)\quad \mathbf{p}(t) = \delta \cdot \mathbf{p}(t-\Delta t) + (1-\delta)\cdot \mathbf{m}(t) \text{ or}$$

$$(ii.)\quad \frac{\Delta \mathbf{p}(t)}{\Delta t} = \frac{(1-\delta)}{\Delta t}\cdot\{\mathbf{m}(t) - \mathbf{p}(t-\Delta t)\} \tag{22}$$

The parameter *delta*, $0 < \delta < 1$, is discussed below. In Appendix A we demonstrate that the rule described in Equations (21) and (22) is optimal under special circumstances. The leap of faith is to assume that the rule is at least "reasonable" under more general conditions.

The parameters δ, ψ_j, mentioned in Equations (21) and (22) depend on the rate of change of the signals as represented by either the raw alphas $\mathbf{a}_j(t)$ or the source portfolios $\mathbf{q}_j(t)$ and on the change in the portfolio $\mathbf{p}(t)$ itself. We now turn our attention to measuring those changes and determining values for these parameters.

A Measure of Signal Speed

We can gauge the rate of change in the signal j between times t and $t-\Delta t$ by measuring the correlation of the positions $\mathbf{q}_j(t)$ and $\mathbf{q}_j(t-\Delta t)$ using the asset covariance, $\mathbf{V}(t)$, at time t. To do the calculation in a sensible way we should tailor the time interval, call it Δt_j, on a signal by signal basis so that a reasonable amount of change takes place resulting in a value for $\gamma_j(t)$ in Equation (23) below in the range of 0.8 to 0.975. This will avoid spurious results if Δt is either too long or too short. Even if we keep daily data, we might want to calculate the correlation over one week, two weeks, or a month so we can see significant changes.

That past correlation is given by:

$$\gamma_j(t) = \frac{\mathbf{q}_j'(t)\cdot\mathbf{V}(t)\cdot\mathbf{q}_j(t-\Delta t_j)}{\sqrt{\mathbf{q}_j'(t)\cdot\mathbf{V}(t)\cdot\mathbf{q}_j(t)}\cdot\sqrt{\mathbf{q}_j'(t-\Delta t_j)\cdot\mathbf{V}(t)\cdot\mathbf{q}_j(t-\Delta t_j)}} \tag{23}$$

We can eliminate the effects of the tailored time interval selection, Δt_j, by calculating a rate of change:

$$g_j(t) = -\frac{\ln(\gamma_j(t))}{\Delta t_j} \text{ or } e^{-g_j(t)\cdot\Delta t_j} = \gamma_j(t). \tag{24}$$

The data will show how the signal has moved in the past. There may be seasonality, such as quarterly or semiannual release of earnings, and there may be a trend, getting faster or slower. The challenge is to use this analysis to choose a point estimate, call it g_j, that will determine how fast (on average) we believe the signal will move in the future. One way to consider this question is in terms of a half-life, that is, the time it will take for the correlation as calculated by Equation (23) to drop to 0.5. Exhibit 3 shows how g_j depends on the half-life.

EXHIBIT 3 Values of g_j for Various Half-Lives

HALF-LIFE	g
1 week	36.0
1 month	8.3
2 months	4.2
1 quarter	2.8
6 months	1.4
9 months	0.9
1 year	0.7

In the example we are following we'll use nine months as the half-life for the SLOW signal, one month for the FAST signal, and six months for the half-life of the INTERMEDIATE signal.

The Pace of Portfolio Change

The parameter *delta* in Equation (22) governs the rate of change of the portfolio *P*. We will express *delta* as $\delta = e^{-d \cdot \Delta t}$, where d measures how fast we attempt to close the gap between where we start, $\mathbf{p}(t - \Delta t)$, and where we would like to be, $\mathbf{m}(t)$. The choice of d, whether it is made explicitly or implicitly, is an attempt to balance two costs:

- Transactions costs. A larger d (thus lower δ) leads to more trading and higher costs.
- Opportunity loss. A smaller d (thus higher δ) implies a less efficient implementation. The fraction of the portfolio *P*'s risk budget directed toward alpha declines and the amount of uncompensated risk increases.

In Appendix A and in an earlier work we show how, under special circumstances, one can make an optimal choice of d.[8] In what follows we first discuss the interpretation of d, which should isolate a reasonable range of values, and then we consider procedures that will help us discover an implied value of d by examining the past behavior of the portfolio.

Interpretation of d

Portfolio *P* chases the model *M*. It is always behind the curve. Indeed, $1/d$ is a measure of how just how much *P* lags *M*. Both *P* and *M* are based on information that has flowed in over previous periods. The age-weighted exposure of *P* to this information is about $1/d$ years longer than the age-weighted exposure of *M* to the same information. Slow trading leaves *P* underexposed

8. "Dynamic Portfolio Analysis," Grinold (2007). This is Chapter 8 in this book.

to recent information and relatively overexposed to older stale information. Exhibit 4 shows lags of one to six months and the corresponding values for d.

EXHIBIT 4 The Relationship Between the Trading Rate *d* and the Lag Between the Average Age of Information in Model Portfolio *M* and Tracking Portfolio *P*

MONTHS LAG	*d*
1 month	12.0
2 months	6.0
3 months	4.0
4 months	3.0
5 months	2.4
6 months	2.0

Estimation of *d*; Revealed Preference

It is possible to get a rough estimate of d by examining the history of the portfolio and the source portfolios. As we indicate in Appendix B, we can use a regression/portfolio optimization approach to estimate parameters $\hat{\delta}(t)$ and $\hat{\beta}_j(t)$ so that:

$$\mathbf{p}(t) = \mathbf{p}(t - \Delta t_0) \cdot \hat{\delta}(t) + \sum_{j=1,J} \mathbf{q}_j(t) \cdot \hat{\beta}_j(t) + \hat{\varepsilon}(t) \tag{25}$$

and the unexplained variance, $\hat{\varepsilon}'(t) \cdot \mathbf{V}(t) \cdot \hat{\varepsilon}(t)$, is minimized. If things are going along relatively smoothly, with no radical changes of policy, and the time interval Δt_0 is selected in a reasonable manner, then one will tend to get estimates $\hat{\delta}(t)$ that are positive and less than one. In those cases, we get an estimate of d:

$$\hat{d}(t) = -\frac{\ln\left(\hat{\delta}(t)\right)}{\Delta t_0}, \quad \hat{\delta}(t) = e^{-\hat{d}(t) \cdot \Delta t_0}. \tag{26}$$

From these estimates of implied past policy along with the intuition that might be gained from Exhibit 4 and future policy plans we settle on values for the parameters d and g_j, $j = 1, \cdots, J$. Then for any rebalance interval Δt we can calculate the risk adjustments ψ_j promised in Equation (21).

$$\begin{aligned} &(i.) \quad \delta = e^{-d \cdot \Delta t}, \gamma_j = e^{-g_j \cdot \Delta t} \\ &(ii.) \quad \psi_j \equiv \frac{1 - \delta}{1 - \delta \cdot \gamma_j} \\ &(iii.) \quad \omega_{M,j} = \psi_j \cdot \omega_{Q,j} \end{aligned} \tag{27}$$

Let's examine how this would work with the example introduced above. The data in Exhibit 5 are based on a value of $d = 4$ and a rebalance interval of one week, $\Delta t = 1/52$; thus $\delta = 0.926$.

EXHIBIT 5 The Assumed Half-Lives of the Three Signals and Corresponding Values of g_j, γ_j and ψ_j Based on $\Delta t = 1/52$, and $\delta = 0.926$

SOURCE	HL MONTHS	g {j}	*gamma* {j}	*psi* {j}	RISK Q	RISK *M*
SLOW	9	0.92	0.982	0.819	1.96%	1.61%
INT.	6	1.39	0.974	0.752	3.78%	2.84%
FAST	1	8.32	0.852	0.351	4.10%	1.44%

In Exhibit 5 the g_j are based on the assumed half-lives. If HL_j is the half-life in months, then $g_j = 12 \cdot \{\ln(2)/HL_j\}$. The γ_j are calculated using item (*i.*) of Equation (27) and the ψ_j are derived from item (*ii.*) of Equation (27). The column Risk *Q* repeats the optimal risk levels, $\omega_{Q,j}$, of the ideal portfolio previously reported in Exhibits 1 and 2. The final column, risk *M*, contains the risk levels, $\psi_j \cdot \omega_{Q,j}$, associated with the model portfolio, as per Equation (21). The risk levels decrease for every signal. The decrease, evident in the *psi* column, is more dramatic for the FAST signal. The risk of model portfolio *M* is 3.06% compared to the 5% risk level for the ideal *Q*. To raise the risk level of *M* to, say, 5%, merely decrease the risk penalty *lambda* from 22.17 to $\{3.06/5\} \cdot 22.17 = 13.57$ and repeat the calculation. This scales up the risk allocation, $\omega_{M,j}$, while it keeps the risk budget allocation and weights the same.

Exhibit 6 compares the results pre (ideal *Q*) and post (model *M*) adjustment for transactions costs.

EXHIBIT 6 The Risk Budgets and Weights for the Zero-Cost Q and the Model/Target *M*

SOURCE	RISK BUDGET Q	RISK BUDGET *M*	WEIGHT Q	WEIGHT *M*
SLOW	14.16%	22.72%	19.95%	27.30%
INT.	34.10%	65.84%	38.42%	48.28%
FAST	51.74%	11.43%	41.64%	24.41%

Opportunity Loss: From Q to M

The adjustment from ideal *Q* to model *M* effectively lowers our sights from one unobtainable goal to another slightly less unobtainable goal. In the process we've left some potential value added on the table.

If we measure the risk-adjusted alpha of *any* portfolio, say *R*, with positions **r**, as:

$$U_R = \boldsymbol{\alpha}' \cdot \mathbf{r} - \frac{\lambda}{2} \cdot \mathbf{r}' \cdot \mathbf{V} \cdot \mathbf{r} = \alpha_R - \frac{\lambda}{2} \cdot v_R^2, \tag{28}$$

then the loss we incur by lowering our sights from *Q* to *R* is:

$$U_Q - U_R = \frac{\lambda}{2} \cdot v_{Q-R}^2. \tag{29}$$

In Equation (32) v_{Q-R} is the risk of a position that is long the zero-cost portfolio Q and short portfolio R. In particular, when R is M, the model/target, we have $v_{Q-M} = 2.58\%$ and the corresponding loss in value added is $U_Q - U_M = 0.74\%$.[9]

The End Result

In Appendix B we examine the consequences of following the rebalancing strategy described in Equation (22). If we let $v_{i,M} \equiv \sum_{j=1,J} \rho_{i,j} \cdot \omega_{M,j}$ be the covariance of source portfolio i with the model portfolio M then we can easily determine the alpha, risk, and implementation efficiency of the implemented strategy P:

$$
\begin{aligned}
&(i.) \quad \alpha_P = \lambda \cdot v_M^2 = \lambda \cdot \sum_{i=1,J} \psi_i \cdot \omega_{Q,i} \cdot v_{i,M} \\
&(ii.) \quad v_P^2 = \sum_{i=1,J} \psi_i^2 \cdot \omega_{Q,i} \cdot v_{i,M} = \sum_{i=1,J} \psi_i \cdot \omega_{M,i} \cdot v_{i,M} \qquad (30) \\
&(iii.) \quad v_{M-P}^2 = \sum_{i=1,J} \psi_i \cdot (1-\psi_i) \cdot \omega_{Q,i} \cdot v_{i,M} = \sum_{i=1,J} (1-\psi_i) \cdot \omega_{M,i} \cdot v_{i,M}
\end{aligned}
$$

Additional Opportunity Lost: From M to P

The opportunity loss described above was due to dropping our sights from Q to M. Because of trading cost the portfolio we actually hold, P, does not capture all the potential value added of the model portfolio M. It is possible to take the analysis a step further (see Appendix B) and look at the efficiency of portfolio P, the portfolio that results from using the updating rule described in Equations (21) and (22). In our example the portfolio P has 2.58% risk. Its correlation (transfer coefficient) with Q is 0.727 and with M is 0.857. The loss in potential value added moving from the ideal Q to the actual P is 1.43%. Given that we lost 0.74% by lowering our sights from the ideal Q to the model M we lose another 0.69% because we cannot track M exactly. That means a certain fraction of portfolio P's risk budget will be residual, that is, not correlated with any source of alpha, and thus risk taken with no expectation of return. Exhibit 7 contains the risk budgets for the three portfolios Q, M, and P.

EXHIBIT 7 Risk Budgets for the Ideal Q, Model *M*, and Actual Portfolio *P*

RISK BUDGET	PORTFOLIO Q IDEAL	PORTFOLIO *M* MODEL	PORTFOLIO *P* ACTUAL
SLOW	14.16%	22.72%	21.49%
INT.	34.10%	65.84%	50.36%
FAST	51.74%	11.43%	2.93%
Residual	0.00%	0.00%	25.22%

9. The portfolio $Q - M$ has positions $\mathbf{q} - \mathbf{m} = \sum_{i=1,J} \mathbf{q}_i \cdot \omega_{Q,i} \cdot (1 - \psi_i)$.

Exhibit 7 shows the magnitude of the compromises forced on us by trading frictions. With no trading costs we would allocate 51.74% of our risk budget to the FAST signal. Taking costs into consideration, we allocate only 2.93% to the FAST signal. This is a huge shift.

Reverse Engineering

If you have a target risk level for the portfolio *P*, say 4.00%, then you can alter the analysis to get that outcome. Change the risk penalty lambda from 22.17 to $22.17 \cdot \{2.58/4.00\} = 14.30$. This will scale up the risk allocations, $\omega_{Q,j}, \omega_{M,j}$. However, the relative risk budget numbers in Exhibit 7 will not change.

Estimate of Costs

We discussed the opportunity losses incurred by lowering our sights from *Q* to *M*, 0.74%, and then in fact lagging behind *M*, 0.69%. We also will incur direct costs either fees and commissions or through market impact. We can estimate these as well (see Appendix A). We'll call the difference between portfolios *M* and *P* the backlog. This is the trade one would make given one period free of transactions costs. We can measure the size of this backlog by its variance, ω_{M-P}^2. A rough estimate of annual transactions costs, c_P, for portfolio *P* is a function of the backlog variance:

$$c_P \approx \frac{\lambda}{2} \cdot \omega_{M-P}^2. \tag{31}$$

For the data this cost comes out as 0.30%. In addition to the 1.43% opportunity loss, this brings the total bill to 1.73% and our annual value added after cost to 1.04%.

Sensitivity Analysis

One of the attractive features of this approach to signal weighting is the ability to do sensitivity analysis. The equations used in the paper can be coded in a spreadsheet in a matter of minutes. As an example, we calculated the weights, Equation (28), of the model portfolio *M* for various values of the trading rate parameter *d*.

EXHIBIT 8 Alpha Weights for the Model Portfolio *M* as the Trading Rate *d* Varies and Other Parameters Are Held Constant

MONTHS LAG	0.5	1	2	4	6	12
d	24	12	6	3	2	1
SLOW	21.66%	23.32%	25.68%	28.52%	30.26%	33.09%
INT.	41.13%	43.55%	46.56%	49.36%	50.55%	51.62%
FAST	37.20%	33.12%	27.76%	22.12%	19.19%	15.30%

The cases in Exhibit 8 bracket the base case with $d = 4$ that is summarized in Exhibit 6. Also, we can consider the zero-cost portfolio Q as the case with d very large. The weight for the ideal is also in Exhibit 6, with 19.95%, 38.42% and 41.64% for SLOW, INTERMEDIATE, and FAST, respectively.

Conclusion

We have presented a relatively straightforward approach to the signal-weighting problem in the face of transactions costs. It has several attractive attributes:

- It is portfolio based. It looks at the signal-weighting problem as an investment problem that links each signal to an investment strategy and then looks for the optimal mix of strategies.
- It is a natural extension of the solution of the signal-weighting problem in the absence of costs.
- It is forward looking. It depends on three properties of the signals: the predicted information ratios, IR_j, the predicted return correlations, $\rho_{i,j}$, and the rate of change of the each signal, g_j. In addition, it depends on two investment strategy parameters: the trading rate of the portfolio, d, a surrogate for turnover, and a risk penalty λ that controls the strategy's level of risk.
- It is easy to perform sensitivity analysis. This is vitally important both to establish a firm understanding of the model and its results and to test the robustness of the answers to reasonable adjustments in the inputs.
- It lends itself to reverse engineering. It is relatively easy to adjust the risk penalty and trading rate to attain a desired level of turnover and active variance.
- It predicts the characteristics of the resulting strategy including its level of risk, risk budget, opportunity loss, and annual trading costs.
- It changes perspective by thinking of each signal as a substrategy and the weights as active risk levels for the substrategy. These risk levels in turn allow the calculation of risk budgets that are a better measure of the importance of each signal.
- It changes perspective by focusing on the dynamics of the signals and the portfolio. The measurement of the rate of change of the signals, g_j, and the trading rate d of the portfolio requires a novel, dynamic look at the signals and the portfolio.

References

Garleanu, Nicolae, and Lasse Heje Pedersen. 2009, 2013. "Dynamic Trading with Predictable Returns and Transactions Costs." Working paper, February 24, 2009, Haas School of Business. Published in *Journal of Finance* 68 (6), December 2013, 2309–2340.

Grinold, Richard C. 2006. "A Dynamic Model of Portfolio Management." *Journal of Investment Management* 4 (2nd quarter): 5–22.
Grinold, Richard C. 2007. "Dynamic Portfolio Analysis." *Journal of Portfolio Management* 34 (Fall): 12–26.
Sneddon, Leigh. 2008. "The Tortoise and the Hare: Portfolio Dynamics for Active Managers." *The Journal of Investing* 17 (Winter): 106–111.

Appendix A

Optimization

We treat the dynamic portfolio management problem using linear-quadratic dynamic programming. We assume the reader has a familiarity with dynamic programming.

In this class of problems, we know that the value function is quadratic in the state variables and that the optimal policy is linear in the state variables. Given that it's an onerous exercise in matrix algebra to find the correct value function and optimal policy, we will take some shortcuts and exploit the special structure of the problem. In particular, we are only interested in the optimal policy function, so we can ignore a large portion of the work.

The paper's results depend on a special case where the transactions costs are proportional to the variance of the basket of stocks being traded. We'll concentrate on that special case and then look at how the results simplify if we allow the trading interval, Δt, to approach zero.

The State

There are N assets and J signals/sources. The information in signal j is represented by a source portfolio, an N element vector, $\mathbf{q}_j$, that represents a mean variance efficient bet on signal j. The state of the system is $\{\mathbf{p}_0, \mathbf{q}_j\}_{j=1J}$, where $\mathbf{p}_0$ is an N vector representing the starting portfolio and the $\mathbf{q}_j$ are the source portfolios.

Alpha and Portfolio q

In the body of the paper we derived the signal weights in the case of zero transactions cost. The result was a risk allocation $\omega_{Q,j}$ where:

$$\begin{aligned} IR_i &= \lambda \cdot \sum_{j=1:J} R_{i,j} \cdot \omega_{Q,j} \\ \mathbf{q} &\equiv \sum_{j=1:J} \mathbf{q}_j \cdot \omega_{Q,j} \\ \alpha &= \lambda \cdot \mathbf{V} \cdot \mathbf{q} \end{aligned} \tag{A1}$$

The Action

The action is to choose a new portfolio; call it **p**.

The Dynamics

The source portfolios are not influenced by our actions:[10]

$$\begin{aligned} &\tilde{\mathbf{q}}_j(t) = \gamma_j \cdot \mathbf{q}_j(t-\Delta t) + \sqrt{1-\gamma_j^2} \cdot \tilde{\mathbf{y}}_j(t), \\ &E\left\langle \tilde{\mathbf{y}}_j(t) \middle| \mathbf{q}_j(t-\Delta t)\right\rangle = 0, \quad E\left\langle \tilde{\mathbf{y}}_j'(t) \cdot \mathbf{V} \cdot \tilde{\mathbf{y}}_j(t)\right\rangle = 1 \\ &E\left\langle \tilde{\mathbf{y}}_j'(t) \cdot \mathbf{V} \cdot \tilde{\mathbf{y}}_k(t)\right\rangle = \Phi_{j,k} \\ &E\left\langle \tilde{\mathbf{q}}_j'(t) \cdot \mathbf{V} \cdot \tilde{\mathbf{q}}_k(t)\right\rangle = R_{j,k} = \frac{\sqrt{1-\gamma_j^2} \cdot \Phi_{j,k} \cdot \sqrt{1-\gamma_j^2}}{1-\gamma_j \cdot \gamma_k} \end{aligned} \tag{A2}$$

From this point on we'll write **Q** to represent the source portfolio portion of the state.

Reward Function

If we are in state $\{\mathbf{p}_0, \mathbf{Q}\}$ and choose portfolio **p**, then we receive a reward:

$$\begin{aligned} &u(\mathbf{p}_0, \mathbf{Q}, \mathbf{p}) \equiv \left\{\boldsymbol{\alpha}'(\mathbf{Q}) \cdot \mathbf{p} - \frac{\lambda}{2} \cdot \mathbf{p}' \cdot \mathbf{V} \cdot \mathbf{p}\right\} \cdot \Delta t \\ &- \frac{\chi}{2 \cdot \Delta t} \cdot (\mathbf{p} - \mathbf{p}_0)' \cdot \mathbf{V} \cdot (\mathbf{p} - \mathbf{p}_0) \end{aligned} \tag{A3}$$

$$\text{where } \boldsymbol{\alpha}(\mathbf{Q}) = \lambda \cdot \mathbf{V} \cdot \sum_{j=1:J} \mathbf{q}_j \cdot \omega_{Q,j}$$

This calls for some interpretation and rearrangement.

The transactions cost looks strange with the Δt in the denominator. Here is how we get there:

$$\begin{aligned} &\frac{\chi}{2} \cdot \dot{\mathbf{p}}' \cdot \mathbf{V} \cdot \dot{\mathbf{p}} \text{ is the annual cost of transacting at rate } \dot{\mathbf{p}} \\ &\frac{\chi}{2} \cdot \dot{\mathbf{p}}' \cdot \mathbf{V} \cdot \dot{\mathbf{p}} \approx \frac{\chi}{2} \cdot \frac{\Delta \mathbf{p}}{\Delta t} \cdot \mathbf{V} \cdot \frac{\Delta \mathbf{p}}{\Delta t} \\ &\text{For one period we have:} \\ &\left\{\frac{\chi}{2} \cdot \dot{\mathbf{p}}' \cdot \mathbf{V} \cdot \dot{\mathbf{p}}\right\} \cdot \Delta t \approx \left\{\frac{\chi}{2} \cdot \frac{\Delta \mathbf{p}}{\Delta t}' \cdot \mathbf{V} \cdot \frac{\Delta \mathbf{p}}{\Delta t}\right\} \cdot \Delta t = \frac{\chi}{2 \cdot \Delta t} \cdot \Delta \mathbf{p}' \cdot \mathbf{V} \cdot \Delta \mathbf{p} \end{aligned} \tag{A4}$$

We will use an ansatz approach: anticipate the solution and then show the guess is correct. This starts with a definition of a model/target portfolio as the place we would like to be if we had a one-period holiday on transactions

10. We provide more detail on the related signal dynamics in Appendix B, Equations B1 through B5.

cost. We assume that the model/target is a linear combination of the source portfolios, and we can easily calculate the expected model portfolio at the start of the next period:

$$\mathbf{m} \equiv \sum_{j=1:J} \mathbf{q}_j \cdot \omega_{M,j} \text{ with } \omega_{M,j} \text{ to be determined}$$
$$\bar{\mathbf{m}}(t+\Delta t) = E\left\langle \mathbf{m}(t+\Delta t) \middle| \mathbf{q}_j(t) \right\rangle \tag{A5}$$
$$\bar{\mathbf{m}}(t+\Delta t) \equiv \sum_{j=1:J} \mathbf{q}_j(t) \cdot \gamma_j \cdot \omega_{M,j}$$

It simplifies matters if we rearrange the one period reward function as follows:

$$u(\mathbf{p}_0, \mathbf{Q}, \mathbf{p}) = \frac{\lambda \cdot \Delta t}{2} \cdot \mathbf{q}' \cdot \mathbf{V} \cdot \mathbf{q}$$
$$- \left\{ \frac{\lambda \cdot \Delta t}{2} \cdot (\mathbf{q} - \mathbf{p})' \cdot \mathbf{V} \cdot (\mathbf{q} - \mathbf{p}) + \frac{\chi}{2 \cdot \Delta t} \cdot (\mathbf{p} - \mathbf{p}_0)' \cdot \mathbf{V} \cdot (\mathbf{p} - \mathbf{p}_0) \right\} \tag{A6}$$
$$\text{where } \mathbf{q} = \sum_{j=1:J} \mathbf{q}_j \cdot \omega_{Q,j}$$

We formulate the dynamic programming in the average growth rate form:

$$\phi \cdot \Delta t + \upsilon(\mathbf{p}_0, \mathbf{Q}) = Max_{\mathbf{p}} \left\{ u(\mathbf{p}_0, \mathbf{Q}, \mathbf{p}) + E\left\langle \upsilon(\mathbf{p}, \tilde{\mathbf{Q}}) \middle| \mathbf{Q} \right\rangle \right\} \tag{A7}$$

The final guess is about the form of $\upsilon(\mathbf{p}_0, \mathbf{Q})$:

$$\upsilon(\mathbf{p}_0, \mathbf{Q}) = f(\mathbf{Q}) - \frac{\kappa}{2} \cdot (\mathbf{m} - \mathbf{p}_0)' \cdot \mathbf{V} \cdot (\mathbf{m} - \mathbf{p}_0)$$
$$\mathbf{m} = \sum_{j=1:J} \mathbf{q}_j \cdot \omega_{M,j} \tag{A8}$$
$$\omega_{M,j} \text{ and } \kappa \text{ to be determined}$$

Note that this says for any **Q** the best place initial position is $\mathbf{p}_0 = \mathbf{m}$.

One more adjustment, and matters will start to simplify.

$$E\left\langle \upsilon(\mathbf{p}, \tilde{\mathbf{Q}}) \mid \mathbf{Q} \right\rangle = -\frac{\kappa}{2} \cdot (\bar{\mathbf{m}} - \mathbf{p})' \cdot \mathbf{V} \cdot (\bar{\mathbf{m}} - \mathbf{p})$$
$$+ E\left\langle f(\tilde{\mathbf{Q}}) \mid \mathbf{Q} \right\rangle + \frac{\kappa}{2} \cdot \bar{\mathbf{m}}' \cdot \mathbf{V} \cdot \bar{\mathbf{m}} - \frac{\kappa}{2} \cdot E\left\langle \tilde{\mathbf{m}}' \cdot \mathbf{V} \cdot \tilde{\mathbf{m}} \mid \mathbf{Q} \right\rangle \tag{A9}$$
$$\text{where } \bar{\mathbf{m}} = \sum_{j=1:J} \mathbf{q}_j \cdot \gamma_j \cdot \omega_{M,j}$$
$$\omega_{M,j} \text{ and } \kappa \text{ to be determined}$$

The second line in Equation (A9) does not depend on **p**. It will not have any influence on the policy decision, so for our purposes we can ignore it.

We are being pulled in three directions. We select the optimal **p** by minimizing:

$$\begin{aligned}
&\frac{\lambda \cdot \Delta t}{2} \cdot (\mathbf{q} - \mathbf{p})' \cdot \mathbf{V} \cdot (\mathbf{q} - \mathbf{p}) && \text{get risk-adjusted alpha} \\
&+ \frac{\chi}{2 \cdot \Delta t} \cdot (\mathbf{p} - \mathbf{p}_0)' \cdot \mathbf{V} \cdot (\mathbf{p} - \mathbf{p}_0) && \text{avoid cost} \\
&+ \frac{\kappa}{2} \cdot (\bar{\mathbf{m}} - \mathbf{p})' \cdot \mathbf{V} \cdot (\bar{\mathbf{m}} - \mathbf{p}) && \text{land in a good place}
\end{aligned} \tag{A10}$$

The optimal solution is a blend of the three:

$$\mathbf{p} = \frac{\lambda \cdot \Delta t \cdot \mathbf{q} + \chi/_{\Delta t} \cdot \mathbf{p}_0 + \kappa \cdot \bar{\mathbf{m}}}{\lambda \cdot \Delta t + \chi/_{\Delta t} + \kappa} \tag{A11}$$

Now let's consider a very special case. Suppose the $\mathbf{Q} = 0$, all the source portfolios are zero. Then $\mathbf{q} = 0$ and $\bar{\mathbf{m}} = \mathbf{0}$, so:

$$\mathbf{p} = \delta \cdot \mathbf{p}_0 \quad \text{where}$$

$$\delta \equiv \frac{\chi/_{\Delta t}}{\lambda \cdot \Delta t + \chi/_{\Delta t} + \kappa} \tag{A12}$$

The left-hand side of Equation (A7) always has a term:

$$-\kappa \cdot \frac{\mathbf{p}_0' \cdot \mathbf{V} \cdot \mathbf{p}_0}{2} \tag{A13}$$

The right-hand side, using the maximum **p** in Equation (A12), will have a term:

$$-\left\{(\lambda \cdot \Delta t + \kappa) \cdot \delta^2 + \frac{\chi}{\Delta t} \cdot (1 - \delta)^2\right\} \cdot \frac{\mathbf{p}_0 \cdot \mathbf{V} \cdot \mathbf{p}_0}{2} \tag{A14}$$

The expression in Equation (A13) should equal the expression in Equation (A14) for any initial position $\mathbf{p}_0$, so we must have:

$$\kappa = (\lambda \cdot \Delta t + \kappa) \cdot \delta^2 + \frac{\chi}{\Delta t} \cdot (1 - \delta)^2 \tag{A15}$$

where delta is defined as per Equation (A12).

If you wrestle with Equations (A12) and (A15) for a while, you can reduce it to a quadratic that defines κ.

$$\kappa^2 + \kappa \cdot \lambda \cdot \Delta t - \chi \cdot \lambda = 0 \tag{A16}$$

Along the way, you will find this useful result:

$$\delta = \frac{\kappa}{\kappa + \lambda \cdot \Delta t}, \quad 1 - \delta = \frac{\lambda \cdot \Delta t}{\kappa + \lambda \cdot \Delta t} \tag{A17}$$

We are halfway. Next, we'll cheat a bit. We show that we can simplify Equation (A11) to end up with:

$$\mathbf{p} = \delta \cdot \mathbf{p}_0 + (1-\delta) \cdot \mathbf{m}$$
$$\text{where } \mathbf{m} = \sum_{j=1:J} \mathbf{q}_j \cdot \omega_{M,j} \tag{A18}$$

For this to work, Equations (A11) and (A18) must give the same answer. That means:

$$(1-\delta) \cdot \sum_{j=1:J} \mathbf{q}_j \cdot \omega_{M,j} = \frac{\lambda \cdot \Delta t \cdot \sum_{j=1:J} \mathbf{q}_j \cdot \omega_{Q,j} + \kappa \cdot \sum_{j=1:J} \mathbf{q}_j \cdot \gamma_j \cdot \omega_{M,j}}{\lambda \cdot \Delta t + \chi/_{\Delta t} + \kappa} \tag{A19}$$

Multiply both sides of Equation (A19) by $\lambda \cdot \Delta t + \chi/_{\Delta t} + \kappa$ and note that:

$$(1-\delta) \cdot \left(\lambda \cdot \Delta t + \chi/_{\Delta t} + \kappa\right) = \lambda \cdot \Delta t + \kappa \tag{A20}$$

The result, after we divide Equation (A20) by $\lambda \cdot \Delta t + \kappa$ and appeal to Equation (A17), is:

$$\sum_{j=1:J} \mathbf{q}_j \cdot \omega_{M,j} = (1-\delta) \cdot \sum_{j=1:J} \mathbf{q}_j \cdot \omega_{Q,j} + \delta \cdot \sum_{j=1:J} \mathbf{q}_j \cdot \gamma_j \cdot \omega_{M,j}$$
$$\Rightarrow \omega_{M,j} = (1-\delta) \cdot \omega_{Q,j} + \delta \cdot \gamma_j \cdot \omega_{M,j} \tag{A21}$$
$$\text{so} \quad \omega_{M,j} = \frac{1-\delta}{1-\delta \cdot \gamma_j} \cdot \omega_{Q,j}$$

To complete the proof, you need to show that these values work. In particular, use $\omega_{M,j}$ defined in Equation (A21) on both sides of the dynamic programming equation, along with the optimal **p** from Equation (A11), and show that the equality holds.

Bottom line:

1. Solve Equation (A16) to get κ.
2. Use κ and Equation (A17) to calculate δ.
3. Use δ, γ_j, $\omega_{Q,j}$ and Equation (A21) to calculate $\omega_{M.j}$.

One additional note. As the time interval shrinks to zero, we have:

$$\kappa \to \sqrt{\lambda \cdot \chi}$$
$$\frac{1-\delta}{\Delta t} \to d = \sqrt{\frac{\lambda}{\chi}}, \quad \chi \cdot d^2 = \lambda \tag{A22}$$
$$\omega_{M,j} = \frac{1-\delta}{1-\gamma_j \cdot \delta} \cdot \omega_{Q,j} \to \frac{d}{d+g_j} \cdot \omega_{Q,j} = \frac{\lambda}{\lambda + g_j \cdot \sqrt{\lambda \cdot \chi}} \cdot \omega_{Q,j}$$

In the case of a single signal, $J = 1$, Equation (A21) corresponds to the analytic solution that we derived in the appendix to the dynamic portfolio analysis and implementation efficiency chapters at the end of Chapter 8.

Appendix B

Policy Analysis

In Appendix A of this chapter we demonstrated that, under special circumstances, a linear decision rule is the optimal policy. We can see this result in Equation (A18). In this appendix, we determine the consequences of rebalancing using *any* linear decision rule similar to the one described in Appendix A or the signal weighting chapter. In addition, we will then present an analytic approach to selecting the best linear decision rules. This direct approach avoids the potential obstacle of dynamic programming and provides an alternative perspective.

Information is contained in J signals that evolve in a relatively straightforward manner, Equation (A2) in Appendix A. Remember what we are calling signals are really single source standardized alphas.

The Signals

$$\begin{aligned} &\tilde{\mathbf{a}}_j(t) = \gamma_j \cdot \mathbf{a}_j(t-\Delta t) + \sqrt{1-\gamma_j^2} \cdot \tilde{\mathbf{u}}_j \quad j = 1, 2, \ldots, J \\ &E\langle \tilde{\mathbf{u}}_j \rangle = 0, \quad E\langle \tilde{\mathbf{u}}_j' \cdot \mathbf{V} \cdot \tilde{\mathbf{u}}_j \rangle = 1, \quad E\langle \tilde{\mathbf{u}}_j | \mathbf{a}_j(t-\Delta t) \rangle = 0 \end{aligned} \tag{B1}$$

Signals are unbiased and placed on a level playing field prior to an allocation of risk to each signal. As a result of Equation (B1):

$$E\langle \tilde{\mathbf{a}}_j(t) \rangle = 0 \;\; \text{no bias} \tag{B2}$$

$$E\langle \tilde{\mathbf{a}}_j'(t) \cdot \mathbf{V}^{-1} \cdot \tilde{\mathbf{a}}_j(t) \rangle = 1 \;\; \text{standardized} \tag{B3}$$

The Source Portfolios

We find it more convenient to deal with portfolios. For each signal $\mathbf{a}_j(t)$, there is a source portfolio, $\mathbf{q}_j(t)$, defined in Equation (B4) below, that efficiently captures the information in $\mathbf{a}_j(t)$:

$$\mathbf{q}_j(t) \equiv \mathbf{V}^{-1} \cdot \mathbf{a}_j(t). \tag{B4}$$

It follows that:[11]

$$\begin{aligned} \tilde{\mathbf{q}}_j(t) &= \gamma_j \cdot \mathbf{q}_j(t-\Delta t) + \sqrt{1-\gamma_j^2} \cdot \tilde{\mathbf{y}}_j, \quad \tilde{\mathbf{y}}_j \equiv \mathbf{V}^{-1} \cdot \tilde{\mathbf{u}}_j \\ R_{i,j} &= E\left\langle \tilde{\mathbf{q}}_i'(t) \cdot \mathbf{V} \cdot \tilde{\mathbf{q}}_j(t) \right\rangle = \frac{\sqrt{1-\gamma_i^2} \cdot \sqrt{1-\gamma_j^2}}{1-\gamma_i \cdot \gamma_j} \cdot E\left\langle \tilde{\mathbf{u}}_i' \cdot \mathbf{V} \cdot \tilde{\mathbf{u}}_j \right\rangle \end{aligned} \tag{B5}$$

A Linear Trading Rule

Suppose portfolio M is a mixture of the source portfolios with positions:

$$\mathbf{m}(t) = \sum_{j=1,J} \mathbf{q}_j(t) \cdot \omega_{M,j} \quad . \tag{B6}$$

It is best to consider the $\omega_{M,j}$ as risk levels. They have that interpretation, and they are not numbers that add to one.

We define portfolio P with positions $\mathbf{p}(t)$ through the process:

$$\mathbf{p}(t) = \delta \cdot \mathbf{p}(t-\Delta t) + (1-\delta) \cdot \mathbf{m}(t) \tag{B7}$$

with $0 \le \delta < 1$.

Our goal is to determine the properties of any portfolio P that is updated using Equation (B7). Many of the properties are linked to the pace of change for portfolio P.

$$\frac{\Delta \mathbf{p}(t)}{\Delta t} \equiv \frac{\mathbf{p}(t) - \mathbf{p}(t-\Delta t)}{\Delta t} = \left\{\frac{1-\delta}{\Delta t}\right\} \cdot \{\mathbf{m}(t) - \mathbf{p}(t-\Delta t)\} \tag{B8}$$

In addition to portfolios M and P we investigate the properties of three other portfolios:

- Portfolio $Z = P(-\Delta t)$ with the pretrade positions $\mathbf{p}(t-\Delta t)$.
- Portfolio $\dot{P}$ (note the dot over the P) with positions equal to the rate of trading, $\Delta \mathbf{p}/\Delta t$ as defined by Equation (B8).
- Portfolio $M - P$, the *backlog*, this is the tracking difference between M and P. It has positions $\mathbf{m}(t) - \mathbf{p}(t)$.

11. The signal portfolios inherit their correlation from the innovations, not the converse.

Notation

The notation we use is:

$$
\begin{aligned}
&\upsilon_{i,M} \equiv E\left\langle \mathbf{q}_i'(t)\cdot \mathbf{V}\cdot \mathbf{m}(t)\right\rangle \\
&\upsilon_{i,P} \equiv E\left\langle \mathbf{q}_i'(t)\cdot \mathbf{V}\cdot \mathbf{p}(t)\right\rangle \\
&\upsilon_{M,P} \equiv E\left\langle \mathbf{m}'(t)\cdot \mathbf{V}\cdot \mathbf{p}(t)\right\rangle \\
&\upsilon_{M,Z} \equiv E\left\langle \mathbf{m}'(t)\cdot \mathbf{V}\cdot \mathbf{p}(t-\Delta t)\right\rangle \\
&\upsilon_{M,\dot{P}} \equiv E\left\langle \mathbf{m}'(t)\cdot \mathbf{V}\cdot \frac{\Delta \mathbf{p}(t)}{\Delta t}\right\rangle \\
&\upsilon_P^2 \equiv E\left\langle \mathbf{p}'(t)\cdot \mathbf{V}\cdot \mathbf{p}(t)\right\rangle \text{ aka } \upsilon_{P,P} \\
&\upsilon_{P,Z} \equiv E\left\langle \mathbf{p}(t)\cdot \mathbf{V}\cdot \mathbf{p}(t-\Delta t)\right\rangle \\
&\upsilon_{M-P}^2 \equiv E\left\langle \left\{\mathbf{m}(t)-\mathbf{p}(t)\right\}'\cdot \mathbf{V}\cdot \left\{\mathbf{m}(t)-\mathbf{p}(t)\right\}\right\rangle \text{ a.k.a. } \upsilon_{M-P,M-P} \\
&\upsilon_{\dot{P}}^2 \equiv E\left\langle \frac{\Delta \mathbf{p}'(t)}{\Delta t}\cdot \mathbf{V}\cdot \frac{\Delta \mathbf{p}(t)}{\Delta t}\right\rangle \text{ a.k.a. } \upsilon_{\dot{P},\dot{P}}
\end{aligned}
\tag{B9}
$$

We can exploit the law of motion and the assumption that the system is in equilibrium to characterize many of its attributes. It is easy to see that:

$$
\upsilon_{i,M} = E\langle \tilde{\mathbf{q}}_i \cdot \mathbf{V} \cdot \tilde{\mathbf{m}}\rangle = \sum_{j=1:J} R_{i,j} \cdot \omega_{M,j} \tag{B10}
$$

The equilibrium assumptions are:

$$
\begin{aligned}
&\upsilon_{P,P} = \upsilon_{Z,Z} \\
&\upsilon_{i,P} = E\langle \mathbf{q}_i'(t-\Delta t)\cdot \mathbf{V}\cdot \mathbf{p}(t-\Delta t)\rangle
\end{aligned}
\tag{B11}
$$

Proposition 1

Let:

$$
\psi_i \equiv (1-\delta)/(1-\delta\cdot\gamma_i), \tag{B12}
$$

and:

$$
\upsilon_{i,M} = \sum_{j=1:J} R_{i,j} \cdot \omega_{M,j} \tag{B13}
$$

Then:

$$
\begin{array}{ll}
(i.) & v_{i,P} = \psi_i \cdot v_{i,M} \\
(ii.) & v_{i,Z} = \gamma_i \cdot \psi_i \cdot v_{i,U} = \gamma_i \cdot v_{i,P} \\
(iii.) & v_{M,P} = \sum_{i=1,J} \omega_{M,i} \cdot \psi_i \cdot v_{i,M} \\
(iv.) & v_{M,Z} = \sum_{i=1,J} \omega_{M,i} \cdot \gamma_i \cdot \psi_i \cdot v_{i,M} \\
(v.) & v_{M,\dot{P}} = \sum_{i=1,J} \omega_{M,i} \cdot \dfrac{(1-\gamma_i)}{\Delta t} \cdot \psi_i \cdot v_{i,M} \\
(vi.) & v_P^2 = \dfrac{v_{M,P} + \delta \cdot v_{M,Z}}{1+\delta} \\
(vii.) & v_{P,Z} = \dfrac{\delta \cdot v_{M,X} + v_{M,Z}}{1+\delta} \\
(viii.) & v_{\dot{P}}^2 = \dfrac{2}{1+\delta} \cdot \dfrac{1-\delta}{\Delta t} \cdot v_{M,\dot{P}} \\
(ix.) & v_{M-P}^2 = \sum_i u_i \cdot (1-\psi_i) \cdot v_{i,M} - \left\{ \dfrac{\delta}{1+\delta} \right\} \cdot v_{M,P-Z}
\end{array}
\tag{B14}
$$

Proof

For (*i.*):

$$v_{i,P} = \delta \cdot v_{i,Z} + (1-\delta) \cdot v_{i,M} \tag{B15}$$

$$v_{i,Z} = \gamma_i \cdot \mathbb{E}\left\langle \mathbf{q}_i (t-\Delta t)' \cdot \mathbf{V} \cdot \mathbf{p}(t-\Delta t) \right\rangle + \sqrt{1-\gamma_i^2} \cdot \mathbb{E}\left\langle \mathbf{u}_i'(t) \cdot \mathbf{V} \cdot \mathbf{p}(t-\Delta t) \right\rangle \tag{B16}$$

However,

$$
\begin{array}{l}
\mathbb{E}\left\langle \mathbf{q}_i (t-\Delta t)' \cdot \mathbf{V} \cdot \mathbf{p}(t-\Delta t) \right\rangle = \mathbb{E}\left\langle \mathbf{q}_i (t)' \cdot \mathbf{V} \cdot \mathbf{p}(t) \right\rangle = v_{i,P} \\
\mathbb{E}\left\langle \mathbf{u}_i'(t) \cdot \mathbf{V} \cdot \mathbf{p}(t-\Delta t) \right\rangle = 0
\end{array}
\tag{B17}
$$

The first of these follows from equilibrium and the second by the nonanticipation of the innovations.

When we combine Equations (B15), (B16), and (B17), we find:

$$v_{i,P} = \delta \cdot \gamma_i \cdot v_{i,P} + (1-\delta) \cdot v_{i,M}. \tag{B18}$$

Equation (B17) together with the definition of ψ_i, Equation (B12), yields our first result (*i.*). In the course of this we also stumbled upon our second result since Equation (B16) implies that $v_{i,Z} = \gamma_i \cdot v_{i,P}$.

Items (*iii.*) through (*v.*) are derived from items (*i.*) and (*ii.*) and the linear nature of covariance calculations.

The calculation of the variance, v_P^2, requires slightly more analysis. If we take the covariance of $\mathbf{p}(t)$ with the terms in Equation (B7), and then the covariance of $\mathbf{p}(t-\Delta t)$ with that same equation, we get two equations.

$$\begin{aligned} v_P^2 &= \delta \cdot v_{P,Z} + (1-\delta) \cdot v_{M,P} \\ v_{P,Z} &= \delta \cdot v_Z^2 + (1-\delta) \cdot v_{M,Z} \end{aligned} \tag{B19}$$

From the equilibrium assumption $v_Z^2 = v_P^2$. Since $v_{M,P}$ and $v_{M,Z}$ are known, Equation (B19) is two equations in two unknowns.

$$\begin{Bmatrix} 1 & -\delta \\ -\delta & 1 \end{Bmatrix} \cdot \begin{Bmatrix} v_P^2 \\ v_{P,Z} \end{Bmatrix} = (1-\delta) \cdot \begin{Bmatrix} v_{M,P} \\ v_{M,Z} \end{Bmatrix}. \tag{B20}$$

Items (*vi.*) and (*vii.*) provide the solution to Equation (B20). Item (*viii.*) follows since $v_{\dot{P}}^2 = 2 \cdot \{v_P^2 - v_{P,Z}\} / \Delta t^2$. For item (*ix.*) we write:

$$v_{M-P}^2 = \{v_M^2 - v_{M,P}\} + \{v_P^2 - v_{M,P}\} \tag{B21}$$

The first expression on the right, from item (*iii.*), is:

$$v_M^2 - v_{M,P} = \sum_i \omega_{M,i} \cdot \{1 - \psi_i\} \cdot v_{i,M} \tag{B22}$$

The second bracketed expression on the right is more complicated:

$$\begin{aligned} v_P^2 - v_{M,P} &= \left\{ \frac{1}{1+\delta} - 1 \right\} \cdot v_{M,P} + \frac{\delta}{1+\delta} \cdot v_{M,Z} \\ &= \frac{\delta}{1+\delta} \cdot \{v_{M,Z} - v_{M,P}\} = -\frac{\delta}{1+\delta} \cdot v_{M,P-Z} \end{aligned} \tag{B23}$$

Result for Small Time Intervals

The results in Proposition 1 simplify as we let the rebalance interval go to zero, $\Delta t \to 0$.

Proposition 2

As $\Delta t \to 0$:

$$
\begin{aligned}
&(i.) \quad v_{i,P} && \to \frac{d}{d+g_i} \cdot v_{i,M} \\
&(ii.) \quad v_{M,P} && \to \sum_{i=1,J} \omega_{M,i} \cdot \frac{d}{d+g_i} \cdot v_{i,M} \\
&(iii.) \quad v_{M.\dot{P}} && \to \sum_{i=1,J} \omega_{M,i} \cdot \frac{d \cdot g_i}{d+g_i} \cdot v_{i,M} \\
&(iv.) \quad v_P^2 && \to \sum_{i=1,J} \omega_{M,i} \cdot \frac{d}{d+g_i} \cdot v_{i,M} = v_{M,P} \\
&(v.) \quad v_{M-P}^2 && \to \sum_{i} \omega_{M,i} \cdot \frac{g_i}{d+g_i} \cdot v_{i,M} \\
&(vi.) \quad v_{\dot{P}}^2 && \to d^2 \cdot \sum_{i=1,J} \omega_{M,i} \cdot \frac{g_i}{d+g_i} \cdot v_{i,M} = d^2 \cdot v_{M-P}^2
\end{aligned}
\tag{B24}
$$

Proof

As $\Delta t \to 0$ we have $(1-\delta)/\Delta t \to d$, $(1-\gamma_i)/\Delta t \to g_i$, $\psi_i \to d/\{d+g_i\}$ and $\omega_{P,Z} \to \omega_{P,P}$. With these relations in mind the results in Equation (B24) are fairly straightforward.

Backlog Variance and Target Correlation

Portfolio P is trying to track portfolio M. One measure of success is the variance of the backlog, v_{M-P}^2. Note that the rate of portfolio change $\omega_{\dot{P}}$ will depend on both the trading rate d and the tracking error, $v_{\dot{P}} = d \cdot v_{M-P}$.[12]

Another measure of implementation efficiency is the target correlation, in this case, $\rho_{M,P} \equiv \{v_{M,P}/v_M \cdot v_p\}$.[13] However, since $v_{M,P} = v_P^2 = v_P \cdot v_P$, we have $\rho_{M,P} = v_P/v_M$.

Projection of the Holdings for Any Portfolio

Any portfolio, say, portfolio H with position **h**, can be represented in terms of the sources and a residual position that is uncorrelated to the sources.

12. This is a variation on the queuing formula, $L = \lambda \cdot W$ where L is the size of the queue, lambda the arrival rate, and W the average time spent in the queue. The queue in our case is the backlog with v_{M-P} a measure of its size, $v_{\dot{P}}$ measuring the arrival (and departure) rate, and $1/d$ the average amount of time an arrival spends in the backlog.

13. This is similar to the transfer coefficient, but since M is not a maximum IR portfolio it does not determine the IR of portfolio P.

$$\mathbf{h} = \sum_j \mathbf{q}_j \cdot \omega_{H,j} + \mathbf{r}_H, \quad \mathbf{r}_H' \cdot \mathbf{V} \cdot \mathbf{q}_j = 0 \text{ for all } j. \tag{B25}$$

For our structure this means:

$$v_{i,H} = \mathbf{q}_i' \cdot \mathbf{V} \cdot \mathbf{h} = \sum_{j=1:J} R_{i,j} \cdot \omega_{H,j} \,. \tag{B26}$$

The Optimal Trading Rate

In Appendix A of this chapter, we used dynamic programming to show that a linear trading rule is the optimal policy, and demonstrated how to select the optimal trade rate d. In this subsection, we will take a direct approach and confirm the hard-won results of Appendix A. This is an extension of the work done in the appendix of Chapter 8, "Dynamic Portfolio Analysis," where we considered the case of $J = 1$ signal. Since this subsection is a bit more technical, we will shift to matrix notation.

$$\begin{array}{lll} \boldsymbol{\upsilon}_P = \left\{ v_{j,P} \right\}_{j=1,J} & \text{covariance of sources and } P & \\ \mathbf{R} = \left\{ R_{i,j} \right\}_{j=1:J,i=1:J} & \text{correlation of the source portfolios} & \text{(B27)} \\ \boldsymbol{\Psi}(d) \;\; J \text{ by } J & \text{diagonal matrix } \psi_j(d) = \dfrac{d}{d+g_j} & \end{array}$$

We need alphas for the signal portfolios. Following the lead of Appendix A, Equation (A3), the alphas of the source portfolios are equal to their information ratios (recall they are scaled to have risk = 1, aka 100%).

$$\begin{array}{ll} IR = \lambda \cdot \mathbf{R} \cdot \boldsymbol{\omega}_Q & \text{source portfolio alphas} \\ \boldsymbol{\omega}_M(d) \equiv \boldsymbol{\Psi}(d) \cdot \boldsymbol{\omega}_Q & \text{target risk weights} \\ \alpha_Q = \lambda \cdot \boldsymbol{\omega}_Q' \cdot \mathbf{R} \cdot \boldsymbol{\omega}_Q & \text{alpha of portfolio } Q \\ \alpha_M(d) = \lambda \cdot \boldsymbol{\omega}_Q' \cdot \mathbf{R} \cdot \boldsymbol{\omega}_M(d) & \text{alpha of portfolio } M \end{array} \tag{B28}$$

Equation (B29) restates some of the results of (B24) using this more compact notation. There is emphasis on the underlying dependence on the trade rate d.

$$\begin{aligned} \boldsymbol{\upsilon}_M(d) &= \mathbf{R} \cdot \boldsymbol{\omega}_M(d) = \mathbf{R} \cdot \boldsymbol{\Psi}(d) \cdot \boldsymbol{\omega}_Q \\ \boldsymbol{\upsilon}_P(d) &= \boldsymbol{\Psi}(d) \cdot \mathbf{R} \cdot \boldsymbol{\omega}_M(d) = \boldsymbol{\Psi}(d) \cdot \mathbf{R} \cdot \boldsymbol{\Psi}(d) \cdot \boldsymbol{\omega}_Q \\ v_M^2(d) &= \boldsymbol{\omega}_M'(d) \cdot \mathbf{R} \cdot \boldsymbol{\omega}_M(d) = \boldsymbol{\omega}_Q' \cdot \left\{ \boldsymbol{\Psi}(d) \cdot \mathbf{R} \cdot \boldsymbol{\Psi}(d) \right\} \cdot \boldsymbol{\omega}_Q \\ v_P^2(d) &= v_{PM}(d) = \boldsymbol{\omega}_M'(d) \cdot \boldsymbol{\Psi}(d) \cdot \mathbf{R} \cdot \boldsymbol{\omega}_M(d) \\ v_B^2(d) &= v_M^2(d) - v_P^2(d) \\ v_{\dot{P}}^2(d) &= d^2 \cdot v_B^2(d) \end{aligned} \tag{B29}$$

Consider Equations (B25) and (B26) for the case where the portfolio in question is portfolio P that results from the linear trading scheme. In that particular case we have:

$$\begin{aligned}
\boldsymbol{\upsilon}_P(d) &= \mathbf{R}\cdot\boldsymbol{\omega}_P(d) = \boldsymbol{\Psi}(d)\cdot\mathbf{R}\cdot\boldsymbol{\omega}_M(d) \\
\boldsymbol{\upsilon}_P(d) &= \boldsymbol{\Psi}(d)\cdot\mathbf{R}\cdot\boldsymbol{\Psi}(d)\cdot\boldsymbol{\omega}_Q \\
\mathbf{R}\cdot\boldsymbol{\omega}_P(d) &= \boldsymbol{\Psi}(d)\cdot\mathbf{R}\cdot\boldsymbol{\omega}_M(d)
\end{aligned} \tag{B30}$$

The third line in Equation (B30) will prove very useful. Its first use is to help us compute the alpha of portfolio P.

$$\begin{aligned}
&\alpha_P(d) = \lambda\cdot\boldsymbol{\omega}'_Q\cdot\mathbf{R}\cdot\boldsymbol{\omega}_P(d) = \lambda\cdot\boldsymbol{\omega}'_Q\cdot\boldsymbol{\Psi}(d)\cdot\mathbf{R}\cdot\boldsymbol{\omega}_M(d) \\
&\boldsymbol{\omega}'_M(d) = \boldsymbol{\omega}'_Q\cdot\boldsymbol{\Psi}(d) \text{ so} \\
&\alpha_P(d) = \lambda\cdot\boldsymbol{\omega}'_M(d)\cdot\mathbf{R}\cdot\boldsymbol{\omega}_M(d) = \lambda\cdot v_M^2(d) \\
&\text{and} \quad v_{QP}(d) = v_M^2(d)
\end{aligned} \tag{B31}$$

Define $c_P(d)$ as our measure of annual transactions cost when we use trade rate d. We have:

$$\begin{aligned}
c_P(d) &= \frac{\chi}{2}\cdot \upsilon_P^2(d) = \frac{\chi}{2}\cdot d^2\cdot \upsilon_B^2(d) \\
c_P(d) &= \frac{\chi}{2}\cdot d^2\cdot\{\upsilon_M^2(d) - \upsilon_P^2(d)\}
\end{aligned} \tag{B32}$$

The objective to be maximized, $V(d)$, is the annual alpha, less the annual transactions cost, less a penalty for risk:

$$\begin{aligned}
U(d) &\equiv \alpha_P(d) - c_P(d) - \frac{\lambda}{2}\cdot \upsilon_P^2(d) \\
\alpha_P(d) &= \lambda\cdot \upsilon_M^2(d) \\
c_P(d) &= \frac{\chi\cdot d^2\cdot\{\upsilon_M^2(d) - \upsilon_P^2(d)\}}{2} \\
U(d) &= \frac{\lambda\cdot \upsilon_M^2(d)}{2} + \frac{\{\lambda - \chi\cdot d^2\}}{2}\cdot\{\upsilon_M^2(d) - \upsilon_P^2(d)\}
\end{aligned} \tag{B33}$$

The last line comes from splitting the alpha term and regrouping. The form suggests the trading rate $\hat{d} = \sqrt{\lambda/\chi}$ so $\lambda - \chi\cdot\hat{d}^2 = 0$. In that case the last line of Equation (B33) becomes:

$$U(\hat{d}) = \frac{\lambda}{2}\cdot \upsilon_M^2(\hat{d}). \tag{B34}$$

From Equation (B34), we know that $U(\hat{d})$ is a lower bound on the optimal value. It turns out we can't do better. To see this, we will show that the partial derivative of V with respect to d is zero when $d = \hat{d}$.[14] That partial derivative is:

14. This is necessary for optimality. It would be sufficient if we also showed that $U(d)$ was quasi-concave. We leave that task to the very ambitious reader. Otherwise Exhibit B1 provides some comfort.

$$\frac{\partial U(d)}{\partial d} = \frac{\lambda}{2} \cdot \frac{\partial v_M^2(d)}{\partial d} - \{\chi \cdot d\} \cdot v_B^2(d) + \frac{\{\lambda - \chi \cdot d^2\}}{2} \cdot \frac{\partial v_B^2(d)}{\partial d} \tag{B35}$$

$$\text{where } v_B^2(d) = v_M^2(d) - v_P^2(d)$$

At $d = \hat{d}$, the term in the second line is zero, so we have:

$$\frac{\partial U(\hat{d})}{\partial d} = \frac{\lambda}{2} \cdot \frac{\partial v_M^2(\hat{d})}{\partial d} - \{\chi \cdot \hat{d}\} \cdot v_B^2(\hat{d}) \cdot \tag{B36}$$

Now comes the heavy lifting to evaluate the two terms in Equation (B36). We start with the matrix derivative of $\mathbf{\Psi}(d)$:

$$\frac{\partial \mathbf{\Psi}(d)}{\partial d} = \frac{\mathbf{\Psi}(d) \cdot (\mathbf{I} - \mathbf{\Psi}(d))}{d} = \frac{(\mathbf{I} - \mathbf{\Psi}(d)) \cdot \mathbf{\Psi}(d)}{d}. \tag{B37}$$

The derivative of the target variance is:

$$\begin{aligned} \frac{\partial v_M^2(d)}{\partial d} &= \frac{\partial \left[\boldsymbol{\omega}_Q' \cdot \{\mathbf{\Psi}(d) \cdot \mathbf{R} \cdot \mathbf{\Psi}(d)\} \cdot \boldsymbol{\omega}_Q\right]}{\partial d} \\ &= \frac{1}{d} \cdot \boldsymbol{\omega}_Q' \cdot \{\mathbf{\Psi} \cdot (\mathbf{I} - \mathbf{\Psi}) \cdot \mathbf{R} \cdot \mathbf{\Psi} + \mathbf{\Psi} \cdot \mathbf{R} \cdot (\mathbf{I} - \mathbf{\Psi}) \cdot \mathbf{\Psi}\} \cdot \boldsymbol{\omega}_Q \\ &= \frac{\boldsymbol{\omega}_M' \cdot \{(\mathbf{I} - \mathbf{\Psi}) \cdot \mathbf{R} + \mathbf{R} \cdot (\mathbf{I} - \mathbf{\Psi})\} \cdot \boldsymbol{\omega}_M}{d} \end{aligned} \tag{B38}$$

In the last line we use $\boldsymbol{\omega}_M = \mathbf{\Psi} \cdot \boldsymbol{\omega}_Q$.

The next effort involves shuffling the backlog variance into a suitable form:

$$\begin{aligned} v_B^2(d) &= v_M^2(d) - v_P^2(d) \\ &= \boldsymbol{\omega}_M' \cdot \mathbf{R} \cdot \boldsymbol{\omega}_M - \boldsymbol{\omega}_M' \cdot \mathbf{R} \cdot \boldsymbol{\omega}_P \\ &= \frac{\{\boldsymbol{\omega}_M' \cdot \mathbf{R} \cdot \boldsymbol{\omega}_M - \boldsymbol{\omega}_M' \cdot \mathbf{R} \cdot \boldsymbol{\omega}_P\}}{2} \\ &\quad + \frac{\{\boldsymbol{\omega}_M' \cdot \mathbf{R} \cdot \boldsymbol{\omega}_M - \boldsymbol{\omega}_P' \cdot \mathbf{R} \cdot \boldsymbol{\omega}_M\}}{2} \\ &\text{recall } \mathbf{R} \cdot \boldsymbol{\omega}_P = \mathbf{\Psi} \cdot \mathbf{R} \cdot \boldsymbol{\omega}_M \text{ so } \boldsymbol{\omega}_P' \cdot \mathbf{R} = \boldsymbol{\omega}_M' \cdot \mathbf{R} \cdot \mathbf{\Psi} \\ v_B^2(d) &= \frac{\{\boldsymbol{\omega}_M' \cdot \mathbf{R} \cdot \boldsymbol{\omega}_M - \boldsymbol{\omega}_M' \cdot \mathbf{\Psi} \cdot \mathbf{R} \cdot \boldsymbol{\omega}_M\}}{2} \\ &\quad + \frac{\{\boldsymbol{\omega}_M' \cdot \mathbf{R} \cdot \boldsymbol{\omega}_M - \boldsymbol{\omega}_M' \cdot \mathbf{R} \cdot \mathbf{\Psi} \cdot \boldsymbol{\omega}_M\}}{2} \\ v_B^2(d) &= \frac{\boldsymbol{\omega}_M' \cdot \{(\mathbf{I} - \mathbf{\Psi}) \cdot \mathbf{R} + \mathbf{R} \cdot (\mathbf{I} - \mathbf{\Psi})\} \cdot \boldsymbol{\omega}_M}{2} \end{aligned} \tag{B39}$$

From Equations (B38) and (B39) we conclude that:

$$\frac{\partial v_M^2(d)}{\partial d} = \frac{2}{d} \cdot v_B^2(d). \tag{B40}$$

If we substitute Equation (B40) into the first-order condition, Equation (B36), we find:

$$\begin{aligned} \frac{\partial U(\hat{d})}{\partial d} &= \frac{\lambda}{2} \cdot \frac{2}{\hat{d}} \cdot v_B^2(\hat{d}) - \{\chi \cdot \hat{d}\} \cdot v_B^2(\hat{d}) \\ \frac{\partial U(\hat{d})}{\partial d} &= \frac{(\lambda - \chi \cdot \hat{d}^2)}{\hat{d}} \cdot v_B^2(\hat{d}) = 0 \end{aligned} \tag{B41}$$

This result is borne out in Exhibit B1 with some ocular calculus.

EXHIBIT B1 Objective Value Sensitivity

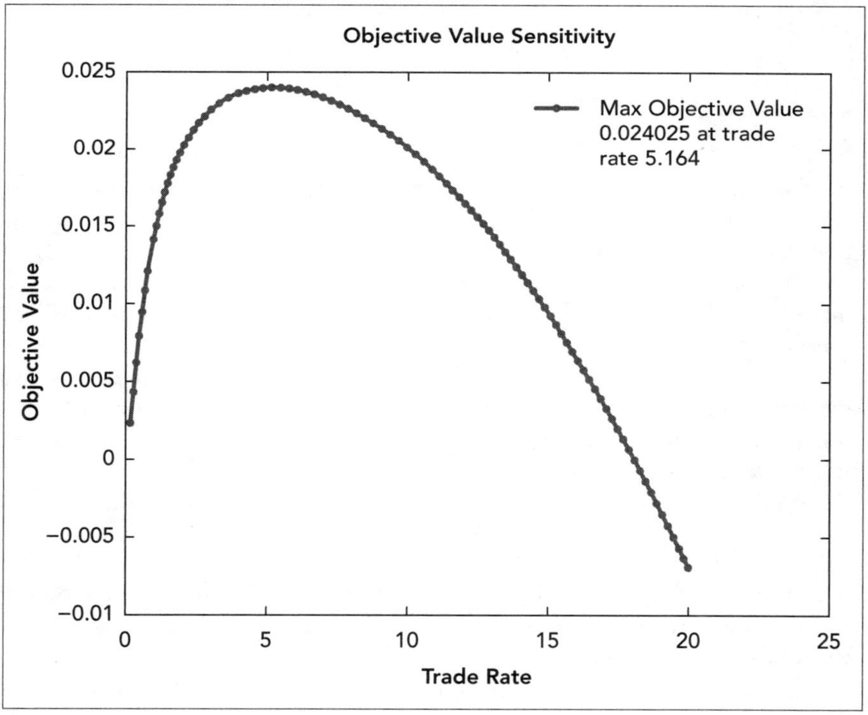

The graph of $U(d)$ is for a case with $\lambda = 20$ and $\chi = 0.75$ with a resulting $\hat{d} = 5.164$.

10

Linear Trading Rules for Portfolio Management[1]

Active portfolio management balances expected returns, the risk of positions, the costs of trading, restrictions on position and trades, and the uncertain way these aspects of the task shift over time. It is a complex problem, so any portfolio management system is at best a compromise. It will make an approximation here, ignore a facet there, concentrate on this, and hope for the best with that—as much art as science.

If we tried to describe the portfolio management challenge with a mathematical model, we would end up with a large constrained dynamic unsolvable stochastic optimization problem. There is, however, a special case where large dynamic stochastic optimization problems are easy to solve. If the objective is quadratic, the process is unconstrained, and the expected returns predictions and portfolio positions change in a linear manner it is called a linear-quadratic dynamic program, LQDP. In a LQDP the optimal policy is summarized by a linear trading rule that tells us our revised positions should be a linear function of our current positions and of other variables that are predictors of returns.

If a linear trading rule is optimal in a special case, then it should be good in a more general case. Our plan is to take that notion and see where it leads. We will start with a linear trading rule and ask what it tells us about the evolution of our portfolio, how the linear trading rule can be improved, and how the linear trading rule can be employed in the context of a more traditional structured portfolio management process.

1. This chapter originally appeared as "Linear Trading Rules for Portfolio Management" by Richard Grinold in 2018 in the special issue of the *Journal of Portfolio Management* dedicated to Stephen A. Ross.

We take the perspective of a portfolio engineer. We have design criteria, say a level of risk and a level of turnover, and subject to those criteria we use linear trading rules to obtain the best possible exposures to the sources of excess return (aka alpha).

Our examination of linear trading rules is based on a dynamic view of portfolio management. We put dynamics at the center of our analysis and hope that the reader will adopt that perspective even if the specific results are ignored.

We start with a description of linear trading rules and stress the crucial role of the trading rate. Then we examine the assumed flow of information about future returns, the rate it arrives, and the rate its forecasting power declines. With a known framework of information flow and a linear trading rule we are able to describe the expected evolution of the portfolio. Simulation results confirm that those predictions are accurate. A sensitivity analysis shows how important predictions change as we vary the trading rate. That sensitivity analysis invites us to tune the linear trading rule to fit our design criteria. One would like to say the linear trading rule is being optimized, but that is too ambitious. In our role as portfolio engineers we should recall that the best rough guide is still a rough guide. In the rough-guiding spirit, we show how the insights we have gained from the study of linear trading rules can be folded into a traditional single or multistage portfolio optimization to give it a dynamic flavor.

The key takeaways are the importance of a dynamic perspective, the crucial role of the trade rate, a systematic procedure for transactions cost-sensitive signal weighting at the asset level, and transformation of a single or multistage optimization into a dynamic (i.e., extremely long horizon) optimization.

There are two technical appendices. Appendix A establishes the link between the linear trading rule and important metrics such as exposure to sources of alpha, risk, turnover, transactions cost, and the efficiency of our risk allocation. Appendix B describes the optimality of linear trading rules in a related dynamic programming problem. This analysis is the motivation for the linear trading rule and the adjusted signal weights used to calculate the model/target position. Appendices A and B are similar to Appendices B and A (respectively) of the signal weighting paper (Chapter 9 in this book), although appendices to this chapter use a single asset bottom-up approach rather than a top-down portfolio approach.

A multistage optimization possesses many of the same features as a dynamic program. See Boyd et al. (2017) for a tour de force. Our suggestion for augmenting a single stage optimization holds for multistage as well. Linear-quadratic dynamic programming (LQDP) was developed in the late 1950s and early 1960s. There is no shortage of literature on LQDP; an Internet search yields about 360,000 hits. For application to portfolio management from an academic perspective see the work of Garleanu and Pederson (2013) and other papers cited there. The approach we have taken is similar to the simulation/optimization algorithm described in Powell's excellent book (2011). This paper is in a similar spirit as some of the author's earlier work. The first, Grinold (2005) (Chapter 7, "Implementation Efficiency," in this book), was an effort to get at the factors that determine a portfolio's transfer coefficient (see Clarke et al. 2002). In Grinold (2007) (Chapter 8, "Dynamic Portfolio Analysis" in this book), we used LQDP to examine the loss in return, from both direct costs and opportunity costs. The effort in Grinold (2010) (Chapter 9, "Signal Weighting," in this book) considered multiple sources of alpha and used LQDP to address the question of signal weighting. This paper takes those ideas from the theoretical/strategic level to the practical/operational level, by asking how linear trading rules can help us manage portfolios.

This chapter follows a different route from the published article. We use a bottom-up approach to signal weighting. For each asset we start with standardized signals, map these into alphas, then to a model position.

As always, the results could be made more complicated. But if we recall that it is better to learn to walk before we try to run, then it is best to start with a case that is both accessible and useful. Once we have mastered the basic idea we can elaborate. In particular, for simplicity we focus on predictions of specific return where information about company A does not tell us anything about company B. This means that the expected covariance between the A and B positions will be zero even if the returns on assets A are B are correlated.

This study, like any other, is based on assumptions that are at best an approximation of reality. We do not know each asset's specific risk, and that elusive specific risk changes over time. Information does not arrive regularly or smoothly. Information that is asset specific is also an ideal. In a zero-sum situation, good news about A is bad news for B. In a win-win framework, A's success is a portend of B's flourishing. The reader can doubtless come up with additional caveats. It can't be perfect.

Linear Trading Rules

Given a starting position and a desired target, we move part of the way toward the target because trading is expensive and it is a moving target.

The linear trading rule is:

$$\begin{Bmatrix} \text{position} \\ \text{of asset } n \\ \text{at time } t \end{Bmatrix} = \delta_n \cdot \begin{Bmatrix} \text{position} \\ \text{of asset } n \\ \text{at time } t-\Delta t \end{Bmatrix} + \left(1-\delta_n\right) \cdot \begin{Bmatrix} \text{target position} \\ \text{of asset } n \\ \text{at time } t \end{Bmatrix}$$

$$p_n(t) = \delta_n \cdot p_n(t-\Delta t) + \left(1-\delta_n\right) \cdot m_n(t), \tag{1}$$

$$\delta_n \equiv e^{-d_n \cdot \Delta t} \leq 1$$

$$d_n \approx {}^{1-\delta_n}\!/_{\Delta t}.$$

where d_n is the trade rate for asset n.

We can also view the linear trading rule in integral and differential form:

Differential Form

$$\dot{p}_n(t) \equiv \frac{\Delta p_n(t)}{\Delta t} \approx d_n \cdot \{m_n(t) - p_n(t)\}$$

Integral Form

$$p_n(t) = (1 - \delta_n) \cdot \sum_{\tau=0:\infty} \delta_n^{\tau} \cdot m_n(t - \tau \cdot \Delta t)$$

The continuous time version of the model generally yields results that are simpler and more revealing. For example, the differential form of the linear trading rule says that we trade to close the *backlog*, $m_n(t) - p_n(t)$, with the trade rate, d_n, indicating how hard we push to close the gap. From the integral form we see that the current position is a weighted average of past target positions. If we calculate the average age in this weighted sum, we find it approximately equal to $1/d_n$ years; thus if $d_n = 3$ we are on average four months behind the model/target.

Information Flow

Information comes from J sources. It is expressed as signals that have, in the long run, mean zero and standard deviation one. The signals have two properties of note: their strength (ability of forecast) as measured by an information ratio, i_j,[2] and their persistence as measured by a half-life, HL_j. The half-life tells the number of trading days it would take for the current signal to lose one-half of its forecasting power. We capture the half-life in three ways, as explained below.

252 trading days/year, 21 per month, 63 per quarter

$\Delta t = 1/252$ years

HL_j number of days until the signal losses 1/2 its strength

$g_j \equiv \dfrac{252 \cdot \ln(2)}{HL_j}$ the rate of loss

$\gamma_j \equiv e^{-g_j \cdot \Delta t}$ the fraction of information retained in one period

$g_j \approx {}^{1-\gamma_j}\!/_{\Delta t}$

2. Note that this symbol i for the information ratio is different from the symbol ι for the information coefficient that appears later in the chapter.

The law of motion for the signals is:

$$\begin{array}{llll} \text{New Signal} = & \text{Retained Old Signal} & + \text{ New Informatio} & \\ s_{n,j}(t) = & \gamma_j \cdot s_{n,j}(t-\Delta t) & + \sqrt{1-\gamma_j^2} \cdot \tilde{y}_{n,j}(t) & (2) \end{array}$$

$$\text{where} \quad E\left\langle \tilde{y}_{n,j}(t) \middle| s_{n,j}(t-\Delta t) \right\rangle = 0 \text{ and } E\left\langle \tilde{y}_{n,j}^2(t) \right\rangle = 1$$

We use this form to bring out the special properties of the information arrival and decay process. The random part of the new signal, the $\tilde{y}_{n,j}(t)$, is for asset n, signal j at time t. The random part has mean zero, standard deviation of one. It is new information and therefore uncorrelated with last period's signal, $s_{n,j}(t-\Delta t)$. Under Equation (2), the long run mean and standard deviation of signals will be, respectively, zero and one.

Our effort is concentrated on predictions of each asset's specific return. We assume that the information we have on one asset does not predict the future return on other assets. However, we will allow for correlation among the signals for any individual asset. The signals inherit this correlation from the correlation of the new information.[3]

$$\phi_{i,j} \equiv Corr\left\langle \tilde{y}_{n,i}, \tilde{y}_{n,j} \right\rangle \text{ then}$$

$$R_{i,j} \equiv Corr\left\langle \tilde{s}_{n,i}, \tilde{s}_{n,j} \right\rangle \approx \frac{\sqrt{g_i \cdot g_j}}{\dfrac{g_i + g_j}{2}} \cdot \phi_{i,j}$$

A basic idea from Grinold and Kahn (2000) is to transform disparate types of asset characteristics into portfolios subtly called characteristic portfolios. We let the characteristic portfolios interact using the rules of variance and covariance. It is an apples-to-apples approach.

In our case we want to transform the signals into positions. There are N assets and we use σ_n to denote the specific risk of asset n. The resulting positions are $b_{n,j}(t)$ and they link with the signals according to the following rule:

$$b_{n,j}(t) = \frac{s_{n,j}(t)}{\sigma_n \cdot \sqrt{N}} \Rightarrow E\left\langle \sigma_n^2 \cdot b_{n,j}^2(t) \right\rangle = 1 \qquad (3)$$

Division by the specific risk is justified since, (*i.*) to go from signal to alpha you multiply by the volatility and (*ii.*) to go from alpha to position you divide by variance. The use of the number of assets to scale the risk is a placeholder, since the weight will be assigned later depending on the trade rate.

Prediction and Simulation

The trade rate, d_n, and the linear trading rule yield predictions of important portfolio outcomes. The predictions are governed by three schemes for

3. The ratio of signal correlation to the correlation of the innovations is the ratio of a geometric mean to an arithmetic mean. It is generally less than one and equal to one only when the decay rates are equal.

weighting the J signals. Each of the three weighting schemes is a J element vector. They are:

- the zero-cost weights $q_n(t)$, $\mathbf{w}_{Q(n)}$,
- the weights for the model (target) position, $m_n(t)$, $\mathbf{w}_{M(n)}$, and
- the resulting weights for the position, $p_n(t)$, $\mathbf{w}_{P(n)}$.

We find the zero-cost weights from first principles as in Grinold and Kahn (2000). See Appendix A of this chapter for details. The zero-cost weights depend on the assumed information coefficients of the sources, $\boldsymbol{\iota}_n = \{\iota_{n,j}\}_{j=1:J}$, for asset n, the variance penalty parameter, λ, and the correlation of the signals, $\mathbf{R}_n$, through the equation:

$$\boldsymbol{\iota}_n = \sigma_n \cdot \lambda \cdot \mathbf{R}_n \cdot \mathbf{w}_{Q(n)} \tag{4}$$

The risk penalty, λ, adjusts the scale. As the subscript n implies all of these quantities can be asset specific.

The zero-cost risk allocation and the positions, $b_{n,j}(t)$, determine the zero-cost positions, $q_n(t)$, and the asset alphas, $\alpha_n(t)$:

$$\begin{aligned} &(i.) \quad q_n(t) \equiv \sum_{j=1:j} b_{n,j}(t) \cdot w_{Q(n),j} \\ &(ii.) \quad \alpha_n(t) \equiv \lambda \cdot \sigma_n^2 \cdot q_n(t) \end{aligned} \tag{5}$$

To get the model/target weights for asset n, $\mathbf{w}_{M(n)}$, we use the trade rate, d_n, and the decay rates of the signals:

$$\psi_{n,j} \equiv \frac{1-\delta_n}{1-\delta_n \cdot \gamma_j} \approx \frac{d_n}{d_n + g_j} \tag{6}$$

$$\boldsymbol{\Psi}_n \text{ a } J \text{ by } J \text{ matrix with } \psi_{n,j} \text{ on the diagonal}$$

According to the logic of Appendix B that describes the dynamic program for one asset and J signals, we obtain the following weights for the target:

$$w_{M(n),j} = \psi_{n,j} \cdot w_{Q(n),j}, \quad \text{or } \mathbf{w}_{M(n)} = \boldsymbol{\Psi}_n \cdot \mathbf{w}_{Q(n)} \tag{7}$$

In Appendix A, we establish the link between the model/target weights, $\mathbf{w}_{M(n)}$, and the resulting effective position weights for the asset, $\mathbf{w}_{P(n)}$. The resulting weights are a direct consequence of the linear trading rule, Equation (1), and the law of motion of the signals, Equation (2). The relationship is:

$$\mathbf{R}_n \cdot \mathbf{w}_{P(n)} = \boldsymbol{\Psi}_n \cdot \mathbf{R}_n \cdot \mathbf{w}_{M(n)} = \boldsymbol{\Psi}_n \cdot \mathbf{R}_n \cdot \boldsymbol{\Psi}_n \cdot \mathbf{w}_{Q(n)} \tag{8}$$

A handy way to think about this is when the signals are uncorrelated. Then we have $w_{P(n),j} = \psi_{n,j} \cdot w_{M(n),j} = \psi_{n,j}^2 \cdot w_{Q(n),j}$. There is a twofold contraction of the risk allocation. For very fast signals this can be dramatic.

An Example

The signals with names, half-lives and information coefficients are detailed in Exhibit 1. In this example, and in all of our calculations, we have assumed, for convenience only, that the information coefficients, $\boldsymbol{\iota}_n$, and correlations,

$\mathbf{R}_n$, are the same for all assets, thus the zero-cost weights, $\mathbf{w}_{Q(n)}$, are the same for all assets.[4]

EXHIBIT 1 Assumed Signal Properties

NAME	HL (DAYS)	INF. COEFF.
FAST	2	0.1785
INT	63	0.0313
SLOW	189	0.0223

In the example, the variance penalty is $\lambda = 25$, and there is some slight correlation, $\mathbf{R}_n$, between the signals, enough to prove the concept but not enough to dominate the results. The asset's specific volatility is 15%.

To illustrate the three weighting schemes, we've included an example using the data in Exhibit 1, Equations (6) through (8), and a trade rate $d = 3$. The time interval is one trading day, $\Delta t = 1/252$.

EXHIBIT 2 Risk Allocations When the Trade Rate Equals 3

d_n=3	$w_Q(n)$	$w_M(n)$	$w_P(n)$	$\psi_{n,j}$
FAST	0.1070	0.00421	0.000282	0.0393
INT.	0.0313	0.01110	0.005860	0.5226
SLOW	0.0223	0.00926	0.007200	0.7659

The FAST signal is too fast for this trade rate. The signal weight drops by more than two orders of magnitude from the zero-cost to the portfolio level.

The Expectations

With risk allocations $\mathbf{w}_{Q(n)}$, $\mathbf{w}_{M(n)}$, $\mathbf{w}_{P(n)}$, we can calculate the following expectations:

- the alpha:
$$\alpha_{P(n)} \equiv E\langle \alpha_n(t) \cdot p_n(t) \rangle = \lambda \cdot \sigma_n^2 \cdot \mathbf{w}'_{Q(n)} \cdot \mathbf{R}_n \cdot \mathbf{w}_{P(n)}$$
- the target variance:
$$\sigma_{M(n)}^2 \equiv E\left\langle \{\sigma_n \cdot m_n(t)\}^2 \right\rangle = \sigma_n^2 \cdot \mathbf{w}'_{M(n)} \cdot \mathbf{R}_n \cdot \mathbf{w}_{M(n)}$$
- the covariance:
$$\sigma_{M(n),P(n)} \equiv E\langle \sigma_n \cdot m_n(t) \cdot \sigma_n \cdot p_n(t) \rangle = \sigma_n^2 \cdot \mathbf{w}'_{M(n)} \cdot \mathbf{R}_n \cdot \mathbf{w}_{P(n)}$$
- the variance:
$$\sigma_{P(n)}^2 \equiv E\left\langle \{\sigma_n \cdot p_n(t)\}^2 \right\rangle \approx \sigma_n^2 \cdot \mathbf{w}'_{M(n)} \cdot \mathbf{R}_n \cdot \mathbf{w}_{P(n)}$$

---

4. In general, the signals will vary in nature and strength in sectors and/or industries, for very large stocks and very small stocks, for highly liquid stocks and stocks that are hard to trade. etc. The bottom-up asset by asset approach we are using is an ideal way to exploit this information. However, this elaboration is a distraction from our stated goal so we will not use it in our examples.

- the backlog variance:

$$\sigma^2_{M(n)-P(n)} \equiv E\left\langle \left\{ \sigma_n \cdot \left[m_n(t) - p_n(t) \right] \right\}^2 \right\rangle \approx \sigma^2_{M(n)} - \sigma^2_{P(n)}$$

- the variance of $\dot{P}(n)$:

$$\sigma^2_{\dot{P}(n)} \equiv E\left\langle \left\{ \sigma_n \cdot \frac{\Delta p_n}{\Delta t} \right\}^2 \right\rangle = d_n^2 \cdot \sigma^2_{M(n)-P(n)}$$

The approximations, ≈, are for the case where Δt is small, that is, where $g_j \approx (1-\gamma_j)/\Delta t$ for all j.

The volatility of the position derivative, $\sigma_{\dot{P}(n)}$, with the nearly imperceptible dot over the P, is key to calculating the expected turnover and transactions cost per year. With an assumption that the trades are normally distributed[5] we can calculate the expected annual turnover (purchases plus sales divided by two) for asset n is:

$$\tau_{P(n)} \equiv \frac{1}{2} \cdot E\left\langle \left| \frac{\Delta p_n}{\Delta t} \right| \right\rangle = \sqrt{\frac{1}{2 \cdot \pi \cdot \sigma_n^2}} \cdot \sigma_{\dot{P}(n)} \tag{9}$$

More work is required for the transactions cost. We use a transactions cost function of the form:

$$tc\,(\Delta p_n) = c_{1,n} \cdot |\Delta p_n| + c_{2,n} \cdot |\Delta p_n|^{\phi}, \tag{10}$$

where the second term is for market impact. The parameter ϕ typically equals 1.5 or 2.

The expected annual transactions cost is then:

$$c_{P(n)} \equiv E\left\langle \frac{tc\,(\Delta p)}{\Delta t} \right\rangle = k_{1,n} \cdot \sigma_{\dot{P}(n)} + k_{2,n} \cdot \sigma^{\phi}_{\dot{P}(n)}$$
$$\text{where } k_{1,n} = \frac{c_{1,n}}{\sigma_n} \cdot \sqrt{\frac{2}{\pi}}, \quad k_{2,n} = \frac{c_{2,n} \cdot \Delta t^{\phi-1}}{\sigma_n^{\phi}} \cdot E\left\langle |Z|^{\phi} \right\rangle \tag{11}$$

If ϕ=1.5 and the distribution is normal, then $E\left\langle |Z|^{1.5} \right\rangle = 0.86$. If ϕ=2, then $E\left\langle |Z|^{2} \right\rangle = 1.00$.

Sensitivity and Maximization

Given a trading rate, d_n, and a linear trading rule, we can predict, with reasonable accuracy, the evolution of the portfolio at both the asset and aggregate level. Exhibits 3, 4, and 5 show how key investment parameters vary as we change the trading rate. In these sensitivity tests, the zero-cost weight, $\mathbf{w}_{Q(n)}$, remains fixed. However, as we change that trading rate, the target weight, $\mathbf{w}_{M(n)}$, and resulting position weight, $\mathbf{w}_{P(n)}$, will change in the manner of Equations (6) through (8). For the sensitivity analysis, we clustered the assets into five buckets according to market impact and used

5. The normality assumption is the simplest case. All that is really required is that the new information, Equation (2), has mean zero, standard deviation 1, and a symmetric distribution. Then we could follow that through the analysis and easily estimate the expectations of the absolute value to any power.

volatility and transactions cost data that were representative of the assets in each bucket. Typical results are shown in Exhibits 3 and 4.

Exhibit 3 shows how the expected alpha, cost, and risk change for a typical asset as a function the trade rate *d*. Of interest are the two bottom curves. Note that the costs accelerate and swamp alpha when the trade rate hits about 7.

EXHIBIT 3 Alpha, Risk, and T-Cost Contribution

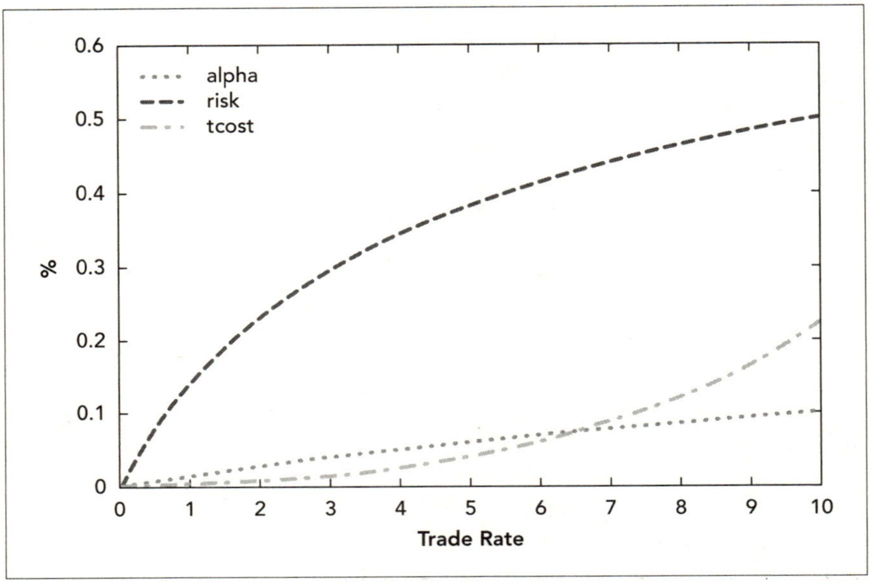

Exhibit 4 illustrates the link between the trade rate *d* and the effective allocation of risk, $\mathbf{w}_{P(n)}$, to the three signals in our example. For the trade rate below 5, the SLOW signal is getting more weight. After that, the intermediate horizon signal INT predominates. The weight assigned to the FAST signal increases at an increasing rate over the interval $0 < d < 10$. This explains the accelerating costs in Exhibit 3.

The objective is annual alpha minus annual cost and minus a penalty for variance:

$$\begin{aligned} O_n &\equiv \left\{\alpha_{P(n)} - c_{P(n)}\right\} - \frac{\lambda}{2} \cdot \sigma_{P(n)}^2 \\ O_P &\equiv \sum_{n=1:N} O_n = \{\alpha_P - c_P\} - \frac{\lambda}{2} \cdot \sigma_P^2 \\ \alpha_P &= \sum_{n=1:N} \alpha_{P(n)}, \quad c_P = \sum_{n=1:N} c_{P(n)}, \quad \sigma_P^2 = \sum_{n=1:N} \sigma_{P(n)}^2 \end{aligned} \tag{12}$$

The individual contributions sum to the aggregate through the assumption of either independent specific returns or uncorrelated signals across assets.

EXHIBIT 4 Expected Position Signal Weights

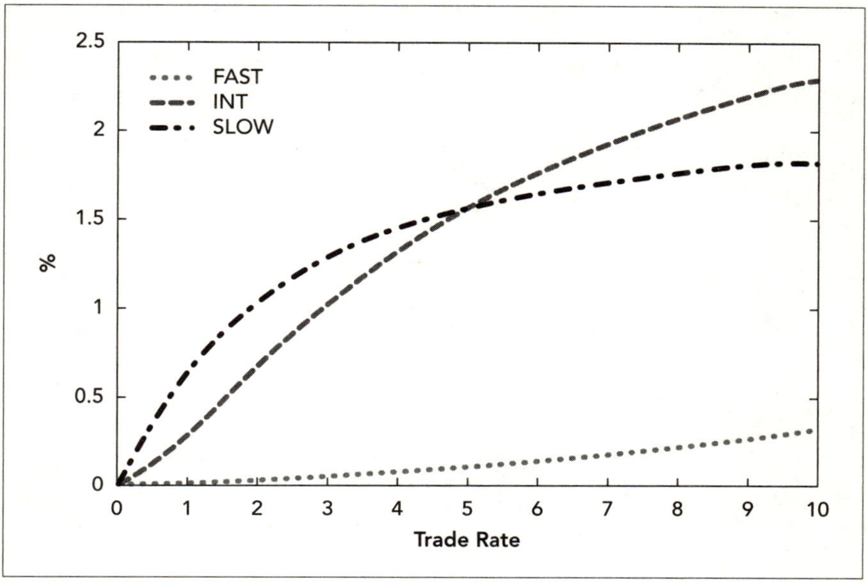

Exhibit 5 looks at the contribution of a representative asset to the objective. In this case it peaks at a trade rate of 2.4. The sensitivity analysis suggests that we use the analytical results to select a trade rate that maximizes expected asset contribution to the overall objective O_P.

Exhibit 6 shows the distribution of the maximizing trade rates for the 200 assets in our sample of Australian data. The average trade rate is 2.68 and they have a standard deviation of 1.25. Only 6 of the 200 assets have a trade rate less than 1, and another 6 have trade rates 5 or more. The resulting trading rates are a major improvement compared to a naive alternative of the same trade rate (2.68) for each asset. The bulk of the improvement comes in savings on transactions cost.

Position Paths

Once we have set the trade rates, we can describe position paths. Starting with an initial position, $p_n(-\Delta t)$, for an asset and the current source positions, $b_{n,j}(0)$, we can use the linear trading rule to plot a series of positions that, in the absence of new information, we should follow in the next few periods.

The equations for the expected position and target in τ periods are:

$$\begin{aligned} \hat{s}_{n,j}(t) &= e^{-g_j \cdot t} \cdot s_{n,j}(0) \\ \hat{m}_n(t) &= \sum_{j=1:J} \hat{s}_{n,j}(t) \cdot w_{M(n),j} \\ \hat{p}_n(t) &= \delta_n \cdot \hat{p}_n(t-\Delta t) + (1-\delta_n) \cdot \hat{m}_n(t) \end{aligned} \tag{13}$$

EXHIBIT 5 Single Asset Objective

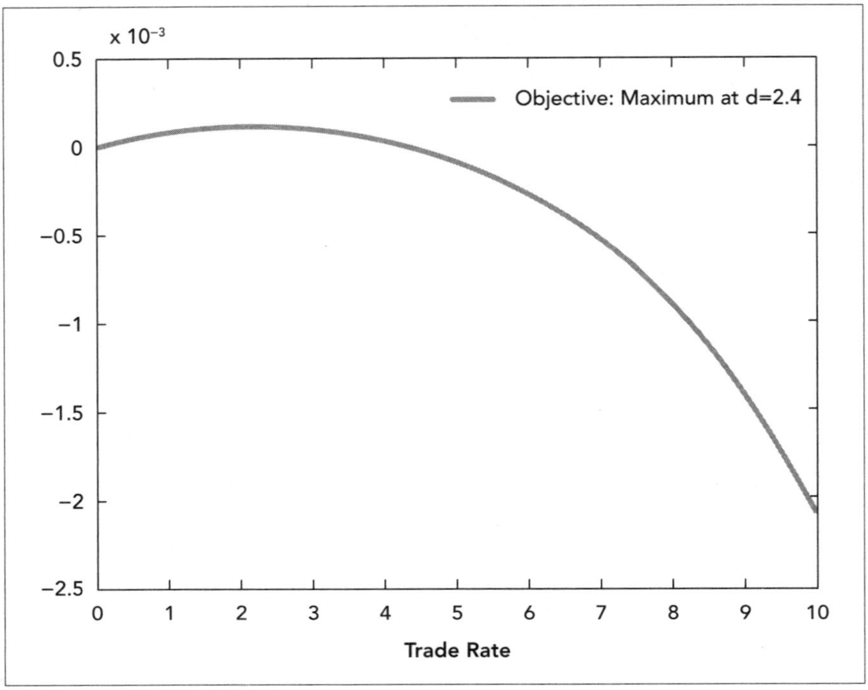

EXHIBIT 6 AUS Objective Maximizing Trade Rates

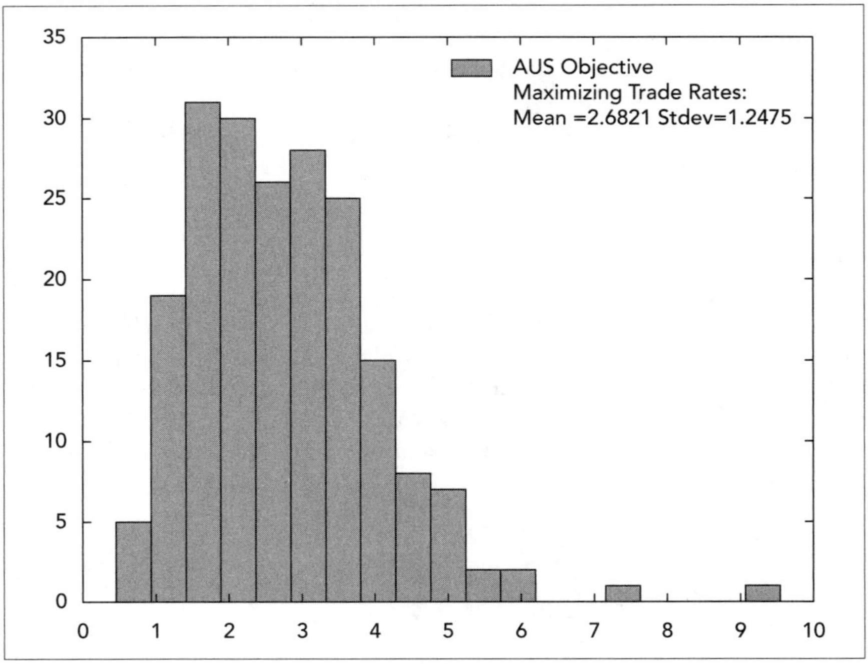

Exhibit 7 shows three position paths depending on different initial conditions. The initial position is zero in all cases. In each of the scenarios the SLOW signal is strong, a two standard deviation event: $s_{n,SLOW}(0) = 2$. The intermediate signal INT is negative, a minus one standard deviation event: $s_{n,INT}(0) = -1$. The scenarios differ in the FAST signal. In the first scenario, it is extremely positive: $s_{n,FAST}(0) = 2$, a two standard deviation event. In the middle scenario, it is zero: $s_{n,FAST}(0) = 0$, there is no short-term information. In the third scenario, the FAST signal is a minus two standard deviation event: $s_{n,FAST}(0) = -2$. When the FAST signal is reinforcing the SLOW signal, we immediately start to build up a position. However, when the FAST signal is strongly negative, we sell for a few periods and then start to build up the position.

EXHIBIT 7 Anticipated Position Paths

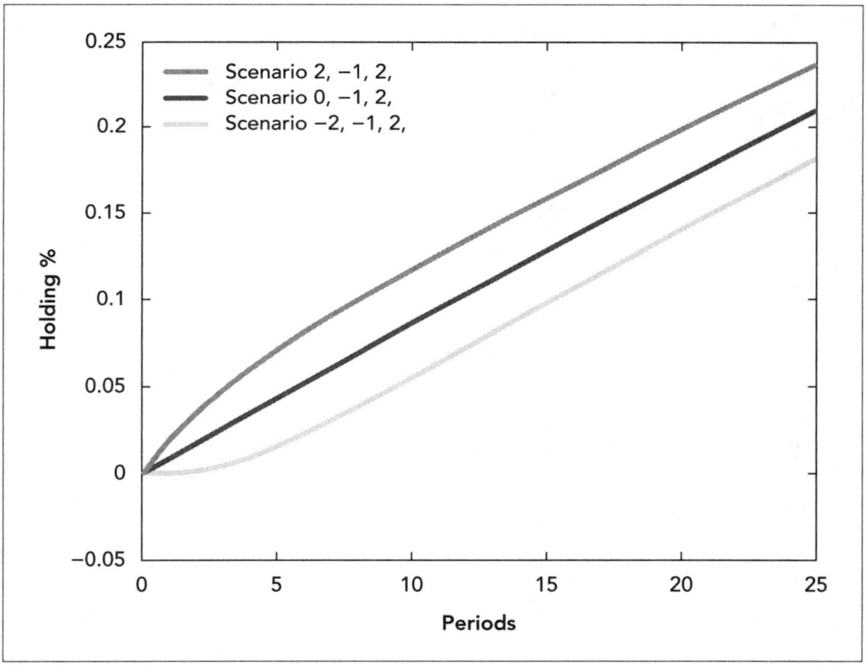

Australian Stock Simulation

The simulation produces signals, sources, positions, alphas, and target positions for 200 stocks and 2,520 dates. We obtained specific volatility and transactions cost data for a sample of Australian stocks. The trading rates differ from asset to asset. They were selected using the maximization process described above. The risk aversion was set at $\lambda = 25$. The time interval was a trading day; 1/252 of a year. The information ratio and half-life data are the same as Exhibit 1.

In our first pass we chose to have a small correlation among the signals for any asset. The correlations are in Exhibit 8.

EXHIBIT 8 Correlation Among the Signals

SIGNAL CORR. R	FAST	INT.	SLOW
FAST	1	−0.0280	0.0043
INT.	−0.0280	1	0.0340
SLOW	0.0043	0.0340	1

This is a lab test. It is not a backtest. No returns are involved. We want to check that predicted levels of turnover, transactions cost, risk, and exposure to sources of alpha agree with the predictions.

In the course of the simulation we gathered data on alpha, risk, cost, and turnover. We also scored the assets on their contribution to the overall objective, Equation (12).

In addition, we calculated the information ratio and the after-cost information ratio, ACIR:

$$IR_P = \frac{\sum_{n=1:N} \alpha_{P(n)}}{\sqrt{\sum_{n=1:N} \sigma^2_{P(n)}}} = \frac{\alpha_P}{\sigma_P}$$
$$ACIR_P \equiv \frac{\sum_{n=1:N} \left\{\alpha_{P(n)} - c_{P(n)}\right\}}{\sqrt{\sum_{n=1:N} \sigma^2_{P(n)}}} = \frac{\alpha_P - c_P}{\sigma_P} \tag{14}$$

Finally, we calculated the correlation with the target:

$$\rho_{P,M} = \frac{\sum_{n=1:N} \sigma_{P(n),M(n)}}{\sqrt{\sum_{n=1:N} \sigma^2_{P(n)}} \cdot \sqrt{\sum_{n=1:N} \sigma^2_{M(n)}}} \approx \frac{\sum_{n=1:N} \sigma^2_{P(n)}}{\sqrt{\sum_{n=1:N} \sigma^2_{P(n)}} \cdot \sqrt{\sum_{n=1:N} \sigma^2_{M(n)}}} = \frac{\sigma_P}{\sigma_M} \tag{15}$$

The approximation above flows from $\sigma_{P(n),M(n)} \approx \sigma^2_{P(n)}$.

Most of the simulation results are sample averages. For example, asset n's contribution to portfolio alpha in the sample is:

$$\frac{1}{T} \cdot \sum_{t=1:T} \alpha_n(t) \cdot p_n(t) \quad \text{the simulation result}$$
$$\alpha_{P(n)} = \lambda \cdot \sigma_n^2 \cdot \mathbf{w}'_{Q(n)} \cdot \mathbf{R}_n \cdot \mathbf{w}_{P(n)} \quad \text{the predicted result} \tag{16}$$

Equation (8) provides a prediction exposure of each asset to each signal. To measure the simulated position risk weights for asset n, we ran a time-series regression:

$$p_n(t) = \hat{a}_{0,n} + \sum_{j=1:J} s_{n,j}(t) \cdot \hat{w}_{n,j} + err_n(t) \tag{17}$$

$\hat{w}_{n,j}$ is the estimated weight of asset n on signal j

The aggregate, portfolio level, results of the simulation presented in Exhibit 9 are excellent:

EXHIBIT 9 Aggregate Properties in a 10-Year Daily Simulation

ITEM	PREDICTION	SIMULATION
Alpha	7.14	6.96
T-Cost/yr.	1.97	1.99
Risk	4.02	3.94
Objective	3.16	3.04
ACIR	1.29	1.26
correlation(*P*,*M*)	0.76	0.75
Target Risk	5.34	5.34

Results at the asset level are, of course, less accurate. We evaluated asset level predictions using:

$$\text{Sim}_n = a_0 + a_1 \cdot \text{Predict}_n + \text{err}_n \quad \text{for } n = 1:N, \tag{18}$$

where Sim_n is the simulated result for asset n and Predict_n is the predicted result for asset n. We want the coefficient a_1 to be close to one and the R^2 to be large.

Exhibit 10 shows the scatter diagram and regression result for transactions cost. Exhibit 11 shows the same scatter diagram and regression result for alpha contribution. The scatter diagram contains the predicted, that is, expected, value on the horizontal axis and the simulated value on the vertical. The transactions cost is the most accurate of the alpha, cost, and risk trio and the alphas are the least accurate. The dashed line is the theoretical ideal with a slope of one and an intercept that adjusts for the simulated average being unequal to the predicted average. The dotted line is the OLS regression line.

EXHIBIT 10 Expected and Realized Annual Transactions Cost

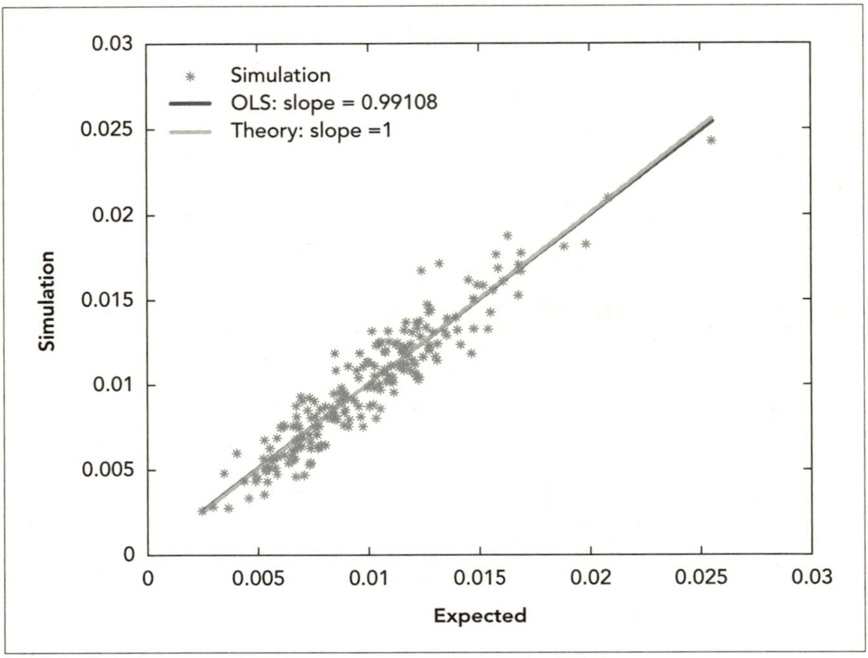

EXHIBIT 11 Expected and Realized Alpha Contribution

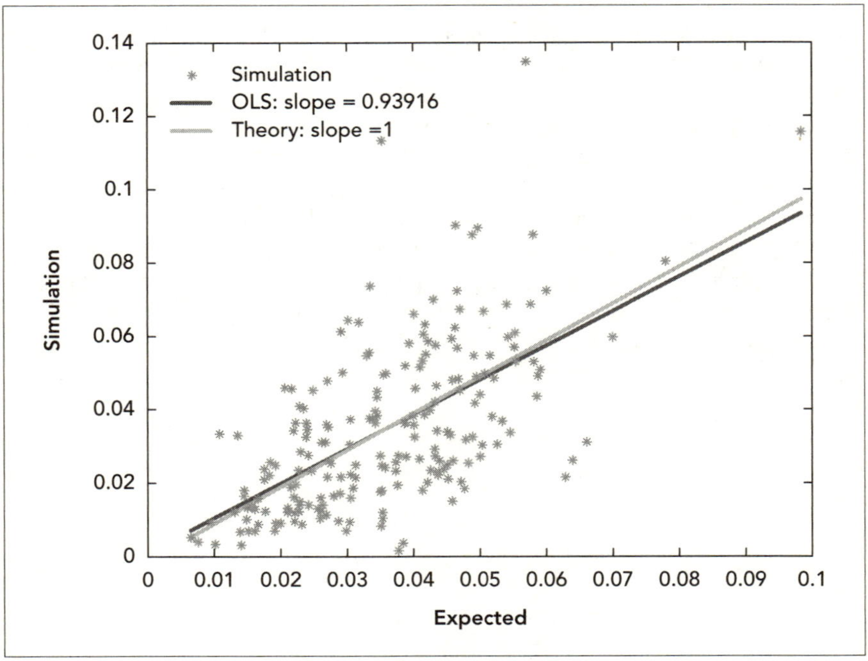

Exhibit 12 shows the results of the regression in Equation (18) for nine important properties of the simulation. At the asset level, the items that involve changes in position (transactions cost, turnover, and $\sigma_{\dot{P}(n)}$) are captured extremely well.

For the other items, two effects make the estimation difficult: the relatively long half-life of some signals allows random departures from the expected to persist for extended periods, and exposure to the FAST signal is small, and tends to get lost in the noise.

EXHIBIT 12 Link Between Expectation and Simulated Averages

VARIABLE	SLOPE	R2
Alpha *P*(*n*)	0.94	0.36
Risk Position *P*(*n*)	1.00	0.60
T-Cost/yr.	0.99	0.89
Risk *P-dot*(*n*)	0.99	0.98
Risk Target *M*(*n*)	0.98	0.69
Cov {*M*(*n*),*P*(*n*)}	0.99	0.55
Omega P(*n*, FAST)	0.86	0.30
Omega P(*n*, INT.)	0.99	0.76
Omega P(*n*, SLOW)	0.95	0.54

We ranked the assets by objective value, O_n, using both the expected values and the outcome of the simulation to construct two Gini curves. Exhibit 13 shows the results.

The value added is not evenly distributed; low t-cost assets have an advantage. On the predicted curve, we have about half of the value added from one-third of the assets. All of the assets are expected to add value. In the Gini curve summarizing the simulation, we find half of the value added with about 22% of the assets, and the last 10% or so of the assets lose value on a cost and risk adjusted basis over the 10 years of the simulation.

Signal Correlation

The results above are for a case with little correlation between the signals. To test whether this was crucial, we did a second simulation where the FAST signal was, by design, uncorrelated with the others and the correlation of the innovations of the INT and SLOW signals was 0.4. This leads to signal correlation of 0.346. Exhibit 14 shows the results.

EXHIBIT 13 AUS: Expected and the Simulated Objective Value

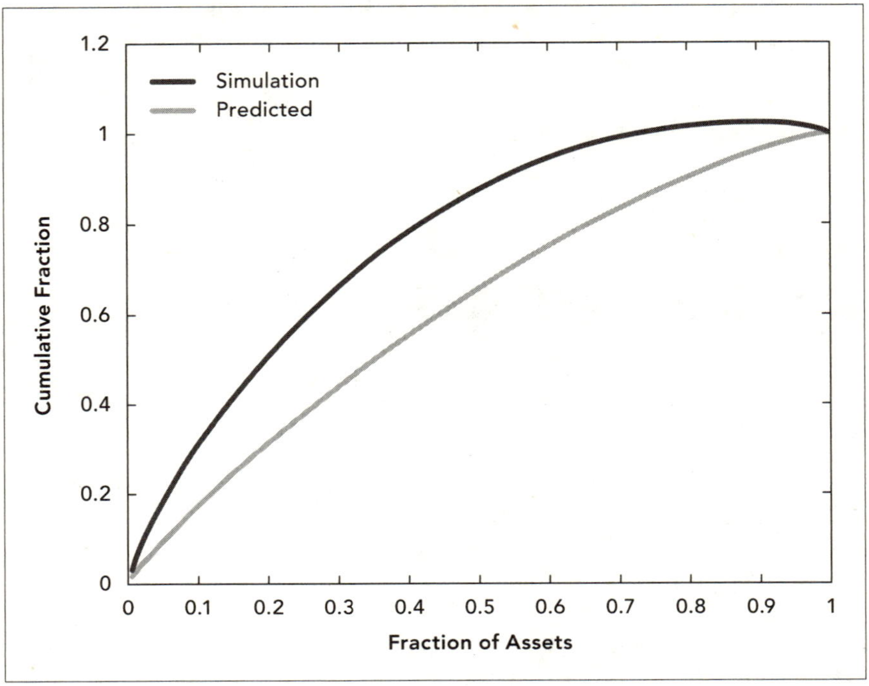

EXHIBIT 14 Aggregate Results with Correlation of 0.346 in INT and SLOW Signals

ITEM	PREDICTION	SIMULATION
Alpha	4.91	4.93
T-Cost/yr	1.60	1.59
Portfolio Risk	3.24	3.26
Objective	2.00	2.02
ACIR	1.02	1.03
Corr(P,M)	0.735	0.738
Target Risk	4.32	4.43

The net result was an overall lowering of the potential information ratio due to redundant information. The predictions are just as accurate.

USA Test

We ran a second simulation using specific risk and transactions cost data on a far larger sample of 3,136 US stocks. The results did not differ much although the average optimal trade rate was lower in the United States, 1.68, compared to 2.68 in Australia. This is understandable, since the Australian sample was the 200 largest stocks and the USA sample includes several thousand illiquid stocks. Exhibit 15 presents a histogram of the optimal trading rates in the USA sample. The USA simulation used the same time period (1/252), risk aversion (25), period (10 years), half-lives, and assumed information ratios. The samples differed in number of assets, trade rates, asset specific risk, and transactions cost data.

EXHIBIT 15 USA: Optimal Trading Rates for 3,136 United States Equities.

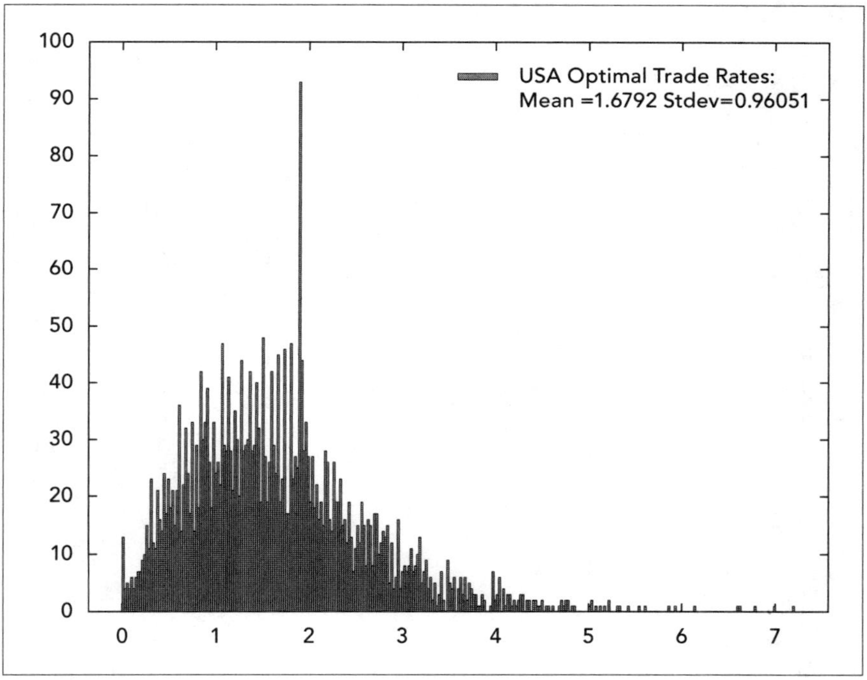

The aggregate results for the United States have no surprises, as Exhibit 16 shows.

EXHIBIT 16 USA: Aggregate Simulation Results.

ITEM	PREDICTION	SIMULATION
Alpha	4.57	4.44
T-Cost/yr.	2.10	2.11
Portfolio Risk	3.06	2.97
Objective	1.30	1.23
ACIR	0.81	0.78
Corr(*P*,*M*)	0.72	0.72
Target Risk	4.27	4.27

There isn't much difference at the aggregate level, with the law of large numbers playing an important role. The relatively high transactions costs have an intimidating effect. There is a larger opportunity loss in this US example.

For comparison with the Australian case we have included the asset-specific regression results. Compare Exhibit 17 and Exhibit 10 on transactions costs, and also Exhibits 18 and 11 on alpha.

EXHIBIT 17 USA: Asset Level Transactions Cost. Prediction vs. Simulation Result

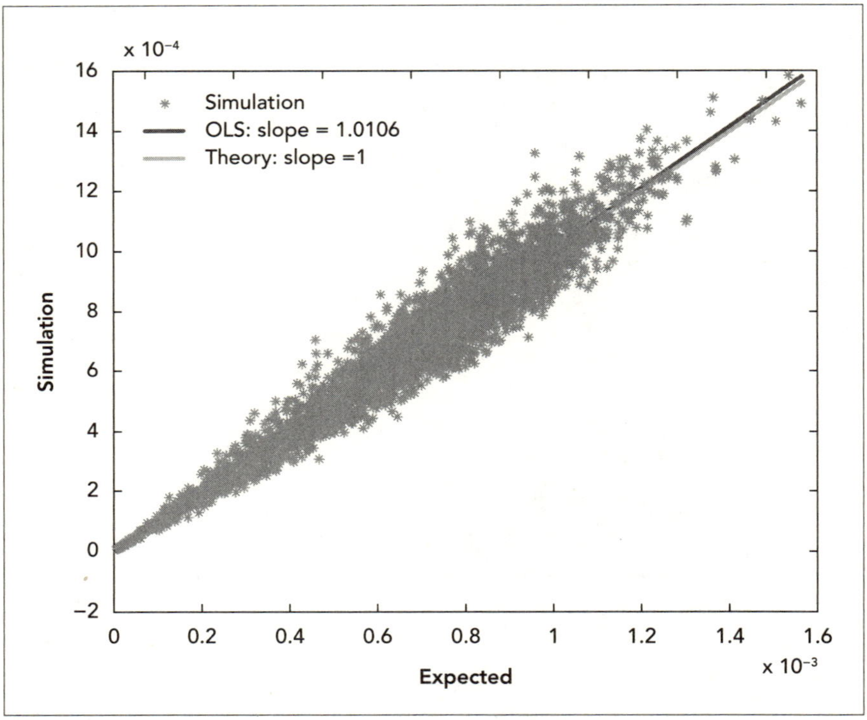

EXHIBIT 18 USA: Asset Level, Average Position Alpha, Prediction vs. Simulation Result.

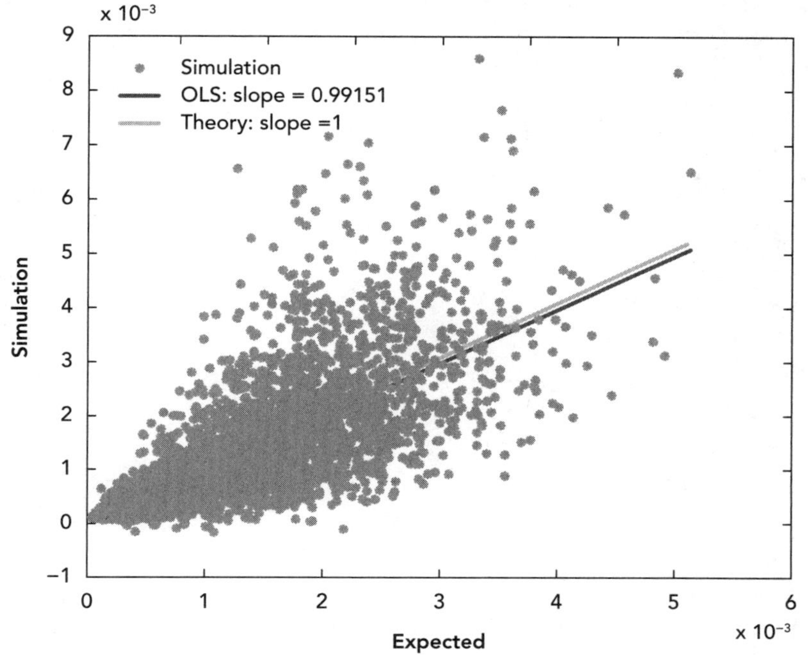

The regression results for all the variables are included in Exhibit 19 (compare with Exhibit 12 for Australia).

EXHIBIT 19 USA: Link Between Expectation and Simulated Averages

VARIABLE	SLOPE	R2
Alpha{*P*(*n*)}	0.99	0.47
Risk{*P*(*n*)}	1.00	0.72
Cost{*P*(*n*)}/yr.	1.01	0.93
Risk *P-dot*(*n*)	1.01	0.98
Target Risk{*M*(*n*)}	1.00	0.81
Cov{*M*(*n*), *P*(*n*)}	1.00	0.60
Omega P(*n*, FAST)	0.89	0.21
Omega P(*n*, INT.)	0.90	0.76
Omega P(*n*, SLOW)	0.93	0.66

Exhibit 19 shows a similar pattern as the Australian sample. It is easy to predict the effect of changes and hard to get a handle on the FAST signal.

EXHIBIT 20 USA: Expected and the Simulated Objective Value

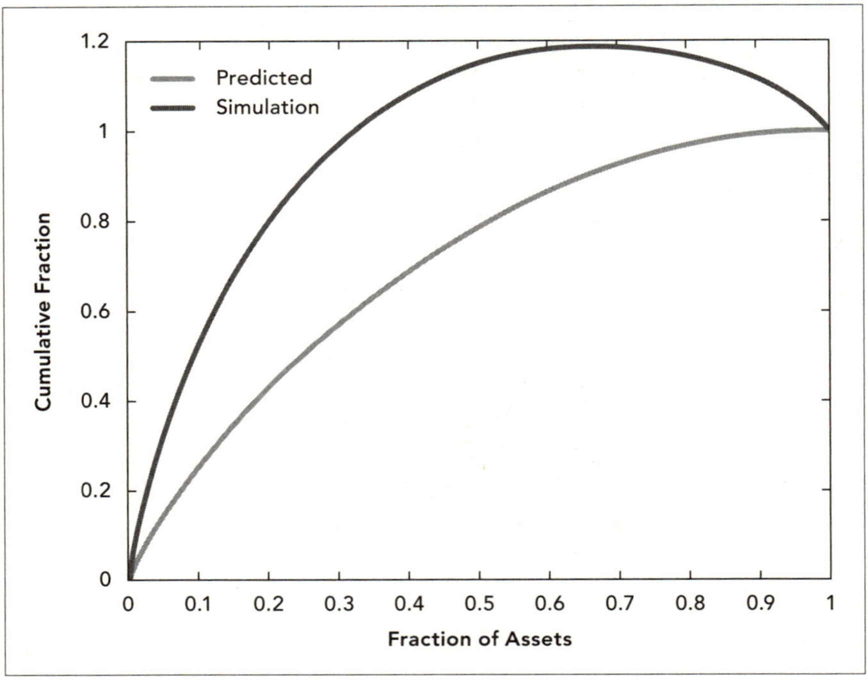

The Gini results, shown in Exhibit 20, are more pronounced than the Australian case. On the predicted curve we have about half of the value added from 30% of the assets and all of the assets are expected to add some value. In the Gini curve summarizing the simulation we get half of the value added with about 10% of the assets, and the last 33% or so of the assets lose value on a cost and risk adjusted basis over the 10 years of the simulation.

Implementation

We can predict the behavior of a system governed by a linear trading rule and use those predictions to choose the trading rate parameter, d_n, for each asset in order to maximize that asset's contribution to an overall objective. To move toward implementation, we must tackle several aspects of the portfolio management problem we have ignored thus far.

- The position $p_n(t)$ is an active position, the deviation between our holding in an asset and the holding of some benchmark or index. There may be constraints on the size of the active positions, requiring the net active position to be zero, long-only constraints requiring the active plus benchmark position to be nonnegative, or constraints associated with a 120-20 portfolio.[6]

- The portfolio may also be taking active factor/smart beta positions in addition to the alphas based on specific return.
- The linear trading rule leads to a large number of small trades, although it is commonly accepted that transactions costs of the type we posited in Equation (10) lead to a no-trade zone for each asset; that is, at each time and for each asset there will be a lower and upper limit such that you sell if your position is above the upper limit and buy if you are below the lower limit and you do not trade if you are between the limits, see Grinold (2018) (Chapter 11, "Nonlinear Trading Rules" in this book). In contrast, the linear trading rule trades all the time.
- The linear trading rule provides average risk control rather than period to period risk control. The active risk of the portfolio tends to drift, and there is nothing to prevent serendipity having signals that favor the preponderance of financial stocks in one period or disliking most of the stocks in extractive industries in another. On average risk control is unsatisfactory.

Traditional single or multistage optimization handles the matters detailed above with relative ease despite a case of shortsightedness. Therefore, our proposal is to take the long-range objective of dynamic programming and harness it to the calculating engine that I refer to as traditional portfolio optimization.

Nonlinear Trading Rules

In the introduction to the "Dynamic Portfolio Analysis" section of this book, we discussed implementation in the more general context of nonlinear trading rules, in particular nonlinear trading rules for general transactions costs, Equation (10).[7] If the nonlinear market impact term in the transactions cost has coefficient $\phi = 1.5$, then we use a nonlinear trading rule called NLTR1.5. If the coefficient is $\phi = 2$, then we use NLTR2. The introduction to this section of the book (Chapter 6) uses NLTR1.5 as an example, so we will use NLTR2 here. We suggest an objective with two components. The first component is derived from the nonlinear trading rule:

Component I

$$\frac{\lambda}{2} \cdot \sum_{n=1:N} \sigma_n^2 \cdot \left\{ \left(b_n - \Delta p_n\right)^2 + z_n \cdot |\Delta p_n| + \frac{k_n}{2} \cdot |\Delta p_n|^2 \right\} \tag{19}$$

where

$b_n = m_n - p_n$ is the backlog: target-initial position

z_n, k_n are the maximizing parameters

6. See Jacobs and Levy (2007).

7. We will cover this topic in more detail in Chapter 11, "Nonlinear Trading Rules for Portfolio Management."

The nonnegative parameters z_n and k_n are selected for asset n in order to maximize its contribution to the overall objective. The nonlinear trading rule article describes the optimization methodology.

We invite the reader to examine the case where the backlog is positive, that is, we are thinking of buying. The question is: how much, if any, do we buy? The answer is nothing if $0 \le b_n \le z_n$. If $z_n < b_n$, then we buy $\Delta p_n = (b_n - z_n)/(1 + k_n)$. Note that $z_n = 0$ and $k_n = \delta_n/(1 - \delta_n)$ will provide the same trades as the linear trading rule.

If component I is the only term in the objective (and we are minimizing), then we will execute the optimal trading rule for each asset. However, there may be concerns pushing the portfolio in other directions.

In particular there is the question of controlling common factor risk and making smart beta/factor forecasts. A discussion requires some additional notation.

$$\begin{aligned} &\mathbf{X} \text{ an } N \text{ by } K \text{ matrix of factor exposures} \\ &\mathbf{x}_T \text{ a } K \text{ element vector of desired active exposures} \\ &\mathbf{F} \text{ a } K \text{ by } K \text{ matrix, covariance plus penalties} \\ &\mathbf{p} = \{p_n\}_{n=1:N} \text{ is the vector of active positions} \\ &\mathbf{x}_P = \mathbf{X}' \cdot \mathbf{p} \text{ a } K \text{ element vector of active exposures} \end{aligned} \tag{20}$$

With this notation the component II is:

$$\frac{\eta}{2} \cdot (\mathbf{x}_T - \mathbf{x}_P)' \cdot \mathbf{F} \cdot (\mathbf{x}_T - \mathbf{x}_P). \tag{21}$$

Two points are in order:

- An alternative or supplement to the common factor penalty, Equation (21), is the use of upper and lower bounds on the deviation, $\mathbf{x}_T - \mathbf{x}_P$. This is, in this author's opinion, a second-best solution. Bounds of this sort should be a safety warning mechanism like a circuit breaker or a guardrail. Hitting the constraint sets off an alarm and indicates that something is out of whack.
- If some desired factor exposures are drifting around too much, say factor k, then consider adding a penalty by increasing the diagonal element, $F_{k,k}$, to tighten things up. In this way we can interpret the parameter η in Equation (21) as a way to tighten and loosen all the penalties and increasing the diagonal elements to tighten up a specific penalty.[8]

This suggested approach is based on theory and experience. It has not been tested. In the least likely case, it may work splendidly the first time it's tried. Otherwise, it may be a dead end, or it may need considerable tweaking before it works. Any test should start as simply as possible, and not add any elaboration until the simpler problem has been thoroughly understood.

8. The penalty, Equation (21), is a convex function. Increasing a diagonal element does not endanger its convex status, but decreasing a diagonal element does.

Summary

Under special circumstances, described in Appendix B, the optimal investment policy for each asset is a linear trading rule that moves from the current position to a new position between the current position and a target. The linear trading rule is our gateway to dynamic portfolio management. We want to know how a linear trading rule can help us manage a portfolio.

We first defined linear trading rules and demonstrated how they predict useful aspects of asset and portfolio behavior. These include risk, transactions cost, turnover, and exposure to various sources of alpha. The predictions are precise at the portfolio level, and the transactions cost and turnover predictions are accurate at the asset level.

Once we have confidence in the predictions, it is a small step to choosing the rate of trading for each asset in order to maximize its contribution to an overall objective. That choice of an optimal trading rate is based on the information ratios of the signals, a penalty on variance, any correlation among the signals, the half-lives of the signals, and the specific volatility and transactions cost of the asset.

A by-product of selecting a trading rate is transactions cost-dependent signal weighting at the asset level. The choice of a trading weight determines the signal weighting for the asset's target ($\mathbf{w}_{M(n)}$ in the text) and a prediction of the resulting exposure of the asset to the signals ($\mathbf{w}_{P(n)}$ in the text).

The information gained in this exercise can be used to replace the objective of a static (one or multistage) portfolio optimization with an objective that will lead us to execute the trading rule if other considerations such as constraints, bounds, desired factor exposures, etc. do not get in the way.

A by-product of this study is a process for transaction cost sensitive signal weighting at the asset level. This opens the door for research that is tailored to a particular segment of the market or in an extreme case to a particular asset.

In Chapter 11, "Nonlinear Trading Rules for Portfolio Management," we carry these ideas forward. In the fifteen months since this article was published we have been able to generalize the results significantly. We can dispense with the requirement that the returns we are forecasting are uncorrelated. We can also allow for signals that effect several assets. For example a WIN-WIN signal that is good (or bad) news for more than one firm; e.g., a b to c firm and its suppliers. We can also allow for WIN-LOSE signals where what portends good news for one company is bad news for its rivals. The calculations become more difficult but the general results hold. There is an optimal linear trade rate for each asset that we can calculate and we can predict the alpha, risk, and cost of the resulting portfolio using those linear trade rates.

Above all we hope that the reader will understand that a portfolio is in motion, it is a dynamic object, and a perceptive portfolio manager will realize where it wants to go, for what benefit, at what cost, and when it might get there.

References

Boyd, Stephen, Enzo Busseti, Steven Diamond, Ronald N. Kahn, Kwangmoo Koh, Peter Nystrup, and Jan Speth. 2017. "Multi-Period Trading via Convex Optimization." *Foundations and Trends in Optimization* 20 (20).

Clarke, Roger, Harindra de Silva, and Steven Thorley. 2002. "Portfolio Constraints and the Fundamental Law of Active Management." *Financial Analysts Journal*, September/October.

Garleanu, Nicolae, and Lasse Pedersen. 2013. "Dynamic Trading with Predictable Returns and Transactions Costs." *Journal of Finance* 68 (December). Previously NBER Working Paper # 15205, 2009.

Grinold, Richard. 2005. "Implementation Efficiency." *Financial Analysts Journal* 61 (September-October): 52–64.

Grinold, Richard. 2007. "Dynamic Portfolio Analysis." *Journal of Portfolio Management* 34 (Fall): 12–26.

Grinold, Richard. "Signal Weighting." 2010. *Journal of Portfolio Management* 36 (Summer): 24–34.

Grinold, Richard. 2018. "Nonlinear Trading Rules for Portfolio Management." *Journal of Portfolio Management* 45 (Fall): 62–70.

Grinold, Richard C., and Ronald N. Kahn. 2000. *Active Portfolio Management*. 2nd ed. New York: McGraw-Hill.

Jacobs, Bruce I., and Kenneth N. Levy. 2007. "20 Myths About Enhanced Active 120–20 Portfolios." *Financial Analysts Journal* 63 (July/August): 19–26.

Powell, William B. 2011. *Approximate Dynamic Programming: Solving the Curses of Dimensionality*. 2nd ed. Wiley Series in Probability and Statistics.

CHAPTER 10

Linear Trading Rules for Portfolio Management

Appendix A

Consequences of Using a Linear Trading Rule

Introduction

The selection of an asset's trade rate d_n allows us to predict the important expected characteristics: alpha, risk, and annual transactions cost, of the asset and therefore of the aggregate strategy. To do this we have to follow three different positions: first an idealized zero-cost position $Q(n)$, second the model (or target) position $M(n)$, and third the resulting invested position, $P(n)$, determined by the linear trading rule.

The Zero Cost Position $Q(n)$

We will follow the section on forecasting in *Active Portfolio Management*, in particular Equation (10.1). For two correlated random variables, say, **x** and **y**, the best linear unbiased estimator (BLUE) of **x** given a value of **y** is:

$$E\langle\tilde{\mathbf{x}}\rangle + Cov\langle\tilde{\mathbf{x}}, \tilde{\mathbf{y}}\rangle \cdot Var^{-1}\langle\tilde{\mathbf{y}}\rangle \cdot \{\mathbf{y} - E\langle\tilde{\mathbf{y}}\rangle\} \tag{A1}$$

This is also the conditional expectation if the variables are normally distributed. In our case $\tilde{\mathbf{x}}$ is the return, $\tilde{\theta}_n$, on asset n over the period $(0,\Delta t)$ and $\tilde{\mathbf{y}} = \tilde{\mathbf{s}}_n$ is the vector of J signals. Both the return and the signals have prior means equal to zero. The signals are standardized to have standard deviation of one.

$$\begin{aligned} &Var\left\langle\tilde{\mathbf{s}}_n\right\rangle = \mathbf{R}_n \quad \text{a correlation matrix} \\ &Cov\left\langle\tilde{\theta}_n, \tilde{\mathbf{s}}_n\right\rangle = Std\left\langle\tilde{\theta}_n\right\rangle \cdot Corr\left\langle\tilde{\theta}_n, \tilde{\mathbf{s}}_n\right\rangle \cdot \mathbf{I} \\ &Std\left\langle\tilde{\theta}_n\right\rangle \cdot Corr\left\langle\tilde{\theta}_n, \tilde{\mathbf{s}}_n\right\rangle \cdot \mathbf{R}_n^{-1} \cdot \mathbf{s}_n \quad \text{is the forecast over } [0, \Delta t] \end{aligned} \tag{A2}$$

Over a short period of time[9] we have:

$$Std\left\langle \tilde{\theta}_n \right\rangle = \sigma_n \cdot \sqrt{\Delta t}$$

$$Corr\left\langle \tilde{\theta}_n, \tilde{s}_n \right\rangle \approx \iota'_n \cdot \sqrt{\Delta t} \tag{A3}$$

$$\left\{\sigma_n \cdot \iota'_n \cdot \mathbf{R}_n^{-1} \cdot \mathbf{s}\right\} \cdot \Delta t \text{ is the forecast over } [0, \Delta t]$$

The alpha is an annualized forecast. So when we divide by Δt, we get:

$$\alpha_n(\mathbf{s}) = \sigma_n \cdot \iota'_n \cdot \mathbf{R}_n^{-1} \cdot \mathbf{s} \quad \text{alpha (annualized)}$$

$$q_n(\mathbf{s}) = \frac{\alpha_n(\mathbf{s})}{\lambda \cdot \sigma_n^2} = \mathbf{w}'_{Q(n)} \cdot \mathbf{s} \quad \text{the zero-cost position} \tag{A4}$$

where

$$\mathbf{w}_{Q(n)} = \frac{\mathbf{R}_n^{-1} \cdot \iota_n}{\lambda \cdot \sigma_n} \quad \text{the zero-cost signal weights}$$

In Equation (A3) ι_n is called the vector of *information coefficients*, which is a fancy name for the correlation of the signal and the return. One way to get notion of a suitable value for the information coefficients is to reverse engineer the fundamental law of active management. First assign an information ratio to each signal. If there are N assets in the forecast then the information ratio divided by the square root of the number of assets will give a reasonable first estimate of the information coefficient. For example with an information ratio of 1.25 and 225 assets we have an information coefficient of 0.083. If you are getting numbers larger than 0.2 for your information coefficients, you may be too optimistic.

The formal method, above, is one way to get at the signal weighting $\mathbf{w}_{Q(n)}$. With some experience with the scale of the problem, one could bypass the formal process and start with a desired $\mathbf{w}_{Q(n)}$. A spreadsheet exercise will help in this regard.

EXERCISE 1 Set the penalty for variance at $\lambda = 18$ and the volatility at $\sigma_n = 0.20$.

Exhibit A1 gives the information coefficients ι and correlation, $\mathbf{R}_n$, of three signals.

EXHIBIT A1

	ic	FAST	INT.	SLOW
FAST	0.25	1	0	0
INT.	0.1	0	1	0.3
SLOW	0.075	0	0.3	1

Compute the signal weights $\mathbf{w}_{Q(n)}$.

9. The risk over a short period of time is $\sigma_n \cdot \sqrt{\Delta t}$. The correlation is $\iota_{n,j} \cdot \left(1 - e^{-g_j \cdot \Delta t}\right) / g_j \cdot \sqrt{\Delta t}$. The product of the two for a very small interval is approximately $\sigma_n \cdot \iota_{n,j} \cdot \Delta t$.

From Equation (A1), we can predict the expected alpha and variance if we trade to hold the position $q_n(t)$ at time t.

$$\begin{aligned}
\alpha_{Q(n)} &\equiv E\langle \alpha_n(t) \cdot q_n(t) \rangle = \lambda \cdot \sigma_n^2 \cdot \mathbf{w}'_{Q(n)} \cdot \mathbf{R}_n \cdot \mathbf{w}_{Q(n)} \\
\sigma_{Q(n)}^2 &\equiv E\langle \sigma_n^2 \cdot q_n^2(t) \rangle = \sigma_n^2 \cdot \mathbf{w}'_{Q(n)} \cdot \mathbf{R}_n \cdot \mathbf{w}_{Q(n)} \Rightarrow \alpha_{Q(n)} = \lambda \cdot \sigma_{Q(n)}^2
\end{aligned} \tag{A5}$$

At the portfolio level:

$$\begin{aligned}
\sigma_Q^2 &\equiv \sum_{n=1:N} \sigma_{Q(n)}^2 && \text{portfolio } Q \text{ variance} \\
\alpha_Q &\equiv \sum_{n=1:N} \alpha_{Q(n)} && \text{portfolio } Q \text{ alpha} \\
IR_Q &= \frac{\alpha_Q}{\sigma_Q} = \lambda \cdot \sigma_Q && \text{portfolio } Q \text{ information ratio}
\end{aligned} \tag{A6}$$

The Model-Target Position *M(n)*

The model will depend on the trade rate d_n. Recall that $\delta_n = e^{-d_n \cdot \Delta t}$ and $\gamma_j = e^{-g_j \cdot \Delta t}$.

Following the dynamic programming results in Appendix B, we define the weight for the target, conditional on the trading rate d_n, as:

$$\begin{aligned}
&\psi_{n,j} \equiv \frac{1-\delta_n}{1-\delta_n \cdot \gamma_j} \to \frac{d_n}{d_n + g_j} \text{ as } \Delta t \searrow 0 \\
&\Psi_n \equiv \text{a } J \text{ by } J \text{ matrix with } \psi_{n,j} \text{ on the diagonal} \\
&\text{thus } \mathbf{w}_{M(n)} = \Psi_n \cdot \mathbf{w}_{Q(n)}
\end{aligned} \tag{A7}$$

It is straightforward to calculate the resulting properties of the target positions and portfolio:

$$\begin{aligned}
&m_n(t) \equiv \sum_{j=1:J} s_{n,j}(t) \cdot w_{M(n),j} = \mathbf{s}'_n(t) \cdot \mathbf{w}_{M(n)} \\
&\alpha_{M(n)} \equiv E\langle \alpha_n(t) \cdot m_n(t) \rangle = \lambda \cdot \sigma_n^2 \cdot \mathbf{w}'_{Q(n)} \cdot \mathbf{R}_n \cdot \mathbf{w}_{M(n)} \\
&\sigma_{M(n)}^2 \equiv E\langle \sigma_n^2 \cdot m_n^2(t) \rangle = \sigma_n^2 \cdot \mathbf{w}'_{M(n)} \cdot \mathbf{R}_n \cdot \mathbf{w}_{M(n)} \\
&\text{and the aggregate results} \\
&\alpha_M \equiv \sum_{n=1:N} \alpha_{M(n)}, \quad \sigma_M^2 \equiv \sum_{n=1:N} \sigma_{M(n)}^2, \quad IR_M = \frac{\alpha_M}{\sqrt{\sigma_M^2}}
\end{aligned} \tag{A8}$$

The Position *P(n)*.

This takes work. First, recall that the linear trading rule is:

$$p_n(t) = \delta_n \cdot p_n(t-\Delta t) + (1-\delta_n) \cdot m_n(t) \tag{A9}$$

The next step is to determine the covariance between $p_n(t)$ and the signals $s_{n,j}(t)$ by multiplying the linear trading rule, Equation (A9), by $s_{n,j}(t)$ and taking expectations:

$$\begin{aligned} E\langle p_n(t)\cdot s_{n,j}(t)\rangle &= \delta_n \cdot E\langle p_n(t-\Delta t)\cdot s_{n,j}(t)\rangle \\ &+ (1-\delta_n)\cdot E\left\langle \sum_{i=1:J} s_{n,j}(t)\cdot s_{n,i}(t)\cdot w_{M(n),i}\right\rangle \end{aligned} \tag{A10}$$

Use the law of motion for the source positions:

$$\begin{aligned} & s_{n,j}(t) = \gamma_j \cdot s_{n,j}(t-\Delta t) + \sqrt{1-\gamma_j^2}\cdot y_{n,j}(t) \Rightarrow \\ & E\langle p_n(t-\Delta t)\cdot s_{n,j}(t)\rangle = E\langle p_n(t-\Delta t)\cdot \gamma_j \cdot s_{n,j}(t-\Delta t)\rangle \\ & \quad + E\left\langle p_n(t-\Delta t)\cdot \sqrt{1-\gamma_j^2}\cdot y_{n,j}(t)\right\rangle \end{aligned} \tag{A11}$$

However, $E\left\langle p_n(t-\Delta t)\cdot \sqrt{1-\gamma_j^2}\cdot y_{n,j}(t)\right\rangle = 0$, so:

$$\begin{aligned} E\langle p_n(t)\cdot s_{n,j}(t)\rangle &= \delta_n \cdot \gamma_j \cdot E\langle p_n(t-\Delta t)\cdot s_{n,j}(t-\Delta t)\rangle \\ &+ (1-\delta_n)\cdot E\left\langle \sum_{i=1:J} s_{n,j}(t)\cdot s_{n,i}(t)\cdot w_{M(n),i}\right\rangle \end{aligned} \tag{A12}$$

In equilibrium $E\langle p_n(t)\cdot s_{n,j}(t)\rangle = E\langle p_n(t-\Delta t)\cdot s_{n,j}(t-\Delta t)\rangle$, thus:

$$E\langle p_n(t)\cdot s_{n,j}(t)\rangle = \psi_{n,j}\cdot \sum_{i=1:J} E\langle s_{n,j}(t)\cdot s_{n,i}(t)\rangle \cdot w_{M(n),i} \tag{A13}$$

As above, $\psi_{n,j} \equiv {}^{1-\delta_n}\!\big/_{1-\delta_n\cdot\gamma_j} \approx {}^{d_n}\!\big/_{d_n+g_j}$. In addition, $E\langle s_{n,i}(t)\cdot s_{n,i}(t)\rangle = R_{i,j}$, so:

$$E\langle p_n(t)\cdot \mathbf{s}_n(t)\rangle = \mathbf{\Psi}_n \cdot \mathbf{R}_n \cdot \mathbf{w}_{M(n)} \tag{A14}$$

Third, project the position $p_n(t)$ onto a space spanned by the signals $s_{n,j}(t)$ leaving a residual $e_n(t)$ that is uncorrelated with the sources:

$$\begin{aligned} &(i.)\quad p_n(t) = \sum_{i=1:J} s_{n,i}(t)\cdot w_{P(n),i} + e_n(t) \text{ where} \\ &(ii)\qquad E\langle e_n(t)\cdot s_{n,j}(t)\rangle = 0 \text{ for all } j \\ &\text{Multiply } (i.) \text{ by } s_{n,j}(t) \text{ and take expectations} \\ &(iii)\quad E\langle p_n(t)\cdot s_{n,j}(t)\rangle = \sum_{i=1:J} s_{n,j}(t)\cdot s_{n,i}(t)\cdot w_{P(n),i} \\ &(iv.)\quad E\langle p_n(t)\cdot \mathbf{s}_n(t)\rangle = \mathbf{R}_n \cdot \mathbf{w}_{P(n)} \end{aligned} \tag{A15}$$

Combine (A14) and (A15) to get:

$$\mathbf{R}_n \cdot \mathbf{w}_{P(n)} = \Psi_n \cdot \mathbf{R}_n \cdot \mathbf{w}_{M(n)} \tag{A16}$$

As a bonus we find that:

$$\sigma_{M(n),P(n)} \equiv E\langle \sigma_n \cdot m_n(t) \cdot \sigma_n \cdot p_n(t) \rangle = \sigma_n^2 \cdot \mathbf{w}'_{M(n)} \cdot \mathbf{R}_n \cdot \mathbf{w}_{P(n)} \tag{A17}$$

To accomplish the fourth step, we introduce yet another strategy. It will play a useful role as a catalyst and then, appropriately, vanish. It is the lagged position, $L(n)$, with holdings $p_n(t - \Delta t)$ at time t. Multiply the linear trading rule first by $\sigma_n^2 \cdot p_n(t)$ and again by $\sigma_n^2 \cdot p_n(t - \Delta t)$ and take expectations. This yields two equations.

$$\begin{aligned}
&\sigma_{P(n)}^2 = \delta_n \cdot \sigma_{P(n),L(n)} + (1-\delta_n) \cdot \sigma_{P(n),M(n)} \\
&\sigma_{P(n),L(n)} = \delta_n \cdot \sigma_{L(n)}^2 + (1-\delta_n) \cdot \sigma_{L(n),M(n)} \\
&\text{where } \sigma_{P(n),L(n)} \equiv E\langle \sigma_n \cdot p_n(t) \cdot \sigma_n \cdot p_n(t-\Delta t) \rangle \\
&\qquad \sigma_{L(n),M(n)} \equiv E\langle \sigma_n \cdot p_n(t-\Delta t) \cdot \sigma_n \cdot m_n(t) \rangle \\
&\text{and} \qquad \sigma_{L(n)}^2 \equiv E\langle \sigma_n \cdot p_n(t-\Delta t) \cdot \sigma_n \cdot p_n(t-\Delta t) \rangle = \sigma_{P(n)}^2
\end{aligned} \tag{A18}$$

Solve Equation (A18) for $\sigma_{P(n)}^2$:

$$\sigma_{P(n)}^2 = \frac{1}{1+\delta_n} \cdot \left\{ \sigma_{P(n),M(n)} + \delta_n \cdot \sigma_{L(n),M(n)} \right\} \tag{A19}$$

As $\Delta t \searrow 0$ we have $\delta_n \nearrow 1$ and $\sigma_{L(n),M(n)} \to \sigma_{P(n),M(n)}$; thus:

$$\sigma_{P(n)}^2 \to \sigma_{M(n),P(n)} = \sigma_n^2 \cdot \mathbf{w}'_{M(n)} \cdot \mathbf{R} \cdot \mathbf{w}_{P(n)} \tag{A20}$$

Again there is a bonus. Let $E(n)$ represent the residual position, with the residual defined in Equation (A15).

$$\begin{aligned}
&(i.) \quad \sigma_{P(n)}^2 = \sigma_n^2 \cdot \mathbf{w}'_{P(n)} \cdot \mathbf{R}_n \cdot \mathbf{w}_{P(n)} + \sigma_{E(n)}^2 \Rightarrow \\
&(ii.) \quad \sigma_{E(n)}^2 \approx \sigma_n^2 \cdot \left\{ \mathbf{w}_{M(n)} - \mathbf{w}_{P(n)} \right\}' \cdot \mathbf{R}_n \cdot \mathbf{w}_{P(n)} \quad \text{the residual variance} \\
&(iii.) \quad \sigma_{M(n)-P(n)}^2 = \sigma_{M(n)}^2 - 2 \cdot \sigma_{P(n),M(n)} + \sigma_{P(n)}^2 \approx \sigma_{M(n)}^2 - \sigma_{P(n)}^2 \quad \text{the backlog variance}
\end{aligned} \tag{A21}$$

Turnover and Transactions Cost

From the differential form of the linear trading rule we have:

$$\begin{aligned}
&\sigma_n \cdot \frac{\Delta p_n(t)}{\Delta t} \approx \sigma_n \cdot d_n \cdot \{ m_n(t) - p_n(t) \} \\
&\Rightarrow \sigma_{\dot{P}(n)}^2 \equiv E\left\langle \left\{ \sigma_n \cdot \frac{\Delta p_n(t)}{\Delta t} \right\}^2 \right\rangle \approx d_n^2 \cdot \sigma_{M(n)-P(n)}^2
\end{aligned} \tag{A22}$$

The expected annual turnover is:

$$E\left\langle\left|\frac{\Delta p_n}{\Delta t}\right|\right\rangle = \frac{1}{\sigma_n} \cdot \sigma_{\dot{P}(n)} \cdot E\langle|X|\rangle \tag{A23}$$

where X has mean zero and standard deviation one. If X is normally distributed, the default choice, then $E\langle|X|\rangle = \sqrt{2/\pi}$. For one-way turnover, divide by two.

Take a similar line with the transactions costs. Suppose the costs and expected annual costs are:

$$\begin{aligned} &tc\,(\Delta p_n) = c_{1,n} \cdot |\Delta p_n| + c_{2,n} \cdot |\Delta p_n|^{\phi} \\ &E\left\langle\frac{tc\,(\Delta p_n)}{\Delta t}\right\rangle = c_{1,n} \cdot E\left\langle\left|\frac{\Delta p_n}{\Delta t}\right|\right\rangle + c_{2,n} \cdot \Delta t^{\phi-1} \cdot E\left\langle\left|\frac{\Delta p_n}{\Delta t}\right|^{\phi}\right\rangle \end{aligned} \tag{A24}$$

If we let:

$$\frac{\Delta p_n}{\Delta t} = \frac{\sigma_{\dot{P}(n)}}{\sigma_n} \cdot X, \quad \text{where } E\langle X\rangle = 0, \quad E\langle X^2\rangle = 1 \tag{A25}$$

then we can write the expected annual transaction cost as:

$$\begin{aligned} &E\left\langle\frac{tc(\Delta p_n)}{\Delta t}\right\rangle = k_{1,n} \cdot \sigma_{\dot{P}(n)} + k_{2,n} \cdot \sigma_{\dot{P}(n)}^{\phi} \\ &\text{where} \\ &k_{1,n} \equiv \frac{c_{1,n}}{\sigma_n} \cdot E\langle|X|\rangle, \quad k_{2,n} \equiv \frac{c_{2,n} \cdot \Delta t^{\phi-1}}{\sigma_n^{\phi}} \cdot E\langle|X|^{\phi}\rangle \end{aligned} \tag{A26}$$

The terms $k_{1,n}, k_{2,n}$ are independent of the trade rate. If X from equation (A25) is normally distributed, then $E\langle|X|\rangle = \sqrt{2/\pi}, \quad E\langle|X|^{1.5}\rangle = 0.86$. For any distribution $E\langle|X|^2\rangle = 1$.

CHAPTER 10
Linear Trading Rules for Portfolio Management

Appendix B

Optimality of Linear Decision Rules

In the main text of the chapter we use three concepts that stem from the analytic solution of a dynamic program. They are:

- The form of the linear trading rule.
- The weights on the model/target position.
- The penalty function used to incorporate the single asset information into a multi-asset one-stage optimization.

This appendix provides the motivation for these three concepts.

A few points before we start:

- We have known linear quadratic dynamic programming leads to a quadratic value function and linear policy rule since 1960. The task of this appendix is to find analytical results in this special case.
- The idea isn't that challenging; it's the horrendous algebra that obscures understanding.
- In our example, the state variables are the current position plus the J signals. The policy variable is the next position, or equivalently, the trade: the change in position.
- If you choose policy variables to maximize a concave quadratic function of state variables and policy variables, then the first order conditions will determine a linear relationship between the state variables and the optimal policy variables. These first-order conditions determine the linear policy rule (linear trading rule in our case).
- When you use the linear first order conditions to substitute for the policy variables in the quadratic objective, you are left with a quadratic function of the state variables.
- If two quadratic functions of the same variables are equal, then the coefficients describing the functions must be equal.
- We are using a steady state version of linear quadratic dynamic programming. In this case there will be an average gain rate each period

and then a quadratic value function that evaluates the benefit of a particular starting state.

- In our case there is symmetry, the optimal value of position and signals $(p, \mathbf{s})$ is exactly the same as the optimal value of positions $(-p, -\mathbf{s})$. Therefore, the optimal value function does not have a linear term, it is a pure quadratic.

Since we are only looking at one asset, we can dispense with the ever-present subscript n.

From the preceding points we conclude that the gain plus value of a starting state, $(p, \mathbf{s})$, must have this form:

$$\sigma^2 \cdot \phi \cdot \Delta t + \frac{\sigma^2}{2} \cdot \mathbf{s}' \cdot \mathbf{H} \cdot \mathbf{s} - \frac{\sigma^2 \cdot \kappa}{2} \cdot \left\{p - \mathbf{w}' \cdot \mathbf{s}\right\}^2$$

σ^2	is the annualized specific variance of the asset	
$\sigma^2 \cdot \phi$	is the annualized gain rate	(B1)
$\mathbf{s}' \cdot \mathbf{H} \cdot \mathbf{s}$	captures the benefit of starting with signals	
$\mathbf{w}' \cdot \mathbf{s}$	is the ideal starting position (the target) if the signals are $\mathbf{s}$	
κ	determines the penalty for being off target	

The object of our exercise is to determine the parameter κ and vector $\mathbf{w}$. The parameter ϕ and matrix $\mathbf{H}$ are not in our sights. A resolute reader can soldier on to determine them. In Appendix A, we defined the zero-cost weight $\mathbf{w}_Q$ that relates the J signals $\mathbf{s}$ to the annualized alpha and the zero-cost position:

$$\alpha(\mathbf{s}) = \lambda \cdot \sigma_n^2 \cdot \mathbf{w}_Q' \cdot \mathbf{s} = \lambda \cdot \sigma_n^2 \cdot q(\mathbf{s}) \tag{B2}$$

In what follows we should be careful to distinguish, $\mathbf{w}_Q$, a known input, from $\mathbf{w}$, an output to be determined.

The transactions cost of moving from an initial p_0 to p is assumed for the purposes of the LQDP to be quadratic of the form:

$$\frac{\chi \cdot \sigma^2}{2} \cdot \left\{\frac{\Delta p}{\Delta t}\right\}^2 \cdot \Delta t, \text{ where } \Delta p = p - p_0 \text{ and}$$

$$\frac{\chi \cdot \sigma^2}{2} \cdot \left\{\frac{\Delta p}{\Delta t}\right\}^2 \text{ is the annual cost of trading at this rate} \tag{B3}$$

Note this assumption is *only for this appendix* where we get the form of the linear decision rule and the weighting for the model/target position. In the main text, we are *not* assuming quadratic transactions costs.

The dynamic programming set-up for a maximum gain rate problem is:

$$\phi \cdot \sigma^2 \cdot \Delta t + V(p_0, \mathbf{s}) = Max_p \left\{ r(p : p_0, \mathbf{s}) \cdot \Delta t + E\langle V(p, \tilde{\mathbf{s}}) | \mathbf{s} \rangle \right\}$$

$$r(p : p_0, \mathbf{s}) \equiv \left\{ \alpha(\mathbf{s}) \cdot p - \frac{\lambda \cdot \sigma^2}{2} \cdot p^2 \right\} - \frac{\chi \cdot \sigma^2}{2} \cdot \left\{ \frac{p - p_0}{\Delta t} \right\}^2 \tag{B4}$$

$$V(p, \mathbf{s}) \equiv \frac{\sigma^2}{2} \cdot \mathbf{s}' \cdot \mathbf{H} \cdot \mathbf{s} - \frac{\kappa \cdot \sigma^2}{2} \cdot \{p - \mathbf{w}' \cdot \mathbf{s}\}^2, \quad \mathbf{w}', \kappa \text{ to be determined}$$

Alternative ways of looking at the constituents are:

$$\mathbf{K} \equiv \mathbf{H} - \kappa \cdot \mathbf{w} \cdot \mathbf{w}'$$

$$V(p, \mathbf{s}) = \kappa \cdot \sigma^2 \cdot \mathbf{w}' \cdot \mathbf{s} \cdot p - \frac{\kappa \cdot \sigma^2}{2} \cdot p^2 + \frac{\sigma^2}{2} \cdot \mathbf{s}' \cdot \mathbf{K} \cdot \mathbf{s} \tag{B5}$$

$$V(p, \mathbf{s}) = \frac{\sigma^2}{2} \cdot \{ p \quad \mathbf{s}' \} \cdot \left\{ \begin{matrix} -\kappa & \kappa \cdot \mathbf{w}' \\ \kappa \cdot \mathbf{w} & \mathbf{K} \end{matrix} \right\} \cdot \left\{ \begin{matrix} p \\ \mathbf{s} \end{matrix} \right\}$$

The reward term can be expressed in a more useful manner by splitting the quadratic transactions cost into three parts.

$$r(p : p_0, \mathbf{s}) \cdot \Delta t = \left[\left\{ \alpha(\mathbf{s}) \cdot p - \frac{\lambda \cdot \sigma^2}{2} \cdot p^2 \right\} - \frac{\chi \cdot \sigma^2}{2} \cdot \left\{ \frac{p - p_0}{\Delta t} \right\}^2 \right] \cdot \Delta t$$

$$\frac{\chi \cdot \sigma^2}{2} \cdot \left\{ \frac{p - p_0}{\Delta t} \right\}^2 \cdot \Delta t = \frac{\chi \cdot \sigma^2}{2 \cdot \Delta t} \cdot p^2 - \frac{\chi \cdot \sigma^2}{\Delta t} \cdot p_0 \cdot p + \frac{\chi \cdot \sigma^2}{2 \cdot \Delta t} \cdot p_0^2$$

$$\Rightarrow r(p : p_0, \mathbf{s}) \cdot \Delta t =$$

$$\sigma^2 \cdot \left\{ \lambda \cdot \Delta t \cdot \mathbf{w}_0' \cdot \mathbf{s} + \frac{\chi}{\Delta t} \cdot p_0 \right\} \cdot p \tag{B6}$$

$$- \frac{\sigma^2}{2} \cdot \left\{ \lambda \cdot \Delta t + \frac{\chi}{\Delta t} \right\} \cdot p^2$$

$$- \frac{\sigma^2}{2} \cdot \frac{\chi}{\Delta t} \cdot p_0^2$$

The final term does not depend on p or $\mathbf{s}$. It can be moved outside of the optimization and subtracted from the left-hand side of the equation.

To evaluate $E\langle V(p, \tilde{\mathbf{s}}) | \mathbf{s} \rangle$ we need to know the dynamics of the signals.

$$\tilde{s}_j(t) = \gamma_j \cdot s_j(t - \Delta t) + \sqrt{1 - \gamma_j^2} \cdot \tilde{y}_j(t),$$

$$E\langle \tilde{y}_j(t) | s_j(t - \Delta t) \rangle = 0, \quad E\langle \tilde{y}_j^2(t) \rangle = 1$$

$$\Gamma \text{ is } J \text{ by } J \text{ diagonal with elements } \gamma_j \tag{B7}$$

$$\Upsilon \text{ is } J \text{ by } J \text{ diagonal with elements } \sqrt{1 - \gamma_j^2} \cdot$$

$$\tilde{\mathbf{s}}(t) = \Gamma \cdot \mathbf{s}(t - \Delta t) + \Upsilon \cdot \tilde{\mathbf{y}}(t)$$

Next determine the expectation $E\langle V(p,\tilde{\mathbf{s}})|\mathbf{s}\rangle$. To do this we'll rely on the form in Equation (B5) and the law of motion above:

$$
\begin{aligned}
E\langle V(p,\tilde{\mathbf{s}})|\mathbf{s}\rangle &= E\left\langle V\left(p, \Gamma\cdot\mathbf{s} + \Upsilon\cdot\tilde{\mathbf{y}}\cdot\sqrt{\Delta t}\right)\right\rangle \\
&= \frac{\sigma^2}{2}\cdot E\left\langle \left\{ p \quad \mathbf{s}'\cdot\Gamma' + \Upsilon\cdot\tilde{\mathbf{y}}\cdot\sqrt{\Delta t} \right\}\cdot\left\{ \begin{matrix} -\kappa & \kappa\cdot\mathbf{w}' \\ \kappa\cdot\mathbf{w} & \mathbf{K} \end{matrix} \right\}\cdot\left\{ \begin{matrix} p \\ \Gamma\cdot\mathbf{s} + \Upsilon\cdot\tilde{\mathbf{y}}\cdot\sqrt{\Delta t} \end{matrix} \right\}\right\rangle \\
&= \sigma^2\cdot\left\{[\kappa\cdot\mathbf{w}'\cdot\Gamma\cdot\mathbf{s}]\cdot p - \frac{\kappa}{2}\cdot p^2\right\} \\
&\quad + \kappa\cdot\sigma^2\cdot p\cdot E\langle\tilde{\mathbf{y}}'\cdot\Upsilon\cdot\mathbf{w}\rangle\cdot\sqrt{\Delta t} \\
&\quad + \frac{\sigma^2}{2}\cdot\mathbf{s}'\cdot\Gamma'\cdot\mathbf{K}\cdot\Gamma\cdot\mathbf{s} \\
&\quad + \sigma^2\cdot E\langle\mathbf{s}'\cdot\Gamma'\cdot\mathbf{K}\cdot\Upsilon\cdot\tilde{\mathbf{y}}\rangle\cdot\sqrt{\Delta t} \\
&\quad + \frac{\sigma^2}{2}\cdot E\langle\cdot\tilde{\mathbf{y}}'\cdot\Upsilon\cdot\mathbf{K}\cdot\Upsilon\cdot\tilde{\mathbf{y}}\rangle\cdot\Delta t
\end{aligned} \tag{B8}
$$

The expectations (second from last and fourth from last terms above) are equal to zero. The last and third from last terms above do not depend on the decision variable p. They can be shifted outside the optimization to the left side of the equation. This results in:

$$
\begin{aligned}
&\phi\cdot\sigma^2\cdot\Delta t + V(p_0,\mathbf{s}) - \frac{\sigma^2}{2}\cdot\mathbf{s}'\cdot\Gamma'\cdot\mathbf{K}\cdot\Gamma\cdot\mathbf{s} \\
&- \frac{\sigma^2}{2}\cdot E\langle\cdot\tilde{\mathbf{y}}'\cdot\Upsilon\cdot\mathbf{K}\cdot\Upsilon\cdot\tilde{\mathbf{y}}\rangle\cdot\Delta t + \frac{\sigma^2}{2}\cdot\frac{\chi}{\Delta t}\cdot p_0^2 \\
&= \sigma^2\cdot Max_p\left\{\left[\lambda\cdot\Delta t\cdot\mathbf{w}_Q'\cdot\mathbf{s} + \frac{\chi}{\Delta t}\cdot p_0 + \kappa\cdot\mathbf{w}'\cdot\Gamma\cdot\mathbf{s}\right]\cdot p - \left[\frac{\lambda\cdot\Delta t + \chi/\Delta t + \kappa}{2}\right]\cdot p^2\right\}
\end{aligned} \tag{B9}
$$

We have attained peak notation. Matters simplify from this point forward.

Consider the very special case when $\{p_0,\mathbf{s}\} = \{0,0\}$ then the optimal new position is $p = 0$, and the right-hand side of Equation (B9) is zero. In addition, $V(0,0)$ equals zero, so we have:

$$\phi\cdot\sigma^2\cdot\Delta t - \frac{\sigma^2}{2}\cdot E\langle\cdot\tilde{\mathbf{y}}'\cdot\Upsilon\cdot\mathbf{K}\cdot\Upsilon\cdot\tilde{\mathbf{y}}\rangle\cdot\Delta t = 0 \tag{B10}$$

Using Equation (B10), the left-hand side of Equation (B9) becomes:

$$\frac{\sigma^2}{2}\cdot\left\{\frac{\chi}{\Delta t} - \kappa\right\}\cdot p_0^2 + \kappa\cdot\sigma^2\cdot\mathbf{w}'\cdot\mathbf{s}\cdot p_0 + \frac{\sigma^2}{2}\cdot\mathbf{s}'\cdot\hat{\mathbf{K}}\cdot\mathbf{s} \tag{B11}$$

where $\hat{\mathbf{K}} \equiv \mathbf{K} - \Gamma'\cdot\mathbf{K}\cdot\Gamma$

Now cancel the omnipresent σ^2 but don't forget about it. This leaves:

$$\frac{1}{2}\cdot\left\{\frac{\chi}{\Delta t}-\kappa\right\}\cdot p_0^2+\kappa\cdot \mathbf{w}'\cdot \mathbf{s}\cdot p_0+\frac{1}{2}\cdot \mathbf{s}'\cdot \hat{\mathbf{K}}\cdot \mathbf{s}$$

$$= Max_p\left\{\left[\lambda\cdot\Delta t\cdot \mathbf{w}_Q'\cdot \mathbf{s}+\frac{\chi}{\Delta t}\cdot p_0+\kappa\cdot \mathbf{w}'\cdot\Gamma\cdot \mathbf{s}\right]\cdot p-\left[\frac{\lambda\cdot\Delta t+\chi/_{\Delta t}+\kappa}{2}\right]\cdot p^2\right\} \quad \text{(B12)}$$

The right-hand side of Equation (B12) has optimal solution and optimal value:

$$\text{Solution}\quad p\,(p_0,\mathbf{s})=\left\{\frac{\frac{\chi}{\Delta t}}{\lambda\cdot\Delta t+\frac{\chi}{\Delta t}+\kappa}\right\}\cdot p_0+\left\{\frac{\lambda\cdot\Delta t\cdot \mathbf{w}_Q'+\kappa\cdot \mathbf{w}'\cdot\Gamma}{\lambda\cdot\Delta t+\frac{\chi}{\Delta t}+\kappa}\right\}\cdot \mathbf{s}$$

$$\text{Value}\quad \left\{\frac{\lambda\cdot\Delta t+\frac{\chi}{\Delta t}+\kappa}{2}\right\}\cdot\{p\,(p_0,\mathbf{s})\}^2 \quad \text{(B13)}$$

The solution in Equation (B13) provides the linear trading rule. It will simplify a great deal in what follows. To get to the form of the linear trading rule we require the first bracketed expression in the solution must be δ. The task will be to show the second bracketed expression in the solution line is $(1-\delta)\cdot \mathbf{w}'$.

The value expression in Equation (B13) will help to get the job done. It contains the linear trading rule, $p\,(p_0, \mathbf{s})$ squared, so it is a quadratic function that will provide three terms: a p_0^2 term, a $p_0\cdot \mathbf{s}$ term, and a quadratic in s. For our purposes we only care about the first two. They must equal the terms with p_0 squared and with $p_0\cdot \mathbf{s}$ on the left side of Equation (B12).

For the quadratic function on the left side of Equation (B12) to be equal to quadratic equation on the value line of Equation (B13) for all values of $(p_0, \mathbf{s})$ means that their coefficients must be equal. This observation yields two relationships:

$$\frac{1}{2}\cdot\left\{\frac{\chi}{\Delta t}-\kappa\right\}=\left\{\frac{\lambda\cdot\Delta t+\frac{\chi}{\Delta t}+\kappa}{2}\right\}\cdot\left\{\frac{\frac{\chi}{\Delta t}}{\lambda\cdot\Delta t+\frac{\chi}{\Delta t}+\kappa}\right\}^2 \quad \text{for the } p_0^2 \text{ term}$$

and for the $\mathbf{s}\cdot p_0$ term: (B14)

$$\kappa\cdot \mathbf{w}=2\cdot\left\{\frac{\lambda\cdot\Delta t+\frac{\chi}{\Delta t}+\kappa}{2}\right\}\cdot\left\{\frac{\frac{\chi}{\Delta t}}{\lambda\cdot\Delta t+\frac{\chi}{\Delta t}+\kappa}\right\}\cdot\left\{\frac{\lambda\cdot\Delta t\cdot \mathbf{w}_Q+\kappa\cdot \mathbf{w}\cdot\Gamma}{\lambda\cdot\Delta t+\frac{\chi}{\Delta t}+\kappa}\right\}$$

Use the first relationship to calculate kappa.

$$\left\{\kappa+\lambda\cdot\Delta t+\frac{\chi}{\Delta t}\right\}\cdot\left\{\frac{\chi}{\Delta t}-\kappa\right\}=\left\{\frac{\chi}{\Delta t}\right\}^2$$

multiply out and cancel we end up with (B15)

$$\kappa^2+\kappa\cdot\lambda\cdot\Delta t-\chi\cdot\lambda=0$$

This quadratic is guaranteed to have two real roots, one positive and one negative. The positive root is our value of kappa. Note for Δt small, $\kappa \approx \sqrt{\lambda \cdot \chi}$.

Now we introduce delta and thus the trading rate.

$$\delta \equiv \frac{\frac{\chi}{\Delta t}}{\lambda \cdot \Delta t + \frac{\chi}{\Delta t} + \kappa} = e^{-d \cdot \Delta t}, \quad 1 - \delta = \frac{\lambda \cdot \Delta t + \kappa}{\lambda \cdot \Delta t + \frac{\chi}{\Delta t} + \kappa} \tag{B16}$$

With sufficient pulling and tugging the reader can establish several results that will be useful further on.

$$\begin{aligned}
&(i.) \quad \frac{\chi}{\Delta t} \cdot (1 - \delta) = \kappa \Rightarrow \frac{1-\delta}{\Delta t} = \frac{\kappa}{\chi} \approx d \\
&(ii.) \quad \kappa \approx \sqrt{\lambda \cdot \chi} \Rightarrow d \approx \sqrt{\frac{\lambda}{\chi}} \\
&(iii.) \quad \kappa + \lambda \cdot \Delta t = \frac{\lambda}{\frac{1-\delta}{\Delta t}} \Rightarrow \kappa \approx \frac{\lambda}{d} \\
&(iv.) \quad 1 - \delta = \frac{\lambda \cdot \Delta t}{\kappa + \lambda \cdot \Delta t} \Rightarrow \delta = \frac{\kappa}{\kappa + \lambda \cdot \Delta t}
\end{aligned} \tag{B17}$$

Now explore the $p_0 \cdot \mathbf{s}$ terms.

$$\begin{aligned}
&\left\{\kappa + \lambda \cdot \Delta t + \frac{\chi}{\Delta t}\right\} \cdot \kappa \cdot \mathbf{w} = \frac{\chi}{\Delta t} \cdot \left[\lambda \cdot \Delta t \cdot \mathbf{w}_Q + \kappa \cdot \Gamma \cdot \mathbf{w}\right], \text{ multiply by } \frac{\Delta t}{\chi} \\
&\left\{\kappa + \lambda \cdot \Delta t + \frac{\chi}{\Delta t}\right\} \cdot \left\{\frac{\kappa \cdot \Delta t}{\chi}\right\} \cdot \mathbf{w} = \{\kappa + \lambda \cdot \Delta t\} \cdot \left[\left\{\frac{\lambda \cdot \Delta t}{\kappa + \lambda \cdot \Delta t}\right\} \cdot \mathbf{w}_Q + \left\{\frac{\kappa}{\kappa + \lambda \cdot \Delta t}\right\} \cdot \Gamma \cdot \mathbf{w}\right] \\
&\text{but } \frac{\kappa \cdot \Delta t}{\chi} = \frac{\kappa + \lambda \cdot \Delta t}{\kappa + \lambda \cdot \Delta t + \frac{\chi}{\Delta t}} = 1 - \delta, \text{ so} \\
&\left\{\frac{\kappa \cdot \Delta t}{\chi}\right\} \cdot \mathbf{w} = \left\{\frac{\kappa + \lambda \cdot \Delta t}{\kappa + \lambda \cdot \Delta t + \frac{\chi}{\Delta t}}\right\} \cdot \left[(1-\delta) \cdot \mathbf{w}_Q + \delta \cdot \Gamma \cdot \mathbf{w}\right] \\
&\Rightarrow \mathbf{w} = (1-\delta) \cdot \mathbf{w}_Q + \delta \cdot \Gamma \cdot \mathbf{w} \\
&\Rightarrow w_j = \frac{1-\delta}{1 - \delta \cdot \gamma_j} \cdot w_{Q,j}
\end{aligned} \tag{B18}$$

Now we'll return to Equation (B13) and the linear trading rule:

$$\begin{aligned}
&p(p_0, \mathbf{s}) = \frac{\alpha(p_0, \mathbf{s})}{\beta} = \left\{\frac{\chi/_{\Delta t}}{\kappa + \lambda \cdot \Delta t + \chi/_{\Delta t}}\right\} \cdot p_0 + \left\{\frac{\lambda \cdot \Delta t \cdot \mathbf{w}'_Q + \kappa \cdot \mathbf{w}' \cdot \Gamma'}{\kappa + \lambda \cdot \Delta t + \chi/_{\Delta t}}\right\} \cdot \mathbf{s} \\
&p(p_0, \mathbf{s}) = \delta \cdot p_0 + \left\{\frac{\kappa + \lambda \cdot \Delta t}{\kappa + \lambda \cdot \Delta t + \chi/_{\Delta t}}\right\} \cdot \left\{\left\{\frac{\lambda \cdot \Delta t}{\kappa + \lambda \cdot \Delta t}\right\} \cdot \mathbf{w}'_Q + \left\{\frac{\kappa}{\kappa + \lambda \cdot \Delta t}\right\} \cdot \mathbf{w}' \cdot \Gamma'\right\} \cdot \mathbf{s} \\
&p(p_0, \mathbf{s}) = \delta \cdot p_0 + (1-\delta) \cdot \left\{(1-\delta) \cdot \mathbf{w}'_Q + \delta \cdot \mathbf{w}' \cdot \Gamma'\right\} \cdot \mathbf{s} \\
&\text{but } (1-\delta) \cdot \mathbf{w}_Q + \delta \cdot \Gamma \cdot \mathbf{w} = \mathbf{w} \text{ so} \\
&\qquad p(p_0, \mathbf{s}) = \delta \cdot p_0 + (1-\delta) \cdot \mathbf{w}' \cdot \mathbf{s}
\end{aligned} \tag{B19}$$

The bottom line using the notation of the chapter is:

$$
\begin{aligned}
&(i.) \quad \text{Given } \chi_n \text{ solve } \kappa_n^2 + \kappa_n \cdot \lambda \cdot \Delta t - \chi_n \cdot \lambda = 0 \text{ for } \kappa_n \\
&(ii.) \quad \text{Calculate } \delta_n = \frac{\kappa_n}{\kappa_n + \lambda \cdot \Delta t} \\
&(iii.) \quad \text{Calculate } w_{M(n),j} = \left\{ \frac{1 - \delta_n}{1 - \delta_n \cdot \gamma_j} \right\} \cdot w_{M(n),j}
\end{aligned}
\tag{B20}
$$

11

Nonlinear Trading Rules for Portfolio Management[1]

In "Linear Trading Rules for Portfolio Management," Grinold (2018) and Chapter 10 in this book, we addressed the challenge of dynamic portfolio management. We showed how an optimized dynamic policy called a linear trading rule (LTR) could be used to manage portfolios on an asset-by-asset basis. We also described how the information gained from the study of LTRs could be folded into a single-stage, multi-asset optimization that also considers factor positions, factor and sector risk, and constraints. We, in effect, harness the static optimization to implement the dynamic policy.

LTRs are optimal in special circumstances and should be a good starting point in more general circumstances. LTRs are also attractive because they come with a theory that provides analytic expressions for key expected attributes of a strategy: the alpha, risk, and transactions cost (t-cost), conditional on the single parameter that determines the LTR.

This article takes the concept further by introducing nonlinear trading rules (henceforth NLTRs). The NLTRs are also motivated by theory. However, they do not lead to formulas for expected alpha, risk, and t-cost. Instead, we rely on simulation to assess the expected performance using any rule. It is heavy-handed but it works.

Despite the technical nature of the material we have tried to keep the equations and related quant jargon to a minimum. The Appendices look at some of the technical aspects in more detail.

1. This chapter originally appeared as "Non-Linear Trading Rules for Portfolio Management" by Richard Grinold in the *Journal of Portfolio Management*, Fall 2018, 62–70.

NLTRs are built on the foundation of the LTRs. A review of LTRs will introduce the notation and terminology used throughout. After this review of LTRs, we consider a motivational example for one asset and one period. This simple example provides the form of the NLTR (Exhibit 1).

EXHIBIT 1 The Nonlinear Trading Rule

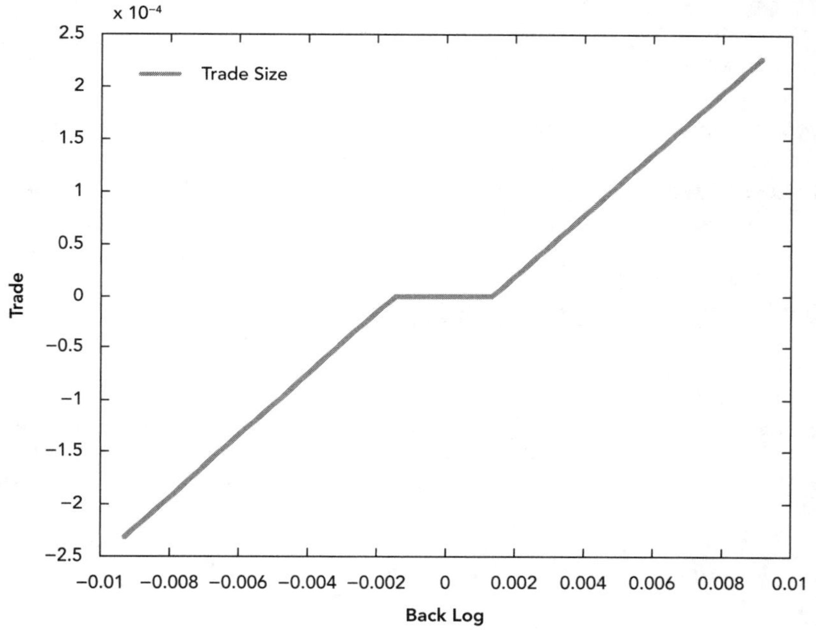

Thus encouraged, we set out to determine the best NLTR for each asset.

The first step is to describe and then validate the simulation/optimization approach. We can do this using LTRs since they, as mentioned above, are accompanied by analytic expressions for key performance measures (alpha, risk, t-cost). This allows us to check simulation results against the analytical results.

Step two is to establish a benchmark. To that end we introduce a quasi-dynamic version of one-stage optimization that we call TCAF. The benchmark is the best TCAF policy. There are now three policy choices in the mix: TCAF, LTR, and NLTR. We select the best policy in each class and compare the results.

Forecasts of future return are derived from a collection of signals, which are represented by standardized random variables with mean zero and standard deviation one. The signals are assumed to contain information about future return. The goal of the active portfolio manager is to obtain the most cost- and risk-effective exposures to the signals.

With the framework established, we test the process on a problem that is complicated enough to illustrate the concept and simple enough to be understood with a small amount of effort. The examples have three uncorrelated signals for each asset. The goal is to illustrate the methodology, not to swamp the reader in output. The technique is scalable. It has been used with up to 32 signals per asset and with significant correlations among the signals.

There are two reasonable measures of aggregate performance. The first is the form of a typical optimization criterion:

$$\text{Objective} \equiv \{\text{Alpha}\} - \frac{\lambda}{2} \cdot \{\text{Risk}\}^2 - \{\text{T-Cost}\}$$

In our case, all three quantities are expressed as annual rates; for example, T-Cost is the total transactions cost incurred for all assets over all periods divided by the number of years in the simulation.

The second measure is the after cost information ratio (ACIR):

$$\left\{\begin{matrix}\text{After Cost} \\ \text{Information Ratio}\end{matrix}\right\} = \frac{\{\text{Alpha}\} - \{\text{T-Cost}\}}{\{\text{Risk}\}}$$

If the risk levels of two strategies are the same, then the two measures will select the same winner in a two-strategy race. If the risk levels differ, then the ACIR is attractive for comparison, since its numerator tells us the expected performance and the ACIR itself provides an estimate of the probability of a negative year.[2] We will concentrate on the ACIR and try to keep the risk levels relatively close when comparing strategies. In the discussion to follow, *benefit* means annual *Alpha minus T-Cost* over the simulation (i.e., the numerator of the ACIR).

For our universe of 3,136 US assets the best LTR policy outperforms TCAF by 0.42% per year and the NLTR outperforms the LTR by 0.60% per year, making a net gain over TCAF of 1.02% per year. However, things didn't turn out quite so well in our universe of 200 Australian assets. The dynamic LTR policy adds 0.66% per year compared to the static TCAF policy, but the NLTR yield a disappointing 0.05% more per year as compared to the LTR, with a net gain of 0.71% per year over TCAF.[3]

In addition to the NLTRs performance, another benefit is restrained trading. An LTR will suggest a trade in each period for each asset—a potential operational nightmare. The typical NLTR used in our results trades 28% of the time, although the trades, when they do occur, are on average about three times larger.

2. If the ACIR equals 0.75 and the active returns minus t-cost are normal, then Prob($Z < -0.75$) = 0.23 gives us the probability of a down year even if our alpha forecasts are as good as we assumed they are.

3. The Australian t-cost model is a linear plus a quadratic term, for example Equation (6). In this case, the LTR model gives the optimal solution if the linear t-cost term is zero and should be close to optimal when the linear t-cost term is small. As a test, we multiplied the linear t-cost coefficient by 5 and solved again. Indeed, we saw a benefit of about 0.40% using the NLTR in that case.

The approach is restricted to predictions of specific asset return. This allows us to consider each asset in isolation.[4] We do not consider factor returns, smart beta tilts, industry timing, or sector returns, although the NLTR can be integrated with a larger process that does consider those aggregate aspects. Aside from the limitation to a single asset, the approach is general. It will work with any number of signals. We need to know about the strength (forecasting potential) of the signal and the nature of the process generating the signal. That process can be smooth, can have jumps, or can allow for different rates of information flow at different points in the year. It must be mean reverting, reflecting the fact that old information eventually loses its value and new information arrives, randomly, to replace it. Otherwise, if you can specify it, you can use it.

There is considerable literature on the topic of portfolio optimization with transactions costs.[5] Most of the theoretical work uses linear (proportional) transactions cost, although Grinold (2018) (Chapter 10 in this book) and Garleanu and Pederson (2009) consider quadratic transactions cost with no proportional (linear) cost. We will follow industry practice and the LTR paper and consider the case with both proportional cost *and* significant nonlinear costs due to market impact. The unique perspective in this and the LTR article is restricting attention to policies with a specified structure and limiting attention to a single asset. This allows us to obtain good solutions to an otherwise intractable stochastic dynamic programming problem.[6] For more on the simulation/optimization approach, see Powell (2011).

Zero Cost and Target Signal Weights

The following results are available in Chapter 10 on LTRs and its technical appendices. The terminology is from Grinold and Kahn (2000).

There are J signals whose forecasting ability is measured by the correlation of the signal with the return. This correlation is called the *information coefficient*. From this information, we can calculate the weights on the signals one would use with no transactions costs. These weights, called the *zero-cost weights*, are denoted $w_{Q(n),j}$ for asset n and signal j. In most of what follows, we will drop the notation n referring to asset n. The reader gets the benefit of cleaner notation and the attendant obligation to remember that all the results are asset specific.

4. In practice, this means we either ignore any significant correlation of signals across assets or find other way to incorporate that information. This is discussed in Grinold (2018), on "Linear Trading Rules for Portfolio Management," Chapter 10 in this book.

5. See Boyd et al (2017) for current practice in portfolio optimization, along with an extensive bibliography.

6. We came to the simulation/optimization approach in a roundabout manner. The LTR parameters could be selected analytically. We used a simulation to demonstrate that the analytic predictions were accurate. They were. Next, we asked if we could choose the trade rate parameter using the simulation, and would it be near the analytic value? We could, and it was. Then the penny dropped, and we cast about for references.

The zero-cost weights $w_{Q,j}$ are determined by the assumed information coefficients, any correlation among the signals, and a risk penalty parameter. Equation (1) shows the calculation.[7]

$$\begin{array}{ll} \iota_j & \text{the information coefficient for signal } j \\ \sigma & \text{specific risk} \\ \lambda & \text{a penalty for risk} \\ R_{j,k} & \text{the correlation between signals } j \text{ and } k \\ w_{Q,j} & \text{the zero-cost weight on signal } j \\ \multicolumn{2}{l}{\iota_k = \lambda \cdot \sigma \cdot \sum_{j=1:J} R_{K,j} \cdot w_{Q,j},\ J \text{ equations to be solved for } w_{Q,j}} \end{array} \tag{1}$$

The zero-cost weights play two roles. The first is the calculation of alpha, as per Equation (2):

$$\begin{aligned} \alpha(t) &= \lambda \cdot \sigma^2 \cdot q(t) \text{ where} \\ q(t) &= \sum_{j=1:J} s_j(t) \cdot w_{Q,j} \end{aligned} \tag{2}$$

The second role for the zero-cost weights is to serve as the foundation in the calculation of the target weights. Both the LTR and NLTR attempt to track a target (or model) position, denoted $m(t)$. The target is determined by a set of weights, $w_{M,j}$. We will take some time to show how these target/model weights are calculated since they are at the heart of the process.

The target weights determine the position that we should hold absent transactions cost on our *next* trade. In contrast, the zero-cost weights, $w_{Q,j}$, determine the position we should hold absent transactions cost in the next period and *all* subsequent periods.

The target weights, $w_{M,j}$, are a discounted version of the zero-cost weights that take into consideration both the rate at which we trade and the rate at which the signals' information gets stale. A description of the target weights requires the notation in Equation (3) and a review of the LTR. As a reminder, the results in Equations (1) to (4), with the exception of the risk penalty λ, are asset specific.

$$\begin{array}{ll} s_j(t) & \text{the value of signal } j \text{ at time } t \\ m(t) & \text{the target position at time } t \\ w_{M,j} & \text{the target weights, to be determined} \\ \multicolumn{2}{l}{m(t) = \sum_{j=1:J} s_j(t) \cdot w_{M,j}} \\ \Delta t & \text{the length of a trading period} \\ p(t - \Delta t) & \text{the initial, pre-trade, position} \\ p(t) & \text{the final, post-trade, position} \\ \Delta p(t) & \text{the trade, } p(t) - p(t - \Delta t) \end{array} \tag{3}$$

7. Grinold (2018) (Chapter 10, "Linear Trading Rules for Portfolio Management" in this book) used a top-down approach to the weighting question in contrast to the bottom-up approach we take here. The Appendix shows how the two approaches are equivalent, subject to certain assumptions.

The LTR depends on a positive trading rate d_ℓ with the ℓ standing for linear. The resulting LTR is described in Equation (4):

$$\begin{aligned}&\delta_\ell \equiv e^{-d_\ell \cdot \Delta t} \text{ is the retention fraction}\\&\Delta p(t) = (1-\delta_\ell)\cdot\{m(t) - p(t-\Delta t)\}\\&\frac{\Delta p(t)}{\Delta t} \approx d_\ell \cdot \{m(t) - p(t)\} \text{ for } \Delta t \text{ small}\end{aligned} \tag{4}$$

The LTR paper shows how to make an optimal choice of d_ℓ hence δ_ℓ.

The third item that influences the target weights is the rate at which information loses its forecasting ability, as measured by the half-lives of the signals.

$$\begin{aligned}&HL_j \quad \text{the half-life of signal } j \text{ in years}\\&e^{-g_j \cdot HL_j} = 0.5 \Rightarrow g_j = \ln(2)/HL_j, \text{ decay rate}\\&\gamma_j \equiv e^{-g_j \cdot \Delta t} \text{ signal retained in one period}\end{aligned} \tag{5}$$

The formula for $w_{M,j}$, developed in the LTR paper, combines these three things—the zero-cost weights $w_{Q,j}$, the trading policy, δ_ℓ, and the decay of information, γ_j—to calculate the target weights:

$$w_{M,j} = \left\{\frac{1-\delta_\ell}{1-\delta_\ell \cdot \gamma_j}\right\} \cdot w_{Q,j} \text{ the target signal weights} \tag{6}$$

These are the weights used throughout the paper to determine the target position as per Equation (3). Again, note that both δ_ℓ and $w_{Q,j}$ are asset specific, and the set of signals could be asset specific as well.

Exhibit 2 contains an example of the signal weight calculation and introduces the three signals used in our illustrative calculations. The numbers in Exhibit 2 are for a universe of 3,136 US stocks and an asset with median volatility and transactions cost. We use 252 trading days per year, so $\Delta t = 1/252$. Note the steep discount in the weight of the FAST signal: the target weight is 4% of the zero-cost weight. Things are not so drastic for the SLOW signal where the discounted target weight is 76% of the zero-cost weight.

EXHIBIT 2 The Signals and Typical Weights

SIGNAL	IC	HL (years)	w_Q	w_M
FAST	0.179	2/252	0.04790	0.00188
INT.	0.036	63/252	0.00951	0.00497
SLOW	0.020	189/252	0.00540	0.00415

The three-signal framework is for illustration only. The technique is scalable. We have solved problems with up to 32 signals per asset and with some significant correlations among the signals. See Grinold (2018), Chapter 10 in this book, for a discussion of natural limitations on signal correlation.

Motivation: A Single-Period Model

The form of the NLTR policy comes from an examination of a one-period problem where the objective is to minimize a penalty for being off target plus the transactions cost due to a change in position. Since this is a one-period problem, we'll drop the time notation and let p_0 represent the initial position. The risk penalty is λ, the asset's specific volatility is σ, and the target position is denoted m.

$$\begin{aligned}
&\kappa(\Delta p \mid m, p_0) \quad \text{the penalty for being off target} \\
&\kappa(\Delta p \mid m, p_0) \equiv \frac{\lambda \cdot \sigma^2}{2} \cdot \{m - (p_0 + \Delta p)\}^2 \\
&c(\Delta p) \qquad \text{the transactions cost} \\
&c(\Delta p) \equiv c_1 \cdot |\Delta p| + \frac{c_2}{2} \cdot |\Delta p|^2 \\
&\kappa(\Delta p \mid m, p_0) + c(\Delta p) \quad \text{The objective}
\end{aligned} \tag{7}$$

The goal is to track the target while keeping transactions costs under control.[8]

If are fortunate enough to start on target ($p_0 = m$), then the best decision is stay put ($\Delta p = 0$). If the starting position is below target ($p_0 < m$), the question is how much to buy, if any. When we start above target ($m < p_0$), we ask how much, if any, to sell. The driver of the decision is the initial deviation from target. That deviation is called the *backlog* as it represents the amount of trading required to get on target.

We leave to the reader to check that that Equation (8) provides the optimal policy:

$$\begin{aligned}
&b \equiv m - p_0 \quad \text{the backlog} \\
&z \equiv \frac{c_1}{\lambda \cdot \sigma^2} \text{ is the size of the no trade zone} \\
&\delta \equiv \frac{c_2}{\lambda \cdot \sigma^2 + c_2} \text{ fraction of the initial position that is retained} \\
&\Delta p = \begin{Bmatrix} (1-\delta)\cdot(b-z) \text{ if } b > z & \text{BUY} \\ 0 \quad \text{if } \; -z \le b \le z & \text{HOLD} \\ (1\text{-}\delta)\cdot(b+z) \;\text{ if } b < -z & \text{SELL} \end{Bmatrix} \text{ the NLTR}
\end{aligned} \tag{8}$$

In Exhibit 1 above, the slope of the lines is $\left(1-\delta\right) \le 1$. The flat part of the curve is the no-trade zone. Two special cases are worth noting: first, the NLTR includes the LTR as a special case (i.e., with $c_1 = 0$ we get $z = 0$); second, in the case where there is no nonlinear term in the transactions cost ($c_2 = 0$), we get $\delta = 0$, and the optimal policy is stay put or move to the closest

8. This expression could be rewritten in the traditional form of an alpha minus a penalty for risk and any transactions cost. However, the alpha in that expression would then be confused with the actual alpha of Equation (2). A penalty for being off track seemed less confusing.

edge of the no-trade zone because $c_2 = 0$ means the slope of the NLTR line is one.

Equation (7) provides the template. The remaining task is to find the best values of the parameters (δ, z) for each asset.[9]

Simulation/Optimization[10]

We use a simulation and optimization process (sim/opt) to select the NLTR parameters, (δ, z). We are tuning the implementation engine for future use conditional on assumed signal strength and behavior. We are not evaluating past signal performance.

The sim/opt algorithm for any asset is:

1. Compute the best LTR, δ_ℓ, using the analytical results presented in the LTR article.
2. Compute the target weights, $w_{M,j}$, using the process described in Equations (3) through (5).
3. Simulate the signals $s_j(t)$ for $j = 1{:}J$ and $t = 0{:}T$. This, combined with the signal weights, provides the time series of target values, $m(t)$ as per Equation (3).
4. Choose a time-zero position, $p(0)$. This can, with no loss in accuracy if T is large, be on target, $p(0) = m(0)$; if you are a purist, you can use the more elaborate process detailed in the LTR article.[11]
5. Systematically explore the space of possible trading rules and select the one with the highest annualized risk-adjusted alpha less transactions cost.

This process works.

Validation

To validate the approach, we compared the results from Chapter 10 on linear trading rules and the sim/opt algorithm detailed above with the no-trade zone set to zero, that is $z = 0$ in Equation (8). When the no-trade zone is zero, we can calculate the optimal trade parameter without resort to simulation. Solving the same problem with the sim/opt approach gives a direct comparison.

9. This motivating discussion is based on the form of transactions cost in Equation (7). For our US assets the nonlinear cost term increases with the 3/2 power, not the square. See Appendix C for an argument boosting the NLTR form in Equation (8) as an approximation when the 3/2 power rule is used.

10. We were tempted to call this *front testing* to emphasize that it has nothing to do with backtesting, a process that can generate more noise than insight.

11. Under an LTR the position, $p(t)$, at any time can be represented as a linear mix of the signals with a third set of weights, w_p, determining the mix plus a residual that is uncorrelated with the signals. Both w_p and the standard deviation of the residual are known, so it is straightforward to generate a time-zero position conditional on the initial value of the signals plus a random residual.

The results are in Exhibit 3. We used a sample of 3,136 US stocks. The risk penalty parameter was $\lambda = 22$. The transactions cost are the 3/2 power variety, and the signals had the properties described in Exhibit 2. The results are based on one rebalance each trading day, with 252 trading days per year and a 100-year simulation. These are aggregate, portfolio-level results. The three columns in Exhibit 3 are, respectively, THEORY where the optimal trade rate is selected analytically, IN SAMPLE, in which the trade rate is selected by the simulation/optimization algorithm described earlier and evaluated using the same sample, and OUT SAMPLE in which the trade rates selected by the sim/opt algorithm are evaluated on a new set of data.

EXHIBIT 3 Validation Results

	THEORY	IN SAMPLE	OUT SAMPLE
Alpha %	4.65	4.56	4.57
Risk %	3.32	3.27	3.29
T-Cost $	2.10	2.06	2.12
Alpha – TC	2.56	2.50	2.46
ACIR	0.77	0.77	0.75

The details of these calculations are in Appendix B.

TCAF: A Static Benchmark

Equation (7) describes an objective that balances between a penalty for being off target and the cost for moving toward the target. The penalty for being off target is annualized, that is, it is the penalty for being a certain distance from target for a year, expressed as a loss in annual return. The transactions cost term represents a loss in return incurred at a point in time. Suppose, for the sake of argument, that the trade keeps us the same distance from the target for four months and then we go back to the initial situation. To get an apples-to-apples annual run-rate comparison, we must reinvest, that is, incur the t-cost again, at four months and again at eight months to stay at the same distance from target for the entire year. In this case the proper objective would be $\kappa(\Delta p \mid m, p_0) + 3 \cdot c(\Delta p)$ because we have to pay the t-cost three times per year to keep up. If, on the other hand, the trade would keep us the same distance from target for two years, then $\kappa(\Delta p \mid m, p_0) + 0.5 \cdot c(\Delta p)$ would be more appropriate. In general, we want to use the criterion:

$$\kappa(\Delta p \mid m, p_0) + \tau \cdot c(\Delta p) \qquad (9)$$

where τ is an amortization factor used to annualize the t-cost.[12] The TCAF strategy uses the simulation/optimization algorithm to find the best value for the amortization factor τ.

12. The choice is inescapable. Ignore it and you have selected $\tau = 1$.

The TCAF strategy works as follows. The sim/opt procedure provides the time series values of the target, $m(t)$. We choose a value of τ. Then we choose Δp at each point in time using Equation (9) as a criterion. Finally, the performance of the resulting sequence of positions and trades is tallied up in the manner described in Appendix B. The value of τ that yields the best performance is selected as the TCAF policy parameter for that asset.

NLTR Results

An LTR does better than the optimized single-stage benchmark TCAF. The NLTR is an improvement over the LTR in the larger universe of US stocks although it only a slight improvement in the smaller universe of 200 Australian assets. The aggregate US results are in Exhibit 4. The risk penalty was varied in each case to get the risk level approximately the same for each type of policy.

EXHIBIT 4 Results for the 3,136 US Assets Using Three Different Policies

USA	TCAF	LTR	NLTR
Alpha %	2.71	4.66	5.14
Risk %	3.27	3.32	3.21
T-Cost %	0.57	2.10	1.98
Alpha – TC	2.14	2.56	3.16
ACIR	0.66	0.77	0.98

The LTR and NLTR rules lead to more trading. With the TCAF rule some 996 high transactions cost assets do not trade at all.

The results for the universe of 200 Australian assets are contained in Exhibit 5. Comparisons of the NLTR results using the sim/opt and model parameters for the United States and Australia are given in Exhibits 6 and 7.

EXHIBIT 5 Results for 200 Australian Assets Using Three Different Policies

AUS	TCAF	LTR	NLTR
Alpha %	4.86	6.65	6.66
Risk %	3.94	3.93	3.91
T-Cost %	0.66	1.79	1.75
Alpha – TC	4.20	4.86	4.91
ACIR	1.07	1.24	1.26

$\lambda = 19$ for TCAF and $\lambda = 25$ for LTR and NLTR.

The Parameter Model

The sim/opt procedure is a blunt instrument doing precision work. The choice of parameters (δ, z) is a delicate matter. For a typical asset the performance benefit of the optimal NLTR over the best policy with $z = 0$ (i.e., the LTR) is about 2 or 3 basis points per century! Because this sensitive choice is based on simulated data, we should expect considerable noise in the chosen policy parameters. To mitigate the noise, we built a cross-sectional model for the parameters using a log-log regression framework.

Subscript n refers to asset n

$$\delta_n = e^{-d_n \cdot \Delta t} \Rightarrow d_n = -\ln(\delta_n) / \Delta t$$

The Cross Sectional Regressions

$$\ln(d_n) = \beta_1 + \beta_2 \cdot \ln(c_{1,n}) + \beta_3 \cdot \ln(c_{2,n}) + \beta_4 \cdot \ln(\sigma_n) + \xi_n \tag{10}$$

$$\ln(z_n) = \phi_1 + \phi_2 \cdot \ln(c_{1,n}) + \phi_3 \cdot \ln(c_{2,n}) + \phi_4 \cdot \ln(\sigma_n) + \varsigma_n$$

The Fitted Values

$$\hat{d}_n = d_n \cdot e^{-\xi_n}, \quad \hat{z}_n = z_n \cdot e^{-\varsigma_n}$$

In Equation (10), d_n, z_n are the parameters selected by the sim/opt algorithm. The idea is that the fitted values will filter the noise from sim/opt process without losing the essence of the NLTR. This turns out to be the case since a NLTR based on the fitted values $\left(\hat{d}_n, \hat{z}_n\right)$ performs just as well as the original parameters, with a lower cross-sectional variation in the parameter values.

The parameter model has the additional benefit of producing a NLTR for a new asset as long as we have t-cost and volatility estimates. In the same fashion, the parameter model can be used to update the trading rules, without resort to sim/opt, when an asset's t-cost and volatility estimates change.[13]

EXHIBIT 6 Comparison of NLTR Results for the US Using the Sim/Opt Parameters and the Model Parameters

USA	NLTR	NLTR FIT
Alpha %	5.14	5.19
Risk %	3.21	3.22
T-Cost %	1.98	2.05
Alpha – TC	3.16	3.14
ACIR	0.98	0.98

13. There are more details on the parameter model in Appendix D.

EXHIBIT 7 Comparison of NLTR Results for Australia Using the Sim/Opt Parameters and the Model Parameters

AUS	NLTR	NLTR FIT
Alpha %	6.66	6.65
Risk %	3.91	1.93
T-Cost %	1.75	1.76
Alpha – TC	4.91	4.90
ACIR	1.26	1.25

Implementation

In the LTR chapter, we discussed at length how the information from an optimized LTR could be exploited to turn a single-stage portfolio optimizer into a dynamic optimizer. The same idea works with the NLTR. In this case, we associate a term for each asset that penalizes deviations from model position and a modified version of the transaction costs.

For each asset there is a penalty

$$\frac{\lambda \cdot \sigma^2}{2}(m - (p_0 + \Delta p))^2 + \hat{c}(\Delta p)$$

where

$$m = \sum_{j=1:J} s_j \cdot w_{M,j} \text{ is the target} \tag{11}$$

$$\hat{c}(\Delta p) = \hat{c}_1 \cdot |\Delta p| + \frac{\hat{c}_2}{2} \cdot |\Delta p|^2 \text{ where}$$

$$\hat{c}_1 = \lambda \cdot \sigma^2 \cdot z, \;\; \hat{c}_2 = \lambda \cdot \sigma^2 \cdot \frac{\delta}{1 - \delta}$$

The first term is unchanged from Equation (7). It is a penalty for the deviation from target. The second term has been altered. The initial transactions costs (c_1, c_2) are gone, and instead the NLTR parameters are used to determine a modified t-cost. The original t-cost information is imbedded in the policy parameters. We use this form even if we started with a 3/2 power transactions cost model.

Summary

This chapter is a continuation of the chapter on linear trading rules. The essential notion in both is a dynamic view of the portfolio optimization challenge. In its full complexity, dynamic portfolio optimization is an overwhelming task, at least with current technology and human capital.[14] However, if we consider the assets one at a time and restrict ourselves to trading policies in a class, such as linear trading rules, or nonlinear trading rules, we gain entry into otherwise obscure space and can optimize the trading policy subject to retaining its form.

Additional key points are as follows:

- Signal weights and trading policy should be asset specific.
- The NLTR and LTR dynamic policies offer significant benefits when compared with an optimized static policy.
- The policy parameter model of Equation (10) is an essential part of the process, akin to a cabinet maker sanding the rough edges.

Aside from these specifics the most significant point is moving from a static mindset to a dynamic one when addressing the portfolio management challenge.

References

Boyd, Stephen, Enzo Busseti, Stephen Diamond, Ronald N. Kahn, Kwangmoo Koh, P. Nystrup, and Jan Speth. 2017. "Multi-Period Trading via Convex Optimization." *Foundations and Trends in Optimization* 3 (1): 1–76.

Garleanu, Nicolae, and Lasse Pedersen. 2009. "Dynamic Trading with Predictable Returns and Transactions Costs." NBER Working Paper # 15205, revised 2013.

Grinold, Richard. "Linear Trading Rules for Portfolio Management." 2018. *Journal of Portfolio Management* 44 (6), Special Stephen Ross Issue, 109–19.

Grinold, Richard, and Ronald N. Kahn. 2000. *Active Portfolio Management.* 2nd ed. New York: McGraw Hill.

Powell, William B. 2011. *Approximate Dynamic Programming: Solving the Curses of Dimensionality.* 2nd ed. Wiley Series in Probability and Statistics. Hoboken: Wiley.

14. For example, with 2,000 assets, 19 signals, and one position per asset, the state space is 20*2,000 = 40,000 real numbers. If you discretize with 10 discrete values along each dimension, then the dynamic programming state space is 10 to the 40,000th power.

CHAPTER 11
Nonlinear Trading Rules for Portfolio Management

Appendix A

Bottom-Up and Top-Down Zero Cost Weights

There are two approaches to getting signal weights. The first is a top-down portfolio approach used in the LTR paper, Grinold (2018) and Chapter 10 in this book. The second is a bottom-up asset-by-asset approach used in the NLTR paper. Beware; the notation can be deceptive. We use the Greek ω for the portfolio level risk allocations and the similar looking Roman **w** for the asset level signal weights.

$$\begin{aligned} &\vec{\omega}_Q = \{\omega_{Q,j}\}_{j=1:J} \text{ signal portfolio } j\text{'s zero-cost risk allocations} \\ &\mathbf{w}_{Q(n)} = \{w_{Q(n),j}\}_{j=1:J} \text{ asset } n\text{'s zero-cost signal weights} \end{aligned} \tag{A1}$$

The signals are:

$$\begin{aligned} &s_{n,j}(t) \text{ signal for asset } n, \text{ signal } j \text{ at time } t. \\ &E\langle s_{n,j}(t)\rangle = 0, \quad E\langle s_{n,j}^2(t)\rangle = 1 \\ &E\langle s_{n,j}(t)\cdot s_{\ell,k}(t)\rangle = \begin{Bmatrix} R_{j,k} & \text{if } n=\ell \\ 0 & \text{if } n\neq\ell \end{Bmatrix} \end{aligned} \tag{A2}$$

Top-Down

We use the signals to construct signal portfolios that have expected risk of 100%:

$$\begin{aligned} &h_{n,j}(t) \text{ position of asset } n, \text{ signal portfolio } j, \text{ time } t \\ &h_{n,j}(t) \equiv \frac{s_{n,j}(t)}{\sigma_n\cdot\sqrt{N}} \Rightarrow E\left\langle \sum_{n=1:N}\{\sigma_n\cdot h_{n,j}(t)\}^2\right\rangle = 1 \\ &E\left\langle \sum_{n=1:N}\{\sigma_n^2\cdot h_{n,j}(t)\cdot h_{n,k}(t)\}\right\rangle = R_{j,k} \end{aligned} \tag{A3}$$

The information ratio for a signal portfolio is the same as its annual alpha since the risk is one. In this spirit we have:

$$\vec{\kappa} = \{\kappa_j\}_{j=1:J} \text{ Annual alpha following strategy } j$$
$$\vec{\omega}_Q = \{\omega_{Q,j}\}_{j=1:J} \text{ Risk allocation to strategy } j$$
$$\vec{\kappa}' \cdot \vec{\omega}_Q = \sum_{j=1:J} \kappa_j \cdot \omega_{Q,j} \text{ Annual alpha with risk allocation } \vec{\omega}_Q \tag{A4}$$
$$\vec{\omega}_Q' \cdot \mathbf{R} \cdot \vec{\omega}_Q \text{ Variance with risk allocation } \vec{\omega}_Q$$

If we use the parameter lambda to penalize variance then we can select an efficient risk allocation by solving:

$$\text{Maximize } \quad \vec{\kappa}' \cdot \vec{\omega} - \frac{\lambda}{2} \cdot \vec{\omega}' \cdot \mathbf{R} \cdot \vec{\omega}$$
$$\text{The solution is } \quad \vec{\omega}_Q = \frac{\mathbf{R}^{-1} \cdot \vec{\kappa}}{\lambda} \text{ with properties}$$
$$\text{Alpha } \quad \vec{\kappa}' \cdot \vec{\omega}_Q = \frac{\vec{\kappa}' \cdot \mathbf{R}^{-1} \cdot \vec{\kappa}}{\lambda} \tag{A5}$$
$$\text{Risk } \quad \sqrt{\vec{\omega}_Q' \cdot \mathbf{R} \cdot \vec{\omega}_Q} = \frac{\sqrt{\vec{\kappa}' \cdot \mathbf{R}^{-1} \cdot \vec{\kappa}}}{\lambda}$$
$$\text{Information Ratio } \quad \frac{\vec{\kappa}' \cdot \vec{\omega}_Q}{\sqrt{\vec{\omega}_Q' \cdot \mathbf{R} \cdot \vec{\omega}_Q}} = \sqrt{\vec{\kappa}' \cdot \mathbf{R}^{-1} \cdot \vec{\kappa}}$$

The zero-cost portfolio at time t is:

$$q_n(t) = \sum_{j=1:J} h_{n,j}(t) \cdot \omega_{Q,j} = \sum_{j=1:J} \frac{s_{n,j}(t)}{\sigma_n \cdot \sqrt{N}} \cdot \omega_{Q,j}$$

or in terms of signal weights

$$q_n(t) = \sum_{j=1:J} s_{n,j}(t) \cdot \left\{ \frac{\omega_{Q,j}}{\sigma_n \cdot \sqrt{N}} \right\} = \sum_{j=1:J} s_{n,j}(t) \cdot w_{Q(n),j} \tag{A6}$$
$$\Rightarrow \mathbf{w}_{Q(n)} = \frac{\vec{\omega}_Q}{\sigma_n \cdot \sqrt{N}} = \frac{\mathbf{R}^{-1} \cdot \vec{\kappa}}{\lambda \cdot \sigma_n \cdot \sqrt{N}}$$

Bottom-Up

We start with the correlations of signals and returns termed *information coefficients.*

$$\vec{\iota}_n = \{\iota_{n,j}\}_{j=1:J} \text{ information coefficients, asset } n \text{, signal } j$$
$$\tilde{\theta}_n \text{ specific return on asset } n \tag{A7}$$
$$\iota_{n,j} = corr\langle \tilde{\theta}_n, \tilde{s}_{n,j} \rangle$$

Use the best linear unbiased estimator to get a forecast of return. We take some liberties and call it a conditional expectation.

$$\begin{aligned}
&\alpha_n(\mathbf{s}) = E\langle\tilde{\theta}_n|\tilde{\mathbf{s}}_n = \mathbf{s}\rangle = Cov\,\langle\tilde{\theta}_n, \tilde{\mathbf{s}}_n\rangle \cdot Var^{-1}\langle\tilde{\mathbf{s}}_n\rangle \cdot \{\mathbf{s}_n - E\langle\tilde{\mathbf{s}}_n\rangle\} \\
&E\langle\tilde{\mathbf{s}}_n\rangle = 0 \\
&Var^{-1}\langle\tilde{\mathbf{s}}_n\rangle = \mathbf{R}^{-1} \\
&Cov\langle\tilde{\theta}_n, \tilde{\mathbf{s}}_n\rangle = \sigma_n \cdot \vec{\iota}_n' \\
&\Rightarrow \alpha_n(\mathbf{s}) = \sigma_n \cdot \vec{\iota}_n' \cdot \mathbf{R}^{-1} \cdot \mathbf{s}
\end{aligned} \tag{A8}$$

Choose the zero-cost position for asset n by solving:

$$\begin{aligned}
&\text{Maximize } \alpha_n(\mathbf{s}) \cdot q - \frac{\lambda}{2} \cdot \sigma_n^2 \cdot q^2 \\
&\Rightarrow q_n(\mathbf{s}) = \frac{\alpha_n(\mathbf{s})}{\lambda \cdot \sigma_n^2} = \frac{\vec{\iota}_n' \cdot \mathbf{R}^{-1} \cdot \mathbf{s}}{\lambda \cdot \sigma_n} = \mathbf{w}_{Q(n)}' \cdot \mathbf{s} \\
&\Rightarrow \mathbf{w}_{Q(n)} = \frac{\mathbf{R}^{-1} \cdot \iota_n}{\lambda \cdot \sigma_n}
\end{aligned} \tag{A9}$$

How do we square the results of Equations (A6) and (A9)? Consider the special case where the information coefficients are not asset dependent, thus $\iota_{n,j} = \iota_j$ for all n. In addition, use the fundamental law approximation in Grinold (1989) for each signal, that is, $\kappa_j \approx \iota_j \cdot \sqrt{N}$. If we take this approximation as gospel then Equation (A6) becomes:

$$\mathbf{w}_{Q(n)} = \frac{\mathbf{R}^{-1} \cdot \vec{\kappa}}{\lambda \cdot \sigma_n \cdot \sqrt{N}} = \frac{\mathbf{R}^{-1} \cdot \vec{\iota} \cdot \sqrt{N}}{\lambda \cdot \sigma_n \cdot \sqrt{N}} = \frac{\mathbf{R}^{-1} \cdot \vec{\iota}}{\lambda \cdot \sigma_n} \tag{A10}$$

which agrees with Equation (A9).

The bottom-up approach allows for more flexibility by allowing signal weights to vary by sector/industry or by type of asset.

CHAPTER 11
Nonlinear Trading Rules for Portfolio Management

Appendix B

Policy Evaluation

We obtain the zero-cost signal weights, $w_{Q(n),j}$, using the bottom-up procedure described in Appendix A. Then we use the LTR paper's results to obtain an optimal LTR trading rate d_n and corresponding retention fraction $\delta_n = \exp\left(-d_n \cdot \Delta t\right)$. Then, in the manner outlined in this chapter's main text, we calculate the target weights:

$$w_{M(n),j} = \frac{1-\delta_n}{1-\delta_n \cdot \gamma_j} \cdot w_{Q(n),j} \tag{B1}$$

Next step is to simulate the signals and an initial position:[15]

$$\begin{aligned} &s_{n,j}\left(t\right) n=1:N, j=1:J, t=0:T \\ &p_n\left(0\right) = \sum_{j=1:J} s_{n,j}\left(0\right) \cdot w_{P(n),j} + r_n\left(0\right) \end{aligned} \tag{B2}$$

This allows us to calculate:

$$\begin{aligned} &q_n\left(t\right) = \sum_{j=1:J} s_{n,j}\left(t\right) \cdot w_{Q(n),j} \quad \text{optimal zero-cost positions} \\ &m_n\left(t\right) = \sum_{j=1:J} s_{n,j}\left(t\right) \cdot w_{M(n),j} \quad \text{target positions} \\ &\alpha_n\left(t\right) = \lambda \cdot \sigma_n^2 \cdot q_n\left(t\right) \qquad \text{alphas} \end{aligned} \tag{B3}$$

A *policy* is a function that takes an initial holding and current signals and determines a new holding:

$$p_n\left(t\right) = f_n\left[s_n\left(t\right), p_n\left(t-\Delta t\right)\right] \tag{B4}$$

15. Appendix A of the LTR chapter shows how to calculate $w_{P(n)}$ and the standard deviation of the residual, $r_n(0)$. The presumption is that you have been using a LTR up to time 0 and then switch to a new policy. If T is large, the initial position is of no importance.

Using any policy along with the initial position and the simulated signals we can determine the sequence of positions and trades:

$$p_n(t) \quad t = 1:T$$
$$\Delta p_n(t) \quad t = 1:T \tag{B5}$$

The history, Equation (B5), allows us to calculate annualized alpha, variance, and cost for each asset:

$$\alpha_{P(n)} = \frac{1}{T} \cdot \sum_{t=1:T} \alpha_n(t) \cdot p_n(t)$$
$$\sigma^2_{P(n)} = \frac{\sigma^2_n}{T} \cdot \sum_{t=1:T} p^2_n(t) \tag{B6}$$
$$c_{P(n)} = \frac{c_{1,n} \cdot \sum_{t=1:T} \left|\Delta p_n(t)\right| + \frac{c_{\phi,n}}{\phi} \cdot \sum_{t=1:T} \left|\Delta p_n(t)\right|^{\phi}}{T \cdot \Delta t}, \quad \phi = 1.5 \text{ or } 2$$

Note that $T \cdot \Delta t$ is the number of years in the simulation, thus $c_{P(n)}$ is the annual rate of t-cost expense for asset n, following this policy.

The figure of merit for asset n is:

$$V_{P(n)} = \alpha_{P(n)} - c_{P(n)} - \frac{\lambda}{2} \cdot \sigma^2_{P(n)} \tag{B7}$$

In the three cases used in the chapter, the policy function depends on:

- MYOPIC (i.e. TCAF): the amortization parameter τ
- LTR: the trade rate parameter d
- NLTR: the no-trade zone z and the slope $(1 - \delta)$

The policy parameters are selected to maximize $V_{P(n)}$.

The aggregate measures of performance are:

$$\alpha_P \equiv \sum_{n=1:N} \alpha_{P(n)}, \quad c_P \equiv \sum_{n=1:N} c_{P(n)}, \quad \sigma^2_P \equiv \sum_{n=1:N} \sigma^2_{P(n)}$$
$$V_P \equiv \alpha_P - c_P - \frac{\lambda}{2} \cdot \sigma^2_P = \sum_{n=1:N} V_{P(n)} \tag{B8}$$
$$\text{ACIR}_P \equiv \frac{\alpha_P - c_P}{\sigma_P}$$

The aggregate variance is the sum of the asset level variances. This flows from our assumption of uncorrelated specific returns. Note it also is true in expectation if we have uncorrelated positions, since for covarying assets $n \neq \ell$ and $\sigma_{n,\ell} \neq 0$:

$$E\langle \tilde{p}_n \cdot \sigma_{n,\ell} \cdot \tilde{p}_\ell \rangle = 0 \text{ if } \tilde{p}_n \text{ is uncorrelated with } \tilde{p}_\ell \tag{B9}$$

There is a potential pitfall in the treatment of the nonlinear component of the transactions cost. Suppose that we looked at trading as a rate, then we could rewrite the transactions cost as:

$$c_{P(n)} = \frac{c_{1,n} \cdot \sum_{t=1:T} \left| \frac{\Delta p_n(t)}{\Delta t} \right| + \left\{ \frac{c_{\phi,n} \cdot \Delta t^{\phi-1}}{\phi} \right\} \cdot \sum_{t=1:T} \left| \frac{\Delta p_n(t)}{\Delta t} \right|^{\phi}}{T}, \quad \phi = 1.5 \text{ or } 2 \tag{B10}$$

The danger lies is in changing the time interval and leaving the nonlinear transactions cost coefficient unchanged.

Appendix C

Transactions Cost with a 3/2 Power Term

We'll take an empirical approach. Consider a case where the penalty for deviation from the target plus the transactions cost is:

$$\begin{aligned} b &= \text{the backlog} \\ \kappa(\Delta p \mid b) &\equiv \frac{\lambda \cdot \sigma^2}{2} \cdot \{b - \Delta p\}^2 \\ c(\Delta p) &= \text{the transactions cost} \\ c(\Delta p) &\equiv c_1 \cdot |\Delta p| + \frac{c_{1.5}}{1.5} \cdot |\Delta p|^{1.5} \\ \kappa(\Delta p \mid b) + c(\Delta p) &= \text{the objective} \end{aligned} \tag{C1}$$

We generated a sample of possible backlog values, normal with mean zero and standard deviation 1.27%. We used median values for the volatility and transactions cost for the universe of 3,136 US assets. Then we minimized the objective, Equation (C1), for each value of the backlog. The result is in Exhibit C1 on the following page.

The figure looks very much like the NLTR figure. See, for example, Exhibit 1, in the main chapter.

If we take the buy part of the curve, $b > z$, and make a linear approximation, we find the result in Exhibit C2.

From the typical results shown in Exhibits C1 and C2 we concluded that a linear approximation of the buy and sell policies would suffice.

We can also examine the analytical properties of the optimal purchase. The first-order conditions when $b > z$ are:

$$\begin{aligned} &-\lambda \cdot \sigma^2 \cdot \{b - \Delta p\} + c_1 + c_{1.5} \cdot \sqrt{\Delta p} = 0 \\ &\text{with } z \equiv \frac{c_1}{\lambda \cdot \sigma^2} \text{ and } k \equiv \frac{c_{1.5}}{\lambda \cdot \sigma^2} \\ &\text{we have} \\ &b - z = \Delta p + k \cdot \sqrt{\Delta p} \end{aligned} \tag{C2}$$

EXHIBIT C1 Nonlinear Trade Rule

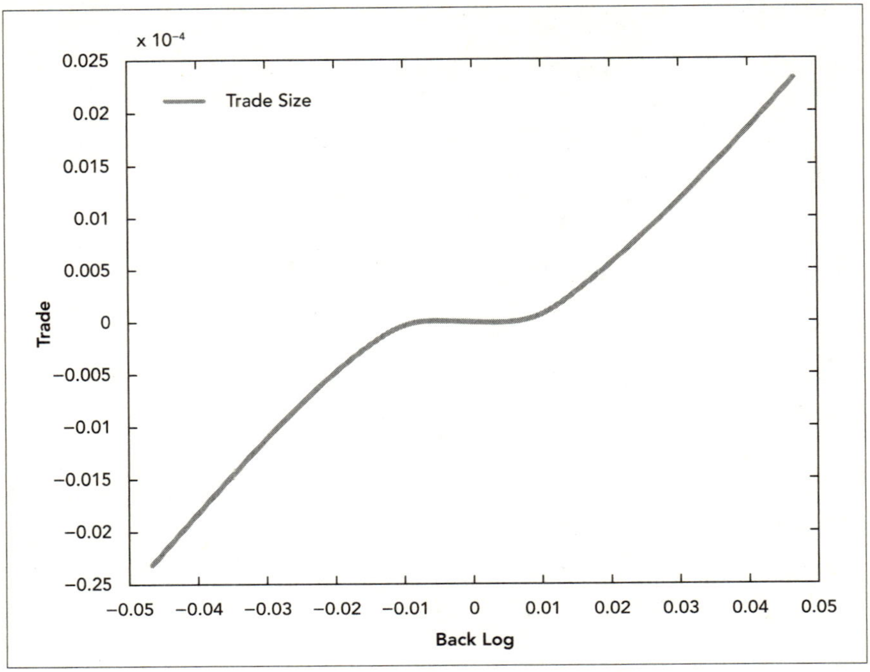

EXHIBIT C2 Linear Regression of Nonlinear Trading Curve

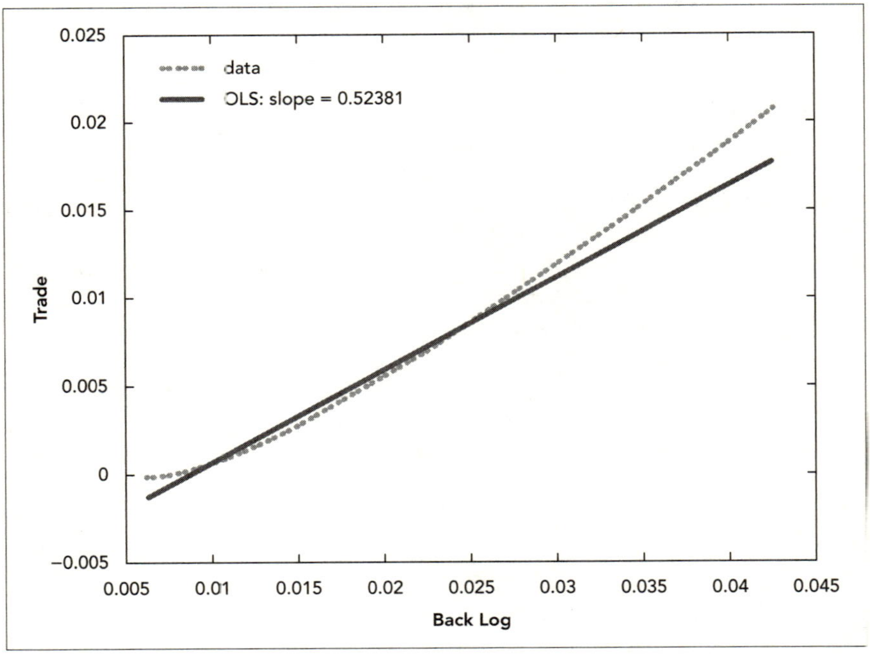

R2 is 97.8

In Equation (C2), z is the size of the no-trade zone. When the backlog, b, exceeds z, $b - z$ is the size of the possible trade. The term Δp is the trade we make, and $k \cdot \sqrt{\Delta p}$ is the trade we forgo due to the market impact cost. In terms of the NLTR:

$$\begin{aligned} \Delta p &= (1-\delta)\cdot(b-z) \\ k\cdot\sqrt{\Delta p} &= \delta\cdot(b-z) \end{aligned} \tag{C3}$$

although the δ in Equation (C3) is not constant. It depends on Δp.

If we differentiate the last line of Equation (C2) with respect to b, we find:

$$\frac{d(\Delta p)}{db} = \frac{2\cdot\Delta p}{2\cdot\Delta p + k\cdot\sqrt{\Delta p}} \tag{C4}$$

This is the derivative of the nonlinear trade line in Exhibit C2. Note that the slope of a line from the edge of the no-trade zone $(z, 0)$ to the trade $(b, \Delta p)$ is:

$$\frac{\Delta p}{b-z} = \frac{\Delta p}{\Delta p + k\cdot\sqrt{\Delta p}} < \frac{d(\Delta p)}{db} \tag{C5}$$

CHAPTER 11
Nonlinear Trading Rules for Portfolio Management

Appendix D

The Parameter Model

As mentioned in the main chapter, we ran regressions on the parameters selected by the simulation/optimization procedure as a noise reduction procedure:

The Cross Sectional Regressions

$$\ln(d_n) = \beta_1 + \beta_2 \cdot \ln(c_{1,n}) + \beta_3 \cdot \ln(c_{2,n}) + \beta_4 \cdot \ln(\sigma_n) + \xi_n$$
$$\ln(z_n) = \phi_1 + \phi_2 \cdot \ln(c_{1,n}) + \phi_3 \cdot \ln(c_{2,n}) + \phi_4 \cdot \ln(\sigma_n) + \zeta_n \quad \text{(D1)}$$
$$\hat{d}_n = d_n \cdot \exp(-\xi_n) \quad \text{fitted (model) value of } d$$
$$\hat{z}_n = z_n \cdot \exp(-\zeta_n) \quad \text{fitted (model) value of } z$$

The results for our collection of US stocks is in Exhibit D1.

EXHIBIT D1 Log-Log Regression Coefficients for the US Assets

USA	CONSTANT	C(1,N)	C(2,N)	SIGMA(N)	R2
ln(d)	6.12	0.73	–1.13	0.98	0.47
ln(z)	–8.82	–0.32	–0.18	–0.35	0.73

Exhibit D2 contains similar results for Australia. In this case the linear t-cost term, $c_1(n)$, was causing collinearity problems with the intercept term, so we dropped it.

EXHIBIT D2 Log-Log Regression Coefficients for the Australian Assets

AUS	CONSTANT	C(2,N)	SIGMA(N)	R2
ln(d)	4.22	–0.55	0.95	0.95
ln(z)	–6.21	–0.42	–0.95	0.80

As part of our evaluation, we used the model fitted values rather than the optimized values and found that they perform just as well. They also are more well behaved since the model tends to bring in outliers and there is a small cross section variance in parameter values. Exhibit D3 shows the results.

EXHIBIT D3 The Averages and Standard Deviations of the Simulation/ Optimization Parameters and Model Parameters

	AVE	AVE FIT	STD	STD FIT
Trade Rate (*d*)	42.1	35.0	40.3	19.0
No-Trade Zone (*z*)	1.43%	1.39%	0.71%	0.62%

Appendix E

General Dynamic Program

Suppose we try a general formulation using dynamic programming. We have N assets and J signals per asset. The state space is $N^*(J + 1)$ real numbers, $\mathbf{p}, \mathbf{S}$ where $\mathbf{p}$ is an N element vector of current positions, and $\mathbf{S}$ is an N by J matrix of signal values. With 2,000 assets and 29 signals per asset, the state space is 60,000 real numbers. If we discretize these, using 10 discrete values along each dimension we have $10^{60{,}000}$ discrete states: a number that MATLAB calls Inf.

If we settle on a single asset, then the state space would be 30 real numbers. A discretization would still be huge. The best approach would be to approximate the transactions cost with a pure quadratic and then use the resulting easily solved linear-quadratic dynamic program. The result would be a linear trading rule.

A general average reward dynamic program for a single asset is of the form:

$$g_0 \cdot \Delta t + V(\mathrm{s}, p_0) = \mathrm{Max}_p \{u(\mathrm{s}, p) \cdot \Delta t - c(p - p_0) + E\langle V(\tilde{\mathrm{s}}, p) | \mathrm{s} \rangle\} \quad \text{(E1)}$$

where g_0 is the annual rate of gain and $V(\mathrm{s}, p_0)$ the benefit of the initial position s, p_0. If things are symmetric, that is, starting (s, p_0) is the same as starting at (–s, $-p_0$), then $V(0, 0) = 0$ and:

$$g_0 \cdot \Delta t = E\left\langle V\left(\tilde{\mathrm{s}}, 0\right) \middle| \mathrm{s} = 0 \right\rangle \quad \text{(E2)}$$

The problem can be simplified further exploiting symmetry in the dynamics of the signals, using the assumption that the signals are mean reverting, and by going to continuous time. The unconstrained nature of the optimization also lends itself to an envelope theorem. Some results along these lines are followed for the linear-quadratic as in Appendix B of the LTR chapter (Chapter 10 in this book).

CHAPTER 11
Nonlinear Trading Rules for Portfolio Management

Appendix F

The Target and Zero Cost Position

In the general context dynamic program, Equation (E1), the zero cost position is $q(\mathrm{s})$, where:

$$u(\mathrm{s}, q(\mathrm{s})) \geq u(\mathrm{s}, p) \quad \text{for all } p$$
$$\frac{\partial u(s, q(\mathrm{s}))}{\partial p} = 0 \quad \text{for all s} \tag{F1}$$

We shall make the very good assumption that $V(p, \mathrm{s})$ has a unique maximizing position for any given s. Call that maximizing position $m(\mathrm{s})$, aka the target position:

$$V(\mathrm{s}, m(\mathrm{s})) \geq V(\mathrm{s}, p) \quad \text{for all } p$$
$$\frac{\partial V(\mathrm{s}, m(\mathrm{s}))}{\partial p} = 0 \text{ for all s} \tag{F2}$$

References

Grinold, Richard. 2018. "Linear Trading Rules for Portfolio Management." *Journal of Portfolio Management* 44 (6), Special Stephen Ross Issue, 109–19. Chapter 10 in this book.

Grinold, R. 1989. "The Fundamental Law of Active Management." *The Journal of Portfolio Management* 15 (Spring): 30–37.

SECTION 2.2

Portfolio Analysis and Attribution

12

Introduction to the Portfolio Analysis and Attribution Section

You load alphas, risk predictions, transactions costs, and constraints into an optimizer and a suggested list of trades emerges. What happened? Why? Are we better off? If so, why? Why am I trading a lot of AAA and not BBB?

Later you observe the results for the day, week, or month and again ask, Why? Was this good luck or excellent work on your behalf? How do you avoid the compelling temptation to assign your defeats to misfortune and your victories to superior portfolio management? The first two questions can be answered by good performance and attribution systems.

The organizational and behavioral question of holding your feet to the fire is more difficult. We won't have much to say on that score, but rants such as the one below may help.[1]

> *I have attended the Performance Committee throughout the year and I've gradually come to the conclusion that we are making the meeting more interesting and simultaneously failing to carry out its mission.*
>
> *I start with three premises.*
>
> 1. *We have a fiduciary responsibility to ourselves and to our clients to understand and to review investment performance.*
> 2. *We prefer evidence to ad hoc explanations.*
> 3. *We have an excellent, albeit not perfect, performance analysis system.*

1. From an anonymous source, modified to protect the guilty.

Despite this I have not seen any serious attention paid to performance analysis. Indeed, when questions of performance arise, they are fobbed off in one or both of the following ways:

- *We endure an elliptical, unenlightening, and eventually futile discussion of the shortcomings of performance analysis. This is blaming the messenger.*
- *Committee members tout various ad hoc explanations:*
  - *All the companies with new, young CEOs did well.*
  - *West Coast retailers had a bad quarter.*
  - *Companies with large inventories of palladium had trouble.*
  - *Etc., etc.*

This is hindsight masquerading as market savvy.

In the end, we do nothing. Portfolio managers receive the message that we will never closely scrutinize them or hold them to account. The committee fails to carry out its central responsibility. This is a failure of leadership.

We hope this helps on the behavioral front and turn to the technical side of the question.

This section describes advances in attribution and performance analysis that provide support when we are willing to hold ourselves accountable. The results extend the material in *Active Portfolio Management* in several ways. First, they are not based on a particular model of asset risk. They work in the context of a currency strategy, an asset allocation strategy, a stock selection strategy, or the management of a portfolio of corporate bonds. The only requirements are a covariance matrix and some imagination. Second, they express a symmetry between ex ante and ex post analysis by treating forecast return and realized return in the same way, treating forecast risk and realized risk in the same way, indeed treating any ex ante question about forecasts with the subsequent realization in the same way. Third, we double down, maybe triple down, on the use of characteristic portfolios as a way of untangling competing explanations.

The two papers included in this section are:

- "Attribution," by Richard C. Grinold
- "The Description of Portfolios," by Richard C. Grinold

Both "Attribution" and "The Description of Portfolios" won Outstanding Paper awards as part of the *Journal of Portfolio Management*'s annual Bernstein Fabozzi/Jacobs Levy Awards for 2008 (volume 33) and 2012 (volume 37), respectively.

In addition, this introduction contains a summary of two related articles:

- "The Opportunity Set," by Richard C. Grinold and Mark B. Taylor, *Journal of Portfolio Management* 35 (Winter 2009): 12–24.
- "Attribution of Performance and Holdings," by Richard C. Grinold and Kelly K. Easton, Chapter 5 in *Worldwide Asset and Liability Modeling*, edited by J. Mulvey and W. T. Ziemba (Cambridge University Press, 1998).

We can consider "The Description of Portfolios" as a continuation of "Attribution," while "The Opportunity Set" is an interesting digression on a topic raised in "Attribution." We will look at "Attribution" and "The Description of Portfolios" first and use the notation of the description paper.

The paper "Attribution of Performance and Holdings" with Kelly Easton takes the attribution idea and combines it with mean-variance portfolio optimization in a manner that allows us to analyze the gap between our ideal cost and constraint-free positions and our optimized positions with both constraints and the transactions cost. This is both a brief tutorial on optimization and a chance to see it in a different light.

The reader might find this strategy advantageous. Start by going through this introduction. It is an overview and a bit of a tutorial as well. The "Attribution" paper has several interesting examples, and the "Descriptions of Portfolios" paper presents the ideas in a more developed form.

Attribution and the Description of Portfolios

The analysis follows from the observation that many interesting portfolio management variables are determined by the correlation between two portfolios. If we develop a method that attributes correlation to sources, then we will have solved several problems in one go. We have succeeded and perhaps succeeded too much since we have developed two ways to address the problem. The two methods agree on the totals, but they can disagree on the allocation (attribution) to the possible sources. The existence of two methods presents an organizational challenge. The suggestion here is to choose one method that makes sense for your application. Stick with it. The bottom line value of such systems is to provide a clue on potential improvements. It is easier to find those clues if you have a history of results calculated in the same manner.

The items we can explain with our methodology fall into two categories: ex ante and ex post.

Ex ante we have portfolio alpha, portfolio variance, opportunity loss, and the transfer coefficient. Ex post we have portfolio return, the opportunity set, and an assessment of the effectiveness of risk controls.

We start with a brief review from *Active Portfolio Management*. The ingredients are alphas for each of N assets, $\boldsymbol{\alpha} = \{\alpha_n\}_{n=1:N}$, a covariance matrix $\mathbf{V}$, and a penalty for active variance λ. We can use these ingredients to define an ideal zero-cost portfolio Q with positions $\mathbf{q} = \{q_n\}_{n=1:N}$ that contains the information incorporated in the alphas.

$$\begin{aligned} \mathbf{q} &= \frac{\mathbf{V}^{-1}\cdot\boldsymbol{\alpha}}{\lambda}, \text{ or } \boldsymbol{\alpha} = \lambda\cdot\mathbf{V}\cdot\mathbf{q} \\ \alpha_Q &= \boldsymbol{\alpha}'\cdot\mathbf{q} = \lambda\cdot\mathbf{q}'\cdot\mathbf{V}\cdot\mathbf{q} = \lambda\cdot\omega_Q^2 \\ IR_Q &\equiv \frac{\alpha_Q}{\omega_Q} = \lambda\cdot\omega_Q \end{aligned} \tag{1}$$

There are several ways to compare *any* portfolio P with positions $\mathbf{p} = \{p_n\}_{n=1:N}$ with Q.[2] The first is the information ratio. Portfolio Q has the highest possible information ratio, denoted $IR = IR_Q$. The math is:

$$
\begin{aligned}
IR \geq IR_P &\equiv \frac{\boldsymbol{\alpha}' \cdot \mathbf{p}}{\sqrt{\mathbf{p}' \cdot \mathbf{V} \cdot \mathbf{p}}} = \frac{\alpha_P}{\omega_P} \\
IR = IR_Q &= \frac{\boldsymbol{\alpha}' \cdot \mathbf{q}}{\sqrt{\mathbf{q}' \cdot \mathbf{V} \cdot \mathbf{q}}} = \sqrt{\boldsymbol{\alpha}' \cdot \mathbf{V}^{-1} \cdot \boldsymbol{\alpha}} = \lambda \cdot \omega_Q \\
\alpha_P &= \lambda \cdot \mathbf{q}' \cdot \mathbf{V} \cdot \mathbf{p} = \lambda \cdot \omega_Q \cdot \rho_{P,Q} \cdot \omega_P = IR \cdot \rho_{P,Q} \cdot \omega_P \\
\frac{\alpha_P}{\omega_P} &= IR_P = IR \cdot \rho_{P,Q}
\end{aligned}
\tag{2}
$$

Any attempt to attribute the alpha α_P or the information ratio IR_P to sources will come down to attributing the correlation (aka the transfer coefficient) ρ_{PQ} to the sources. In a similar line we could attempt to explain the variance of portfolio P. In that case we know that $\rho_{P,P} = 1$; there is no mystery on that account. The useful question is what are the linkages that make it equal to one.

We can also analyze pre–transactions cost objective value and its counterpart the opportunity loss.

The precost objective for any portfolio P is:

$$
\begin{aligned}
O_P &\equiv \boldsymbol{\alpha}' \cdot \mathbf{p} - \frac{\lambda}{2} \cdot \mathbf{p}' \cdot \mathbf{V} \cdot \mathbf{p} = \alpha_P - \frac{\lambda}{2} \cdot \omega_P^2 \\
O_Q &= \frac{\lambda}{2} \cdot \omega_Q^2 \\
L_P &\equiv \frac{\lambda}{2} \cdot (\mathbf{q} - \mathbf{p})' \cdot \mathbf{V} \cdot (\mathbf{q} - \mathbf{p}) = \frac{\lambda}{2} \cdot \omega_{Q-P}^2 \quad \text{opportunity loss} \\
L_P + O_P &= O_Q
\end{aligned}
\tag{3}
$$

Note that maximizing the objective O_P is the same as minimizing the opportunity loss L_P. We will find it useful later to define the backlog portfolio, B, as $B = P - Q$.

EXERCISE 1 Derive the expressions in the second and fourth lines of Equation (3). Hint: Use $\boldsymbol{\alpha} = \lambda \cdot \mathbf{V} \cdot \mathbf{q}$ from Equation (1).

From Equation (3) we see that attributing the objective value of any portfolio P consists of first explaining the variance for portfolio Q and second explaining the opportunity loss that is proportional to the variance of the backlog, B.

2. Portfolios are not constrained to add to one, to add to zero, or to be nonnegative. They can be quite general with long positions and short positions.

Ex Post Attribution

Ex ante measures are generally annual. Ex post measures tend to be of shorter periods, so the length of the period will have to feature in our discussion.[3] Suppose that $\boldsymbol{\theta}$ is the N vector of returns over a period $[0, \Delta t]$. We can associate a portfolio H, called the *hindsight* portfolio, with these returns through:

$$\begin{aligned} \boldsymbol{\theta} &= \sqrt{\Delta t} \cdot \mathbf{V} \cdot \mathbf{h} \\ \theta_H &= \boldsymbol{\theta}' \cdot \mathbf{h} = \omega_H^2 \cdot \sqrt{\Delta t} \\ \boldsymbol{\theta}' \cdot \mathbf{V}^{-1} \cdot \boldsymbol{\theta} &= \omega_H^2 \cdot \Delta t \end{aligned} \tag{4}$$

For any portfolio P, the returns over the period are:

$$\boldsymbol{\theta}' \cdot \mathbf{p} = \theta_P = \mathbf{h}' \cdot \mathbf{V} \cdot \mathbf{p} \cdot \sqrt{\Delta t} = \omega_H \cdot \rho_{H,P} \cdot \omega_P \cdot \sqrt{\Delta t}$$

$$\frac{\theta_P}{\omega_P \cdot \sqrt{\Delta t}} = \omega_H \cdot \rho_{H,P} \qquad \frac{\{\text{return realized } [0, \Delta t]\}}{\{\text{predicted risk } [0, \Delta t]\}}$$

$$\text{or} \quad \frac{\theta_P}{\omega_P \cdot \sqrt{\Delta t}} = OS \cdot IC_P \tag{5}$$

OS is the opportunity set, $OS = \omega_H = \sqrt{\dfrac{\boldsymbol{\theta}' \cdot \mathbf{V}^{-1} \cdot \boldsymbol{\theta}}{\Delta t}} = \sqrt{\mathbf{h}' \cdot \mathbf{V} \cdot \mathbf{h}}$

IC_P is the realized information coefficient, $IC_P = \rho_{H,P}$

Note that the size of the opportunity set, OS, is independent of the portfolio P. Attribution of performance has to focus on explaining the correlation, $\rho_{H,P}$ of portfolios H and P.[4] (See Exhibit 1.)

EXHIBIT 1 Summary of Items We Can Attribute to Sources by Explaining a Correlation

ITEM	NOTATION	FORMULA	CORRELATION
Info. Ratio Sq.	IR^2	$\lambda^2 \cdot \omega_Q^2$	$\rho_{Q,Q}$
Variance P	ω_P^2	ω_P^2	$\rho_{P,P}$
Alpha P	α_P	$\lambda \cdot \omega_{P,Q}$	$\rho_{P,Q}$
Opp. Loss P	L_P	$\frac{\lambda}{2} \cdot \omega_B^2$	$\rho_{B,B}$
Return P	θ_P	$\omega_{P,H} \cdot \sqrt{\Delta t}$	$\rho_{P,H}$
Opp. Set Sq.	OS^2	ω_H^2	$\rho_{H,H}$

3. This point about the time period is not as clear as it could be in the two articles included in this section, so we are stressing it here.
4. We define the opportunity set in an equivalent but slightly different way later on in this chapter. The description above avoids details it is better to postpone.

Explanatory Variables

We have established the point that several interesting attribution questions boil down to explaining the correlation between two portfolios or, in the case of variance, of the portfolio with itself. The task of the attribution is to sort out that correlation using a set of explanatory variables. This raises the question: what are the explanatory variables? They don't have to be the same in every case, they can be tailored to the task. The sources of alpha are an excellent starting point. Also, if the portfolio has a tendency to get exposed to sources of risk that are not associated with any expectation of added return then these should make it on the list. In general, assembling a list of potential explanatory variables is, as in a regression analysis, the creative step.

We will represent our set of explanatory variables by an N (number of assets) by J (number of variables) matrix $\mathbf{X}$ with $X_{n,j}$ the exposure of asset n to variable j.

Representing Variables as Portfolios

The explanatory variables are a disparate group: apples, oranges, kumquats, and figs. We can put them on a common footing by representing them as portfolios. There are two ways to do this. We can use context-free single factor portfolios, or multiple factor portfolios that take into account all the other factors. First, consider the single factor approach.

$$\begin{aligned} &S_j = \text{the single factor portfolio for factor } j \\ &\mathbf{V}\cdot\mathbf{s}_j = \mathbf{x}_j, \quad \mathbf{s}_j = \mathbf{V}^{-1}\cdot\mathbf{x}_j \\ &\mathbf{S} \ \text{ the } N \text{ by } J \text{ matrix with columns } \mathbf{s}_j \\ &\mathbf{V}\cdot\mathbf{S} = \mathbf{X} \end{aligned} \tag{6}$$

Now, consider the multiple factor approach, which is a repackaging of the single factor portfolios. Multiple factor portfolio j is called M_j. It has holdings $\mathbf{m}_j = \{m_{n,j}\}_{n=1:N}$. Portfolio M_j is uncorrelated with the single factor portfolios S_k for k not equal to j and has a unit covariance with single factor portfolio S_j.

Similar to matrix $\mathbf{X}$, the matrix $\mathbf{M}$ is the N by J matrix with the multiple factor (mimicking) portfolios as columns. In math terms we have:

$$\begin{aligned} &\mathbf{M} \equiv \mathbf{S}\cdot(\mathbf{S}'\cdot\mathbf{V}\cdot\mathbf{S})^{-1} \\ &\mathbf{M}'\cdot\mathbf{V}\cdot\mathbf{S} = \mathbf{I} \text{ where } \mathbf{I} \text{ is a } J \text{ by } J \text{ identity matrix} \\ &\mathbf{m}'_j\cdot\mathbf{V}\cdot\mathbf{s}_j = 1 = \omega_{M_j}\cdot\rho_{M_j,S_j}\cdot\omega_{S_j} \\ &\Rightarrow \rho_{M_j,S_k} = \left\{ \begin{array}{c} 0 \ \text{ if } k \neq j \\ \dfrac{1}{\omega_{M_j}\cdot\omega_{S_j}} \text{ if } k = j \end{array} \right\} \end{aligned} \tag{7}$$

With this as background, let's consider a traditional approach to the attribution of returns.

The traditional model is based on a GLS regression:

$$\begin{aligned}
&\boldsymbol{\theta} = \mathbf{X}\cdot\mathbf{f} + \boldsymbol{\xi} \text{ where}\\
&\boldsymbol{\theta} \text{ is the } N \text{ vector of asset returns over } [0, \Delta t]\\
&\mathbf{X} \text{ is an } N \text{ by } J \text{ matrix of asset factor exposures}\\
&\mathbf{f} \text{ is a } J \text{ element vector of estimated factor returns}\\
&\boldsymbol{\xi} \text{ is an } N \text{ vector of estimated asset residual returns}
\end{aligned} \tag{8}$$

The estimates of f and the residual ξ are:

$$\begin{aligned}
&\mathbf{f} = \left(\mathbf{X}'\cdot\mathbf{V}^{-1}\cdot\mathbf{X}\right)^{-1}\cdot\mathbf{X}'\cdot\mathbf{V}^{-1}\cdot\boldsymbol{\theta}\\
&\boldsymbol{\xi} = \boldsymbol{\theta} - \mathbf{X}\cdot\mathbf{f}\\
&\mathbf{X}'\cdot\mathbf{V}^{-1}\cdot\boldsymbol{\xi} = 0
\end{aligned} \tag{9}$$

Now, let's look again at the return attribution, Equations (8) and (9), from a portfolio perspective. To do this we have to transform the factor exposures and the returns into portfolios:

$$\begin{aligned}
&\boldsymbol{\theta} = \mathbf{V}\cdot\mathbf{h}\cdot\sqrt{\Delta t} && H \text{ is the hindsight portfolio}\\
&\mathbf{X} = \mathbf{V}\cdot\mathbf{S} && \text{The source portfolios } S_j\\
&\boldsymbol{\xi} = \mathbf{V}\cdot\mathbf{r}\cdot\sqrt{\Delta t} && R \text{ is the residual portfolio}
\end{aligned} \tag{10}$$

The holdings in the *hindsight* portfolio are proportional to the portfolio you would hold if your alphas were equal to the realized returns $\boldsymbol{\theta}$. In the same spirit, the vector **r** contains the holdings in the residual portfolio. The J columns of S are the factor or *source* portfolios, S_j.

EXERCISE 2 Show that the estimated factor returns, f, in Equation (9) are the returns on the multiple factor portfolios, Equation (7), and that the residual portfolio R is uncorrelated with the source portfolios; that is, that:

$$\begin{aligned}
&(i.) \quad \mathbf{f} = \mathbf{M}'\cdot\boldsymbol{\theta}\\
&(ii.) \quad \mathbf{S}'\cdot\mathbf{V}\cdot\mathbf{r} = 0
\end{aligned} \tag{11}$$

Starting with any portfolio P, the portfolio will have returns and factor exposures:

$$\begin{aligned}
&\theta_P = \boldsymbol{\theta}'\cdot\mathbf{p} = \mathbf{h}'\cdot\mathbf{V}\cdot\mathbf{p}\cdot\sqrt{\Delta t}\\
&\mathbf{x}_P = \mathbf{X}'\cdot\mathbf{p} = \mathbf{S}'\cdot\mathbf{V}\cdot\mathbf{p}
\end{aligned} \tag{12}$$

Putting together Equations (10), (11), and (12), we have:

$$\begin{aligned}
&\theta_P = \mathbf{x}'_P\cdot\mathbf{f} + \xi_P\\
&\mathbf{h}'\cdot\mathbf{V}\cdot\mathbf{p}\cdot\sqrt{\Delta t} = (\mathbf{p}'\cdot\mathbf{V}\cdot\mathbf{S})\cdot\left(\mathbf{M}'\cdot\mathbf{V}\cdot\mathbf{h}\cdot\sqrt{\Delta t}\right) + \left(\mathbf{p}'\cdot\mathbf{V}\cdot\mathbf{r}\cdot\sqrt{\Delta t}\right)
\end{aligned} \tag{13}$$

Notice that all of the terms in the second line of Equation (13) are covariances:

(*i.*) $\mathbf{h}' \cdot \mathbf{V} \cdot \mathbf{p}$ portfolio P and the hindsight portfolio H

(*ii.*) $\mathbf{p}' \cdot \mathbf{V} \cdot \mathbf{S}$ portfolio P with the source portfolios S_j

(*iii.*) $\mathbf{M}' \cdot \mathbf{V} \cdot \mathbf{h}$ multiple factor portfolios M_j and portfolio H

(*iv.*) $\mathbf{p}' \cdot \mathbf{V} \cdot \mathbf{r}$ portfolio P and residual return portfolio R

This is apples to apples, and it is not a radical departure from *Active Portfolio Management*. It will lead to the same answer if you use the same factors. If the traditional approach led to large unexplained residuals, this approach, using the same factors, will lead to the same unexplained residuals. It is, at worst, old wine in new bottles, and, at best, a more useful and flexible perspective. In article "The Description of Portfolios," we call it method MX. There is another approach.

Method SY

We start with portfolio P and consider the source portfolios as building blocks. We want to use these building blocks to assemble a portfolio close to P by making the variance of the residual as small as possible:

$$\begin{aligned}&\text{Find } \gamma_P \text{ so that}\\ &\mathbf{p} = \mathbf{S} \cdot \gamma_P + \mathbf{u} \text{ and}\\ &\mathbf{u}' \cdot \mathbf{V} \cdot \mathbf{u} \text{ is minimized}\end{aligned} \tag{14}$$

The solution is:

$$\begin{aligned}&\gamma_P = \mathbf{M}' \cdot \mathbf{V} \cdot \mathbf{p}\\ &\Rightarrow \mathbf{S}' \cdot \mathbf{V} \cdot \mathbf{u} = 0 \text{ the residual position is uncorrelated with the sources}\end{aligned} \tag{15}$$

With this perspective, the return on portfolio P can again be expressed in terms of portfolios and covariances:

$$\begin{aligned}&\theta_P = \theta' \cdot \mathbf{p} = \theta' \cdot \mathbf{S} \cdot \gamma_P + \theta' \cdot \mathbf{u} \text{ or}\\ &\mathbf{h}' \cdot \mathbf{V} \cdot \mathbf{p} \cdot \sqrt{\Delta t} = \left(\mathbf{h}' \cdot \mathbf{V} \cdot \mathbf{S} \cdot \sqrt{\Delta t}\right) \cdot \left(\mathbf{M}' \cdot \mathbf{V} \cdot \mathbf{p}\right) + \mathbf{h}' \cdot \mathbf{V} \cdot \mathbf{u}_P \cdot \sqrt{\Delta t}\end{aligned} \tag{16}$$

Note the similarity and differences between Equations (16) and (13).

EXERCISE 3 In Equation (16), $\mathbf{h}' \cdot \mathbf{V} \cdot \mathbf{u} = \omega_H \cdot \rho_{H,U} \cdot \omega_U$, and in Equation (13), $\mathbf{p}' \cdot \mathbf{V} \cdot \mathbf{r} = \omega_P \cdot \rho_{P,R} \cdot \omega_R$. Show:

(*i.*) $\mathbf{h}' \cdot \mathbf{V} \cdot \mathbf{u} = \mathbf{p}' \cdot \mathbf{V} \cdot \mathbf{r}$

(*ii.*) $\omega_U = \rho_{U,P} \cdot \omega_P$

(*iii.*) $\omega_R = \rho_{R,H} \cdot \omega_H$

We can take Equation (16) or Equation (13) and boil it down to an equation about correlation.

If we divide Equation (16) by $\sqrt{\Delta t}$ and express all the covariances as risk · correlation · risk, we find:

$$\omega_H \cdot \rho_{H,P} \cdot \omega_P = \sum_{j=1:J} \left\{\omega_H \cdot \rho_{H,S_j} \cdot \omega_{S_j}\right\} \cdot \left\{\omega_{M_j} \cdot \rho_{M_j,P} \cdot \omega_P\right\} + \omega_H \cdot \rho_{H,U} \cdot \omega_U$$

$$\rho_{H,P} = \sum_{j=1:J} \rho_{H,S_j} \cdot \left\{\omega_{S_j} \cdot \omega_{M_j}\right\} \cdot \rho_{M_j,P} + \rho_{H,U} \cdot \rho_{U,P} \qquad (17)$$

but $\omega_{S_j} \cdot \omega_{M_j} = \dfrac{1}{\rho_{S_j,M_j}}$ so

$$\rho_{H,P} = \sum_{j=1:J} \frac{\rho_{H,S_j} \cdot \rho_{M_j,P}}{\rho_{S_j,M_j}} + \rho_{H,U} \cdot \rho_{U,P} \quad \text{method } SY$$

EXERCISE 4 Do the same analysis for Equation (13) and show that:

$$\rho_{H,P} = \sum_{j=1:J} \frac{\rho_{H,M_j} \cdot \rho_{S_j,P}}{\rho_{S_j,M_j}} + \rho_{H,R} \cdot \rho_{R,P} \quad \text{method MX} \qquad (18)$$

EXERCISE 5 Show that the size of the residual is the same in each case:

$$\rho_{H,R} \cdot \rho_{R,P} = \rho_{H,U} \cdot \rho_{U,P}$$

so each method explains the same fraction of the correlation.

EXERCISE 6 Suppose we chose to attribute the holdings using the multiple portfolios **M**, rather than the single source portfolios **S**; that is,

$$\begin{aligned} &\text{Find } \boldsymbol{\beta}_P \text{ so that} \\ &\mathbf{p} = \mathbf{M} \cdot \boldsymbol{\beta}_P + \mathbf{u} \text{ and} \\ &\mathbf{u}' \cdot \mathbf{V} \cdot \mathbf{u} \text{ is minimized} \end{aligned} \qquad (19)$$

Show that we end with Equations (13) and (18); that is, this is method MX starting with holdings attribution Equation (19) rather than returns attribution Equation (9).

The methods differ in how they attribute to the sources. The choice of method rests on how you want to use the result: in particular, what variables do you control, and how would changing them influence the allocation? That said, the article "Attribution" has both feet in the SY camp.

This can be seen as part of an evolutionary process since the same author is in the MX camp three years later in "The Description of Portfolios."

The decompositions above have the pleasant feature that each component is a correlation. In addition, the new actor, ρ_{M_j,S_j}, which is always positive, has a useful interpretation. The inverse of ρ_{M_j,S_j} is called the *variance inflation factor*, or VIF. High values of VIF (low values of ρ_{M_j,S_j}) can signal multicollinearity. A rough rule of thumb is that you have concerns if $\rho_{M_j,S_j} < 0.25$, and you have problems if $\rho_{M_j,S_j} < 0.1$.

The Opportunity Set

The article "The Opportunity Set" was joint work with Mark P. Taylor, the polymath professor and dean who is an expert on currency markets, statistics, Shakespeare, economics, and much more.[5]

In "Attribution" we stressed the similarity in treatment for the ex ante alpha and ex post return. Recall that portfolio H is the hindsight portfolio, see Equation (10). The results are:

$$\begin{aligned} &(i.) \quad \alpha_P = IR \cdot \omega_P \cdot \rho_{P,Q} \quad \text{ex ante} \\ &(ii.) \quad \theta_P = OS \cdot \omega_P \cdot \rho_{P,H} \quad \text{ex post} \end{aligned} \tag{20}$$

In item (*i.*) above, $\rho_{P,Q}$ is the transfer coefficient and IR is the maximum attainable ex ante information ratio, that is, the information ratio of portfolio Q. The second equation is an ex post analog. The new actor, OS, is called the *opportunity set*. It is the maximum possible ratio of realized return to predicted risk.

The Time Interval

The alphas and the covariance matrix are stated in annual terms. However, the returns, $\boldsymbol{\theta}$, generally will be from a shorter period: a month, a week, or a day. The similarity of items (*i.*) and (*ii.*) in the equations above can be deceptive since the ω_P in item (*i.*) is annual while the same notation is used in item (*ii.*) for a risk prediction over a different time horizon. The challenge is to recall that the risk is for the same period of time as the returns. In the case of the ex ante alpha, the period is always one year, so there is no possibility of confusion. In the ex post case, the period is generally shorter. We could clutter up the notation with $\Omega(\Delta t)$, $\omega_P(\Delta t)$, $\theta_P(\Delta t)$. However, the idea of a period is usually clearly established in any evaluation of returns, so the additional notation seems superfluous.

A Model for Returns

We are going to assume that the returns are independent and identically distributed from period to period. In that case we can scale the annual covariance matrix $\mathbf{V}$ to get the appropriate covariance matrix for any time period:

$$\begin{aligned} &\Omega \equiv \mathbf{V} \cdot \Delta t && \text{predicted } N \text{ by } N \text{ covariance over } [0, \Delta t] \\ &\boldsymbol{\theta} && N \text{ vector of returns over } [0, \Delta t] \\ &OS \equiv \sqrt{\boldsymbol{\theta}' \cdot \Omega^{-1} \cdot \boldsymbol{\theta}} && \text{Opportunity Set for realized returns } \boldsymbol{\theta} \text{ in } [0, \Delta t] \end{aligned} \tag{21}$$

5. Professor Taylor is at the time of this writing the Dean of the Olin School of Business at Washington University.

EXERCISE 7 Suppose the annual predicted risk of a portfolio is 5%. What is the predicted risk over a month, a week, or a day (252 trading days per year)?

We can break up the annual covariance matrix into its risk and correlation components:

$$\begin{aligned}
&\mathbf{V} = \Sigma \cdot \mathbf{R} \cdot \Sigma \\
&\Sigma \text{ is an diagonal } N \text{ matrix} \\
&\mathbf{R} \text{ is an } N \text{ by } N \text{ correlation matrix} \\
&\Omega = \sqrt{\Delta t} \cdot \Sigma \cdot \mathbf{R} \cdot \Sigma \cdot \sqrt{\Delta t} \\
&\sqrt{\Delta t} \cdot \Sigma \text{ is the asset risk over } [0, \Delta t]
\end{aligned} \tag{22}$$

We can go one step further and represent the correlation matrix **R** in terms of its Cholesky decomposition:

$$\begin{aligned}
&\mathbf{R} = \mathbf{C} \cdot \mathbf{C}' \\
&\mathbf{C} \quad \text{is a lower triangular matrix} \\
&\mathbf{C}' \quad \text{is the transpose of } \mathbf{C}, \text{ so} \\
&\Omega = \sqrt{\Delta t} \cdot \Sigma \cdot \mathbf{C} \cdot \mathbf{C}' \cdot \Sigma \cdot \sqrt{\Delta t}, \text{ and} \\
&\Omega^{-1} = \frac{\Sigma^{-1} \cdot [\mathbf{C}']^{-1} \cdot [\mathbf{C}]^{-1} \cdot \Sigma^{-1}}{\Delta t}
\end{aligned} \tag{23}$$

EXERCISE 8 What is the Cholesky decomposition of the two-by-two correlation matrix:

$$\mathbf{R} = \begin{Bmatrix} 1 & \rho \\ \rho & 1 \end{Bmatrix}$$

EXERCISE 9 Suppose that **C** is the Cholesky matrix for the N by N correlation matrix **R**. Show how to calculate the Cholesky matrix for the $N + 1$ by $N + 1$ correlation matrix:

$$\mathbf{R}_{N+1} = \begin{Bmatrix} \mathbf{R} & \boldsymbol{\phi} \\ \boldsymbol{\phi}' & 1 \end{Bmatrix}, \text{ where } \boldsymbol{\phi}' = \{\phi_1, \phi_2, \ldots \phi_N\}$$

$$\begin{aligned}
&\text{where } \phi_n = \rho_{n,N+1}, \text{ the return correlation} \\
&\text{of assets } n \text{ and } N+1
\end{aligned}$$

If the unconditional mean of the returns is zero or we are defining the return as net of some mean, then the covariance matrix Ω is consistent with the following return generating process:

$$\begin{aligned}
&\boldsymbol{\theta} = \Sigma \cdot \mathbf{C} \cdot \mathbf{z} \cdot \sqrt{\Delta t} \text{ where} \\
&E\{\mathbf{z}\} = 0, \quad E\{\mathbf{z} \cdot \mathbf{z}'\} = \mathbf{I} \\
&E\{\boldsymbol{\theta} \cdot \boldsymbol{\theta}'\} = E\{\Sigma \cdot \mathbf{C} \cdot \mathbf{z} \cdot \mathbf{z}' \cdot \mathbf{C}' \cdot \Sigma\} \cdot \Delta t = \Omega
\end{aligned} \tag{24}$$

Note there is no assumption of normality, just the existence of the first and second moment.

If we combine the return generation process, Equation (24), and the model of covariance, Equation (22), and follow through the massive number of cancellations we arrive at:

$$OS^2 = \boldsymbol{\theta}' \cdot \Omega^{-1} \cdot \boldsymbol{\theta} = \mathbf{z}' \cdot \mathbf{z} \text{ and}$$
$$E\{OS^2\} = N \tag{25}$$

The article "The Opportunity Set" takes this analysis several steps further since we are actually more interested in $E\{OS\}$. The article's result is:

$$\frac{E\{OS\}}{\sqrt{N}} \to 1 \text{ as } N \text{ gets large}$$

This is not altogether obvious. It is a case where an analysis of the simplest example can lead you astray. If $N = 1$ and returns are normal, then $E\{OS\} = \sqrt{2/\pi} \approx 0.798$. This is not encouraging. However, as we show the approximation improves rapidly as N grows larger and is generally "good enough" for N larger than 10.

One can also separate the square of the opportunity set, Equation (25), into benchmark (market) and residual components: MOS and ROS. These combine in Pythagorean fashion.

$$OS^2 = MOS^2 + ROS^2$$

The expected size of the MOS^2 is one. The data sample used in the article includes the market crash of October 1987. The MOS hit its maximum value of 4.93 in that month, which is no surprise. What is surprising is that there was very little residual opportunity that month. There was little chance to separate losers and winners; every stock was a loser.

The opportunity set can also serve as a measure of our risk predictions. If the OS^2 is consistently above N then it suggests that you might be underpredicting risk.

There is a third and of course related interpretation of the opportunity set. If we use the annual covariance matrix V from Equation (22) rather than the per period covariance matrix we have

$$\upsilon(\theta) = \frac{\theta' \cdot \mathbf{V}^{-1} \cdot \theta}{N}$$

which has an expected value equal to the length of the time period. One can use this to gauge the pace of the market. For example, if the returns θ are measure on a weekly basis and $\upsilon(\theta) > 1/52$ we say the market is moving faster than usual. This interpretation has appeal for those who have experienced intermittent frenetic and torpid periods on a trading desk.

The article includes three illustrations that demonstrate the robustness of the result. One considers the US equity market where N is roughly 1,000.

A second considers the world's major equity markets where $N = 13$. Finally, in Appendix B, the article considers the world's major currencies with $N = 9$.

We also show analytically and by example that the returns having a nonzero mean does not materially affect the result. And in Appendix B we show, by a Monte Carlo illustration, that the result stays valid even with nonnormal fat-tailed distributions.

Attribution and Optimization

We start with two cautions. First, you can skip this section if you are not extremely interested in optimization, or if optimization is new to you.

If you got this far, the second caution is that we are using marginal analysis, the first-order conditions, to make a total allocation. This is not perfect, but in the absence of alternatives, it is the best we can do. If you establish a system similar to the one suggested below, the important thing is to use it consistently and prudently. If certain constraints are consistently hurting either ex ante or ex post, consider changing them. If transactions costs are eating up your returns, consider a lower level of turnover or additional research into reducing cost.

Our goal is to briefly describe a single stage portfolio optimization problem, and then use the first-order conditions to present some interesting and investment relevant information that is a by-product of the optimization. As always, when we refer to a portfolio, we are using a general concept. There is no requirement that the positions are positive, or that they sum to one or zero.

The description below relies heavily on the article "Attribution of Performance and Holdings," by Richard Grinold and Kelly Easton.[6]

We start with a brief review of one-stage portfolio optimization. First the notation and terminology in our problem:

$\mathbf{p}_0$ the initial portfolio, an N element vector

$\mathbf{p}$ the new portfolio, an N element vector

$\boldsymbol{\alpha}$ the return forecasts, an N element vector

$\mathbf{V}$ a covariance matrix, an N by N matrix

λ a parameter used to penalize variance (26)

$\mathbf{q} \equiv \dfrac{\mathbf{V}^{-1} \cdot \boldsymbol{\alpha}}{\lambda}$ the ideal, zero-cost portfolio

$L_P = \dfrac{\lambda}{2} \cdot (\mathbf{q} - \mathbf{p})' \cdot \mathbf{V} \cdot (\mathbf{q} - p)$ the opportunity loss

$c_P = c \cdot (\mathbf{p} - \mathbf{p}_0)$ the transactions costs of moving from $\mathbf{p}_0$ to $\mathbf{p}$.

$\mathbf{A} \cdot \mathbf{p} \le \mathbf{d}$ J constraints

6. Chapter 5, pp. 87–113, in *Worldwide Asset and Liability Modeling*, edited by J. Mulvey and W. T. Ziemba. Cambridge University Press, 1998.

It is easier to understand the first-order conditions if we add the following N accounting constraints:

$$\begin{aligned} \mathbf{p}-\mathbf{b}+\mathbf{s}=\mathbf{p}_0 &\quad N \text{ accounting constraints} \\ \mathbf{b}\geq 0 &\quad \text{an } N \text{ element vector of buys} \\ \mathbf{s}\geq 0 &\quad \text{an } N \text{ element vector of sells} \end{aligned} \tag{27}$$

EXERCISE 10 (Spread Sheet): Consider a one-asset problem with the following data: risk penalty $\lambda = 20$, volatility $\sigma = 15\%$, alpha $\alpha = 1.8\%$, initial position $p_0 = 0.01$, with buy and sell cost for a trade Δp:

$$c(\Delta p) = 0.0008 \cdot |\Delta p| + \frac{0.1}{2} \cdot (\Delta p)^2$$

There are no constraints. Find the optimal solution q in the absence of transactions cost and the optimal solution $\hat{p}$ with transactions costs.

Starting with Equations (26) and (27), we can write out the transactions cost in more detail:

$$\begin{aligned} & c(\mathbf{p}-\mathbf{z}) = \sum_{n=1}^{N} c_{1,n} \cdot b_n + c_{2,n}(b_n) + \sum_{n=1}^{N} c_{1,n} \cdot s_n + c_{2,n}(s_n) \\ & c_{1,n} = \text{a proportional cost for purchases and sales} \\ & c_{2,n} = \text{market impact cost functions of purchases and sales} \\ & \text{For example:} \\ & c_{2,n}(b_n) = \frac{2}{3} \cdot k_n \cdot b_n^{3/2} \ \ or \ \ c_{2,n}(b_n) = \frac{1}{2} \cdot k_n \cdot b_n^2, \quad k_n \geq 0 \\ & \text{In general, we assume the costs are increasing and convex.} \end{aligned} \tag{28}$$

As we established earlier, in Equation (3), the risk-adjusted alpha plus the opportunity loss is a constant, so minimizing opportunity loss is equivalent to maximizing risk-adjusted alpha. We will use that to make our optimization problem one of minimizing losses:

$$\begin{aligned} & U(\mathbf{p}_0, \mathbf{d}) = \text{Minimum}\{\, L_P + c(\mathbf{p} - \mathbf{p}_0)\} \\ & \text{Subject to } \mathbf{A} \cdot \mathbf{p} \leq \mathbf{d} \\ & \text{where} \quad L_P \equiv \frac{\lambda}{2}(\mathbf{q} - \mathbf{p})' \cdot \mathbf{V} \cdot (\mathbf{q} - \mathbf{p}) \quad \text{the opportunity loss} \\ & \text{and} \quad c(\mathbf{p} - \mathbf{p}_0) \quad \text{the transactions cost} \end{aligned} \tag{29}$$

EXERCISE 11 (Continuation of spreadsheet exercise.) Formulate the problem described in Exercise 10 in the form of Equation (29) and show that you get the same answer as the more traditional alpha minus a penalty for variance and minus t-cost.

The constraints and associated Lagrange multipliers (dual variables) are:

$$\begin{array}{cc} \text{Constraint} & \text{Multiplier} \\ \mathbf{p} - \mathbf{b} + \mathbf{s} = \mathbf{p}_0 & \upsilon \\ \mathbf{b} \geq 0 & \phi \geq 0 \\ \mathbf{s} \geq 0 & \psi \geq 0 \\ \mathbf{A} \cdot \mathbf{p} \leq \mathbf{d} & \pi \geq 0 \end{array} \tag{30}$$

The optimality conditions are:[7]

$$\begin{aligned} &\lambda \cdot \mathbf{V} \cdot (\mathbf{q} - \mathbf{p}) - \mathbf{A}' \cdot \pi - \upsilon = 0 \quad \text{for } \mathbf{p} \\ &-\{\mathbf{c}_1 + \nabla c_2(\mathbf{b})\} + \upsilon + \phi = 0 \quad \text{for } \mathbf{b} \\ &-\{\mathbf{c}_1 + \nabla c_2(\mathbf{s})\} - \upsilon + \psi = 0 \quad \text{for } \mathbf{s} \end{aligned} \tag{31}$$

Finally, the complementary slackness conditions for the inequality constraints are:

$$\begin{array}{ll} \sum_{n=1:N} A_{j,n} \cdot p_n < d_j \Rightarrow \pi_j = 0 & \pi_j > 0 \Rightarrow \sum_{n=1:N} A_{j,n} \cdot p_n = d_j \\ b_n > 0 \Rightarrow \phi_n = 0 & \phi_n > 0 \Rightarrow b_n = 0 \\ s_n > 0 \Rightarrow \psi_n = 0 & \psi_n > 0 \Rightarrow s_n = 0 \end{array} \tag{32}$$

This lays out the general framework. Our next effort is to show that the multiplier υ_n can be interpreted as the marginal cost of increasing the optimal position p_n either by buying more or selling less. This will require a detailed look at the first-order conditions.

At optimality each asset is either a buy, a sell, or a hold:

$$\begin{aligned} &\text{buy } b_n > 0 \Rightarrow \phi_n = 0 \Rightarrow \upsilon_n = c_{1,n} + \frac{dc_{2,n}(b_n)}{db_n} \\ &\text{sell } s_n > 0 \Rightarrow \psi_n = 0 \Rightarrow \upsilon_n = -\left\{ c_{1,n} + \frac{dc_{2,n}(s_n)}{db_n} \right\} \\ &\text{hold } b_n = s_n = 0 \Rightarrow -c_{1,n} \leq -c_{1,n} + \psi_n = \upsilon_n = c_{1,n} - \phi_n \leq c_{1,n} \end{aligned} \tag{33}$$

From this we can see that υ_n is the marginal cost of increasing p_n either by buying more or selling less. Equivalently, it is the marginal cost of decreasing the initial position thus pushing us to buy more or sell less. If the asset is a hold, then υ_n is less than the linear transactions cost, $c_{1,n}$, in absolute value.

EXERCISE 12 (Continuation of spreadsheet exercise.) Examine the same problem as in Exercise 10 and add the constraints $p \leq \bar{p}$ and $-p \leq \bar{p}$. See how the optimal solution varies as the bound $\bar{p}$ increases from 0.03 to 0.04.

7. To suit our special purpose, we have flipped the sign of the multipliers associated with the accounting constraints.

EXERCISE 13 (This is Exercise 12 continued.) Show that the multipliers associated with the upper bound constraint are:

$$\pi = \{\lambda \cdot \sigma^2 + c_2\} \cdot \max\{0, \hat{p} - \bar{p}\}$$

Our main result comes from the first equation in (31):

$$\begin{aligned} &(i.) \quad \lambda \cdot \mathbf{V} \cdot (\mathbf{q} - \mathbf{p}) = \mathbf{A}' \cdot \boldsymbol{\pi} + \boldsymbol{\upsilon} \\ &\qquad \lambda \cdot \mathbf{V} \cdot \mathbf{q} = \boldsymbol{\alpha} \Rightarrow \\ &(ii.) \quad \boldsymbol{\alpha} = \lambda \cdot \mathbf{V} \cdot \mathbf{p} + \mathbf{A}' \cdot \boldsymbol{\pi} + \boldsymbol{\upsilon} \text{ Allocation of Alpha} \end{aligned} \tag{34}$$

From item (*ii.*) we get an allocation of alpha for each asset:

$$\begin{array}{cccc} \text{Alpha}_n & \text{In portfolio} & \text{Loss to constraints} & \text{Loss to t-cost} \\ \alpha_n = & \lambda \cdot \sum\limits_{k=1:N} V_{n,k} \cdot p_k & + \sum\limits_{j=1:J} A_{n,j} \cdot \pi_j & + \upsilon_n \end{array} \tag{35}$$

EXERCISE 14 (Continuation of spreadsheet exercise.) Show how the alpha is allocated as the upper bound $\bar{p}$ increases from 0.03 to 0.04.

Equation (35) allows for a constraint-by-constraint and asset-by-asset breakdown of the alpha absorbed by the constraint. In addition, from Equation (33) for buys and sells we can split out the linear and market impact costs. Finally, note that the "In portfolio" term in Equation (35) is the risk penalty λ times the covariance of the return on asset n, θ_n, with the return on portfolio P, θ_P, *i.e.* $\lambda \cdot Cov\langle \theta_n, \theta_P \rangle$.

Recall that the opportunity loss for portfolio P is:

$$L_P = \frac{\lambda}{2} \cdot (\mathbf{q} - \mathbf{p})' \cdot \mathbf{V} \cdot (\mathbf{q} - \mathbf{p}) \tag{36}$$

also known as the risk penalty applied to the backlog variance.

If we premultiply item (*i.*) of Equation (34) by $(\mathbf{q} - \mathbf{p})'$ and divide by 2 we can, with some manipulation, allocate the opportunity loss to the constraints and the transactions cost:

$$L_P = \left\{ \begin{array}{ccc} \dfrac{\boldsymbol{\pi}' \cdot (\mathbf{A} \cdot (\mathbf{q} - \mathbf{p}))}{2} & + & \dfrac{(\mathbf{q} - \mathbf{p})' \cdot \boldsymbol{\upsilon}}{2} \\ \text{Constraints} & + & \text{Transaction Costs} \end{array} \right\} \tag{37}$$

Note that we already have accounted for the transactions cost paid as the other term in the objective. We can view the transactions cost allocation in Equation (37) as the cost of intimidation. The existence of the costs means that we forgo many trades that would otherwise be advantageous.

EXERCISE 15 Use the complementary slackness conditions, Equation (32), to establish Equation (37).

EXERCISE 16 (Continuation of spreadsheet exercise.) Show how the allocation to opportunity loss Equation (37) varies as the upper bound increases from 0.03 to 0.04.

The constraint part of Equation (37) can be broken down constraint by constraint and the transactions cost by proportional costs and market impact. For the transactions cost, the opportunity loss is the product of the backlog trade to the ideal zero-cost unconstrained solution and the marginal transactions cost. For the constraints, the opportunity loss is proportional to the marginal value of what is being constrained, the π_j, and also proportional to the amount of the resource used by the ideal **q** as opposed to the constrained optimal **p**.

The final way we can use Equation (34) is to allocate the holdings in P to alpha, the constraints and the t-costs. Simply multiply item (*i.*) by $\mathbf{V}^{-1}/\lambda$ and we find:

$$\begin{array}{cccc} \text{zero cost} = & \text{portfolio} & + \text{constraint} & + \text{t-cost} \\ \mathbf{q} = & \mathbf{p} & + \ \mathbf{f} & + \ \mathbf{g} \end{array}$$

$$\text{where } \mathbf{f} \equiv \sum_{j=1:J} \mathbf{f}_j \text{ and } \mathbf{g} \equiv \frac{\mathbf{V}^{-1} \cdot \upsilon}{\lambda} \tag{38}$$

$$\mathbf{f}_j = \frac{\mathbf{V}^{-1} \cdot \mathbf{a}'_j \cdot \pi_j}{\lambda}, \quad \mathbf{a}'_j \text{ is the } j\text{-th row of } \mathbf{A}\text{, transposed}$$

This attribution in terms of position makes it possible to consider the realized cost and benefits of the constraints. If we do the breakdown (Equation (38)) at the start of each period to portfolios—call them Q, P, F_j for the jth constraint, and G for the t-cost—then we can calculate the return on those portfolios. Over a reasonable period of time, say a quarter or a year, we should start to observe patterns. We can determine if the constraints are hurting or helping. We can estimate how much, if any, the intimidation of transactions cost, portfolio G, is detracting from performance. Of course, in any period where performance is poor, that is, portfolios Q and P underperform, then the constraints and intimidation will generally help.

EXERCISE 17 (Continuation of spreadsheet exercise.) show how attribution of the zero-cost optimal position varies, see Equation (38), as to the upper bound increase from 0.03 to 0.04.

Example

In this example we are rebalancing a pure long-short portfolio allocating to the equity markets in 13 countries. There is an upper and lower bound of 15% on all positions and there are four constraints. Two constraints are upper and lower limits on the total active position at 1%. The other two constraints are upper and lower limits of 1% on the aggregate exposure to the eight European countries ($n \in E$ indicates the subset of countries in

Europe). This constraint does not allow any large Europe versus the rest of the world position. Thus, we have a total of 30 constraints and bounds. Since all the constraints and bounds are symmetrical, at most 15 will be binding at any time.

$$(i.)\quad p_n \le 0.15 \quad \text{for all } n$$

$$(ii.)\quad -p_n \le 0.15 \quad \text{for all } n$$

$$(iii.)\quad \sum_{n=1:N} p_n \le 0.01 \text{ net position upper limit}$$

$$(iv.)\quad -\sum_{n=1:N} p_n \le 0.01 \text{ net position lower limit}$$

$$(v.)\quad \sum_{n\in E} p_n \le 0.01 \text{ net Europe upper limit}$$

$$(vi.)\quad -\sum_{n\in E} p_n \le 0.01 \text{ net Europe lower limit}$$

The transactions cost consists of a linear term and a quadratic market impact term.

Here is the scenario. The portfolio has a large underweight of the European (including the UK) markets of –7.78% that was considered too risky. Imposing constraints (*v.*) and (*vi.*) will make the portfolio roughly net zero in Europe. We rebalance with these additional constraints.

Exhibit 2 contains the initial position, the buys, the sells, and the resulting positions.

EXHIBIT 2 The Positions *P*, *Z*, *B*, and *S*

COUNTRY	POSITION (P)	INITIAL (Z)	BUYS	SELLS
FRA	–1.59	–0.22	0.00	1.37
GER	3.31	1.61	1.71	0.00
NTH	9.73	10.64	0.00	0.91
SPA	–4.87	–4.46	0.00	0.41
ITA	–15.00	–15.00	0.00	0.00
SWE	8.30	7.59	0.71	0.00
SWI	3.65	3.00	0.65	0.00
UKI	–4.53	–10.94	6.41	0.00
USA	–15.00	–15.00	0.00	0.00
CAN	–2.45	1.01	0.00	3.46
AUS	5.91	7.16	0.00	1.25
HKG	–1.09	–0.38	0.00	0.71
JPN	12.64	15.00	0.00	2.36

There is a net buying of 6.78% of the European countries in order to meet the constraint. Despite that move to Europe, the portfolio does go further short the French and Spanish markets. Initially two markets, Italy and the United States (USA), are at the lower limit and Japan is at upper limit on holdings. After rebalancing Japan has come off its upper bound although it remains the largest active position. Only two countries, the United States and Italy, do not trade.

Exhibit 3 gives us the allocation of alpha to the portfolio *P*, the constraints and bounds *F*, and transactions cost *G*.

EXHIBIT 3 Alpha Allocation

COUNTRY	ALPHA	PORTFOLIO	CONSTRAINTS	T COSTS
FRA	–1.56	0.02	–1.38	–0.19
GER	–0.74	0.54	–1.38	0.11
NTH	0.35	1.90	–1.38	–0.17
SPA	–2.22	–0.72	–1.38	–0.11
ITA	–4.12	–2.23	–1.90	0.01
SWE	2.82	3.89	–1.38	0.31
SWI	–0.65	0.61	–1.38	0.13
UKI	–0.77	0.15	–1.38	0.47
USA	–2.83	–1.41	–1.43	0.01
CAN	–1.47	–0.37	–0.64	–0.46
AUS	2.24	3.17	–0.64	–0.28
HKG	1.91	2.71	–0.64	–0.16
JPN	7.83	8.85	–0.64	–0.39

Although is not apparent, the potential alpha, column 2, and the alpha in the portfolio, column 3, are highly correlated; the correlation is 0.996. The mean of the alphas, column 2, is about 6 basis points. The mean of the alphas in the portfolio, column 3, is 132 basis points. That shift in mean of 126 basis points is due to 110 basis points in the constraints, 10 basis points in the bounds, and 6 basis points in costs. Note that Italy and USA, the countries that do not trade, have negligible contributions in the transactions costs, but their hitting the –0.15 limit registers in the constraint column.

Exhibit 4 has the aggregate measures of performance.

EXHIBIT 4 Aggregate Measure of Performance

SOURCE	VALUE (BASIS POINTS)
Improvement $O_P - O_Z$	6
Opp. Loss Z L_Z	14.68
Opp. Loss P L_P	4.33
Reduce Opp. Loss $L_Z - L_P$	10.35
T-Cost	4.17
Opp. Loss T-Cost	1.39
Opp. Loss Constraints	2.94

We spent 4.17 basis points to rebalance and satisfied the new constraint on the net European position and at the same time manage to tighten up so the opportunity loss of 14.68 basis points at the initial position Z is reduced to 4.33 basis points.

That opportunity loss, in turn, can be attributed in the fashion of Equation (37) as 2.94 basis points for the constraints and 1.39 basis points for the intimidation factor of transactions cost. Thus, the net impact of the transactions cost is the 4.17 direct cost plus 1.39 intimidation or 5.56 basis points. Of the opportunity loss due to transactions cost, the UK is responsible for 52% of the total. It makes the largest trade, a 6.41% purchase, and still has a backlog of 3.07%. For the constants the lower bounds on the USA (1.2 bps) and Italy (0.8 bps) are responsible for 68% of the opportunity loss.

Exhibit 5 shows the positions allocated as per Equation (38):

EXHIBIT 5 Portfolio Positions

COUNTRY	ZERO COST Q	PORTFOLIO *P*	CONSTRAINT *F*	T. COST G
FRA	–2.03	–1.59	2.20	–2.65
GER	5.13	3.31	0.46	1.36
NTH	8.95	9.73	1.78	–2.55
SPA	–6.41	–4.87	–0.94	–0.59
ITA	–18.12	–15.00	–3.43	0.30
SWE	9.68	8.30	0.23	1.16
SWI	3.71	3.65	–0.53	0.59
UKI	–1.46	–4.53	–1.76	4.83
USA	–18.07	–15.00	–4.11	1.04
CAN	–2.65	–2.45	2.39	–2.58
AUS	4.45	5.91	–0.53	–0.92
HKG	–0.34	–1.09	0.56	0.19
JPN	12.71	12.64	0.43	–0.36

Note that all the countries where we buy have positive positions in the T. Cost G column and all sells have negative positions. The biggest buy, the UK, and the biggest sell, Canada, clearly register. Similarly, Italy and the USA hit the lower limit, but the zero-cost unconstrained portfolio would like to go deeper into negative territory, –18.12% for Italy and –18.07% for the USA. The constraint position *F* picks up the bulk of the difference, –3.43% for Italy and –4.11% for the USA.

These are best analyzed through the lens of the covariance matrix. Exhibit 6 has the predicted risk of each portfolio on the diagonal and the predicted correlation of returns on the off diagonal.

EXHIBIT 6 Risk (on the Diagonal) and Correlation of the Portfolios *Q*, *P*, *F*, and *G*

	PORT Q	PORT P	PORT F	PORT G
Port *Q*	3.75%	0.986	0.546	–0.056
Port *P*	0.986	3.47%	0.460	–0.138
Port *F*	0.546	0.46	0.65%	–0.390
Port *G*	–0.056	–0.138	–0.390	0.52%

Summary

This chapter serves as an introduction to the following two chapters on attribution. They present a unified format for answering questions about portfolios on both an ex ante and ex post basis.

The introduction also described two related papers not included in this collection. "The Opportunity Set" is devoted to ex post return analysis and examines the realized potential for choosing among the assets. The "Attribution of Performance and Holdings" shows how these ideas can be linked to a portfolio optimization and used to explain the impact of constraints, bounds, and transactions cost on positions and outcomes.

13

Attribution[1]

Modeling Asset Characteristics as Portfolios

Introduction

This chapter presents a flexible, unified, and portfolio-centered approach to attribution. It treats attribution questions that occur before the fact (ex ante) and after the fact (ex post) in an entirely symmetric manner. Ex ante we are concerned with the sources of risk in the portfolio, the sources of possible outperformance, and whatever may be hindering us from a more efficient implementation. Ex post we are concerned with the performance of our forecasts, the performance of the portfolio, and the efficacy of our risk control.

In this chapter, we look at all of these questions in terms of an analysis of the covariance (or correlation) of the return between two portfolios. This requires an unusual step to model asset characteristics like alphas and returns as portfolios. Then we model the covariance of those characteristic portfolios and the portfolios that we actually hold.

The benefit in making this unfamiliar step of modeling asset characteristics as portfolios is an ability to look at all questions in a similar way. There is great economy of thought and software to be gained by concentrating in the portfolio domain.

There are two main thrusts to the chapter:

1. This chapter originally appeared as "Attribution" by Richard Grinold in the *Journal of Portfolio Management*, Winter 2006, 9–22. It was recognized with an Outstanding Paper Award as part of the 2007 Bernstein Fabozzi/Jacobs Levy Awards.

- Framing interesting portfolio management questions in terms of an analysis of covariance
- Analyzing the covariance

We start by showing how to model several aspects of a portfolio: risk, alpha, the transfer coefficient, and expected loss in utility as proportional to a covariance. Then we present a rudimentary analysis of risk predictions in a case where there is very little structure available. Next, we add structure by detailing a set of possible sources that are likely to be of help in explaining the composition of our portfolio. The same analysis that we have used to attribute alpha and risk ex ante can be used ex post to attribute return. Finally, we demonstrate the flexibility of the idea by showing other possible attribution schemes and also show how other return-regression schemes fall into this framework.

There is a vast amount of information available on attribution. A Google search on *portfolio attribution* gets 172,000 hits. This paper stems from the cross-sectional return-regression framework of Rosenberg and McKibben (1973), Fama and McBeth (1973), and Fama and French (1993). This paper uses the insight of Clarke, de Silva, and Thorley (2002, 2005) that implementation efficiency is neatly captured by the predicted return correlation between the portfolio you hold and the portfolio you would like to hold absent cost and constraints. In particular, Clarke, de Silva, and Thorley link the ex ante with the ex post and use the realized information coefficient as the ex post analogue of the transfer coefficient. Our notion of the backlog is similar in sprit to their "optimal active weight not taken," and our concept of the opportunity set is akin to their realized dispersion measure. However, our motivation and approach are different. We are trying to provide a framework—think of laboratory test equipment—that will facilitate studies of a wide range of topics on risk, implementation efficiency, and return. In fact, the initial motivation for the paper was the alpha vintage model mentioned below. In addition, the portfolio-centered approach that defines our correlations as the expected return correlation between two portfolios allows us to obtain exact results and effect a simplification of some of the notions.

Ex Ante

In this section, we review a few simple results from portfolio theory[2] to show how many ex ante aspects of a portfolio can be captured as a covariance, variance, volatility, or correlation. This allows us to gather several seemingly disparate facets of the portfolio in a unified framework.

We consider a collection of N assets and an N by N covariance matrix $\mathbf{V}$ whose n,mth element, $V_{n,m}$, is the predicted covariance of the return to assets n and m. Risk predictions are annualized. A portfolio, say portfolio P, is a vector of holdings $\mathbf{p} = \{p_1, p_2, \cdots, p_N\}$ that does *not* have to sum to

2. These can be found in Grinold and Kahn (2000) or in a more concentrated form in Grinold (2005), Chapter 7 in this book.

one and does *not* have to be nonnegative. Thus, we can represent long-short portfolios and the active portion of a long-only mandate as a portfolio. The variance and risk of this portfolio are given, respectively, by:

$$\omega_{P,P} = \sum_{n=1,N} \sum_{m=1,N} p_n \cdot V_{n,m} \cdot p_m; \quad \omega_P = \sqrt{\sum_{n=1,N} \sum_{m=1,N} p_n \cdot V_{n,m} \cdot p_m} . \tag{1}$$

For two portfolios, call them X and Y, the covariance, $\omega_{X,Y}$, and correlation, $\rho_{X,Y}$, are given by:

$$\omega_{X,Y} = \sum_{n=1,N} \sum_{m=1,N} x_n \cdot V_{n,m} \cdot x_m; \quad \omega_{X,Y} = \omega_X \cdot \rho_{X,Y} \cdot \omega_Y . \tag{2}$$

At any time, we have a forecast of annualized asset exceptional return that we call alpha; $\boldsymbol{\alpha} = \{\alpha_1, \alpha_2, \cdots, \alpha_N\}$. The alpha of portfolio P is:

$$\alpha_P = \sum_{n=1,N} \alpha \cdot p_n . \tag{3}$$

The information ratio of portfolio P, IR_P, is defined as the amount of alpha we expect to obtain in a year per unit of risk undertaken in pursuit of that alpha.

$$IR_P \equiv \frac{\alpha_P}{\omega_P}. \tag{4}$$

Our investment objective is to maximize what we call risk-adjusted or certainty equivalent return:

$$U_P = \alpha_P - \frac{\lambda}{2} \cdot \omega_{P,P}. \tag{5}$$

This is alpha less a penalty for risk. Of course, our overall objective must consider transactions costs and any limitations or constraints that might be imposed on the portfolio.

We start with the optimal solution to Equation (5) in the absence of constraints or transactions costs. We'll call that *ideal* portfolio Q. One can obtain Q's holdings $\mathbf{q} = \{q_1, q_2, \cdots, q_N\}$ by solving the equations:

$$\alpha_n = \lambda \cdot \sum_{m=1,N} V_{n,m} \cdot q_m, \tag{6}$$

where the sum $\sum_{m=1,N} V_{n,m} \cdot q_m$ is the covariance of asset n with portfolio Q. We write it as $\omega_{n,Q}$. Thus, we can write Equation (6) as:

$$\alpha_n = \lambda \cdot \omega_{n,Q} . \tag{7}$$

The alpha and risk-adjusted expected return of the ideal portfolio Q are:

$$\alpha_Q = \lambda \cdot \omega_{Q,Q} ; \; U_Q = \frac{\lambda}{2} \cdot \omega_{Q,Q} . \tag{8}$$

If we combine Equations (3), (7), and the fact that $\sum_{n=1,N} p_n \cdot \omega_{n,Q} = \omega_{P,Q}$, we see that the alpha and information ratio for any portfolio P are given by:

$$\alpha_P = \lambda \cdot \omega_{P,Q} = \lambda \cdot \omega_Q \cdot \rho_{P,Q} \cdot \omega_P . \tag{9}$$

After dividing Equation (9) through by ω_P, we have:

$$IR_P = \lambda \cdot \omega_Q \cdot \rho_{P,Q} . \tag{10}$$

The correlation, $\rho_{P,Q}$, of any portfolio P with the ideal portfolio Q is called the *transfer coefficient.*[3] It is a measure of implementation efficiency.

Notice that Equation (10) implies:

- The information ratio of portfolio Q is equal to $\lambda \cdot \omega_Q$. This follows by setting $P=Q$ and noting $\rho_{Q,Q} = 1$.
- Portfolio Q has the highest possible information ratio since $\rho_{P,Q} \leq 1$. That highest information ratio is given by:

$$IR \equiv IR_Q = \lambda \cdot \omega_Q . \tag{11}$$

The Backlog

Let portfolio B be the difference between P and Q. Portfolio B is called the *backlog*. It is the basket trade that we would need to make to take us from P to the ideal Q. The loss in objective value, also known as opportunity loss, from holding P rather that Q is proportional to the variance of the backlog:

$$U_Q - U_P = \frac{\lambda}{2} \cdot \omega_{B,B} . \tag{12}$$

What, one may ask, does this have to do with attribution? The key idea is that the risk, alpha, implementation efficiency, and loss in certainty equivalent return can be expressed as proportional to, respectively, a risk, a covariance, a correlation, and a variance. And, as we will show later, it is possible to model other aspects the any portfolio in terms of covariance and correlation as well. Thus, we should turn our thinking toward a general ability to explain covariance and correlation if we want a flexible and unified notion of attribution.

With No Structure

We start with little structure save the assets themselves. In this relatively simple environment, we can lay out the basic ideas that play a role in the more interesting and less transparent cases that follow.

3. See Clarke, de Silva, and Thorley (2001) and Grinold (2005).

Let X and Y represent two portfolios each captured as an N element vector of possibly long and short holdings; $\mathbf{x} = \{x_1, x_2, \cdots, x_N\}$ and $\mathbf{y} = \{y_1, y_2, \cdots, y_N\}$. The covariance of portfolios X and Y is:

$$\omega_{X,Y} = \sum_{n=1,N} \sum_{m=1,N} x_n \cdot V_{n,m} \cdot y_m . \tag{13}$$

We can rewrite this as:

$$\omega_{X,Y} = \sum_{n=1,N} x_n \cdot \sum_{m=1,N} V_{n,m} \cdot y_m = \sum_{n=1,N} x_n \cdot \omega_{n,Y}, \tag{14}$$

where $\omega_{n,Y}$ is the covariance of asset n's return with the return on portfolio Y.

We can think of x_n as our exposure to asset n and then $\omega_{n,Y}$ as expressing the link between asset n and the portfolio Y. Note that this is correct at the margin as:

$$\frac{\partial \omega_{X,Y}}{\partial x_n} = \omega_{n,Y} . \tag{15}$$

Of course, there is nothing special about either X or Y, so we could also write:

$$\omega_{X,Y} = \omega_{Y,X} = \sum_{n=1,N} y_n \cdot \omega_{n,X} . \tag{16}$$

This seemingly innocent and ad hoc procedure of allocating the component $x_n \cdot \omega_{n,Y}$ (or $y_n \cdot \omega_{n,X}$) of $\omega_{X,Y}$ to asset n is exactly what we will do in more structured (i.e., complicated) situations. There, under cover of a smidgen of theory and statistical technique, this procedure will look more elegant. Nevertheless, it is the same.

Risk Budgeting

Suppose that X and Y are both equal to a portfolio P. Then the variance, $\omega_{P,P} = \omega_P^2$, and risk, ω_P of portfolio P are given, respectively, by:

$$\omega_{P,P} = \sum_{n=1,N} \sum_{m=1,N} p_n \cdot V_{n,m} \cdot p_m; \quad \omega_P = \sqrt{\sum_{n=1,N} \sum_{m=1,N} p_n \cdot V_{n,m} \cdot p_m} . \tag{17}$$

Using the logic of Equation (2), we can write:

$$\omega_{P,P} = \sum_{n=1,N} p_n \cdot \omega_{n,P} . \tag{18}$$

We will attribute an amount of variance $p_n \cdot \omega_{n,P}$ to asset n and, similarly, a fraction of the variance, $p_n \cdot \omega_{n,P} / \omega_{P,P}$, to asset n.

Exhibit 1 shows an example using a 10-asset long and short portfolio of 10 major currencies.[4] The currencies are ordered so that the first currency, in

4. The US dollar is the base currency and is viewed as risk-free.

our case the yen, consumes the largest fraction of the budget. If we wish to decrease the portfolio risk, then decreasing the size of our active portfolio in the yen, Swiss franc, or Swedish kroner, would be a reasonable place to start. Note that both the euro and the Norwegian kroner are diversifying. Increasing our active positions in those assets will decrease overall risk as they are acting as counterweight to other positions in the portfolio.

EXHIBIT 1 Contribution to Risk of Each Asset

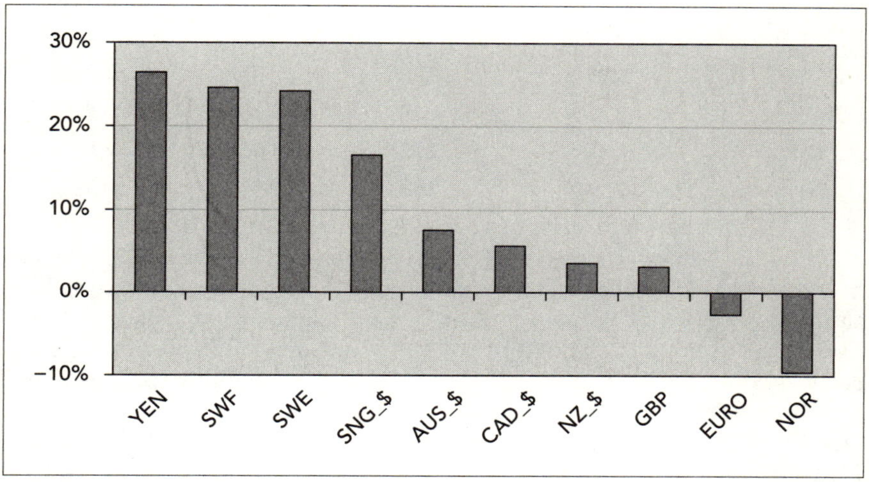

We'll look at two ways to interpret the allocation of risk in Equation (18). The first is based on correlation. Let's recall that we can break the covariance of asset n and portfolio P into components:

$$\omega_{n,P} = \omega_n \cdot \rho_{n,P} \cdot \omega_P \tag{19}$$

where ω_n is the risk of asset n, ω_P is the risk of portfolio P, and $\rho_{n,P}$ is the correlation of asset n and portfolio P.

If we define:

$$\psi_{P,n} \equiv \frac{p_n \cdot \omega_n}{\omega_P}, \tag{20}$$

then the fraction of variance attributed to asset n can be written as:

$$\frac{p_n \cdot \omega_{n,P}}{\omega_{P,P}} = \psi_{P,n} \cdot \rho_{n,P}, \text{ where } \sum_{n=1,N} \psi_{p,n} \cdot \rho_{n,p} = 1. \tag{21}$$

We can think of $\psi_{P,n}$ as being a standardized measure of portfolio P's exposure to asset n and, of course, $\rho_{n,P}$ is the correlation of asset n with portfolio P. $\psi_{P,n}$ has many of the attributes of a correlation. Indeed, in the case where all the N assets are uncorrelated, then $\psi_{P,n}$ is equal to the correlation $\rho_{n,P}$.

The numbers behind Exhibit 1 are included in Exhibit 2.

EXHIBIT 2 Risk Attribution for Currency Portfolio

	p(*n*)	rho(*n*,*P*)	psi(*P*,*n*)	PRODUCT
YEN	–9.62%	–0.554	–0.477	26.44%
SWF	–10.47%	–0.472	–0.522	24.62%
SWE	–12.14%	–0.425	–0.57	24.25%
SNG_$	–11.65%	–0,435	–0.379	16.48%
AUS_$	8.54%	0.184	0.413	7.60%
CAD_$	9.38%	0.175	0.327	5.74%
NZ_$	5.39%	0.132	0.272	3.60%
GBP	–2.45%	–0.315	–0.102	3.22%
EURO	1.40%	–0.378	0.067	–2.53%
NOR	12.94%	–0.156	0.606	–9.43%

Exhibit 2 has the long/short holdings of each asset in column 1. The holding in the US dollar is minus the sum of these holdings, about +8% in this case. The second column contains the correlation of each asset with the overall portfolio, $\rho_{n,P}$. The third column is our derived exposure $\psi_{P,n}$ and the last column the product $\psi_{P,n} \cdot \rho_{n,P}$. These are the numbers depicted in Exhibit 1; they sum to one. Note the apparent paradox that increasing the largest position, the Norwegian kroner, will actually reduce risk. The source is readily identified. We are short about 25% in European currency, and the long euro and Norway is not enough to counterbalance.

Structure

In this section we add structure to the attribution scheme.[5] We will attribute the risk, alpha, information ratio, transfer coefficient, and loss in utility of any portfolio P to specific sources rather than the assets themselves. In a departure from the norm, we will think of these sources as portfolios rather than asset groups such as sectors or common factors such as value, size, and momentum. The idea is to take abstract concepts such as liquidity and growth and give them an investment persona. Then we can answer questions about the relationship between our portfolio and liquidity and growth by examining the predicted return correlation between our portfolio and the liquidity and growth portfolios. In a later section we will illustrate some alternative specifications of the sources.

Let $S_j; j = 1, \cdots J$ be J possible sources. Each source is represented by a portfolio called S_j. The holdings in these portfolios are $\mathbf{s}'_j = \{s_{1,j}, s_{2,j}, \cdots, s_{N,j}\}$ where $s_{n,j}$ is the holding of asset n in source portfolio j. Each source, as a portfolio, will have its easily calculated predicted risk, alpha, and information

5. Results are derived in the Appendix.

ratio. The predicted covariance and correlation between any two sources is calculated in the usual manner:

$$\omega_{j,k} = \sum_{n=1,N} \sum_{m=1,N} s_{n,j} \cdot V_{n,m} \cdot s_{m,k}; \quad \omega_{j,k} = \omega_j \cdot \rho_{j,k} \cdot \omega_k . \tag{22}$$

We will make consistent use of a representative example to illustrate the points. In this example, we have chosen to partition our alpha sources into three groups according to their rate of change: FAST for the signals that change quickly, SLOW for the signals that change slowly, and INT for those that are somewhat in between. We can think of the FAST source as a model portfolio built entirely from the rapidly changing signals and a similar notion for SLOW and INT. In addition to the three sources, we have, the ideal portfolio *Q* and a less-than-ideal actual portfolio *P*. The forecasted risk, alpha, and *IR* of these five portfolios in our example are given in Exhibit 3.[6]

EXHIBIT 3 Forecast Properties (columns) of the Portfolios (rows).

POSITION	RISK %	ALPHA %	*IR*
FAST	4.00	4.00	1.00
INT.	3.00	2.25	0.75
SLOW	2.00	1.00	0.50
Ideal Q	6.65	11.07	1.66
Actual *P*	4.77	6.82	1.43

Exhibit 4 shows the correlations between the portfolios *Q* and *P* and the three source portfolios.

EXHIBIT 4 Correlation of Ideal Portfolio Q with the Source Portfolios (Row 1) and Correlation of Portfolio P with the Source Portfolios (Row 2)

CORRELATIONS	FAST	INT.	SLOW
$\rho_{j,Q}$	0.601	0.451	0.301
$\rho_{j,P}$	0.231	0.584	0.536

These results are in line with the general thrust of our example. Portfolio *Q*, unencumbered by trading costs, pursues the stronger FAST source aggressively and pays less attention to the SLOW and INT sources. Our actual implementation is deterred by transactions costs, so it moves more slowly. Portfolio *P* has a higher correlation with the slower moving signals. The line $\rho_{j,Q}$ is of special interest since these are the transfer coefficients of the source portfolios.

6. In the published article, this exhibit incorrectly has the alpha of portfolio *P* as 5.81% and the resulting *IR* as 1.22.

To analyze any portfolio, we use a regression to parse out the aspects of our holdings that are explained by each of the sources. The regression for a generic portfolio X is:

$$x_n = \sum_{j=1,J} s_{n,j} \cdot \beta_{X,j} + \varepsilon_{X,n}. \tag{23}$$

The regression splits the portfolio X into a component—let's call it $\hat{x}_n = \sum_{j=1,J} s_{n,j} \cdot \beta_{X,j}$—that is explained by the sources and a residual portfolio, $\varepsilon_X = \{\varepsilon_{X,1}, \varepsilon_{X,2}, \cdots, \varepsilon_{X,N}\}$, that is not explained by the sources. The regression is designed so that the residual and each of the source portfolios are uncorrelated:

$$0 = \sum_{n=1,N} \sum_{m=1,N} s_{n,j} \cdot V_{n,m} \cdot \varepsilon_{X,m} \text{ for } j = 1, 2, \ldots, J. \tag{24}$$

Exhibit 5 displays the regression results for portfolios P and Q. In our example, the ideal portfolio Q is a mixture of the three sources, so the regression R-squared is one. For the actual portfolio, P, the regression can only explain 87.34% of the portfolio's risk.

EXHIBIT 5 Regression Coefficients from Equation (23) and R-Squared of the Regression. Row 1 Is for the Ideal Portfolio Q and Row 2 for Portfolio P.

	FAST	INT.	SLOW	R-SQUARED %
$\beta_{j,Q}$	1.581	1.223	1.990	100.0
$\beta_{j,P}$	0.753	0.964	1.664	87.34

Let's return to our regression Equation (23). The residual portion is, as we note in Equation (24), uncorrelated with all of the sources. We will make frequent use of the relationship between the risk of X, the risk of the residual $\varepsilon(X)$, and the correlation between the two as captured in Equation (25).

$$\omega_{\varepsilon(X)} = \omega_X \cdot \rho_{X,\varepsilon(X)} \tag{25}$$

where (*i.*) $\omega_{\varepsilon(X)}$ is the risk of the residual portfolio ε_X, (*ii.*) ω_X is the risk of portfolio X, and (*iii.*) $\rho_{X,\varepsilon(X)}$ is the correlation between X and its residual ε_X.

In our example, $\rho_{P,\varepsilon(P)} = 0.355$. We can think of the regression R^2 as $\sqrt{1 - \rho^2_{X,\varepsilon(X)}}$.[7]

7. Not adjusting for degrees of freedom.

Within this framework, the covariance of any two portfolios X and Y can be written as:

$$\omega_{X,Y} = \sum_{j=1,J} \beta_{X,j} \cdot \omega_{j,Y} + \omega_{\varepsilon(X),\varepsilon(Y)}, \tag{26}$$

where $\beta_{X,j}$ is the regression coefficient for portfolio X and source j, $\omega_{j,Y}$ is the covariance between portfolio Y and source j, and $\omega_{\varepsilon(X),\varepsilon(Y)}$ is the covariance between the residual portfolios of X and Y. The component $\sum_{j=1,J} \beta_{X,j} \cdot \omega_{j,Y}$ is the fraction of covariance explained by the sources, and the component, $\omega_{\varepsilon(X),\varepsilon(Y)}$ is the covariance of the residuals and consequently not explained by the sources.

We can, again as we demonstrate in the Appendix, go a step further and attribute the *correlation* between X and Y to the sources:

$$\rho_{X,Y} = \sum_{j=1,J} \psi_{X,j} \cdot \rho_{j,Y} + \rho_{X,\varepsilon(X)} \cdot \rho_{\varepsilon(X),Y}. \tag{27}$$

In Equation (27):

$$\psi_{X,j} \equiv \frac{\beta_{X,j} \cdot \omega_j}{\omega_X} \tag{28}$$

is a standardized version of the regression coefficient that adjusts for the different levels of risk in source portfolio j and portfolio X. If we rescale the source portfolios so they all have the same risk as portfolio X, then $\psi_{X,j}$ would be the resulting regression coefficient.

We can also think of $\psi_{X,j}$ as a *pseudo-correlation*. Note that $\psi_{X,j}$ is dimensionless, as $\beta_{X,j}$ is in units of X per unit of j and that $\psi_{X,j}$ is indeed a correlation in the special case where the source are uncorrelated; that is, $\omega_{j,k} = 0$ if $j \neq k$. Notice also that the risk of the component $\beta_{P,j} \cdot s_j$ of portfolio P is $\omega_j \cdot \beta_{P,j} = \omega_P \cdot \psi_{P,j}$. Thus, at least in isolation, we can consider this product a risk allocation to source j.

Risk

We can use Equation (27) to attribute the variance of portfolios Q and P to the three sources. When $X = Y$ the sum in Equation (27) is necessarily equal to one, so we can account for all of the risk. The breakdown in our example is shown in Exhibit 6.

EXHIBIT 6 Attribution of the Variance of Portfolios Q in Row 1 and *P* in Row 2 to the Sources and a Residual

RISK BUDGET %	FAST	INT	SLOW	RESIDUAL
Ideal Q	57.16	24.86	17.98	0
Actual *P*	14.59	35.41	37.34	12.66

The numbers in each row of Exhibit 6 sum to 100%. The risk in portfolio Q is all explained by the sources, so the residual is 0.0. For the actual portfolio P, 12.66% is not explained by the sources. Once again, we can see how transactions costs slow down an actual implementation. For Q, 57.16% of its risk is explained by the FAST signal while that accounts for slightly less than 15% of the risk in the actual implementation.

Alpha and the Information Ratio

If we are trying to explain portfolio alpha, then we know from Equation (9) that:

$$\alpha_P = \lambda \cdot \omega_{P,Q} = \lambda \cdot \omega_Q \cdot \rho_{P,Q} \cdot \omega_P = IR \cdot \omega_P \cdot \rho_{P,Q}. \tag{29}$$

In particular for source j,

$$\alpha_j = \lambda \cdot \omega_{j,Q} = \lambda \cdot \omega_Q \cdot \rho_{j,Q} \cdot \omega_j = IR \cdot \omega_j \cdot \rho_{j,Q}. \tag{30}$$

If we apply Equation (27) to the transfer coefficient $\rho_{P,Q}$ we obtain:

$$\alpha_P = IR \cdot \omega_P \cdot \left\{ \sum_{j=1,J} \psi_{P,j} \cdot \rho_{j,Q} + \rho_{P,\varepsilon(P)} \cdot \rho_{\varepsilon(P),Q} \right\}. \tag{31}$$

In this breakdown alpha depends on three things:

- The environment in terms of the overall potential of the alphas captured by IR
- The level of risk in the portfolio ω_P
- The transfer coefficient $\rho_{Q,P}$

The transfer coefficient is in turn attributed to three sources and a residual. The part attributed to source j is $\psi_{P,j} \cdot \rho_{j,Q}$ where $\rho_{j,Q}$ is the transfer coefficient of source j and $\psi_{P,j}$ is the standardized exposure of portfolio P to source j.

Exhibit 7 describes the breakdown for portfolio P. The total alpha is 6.85%; it is all from the sources, no residual. Portfolio IR is 1.43 compared to a potential IR of 1.66. The transfer coefficient is 0.86.

The top panel tells what is possible. From the alphas we can calculate the highest possible IR, 1.66 which is the IR of portfolio Q. The second panel of Exhibit 7 details the alpha contributions by source. For source j, the contribution is $IR \cdot \omega_P \cdot \{\psi_{P,j} \cdot \rho_{j,Q}\}$, where $IR \cdot \omega_P$ is the potential, $\psi_{P,j}$ the standardized exposure, and $\rho_{j,Q}$ the transfer coefficient of source j. In our case, $IR = 1.66$ and $\omega_P = 4.77\%$, so $IR \cdot \omega_P = 7.92\%$. For example, our exposure to the INT source is $\psi_{P,INT.} = 0.606$, the transfer coefficient of the INT source is $\rho_{INT.,Q} = 0.451$, thus we attribute $7.94\% \cdot \{0.606 \cdot 0.451\} = 2.17\%$ to the INT source.

EXHIBIT 7 Analysis of Alpha for Portfolio *P*. Top Panel, Aggregates. Bottom Panel, by Source.

AGGREGATE RESULTS	PORTFOLIO Q	PORTFOLIO P
Alpha	11.07	6.85
Risk	6.65	4.77
Information Ratio	1.66	1.43
Transfer Coefficient	1	0.86

SOURCE RESULTS	FAST	INT.	SLOW	RESIDUAL	TOTAL
Exposure $\psi_{P,j}$	0.631	0.606	0.697	0.356	
Correlation $\rho_{j,Q}$	0.601	0.451	0.301	0	
Product $\psi_{P,j} \cdot \rho_{j,Q}$	0.379	0.273	0.209	0	0.86
Times $IR \cdot \omega_P$ %	3.01	2.17	1.66	0	6.85

Loss in Value Added

We can switch from the glass is two-thirds full perspective and move to the glass is one-third empty perspective, and ask how much of our potential value added are we giving up by holding *P* rather than *Q*. Recall that we define the backlog as $B = Q - P$ then the loss in objective value, also known as the opportunity loss, is proportional to the variance of the backlog portfolio:

$$\text{Opportunity Loss} \equiv U_Q - U_P = \frac{\lambda}{2} \cdot \omega_{B,B} . \tag{32}$$

In our example, $\lambda = 25$, so all we need do is explain the variance of the backlog as per Equation (6) with both *X* and *Y* equal to *B*. The backlog variance in Exhibit 8 stems predominantly from being behind the curve on the FAST signal and the residual risk in portfolio *P*. The expected loss in terms of risk-adjusted return is 1.54%.

EXHIBIT 8 Opportunity Loss

BACKLOG	FAST	INT.	SLOW	RESIDUAL	TOTAL
Opp. Loss %	1.20	0.02	–0.05	0.36	1.54
$\rho_{j,B}$	0.781	0.013	–0.030	0.235	1.00

Ex Post

Our goal is a unified and portfolio-centered view of both ex post and ex ante attribution. This unified perspective allows us to approach both aspects in the same way. We can put expectations alongside realizations and sort out what worked, what didn't, and why.

This pleasing symmetry has a price. We must represent those returns with a portfolio. This is done in exactly the same manner we used to capture the ex ante forecasts as an ideal portfolio. This time it will be an ex post ideal or *hindsight* portfolio. After we have made that small leap the ex post attribution will proceed in a manner that is analogous to the ex ante cases discussed previously.

Ex Post Ideal

We will let θ_n be the return on asset n.[8] Suppose that our forecast of alpha was a spot-on θ_n. What portfolio we would have built with those perfect forecasts? Call that hindsight portfolio R. Portfolio R has holdings $\mathbf{r} = \{r_1, r_2, \cdots, r_N\}$ that are calculated in the same manner as the holdings of the ex ante ideal portfolio Q:[9]

$$\theta_n = \lambda \cdot \sum_{n=1,N} V_{n,m} \cdot r_m. \tag{33}$$

As in Equation (9), we can write Equation (33) as:

$$\theta_n = \lambda \cdot \omega_{n,R} = \lambda \cdot \omega_R \cdot \rho_{n,R} \cdot \omega_n. \tag{34}$$

We can then aggregate Equation (34) and represent the return on any portfolio P in terms of its covariance with R:

$$\theta_P = \sum_{n=1,N} \theta_n \cdot p_n = \lambda \cdot \omega_{P,R} = \lambda \cdot \omega_R \cdot \omega_P \cdot \rho_{P,R}. \tag{35}$$

The Opportunity Set and Realized IC

From Equation (35) we see that the realized return on any portfolio P will be proportional to its risk, ω_P, and its correlation with the ex post ideal $\rho_{P,R}$. Equation (35) tells us three things:

- The ratio θ_R/ω_R equals $\lambda \cdot \omega_R$ since $\rho_{R,R} = 1$.
- The ratio θ_P/ω_P for any portfolio P is less than $\lambda \cdot \omega_R$ since $\rho_{P,R} \le 1$.
- The correlation $\rho_{P,R}$ is the ex post analogue of the transfer coefficient $\rho_{P,Q}$.

8. The θ_n are the returns we are forecasting. Thus, alpha is the forecast or expectation of theta: $\alpha_n = E\langle\theta_n\rangle$. In most cases, the theta is return less market return or could be net of components of return where we are not looking for potential value added but to control risk. For example, in an equity portfolio we many not want to take any active industry positions. In that context, θ_n would be returns net of industry.

9. See Equation (6).

We'll call $\rho_{P,R}$ the *realized information coefficient* or realized *IC* of portfolio *P*. We will call the maximum ratio that can be obtained the *opportunity set*.[10] It is:

$$OS = \frac{\theta_R}{\omega_R} = \lambda \cdot \omega_R \,. \tag{36}$$

Thus, explaining performance for portfolio *P* is equivalent to explaining the correlation $\rho_{P,R}$ since:

$$\theta_P = OS \cdot \omega_P \cdot \rho_{P,R} \,. \tag{37}$$

The product in Equation (37) neatly partitions the return into three buckets: *OS* representing the maximum opportunity available, ω_P representing the portfolio's aggressiveness, and finally the realized *IC*, $\rho_{P,R}$, which measures how effective we were in aligning our portfolio with the ex post ideal *R*.

For the source portfolios S_j; $j = 1, J$ introduced above we have:

$$\theta_j = OS \cdot \omega_j \cdot \rho_{j,R} \,. \tag{38}$$

The correlation $\rho_{j,R}$ is the realized *IC* for source *j*. It tells us in a standardized way how well our forecasts have done in this particular case. If we put Equation (37) together with our analysis of correlation, Equation (27), then we have the ex post analogue of Equation (31):

$$\theta_P = OS \cdot \omega_P \cdot \left\{ \sum_{j=1,J} \psi_{P,j} \cdot \rho_{j,R} + \rho_{P,\varepsilon(P)} \cdot \rho_{\varepsilon(P),R} \right\} \,. \tag{39}$$

Let's return to our example and see how this might work. In our case, we will need only five pieces of data to do the ex post analysis. These are: the size of the opportunity set *OS*, the realized information coefficients of the three source portfolios, $\rho_{j,R}$, and the correlation between the residual component of portfolio *P* and the return portfolio *R*, $\rho_{\varepsilon(P),R}$. In this example, using monthly residual returns, we have $OS = 10.51$. The correlation of the residual component of *P* with the return component is $\rho_{\varepsilon(P),R} = -0.117$, so we will lose on the residual. Exhibit 9 (see next page), gives the performance for the three sources, as per Equation (38).

10. This can be calculated directly: $OS = \sqrt{\sum_{n=1,N} \sum_{m=1,N} \theta_n \cdot V^{-1}_{n,m} \cdot \theta_m}$ where $V^{-1}_{n,m}$ is the *n,m*th element of the inverse of the covariance matrix **V**. A similar calculation holds for the maximum information ratio; $IR = IR_Q = \sqrt{\sum_{n=1,N} \sum_{m=1,N} \alpha_n \cdot V^{-1}_{n,m} \cdot \alpha_m}$. In subsequent work, the "Opportunity Set" paper (Grinold and Taylor (2009)), we adjust the definition to the length of the period and show that the expected size of the opportunity set is approximately $\sqrt{N}$ where *N* is the number of assets.

EXHIBIT 9 Performance of the Source Portfolios

SOURCE	FAST	INT.	SLOW
Risk ω_j %	4.00	3.00	2.00
Realized *IC*, $\rho_{j,R}$	0.087	–0.045	0.096
$\theta_j = OS \cdot \rho_{j,R} \cdot \omega_j$	3.66	–1.42	2.02

Row 1 is the risk, row 2 is the realized information coefficient, and row three is the return. The product of the number in row 1 times the number in row 2 and the opportunity set, in this case $OS = 10.51$, give us the number in row 3, the return attributed to the signal in that period.

As we can see, the FAST and SLOW signals were successful as predictions. Thus the 3.66% return attributed to the FAST source is the product of the opportunity set, 10.51, the risk of the FAST source, 4.00%, and the realized *IC* of the fast source, 0.087. The intermediate horizon source, INT, was less fortunate. An investment in source INT would lose 1.42%.

With this structure we can analyze the return on our portfolio in exactly the same manner we examine the properties of our alpha forecasts in Exhibit 7. The opportunity set is 10.51. The risk of our portfolio is 4.77%, so the potential return capture is $OS \cdot \omega_P = 50.18\%$.

Faced with this huge number we have to summon up our humility at this point and realize that capturing one-twentieth of the potential will be an outstanding outcome.

EXHIBIT 10 Attribution of Return to the Source Portfolios and Residual

SOURCE	FAST	INT.	SLOW	RESIDUAL	TOTAL
Exposure $\psi_{P,j}$	0.631	0.606	0.6970	0.3560	
Realized *IC* $\rho_{j,R}$	0.087	–0.045	0.0960	–0.1170	
Product $\psi_{P,j} \cdot \rho_{j,R}$	0.0549	–0.0273	0.0669	–0.0417	0.0528
$OS \cdot \omega_P \cdot \psi_{P,j} \cdot \rho_{j,R}$ %	2.76	–1.37	3.3600	–2.090	2.66

The standardized exposures to the three return sources are exactly the same as our standardized exposures to the three alpha sources. As we indicated above, the FAST and SLOW signals were successful while the INT was not. For the slow signal, our exposure is 0.697 and the realized *IC* as we see in Exhibits 9 and 10 is 0.096. Thus, we attribute a fraction $0.697 \cdot 0.096 = 0.067$ of the total potential return to the SLOW source. In this case the total potential is 50.18%, so we attribute $0.067 \cdot 50.18\% = 3.36\%$ to the SLOW source. In the same manner, we attribute to the FAST and INT sources and find a net contribution from the sources of 4.75%. As for the residual, our residual exposure is $\rho_{P,\varepsilon(P)} = 0.356$. This means our residual risk is $\omega_P \cdot \rho_{P,\varepsilon(P)} = 4.77\% \cdot 0.356 = 1.70\%$. As it turns out this residual portfolio has a realized *IC* of $\rho_{\varepsilon(P),R} = -0.117$ so we lose

$10.51 \cdot \{1.70\%\} \cdot \{-0.117\} = -2.09\%$ due to our residual position. All in, we are ahead, $4.75\% - 2.09\% = 2.66\%$. The realized *IC* for the entire portfolio is 0.06.

We can do the same analysis for the ideal portfolio *Q* and the backlog *B*. In the first case, we are asking how our model performed, and in the second we are asking how our implementation influenced performance.

Additional Points

In this section, we illustrate additional applications and discuss nuances of the scheme.

Risk Control

Up to this point we have concentrated on that element of return, θ_n, that we were attempting to forecast. We also want to control risk in the other components of return. Let's say that the total excess return on asset *n* is $\chi_n = \phi_n + \theta_n$ where θ_n is the component of return where we hope to add value and ϕ_n is the part of the return that we wish to control.

For example, in an industry neutral strategy ϕ_n would be the industry return. The Appendix indicates how one can separate these two elements of return. The total return to portfolio *P* is:

$$\chi_P = \phi_P + \theta_P; \quad \phi_P = \sum_{n=1,N} \phi_n \cdot p_n, \quad \theta_P = \sum_{n=1,N} \theta_n \cdot p_n. \tag{40}$$

We can identify sources of risk, portfolios $\hat{\mathrm{s}}_k$ $k = 1, \ldots, K$, which may or may not overlap with the sources of alpha. To continue the example mentioned above, these *K* sources could be *K* industry portfolios.[11] We can analyze portfolio *P* with respect to those sources of risk in exactly the same way as we analyzed it against the alpha sources; recall Equation (23):

$$p_n = \sum_{k=1,K} \hat{s}_{n,k} \cdot \hat{\beta}_{P,k} + \hat{\varepsilon}_{P,n}. \tag{41}$$

The exposures $\hat{\beta}_{P,k}$ and residual $\hat{\varepsilon}_P$ are, of course, distinct from the exposures and residuals that we obtained with the regression against alpha sources.

We then build an ex post risk portfolio *F* with holdings $\mathrm{f} = \{f_1, f_2, \cdots, f_N\}$ determined by:

$$\phi_n = \lambda \cdot \sum_{n=1,N} V_{n,m} \cdot f_m. \tag{42}$$

11. If we wish to control industry risk and market risk (i.e., little or no beta exposure), then we have to be a bit clever since the market portfolio is a mix of the industry portfolios. Controlling for the market and *K* – 1 of the industries is one approach.

Then, following the logic of the previous sections, the risk-controlled component of return for portfolio P is:

$$\phi_P = \lambda \cdot \omega_{F,P} = \lambda \cdot \omega_F \cdot \rho_{F,P} \cdot \omega_P . \tag{43}$$

Portfolio F has the maximum ratio of this controlled return per unit of predicted risk. That ratio is $CR = \lambda \cdot \omega_F$. Thus, we can write:

$$\phi_P = \lambda \cdot \omega_{F,P} = CR \cdot \omega_P \cdot \left\{ \sum_{k=1,K} \hat{\psi}_{P,k} \cdot \rho_{k,F} + \rho_{P,e(P)} \cdot \hat{\rho}_{e(P),F} \right\} \tag{44}$$

where, to distinguish them from exposures to alpha sources, I have placed hats over the standardized exposures, $\hat{\psi}_{P,k}$, to the sources of risk. Note you could do much of the same analysis of the alpha sources themselves along with the ex ante ideal Q and the residual ε_P of portfolio P to the alpha sources.

Indeed, the flexibility one has in this regard is a blessing and a curse: a curse since the ability to whimsically disgorge a mass of data can obscure understanding as much as help it. The great flexibility means that questions should be thought through in advance, and priors established, and then the attribution scheme set up in the light of those questions and priors.

Purists may recoil at the suggestion of one attribution for our pursuit of alpha and another for our efforts at risk control. I have taken to heart the proverb that "The hunter who chases two rabbits won't catch either."

Vintage Alpha Sources

Up to this point we have considered alpha by source. It is also possible to analyze alpha along the time dimension, that is, by date of arrival. At time t we have N alphas $\alpha_n(t)$. In addition, we know the alphas that were current for those N assets at earlier times $\alpha_n(t-\tau)$ for $\tau = 1, 2, \ldots, T$.[12] We can consider the portfolios $Q(t-\tau)$ with holdings $\mathbf{q}(t-\tau)$ that we would hold today based on the information of τ periods ago.[13] It is possible to separate today's ideal holding $\mathbf{q}(t)$ into (see the Appendix for details):

- An initial position $\mathbf{q}(t-T)$ where $\mathbf{q}(t-T)$ is the portfolio we would hold today based on the all the information available at time $t-T$.
- And T increments, $\mathbf{u}(t-\tau)$, where $\mathbf{u}(t-\tau)$ is the portfolio we would hold today based solely on the *new* information that flowed in during the time interval from $t-(\tau+1)$ to $t-\tau$.

If, for example, we are considering monthly periods over a year then T is 12. There are 12 increments of information and a portfolio $\mathbf{q}(t-12)$ that we would ideally hold today if we were using the information, $\boldsymbol{\alpha}(t-12)$

12. If the asset did not exist or was not in our data set in prior period, use zero.

13. This is to finesse the issue of changes in the covariance matrix from one date to the next. This question can be treated separately by having your sources be portfolio $\mathbf{q}_1$ as produced by a past covariance matrix and portfolio $\mathbf{q}_2$ as produced by the current covariance matrix. Then you could look at sources as the information as captured by $\mathbf{q}_1$ and the change in risk prediction as captured by, $\mathbf{q}_2 - \mathbf{q}_1$.

that was available one year ago. The base position, $\mathbf{q}(t-12)$, and the twelve increments, $\mathbf{u}(t-\tau)\ \tau=0,1,\ldots,11$, can be used as the sources. They will, by construction, explain 100% of the current ideal $\mathbf{q}(t)$.

The ex ante analysis will then tell us how exposed we are to information sorted by its date of arrival. The ex post analysis will tell us how well we fared in each time segment. We can compare the risk budget of the ideal, $\mathbf{q}(t)$, with any actual portfolio to gauge our exposure to dated rather than current information.

X,Y *or* Y,X

We have shown how to model ex ante alpha and ex post returns (among other things) as proportional to a covariance or correlation. With the introduction of various sources, we can decompose the correlation into a sum of standardized exposures of one portfolio to the sources multiplied by correlations of the other portfolio with the sources. The exposures are multivariate; they come from the regression. The transfer coefficients and realized *IC*s are bivariate; they are the correlations between two portfolios. We have chosen to do this in such a way that we can interpret the correlations as transfer coefficients ex ante and realized information coefficients ex post while the exposures are the same in both cases.

We could have chosen to go the other route and model the standardized exposures to the sources of the ex ante ideal *Q* and ex post ideal *R* and used the correlations of actual portfolio *P*. For alpha this yields:

$$\alpha_P = IR \cdot \omega_P \cdot \left\{ \sum_{j=1,J} \psi_{Q,j} \cdot \rho_{j,P} + \rho_{P,e(P)} \cdot \rho_{e(P),Q} \right\}. \tag{45}$$

Compare Equation (45) with Equation (31). For ex post return, we find:

$$\theta_P = OS \cdot \omega_P \cdot \left\{ \sum_{j=1,J} \psi_{R,j} \cdot \rho_{j,P} + \rho_{P,e(P)} \cdot \rho_{e(P),R} \right\}. \tag{46}$$

Compare Equation (46) with equation (39).

A most interesting comparison is when *P* is one of the source portfolios, say, S_ℓ. Then Equations (45) and (46) become:

$$\alpha_\ell = IR \cdot \omega_\ell \cdot \left\{ \sum_{j=1,J} \psi_{Q,j} \cdot \rho_{j,\ell} \right\} \text{ and } \theta_\ell = OS \cdot \omega_\ell \cdot \left\{ \sum_{j=1,J} \psi_{R,j} \cdot \rho_{j,\ell} \right\}. \tag{47}$$

If we use Equation (31), we have what appears to be a simpler and more reasonable result. The exposures and standardized exposures to a source S_ℓ are $\beta_{\ell,j} = \psi_{\ell,j} = 0$ if $j \neq \ell$ and $\beta_{\ell,\ell} = \psi_{\ell,\ell} = 1$. Therefore we have expressions:

$$\alpha_\ell = IR \cdot \omega_\ell \cdot \rho_{\ell,Q} \text{ and } \theta_\ell = OS \cdot \omega_\ell \cdot \rho_{\ell,R} \tag{48}$$

that rely heavily on the transfer coefficient $\rho_{\ell,Q}$ and realized information coefficient $\rho_{\ell,R}$.

Industry Practice

The author is familiar with one venerable and widely used ex post attribution system based on returns regression. We start with a group of K factors representing industries and common characteristics such as size, valuation, liquidity, and volatility. The factors are captured in an N by K matrix with coefficients $x_{n,k}$. We associate returns with the factors by regressing the asset returns θ_n against the factors:[14]

$$\theta_n = \sum_{k=1,K} x_{n,k} \cdot f_k + u_n \quad . \tag{49}$$

The estimated coefficients f_k are called factor returns and can be interpreted as the return on a portfolio.[15]

Given a portfolio P that we wish to analyze with holdings $\mathbf{p} = \{p_1, p_2, \ldots, p_N\}$, we calculate the exposures as:

$$x_{P,k} \equiv \sum_{n=1,N} p_n \cdot x_{n,k} \tag{50}$$

of portfolio P to common factor k. The return on portfolio P is then:

$$\theta_P = \sum_{k=1,K} x_{P,k} \cdot f_k + \sum_{n=1,N} p_n \cdot u_n . \tag{51}$$

We attribute the amount $x_{P,k} \cdot f_k$ (exposure $x_{P,k}$ times factor return f_k) to factor k. The remainder, $\sum_{n=1,N} p_n \cdot u_n$, is residual.

There is another way to interpret this procedure and link it with the method touted here. For each of the K factors, we can associate a source portfolio S_k with holdings $s_{k,n}$ by solving the equations:

$$x_{n,k} = \lambda \cdot \sum_{m=1,N} V_{n,m} \cdot s_{k,m} = \lambda \cdot \omega_{n,k} . \tag{52}$$

In this context, we can think of portfolio P's exposures as (see Equation (50)):

$$x_{P,k} = \lambda \cdot \omega_{P,k} = \lambda \cdot \omega_k \cdot \rho_{k,P} \cdot \omega_P . \tag{53}$$

Thus, the factor exposure is the risk penalty times a covariance of the source portfolio and the portfolio P that we wish to analyze. If we regress the ex post ideal portfolio R as in Equation (23) against the source portfolios:

$$r_n = \sum_{k=1,K} s_{n,k} \cdot \beta_{R,k} + \varepsilon_{R(n)}, \tag{54}$$

we find, as is demonstrated in the Appendix, that the resulting estimates, $\beta_{R,k}$, are exactly equal to the factor returns f_k obtained from Equation (49). Thus:

$$f_k = \beta_{R,k} = \frac{\omega_R}{\omega_k} \cdot \psi_{R,k} \tag{55}$$

---

14. A GLS regression.

15. It is a portfolio with holdings h_n with $\sum_{n=1,N} h_n \cdot x_{n,k} = 1$ and $\sum_{n=1,N} h_n \cdot x_{n,j} = 0$ for $j \neq k$ and minimal risk among all portfolios with those attributes.

where $\psi_{R,j}$ is the standardized exposure introduced above. Therefore, the return attributed to factor (source) k can be written in several ways:

$$x_{P,k} \cdot f_k = x_{P,k} \cdot \beta_{R,k} = \lambda \cdot \omega_R \cdot \omega_P \cdot \psi_{R,k} \cdot \rho_{k,P} = OS \cdot \omega_P \cdot \psi_{R,k} \cdot \rho_{k,P} \quad (56)$$

where, as in the previous section, $OS = \lambda \cdot \omega_R$ is the size of the opportunity set.

If we compare this with Equation (46), we see that this is just the Y,X method of splitting up the covariance rather that the X,Y method suggested in this chapter.

Another Perspective

The risk of the residual component of a portfolio is $\omega_P \cdot \rho_{P,\varepsilon(P)}$. Also, the risk of the jth source portfolio times its exposure $\beta_{P,j}$ is $\omega_j \cdot \beta_{P,j} = \omega_P \cdot \psi_{P,j}$. We can think of these products as risk allocations as in the formulae for portfolio risk, portfolio alpha, and portfolio return:

$$\begin{aligned}
\omega_P &= 1 \cdot \left\{ \sum_{j=1,J} \left(\omega_P \cdot \psi_{P,j}\right) \cdot \rho_{j,P} + \left(\omega_P \cdot \rho_{P,\varepsilon(P)}\right) \cdot \rho_{\varepsilon(P),P} \right\} \\
\alpha_P &= IR \cdot \left\{ \sum_{j=1,J} \left(\omega_P \cdot \psi_{P,j}\right) \cdot \rho_{j,Q} + \left(\omega_P \cdot \rho_{P,\varepsilon(P)}\right) \cdot \rho_{\varepsilon(P),Q} \right\} . \quad (57) \\
\theta_P &= OS \cdot \left\{ \sum_{j=1,J} \left(\omega_P \cdot \psi_{P,j}\right) \cdot \rho_{j,R} + \left(\omega_P \cdot \rho_{P,\varepsilon(P)}\right) \cdot \rho_{\varepsilon(P),R} \right\}
\end{aligned}$$

We see that the risk from each source and the risk from the residual are consistently represented in the equations allocating portfolio risk, portfolio alpha, and portfolio return. The whole *and each part* can be considered as the product of three entities:

- A constant that is independent of the portfolio or part; for Example 1, IR or OS.
- A stand-alone risk; for example, ω_P for the whole, $\omega_P \cdot \psi_{P,j}$ for source j, or $\omega_P \cdot \rho_{P,\varepsilon(P)}$ for the residual.
- A correlation such as $\rho_{P,R}$ for the whole, $\rho_{j,R}$ for source j, and $\rho_{\varepsilon(P),R}$ for the residual.

Conclusion

This chapter has presented a flexible, unified, and portfolio-centered approach to attribution. The key to the analysis is to pose the relevant question in portfolio terms. This perspective allows attribution by examination of the covariance or correlation of return between two portfolios. We demonstrated how to use this idea in situations with little structure and in situations with where it is possible to identify possible sources of expected return (alpha) and risk.

We showed how the same procedure that allowed us to do an ex ante analysis of a portfolio's alpha and predicted risk could also be used ex post to look at returns in much the same format. The procedure highlights the role of the transfer coefficient ex ante as the correlation of any portfolio's predicted return with the predicted return on an ex ante ideal portfolio. For the ex post analysis, we simply use an ex post ideal portfolio and refer to the correlation of any portfolio's return with the return on that ex post ideal as the realized information coefficient; which is the ex post analogue of the transfer coefficient.

In the final section we compared the approach suggested here with more traditional methods and find they are, in a sense, equivalent. Both attribute return (or alpha) to a source through a notion of exposure times result. In the traditional return regression models, the exposure to a source is bivariate and based on the relationship between that source and the portfolio being analyzed. The results (factor returns) are obtained through a multivariate manner through regression. In the methods suggested here, the exposures are obtained in a multivariate manner and the results are bivariate.

References

Clarke, Roger, Harindra de Silva, and Steven Thorley. 2005. "Performance Attribution and the Fundamental Law of Active Management." *Financial Analysts Journal* 61 (September/October): 70–82. Also, working paper, February 2005.

Clarke, Roger, Harindra de Silva, and Steven Thorley. 2002. "Portfolio Constraints and the Fundamental Law of Active Management." *Financial Analysts Journal*, September/October, 48–66.

Fama, Eugene F., and Kenneth R. French. 1993. "Common Risk Factors in the Returns on Stocks and Bonds." *Journal of Financial Economics* 33 (1): 3–56.

Fama, Eugene F., and James MacBeth. 1973. "Risk, Return, and Equilibrium: Empirical Tests." *Journal of Political Economy* 81 (May-June): 987–1008.

Grinold, Richard. 2005. "Implementation Efficiency." *Financial Analysts Journal*, September/October, 52–64.

Grinold, Richard C., and Ronald N. Kahn. 2000. *Active Portfolio Management.* 2nd ed. New York: McGraw-Hill.

Rosenberg, Barr, and Walt McKibben. 1973. "The Prediction of Systematic and Specific Risk in Common Stocks." *The Journal of Financial and Quantitative Analysis* 8 (March): 317–33.

Appendix

This appendix contains support for assertions made in the text that are more technical in nature. There are five parts:

- Description of the regression used in Section IV
- Derivation of Equation (27) in Section IV
- Separation of the risk controlled and forecast returns in Section VI
- Determining the new information flows in each period in Section VI
- Equivalence of the returns regression, Equation (49), and the portfolio regression, Equation (54)

Portfolio Regression

Equation (23), in matrix notation, is:

$$\mathbf{x} = \mathbf{S} \cdot \boldsymbol{\beta}_x + \boldsymbol{\varepsilon}_x. \tag{A1}$$

If we premultiply this by $\mathbf{S}' \cdot \mathbf{V}$ we find:

$$\mathbf{S}' \cdot \mathbf{V} \cdot \mathbf{x} = \{\mathbf{S}' \cdot \mathbf{V} \cdot \mathbf{S}\} \cdot \boldsymbol{\beta}_x + \mathbf{S}' \cdot \mathbf{V} \cdot \boldsymbol{\varepsilon}_x. \tag{A2}$$

Our goal is to have the residual uncorrelated with the sources, thus $\mathbf{S}' \cdot \mathbf{V} \cdot \boldsymbol{\varepsilon}_X = 0$ and we have:

$$\boldsymbol{\beta}_x = \{\mathbf{S}' \cdot \mathbf{V} \cdot \mathbf{S}\}^{-1} \cdot \mathbf{S}' \cdot \mathbf{V} \cdot \mathbf{x}. \tag{A3}$$

Note that $\{\mathbf{S}' \cdot \mathbf{V} \cdot \mathbf{S}\}$ is the J by J covariance of the source portfolios.

The risk of the residual holdings is:[16]

$$\omega_{\varepsilon(X)} = \sqrt{\boldsymbol{\varepsilon}_x' \cdot \mathbf{V} \cdot \boldsymbol{\varepsilon}_x}. \tag{A4}$$

For any portfolio Y, the covariance with this residual is:

$$\omega_{Y,\varepsilon(X)} = \mathbf{y}' \cdot \mathbf{V} \cdot \boldsymbol{\varepsilon}_x = \omega_Y \cdot \rho_{Y,\varepsilon(X)} \cdot \omega_{\varepsilon(X)}. \tag{A5}$$

16. This is corrected from the version in the published paper, which used the wrong Equation (A4).

Since $\mathbf{x}' \cdot \mathbf{V} \cdot \boldsymbol{\varepsilon}_X = \boldsymbol{\varepsilon}_X' \cdot \mathbf{V} \cdot \boldsymbol{\varepsilon}_X$,we can easily establish that:

$$\omega_X \cdot \rho_{X,\varepsilon(X)} = \omega_{\varepsilon(X)} \cdot \tag{A6}$$

Derivation of Equation (27)

We start with a slight variant of Equation (26):[17]

$$\omega_{X,Y} = \sum_{j=1,J} \beta_{X,j} \cdot \omega_{j,Y} + \omega_{\varepsilon(X)} \cdot \rho_{\varepsilon(X),Y} \cdot \omega_Y. \tag{A7}$$

We can write $\omega_{j,Y} = \omega_j \cdot \rho_{j,Y} \cdot \omega_Y$ and use the definition $\omega_X \cdot \psi_{X,j} = \beta_{X,j} \cdot \omega_j$ of $\psi_{X,j}$. Then Equation (A7) becomes:

$$\omega_{X,Y} = \omega_X \cdot \left\{ \sum_{j=1,J} \psi_{X,j} \cdot \rho_{j,Y} \right\} \cdot \omega_Y + \omega_{\varepsilon(X)} \cdot \rho_{\varepsilon(X),Y} \cdot \omega_Y. \tag{A8}$$

In addition, recall from Equation (A6) that $\omega_{\varepsilon(X)} = \omega_X \cdot \rho_{X,\varepsilon(X)}$, so:

$$\omega_{X,Y} = \omega_X \cdot \left\{ \sum_{j=1,J} \psi_{X,j} \cdot \rho_{j,Y} + \rho_{X,\varepsilon(X)} \cdot \rho_{\varepsilon(X),Y} \right\} \cdot \omega_Y. \tag{A9}$$

Separation of Return Components

Let $\hat{\mathbf{S}}$ be the N by K matrix where each column is a source of risk that we wish to control. Let $\boldsymbol{\chi}$ be the excess return and define portfolio Y as $\boldsymbol{\chi} = \lambda \cdot \mathbf{V} \cdot \mathbf{y}$. A regression as in Equation (A1),

$$\mathbf{y} = \hat{\mathbf{S}} \cdot \boldsymbol{\beta}_Y + \boldsymbol{\varepsilon}_Y$$

gives us returns we wish to control, $\boldsymbol{\phi} = \lambda \cdot \mathbf{V} \cdot \hat{\mathbf{S}} \cdot \boldsymbol{\beta}_Y$ and the residual we are trying to predict: $\boldsymbol{\theta} = \lambda \cdot \mathbf{V} \cdot \boldsymbol{\varepsilon}_Y$. The portfolios $\mathbf{f} = \hat{\mathbf{S}} \cdot \boldsymbol{\beta}_Y$ and $\mathbf{r} = \boldsymbol{\varepsilon}_Y$ are uncorrelated and $\boldsymbol{\theta}' \cdot \mathbf{V}^{-1} \cdot \boldsymbol{\phi} = 0$.

New Information Flows in Vintage Example

For each $\tau = 0, T$ calculate $\mathbf{q}(t-\tau)$ by solving $\boldsymbol{\alpha}(t-\tau) = \lambda \cdot \mathbf{V} \cdot \mathbf{q}(t-\tau)$. Then define:

$$\gamma(t-\tau) = \frac{\mathbf{q}'(t-\tau) \cdot \mathbf{V} \cdot \mathbf{q}(t-\tau-1)}{\mathbf{q}'(t-\tau-1) \cdot \mathbf{V} \cdot \mathbf{q}(t-\tau-1)}. \tag{A10}$$

Our incremental portfolio is:

$$\mathbf{u}(t-\tau) = \mathbf{q}(t-\tau) - \gamma(t-\tau) \cdot \mathbf{q}(t-\tau-1). \tag{A11}$$

17. Equation (26) involves the covariance of $\varepsilon(X)$ with $\varepsilon(Y)$. Since the sources are uncorrelated with the residuals, $\omega_{\varepsilon(X),\varepsilon(Y)} = \omega_{\varepsilon(X),Y} \Rightarrow \omega_{\varepsilon(X)} \cdot \rho_{\varepsilon(X),Y} \cdot \omega_Y$.

The condition (A10) guarantees that the new positions are uncorrelated with the preceding portfolio, that is, $\mathbf{u}'(t-\tau)\cdot\mathbf{V}\cdot\mathbf{q}(t-\tau-1)=0$.[18]

Equivalence of the Returns Regression, Equation (49), and the Portfolio Regression, Equation (54)

If we start with the returns regression:

$$\boldsymbol{\theta}=\mathbf{X}\cdot\mathbf{f}+\mathbf{u},\quad \mathbf{f}=\left\{\mathbf{X}'\cdot\mathbf{V}^{-1}\cdot\mathbf{X}\right\}^{-1}\cdot\mathbf{X}'\cdot\mathbf{V}^{-1}\cdot\boldsymbol{\theta} \qquad \text{(A12)}$$

as compared to the portfolio regression:

$$\mathbf{r}=\mathbf{S}\cdot\boldsymbol{\beta}_R+\boldsymbol{\varepsilon}_R,\quad \boldsymbol{\beta}_R=\{\mathbf{S}'\cdot\mathbf{V}\cdot\mathbf{S}\}^{-1}\cdot\mathbf{S}'\cdot\mathbf{V}\cdot\mathbf{r}. \qquad \text{(A13)}$$

The most direct way is just to substitute $\boldsymbol{\theta}=\lambda\cdot\mathbf{V}\cdot\mathbf{r}$ and $\mathbf{X}=\lambda\cdot\mathbf{V}\cdot\mathbf{S}$ into parts of the formula (A12) for **f**.[19] We obtain:

$$\mathbf{X}'\cdot\mathbf{V}^{-1}\cdot\mathbf{X}=\lambda^2\cdot\mathbf{S}'\cdot\mathbf{V}\cdot\mathbf{S},\quad \mathbf{X}'\cdot\mathbf{V}^{-1}\cdot\boldsymbol{\theta}=\lambda^2\cdot\mathbf{S}'\cdot\mathbf{V}\cdot\mathbf{r}. \qquad \text{(A14)}$$

Note the risk aversion cancels and plays no role in the calculation, thus $\boldsymbol{\beta}_R=\mathbf{f}$.

18. The published paper incorrectly referenced Equation (A9).
19. The published paper incorrectly referenced Equation (A11).

14

The Description of Portfolios[1]

Top-level descriptions of portfolios are clear-cut. We calculate the predicted risk, the predicted return, trades, and subsequent realized returns with formulae that are widely used and understood.

Matters become obscure when we attempt to reveal the numbers behind the numbers. In this chapter, we present a general and flexible method to describe important aspects of portfolio and related investment process in terms of an underlying set of factors that can be customized to suit the question at hand. It may not appear to be the case, but the results in this paper are consistent the type of return attribution described in Grinold and Kahn (2000). This is old wine in an assortment of new bottles. The approach is very different, it is much more general, and the results are presented in a different manner.

The idea is to use portfolio theory to describe portfolios. The tools are a mix of portfolios and factors. Our factors are not mystical forces that are sensed and unseen. They are visible. Indeed any list of numbers, one for each asset, will serve as a factor. Examples are the asset's earnings yield, the asset's return in some past period, the asset's expected return, the asset's realized return in a subsequent period, and so on.

We distinguish two types of factors: *target factors* that we would like to explain, such as alpha (expected residual return) and realized return, and *explanatory factors* that we think will assist us in making that description. We carry a small model having 10 assets and three explanatory factors through the chapter to provide a specific example.

1. This chapter originally appeared as "The Description of Portfolios" by Richard Grinold in the *Journal of Portfolio Management*, Winter 2011, 15–30. It was recognized with an Outstanding Paper Award as part of the 2007 Bernstein Fabozzi/Jacobs Levy Awards.

For every factor, there is a portfolio. Call it the factor portfolio. This leads to three types of portfolios:

1. The portfolio you wish to analyze. Think of this as the portfolio you hold. Call it *P*.
2. The factor portfolio linked to the factor we wish to analyze, such as alpha or return. Call this the target portfolio *T*.
3. A collection of *K* factor portfolios associated with the explanatory factors we presume will help in revealing the links between *P* and *T*. Call these $S_1, S_2, \cdots, S_K$.

The beauty of this structure is in its generality. For instance, we can make the target portfolio *T* and the portfolio we wish to analyze, *P*, the same portfolio, that is, set $T = P$. In that case we are analyzing the variance of portfolio *P*. If the target *T* is associated with some factor of great interest, say alpha or realized return, then we can work the system backward and have *P* be the same portfolio, that is, set $P = T$. Then we can examine the sources of alpha and return in a context independent of any particular portfolio.

To get the job done we need a fourth type of portfolio that we call the factor-mimicking portfolio. There is one mimicking portfolio for each of the *K* explanatory factors. The factor-mimicking portfolios are not entirely new. They are a repackaged form of the factor portfolios $S_1, S_2, \cdots, S_K$. Each mimicking portfolio is assembled so it is exposed to one and only one of the *K* factors. Call the mimicking portfolios $M_1, M_2, \cdots, M_K$.

The main contributions of this chapter are:

- Moving beyond the question of return attribution to the more general problem of portfolio description.
- Showing that many disparate portfolio description problems are variations on a common problem of explaining the covariance between two portfolios.
- Using mimicking portfolios to explain the positions held by any portfolio and the covariance of that portfolio with the assets.
- Interpreting a portfolio's factor exposure as a covariance.
- Developing the risk and correlation based (*risk-corr*) method of presenting results. Risk-corr places the correlations between the portfolios front and center.

In the next section, we present the idea of factors and their representation as factor portfolios. We also define the factor-mimicking portfolios and associate a set of mimicking factors with them. These two sets of factor portfolios and two sets of factors are the building blocks for later results. We then show how to represent the positions in any portfolio *P* as a mixture of the mimicking portfolios and a residual portfolio. The weights in the mixture are portfolio *P*'s exposures to the factors. The same idea, and the same weights, can be used to represent the covariance of portfolio *P* with the assets as a mixture of the mimicking factors. These two relationships are the key to explaining variance and covariance using the factor structure.

We then turn to the risk-corr interpretation of the results. Previously, we measured the contribution of factor k to the total as the product of two exposures: the exposure of portfolio P to factor k and the exposure of the target portfolio T to mimicking factor k. It is possible to tear that product apart and replace it with a more portfolio theory–oriented function of five pieces. The pieces are the risks of portfolios P and T and three correlations:

- the correlation between portfolio P and factor portfolio k, S_k,
- the correlation between factor portfolio S_k and mimicking portfolio M_k, and
- the correlation between mimicking portfolio M_k and target portfolio T.

The relations are indicated in Exhibit 1.

EXHIBIT 1 The Relationship Path for Factor k Linking the Portfolio P and the Target Portfolio T

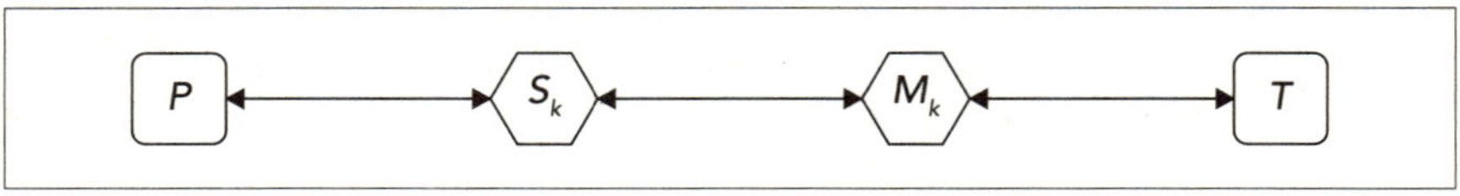

This in-depth look lets us view the key drivers of the results and also flag suspicious results since the correlation between factor portfolio S_k and mimicking portfolio M_k is also a diagnostic for collinearity among the factors. We conclude with a summary and two appendices. Appendix A shows how results specialize when there is a second factor structure underlying the prediction of risk. Appendix B tells us what happens if we switch the roles of factor portfolios and mimicking portfolios (switch S_k and M_k in Exhibit 1).

This paper continues a line of reasoning that started in Grinold (2006), which is Chapter 13, "Attribution." That in turn was stimulated by the work of Clarke, de Silva, and Thorley (2002). The subject is related to the question of return attribution (performance measurement). There is a vast literature on that topic, indeed a special journal. I shall not try to represent it here.

Factors, Source Portfolios, and Mimicking Portfolios

In this section, we introduce the notion of factors and the four ways they can be represented. All four play a significant role in what follows.

We consider an investment universe of N assets. A factor is a measurable attribute of the assets. At the crudest level, it is a list of N numbers, one for each asset. Examples are the earnings-to-price ratio, last period's return, next period's return (you have to wait for this one), the predicted return from some sell-side sage, the fraction of sales outside the home country, a consensus estimate of earnings growth, the debt-to-equity ratio, the fraction of revenue derived from the technology sector, and so on.

We usually consider more than one factor, so we'll use the matrix notation $x_{n,k}$ to describe the exposure of asset $n = 1, N$ to factor $k = 1, K$. There are fewer, usually far fewer, factors than assets. In no case will there be more factors than assets; that is, $K \leq N$. Exhibit 2 introduces the example we follow throughout. There are, for limitations of space, just 10 assets. There are three factors. In this example the factors are investment themes: VALUE, QUALITY, and SENTIMENT (abbreviated SENT.).

EXHIBIT 2 **Scores of 10 Assets on Three Investment Themes**

X	VALUE	QUALITY	SENT.
A1	–1.772	–0.594	–0.181
A2	0.609	–0.370	–0.524
A3	–0.383	1.117	1.502
A4	–0.176	0.203	–0.451
A5	–0.346	–0.552	–1.117
A6	1.329	–0.329	1.582
A7	–0.143	–0.650	–1.298
A8	–0.090	1.031	0.117
A9	1.695	–0.390	–0.413
A10	–0.724	1.940	0.784

In this particular example, the assets are scored on the three investment themes. That means the average in each column is zero and the standard deviation is one. The scoring is just for convenience. Indeed, one of our main points is that scale does not matter. We could multiply the VALUE numbers by 3.2, the QUALITY numbers by 0.4, and the SENTIMENT numbers by 0.74 and the results will be the same.

The Source Portfolios

The factors have a portfolio representation. This link between factor and portfolio flows through an N by N covariance matrix **V**.[2] Suppose that $\mathbf{x}_k$ is the kth column of the matrix **X**, the kth factor. We can tie $\mathbf{x}_k$ to a portfolio by finding the portfolio, call it S_k with positions $\mathbf{s}_k$, that solves:

$$\mathbf{x}_k = \mathbf{V} \cdot \mathbf{s}_k. \tag{1}$$

The connection in Equation (1) has an efficiency interpretation. Suppose we considered any portfolio, call it P, with positions **p** in the N assets. The

2. This covariance matrix may or may not be based on the factor structure **X** or some other collection of $J \neq K$ factors. One of our objectives is to liberate the choices of factors used to answer often ad hoc questions about portfolios from the set of factors used to effectively capture risk. See Appendix A for an analysis of the intersection of risk factors and explanatory factors.

exposure of portfolio P to factor k and the predicted risk of portfolio P are, respectively:

$$x_{P,k} = \sum_{n=1,N} p_n \cdot x_{n,k} = \mathbf{p}' \cdot \mathbf{x}_k, \quad \omega_P = \sqrt{\mathbf{p}' \cdot \mathbf{V} \cdot \mathbf{p}}. \tag{2}$$

Portfolio S_k defined in Equation (1) has the highest ratio of exposure to factor k divided by risk, $x_{P,k}/\omega_p$. Portfolio S_k is an efficient manifestation of factor k.

The matrix **S** consists of the portfolios $\mathbf{s}_1$ in column one, $\mathbf{s}_2$ in column two and so forth up to $\mathbf{s}_K$ in the last column K. The relationship between the factor exposures contained in the matrix **X** and the source portfolios in the matrix **S** is the matrix generalization of Equation (1):

$$\mathbf{X} = \mathbf{V} \cdot \mathbf{S}, \quad \mathbf{S} = \mathbf{V}^{-1} \cdot \mathbf{X}. \tag{3}$$

For the sample data given in Exhibit 2, the values for the source portfolios are reported in Exhibit 3.

EXHIBIT 3 The Source Portfolios

S	VALUE	QUALITY	SENT.
A1	–32.19	–10.87	–4.24
A2	18.41	–12.90	–18.77
A3	–12.43	30.96	41.13
A4	–6.09	–31.90	–13.03
A5	–8.77	–12.34	–25.02
A6	42.87	–11.73	51.60
A7	–3.73	–11.81	–23.66
A8	–4.22	29.30	2.02
A9	45.42	–11.43	–12.80
A10	–20.12	49.28	18.87

The K source portfolios are composite assets used to construct more general portfolios. The K by K covariance matrix of those composites is:

$$\Omega = \mathbf{S}' \cdot \mathbf{V} \cdot \mathbf{S}. \tag{4}$$

Exhibit 4 shows the three-by-three matrix Omega for our example.

EXHIBIT 4 Covariance of the Source Portfolios

OMEGA	VALUE	QUALITY	SENT.
Value	**15.05**	*–62.15*	*27.69*
Quality	–0.271	**15.26**	*126.97*
Sent.	0.119	0.538	**15.45**

The diagonals (**bold**) are the standard deviations. The numbers in the upper triangle (*italics*) are the covariances, and the numbers in the lower triangle are the correlations.

The Mimicking Portfolios

The source portfolios described above are linked to the factors on a one-to-one basis. A change in asset A6's exposures to the QUALITY factor would not change the position of asset A6 in the VALUE or the SENTIMENT source portfolio. The mimicking portfolios are a second collection of portfolios that view the factors in context.

Recall that the source portfolio k has the most of factor k per unit of risk. Mimicking portfolio k has the highest possible exposure to factor k per unit of risk with the added proviso that it has zero exposure to the other factors $j \neq k$. In the context of the example, we want a QUALITY mimicking portfolio that has a zero exposure to VALUE and SENTIMENT and at the same time captures QUALITY efficiently—that is, the most QUALITY per unit of risk. More technically, we look for a minimal risk portfolio M_k that has exposures $x_{M_k,k} = 1$ and $x_{M_k,j} = 0$ for each factor j not equal to k.

Let $\mathbf{m}_k$ be the positions in portfolio M_k that do the trick and let $\mathbf{M}$ be the N by K matrix with $\mathbf{m}_k$ in column k.[3] The formula for $\mathbf{M}$ is straightforward,

$$\mathbf{M} = \mathbf{S} \cdot \Omega^{-1}. \tag{5}$$

Recall that Ω is the K by K covariance matrix of the source portfolios.

Each mimicking portfolio is a weighted (possibly long and short) mixture of the source portfolios. Thus, the mimicking portfolios do not open up new territory; they are a more focused description of the old territory.

For the example, Exhibit 5 displays the values of the mimicking portfolios.

EXHIBIT 5 The mimicking portfolios

M	VALUE	QUALITY	SENT.
A1	−0.190	−0.141	0.079
A2	0.102	0.030	−0.106
A3	−0.069	0.023	0.168
A4	−0.086	−0.191	0.057
A5	−0.029	−0.008	−0.097
A6	0.100	−0.191	0.306
A7	−0.003	0.003	−0.100
A8	−0.046	0.192	−0.099
A9	0.239	0.083	−0.125
A10	−0.022	0.227	−0.039

The mimicking portfolios certainly differ in scale from the source portfolios, as shown in Exhibit 3. They are similar in structure: the correlations

3. Let $\mathbf{u}_k$ be a vector with kth element equal to one and all the other elements equal to zero. Find a portfolio $\mathbf{m}$ so that $\mathbf{m}' \cdot \mathbf{V} \cdot \mathbf{m}$ is minimized with constraints $\mathbf{X}' \cdot \mathbf{m} = \mathbf{u}_k$. The solution is the kth mimicking portfolio.

of positions are 89% for VALUE, 77% for QUALITY, and 82% for SENTIMENT. Only 6 of the 10 positions in the mimicking SENTIMENT portfolio have the same sign as the positions in the source SENTIMENT portfolio.

The mimicking portfolios serve as a second group of composites, or building blocks, which we can use to construct or to represent the holdings in any portfolio. The covariance matrix of the mimicking portfolios is

$$\Psi = \mathbf{M}' \cdot \mathbf{V} \cdot \mathbf{M}. \tag{6}$$

For the example, Exhibit 6 displays the covariance matrix of the mimicking portfolios.

EXHIBIT 6 Covariance of the Mimicking Portfolios

PSI	VALUE	QUALITY	SENT.
Value	**0.073**	*0.0025*	*–0.0019*
Quality	0.400	**0.0849**	*–0.0041*
Sent.	–0.326	–0.597	**0.0812**

The diagonals (**bold**) are the standard deviations. The numbers in the upper triangle (*italics*) are the covariances, and the numbers in the lower triangle are the correlations.

Three things are of note in Exhibit 6. First, the standard deviations are on a vastly different scale than the standard deviations of the source portfolios, as shown in Exhibit 4. Second, while the VALUE mimicking portfolio has zero exposure to QUALITY and SENTIMENT factors, it can be correlated with the QUALITY and SENTIMENT mimicking portfolios. Third, notice that the correlations of the mimicking portfolios have the opposite signs of the correlations of the source portfolios in Exhibit 4. We discuss this inverse relationship later.

Mimicking Factors

The original set of factors, **X**, implied a collection of efficient source portfolios, **S**. In the same fashion, the mimicking portfolios **M** can be used to imply a collection of K mimicking factors. We will let **Y** be the N by K matrix with mimicking factor k in the kth column. The relationship between **M** and **Y** is a direct analogy with the relationship between **X** and **S** in Equation (3):

$$\mathbf{Y} = \mathbf{V} \cdot \mathbf{M}, \quad \mathbf{M} = \mathbf{V}^{-1} \cdot \mathbf{Y}. \tag{7}$$

To complete the example, the mimicking factors are reported in Exhibit 7.

EXHIBIT 7 The Mimicking Factor Exposure

Y	VALUE	QUALITY	SENT.
A1	−0.01057	−0.00793	0.00468
A2	0.00335	0.00100	−0.00311
A3	−0.00218	0.00091	0.00605
A4	−0.00304	−0.00724	0.00231
A5	−0.00105	−0.00024	−0.00443
A6	0.00321	−0.00558	0.00922
A7	0.00014	0.00031	−0.00562
A8	0.00185	0.00672	−0.0033
A9	0.00887	0.00309	−0.0044
A10	−0.00057	0.00895	−0.00141

The mimicking factor exposures **Y** are remarkably different in scale to the factor exposures **X** in Exhibit 2. They are, however, similar in texture. The correlation between the two is 0.82, and they agree on sign in 70% of the cases (21 of 30).

Exhibit 8 summarizes the names and notation introduced to this point.

EXHIBIT 8 Summary of Notation and Definitions

	SOURCES	MIMICKING
Factors (*N by K*)	X	Y
Ports (*N by K*)	S	M
F & P Connection	$X = V \cdot S$	$Y = V \cdot M$
Covar. (*K by K*)	$\Omega = S' \cdot V \cdot S$	$\Psi = M' \cdot V \cdot M$

Thus, we have a foursome: two sets of factors, **X** and **Y**, and two sets of portfolios, **S** and **M**. Exhibit 9 illustrates the relationships between these four elements.

EXHIBIT 9 Graphic Summary of the Relationships Among the Factors X, Source Portfolios S, Mimicking Portfolios M, and Mimicking Factors Y

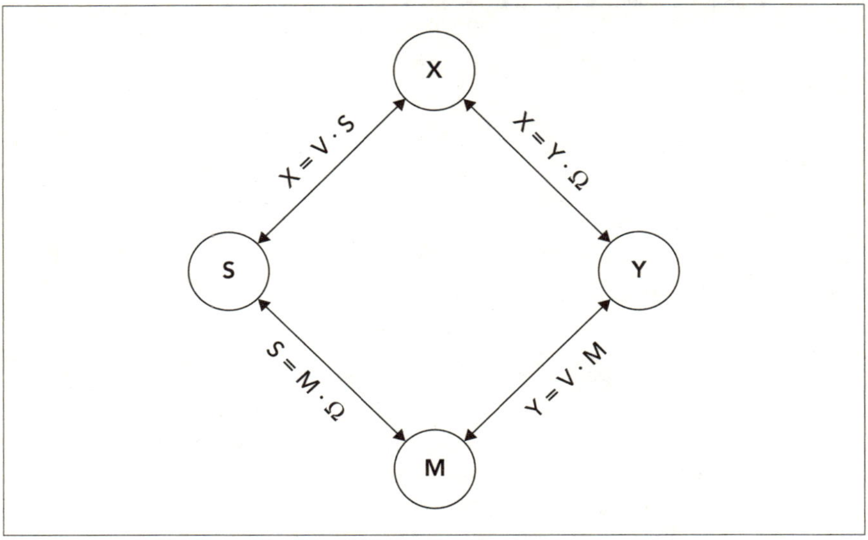

Special Links

There are three links between the factors **X** and sources portfolio, **S**, and the mimicking factors **Y** and the mimicking portfolios **M**. They are illustrated in Exhibit 10.

EXHIBIT 10 The Key Linkages Between the Factor-Source Portfolios (X,S) and Mimicking Factors and Portfolios (Y,M)

	PORTFOLIO LINKS
Projection	$S \cdot Y' = M \cdot X'$
Covariance	$M' \cdot V \cdot S = \mathbf{I}$
Scale	$M' \cdot V \cdot M = \Psi = \Omega^{-1} = \{S' \cdot V \cdot S\}^{-1}$

The projection relationship is used to represent portfolios in terms of the source or mimicking composites. More on this theme will follow.

The covariance relationship says that the mimicking portfolio for the kth factor, M_k, is uncorrelated with the source portfolios, S_j, for the other factors j not equal to k. This is indeed the rule we used to construct the mimicking portfolios, although it is stated here in terms of covariance rather than exposure. We lean heavily on this relationship in the following sections, stressing the risk-corr interpretation of the results. Notice this is equivalent to saying that each of the mimicking portfolios has a unit exposure to a single factor and zero to the other factors, $\mathbf{X}' \cdot \mathbf{M} = \mathbf{I}$. It also the case that the source portfolios have a unit exposure to a single mimicking factor and zero to the mimicking other factors, $\mathbf{Y}' \cdot \mathbf{S} = \mathbf{I}$.

The third relationship, called scale, says that the *K* by *K* covariance of the mimicking portfolios, Ψ, is the inverse of the covariance of the source portfolios, Ω. We illustrate in the following sections that it is the product of the source and the mimicking factors (or portfolios) that matters. The size of source and mimicking factors is inversely related, so the product of the two is independent of scale. For an example, if we double the size of the QUALITY exposures for all assets, then the risk of the QUALITY source portfolio will double as well. However, the risk of the QUALITY mimicking portfolio is cut in half, and the mimicking QUALITY factor exposures are halved as well. What is given by one hand is taken away by the other.

Is this too elaborate? Is William of Ockham getting edgy? After all, as Exhibit 9 shows, with **X** we can discover **S**, **M**, and **Y**. This is indeed true, but as we endeavor to demonstrate below, the foursome of **X**, **S**, **M**, and **Y** all play a natural role in the description of portfolios and their properties.

Representation of Holdings

The structure described in the last section can be used to split the positions in any portfolio into one part that is made up of the source portfolios and a second part we call, for want of a better name, the residual portfolio. We can do this in either of two ways. Method MX uses the mimicking portfolios **M** as composite assets and the factors **X** to determine the weight on the composites. Method SY uses the source portfolios **S** as composite assets and the mimicking factors **Y** to determine the weight on the composites. We run through the analysis using method MX. Appendix B briefly indicates how the results differ had we used method SY.

We start with a general portfolio *P* with positions **p**. The exposure of portfolio *P* to the factors is $\mathbf{x}_P = \mathbf{X}' \cdot \mathbf{p}$ with $x_{P,k}$ as the exposure of portfolio *P* to source *k*. We can split portfolio *P* as follows:

$$\mathbf{p} = \sum_{k=1,K} \mathbf{m}_k \cdot x_{P,k} + \varepsilon_P = \mathbf{M} \cdot \mathbf{x}_P + \varepsilon_P . \qquad (8)$$

The notation ε_P refers to the residual part of portfolio *P*. The partition of portfolio *P* in Equation (8) has the attractive feature that it minimizes the amount of portfolio *P*'s predicted variance that comes from the residual. For much the same reason, this means that the residual portfolio ε_P is uncorrelated with the composites **M** and the sources **S**. Therefore, the residual portfolio ε_P has zero exposure to both the factors **X** and mimicking factors **Y**, that is, $\mathbf{X}' \cdot \varepsilon_P = 0$ and $\mathbf{Y}' \cdot \varepsilon_P = 0$.[4]

Exhibit 11 shows a typical portfolio and its partition using the example of 10 assets and three factors introduced earlier. The portfolio has long and short positions. Its forecast risk is 4.5%. As we shall see, the three sources

4. If we premultiply Equation (8) by $\mathbf{X}' = \mathbf{S}' \cdot \mathbf{V}$ we get $\mathbf{X}' \cdot \mathbf{p} = \mathbf{x}_P = \{\mathbf{S}' \cdot \mathbf{V} \cdot \mathbf{M}\} \cdot \mathbf{x}_P + \mathbf{X}' \cdot \varepsilon_P$. Then use $\mathbf{S}' \cdot \mathbf{V} \cdot \mathbf{M} = \mathbf{I}$, to obtain $\mathbf{X}' \cdot \varepsilon_P = 0$.

explain roughly two-thirds of the variance of this portfolio with the remaining one-third attributed to the residual.

EXHIBIT 11 Decomposition of the Holdings in a Typical Active Portfolio Expressed in Percentage Terms

M*X′	VALUE	QUALITY	SENT.	ε_P	P
A1	−7.12%	−0.88%	3.59%	0.43%	−5.85%
A2	3.83%	0.19%	−4.82%	8.60%	7.80%
A3	−2.59%	0.14%	7.62%	−2.56%	2.62%
A4	−3.23%	1.20%	2.59%	5.88%	4.04%
A5	−1.08%	−0.05%	−4.41%	−5.94%	−11.49%
A6	3.72%	1.20%	13.86%	−0.46%	15.94%
A7	−0.13%	0.02%	−4.55%	−0.42%	−5.07%
A8	1.73%	1.21%	−4.49%	0.70%	−0.85%
A9	8.93%	0.52%	−5.68%	−4.03%	−0.27%
A10	−0.81%	1.43%	−1.78%	3.23%	2.06%
x_P	0.374	0.063	0.453	1	1

The last column in Exhibit 11 contains the portfolio's positions. The next to last column contains the residual, unexplained holdings. The bottom row for the first three columns reports the factor exposures $\mathbf{x}_P$. The holdings in columns one through three are the positions in the mimicking portfolios, as shown in Exhibit 5, multiplied by the corresponding exposure. For example, as Exhibit 5 shows, in the mimicking VALUE portfolio, the position for asset A9 is 0.239. When we multiply this by portfolio *P*'s exposure to mimicking VALUE, 0.374, we get 0.0893, or 8.93%.

Although the residual holdings contribute just one-third of the variance, they remain as a significant source of risk for some assets. Indeed, for assets A2, A4, and A10 the residual position is dominant. With this representation of holdings, it is easy to describe the source's contribution to various portfolio properties. We will consider, by way of example, two of these: alpha and return. A third, variance, takes slightly more work.

Description of Portfolio Alpha and Return

The first feature of the portfolio that we wish to describe is the portfolio's alpha. The term alpha indicates a forecast of asset residual return. The alpha notation is $\boldsymbol{\alpha}$, α_n, α_P for, respectively, the *N* element vector of alphas, the alpha of asset *n*, and the alpha of portfolio *P*.

A second facet of the portfolio we wish to describe is the realized return.[5] The return notation is θ, θ_n, θ_P for, respectively, the *N* element vector of asset returns, the returns of asset *n*, and the return of portfolio *P*.

With this notation we have α_{M_k} and θ_{M_k} for the alpha and return of mimicking portfolio *k*, M_k. We also have α_{ε_P} and θ_{ε_P} for the alpha and return of the residual positions ε_P.

The result follows directly by premultiplying the representation of *P* in Equation (8) by either α' or θ. For alpha we obtain:

$$\alpha_P = \sum_{k=1,K} \alpha_{M_k} \cdot x_{P,k} + \alpha_{\varepsilon_P}. \tag{9}$$

There is a similar result for the return:

$$\theta_P = \sum_{k=1,K} \theta_{M_k} \cdot x_{P,k} + \theta_{\varepsilon_P}. \tag{10}$$

The numerical results using the example are reported in Exhibit 12.

EXHIBIT 12 Description of Portfolio Alpha and Return

ALPHA	VALUE	QUALITY	SENT.	ε_P	P
x_P	**0.374**	**0.063**	**0.453**	1	1
Alpha_M	6.01%	4.46%	2.69%	0.19%	3.94%
Contribution	2.25%	0.28%	1.22%	0.19%	3.94%

RETURN	VALUE	QUALITY	SENT.	ε_P	P
x_P	**0.374**	**0.063**	**0.453**	1	1
Return_M	0.50%	0.37%	0.22%	0.15%	0.46%
Contribution	0.19%	0.02%	0.10%	0.15%	0.46%

In each table the bottom line is the product of the two lines above.

The alpha of the assets is mainly generated by the three themes, so it is not surprising that the bulk (about 95%) of the alpha stems from the themes. The return result is more surprising and demonstrates the hazard of using a single sample to illustrate a more general process. Everything works! All three themes and the residual deliver positive returns. This is not typical. In fact, we did a 12,000-month simulation with an anticipated annual information ratio of 0.875 and found the "everything works" scenario 6.34% of the months, or roughly once every year and a half. In about 40% of the cases, the portfolio's return was negative, and we find the "nothing works" scenario in 2.4% of the months, or about once every three and a half years.

5. These may be residual returns. If the strategy is neutral on some major contributors to risk, e.g., the market as a whole, or major sectors, then these may be filtered from the returns prior to the analysis.

What Do These Numbers Mean? Part I

The numbers in Exhibit 12 have an "off-the-top" interpretation. Consider an alternative portfolio that drops the SENTIMENT theme, that is, move from $\mathbf{p}$ to $\mathbf{p} - \mathbf{m}_3 \cdot 0.453$, then the alpha would drop by 1.22%, and the return would drop by 0.10%.

Portfolio Variance

The description of portfolio variance in terms of sources is slightly more complicated than the attribution of either alpha or return—or whatever—to sources and a residual. It requires a two-step process.

The first step is to premultiply the representation of the position $\mathbf{p}$ in terms of mimicking portfolios, as shown in Equation (8), by the asset covariance matrix $\mathbf{V}$, and use the relationship, $\mathbf{V} \cdot \mathbf{M} = \mathbf{Y}$. We find:

$$\mathbf{V} \cdot \mathbf{p} = \mathbf{Y} \cdot \mathbf{x}_P + \mathbf{V} \cdot \boldsymbol{\varepsilon}_P. \tag{11}$$

Equation (11) says that the representation of the covariance of any portfolio with the assets requires using *both* the original factors $\mathbf{X}$ and the mimicking factors $\mathbf{Y}$. It also suggests that the factors $\mathbf{X}$ and mimicking factors $\mathbf{Y}$ can be interpreted as covariances. We will follow up on that suggestion in the next section.

The second step is to premultiply Equation (11) by $\mathbf{p}'$ to arrive at the slicing up of the variance $\omega_P^2 = \mathbf{p}' \cdot \mathbf{V} \cdot \mathbf{p}$. From there we have two easy substeps as follows:[6]

$$\omega_P^2 = \mathbf{p}' \cdot \{\mathbf{Y} \cdot \mathbf{x}_P + \mathbf{V} \cdot \boldsymbol{\varepsilon}_P\} = \mathbf{y}'_P \cdot \mathbf{x}_P + \mathbf{p}' \cdot \mathbf{V} \cdot \boldsymbol{\varepsilon}_P = \sum_{k=1,K} y_{P,k} \cdot x_{P,k} + \boldsymbol{\varepsilon}'_P \cdot \mathbf{V} \cdot \boldsymbol{\varepsilon}_P. \tag{12}$$

The contribution of source k to the variance is the product, $y_{P,k} \cdot x_{P,k}$, of two exposures: exposure of portfolio P to the mimicking factor k, $y_{P,k}$, and exposure of portfolio P to factor k, $x_{P,k}$.

EXHIBIT 13 Attribution of Portfolio Variance to the Factors and a Residual

VARIANCE	VALUE	QUALITY	SENT.	ε_P	P
x_P times 100	37.41	6.28	45.33	100	100
y_P times 100	0.127	−0.049	0.201	0.0669	0.2025
Contribution	4.76	−0.31%	9.11	6.69	20.25

Lines 1 and 2 contain the exposures to the source and mimicking portfolios multiplied by 100. Line 3, the contribution, is the product of lines 1 and 2. The variance numbers are scaled up by a factor of 100·100; thus the square root of the total variance, 20.25, is the risk of the portfolio, 4.5%, in percentage terms.

Exhibit 13 shows the breakdown of the variance for the sample portfolio.

6. Substep one, premultiply Equation (11) by $\boldsymbol{\varepsilon}'_P$ and use $\boldsymbol{\varepsilon}'_P \cdot \mathbf{Y} = 0$ to get $\boldsymbol{\varepsilon}'_P \cdot \mathbf{V} \cdot \mathbf{p} = \boldsymbol{\varepsilon}'_P \cdot \mathbf{V} \cdot \boldsymbol{\varepsilon}_P$. Substep two, premultiply Equation (11) by $\mathbf{p}'$. The first term is $\mathbf{y}'_P \cdot \mathbf{x}_P$; the second is $\mathbf{p}' \cdot \mathbf{V} \cdot \boldsymbol{\varepsilon}_P$ and that we know from substep one is equal to $\boldsymbol{\varepsilon}'_P \cdot \mathbf{V} \cdot \boldsymbol{\varepsilon}_P$.

What Do These Numbers Mean? Part II

The numbers in the third row of Exhibit 13 add nicely to the correct portfolio variance. However, they do not have the convenient "off-the-top" interpretation described in part I.[7] The data serve as a makeshift accounting scheme. Consider an illustrative example without factors.[8] There are two assets. The variance of a portfolio P with positions $\mathbf{p}$ is:

$$\omega_P^2 = \{p_1 \cdot V_{1,1} \cdot p_1 + p_1 \cdot V_{1,2} \cdot p_2\} + \{p_2 \cdot V_{2,1} \cdot p_1 + p_2 \cdot V_{2,2} \cdot p_2\}. \qquad (13)$$

The curly brackets in Equation (13) indicate the variance allocated to assets one and two. We are taking the covariance between the two and splitting it down the middle. This is not the most exciting result and certainly not one that is tied to an off-the-top alternative. For example, if we drop the position in asset one, p_1, to zero then the first term in Equation (13) disappears but the second term is altered as well. In the following risk-corr section, we present a slightly more encouraging view of the allocation of variance.

The Risk-Corr Interpretation

The previous results are straightforward and useful. In this section, we present a deeper interpretation of the results using the language of portfolio theory (covariance, correlation, and risk). The idea is to uncover and focus on the relationships behind the results. This is an alternative interpretation. The answers will not change, but our perspective changes and our ability to interpret and frame the analysis is altered as well.

We start with the observation that a portfolio's exposure to any factor, $\mathbf{X}$, or mimicking factor, $\mathbf{Y}$, can be viewed as a covariance. Indeed:

$$\begin{aligned} &(i.) \quad \mathbf{X}' \cdot \mathbf{p} = \mathbf{S}' \cdot \mathbf{V} \cdot \mathbf{p} \Rightarrow x_{P,k} = \omega_{S_k} \cdot \rho_{S_k,P} \cdot \omega_P \\ &(ii.) \quad \mathbf{Y}' \cdot \mathbf{p} = \mathbf{M}' \cdot \mathbf{V} \cdot \mathbf{p} \Rightarrow y_{P,k} = \omega_{M_k} \cdot \rho_{M_k,P} \cdot \omega_P \end{aligned} \qquad (14)$$

where the omega, ω, and rho, ρ, notations are predicted risks and correlations, respectively,

$$\begin{aligned} &(i.) \quad \omega_{S_k} \equiv \sqrt{\mathbf{s}_k' \cdot \mathbf{V} \cdot \mathbf{s}_k},\ \omega_{M_k} \equiv \sqrt{\mathbf{m}_k' \cdot \mathbf{V} \cdot \mathbf{m}_k},\ \omega_P \equiv \sqrt{\mathbf{p}' \cdot \mathbf{V} \cdot \mathbf{p}} \\ &(ii.) \quad \rho_{S_k,P} \equiv \frac{\mathbf{s}_k' \cdot \mathbf{V} \cdot \mathbf{p}}{\omega_{S_k} \cdot \omega_P},\ \rho_{M_k,P} \equiv \frac{\mathbf{m}_k' \cdot \mathbf{V} \cdot \mathbf{p}}{\omega_{M_k} \cdot \omega_P},\ \rho_{S_k,M_k} \equiv \frac{\mathbf{s}_k' \cdot \mathbf{V} \cdot \mathbf{m}_k}{\omega_{S_k} \cdot \omega_{M_k}}. \end{aligned} \qquad (15)$$

7. Except for the residual. If we eliminate the residual, the sum $\sum_k x_{P,k} \cdot y_{P,k}$ will give us the variance of the remaining portfolio.

8. The inner product $\mathbf{y}_P' \cdot \mathbf{x}_P$ can be considered a variance, since $\mathbf{y}_P = \Psi \cdot \mathbf{x}_P$ and $\mathbf{x}_P = \Omega \cdot \mathbf{y}_P$, and hence $\mathbf{y}_P' \cdot \mathbf{x}_P = \mathbf{y}_P' \cdot \Omega \cdot \mathbf{y}_P$ or $\mathbf{y}_P' \cdot \mathbf{x}_P = \mathbf{x}_P' \cdot \Psi \cdot \mathbf{x}_P$. If we split the covariance terms in these expressions, we get the results of Exhibit 13.

Recall from the previous section that the contribution of factor k to portfolio P's variance is the product $y_{P,k} \cdot x_{P,k}$. With the result in Equation (14), the notation of Equation (15), and a bit of rearranging,[9] we have:

$$y_{P,k} \cdot x_{P,k} = \omega_P \cdot \left\{ \frac{\rho_{S_k,P} \cdot \rho_{M_k,P}}{\rho_{S_k,M_k}} \right\} \cdot \omega_P. \tag{16}$$

The term in brackets, made up of three correlations, represents the fraction of total variance that is associated with source k. As we know from the variance example in Exhibit 13, this fraction can be negative.

There is a symmetric treatment of the source and mimicking portfolios in Equation (16). The correlation of the portfolio P with both the source S_k, ρ_{P,S_k}, and the correlation with the mimicking portfolio M_k, $\rho_{M_k,P}$, will contribute equally.

The correlation between the source and mimicking portfolios for factor k, ρ_{S_k,M_k} is always positive.[10] It is a measure of collinearity. If ρ_{S_k,M_k} equals one, the source portfolio S_k is uncorrelated with the other sources, S_j $j \neq k$. If the correlation ρ_{S_k,M_k} is small, it means that source k is more or less a repackaged form of the other sources. Division by ρ_{S_k,M_k} in Equation (16) implies that a small value of ρ_{S_k,M_k} increases the influence of factor k. Moreover, if ρ_{S_k,M_k} is small for factor k, it is likely to be small for some other factors as well. In those cases, the results tend to be vexing and useless. For example, the portfolio's alpha is 1.50%. Source number one contributes 13.00%, and source number two contributes –11.50%. This suggests that we have an unfortunate choice of sources/factors and that a visit to the drawing board is in order.[11]

Let's turn to the residual component. The residual variance can be expressed in a similar style to the factor description in Equation (16). Since $\omega_{\varepsilon_P} = \omega_P \cdot \rho_{P,\varepsilon_P}$, we have:

$$\omega_{\varepsilon_P}^2 = \omega_P \cdot \left\{ \rho_{P,\varepsilon_P} \cdot \rho_{\varepsilon_P,P} \right\} \cdot \omega_P. \tag{17}$$

The total, therefore, is:

$$\omega_P^2 = \omega_P \cdot \left\{ \sum_{k=1,K} \frac{\rho_{S_k,P} \cdot \rho_{M_k,P}}{\rho_{S_k,M_k}} + \rho_{P,\varepsilon_P} \cdot \rho_{\varepsilon_P,P} \right\} \cdot \omega_P. \tag{18}$$

---

9. If we substitute for $y_{P,k}$ and $x_{P,K}$ from Equation (14), and use the notation of Equation (15), we get $y_{P,k} \cdot x_{P,k} = \omega_P \cdot \left\{ \rho_{S_k,P} \cdot \left[\omega_{S_k} \cdot \omega_{M_k} \right] \cdot \rho_{M_k,P} \right\} \cdot \omega_P$. Next, recall that the mimicking portfolio k was selected to have a unit exposure to factor k and a zero exposure to the other factors. In covariance terms, see the covariance row in Exhibit 10, we have $\omega_{S_k,M_k} = \omega_{S_k} \cdot \rho_{S_k,M_k} \cdot \omega_{M_k} = 1$. This in turn means that $\omega_{S_k} \cdot \omega_{M_k} = 1/\rho_{S_k,M_k}$.

10. It might be zero if one factor was a repackaging of the others. We are assuming that the selection of factors was not that foolish.

11. If we attempted to explain portfolio S_k in terms of the other sources S_j $j \neq k$ in the same fashion as Equation (B1) in Appendix B, then the fraction of the variance of S_k that is *not* explained by the other sources is ρ_{S_k,M_k}^2. The standard measure of multicollinearity is the variance inflation factor, VIF_k for factor k. The relationship between VIF_k and ρ_{S_k,M_k} is $\rho_{S_k,M_k} = \sqrt{1/VIF_k}$. A value of VIF_k above 4 or 5 is considered a red flag. That means that a value of ρ_{S_k,M_k} below 0.5 is a similar sign of trouble.

The sum in the curly brackets in Equation (18) is, of course, equal to one. It allocates the variance to the factors and a residual expressed in terms of correlations. Exhibit 14 shows the result for our example.

EXHIBIT 14 The Decomposition of Portfolio Variance

VARIANCE	VALUE	QUALITY	SENT	ε_P	P
rho_P_Sk	0.552	0.091	0.652	0.575	1
rho_Sk_Mk	0.910	0.772	0.797	1	1
rho_Mk_P	0.387	−0.127	0.550	0.575	1
Contribution	0.235	−0.015	0.450	0.330	1

This contains the same information as Exhibit 13 although it is expressed in a different manner. The bottom row, labeled Contribution, is the product of rows 1 and 3 divided by correlation in row 2.

What Do These Numbers Mean? Part III

In the discussion of the previous variance result, we concluded that the allocation of variance to each factor stemmed from simply sharing covariance terms. The risk-corr interpretation reveals a significant marginal interpretation of the results as well. Suppose we make a fractional increase in the portfolio's exposure to any factor; from $x_{P,k}$ to $\hat{x}_{P,k} = \{1+\delta\} \cdot x_{P,k}$. If the exposure to factor k, $x_{P,k}$ is zero, there is no change. Otherwise, when the exposure to factor k, $x_{P,k}$ is not zero we have $\Delta x_{P,k} = \hat{x}_{P,k} - x_{P,k} = \delta \cdot x_{P,k} \neq 0$. The resulting change in portfolio risk is:

$$\frac{\Delta\omega_P}{\omega_P} \approx \left\{ \frac{\rho_{P,S_k} \cdot \rho_{P,M_k}}{\rho_{S_k,M_k}} \right\} \cdot \frac{\Delta x_{P,k}}{x_{P,k}}. \tag{19}$$

For example, a 10% increase in the VALUE exposure from 0.374 to $0.4114 = 0.374 + 0.0374$ should, according to Exhibit 14 and Equation (19), cause a 2.35% increase in the portfolio's risk. The actual number is 2.50%. A 10% SENTIMENT exposure increase from 0.453 to 0.499 leads to a 4.72% increase in portfolio risk; Equation (19) predicts 4.50%. Things go the other way for QUALITY since $\rho_{M_2,P} < 0$. A 10% increase in the QUALITY exposure from 0.063 the 0.069 yields a 0.14% decrease in risk. Equation (19) predicts a decrease of 0.15%.

The Risk-Corr Description of a Portfolio's Interaction with Other Factors

The discussion above used the risk-corr framework to explain a portfolio's variance. We now turn to the risk-corr interpretation of other portfolio attributes. For the purpose of illustration, the attributes are forecast alpha and realized return. The approach is not limited to those applications. It could be any attribute of the portfolio.

Recall that we have two types of factors:

- Factors in want of explanation; such as the vector of asset alphas, $\boldsymbol{\alpha}$, or the vector of asset returns, $\boldsymbol{\theta}$, and
- Factors that are used to make the explanation; such as the VALUE, QUALITY and SENTIMENT themes.

We treat the factors that we want to explain in exactly the same manner as we treated the descriptive factors **X**. Turn the factors into portfolios. This represents all the elements of the problem as portfolios. On that common ground, standard deviation measures scale and correlation measures relationship.

In the context of the example, for the alpha, $\boldsymbol{\alpha}$, and return, $\boldsymbol{\theta}$, we create portfolios *Q* and *H* with positions **q** and **h** given by:

$$\boldsymbol{\alpha} = \mathbf{V} \cdot \mathbf{q}, \quad \boldsymbol{\theta} = \mathbf{V} \cdot \mathbf{h}. \tag{20}$$

The notion of efficiency (see the discussion immediately following Equation (2)), tells us that portfolio *Q* gets the most alpha per unit of forecast risk. In other words, portfolio *Q* has the highest possible information ratio. In the same way portfolio *H* has the highest ratio of realized return per unit of forecast risk. The *H* stands for *hindsight* as a reminder that we can only create this portfolio after we observe the returns, in other words, too late.

With the factor portfolio concept extended to cover the alpha and returns we have:

$$\begin{aligned} &(i.) \quad \alpha_P = \boldsymbol{\alpha}' \cdot \mathbf{p} = \mathbf{q}' \cdot \mathbf{V} \cdot \mathbf{p} = \omega_P \cdot \rho_{P,Q} \cdot \omega_Q \\ &(ii.) \quad \theta_P = \boldsymbol{\theta}' \cdot \mathbf{p} = \mathbf{h}' \cdot \mathbf{V} \cdot \mathbf{p} = \omega_P \cdot \rho_{P,H} \cdot \omega_H \end{aligned}. \tag{21}$$

Equation (21) introduces several significant concepts:

- ω_Q is the forecast risk of portfolio *Q and* the highest possible *information ratio*, *IR*, that can be obtained using the alphas, $\boldsymbol{\alpha}$.[12] In equation form, $\alpha_Q / \omega_Q = \omega_Q = IR$.
- ω_H is the predicted risk of portfolio *H and* the highest possible ratio of realized return to forecast risk that we can obtain. We call this highest realized return/predicted risk ratio the *opportunity set*, *OS*.[13] In equation form, $\theta_H / \omega_H = \omega_H = OS$.
- $\rho_{P,Q}$ is the correlation of portfolios *P* and *Q*. This correlation is also known as the *transfer coefficient*.[14] The information ratio of any portfolio *P*, $IR_P = \alpha_P / \omega_P$ is equal to $\rho_{P,Q} \cdot IR$.

12. We can get this result directly. The information ratio is generally defined as $IR = \sqrt{\boldsymbol{\alpha}' \cdot \mathbf{V} \cdot \boldsymbol{\alpha}}$. If we substitute $\boldsymbol{\alpha} = \mathbf{V} \cdot \mathbf{q}$ into this relationship we get $IR = \sqrt{\mathbf{q}' \cdot \mathbf{V} \cdot \mathbf{q}} = \omega_Q$.
13. See Grinold and Taylor (2009). The opportunity set is defined as $OS = \sqrt{\boldsymbol{\theta}' \cdot \mathbf{V}^{-1} \cdot \boldsymbol{\theta}}$. If we substitute $\boldsymbol{\theta} = \mathbf{V} \cdot \mathbf{h}$ in this relationship, we get $\omega_H = \sqrt{\mathbf{h}' \cdot \mathbf{V} \cdot \mathbf{h}} = OS$.
14. See Clarke, de Silva, and Thorley (2002).

- $\rho_{P,H}$ is the correlation of portfolios *P* and *H*. This correlation is also known as the *realized information coefficient*, or realized *ic*.[15] The ratio of realized return to forecast risk for portfolio *P*, θ_P / ω_P, is equal to $\rho_{P,H} \cdot OS$.

Assembling the Pieces

From Equation (11), we can get a factor representation for $\mathbf{V} \cdot \mathbf{p}$. If we premultiply this by **q** and **h**, respectively, we get:

$$
\begin{aligned}
&(i.) \quad \alpha_P = \mathbf{q}' \cdot \{\mathbf{Y} \cdot \mathbf{x}_P + \mathbf{V} \cdot \boldsymbol{\varepsilon}_P\} = \mathbf{y}'_Q \cdot \mathbf{x}_P + \mathbf{q}' \cdot \mathbf{V} \cdot \boldsymbol{\varepsilon}_P = \sum_{k=1,K} y_{Q,k} \cdot x_{P,k} + \omega_{\varepsilon_P,Q} \\
&(ii.) \quad \theta_P = \mathbf{h}' \cdot \{\mathbf{Y} \cdot \mathbf{x}_P + \mathbf{V} \cdot \boldsymbol{\varepsilon}_P\} = \mathbf{y}'_H \cdot \mathbf{x}_P + \mathbf{h}' \cdot \mathbf{V} \cdot \boldsymbol{\varepsilon}_P = \sum_{k=1,K} y_{H,k} \cdot x_{P,k} + \omega_{\varepsilon_P,H}
\end{aligned}
\tag{22}
$$

In the fashion of Equation (14), we can express the exposures of portfolios *Q* and *H* to the mimicking factors as $y_{Q,k} = \omega_Q \cdot \rho_{Q,M_k} \cdot \omega_{M_k}$ and $y_{H,k} = \omega_H \cdot \rho_{H,M_k} \cdot \omega_{M_k}$, respectively. Using the same approach as we used before, we arrive at:

$$
\begin{aligned}
&(i.) \quad \alpha_P = \omega_P \cdot \left\{ \sum_{k=1,K} \frac{\rho_{P,S_k} \cdot \rho_{M_k,Q}}{\rho_{S_k,M_k}} + \rho_{P,\varepsilon_P} \cdot \rho_{\varepsilon_P,Q} \right\} \cdot \omega_Q \\
&(ii.) \quad \theta_P = \omega_P \cdot \left\{ \sum_{k=1,K} \frac{\rho_{P,S_k} \cdot \rho_{M_k,H}}{\rho_{S_k,M_k}} + \rho_{P,\varepsilon_P} \cdot \rho_{\varepsilon_P,H} \right\} \cdot \omega_H
\end{aligned}
\tag{23}
$$

The expressions in the curly brackets in Equation (23) are, respectively, the transfer coefficient and the realized *ic* attributed to the *K* factors and a residual. The scale factors $\omega_Q = IR$ and $\omega_H = OS$ are common to all portfolios. The scale factor ω_P assures us that the alpha and return are being measured relative to the predicted risk in the portfolio. Exhibit 15 (see next page) contains the results for the example we have followed throughout. This is the risk-corr equivalent of the results in Exhibit 12.

As in Exhibit 14, the first three rows measure correlations. Note how the first two rows in both tables of Exhibit 15 are the same as the first two rows in the table describing variance in Exhibit 14.

15. Another formula for the realized *ic* is $\rho_{P,H} = \dfrac{\boldsymbol{\theta}' \cdot \mathbf{p}}{\left\{\sqrt{\boldsymbol{\theta}' \cdot \mathbf{V}^{-1} \cdot \boldsymbol{\theta}} \cdot \sqrt{\mathbf{p}' \cdot \mathbf{V} \cdot \mathbf{p}}\right\}}$.

EXHIBIT 15 The Factor Attribution of the Transfer Coefficient and the Realized Information Coefficient

TRANS. COEFF.	VALUE	QUALITY	SENT.	ε_P	P
rho_P_Sk	0.552	0.091	0.652	0.575	1
rho_Sk_Mk	0.910	0.772	0.797	1	1
rho_Mk_Q	0.659	0.420	0.265	0.058	0.70
Contribution	0.400	0.050	0.217	0.034	0.70

REALIZED IC	VALUE	QUALITY	SENT.	ε_P	P
rho_P_Sk	0.552	0.091	0.652	0.575	1
rho_Sk_Mk	0.910	0.772	0.797	1	1
rho_Mk_H	0.075	0.048	0.030	0.064	0.113
Contribution	0.046	0.006	0.025	0.037	0.113

The bottom row is the product of the correlations in rows 1 and three divided by the correlation in row 2.

What Do These Numbers Mean? Part IV

All of the numbers in row three of Exhibit 15 are transfer coefficients.[16] The first three are the transfer coefficients of the mimicking portfolios. The fourth number along row three is the transfer coefficient of the residual portfolio, $\rho_{\varepsilon_P,Q} = 0.0575$, and the last number is the transfer coefficient of portfolio *P*, $\rho_{P,Q} = 0.700$. The sum of the first four numbers in fourth row is equal to the transfer coefficient $\rho_{P,Q}$. In the case where the portfolio *P*'s alpha is not zero, $\alpha_P \neq 0$, and the exposure to factor *k* is not zero as well, $x_{P,k} \neq 0$, one can show that:

$$\frac{\Delta\alpha_P}{\alpha_P} \approx \left\{\frac{1}{\rho_{P,Q}} \cdot \frac{\rho_{P,S_k} \cdot \rho_{M_k,Q}}{\rho_{S_k,M_k}}\right\} \cdot \frac{\Delta x_{P,k}}{x_{P,k}}. \tag{24}$$

The expression in the curly brackets is the fraction of the transfer coefficient attributed to factor *k*. For the numbers in Exhibit 15, 57.12% of the transfer coefficient comes from VALUE. A 10% increase in the value exposure from 0.374 to 0.4114 should lead to a 5.712% increase in alpha. This approximation is very accurate.[17] The off-the-top interpretation of the results still applies (see the discussion following Exhibit 12). The loss of alpha if we, for example, took the SENTIMENT exposure to zero would be

16. There is yet another way to display these results. For any portfolio *P*, the information ratio is $IR_P = \rho_{P,Q} \cdot \omega_Q$. Then divide Equation (23) (*i.*) by ω_P. We obtain:

$$IR_P = \sum_{k=1,K}\left\{\frac{\rho_{P,S_k}}{\rho_{S_k,M_k}}\right\} \cdot IR_{M_k} + \rho_{P,\varepsilon_P} \cdot IR_{\varepsilon_P}.$$

17. One can carry this analysis further to measure the impact of changes on portfolio *P*'s information ratio IR_P and transfer coefficient $\rho_{P,Q}$ since $\Delta\alpha_P/\alpha_P = \Delta\rho_{P,Q}/\rho_{P,Q} + \Delta\omega_P/\omega_P$ and $\Delta\alpha_P/\alpha_P = \Delta IR_P/IR_P + \Delta\omega_P/\omega_P$.

$0.217 \cdot \omega_P \cdot IR = 0.217 \cdot 0.045 \cdot 1.25 = 1.22\%$, which agrees with the numbers in Exhibit 12.

The scheme for this three-factor example is shown in Exhibit 16. In this case, we have the generic symbol T for the target portfolio. Recall that T could equal either P for variance, Q for alpha, H for return, or some other aspect of the portfolio not discussed above.

EXHIBIT 16 Schematic of Risk-Corr Description

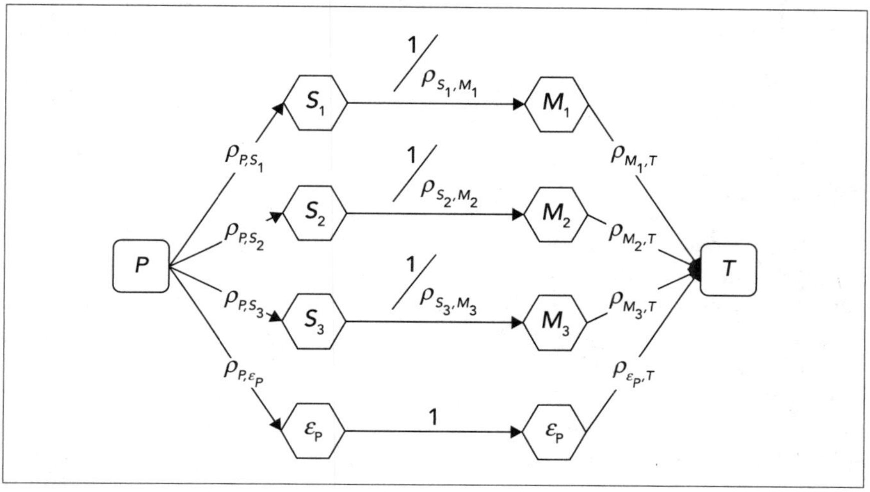

Explanation of the correlation of portfolios *P* and *T*.

In Exhibit 16, we show the $K+1$ paths from P to T.[18] Recall that:

- $T = Q$ indicates we are explaining alpha and the transfer coefficient,
- $T = H$ indicates we are explaining return and the realized information coefficient, and
- $T = P$ indicates we are allocation the variance of P to factors and a residual.

Each factor path from P to T consists of three links. Each link has an associated correlation. The links from P to the sources (and the residual ε_P) are the correlations between those portfolios, $\rho_{P,S_k}, \rho_{P,\varepsilon_P}$. The links from the mimicking portfolios (and residual) to the target T are the correlations between those portfolios and T, $\rho_{M_k,T}, \rho_{\varepsilon_P,T}$. The middle link has the inverse of the correlation between the source and mimicking portfolio for that factor. The amount of the correlation between P and T explained by a path is the product of the numbers on that path. The correlation between P and T is the sum of the correlations identified with each path.

Do the benefits of the risk-corr approach outweigh the burden of its added complexity? We believe so. Here are some of the benefits:

18. You can consider the residual an ad hoc $K+1$st factor used only in the description of portfolio P. Since the residual is uncorrelated with the other factors it has a correlation of one with its mimicking portfolio.

- Identifies and exhibits the three crucial ingredients in the factor relationship:
  - correlation of the portfolio P with the source portfolios S_k
  - correlation of the source portfolios S_k and mimicking portfolios M_k
  - correlation of the mimicking portfolios M_k and the target (e.g., Q, H, P) portfolio
- Separates the scale and relationship aspects of the problem.
- Puts all description questions on the same footing.
- Places possible multicollinearity problems up front by displaying the correlations ρ_{S_k,M_k}.
- Enlarges our perspective on what type of questions we can ask. Some examples are included below.

Added Benefits

The risk-corr perspective quickly shows one how to answer new questions within the same framework. Since we have linked alpha to portfolio Q and shown that the information ratio squared is equal to the variance of portfolio Q, $IR^2 = \omega_Q^2$, we can substitute Q for P in the variance calculation, as depicted in Exhibit 14, and allocate the information ratio to the various factors and a residual. In the same fashion, the returns are associated with portfolio H so the squared opportunity set is the variance $OS^2 = \omega_H^2$. Exhibit 17 shows the explanation of the squared information ratio and squared opportunity set for the example.

EXHIBIT 17 Factor Description of the Information Ratio and Opportunity Set

IR^2	VALUE	QUALITY	SENT.	e_Q	Q
rho_Q_Sk	0.616	0.527	0.712	0.174	1
rho_Sk_Mk	0.910	0.772	0.797	1	1
rho_Mk_Q	0.659	0.420	0.265	0.174	1
Contribution	0.446	0.287	0.237	0.030	1

OS^2	VALUE	QUALITY	SENT.	e_H	H
rho_H_Sk	0.070	0.060	0.081	0.994	1
rho_Sk_Mk	0.910	0.772	0.797	1	1
rho_Mk_H	0.075	0.048	0.030	0.994	1
Contribution	0.0058	0.0037	0.0031	0.9874	1

The numbers in Exhibit 17 have the same interpretation as the explanation of variance in the "What Do These Numbers Mean? Part III" section. There are no great surprises in the description of alpha. We selected the factors because they were the important drivers of the forecasts. Together the factors describe 97% of the (squared) information ratio. There should be no surprises in the description of the (squared) opportunity set, but there is a strong reminder that even with a significant alleged forecasting advantage, $IR = 1.25$ and a sample period where "everything works," most of what happens is beyond our reach. In this instance 98.74% of the return is attributed to residual, nonfactor sources.

Other Applications

We have concentrated on the description of portfolio risk, alpha, and return. The procedures described above are more general than those examples might indicate. Here are two outside-the-box applications.

Information Vintage Profile

An active manager builds a portfolio based on the flow of information. Transactions costs serve as a friction that keeps the portfolio behind the curve. The portfolio does not fully embody the latest information, and it retains positions that were based on stale information. We can classify information with the alphas that are used to forecast return at different times. It is relatively easy to split these alphas into to initial alpha;[19] say the alphas used one year ago, $\boldsymbol{\alpha}(t-12)$, and the new information added, call it $\mathbf{u}(t-j)$, in each of the 12 succeeding months for $j = 0, 1, \cdots, 11$. That would give us 13 factors, $\mathbf{u}(t), \mathbf{u}(t-1), \cdots, \mathbf{u}(t-11), \boldsymbol{\alpha}(t-12)$: the original year-old alphas and the 12 bundles of new information. These factors should be relatively uncorrelated since the essence of *new* information is that it cannot be predicted using old information.

Trades

Think of $\mathbf{p}(t), \mathbf{p}(t-1)$ as the positions held at the start of period t and period $t - 1$. Then $\mathbf{d} = \mathbf{p}(t) - \mathbf{p}(t-1)$ are the changes in the portfolio during the period.[20] At any time t, the ideal portfolio, $\mathbf{i}(t)$, represents the positions we would hold if we were given a holiday on transactions costs, and $\mathbf{b}(t) \equiv \mathbf{i}(t) - \mathbf{p}(t)$ represents the backlog, that is, how far we are from the ideal or how much we would trade if it was costless. In addition, suppose we follow J different information sources. As in the previous example, let $\mathbf{u}_j(t)$ be the new information flowing in from source j during the most recent period. Then the $K = 1 + J$ items used to explain the trades $\mathbf{d}$ are $\mathbf{u}_1(t), \mathbf{u}_2(t), \cdots, \mathbf{u}_J(t), \mathbf{b}(t-1)$.[21] Note, in this example, we start with $\mathbf{x}_j = \mathbf{u}_j(t)$ for $j = 1, J$ and $\mathbf{x}_{J+1} = \mathbf{V}(t) \cdot \mathbf{b}(t-1)$, since $\mathbf{b}(t-1)$ is already a portfolio.

19. If $\mathbf{V}(t), \boldsymbol{\alpha}(t), \boldsymbol{\alpha}(t-1)$ are, respectively, the covariance matrix at time t, the alphas at time t, and the alphas at time $t - 1$, then let $\gamma_t \equiv \boldsymbol{\alpha}(t) \cdot \mathbf{V}(t) \cdot \boldsymbol{\alpha}(t-1) / \boldsymbol{\alpha}(t-1) \cdot \mathbf{V}(t) \cdot \boldsymbol{\alpha}(t-1)$. The term $\mathbf{u}(t) \equiv \boldsymbol{\alpha}(t) - \gamma_t \cdot \boldsymbol{\alpha}(t-1)$ is the new information that arrives between $t - 1$ and t. The factors in this case would be $\mathbf{u}(t), \mathbf{u}(t-1), \cdots, \mathbf{u}(t-11), \boldsymbol{\alpha}(t-12)$.

20. We could take this one level higher and separate changes due to price movement and changes due to trades. In practice this makes a small difference and would obscure the thrust of the example.

21. One might also add a signed transactions cost to the list. If we buy the asset, use the forecast marginal (or average) cost of a purchase. If we sell the asset, use the negative of the marginal (or average) cost of a sale. If we don't trade, use zero.

Summary and Conclusions

This chapter is based on one notion: use portfolio theory to describe portfolios. We do this by treating the subjects we would like to portray, and the palette of factors we use to depict them, in the same way. Factors are represented as portfolios, indeed as a portfolio that has the highest exposure to the factor per unit of risk. This notion is reversible. If we start with a portfolio, we can create a factor that is efficiently captured by that portfolio. Readers will be cheered to know that every portfolio is good for something.

Instead of considering the intersection of portfolios and factors, we can focus solely on portfolios and their covariance with other portfolios. This allows us to crank up the machinery of portfolio theory and shift from the analysis of portfolios and factors to the explanation of covariance.

Covariance depends on the risk of both portfolios and the correlation between them. Risk is a matter of scale and the correlation is a measure of relationship. When we introduce descriptive factors and their factor portfolios, we find we must also introduce a cousin of the factor portfolios that we call the mimicking portfolios. The mimicking portfolio is the most efficient embodiment of the factor with the added stipulation that it is not linked to any the other factors.

We can represent the positions held by any portfolio P as a mix of the mimicking portfolios weighted by the portfolio P's exposure to the factors and a residual (see Equation (8)). We use the same ideas to represent the covariance of any portfolio (aka a factor) in terms of the mimicking factors, the portfolio's exposure to the factors, and a residual factor (see Equation (11)). This provides a general model for depicting the portfolio's variance and the portfolio's exposure to certain other factors, such as alpha and return.

We can dig deeper, however. The sections on risk-corr analysis are based on the observation, made explicit in Equations (21) and (14), that an exposure to a factor can be represented as a covariance.[22] That allows us to separate the problem of explaining variance (scale squared) and correlation. Suppose that we are trying to describe the linkage (correlation) between the portfolio, P, and another portfolio T. The contribution of factor k in explaining the correlation between P and T is the product of three terms:

1. The correlation, ρ_{P,S_k} between portfolio P and the kth factor portfolio S_k
2. The inverse of the correlation, ρ_{S_k,M_k}, between factor portfolio S_k and the kth mimicking portfolio M_k
3. The correlation, $\rho_{M_k,T}$ between mimicking portfolio M_k and portfolio T

The contribution to the correlation $\rho_{P,T}$ from factor k is then:

$$\frac{\rho_{P,S_k} \cdot \rho_{M_k,T}}{\rho_{S_k,M_k}}. \tag{25}$$

22. The original article incorrectly references Equations (16) and (23).

The schematic in Exhibit 18 shows the links.

EXHIBIT 18 Schematic of the Contribution of One Factor to the Correlation Between Portfolios *P* and *T*

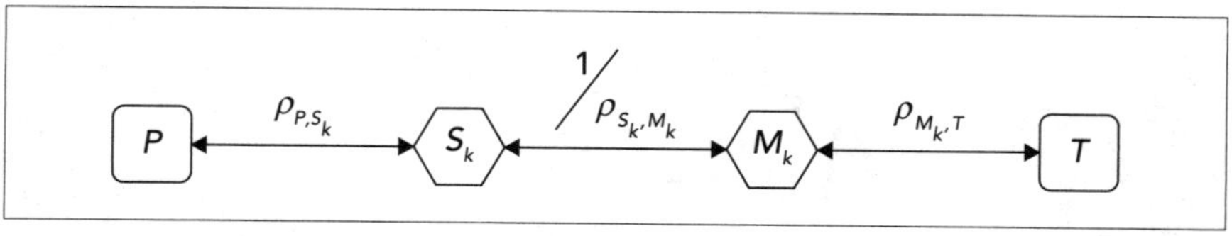

The risk-corr method of decomposing alpha, risk, and return does not produce new answers. It does alter and enlarge our perspective by greatly expanding the possible questions we might ask, providing a unified approach to answering those questions, and digging deeper to uncover the linkages, shown in Exhibit 18, that support those answers.

References

Clarke, Roger, Harindra de Silva, and Steven Thorley. 2002. "Portfolio Constraints and the Fundamental Law of Active Management." *Financial Analysts Journal* 58 (September/October): 48–66.

Grinold, Richard C., and Ronald N. Kahn. 2000. *Active Portfolio Management: Quantitative Theory and Applications.* 2nd ed. New York: McGraw-Hill.

Grinold, Richard. "Attribution." 2006. *Journal of Portfolio Management* 33 (Winter): 9–24.

Grinold, Richard, and Mark P. Taylor. 2009. "The Opportunity Set." *Journal of Portfolio Management* 35 (Winter): 12–24.

Menchero, Jose, and Vijay Poduri. 2008. "Custom Factor Attribution." *Financial Analysts Journal* 64 (March/April): 81–92.

Tien, D., Paul Pfleiderer, R. Maxim, and Terry Marsh. 2005. "Decomposing Factor Exposures for Equity Portfolios." In *Linear Economic Models in Finance*, edited by John Knight and Stephen Satchell. Elsevier, Amsterdam.

Appendix A

Portfolio Description and Factor Risk Models

Suppose **X** is *N* by *K* of rank *K* and that the covariance matrix **V** is based on the factors **X**:

$$\mathbf{V} = \mathbf{X} \cdot \mathbf{F} \cdot \mathbf{X}' + \Delta \tag{A1)}$$

where Δ is *N* by *N* and invertible.

The general formulae for the source portfolios and mimicking portfolios are:

$$\begin{aligned} &(i.) \quad \mathbf{S} = \mathbf{V}^{-1} \cdot \mathbf{X}, \ \ \Omega = \mathbf{S}' \cdot \mathbf{V} \cdot \mathbf{S}, \ \ \Psi = \Omega^{-1} \\ &(ii.) \quad \mathbf{M} = \mathbf{S} \cdot \Psi \\ &(iii.) \quad \mathbf{Y} = \mathbf{V} \cdot \mathbf{M} \end{aligned} \tag{A2}$$

With the covariance matrix **V** in the form of Equation (A1), the results specialize as follows.

Proposition

If **V** is in the form specified by Equation (A1), and if we define **G** by:

$$\mathbf{G} \equiv \{\mathbf{X}' \cdot \Delta^{-1} \cdot \mathbf{X}\}^{-1} \tag{A3}$$

then:

$$
\begin{aligned}
&(i.) \quad \mathbf{S} = \Delta^{-1} \cdot \mathbf{X} \cdot \mathbf{G} \cdot \{\mathbf{F} + \mathbf{G}\}^{-1} \\
&(ii.) \quad \Omega = \{\mathbf{F} + \mathbf{G}\}^{-1}, \Psi = \mathbf{F} + \mathbf{G} \\
&(iii.) \quad \mathbf{M}' = \{\mathbf{X}' \cdot \mathbf{V}^{-1} \cdot \mathbf{X}\}^{-1} \cdot \mathbf{X}' \cdot \mathbf{V}^{-1} = \{\mathbf{X}' \cdot \Delta^{-1} \cdot \mathbf{X}\}^{-1} \cdot \mathbf{X}' \cdot \Delta^{-1} \\
&(iv.) \quad \mathbf{Y} = \mathbf{X} \cdot \{\mathbf{F} + \mathbf{G}\}^{-1} \\
&(v.) \quad \mathbf{S}' \cdot \{\mathbf{X} \cdot \mathbf{F} \cdot \mathbf{X}'\} \cdot \mathbf{S} = \{\mathbf{F} + \mathbf{G}\}^{-1} \cdot \mathbf{F} \cdot \{\mathbf{F} + \mathbf{G}\}^{-1}, \\
&\qquad \mathbf{S}' \cdot \Delta \cdot \mathbf{S} = \{\mathbf{F} + \mathbf{G}\}^{-1} \cdot \mathbf{G} \cdot \{\mathbf{F} + \mathbf{G}\}^{-1} \\
&(vi.) \quad \mathbf{M}' \cdot \{\mathbf{X} \cdot \mathbf{F} \cdot \mathbf{X}'\} \cdot \mathbf{M} = \mathbf{F}, \ \mathbf{M}' \cdot \Delta \cdot \mathbf{M} = \mathbf{G}
\end{aligned}
\tag{A4}
$$

Proof

Items (*i.*) and (*ii.*) can be easily verified by direct substitution. Some work is needed for item (*iii.*). First, $\mathbf{S}' = \mathbf{X}' \cdot \mathbf{V}^{-1}$ and $\{\mathbf{S}' \cdot \mathbf{V} \cdot \mathbf{S}\}^{-1} = \{\mathbf{X}' \cdot \mathbf{V}^{-1} \cdot \mathbf{X}\}^{-1}$ indicates that the first equality in item (*iii.*) of Equation (A4) is always true. To verify the second equality in item (*iii.*) of Equation (A4)), we exploit the factor structure of the covariance matrix:

$$\{\mathbf{X} \cdot \mathbf{F} \cdot \mathbf{X}' + \Delta\} \cdot \mathbf{V}^{-1} = \mathbf{I} \tag{A5}$$

Premultiply Equation (A5) by $\mathbf{X}' \cdot \Delta^{-1}$,

$$\{\mathbf{X}' \cdot \Delta^{-1} \cdot \mathbf{X} \cdot \mathbf{F} + \mathbf{I}\} \cdot \mathbf{X}' \cdot \mathbf{V}^{-1} = \mathbf{X}' \cdot \Delta^{-1} \tag{A6}$$

Premultiply Equation (A6) by **G** from Equation (A3):

$$\{\mathbf{F} + \mathbf{G}\} \cdot \mathbf{X}' \cdot \mathbf{V}^{-1} = \{\mathbf{X}' \cdot \Delta^{-1} \cdot \mathbf{X}\}^{-1} \cdot \mathbf{X}' \cdot \Delta^{-1}. \tag{A7}$$

From item (*ii.*) of Equation (A4), we have $\Psi = \{\mathbf{F} + \mathbf{G}\}$. Combine this with $\mathbf{X}' \cdot \mathbf{V}^{-1} = \mathbf{S}'$ and $\mathbf{M}' = \Psi \cdot \mathbf{S}'$ to get:

$$\mathbf{M}' = \{\mathbf{X}' \cdot \Delta^{-1} \cdot \mathbf{X}\}^{-1} \cdot \mathbf{X}' \cdot \Delta^{-1}. \tag{A8}$$

The remaining items in Equation (A4) can be verified by direct substitution.

Factor Return Regression

This proposition implies that the estimated factor returns in a GLS regression are the same as the returns on the mimicking portfolios. The regression is:

$$\boldsymbol{\theta} = \mathbf{X} \cdot \mathbf{f} + \mathbf{u}. \tag{A9}$$

If we do a GLS regression with the variance of the residuals either **V** or Δ, then according to item (*iii.*) of Equation (A4), the estimated factor returns are:

$$\hat{\mathbf{f}} = \mathbf{M}' \cdot \boldsymbol{\theta}. \tag{A10}$$

Two Sets of Factors

Suppose we have a second set of factors, call them $\hat{\mathbf{X}}$, that are not equal to the factors $\mathbf{X}$ used in the risk model. We can calculate the related source portfolios, $\hat{\mathbf{S}}$, mimicking portfolios, $\hat{\mathbf{M}}$, and mimicking factors, $\hat{\mathbf{Y}}$, using the methods described in the text. The relation of the foursome $\left\{\hat{\mathbf{X}}, \hat{\mathbf{S}}, \hat{\mathbf{M}}, \hat{\mathbf{Y}}\right\}$ to the risk model quartet $\{\mathbf{X}, \mathbf{S}, \mathbf{M}, \mathbf{Y}\}$ is straightforward using Equation (8) for each portfolio in $\hat{\mathbf{S}}$ and $\hat{\mathbf{M}}$.[23]

$$\begin{aligned} &(i.) \qquad \hat{\mathbf{S}} = \mathbf{M}\cdot\left(\mathbf{S}'\cdot\hat{\mathbf{X}}\right) + \mathbf{E}, \quad \mathbf{M}'\cdot\mathbf{V}\cdot\mathbf{E} = 0 \\ &(ii.) \qquad \hat{\mathbf{M}} = \mathbf{M}\cdot\left(\mathbf{S}'\cdot\hat{\mathbf{Y}}\right) + \mathbf{F}, \quad \mathbf{M}'\cdot\mathbf{V}\cdot\mathbf{F} = 0 \end{aligned} \tag{A11}$$

Thus, the residual portfolios in the columns of **E** and **F** have zero covariance with the portfolios in **S** and **M**.

This works in reverse as well:

$$\begin{aligned} &(i.) \qquad \mathbf{S} = \hat{\mathbf{M}}\cdot\left(\hat{\mathbf{S}}'\cdot\mathbf{X}\right) + \mathbf{G}, \quad \hat{\mathbf{M}}'\cdot\mathbf{V}\cdot\mathbf{G} = 0 \\ &(ii.) \qquad \mathbf{M} = \hat{\mathbf{M}}\cdot\left(\hat{\mathbf{S}}'\cdot\mathbf{Y}\right) + \mathbf{L}, \quad \hat{\mathbf{M}}'\cdot\mathbf{V}\cdot\mathbf{L} = 0 \end{aligned} \tag{A12}$$

In this case, the residual portfolios, columns of **G** and **L**, are not correlated with the portfolios $\hat{\mathbf{S}}$ and $\hat{\mathbf{M}}$.

For a similar analysis, see Appendix B of Menchero and Poduri (2008) and Tien et al. (2005).

23. We have used $\mathbf{X}'\cdot\hat{\mathbf{S}} = \mathbf{S}'\cdot\mathbf{V}\cdot\hat{\mathbf{S}} = \hat{\mathbf{S}}\cdot\mathbf{X}'$ to calculate the exposures of the $\hat{\mathbf{S}}$ portfolios to the $\mathbf{X}$ factors.

Appendix B

The SY Method

The linkage diagram in Exhibit 9 illustrates that $\mathbf{M} \cdot \mathbf{X}' = \mathbf{S} \cdot \mathbf{Y}'$. To verify this, recall that $\mathbf{Y}' = \Psi \cdot \mathbf{X}'$ and $\mathbf{S} \cdot \Psi = \mathbf{M}$. Method MX uses the mimicking portfolios as building blocks and the portfolio's exposure to the factors, $\mathbf{X}' \cdot \mathbf{p} = \mathbf{x}_P$, as the weights. Method SY uses the source portfolios as building blocks, and the exposures to the mimicking factors $\mathbf{Y}$ as the weights. The residual portfolio, ε_P, is the same in either case.

The key results are

$$\begin{aligned} &(i.) \quad \mathbf{p} = \mathbf{S} \cdot \mathbf{y}_P + \varepsilon_P, \quad \mathbf{y}_P = \mathbf{Y}' \cdot \mathbf{p} \\ &(ii.) \quad \mathbf{V} \cdot \mathbf{p} = \mathbf{X} \cdot \mathbf{y}_P + \mathbf{V} \cdot \varepsilon_P \end{aligned} \qquad (B1)$$

The breakdown among the factors is different in the case of the alpha and return. The total allocated to the factors is the same, since the residual portfolio does not change when we switch from method MX to method SY. You can see the differences in breakdown and similarity in total allocated in our example by comparing Exhibit 15 in the main text with Exhibit B1. In the example, we have a negative mimicking factor exposure to QUALITY (see Exhibit 13). Even though the QUALITY source portfolio has a positive alpha and a positive return, there is a negative contribution.

EXHIBIT B1 The Description of Alpha and Return Using the SY Method

TRANS. COEFF.	VALUE	QUALITY	SENT.	*e_P*	*P*
rho_P_Mk	0.387	–0.127	0.550	0.575	1
rho_Sk_Mk	0.910	0.772	0.797	1	1
rho_Sk_Q	0.616	0.527	0.712	0.058	0.70
Contribution	0.262	–0.087	0.491	0.034	0.70
Method MX′	0.400	0.050	0.217		

REALIZED IC	VALUE	QUALITY	SENT.	*e_P*	*P*
rho_P_Mk	0.387	–0.127	0.550	0.575	1
rho_Sk_Mk	0.910	0.772	0.797	1	1
rho _Sk_H	0.070	0.060	0.081	0.064	0.113
Contribution	0.0299	–0.0099	0.0560	0.037	0.113
Method MX′	0.0456	0.0057	0.0247		

SECTION 3

Applications of Active Portfolio Management

SECTION 3.1

Expected Return: The Equity Risk Premium and Market Efficiency

15

Introduction to "A Supply Model of the Equity Premium"

This article was published by the CFA institute in a collection of similar efforts titled *Rethinking the Equity Risk Premium*.[1] The work was written by Richard Grinold along with coauthors Kenneth Kroner and Laurence Siegel.[2]

The collection examines the equity risk premium from a variety of perspectives. Our particular effort is constructive and operational: it describes a process for forecasting the equity risk premium over the following decade.

This is important work for a pension fund, an endowment, or foundation's strategic asset allocation effort. It also provides the context for any efforts at tactical asset allocation.

The process we describe is not perfect. It is, however, a framework for approaching the problem and should be relatively free of whimsy. Like any process, it can be and should be improved. In fact, the improvement should be imbedded into the framework. With structure, discipline, learning from others, and learning from experience, one can obtain exceptional results.

The reader who is interested in this topic should take a skeptical approach. Would you do things differently: why, how? If you are engaged at that level, you are on the way to constructing your process. It's all about process.

1. 2011, CFA Institute Research Foundation, Charlottesville, VA. Edited by P. Brett Hammond, Martin L. Leibowitz, and Laurence B. Siegel.
2. Kenneth Kroner is CEO of Pluribus Labs, San Francisco, California. Laurence B. Siegel is the Gary P. Brinson Director of Research, CFA Institute Research Foundation.

16

A Supply Model of the Equity Premium[1]

The equity risk premium is almost certainly the most important variable in finance. It tells you how much you need to save, what you can spend, and how to allocate your assets between equities and bonds. Yet, recognized experts cannot agree on a value for the equity risk premium (ERP) within an order of magnitude, or even get the signs of their estimates to agree. In a 2001 symposium that was the predecessor of the one that is documented in the book that contained this article, Robert Arnott and Ronald Ryan set forth an ERP estimate of –0.9%, while Roger Ibbotson and Peng Chen proposed +6%.[2] There remains considerable disagreement about the size of the premium and how to estimate it.

In 2002, two of us (Grinold and Kroner) proposed a model of the ERP that linked equity returns to gross domestic product (GDP) growth.[3] The key insight, which draws on earlier work by a number of authors, is that aggregate corporate profits cannot grow much faster—or much slower—than GDP indefinitely. (And, as Herbert Stein was fond of reminding us, any economic trend that cannot continue forever, will not.) If profits grow faster than GDP, they eventually take over the economy, leaving nothing for labor, government, natural resource owners, or other claimants. If profits grow more slowly than GDP for long enough, they eventually disappear and there

1. This chapter originally appeared as "A Supply Model of the Equity Premium" by Richard C. Grinold, Kenneth F. Kroner, and Laurence B. Siegel in *Rethinking the Equity Risk Premium*, edited by P. Brett Hammond, Martin L. Leibowitz, and Laurence B. Siegel (Charlottesville VA: CFA Institute Research Foundation, 2011). The authors thank Antti Ilmanen for his very generous contribution of a number of different data sources, and for his wise counsel. Paul Kaplan also provided helpful advice and contributed invaluable data.

2. See Arnott and Ryan (2001) and Ibbotson and Chen (2003). The Ibbotson and Chen estimate of 6% is an arithmetic mean expectation; their geometric mean expectation was 4%.

3. Grinold and Kroner (2002).

is no profit motive for businesses to continue operating. Thus, in the very long run, the ratio of profits to GDP is roughly a constant.

The title of this shortened and updated version of Grinold and Kroner (2002) refers to the "Supply Model" of Diermeier, Ibbotson, and Siegel (1984), who differentiated between the demand for capital market returns (what investors need to compensate them for risk) and the supply of returns (what the macroeconomy makes available). The original supply model likewise made use of a link between profits and GDP. Although our method is designed to produce an ERP estimate that reflects both supply and demand, the link to macroeconomic performance gives it a supply-side flavor.[4]

When we updated the estimates, we found that not all of the components could be updated with equal accuracy, so the ERP estimate provided here is subject to some important caveats regarding data adequacy. The method that we recommend, however, remains largely unchanged from our earlier work.

The Equity Risk Premium Model

We define the equity risk premium as the expected total return differential between the S&P 500 index of US equities and a 10-year par US government bond, over the next 10 years. Our forecast of the return to the 10-year government bond over the next 10 years is just the yield on that bond. Therefore, the equity risk premium becomes:

$$E(R_S - R_B) = \textit{expected S \& P 500 return} - \textit{10 year bond yield}. \qquad (1)$$

A purer and more "modern" approach would be to conduct the whole analysis in real terms, and to use the yield on a 10-year par TIPS bond or, alternatively, a 10-year TIPS strip as the relevant bond yield. The authors of some of the other articles in the original book do that. We estimate the ERP over 10-year nominal bonds because that is what Grinold and Kroner (2002) did. The numerical difference between the results of the two methods, real and nominal, is not large.

Forecasting the return on the S&P 500 over the next 10 years is more difficult, and therefore gets most of the attention of this paper. The framework we use is to decompose equity returns into several understandable pieces, then examine each piece separately.

The return to equities over a single period can always be decomposed into:

$$R_S = \textit{income return} + \textit{nominal earnings growth} + \textit{repricing}. \qquad (2)$$

4. A more detailed history of the estimation of the ERP is in the Foreword (by Laurence B. Siegel) to Paul D. Kaplan, *Frontiers of Modern Asset Allocation* (John Wiley & Sons, 2012).

The income return is the percentage of market value that is distributed to shareholders as cash. If dividends are the only source of income, then this is equivalent to the dividend yield. Today, share repurchase programs (buybacks) are another common means of distributing cash to shareholders. Cash takeovers (by one company of another) should also be counted in the income return of an index that includes the stock of the acquired company.

The next two terms in Equation (2) are the capital gain. Capital gains come from a combination of earnings growth and P/E expansion or contraction, which we call "repricing."

For expository purposes, we decompose the components further and we use more precise notation. The return over a single period is:

$$R = \underbrace{\frac{D}{P} - \Delta S}_{income} + \underbrace{i + g}_{earnings\ growth} + \underbrace{\Delta PE}_{repricing} \quad . \tag{3}$$

The first term, D/P, is simply the dividend yield. The second term,$-\Delta S$, is the percent change in the number of shares outstanding. The percent change in the number of shares outstanding is equal to the "repurchase yield" (theoretically also including cash takeovers), minus new shares issued (dilution); it sports a negative sign because a decrease in the number of shares outstanding is additive to return, and an increase is subtractive to return.[5] Together, the terms D / P and $-\Delta S$ measure the fraction of market capitalization that the firms in an index, in aggregate, give back to shareholders in cash. Therefore, we will refer to the sum of these two terms as the "income return."

The remaining terms, $i + g + \Delta PE$, make up the capital gain. The term i is the inflation rate. The term g is the real earnings (not earnings per share) growth rate over the period of measurement. The final term, ΔPE, is the percent change in the P/E multiple over the period. We refer to this last piece as the "repricing" part of the return.

It is important to realize that this decomposition of returns is essentially an identity, not an assumption, *so any view on the equity risk premium can be mapped into these components*. To illustrate, if the current 10-year bond yield is 3%, anyone who believes that the equity risk premium is currently 4% must believe that the income return, nominal earnings growth, and repricing will sum to 7%.

5. Share buybacks may be viewed either as a component of income return or as a component of capital gain. The owner of a single share, who holds onto the share through the share buyback program, experiences the buyback as a component of capital gain because the same earnings are divided among fewer shares, causing EPS to rise although earnings (not per share) have not changed; if the P/E ratio of the stock and all other things are held equal, then, the stock price rises. An index fund investor, however, experiences the share buyback as cash income, since the index fund manager—who tenders some of the shares to the issuer in order to keep the weight of the stock in the fund proportionate to the weight of the stock in the index—receives cash, which is then distributed to, or held by, fund shareholders like any other cash (tax considerations aside). We choose to view share buybacks as a component of the income return.

Historical Returns

Let us consider briefly what risk premium markets have provided historically. During the 85 years from 1926 to 2010, the US stock market delivered a compound annual nominal return of 9.9% and the intermediate-term US Treasury bond market delivered a compound annual nominal return of 5.4%.[6] So the realized premium that stocks delivered over bonds was 4.5%.[7] The historical return decomposition in Exhibit 1 can be used to better understand this 9.9% per year equity return.

EXHIBIT 1 Decomposition of Total Returns on the S&P 500 from 1926 to 2010*

Income return	4.10%
Real EPS growth	1.91%
Inflation	2.99%
P/E repricing	0.58%
Within-year reinvestment return**	0.28%
Total return	9.87%

* S&P 90 from January 1926 to February 1957; S&P 500 from March 1957 to present.
** Reinvestment of dividends paid during the year in the capital gain index (which consists of real EPS growth plus inflation plus P/E repricing).
Source: Morningstar/Ibbotson. Used by permission.

The income return (through dividends only, not share buybacks) on the S&P 500 was 4.1% annualized over this 85-year period. In this decomposition, we adjusted earnings growth for increases in the number of shares to arrive at *earnings per share (EPS) growth.* EPS grew at a rate of about 4.9% per year (1.9% real growth and 3.0% inflation) over the 85 years.

The remainder of the total return on equities was due to repricing. The price/earnings (P/E) ratio of the market, measured as the end-of-year price divided by trailing 12-month earnings, grew from 11.3 at year-end 1925 to 18.5 at year-end 2010.[8] This repricing works out to an additional return, or P/E expansion, of 0.58% per year. A common view is that this P/E expansion was understandable and rational in light of the technological and financial innovations over this long period. For example, accounting standards became more transparent. Innovations such as the index fund make it easier for investors to diversify security-specific risk and to save on costs. Mutual fund complexes provide easier access to institutional-quality active

6. Morningstar Inc., *Ibbotson SBBI 2011 Classic Yearbook,* p. 32 (table 2.1), data for large-company stocks (the S&P 90 from January 1926 through February 1957, and the S&P 500 thereafter). Returns are before fees, transaction costs, taxes, and other costs.

7. This amount, 4.5%, is the arithmetic difference of geometric means. The geometric difference of geometric means, or compound annual rate at which stocks out-returned bonds, is given by $(1+.099) / (1+.054) - 1 = 4.27\%$.

8. Because earnings were growing very quickly at the end of 2010, the more familiar P/E calculated as the current price divided by 12 months *forward* (forecast) earnings was lower than the 18.5 shown here.

management. Finally, the business cycle is perceived to be under better control than in the 1920s and 1930s, making expected earnings smoother; the 2008–2009 near-depression and quick recovery, at least in corporate profits and the stock market, supports this view somewhat. All of these factors have made equity investing less risky and contributed to the repricing that we saw over this 85-year period.

But the presence of these factors in the past does not mean that we should build continued upward repricing into our forecasts. This question is considered later in this chapter.

The return decomposition in Exhibit 1 is further dissected into annual return contributions, shown in Chart 1 of Grinold and Kroner (2002) but not here. Their graph demonstrates that the noisiest component of returns is clearly the P/E repricing component, followed by the real earnings growth component. Inflation and income returns are relatively stable through time. This observation implies that our real earnings growth and repricing forecasts are likely to be the least accurate, while our inflation and income return forecasts are likely to be more accurate.

Rajnish Mehra and Edward C. Prescott (1985), and many others, have argued that this 4.5% equity premium was a multiple of the amount that should have been necessary to entice investors to hold onto the risky cash flows offered by equities instead of the certain cash flows offered by bonds. This contention has spawned a huge literature on the "equity risk premium puzzle."[9] We have always been puzzled by a debate that suggests that investors were wrong while a specific macroeconomic theory is right, but Professor Mehra shed additional light on this question in his article in the same book as this chapter originally appeared.

Looking to the Future

We now examine each of the terms of Equation (3) to determine what data are needed to forecast them over the moderately long run (10 years). We then combine the elements to estimate, or forecast, the total return on the S&P 500 over that time frame. Finally, we subtract the 10-year Treasury bond yield to arrive at the expected equity risk premium.

Income Return

The income return is the percentage of market capitalization that is distributed to shareholders in cash. Currently, there are two principal means of distributing cash to shareholders: dividend payments and share repurchases. A third method, buying other companies for cash, "works" at the index level, since index investors hold the acquired as well as the acquiring company if the index is broad enough.

9. For surveys of this literature, see Kocherlakota (1996) and Mehra (2003).

Until the mid-1980s, dividends were essentially the only means of distributing earnings. Since then, repurchases have skyrocketed in popularity, in part because they are a more tax-effective means of distributing earnings and in part because companies with cash to distribute may not want to induce investors to expect a distribution every quarter (and cutting dividends is painful, often causing the stock price to decline). In addition, there may be a stigma that dividend-paying companies tend not to be "growth" companies.

In fact, according to Grullon and Michaely (2000), the nominal growth rate of repurchases between 1980 and 1998 was 28.3%. Numerous other studies show that, over the broad market, share repurchases have surpassed dividends as the preferred means of distributing earnings.[10] According to Fama and French (2001), only about a fifth of publicly traded (nonfinancial and nonutility) firms paid any dividends at the time of their study, compared to about two-thirds as recently as 1978. So the "repurchase yield" now exceeds the dividend yield.

As of March 18, 2011 (when this article was being written), the dividend yield was 1.78%.[11] Like a bond yield, the current (not historical average) dividend yield is likely to be the best estimate of the income return over the near to intermediate future, so we use 1.78% as our estimate of D/P in estimating Equation (3).

To estimate the repurchase yield, we use historical data over the longest period for which data were available from Standard and Poor's, the 12 years from the beginning of 1998 to the end of 2009. We calculated the annual repurchase yield as the sum of a given year's share repurchases, divided by the end-of-year capitalization of the market. The data are shown in Exhibit 2 (see next page). The average of the 12 annual repurchase yields is 2.2%, and we use this number in our ERP estimate.

It is possible to make the case for a much higher repurchase yield forecast, by giving greater weight to more recent information (which is basically what we did with the dividend yield). Standard and Poor's wrote, in June 2008: "Over the past fourteen quarters, since the buyback boom began during the fourth quarter of 2004, S&P 500 issues have spent approximately $1.55 trillion on stock buybacks compared to . . . $783 billion on dividends."[12] While buybacks collapsed in 2009, they rebounded in 2010 and 2011. If the two-to-one ratio of buybacks to dividend payments observed by Standard & Poor's over 2004–2008 persists in the future, the repurchase yield will be as high as 3.5% or 3.6%. Aiming for a "fair and balanced"

---

10. See, for example: (1) Fama and French (2001), (2) Grullon and Michaely (2000), (3) Fenn and Liang (2000).

11. Data accessed at http://www.multpl.com/s-p-500-dividend-yield on March 18, 2011.

12. "S&P 500 Stock Buybacks Retreat in Q1 But Remain Strong," Standard and Poor's press release, June 18, 2008, accessed at http://www2.standardandpoors.com/spf/pdf/index/061808_SP500_BUYBACK_PR.pdf, on March 18, 2011.

EXHIBIT 2 Repurchase Return of the S&P 500, 1998–2009

	Year-end market capitalization ($ billions)	Share repurchases during Year ($ billions)	Share repurchases return
1998	9,942.37	125	1.26%
1999	12,314.99	142	1.15%
2000	11,714.55	151	1.29%
2001	10,463.39	132.21	1.26%
2002	8,107.41	127.25	1.57%
2003	10,285.83	131.05	1.27%
2004	11,288.60	197.48	1.75%
2005	11,254.54	349.22	3.10%
2006	12,728.86	431.83	3.39%
2007	12,867.86	589.12	4.58%
2008	7,851.81	339.61	4.33%
2009	9,927.56	137.60	1.39%
Average			2.20%

Source: Standard and Poor's.

estimate, we use the lower 2.2% number arrived at by weighting all 12 years of historical share-repurchase data equally.[13]

Cash buyouts. We have not included cash buyouts in this estimate of the repurchase yield. From the standpoint of an investor who holds an index containing companies A, B, C, and so forth, a cash buyout or takeover—a payment by company A to an investor holding shares of company B, in exchange for tender of those shares—is no different from a share buyback, which is a payment by company A to an investor holding shares of A in exchange for a tender of *those* shares. Thus, the "cash buyout yield" needs to be added to the repurchase yield when summing all the pieces of—ΔS. However, we do not have data for cash buyouts. If we did, they would increase our forecast of the equity risk premium (because cash buyouts must be a positive number and no other component of the ERP would change).

13. Use of this lower number is neutral, not conservative in the sense of numerically minimizing the ERP estimate. The reason is that there are offsetting biases. Our buyback estimate of 2.2% is too high because we do not subtract the historical contribution of buybacks to the dilution estimate, discussed later; and it is too low because very recent buyback rates have been much higher than 2.2%, plus we fully ignore the cash takeover yield.

The Effect of Dilution on Income Return

Dilution is the effect of new issuance of shares by existing companies and takes place through secondary offerings and the exercise of stock options. Dilution may be regarded as reflecting capital that needs to be injected from the labor market (or from elsewhere) into the stock market in order that investors can participate fully in the real economic growth described in the next section. Formally, dilution (expressed as an annual rate, or decrement to the expected equity total return) is the difference between the growth rate of dividends and the growth rate of dividends per share. If the payout ratio is assumed constant, dilution is also equal to the difference between the growth rate of earnings and the growth rate of EPS.

Grinold and Kroner (2002) estimated dilution from secondary offerings using historical data and dealt with stock options separately. Here, because we do not have the data to properly update the dilution estimates in Grinold and Kroner (2002), we use a shortcut: we directly adopt the 2% per year dilution estimate in Bernstein and Arnott (2003).

Bernstein and Arnott studied the United States from 1871 to 2000, and other countries over shorter periods. Instead of measuring the difference between the growth rate of earnings and that of EPS, they used a proxy: they measured the difference between the growth rate of total market capitalization and the capital appreciation return (price return) on existing shares. Dilution thus measured is net of share buybacks and cash buyouts (which are forms of negative dilution—companies giving cash back to shareholders being the opposite of raising capital by selling shares). The 2% dilution estimate for the United States is supported by evidence from other countries.[14]

We should then subtract from the 2% dilution estimate that part of historical dilution that was due to buybacks and cash takeovers (but *not* the part of dilution that was due to stock option issuance, since these cash flows went to employees, not shareholders). However, we do not have the data to perform these adjustments, so we do not attempt them. (Note that buybacks were tiny until the mid-1980s, that is, over about the first 115 years of the 130-year sample, so historical buybacks probably had a minimal impact on the whole-period average rate of dilution.) We just use the 2% estimate.

Income Return: Numerical Estimate

The income return forecast consists of the expected dividend yield, *D*/*P*, minus the expected rate of change in the number of shares outstanding,

14. For a fuller discussion of dilution and an excellent description of the Bernstein and Arnott (2003) method, see also Cornell (2010). Cornell writes (p. 60): "Bernstein and Arnott (2003) suggest an ingenious procedure for estimating the combined impact of both effects (the need of existing corporations to issue new shares, and the effect of start-ups) on the rate of growth of earnings to which current investors have a claim. They note that total dilution on a market-wide basis can be measured by the ratio of the proportionate increase in market capitalization to the value-weighted proportionate increase in stock price. More precisely, each period net dilution is given by the equation, *net dilution* = $(1 + c) / (1 + k) - 1$, where c is the percentage capitalization increase and k is the percentage increase in the value weighted price index. It should be noted that this dilution measure holds exactly only for the aggregate market portfolio."

ΔS. The expected dividend yield is 1.78%. The number of new shares is expected to grow at a –0.2% annual rate, consisting of 2% dilution minus a 2.2% repurchase yield. Adding up all the pieces, the income return forecast is 1.98%.

Expected Real Earnings Growth

We expect real dividend growth, real earnings growth, and real GDP growth (all of these expressed in aggregate, not per share or *per capita*, terms) to be equal to each other.

We expect dividend and earnings growth to be equal because we assume a constant payout ratio. While the payout ratio has fluctuated widely in the past, the ratio has trended downward over time, presumably due to tax and corporate liquidity considerations. However, the decline has effectively stopped. Exhibit 3 shows the dividend payout ratio for the S&P index for 1900–2010; this curious series looks as though it has been bouncing between a declining lower bound (which has now leveled off near 30%) and an almost unlimited upper bound. The very high values of the payout ratio are achieved when there is an earnings collapse (as in 2008–2009) but companies are loath to cut dividends more than they have to.[15] The lower bound reflects payout policy during normally prosperous times.

The current lower bound of about 30% would be a reasonable forecast of the payout ratio, but we do not need an explicit forecast because we have already assumed that it will be constant over the 10-year term of our ERP estimate. However, it is helpful to have empirical support for our assumption of a constant payout ratio, and the recent relative recent stability of the lower bound in Exhibit 3 provides this support.

We expect real earnings growth to equal real GDP growth for the macroconsistency reason stated earlier: any other result would, in the very long run, lead to an absurdity, corporate profits either taking over national income entirely or disappearing. Exhibit 4 shows the (trendless) fluctuations in the corporate profit share of GDP since 1947.

These observations leave us with the puzzle of forecasting real GDP growth. Grinold and Kroner (2002) engaged in a fairly typical macroeconomic analysis that involved productivity growth, labor force growth, and the expected difference between S&P earnings and overall corporate profits. They did not use historical averages or trends directly as forecasts but argued that the data plus other factors justified the conclusion that real GDP would most likely grow at 3% over the relevant forecast period, and that real S&P 500 earnings would grow at 3.5%.

15. The all-time high level of the payout ratio, 397%, was reached in March 2009 when annualized monthly dividends per "share" of the S&P 500 index were $27.25 and annualized monthly earnings per "share" were $6.86.

EXHIBIT 3 **Payout Ratio of US Equity Market, 1900–2010**

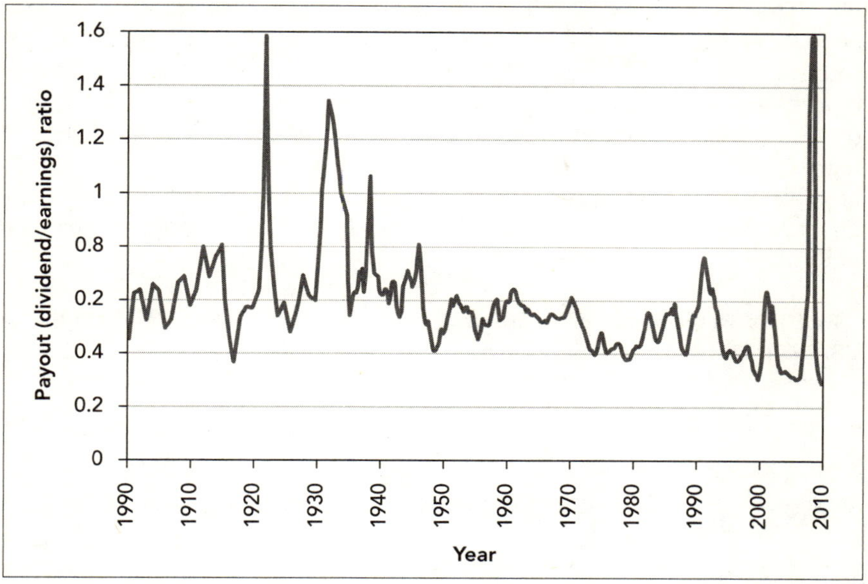

Source: Robert Shiller (raw data). Calculations by the authors.

EXHIBIT 4 **US Corporate Profits as Percentage of GDP, Quarterly, 1947–2010**

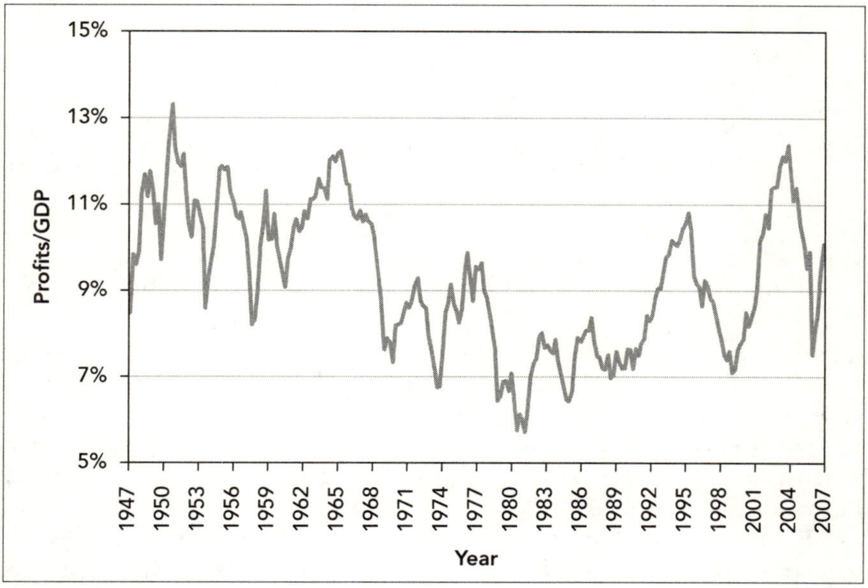

Source: Haver Analytics, citing US National Accounts data. Profits are pretax.

Real economic growth, by definition, equals real productivity growth plus labor force growth. While we can update the historical productivity and labor force growth numbers, these do not produce an especially helpful forecast, any more than they did for Grinold and Kroner (2002), who distanced themselves from it somewhat. The reason is that extrapolating recent trends in these components of economic growth can produce unrealistically high or low expectations, while using historical averages gives no insight into possible future changes in the components, which are important. Nevertheless, updates of these components are provided for informational purposes in Exhibit 5.

EXHIBIT 5 Real Productivity Growth and Labor Force Growth Rates in the US, 1971–2009

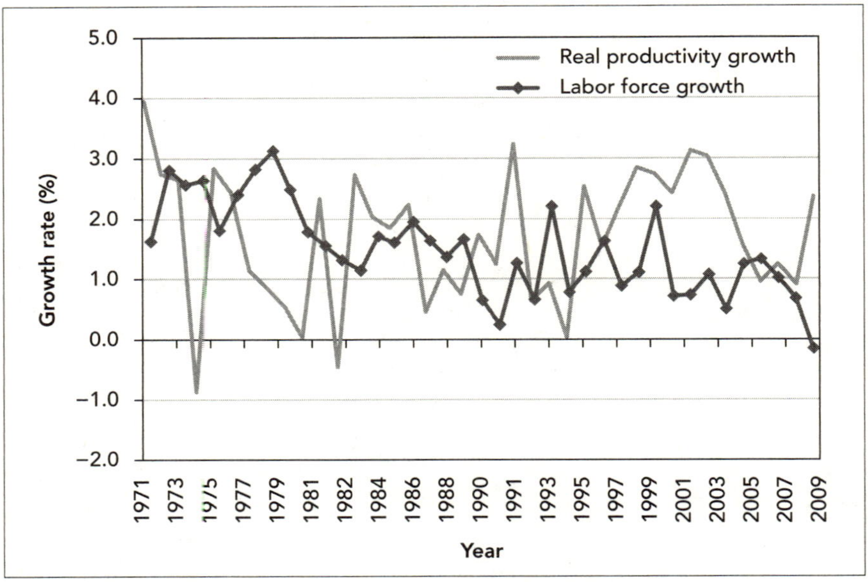

Source: Organisation for Economic Co-Operation and Development, OECD StatExtracts (http://stats.oecd.org/Index.aspx as of November 14, 2011: total labor force, US, and labor productivity annual growth rate, US).

We can, however, use a different decomposition of real economic growth, also definitional. Expected GDP growth equals expected *per capita* GDP growth plus expected population growth. We believe that population growth is easier to forecast than labor force growth because the latter is partly endogenous (for example, people work longer if they need the money due to a weak economy).[16]

Exhibit 6 shows that, in the United States since 1789, real *per capita* GDP growth exhibits a fairly tight fit to a 1.8% compound annual growth rate.

16. Population growth is also partly endogenous (because the decision of how many children to have, whether to immigrate, and so forth, may depend on economic performance). However, these effects operate with long lags and tend to move the population growth rate only slowly.

A global estimate taken by Cornell (2010) from the growth-happy postwar (1960–2006) period in the twentieth century is higher but not dramatically so (2.42% for mature economies and 2.79% for emerging economies). A cautious forecast is that the 1.8% growth rate will continue. If there is substantial risk to this forecast, it is to the upside because an investment in the S&P 500 is not a pure bet on the United States; many, if not most, of the companies in the index are global companies selling into markets that are growing more rapidly than the US market.

EXHIBIT 6 Real US GDP per Capita, 1789–2008

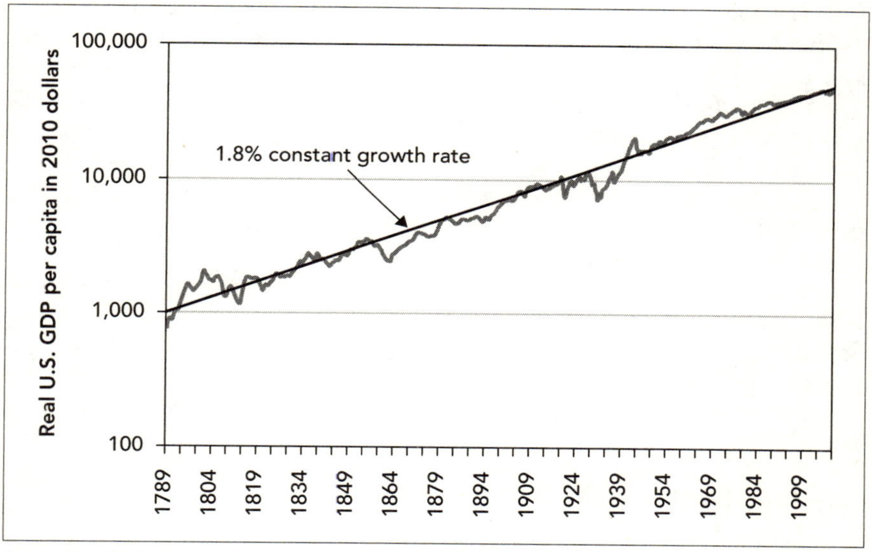

Source: Data from Robert D. Arnott (personal communication), graphed by the authors.

To this 1.8% real per capita GDP growth estimate, we add the Economist Intelligence Unit 10-year US population growth estimate of 0.85%, for a total real GDP growth forecast of 2.65%.[17] This number is a little below current consensus estimates.

This simplified method is somewhat problematic in that, if the rate of dilution is 2% at all population growth rates, then population growth has a one-for-one effect on the estimate of the expected return on equities and thus on the ERP. This suggests an easy beat-the-market strategy: invest only in countries with the fastest population growth. This strategy has not worked well in the past and, even if it did over some sample periods, easy beat-the-market strategies are usually illusory. Thus, the dilution estimate should probably be higher for countries with higher population growth rates, or for a country during periods when it has a higher population growth rate. While

17. Accessed at http://7marketspot.com/archives/2276 on May 2, 2011, under the heading "USA economy: Ten-year growth outlook," in the column "2011–20." If, instead, we used real productivity growth plus labor force growth to estimate real GDP growth, we would get a slightly higher number for real productivity growth and a slightly lower number for labor force growth, for a very similar overall real GDP forecast.

the logic of using a link to real GDP growth to forecast the stock market has great intuitive appeal, putting it into practice with any precision will take more work and more thought regarding dilution.[18]

Expected Inflation

Because we are deriving the ERP relative to Treasury bonds, we do not need our own inflation forecast as much as we need an estimate of the inflation rate that is priced into the 10-year Treasury bond market. Historical inflation rates have no bearing on this number, so we do not present them. Fortunately, the yield spread between 10-year nominal US Treasury bonds and 10-year TIPS is a direct, although volatile, measure of the inflation rate that is expected by bondholders. (The spread also includes an inflation risk premium, present in nominal bond yields but not in TIPS yields, for which we need to adjust.)

On April 22, 2011, the breakeven inflation rate (the yield spread described above) was 2.60%.[19] This rate is high by recent standards—it was as low as 1.5% in September 2010—but is typical of the longer history of the series. Recent concerns about very high and rapidly growing levels of public indebtedness (of the US government, of local governments in the United States, and of non-US governments) have contributed to the increase in inflation expectations. We subtract 0.2% for the inflation risk premium to arrive at a 2.4% compound annual inflation forecast over the next 10 years.[20]

Expected Repricing

Grinold and Kroner (2002, p. 15, chart 8) conducted an analysis of the market's P/E ratio that led them to include a nonzero (–0.75% per year) value for the repricing term, ΔPE, in Equation (3). At the time the analysis was conducted, November 2001, the conventional trailing P/E of the market (price divided by trailing year's earnings) was a lofty 29.7 and the "Shiller P/E" (price divided by 10 years' trailing real earnings) was 30.0, prompting the

18. Our simplified method has some further characteristics worth noting. It does not take specific account of the wedge between population growth and labor force growth if the proportion of retirees (or children) in the population is expected to change. A growing unproductive retiree population should be considered bearish. However, many would-be retirees are not financially prepared for retirement and, willingly or not, will work longer than they originally anticipated, contributing to GDP.

In addition, in an advanced technological society, an aging population distribution within the workforce is not all bad! We are accustomed to thinking of young workers as productive and older workers as unproductive, but this is only the case in a fairly primitive economy where the primary job description is "lift this and put it over there." In a technological society, young workers are unproductive—often startlingly so, earning the minimum wage—and older workers produce most of the value added and make the lion's share of the money.

Nevertheless, young workers' productivity grows quickly and older workers' productivity grows slowly or shrinks, so that the impact of an aging workforce on *rates of change* in productivity may be less salutary than its impact on the *level* of productivity.

19. http://www.bloomberg.com/apps/quote?ticker=USGGBE10:IND.

20. This estimate of the inflation risk premium is taken from page 31 (graph 2) of Hördahl (2008).

authors to conclude that the P/E was likely to decline. (The Shiller P/E is designed to smooth out fluctuations caused by changes in year-to-year earnings.) And decline it did.

EXHIBIT 7 Conventional and Shiller P/E Rations of the US Equity Market, 1900–2010

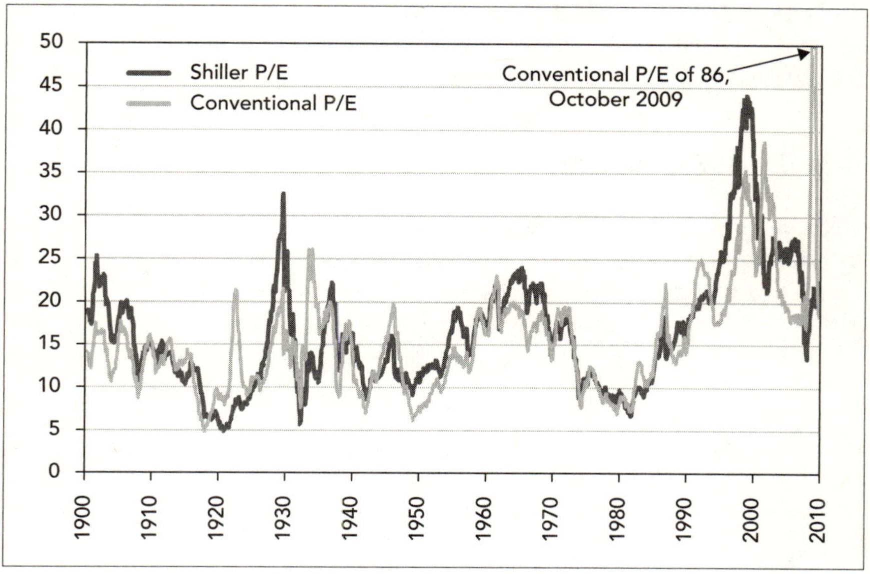

Today, the situation is different. Exhibit 7 shows the conventional P/E and Shiller P/E of the US market.[21] Today's conventional P/E of 18.5 is only modestly above the very long-run (1900–2010) average P/E of 15.7, and it is below the more recent long-run (1970–2010) average P/E of 18.9. The Shiller P/E tells a slightly less favorable story— the current value is 22.4 compared to an average of 16.3 over 1900–2010 and 19.2 over 1970–2010.[22] It should be remembered, however, that the current Shiller P/E, by averaging 10 years of trailing earnings, includes an earnings collapse in 2008–2009 that is almost literally unprecedented; even the Great Depression did not see as sharp a contraction in S&P earnings, although overall corporate profits in 1932 were negative. (Huge losses in a few large companies, such as occurred in 2008–2009, go a long way toward erasing the profits of the other companies when summed across an index.) Only the depression of 1920–1921 is comparable.

Thus, we do not see any justification for using a nonzero value for the repricing term in Equation (3). The current level of the market is already reflected in the (low) dividend yield. Speaking theoretically, it is not double

21. The Shiller P/E is described in Shiller (2000), p. 7.
22. In this section, "current" values are as of December 2010.

counting to have a repricing term when the dividend yield already incorporates the market's valuation, because the influence of the dividend yield is amortized over the infinite run, while our forecast is only for the next 10 years. Thus, if we believe that the market is mispriced in such a way that it will be fully corrected within 10 years, a nonzero repricing term is warranted. While Grinold and Kroner (2002) argued that the market P/E was too high at that time and would decline at an expected rate of 0.75% per year over the forecast horizon, we do not think the market is currently too high (or too low) and our repricing forecast is zero.

Bringing It All Together

Here, we estimate the expected total nominal return on equities, as expressed in Equation (3), using the inputs we derived in the foregoing sections. We then subtract the 10-year nominal US Treasury bond yield to arrive at our estimate of the equity risk premium, ERP, over the next 10 years.

Income return, $\frac{D}{P} - \Delta S$

= 1.78% dividend yield −(−0.2% repurchase yield net of dilution)
= 1.98%

Capital gain, $i + g + \Delta PE$

= 2.4% inflation + 1.8% real per capita GDP growth + 0.85% population growth
= 5.05%

Total expected equity return

= 1.98% + 5.05%
= 7.03% (rounding, 7%)

− 10-year Treasury bond on April 22, 2011: 3.40%[23]
= Expected ERP over 10-year Treasuries: 3.6%

Arithmetic vs. Geometric Mean Forecasts

The above forecasts are geometric means (r_G). To estimate the equivalent arithmetic mean return expectation (r_A) for use as inputs into an optimizer, we rely on the approximation:

$$1 + r_G \approx (1 + r_A) - \frac{\sigma^2}{2} . \quad (4)$$

23. http://finance.yahoo.com/q?s=%5ETNX on April 22, 2011.

We use standard deviations drawn from 1970–2010 because we do not necessarily expect bond returns to be as placid as they have been recently; thus, for the purpose of estimating standard deviations only, we include this long period because it includes the bond bear market of 1970–1980 and the dramatic subsequent recovery.[24] We obtain:

Expected arithmetic mean equity total return:	8.59%
Expected arithmetic mean 10-year Treasury bond total return:	3.96%
Difference (expected arithmetic mean ERP):	4.63%

A limitation of this study is that we use US, not global, macroeconomic data in our estimate of the expected return on the S&P 500. The S&P 500 is a global index, in that it contains many companies that earn most, or a substantial share, of their profits outside the United States. Perhaps global economic growth rates are more relevant than US growth rates to the expected return on the S&P. Future work should take this possibility into consideration.

Assessing the Grinold and Kroner (2002) Forecast

In our 2002 article, we identified three camps of ERP forecasters: "risk premium is dead," "rational exuberance," and "risk is rewarded." We called the first two views "extreme" and wished to be counted among the moderate "risk is rewarded" camp, in keeping with our belief that markets are generally efficient and that prices therefore do not get very far out of line with value for very long.

Our forecast, evaluated over 2002–2011, was too high. The main problem was the volatile repricing term. We seriously underestimated the speed with which the unusually high P/E ratios that then prevailed would revert toward their historical mean. Today, we are forecasting repricing of zero, consistent with our view that the market is, finally, after two bear markets and two recoveries, roughly fairly priced. Because the repricing term is noisy, we know that our current forecast is more likely to be too high or too low than it is to be just right, when evaluated over the next 10 years. However, we believe we have identified the middle of the range of likely outcomes. While black swans, fat tails, and tsunamis are the talk of the day, such large unexpected events tend to fade in importance as they are averaged in with less dramatic events over extended periods, and the underlying long-term trends reveal themselves once more.[25] We expect moderate growth in the stock market.

24. Stocks, 17.68%; bonds 9.73%. (Source: Aswath Damodaran, http://pages.stern.nyu.edu/~adamodar, accessed on June 3, 2011.)
25. A skeptical look at the phenomenon of black swans is provided by one of us in Siegel (2010).

References

Arnott, Robert D., and Ronald J. Ryan. 2001. "The Death of the Risk Premium." *Journal of Portfolio Management* (Spring): 61–74.

Bernstein, William J., and Robert D. Arnott. 2003. "Earnings Growth: The Two Percent Dilution." *Financial Analysts Journal* 59 (September/October): 47–55.

Cornell, Bradford. 2010. "Economic Growth and Equity Investing." *Financial Analysts Journal* 66 (January/February): 54–64.

Diermeier, Jeffrey J., Roger G. Ibbotson, and Laurence B. Siegel. 1984. "The Supply of Capital Market Returns." *Financial Analysts Journal* (March/April): 74–80.

Fama, Eugene F., and Kenneth R. French. 2001. "Disappearing Dividends: Changing Firm Characteristics or Lower Propensity to Pay?" *Journal of Financial Economics* 60 (April), 3–43.

Fenn, George W., and Nellie Liang. 2000. "Corporate Payout Policy and Managerial Stock Incentives." Federal Reserve Board working paper (March).

Grinold, Richard C., and Kenneth F. Kroner. 2002. "The Equity Risk Premium: Analyzing the Long-Run Prospects for the Stock Market." *Investment Insights* 5 (July), Barclays Global Investors, San Francisco. Second printing 2004. Available online at http://www.cfapubs.org/userimages/ContentEditor/1141674677679/equity_risk_premium.pdf.

Grullon, Gustavo, and Roni Michaely. 2000. "Dividends, Share Repurchases and the Substitution Hypothesis." Unpublished manuscript, Johnson Graduate School of Management, Cornell University (April).

Hördahl, Peter. "The Inflation Risk Premium in the Term Structure of Interest Rates." *BIS Quarterly Review*, September 2008, 23–38. Bank for International Settlements. http://www.bis.org/publ/qtrpdf/r_qt0809e.pdf.

Ibbotson, Roger G., and Peng Chen. 2003. "Long-Run Stock Returns: Participating in the Real Economy." *Financial Analysts Journal*, January/February, 88–98.

Ibbotson SBBI. 2011. *2011 Classic Yearbook: Market Results for Stocks, Bonds, Bills, and Inflation, 1926–2010*. Chicago: Morningstar.

Kaplan, Paul D. 2011. *Frontiers of Modern Asset Allocation*. Hoboken, NJ: John Wiley & Sons.

Kocherlakota, Narayana R. 1996. "The Equity Premium: It's Still a Puzzle," *Journal of Economic Literature* 34: 42–71.

Mehra, Rajnish. 2003. "The Equity Premium: Why Is It a Puzzle?" *Financial Analysts Journal* 59 (January /February): 54–69.

Mehra, Rajnish, and Edward C. Prescott. 1985. "The Equity Premium: A Puzzle." *Journal of Monetary Economics* 15 (March): 145–61.

Shiller, Robert J. 2000. *Irrational Exuberance*. 2nd. ed. Princeton University Press, Princeton.

Siegel, Laurence B. 2010. "Black Swan or Black Turkey? The State of Economic Knowledge and the Crash of 2007–2009." *Financial Analysts Journal* 66 (July/August): 6–10.

Standard & Poor's. 2008. "S&P 500 Stock Buybacks Retreat in Q1 but Remain Strong." Press release (June 18).

17

Introduction to "Is Beta Dead Again?"

The chapter "Is Beta Dead Again?" was originally published during a periodic furor over the economic message contained in Sharpe's capital asset pricing model (CAPM) and its implication for the efficiency of equity markets, specifically the US equity market.

That furor has subsided. The current fuss centers on Sharpe's "Arithmetic of Active Management," a simpler and more dangerous challenge to the active manager.[1] That controversy is still generating some steam. See Lasse Pedersen's "Sharpening the Arithmetic of Active Management" for a counterargument and a large list of references.[2]

The paper was motivated by the author's conviction that if you ignore the CAPM you should not do away with the notion of beta. Beta is just too useful a part of the portfolio engineer's kit. Those uses are set out in the chapter.

The chapter contains work with mean-variance efficiency diagrams and does a crude test of the efficiency of an equity benchmark in the US equity market. The benchmark, BARRA's US HICAP, looks bad on the efficiency dimension mostly due to the exceptional performance of low volatility stocks.[3]

In the chapter we also refer to the best linear unbiased estimator, *BLUE*, and what we call the forecasting equation. In the remainder of this introduction we present a brief tutorial on the forecasting equation.

$$\tilde{\theta} \quad N \text{ vector of returns we want to forecast} \tag{1}$$

$$\tilde{s} \quad J \text{ vector of signals that we believe will help}$$

1. W. F. Sharpe, "The Arithmetic of Active Management," *Financial Analysts Journal* 47, no. 1 (Jan–Feb): 7–9.
2. L. H. Pedersen, "Sharpening the Arithmetic of Active Management," *Financial Analysts Journal* 47, no. 1 (Q1, 2018): 21–36.
3. The BARRA HICAP is a roughly equivalent to the Russell 1000 index.

The discussion of the best linear unbiased estimator is usually presented in terms of a linear regression. We are going to take a different tack. We will assume that we know the expected values of our returns and signals and the covariances among them. We have two sets of variables—the returns $\tilde{\theta}$ and the signals $\tilde{s}$—that we hope will help us forecast the returns. We observe the signal and then the return.

We assume that we know the unconditional expected values of $\tilde{\theta}$ and $\tilde{s}$, and the covariances among them:

$\bar{\theta}$	the unconditional expected value of $\tilde{\theta}$	
$\bar{s}$	the unconditional expected value of $\tilde{s}$	
$\Psi(s,s)$	the J by J covariance of the signals $\tilde{s}$	(2)
$\Psi(\theta,\theta)$	the N by N covariance of the returns $\tilde{\theta}$	
$\Psi(\theta,s)$	the N by J covariance of $\tilde{\theta}$ and $\tilde{s}$	

The forecasting equation tells us how our expectation of the returns *changes* if we have knowledge of the signals. We will use the notation and language of conditional expectation. This is valid if all the variables are normal and in some other cases. In any case, what we are calling the change in expectation is:

$$\left\{E\langle\tilde{\theta}\,|\,\tilde{s}=s\rangle-\bar{\theta}\right\}=\Psi(\theta,s)\cdot\Psi^{-1}(s,s)\cdot\{s-\bar{s}\}. \tag{3}$$

On the left side of Equation (3) we have the change in expectation due to our knowledge of the signals. In the context of *Active Portfolio Management*, this is the alpha forecast. Note that $\Psi(\theta,s)\cdot\Psi^{-1}(s,s)$ is similar to a beta; it is a covariance divided by a variance.

We can dig a bit deeper and find a useful message in the formula. If you are a deep digger, read on.

Let's look at the covariances in terms of standard deviations and correlations:

$\Psi(\theta,\theta)=\Sigma(\theta)\cdot\Phi(\theta,\theta)\cdot\Sigma(\theta)$

$\Sigma(\theta)$ diagonal matrix giving the standard deviations of the returns

$\Phi(\theta,\theta)$ N by N matrix giving the correlations of the returns

$\Psi(s,s)=\Sigma(s)\cdot\Phi(s,s)\cdot\Sigma(s)$ similar split for the signals (4)

$\Psi(\theta,s)=\Sigma(\theta)\cdot\Phi(\theta,s)\cdot\Sigma(s)$

$\Phi(\theta,s)$ N by J matrix giving the correlations of the returns and signals

In the terminology of *Active Portfolio Management*, the matrix $\Phi(\theta, s)$ is the matrix of *information coefficients* or *IC*s. With this notation the forecasting equation becomes:

$$\{E\langle\tilde{\theta}|\tilde{s}=s\rangle-\bar{\theta}\}=\Sigma(\theta)\cdot\{\Phi(\theta,s)\cdot\Phi^{-1}(s,s)\}\cdot\{\Sigma^{-1}(s)\cdot[s-\bar{s}]\}$$

$\Sigma(\theta)$	Volatility	
$\{\Phi(\theta,s)\cdot\Phi^{-1}(s,s)\}$	*IC* corrected for signal correlation	(5)
$\{\Sigma^{-1}(s)\cdot[s-\bar{s}]\}$	Score; The signals standardized; mean 0, stdev. 1	

This is the familiar *Volatility* · *IC* · *Score* message touted in *Active Portfolio Management*, Chapter 10. For devotees of the Black-Litterman approach,[4] be assured that the forecast in Equation (5) is equivalent and, in our view, a great deal easier to understand and use. It is also equivalent to a maximum likelihood estimation approach and a Bayesian regression approach, but those are stories for another day.

4. Fischer Black and Robert Litterman, "Asset Allocation Combining Investor Views with Market Equilibrium," *Journal of Fixed Income* 1, no. 2 (September 1991): 7–18; and Fischer Black and Robert Litterman, "Global Portfolio Optimization," *Financial Analysts Journal* 48, no. 5 (September/October 1992): 28–43.

18

Is Beta Dead Again?[1]

Beta splits a security's return into a part that is perfectly correlated with a benchmark portfolio and an uncorrelated residual. Beta is used to analyze performance, control risk, make conditional forecasts, and set a priori expected returns. It is primarily beta's role in the capital asset pricing model (CAPM), which says expected residual returns should be zero, that makes beta controversial.

Concern for beta's vitality dates from the feature article "Is Beta Dead?" in the July 1980 issue of *Institutional Investor*. That story was based on some mid-1970s academic assaults on the capital asset pricing model. Early in 1992, the *New York Times* and the *Economist* reported on research by professors Fama and French that mounted a renewed attack on beta.[2] What is going on? Is this a late hit on an already dead beta? A born-again beta put to the sword once more? An arcane academic battle that surfaces once a decade?

This article addresses these questions. Our conclusion is that beta suffered collateral damage in an attack on the CAPM. If we view that attack from one angle, beta appears to be severely injured. If we see that attack from other angles, beta escapes unscathed, although the CAPM remains on the defensive.

The question remains, can beta live if the CAPM dies? The answer is yes, because beta has several uses that are separate from the CAPM. Consider the tale of the three portfolios. The first has $50 million in Treasury bills (the risk-free asset), the second $50 million in an S&P 500 index fund, and the third $50 million in the S&P 500 portfolio plus a $50 million long exposure to S&P 500 futures. These portfolios are one-dimensional, and that dimension is beta. The betas of these three portfolios (with the S&P 500

1. This chapter originally appeared as "Is Beta Dead Again?" by Richard C. Grinold in the *Financial Analysts Journal*, July/August 1993, 28–34. In October 2018, the author revised the article for this chapter.
2. Fama and French (1992).

as the benchmark) are 0, 1, and 2, respectively. Each of these portfolios will earn the T-bill (risk-free) return plus the portfolio's beta times the excess return on the S&P 500, so the expected return on each portfolio will be the risk-free return plus beta times the expected excess return on the S&P 500.[3] The volatility of each portfolio will be its beta times the volatility of the S&P 500. Beta is the crucial determinant of the risk and expected return of each of these portfolios.

Betas and Elephants

One of the difficulties in discussing the term *beta* is that beta means different things to different people. Recall the parable about the elephant and the blind men. Five blind men are presented with an elephant and are asked to describe it. The first, clutching a leg, concludes that the elephant is like a tree. Another, latched on to the tail, determines the elephant is like a rope. A third man, pressed against the elephant's flank, thinks it is like a wall. The fourth has grabbed the trunk and concludes he is holding a snake, while the fifth, grasping a tusk, thinks the elephant is a spear. There is a tree, rope, wall, snake, and spear quality to beta, too! Let's look at some of the ways we use the term *beta* and see if the entire elephant emerges.[4]

Beta #1: A Regression Coefficient

The term *beta* is borrowed from linear regression. Consider a time series regression of portfolio excess return, $r_P(t)$, against some benchmark excess return, $r_B(t)$:

$$r_P(t) = \alpha_P + \beta_P \cdot r_B(t) + \varepsilon_P(t), \quad \text{for } t = 1, 2, \ldots, T \tag{1}$$

Estimates of the parameters alpha and beta in Equation (1) are selected by minimizing the sum of the squared residuals, $\varepsilon_P(t)$. These estimated coefficients are the realized, or historical, alphas and betas, since they are an ex post evaluation of the returns.

3. The excess return is return less the return on a nominally risk-free asset (such as a Treasury bill) that matures at the end of the period.

4. This task is made more complicated because statisticians, econometricians, and the like use the term *beta* for any estimated coefficients in any model (e.g., star luminosity and distance; smoking and health, etc.).

EXHIBIT 1 **Excess Returns on the MMI vs. Excess Returns on the S&P 500**

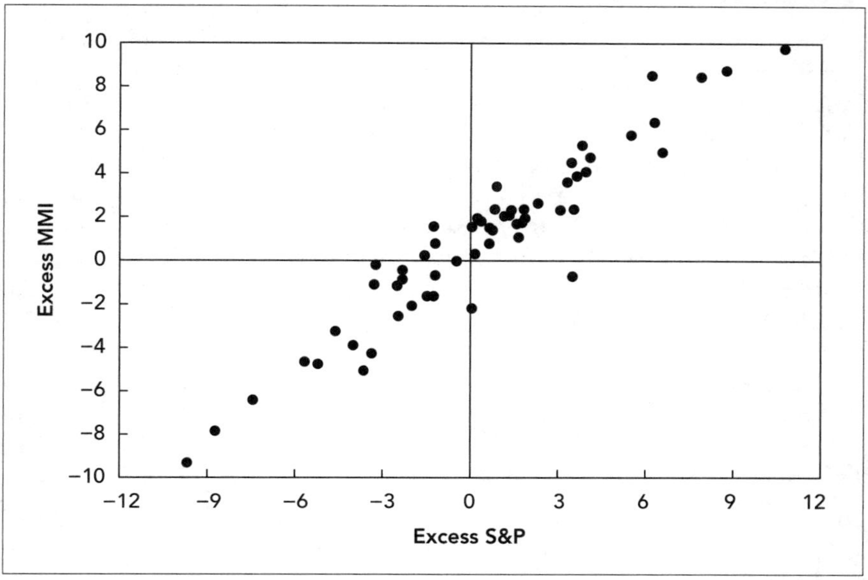

Exhibit 1 is a scatterplot showing excess return pairs for the MMI and the S&P 500. The S&P 500 is playing the role of the benchmark. The excess returns are for 60 months from November 1987 through October 1992. The two series have average monthly excess returns of 0.66% and 0.69%, respectively. The coefficient β_{MMI} is the estimated slope of the regression line (in this case, 0.91 ± 0.037). The coefficient α_{MMI} is the intercept (in this case, 0.032% ± 0.15%). Exhibit 1 shows the role of beta in explaining (ex post) the co-movement of the MMI and the S&P 500. If you picked up all the points on the scatterplot and moved them up, down, left, or right (no twisting!), the estimated beta would not change. The average returns on the portfolios and the alpha would change, but beta, the co-movement of the two portfolios, would remain unchanged. The purpose of the regression given in Equation (1) is to break returns down into a component that is perfectly correlated with the benchmark, $\beta_P \cdot r_B(t)$, and another component, $\alpha_P + \varepsilon_P(t)$, that is uncorrelated with the benchmark. There is an investment idea behind this regression.[5] An investor could obtain an excess return equal to $\beta_P \cdot r_B(t)$ simply by rebalancing the portfolio at the beginning of each period, so that a fraction, β_P, is invested in the benchmark, with the remainder, $1 - \beta_P$, held in the risk free asset. The remaining component, $\alpha_P + \varepsilon_P(t)$, is a measure of value added to that simple strategy of rebalancing to the fixed beta level of β_P each period.

5. Jensen (1968).

Beta #2: Predicted Beta

The regression beta is a statistical construct. It tells what happened over a certain period with a particular sample of data. The regression beta can be interpreted as the sample covariance of the portfolio and benchmark return divided by the sample variance of the benchmark return.

When we look forward and attempt to forecast beta, we use the same notion of a covariance divided by a variance. Any model for predicting asset variance and covariance can be used to predict the variance of a benchmark and the covariance of any portfolio with that benchmark. The ratio of those two quantities is the portfolio's predicted beta with respect to the benchmark.[6] An investment manager can build or rent a model of investment risk. The basic product is an N by N covariance matrix, call it $\mathbf{V}$, where $V_{n,m}$ represents a forecast of the covariance of the annual returns of assets n and m. If P and B are portfolios with respective positions $\mathbf{p} = \{p_n\}_{n=1:n}$ and $\mathbf{b} = \{b_n\}_{n=1:N}$, and r_P and r_B are the excess returns on the portfolio P and the benchmark portfolio B, then the formula is:

$$\beta_P = \frac{\text{Cov}\langle r_P, r_B \rangle}{\text{Var}\langle r_B \rangle} = \frac{\mathbf{b}' \cdot \mathbf{V} \cdot \mathbf{p}}{\mathbf{b}' \cdot \mathbf{V} \cdot \mathbf{b}}$$

$$\text{where } \mathbf{b}' \cdot \mathbf{V} \cdot \mathbf{p} = \text{Cov}\langle r_P, r_B \rangle = \sigma_{P,B} \tag{2}$$

$$\mathbf{b}' \cdot \mathbf{V} \cdot \mathbf{b} = \text{Var}\langle r_B \rangle = \sigma_{B,B} = \sigma_B^2$$

$$\boldsymbol{\beta} = \frac{\mathbf{V} \cdot \mathbf{b}}{\mathbf{b}' \cdot \mathbf{V} \cdot \mathbf{b}} = \{\beta_n\}_{n=1:N}$$

Beta #3: Residual Risk

The predicted beta of Equation (2) measures exposure to benchmark risk. Like the historical regression beta, it can be used to break the portfolio's excess return, r_P, into one component, $\beta_P \cdot r_B$, that is perfectly correlated with the benchmark and another component (the residual return), $r_P - \beta_P \cdot r_B$, that is not correlated with the benchmark return.[7] If we use the predicted beta of Equation (2), we can split the holdings in any portfolio P into a component that is correlated with the benchmark and a second, residual component, call it portfolio S_P, for the surplus (residual, but r is taken for returns) component of portfolio P. S_P is uncorrelated with the benchmark. Since the benchmark component and the residual component are uncorrelated, we can easily separate the portfolio's variance, σ_P^2, into benchmark and residual terms:

6. One approach to making this forecast is to use the historical beta obtained from Equation (1). However, it is possible to do much better, since we may know a lot more about stocks and portfolios than we can obtain by restricting our attention to historical returns.
7. The portfolio's alpha is the expected residual return.

$$
\begin{aligned}
&\mathbf{s}_P = \mathbf{p} - \beta_P \cdot \mathbf{b} \;\Rightarrow \mathbf{b}' \cdot \mathbf{V} \cdot \mathbf{s}_P = 0 \\
&\sigma_P^2 = \left(\beta_P \cdot \mathbf{b} + \mathbf{s}_P\right)' \cdot \mathbf{V} \cdot \left(\beta_P \cdot \mathbf{b} + \mathbf{s}_P\right) \\
&\sigma_P^2 = \beta_P^2 \cdot \sigma_B^2 + \omega_P^2 \;\text{ where} \\
&\omega_P^2 = \mathbf{s}_P' \cdot \mathbf{V} \cdot \mathbf{s}_P \;\text{ is the residual variance of } P.
\end{aligned} \tag{3}
$$

In Equation (3), σ_B^2 is the variance of the benchmark portfolio. We see that beta determines the benchmark component of risk. Thus, if there is a futures contract on the benchmark portfolio, one can use it to alter the portfolio's beta, leaving the residual component unchanged. In fact, by selling futures contracts equal in value to β_P times the value of portfolio P, one could hedge all the portfolio's benchmark risk; only the residual risk would remain.

Another valuable measure of risk is the active (tracking) variance, σ_{P-B}^2, which predicts the variance of the active return (also known as the tracking error) between the portfolio return and benchmark return, $r_P - r_B$. We can use beta to split the active return into a component that is correlated with the benchmark and a residual component. The active variance is then the sum of the variances of these two uncorrelated parts:

$$
\sigma_{P-B}^2 = (\mathbf{p} - \mathbf{b})' \cdot \mathbf{V} \cdot (\mathbf{p} - \mathbf{b}) = (1 - \beta_P)^2 \cdot \sigma_B^2 + \omega_P^2 . \tag{4}
$$

Beta is a key determinant of both the total variance (Equation (3)) and the active variance (Equation (4)).

Institutional portfolio managers whose performance is judged relative to a benchmark use beta as a risk control to neutralize the portfolio's relative performance against any radical moves of the benchmark.

Beta #4: Conditional Expected Returns

Beta can be used to forecast expected returns on an asset or a portfolio of assets conditional on some information about the return of any other asset or portfolio of assets. For example, let's consider a simple world of two assets, STOCKS and BONDS, with BONDS playing the role as the benchmark. The bond market is initially yielding 2.5% over T-bills, which provides a conventional expected return on bonds. Suppose our proprietary research says the bond market will be down 1% in the next year due to otherwise unanticipated inflation and rate increases. What does that insight about the bond market tell us about the expected return on stocks? Beta can help us answer that question. If we measure our betas as in Equation (2), with the B = BONDS as the benchmark, then the best linear unbiased estimate of the change in the expected return on STOCKS for our example is:[8]

8. I have taken the liberty of using notation for the conditional expectation for the *BLUE* estimate. The *BLUE* estimate will be the conditional expectation if the distributions are joint normal. It is the best linear unbiased estimate in any case. For details, see Theil (1971), pp. 123–4.

$$
\begin{aligned}
&E\langle r_{STOCKS} | r_{BONDS} = -0.01\rangle - E\langle r_{STOCKS}\rangle \\
&= \beta_{STOCKS} \cdot \{-0.01 - E\langle r_{BONDS}\rangle\} \\
&\text{where} \\
&\beta_{STOCKS} = \frac{Cov\,\langle r_{STOCKS}, r_{BONDS}\rangle}{Var\,\langle r_{BONDS}\rangle}
\end{aligned} \tag{5}
$$

In this formula, $E\langle r_{STOCKS}\rangle$ and $E\langle r_{BONDS}\rangle$ are the unconditional expected excess returns on the STOCKS and BONDS. In our example case, we have $E\langle r_{BONDS}\rangle = 0.025$. The expression $E\langle r_{STOCKS} | r_{BONDS} = -0.01\rangle$ should be read as the expected excess return on STOCKS, conditional on knowing that the excess return on the BOND market will be –1%. Using a reasonable estimate of 1.4 for β_{STOCKS}, we get a *change* in the STOCKS prediction of –4.9%.

Beta #5: The CAPM

The CAPM is an economic result that can be used to obtain unconditional expected returns.[9] The CAPM breaks expected return into two parts: a time premium (the risk-free return) that an investor obtains for parting with the money for an interval of time and an expected excess return (also called a risk premium) that the investor expects to earn for taking on risk. There is no premium for taking on residual risk since it can be diversified away. The CAPM maintains that a portfolio's expected excess returns are proportional to that portfolio's beta with respect to the market portfolio of all assets. It is an important distinction that we say *the* market as opposed to *a* benchmark. In the equations below, the *M* for market has replaced the *B* for benchmark. There is no alternative version of the market; it is the all-embracing, universal portfolio. A well-diversified index of domestic equities is sometimes used as a surrogate for the market even though it will fall far short of the universal ideal.

The CAPM formula is:

$$
\begin{aligned}
&E\langle r_P\rangle = \beta_P \cdot E\langle r_M\rangle \\
&\text{where } \beta_P = \frac{Cov\langle r_P, r_M\rangle}{Var\langle r_M\rangle} = \boldsymbol{\beta}' \cdot \mathbf{p} = \left\{\frac{\mathbf{m}' \cdot \mathbf{V}}{\mathbf{m}' \cdot \mathbf{V} \cdot \mathbf{m}}\right\} \cdot \mathbf{p}
\end{aligned} \tag{6}
$$

Under the CAPM, beta and the market's risk premium $E\langle r_M\rangle$ are the sole factors that explain expected excess return.[10] The CAPM idea is equivalent to the notion that the market portfolio, the sum total of all holdings, is a mean-variance efficient portfolio that offers the highest attainable expected excess return per unit of predicted risk. The CAPM illustrates both the power of economics and its reputation as the dismal science. The advent of the CAPM

9. Sharpe (1964).

10. This is the simplest version of the CAPM. As we will see below, there is a more general zero beta version of the CAPM.

started a very slow process of shifting the burden of relative performance proof onto the active managers.

The CAPM as captured by Equation (6) has been on the defensive for quite a while. The theoretical efforts of Merton and Ross were key events.[11] These authors, using quite different approaches, end up suggesting a multiple factor approach for explaining expected excess returns. Multiple factor models are a recurring theme in academic circles.[12] The conventional wisdom has shifted to say that beta and several other factors (size, value, and volatility, or exposure to unanticipated changes in interest rates, oil prices, inflation, and industrial production) are important in determining expected excess returns. That debate has been rekindled by the Fama and French article.[13] In the latter part of this chapter, we will return to the CAPM and perform a simple experiment to test the efficiency of a value-weighted large-cap benchmark in the US equity market.

Beta #6: The Post-Processed Forecast

Many institutional investors prefer to manage their portfolios relative to an investment benchmark such as the S&P 500. Those managers can make the useful assumption, without any special insights, that the benchmark portfolio is mean-variance efficient. The upshot of this assumption is that, absent any proprietary information, the manager will hold the benchmark portfolio. This is reasonable and in line with the management objective. The assumption also means that the manager sets unconditional expected excess returns of all assets and portfolios by:

$$E\langle r_P \rangle = \beta_P \cdot E\langle r_B \rangle \quad \text{where } \beta_P = \frac{Cov\langle r_P, r_B \rangle}{Var\langle r_B \rangle}. \tag{7}$$

In Equation (7), beta is measured with respect to the benchmark. This is Equation (6) with *a* benchmark filling in for *the* market. The similarity is deceptive. Equation (6), the CAPM, is an economic statement. Equation (7) is a portfolio engineer's method for anchoring the portfolio to the benchmark.

Exhibit 2 illustrates the situation where the (naive) investor has no special information. This absence of information means that the benchmark portfolio, *B*, is efficient in the sense of offering the highest mean return for its level of risk as measured by standard deviation.

11. Merton (1973) and Ross (1976).
12. See Sharpe (1984) and Shanken (1985).
13. Fama and French (1992).

EXHIBIT 2 The Naive Forecast

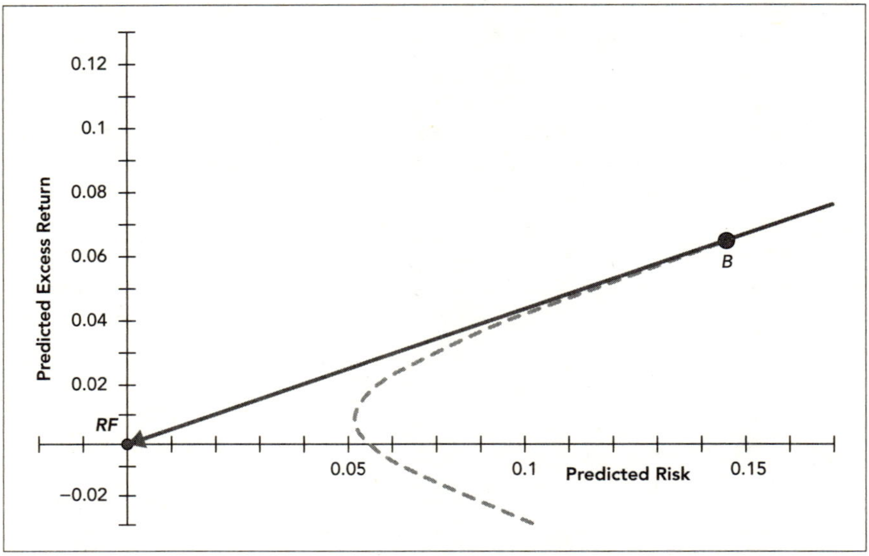

Exhibit 3 shows the same benchmark portfolio, but this time in the context of an investor who possesses special information. That information has expanded the possible risk and return options open to the investor. As a result, the benchmark *B* is well inside the efficient frontier.

EXHIBIT 3 The Informed Forecast

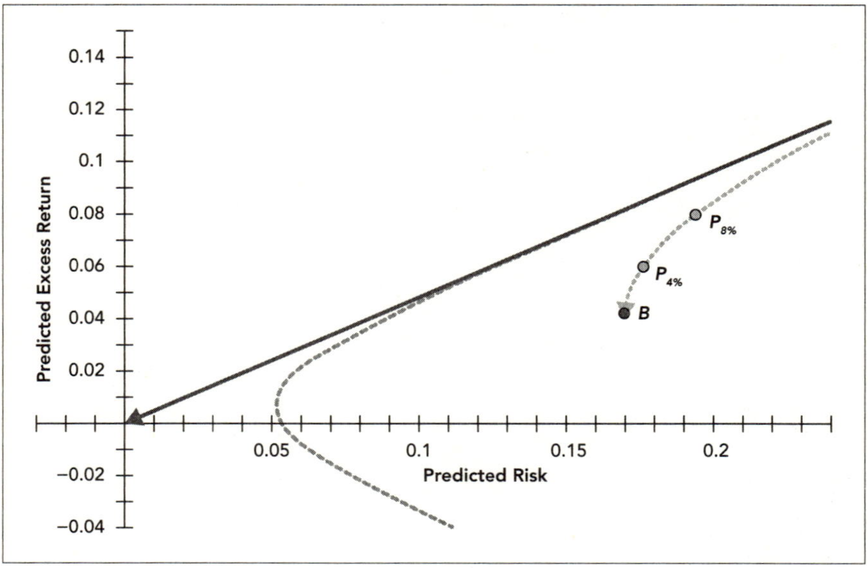

We can consider the research process as process for calculating conditional expectations.[14] The output of that process is a forecast, f, of the residual returns $\tilde{\mathbf{r}} - \boldsymbol{\beta} \cdot \tilde{r}_B$ on the *N* assets.

$$\mathbf{f} = E\langle \tilde{\mathbf{r}} - \boldsymbol{\beta} \cdot \tilde{r}_B \,|\, INFO \rangle. \tag{8}$$

Read Equation (8) as conditional on our proprietary INFO, we expect the residual return on the assets to be **f**.

Let $f_B = \mathbf{f}' \cdot \mathbf{b}$ be the resulting forecast of the benchmark return from Equation (8). If Equation (8) is an unbiased forecast, then we expect f_B to be zero. However, there is no guarantee that the forecasting process is in fact unbiased, and even if f_B is expected to be zero, that is not good enough. We can ensure that we have a residual forecast by post-processing the forecast and splitting it into a benchmark and component in the same way we split a portfolio's positions, Equation (3), into benchmark and residual parts. Beta plays a key role in this filtering operation, which produces a forecast, $\boldsymbol{\alpha}$, that is guaranteed to be benchmark neutral.

$$\begin{aligned} &\boldsymbol{\alpha} = \mathbf{f} - f_B \cdot \boldsymbol{\beta} \quad \text{where} \\ &\boldsymbol{\beta} \equiv \frac{\mathbf{V} \cdot \mathbf{b}}{\sigma_B^2} \quad \text{and therefore} \\ &\boldsymbol{\alpha}' \cdot \mathbf{b} = 0. \end{aligned} \tag{9}$$

The objective of this relative performance manager is to maximize portfolio alpha less a penalty for active variance:

$$\text{Maximize } \boldsymbol{\alpha}' \cdot \mathbf{p} - \frac{\lambda}{2} \cdot (\mathbf{p} - \mathbf{b})' \cdot \mathbf{V} \cdot (\mathbf{p} - \mathbf{b}). \tag{10}$$

The objective in the optimization, Equation (10), will tempt us to take on additional residual risk but to maintain a portfolio beta of one. You can see the situation in Exhibit 3. The efficient frontier has been expanded by the proprietary information. The benchmark *B* is inside the frontier. The dotted line from the benchmark moving up and to the right consists of portfolios that have a beta of one and an increasing amount of residual risk. We have marked the points with 4% and 8% residual risk. The vertical distance of the 4% and 8% portfolios above the benchmark is the size of the alpha we expect by increasing the residual risk ω_P.

What to do with the component of our forecast, f_B, that has been discarded by the post-processor, Equation (9)? We should follow up and see if it is an effective forecast of benchmark return, or noise we were fortunate to have removed from our forecast. If f_B appears helpful in forecasting the benchmark's return and there is another strategy, say asset allocation, that does take positions in aggregates, then this bottom-up benchmark forecast might be of interest in that strategy.

14. See the appendix to Chapter 10 in Grinold and Kahn (2000).

Summary to this Point

Beta can be defined as the slope of an ex post regression line (#1) or as an ex ante prediction (#2). Beta's role in predicting risk (#3) and in developing conditional expectations (#4 and #6) depend on using beta as a measure of comovement. Investment managers who wish to add value relative to some benchmark portfolio can use beta to obtain an a priori forecast of excess returns, Equation (7), and to ensure that all active risk is residual to the benchmark; see Exhibit 3. These uses of beta are noncontroversial.

Controversy surrounds the CAPM's use of beta (#5) as the sole measure of expected excess return. The CAPM is a powerful economic idea that revolves around the notion of the market. Its practical effect has been to shift the burden of proof to the active manager. If active managers can't say why their product is superior to an index fund, they are unlikely to succeed.

Academics would like to test the CAPM to see if its predictions align with reality. These tests face a large hurdle; *the* market is an elusive concept therefore hard to identify let alone test.

Is the Benchmark Efficient?

We can try to answer a related question. Is a particular investment benchmark an efficient portfolio? We consider that question in Chapter 20 of this book, "Are Benchmark Portfolios Efficient?"

In what follows, we'll describe another approach to the benchmark efficiency question. The discussion does not pretend to be a definitive statistical test. It is interesting in the context of this chapter since it provides another example of beta's utility. In this case, it's the absence of beta since the test centers on a portfolio with a beta of zero.

A portfolio is *fully invested* if all of its positions are risky and the net sum of its holdings, the longs minus the shorts, is positive. We can normalize those holdings, divide by the total value, so that they sum to one.

A portfolio's predicted *Sharpe ratio* is the ratio of its expected excess return divided by its predicted risk. The realized Sharpe ratio is the realized excess return divided by the realized risk. In a well-defined universe of risky assets, we generally can find a fully invested portfolio that has a maximum Sharpe ratio.[15] Call that fully invested portfolio with the maximum Sharpe ratio portfolio X for unknown; that is, we know such a portfolio exists, we just don't know what it is. Then, using an argument similar to the one used in the original CAPM paper, we can establish that:

$$\mu_P = \beta_P \cdot \mu_X$$

where

$$\beta_P \equiv \frac{Cov\langle r_P, r_X\rangle}{Var\langle r_X\rangle} = \frac{\sigma_{P,X}}{\sigma_X^2} \tag{11}$$

15. The stipulation is that the minimum risk fully invested portfolio C, to be introduced below, has a positive expected excess return.

Equation (11) says the expected excess returns on any portfolio (or asset) are proportional to that portfolio's (or asset's) beta with portfolio X standing in for the market.[16]

If we can show that the unknown X is in fact equal to the benchmark B, as in Exhibit 2, then the benchmark is an efficient portfolio and we can replace X with B in Equation (11).

The Zero Beta Portfolio

The zero beta version of the CAPM was developed by Fischer Black.[17] The zero beta theory was designed to establish a CAPM-like result under more general conditions, in particular, in the case where there is no risk-free asset due to uncertain inflation and other market imperfections.

We are going to hijack the zero beta concept and use it as a crude test of the efficiency of a benchmark portfolio. We identify a portfolio, call it portfolio Z, that is fully invested, has a beta of zero, and has minimum risk. If the benchmark is the portfolio with the maximum Sharpe ratio, that is, if $X = B$, then the expected excess return on the zero beta portfolio Z should be zero.

We can determine the zero beta portfolio Z in two steps. The first step is to compute the minimum risk fully invested portfolio. Call it portfolio C.[18] Some of the properties of portfolio C are summarized in Equation (12). We assume there are N risky assets. Every element in the vector $\mathbf{e}$ is equal to one, so for portfolio P with holdings $\mathbf{p}$ in the risky assets $\mathbf{e}' \cdot \mathbf{p} = \sum_{n=1:N} p_n$ is the sum of the risky positions. The N by N predictive covariance matrix $\mathbf{V}$ is known at the beginning of the period.

$$\begin{gathered}\text{A portfolio } P \text{ is } \textit{fully invested} \text{ if } \mathbf{e}' \cdot \mathbf{p} = 1 \\ \text{portfolio C is } \textit{the} \text{ fully invested portfolio} \\ \text{with minimum risk.} \Rightarrow \mathbf{c} = \frac{\mathbf{V}^{-1} \cdot \mathbf{e}}{\mathbf{e}' \cdot \mathbf{V}^{-1} \cdot \mathbf{e}} \\ \sigma_C^2 = \frac{1}{\mathbf{e}' \cdot \mathbf{V}^{-1} \cdot \mathbf{e}}, \quad \beta_C = \frac{\sigma_C^2}{\sigma_B^2} < 1\end{gathered} \qquad (12)$$

In Exhibit 4, portfolio C is the point on the dashed curve (a hyperbola) with minimum risk, about 5%.

16. The idea is to consider all mixtures of asset n and portfolio X. Those mixtures form a smooth curve in mean standard deviation space. The curve has to be tangent to the efficient frontier at portfolio X. The tangency condition, after some pushing and shoving, leads to Equation (11).
17. Black (1972).
18. There is a great deal said about portfolio C in the second chapter of Grinold and Kahn (2000).

EXHIBIT 4 **Ex Ante View with an Efficient Benchmark**

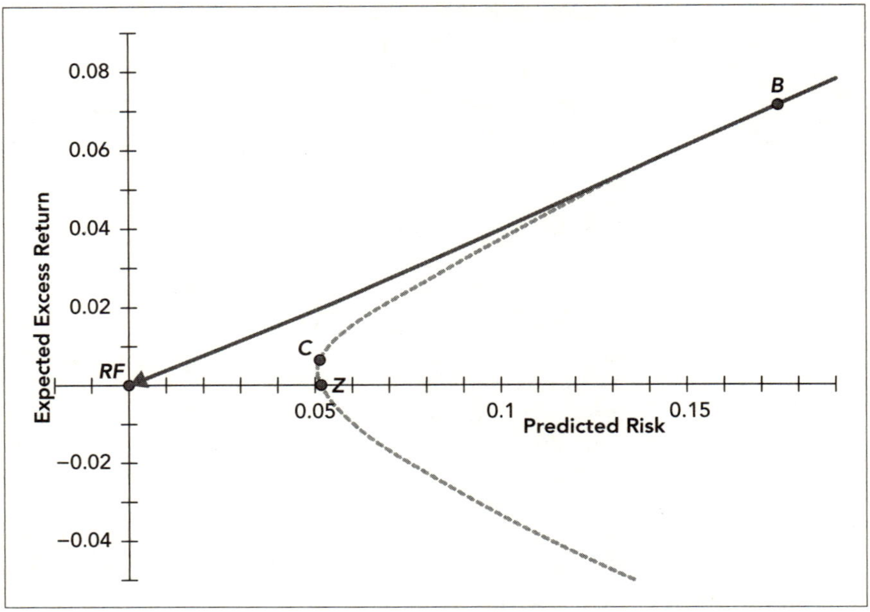

If we exclude the very strange case where all assets have identical expected excess returns, and we assume the benchmark has maximum Sharpe ratio, $X = B$, then we should see something like Exhibit 4.

The second step in finding portfolio Z is to split portfolio C into a part that is aligned with the benchmark and a portion, S_C, that is residual to the benchmark (see Equation (3)). Portfolio Z is that residual component of portfolio C that is scaled up to have full investment.

$$\begin{aligned} \mathbf{c} &= \beta_C \cdot \mathbf{b} + \mathbf{s}_C \\ \mathbf{z} &= \frac{\mathbf{s}_C}{1-\beta_C}, \quad \beta_Z = 0 \\ \sigma_Z^2 &= \frac{\sigma_C^2}{1-\beta_C} \end{aligned} \tag{13}$$

We will attempt to show a benchmark is not efficient, $B \neq X$, using a proof by statistical contradiction. It goes as follows.

1. *Assume* the benchmark is efficient. Since the benchmark is efficient, then a fully invested portfolio with zero beta should have zero expected excess return.
2. Calculate beta relative to the benchmark: $\beta_P = Cov\langle r_P, r_B\rangle / Var\langle r_B\rangle$.
3. For time periods $t = 1{:}T$, use Equations (12) and (13) to determine the portfolio at time t, call it $Z(t)$, that is fully invested, has zero beta and minimum risk.

4. Calculate the return on portfolio $Z(t)$ over the next time interval.
5. Use statistics to determine if the average return on the portfolio's $Z(t)$ for $t = 1{:}T$ is statistically different from zero.

There is nothing in this test for the benchmark; it can only lose. If the average returns on the $Z(t)$ aren't much different from zero, the benchmark is not off the hook. Not guilty does not mean innocent. There is no protection against double or multiple jeopardy. Other researchers will dream up tests and eventually the benchmark will lose.

What the Data Show

Exhibit 5 contains the actual data for the US equity market monthly returns from January 1973 through July 1992, with the value weighted BARRA HICAP universe playing the role of the benchmark.[19]

EXHIBIT 5 Results of a Test January 1973 Through July 1992

PORTFOLIO	EXCESS RETURN %	RISK %	SHARPE RATIO	T-STAT
Portfolio *B*	4.20	16.62	0.25	1.12
Portfolio C	6.24	11.00	0.57	2.51
Portfolio Z	8.28	15.5	0.53	2.36

These data are graphed in Exhibit 6.[20]

Exhibit 6, in contrast to exhibits 2,3, and 4, shows the annualized realized risks and excess returns over the January 1973 through July 1992 period. The points *B*, *C*, and *Z* are what did occur, as per Exhibit 5. The frontier is drawn in Exhibit 6 to show what should have happened if (i.) the benchmark was efficient and (ii.) portfolio *C* was indeed the minimum risk fully invested portfolio. The point C^* has the same realized risk as *C* and a realized excess return that is consistent with the benchmark being efficient. Portfolio Z^* is derived from the benchmark and C^* using the method specified in Equation (13). C^* and Z^* are what should have happened and *C* and *Z* are what did transpire.

The most striking thing about Exhibits 5 and 6 is that the average excess return on portfolio *C* is higher than the average excess return on the benchmark! Because *C* is a mixture of *Z* and *B*, the excess return on the zero beta portfolio *Z* is higher still! Portfolio *Z* that is supposed to have an expected excess return of zero has a realized excess return that is statistically significant. Even more remarkable, it is difficult to establish with nearly 20 years of data that the benchmark has a positive expected excess return.

19. The HICAP universe is comprised of about 1,200 of the largest capitalization stocks in the US market. We get similar results if we use the S&P 500.
20. The data are approximate. Gleaned from the original article and Figure E in that article. The data set did not survive the 25 years from initial publication to this revision.

EXHIBIT 6 Realized Results

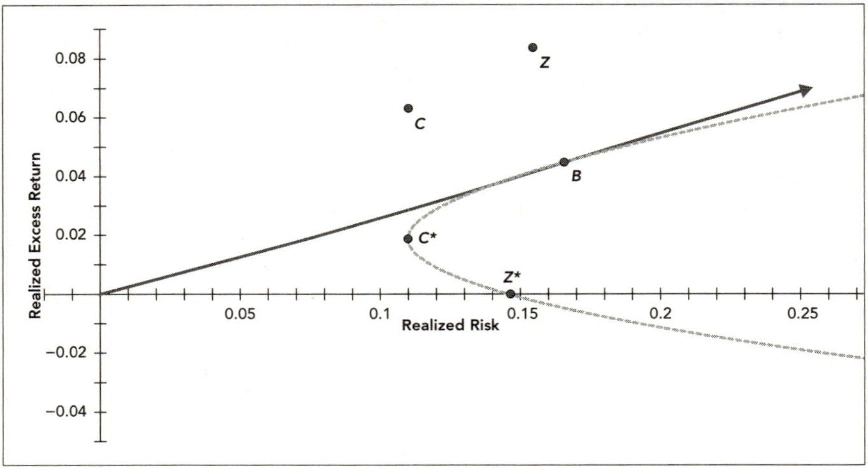

The remarkable fact is not that *B* is doing badly. A market Sharpe ratio in the 0.25 to 0.35 range is not unusual. It is remarkable that *C* and *Z* are doing so well! This is another way to capture the notion that assets with low predicted volatility tend to be relatively good performers.

It is easy to grouse about these results and grouse for good reason. One reason is our heavy reliance on the ex ante prediction of beta and consequent identification of portfolio *Z*. That will be as good as the risk model we use, and that risk model will not be perfect. In particular, notice that the realized risk of portfolio *C* is higher than the average predicted level of about 7%. Choosing portfolio *C* is an excellent stress test for a model of covariance. The optimization will like all the assets whose risk has been underestimated and tend to stay away from all the assets whose risk has been overestimated.

Lessons for Investment Managers

Our first lesson is the reminder that beta plays multiple roles. It is the portfolio engineer's version of the Swiss Army knife. We should be careful to distinguish beta's use in the economic theory from its indisputable role as a measure of risk and comovement for portfolios, and its ability to split returns, positions, and forecasts into benchmark and residual components.

The second lesson is a reminder of the continued academic siege of the CAPM. That siege has continued and morphed into the smart beta movement. Cynics contend that these results are produced on one set of data through the collective efforts of legions of researchers. Each legionnaire is equipped with a powerful computer, is fully aware of the results produced by others, and has an urgent need to publish. What data set could stand up to that level of scrutiny?

A Paradox?

Consider two questions: (1) Do you think that the S&P 500 is an ex ante efficient portfolio? and (2) Do you believe that there is a systematic way that investors can build portfolios using S&P 500 stocks that consistently outperform the index? It is possible that the answer to both questions is no. The S&P 500 may be an inefficient portfolio, but that there is no systematic way to find a better portfolio? We are left with the tantalizing conclusion that the benchmark may well be inefficient, but it is very difficult to outperform.[21]

References

Black, Fischer. 1972. "Capital Market Equilibrium with Restricted Borrowing." *Journal of Business* 45: 444–54.

Fama, Eugene, and Kenneth E. French. 1992. "The Cross-Section of Expected Stock Returns." *Journal of Finance*, June.

Grinold, Richard C., and Ronald N. Kahn. 2000. *Active Portfolio Management*. 2nd ed. New York: McGraw Hill.

Jensen, Michael C. 1968. "The Performance of Mutual Funds in the Period 1945–64." *Journal of Finance*, May.

Merton, Robert. 1973. "An Inter-temporal Capital Asset Pricing Model." *Econometrica* 41: 867–87.

Ross, Stephen. 1976. "The Arbitrage Pricing Theory of Capital Asset Pricing." *Journal of Economic Theory*, December.

Shanken, Jay. 1985. "Multi-Beta CAPM or Equilibrium APT? A Reply." *Journal of Finance* 60: 1189–96.

Sharpe, William F. 1964. "Capital Asset Prices: A Theory of Market Equilibrium Under Conditions of Risk." *Journal of Finance* 19: 425–42.

Sharpe, William F. 1984. "Factor Models, CAPMs and the APT." *Journal of Portfolio Management*, Fall.

Theil, H. 1971. *Principles of Econometrics*. New York: John Wiley.

21. The author would like to thank Jay Shanken and Andrew Rudd for valuable comments.

19

Introduction to "Are Benchmark Portfolios Efficient?"

Do active managers add value? The answer from both the logic of Sharpe's "Arithmetic of Active Management" and the track record of active managers taken as a group appears to be no.[1] Can active managers add value? Is it possible? This is a somewhat different and knotty question that needs to be answered in some context. The academics Michael Gibbons, Stephen Ross, and Jay Shanken (GRS) have developed a test that will give a statistician's highly qualified answer to the question as long as we provide the context.

The GRS test works with a set of N assets and T time periods. In our case one asset is the benchmark portfolio, for example the S&P 500. The other $N - 1$ assets are active strategies that are easily described before inspecting the data. The test's statistical power increases with $T - N$, so it is better to have T large and N small. For that reason, it makes sense to use substrategies for assets. GRS used examples of $N = 12$ sector portfolios, $N = 10$ capitalization decile portfolios, and again, $N = 10$ decile portfolios ordered by historical (regression) beta. We take a different approach and use four factor tilt strategies along with the benchmark to flesh out the investment choices.

The strategies could be much more general. The only limitation on the portfolios is that they be specified before inspecting the data. No peeking ahead. However, this generality can be a trap, since testing 20 strategies will most likely produce one that is statistically significant even if they are all nonsense. For that reason, it is best to stick with something simple; think twice, test once.

1. W. F. Sharpe, "The Arithmetic of Active Management," *Financial Analysts Journal* 47, no. 1 (January–February 1991).

Our article uses four tilt portfolios where the tilts are toward SIZE, VALUE, MOMENTUM, and VOLATILITY. It is not possible to reproduce the benchmark using the SIZE, VALUE, MOMENTUM, and VOLATILITY tilt portfolios. For that reason, we added the benchmark to the mix, giving us $N = 5$ in all. This distinction was not as clear as it should be in the original version of the published article, although it will be in the chapter in this volume.

The SIZE, VALUE, MOMENTUM, and VOLATILITY factors were well known in the United States since the mid 1970s, and the notion of factor investing became internationalized in the late 1980s as factor-based models of portfolio risk became available in the United Kingdom (early 80s), Japan (mid 80s), Australia (late 80s), and Europe (about 1990).

If we look over the T periods (each of length Δt) and compute the returns of each strategy in each period and then the subtract off the risk-free return in that country for that period we will have a data set of $N \cdot T$ excess returns for the strategies and the benchmark. With these realized returns we can calculate average annual excess returns, μ_n, and an annual N by N return covariance matrix, V, also based on the realized returns. We assume that the assets are defined in a sensible way and therefore the covariance matrix is not singular.

The realized *Sharpe ratio* for any portfolio is the realized annual excess return divided by the realized annual risk. The realized efficient frontier consists of portfolios with positive risk and the largest possible Sharpe ratio.[2] In the article we calculate a portfolio with maximum Sharpe ratio by fixing the level of realized excess return to a target level, μ_{target}, and then finding the portfolio with that level of realized excess return and minimum risk.

This leads to the optimization problem described in Equation (1):

$$\begin{aligned} &\text{Minimize} && \frac{1}{2} \cdot \mathbf{h}' \cdot \mathbf{V} \cdot \mathbf{h} \\ &\text{Subject to} && \boldsymbol{\mu}' \cdot \mathbf{h} = \mu_{\text{target}} \\ &\text{Solution} && \mathbf{h} = \left\{ \frac{\mu_{\text{target}}}{\boldsymbol{\mu}' \cdot \mathbf{V}^{-1} \cdot \boldsymbol{\mu}} \right\} \cdot \mathbf{V}^{-1} \cdot \boldsymbol{\mu} \\ &\text{Sharpe ratio} && SR_H = \sqrt{\boldsymbol{\mu}' \cdot \mathbf{V}^{-1} \cdot \boldsymbol{\mu}} \end{aligned} \tag{1}$$

An appealing alternative to Equation (1) is described in Exercise 1.

EXERCISE 1 Suppose that σ_B^2 is the annual realized variance of the benchmark. Show that:

$$\mathbf{h} = \left\{ \frac{\sigma_B}{\sqrt{\boldsymbol{\mu}' \cdot \mathbf{V}^{-1} \cdot \boldsymbol{\mu}}} \right\} \cdot \mathbf{V}^{-1} \cdot \boldsymbol{\mu} \tag{2}$$

is also on the realized efficient frontier and has the same realized risk as the benchmark.

2. The realized Sharpe ratio is similar to the notion of the *opportunity set*. The opportunity set uses realized returns and *a priori* forecasts of asset covariances and is generally calculated over short periods: a day, a week, a month, etc. The realized Sharpe ratio uses realized returns and covariance calculated from realized returns and generally applies for longer period: years, decades, etc.

Whether it is calculated via Equation (1) or (2), we will call this ex post efficient mixture portfolio H where the H stands for *hindsight* to recall its provenance. Portfolio H can have short positions, and the sum of the h_n is not constrained to be one. We assume that the risk-free asset is used to make up any shortfall if $\sum_{n=1:N} h_n < 1$ or we borrow the excess at the risk-free rate if the sum exceeds one.

The framework should be structured to allow for the choice of a vector **b** so that:

$$\begin{aligned} &\mu' \cdot \mathbf{b} = \mu_B && \text{The benchmark's realized annual excess return} \\ &\sqrt{\mathbf{b} \cdot \mathbf{V} \cdot \mathbf{b}} = \sigma_B && \text{The benchmark's realized annual risk} \\ &SR_B \equiv \mu_B / \sigma_B && \text{The benchmark's realized Sharpe ratio} \end{aligned} \tag{3}$$

In our case, with the benchmark being one of the substrategies, this requirement is automatically satisfied.

The after-the-fact optimization has reduced N assets to two, the benchmark portfolio B and hindsight portfolio H. The benchmark is defined without prior knowledge of the returns. Portfolio H, in contrast, is selected after the fact by mixing the N substrategies. The hindsight portfolio should perform much better than the benchmark, since by Equation (3), the benchmark was one possible choice. The GRS test pits H against B and adjusts for the advantage H has due to its ex post origins.

EXERCISE 2 Continuation of Exercise 1 where $\sigma_B = \sigma_H$. Let ρ_{BH} be the realized return correlation between portfolios B and H. Consider a new portfolio Z that has positions $\mathbf{z} = \mathbf{b} - \rho_{BH} \cdot \mathbf{h}$. Show that the realized excess return on Z is zero. Draw a graph with realized risk on the x-axis and realized excess return on the y-axis and plot B, H, and Z.

The GRS article uses the relationship:

$$SR_H^2 = SR_B^2 + IR_H^2 \tag{4}$$

to define the information ratio. See the appendix to Chapter 5 of *Active Portfolio Management* for a derivation of this equation along with an extensive discussion of information ratios.

The GRS test is based on the realized Sharpe ratio of the benchmark, the realized information ratio of the hindsight portfolio, IR_H, the time interval Δt, the number of substrategies, N, and number of periods T. The GRS test statistic is proportional to:

$$\frac{IR_H^2 \cdot \Delta t}{1 + SR_B^2 \cdot \Delta t} \tag{5}$$

An Alternative Test[3]

A less elegant but more direct and intelligible test could be applied. All one needs is the ability to simulate the residual returns on the assets. The GRS test assumes the residuals are normal, so a simulation can do that well and better if we have some superior insight into the higher moments of the residual returns of the substrategies.

We can split the in-sample covariance matrix **V** into benchmark and residual components as per Equation (6):

$$\begin{aligned} &\mathbf{V} = \sigma_B^2 \cdot \boldsymbol{\beta} \cdot \boldsymbol{\beta}' + \mathbf{R} \\ &\text{where } \boldsymbol{\beta} \equiv \frac{\mathbf{V} \cdot \mathbf{b}}{\sigma_B^2} \\ &\text{Note} \quad \mathbf{b}' \cdot \mathbf{R} = 0 \end{aligned} \tag{6}$$

In our case with the benchmark as one of the assets, say asset #1, we have $\mathbf{b}' = (1,0,0,0,0)$ and the first row and column of **R** will be zero.

The residual covariance matrix **R** is symmetric and positive semidefinite, and of rank $N - 1$.

We can do an eigenvalue decomposition of $\mathbf{R} \cdot \Delta t$ as follows:

$$\begin{aligned} &\mathbf{R} \cdot \Delta t = \mathbf{E} \cdot \mathbf{D} \cdot \mathbf{D} \cdot \mathbf{E}' \\ &\mathbf{D} \ \text{ is an } N \text{ by } N \text{ diagonal matrix with one diagonal} \\ &\quad \text{element equal to zero the rest positive} \\ &\mathbf{E} \ \text{ is an } N \text{ by } N \text{ matrix} \\ &\mathbf{E}' \ \text{ is the transpose \textbf{and} inverse of } \mathbf{E} \\ &\mathbf{b}' \cdot \mathbf{R} = 0 \Rightarrow \mathbf{b}' \cdot \mathbf{E} \cdot \mathbf{D} = 0 \end{aligned} \tag{7}$$

With the structure provided by Equation (7), we can generate an N element vector of residual returns as follows:[4]

$$\begin{aligned} &\text{Select a random } N \text{ element vector } \mathbf{s} \text{ so that} \\ &E\langle \mathbf{s} \rangle = 0, \quad E\langle \mathbf{s} \cdot \mathbf{s}' \rangle = \mathbf{I} \\ &\text{Define the } N \text{ element residual return vector } \boldsymbol{\varepsilon} \text{ as} \\ &\boldsymbol{\varepsilon} = \mathbf{E} \cdot \mathbf{D} \cdot \mathbf{s} \\ &\text{So that } E\langle \boldsymbol{\varepsilon} \rangle = 0, \quad E\langle \boldsymbol{\varepsilon} \cdot \boldsymbol{\varepsilon}' \rangle = \mathbf{R} \cdot \Delta t \\ &\text{and } \mathbf{b}' \cdot \boldsymbol{\varepsilon} = 0 \end{aligned} \tag{8}$$

This ability to generate residuals with zero expected return and the same correlation as our sample is the foundation of the ad hoc test.

Choose J to be the number of decimal places of accuracy desired, for example $J = 4$ implies 0.0001. We will generate 10^J sets of residual returns

3. This section is supplementary to the material in the "Are Benchmark Portfolios Efficient?" article. It can be skipped.

4. If we know, for example, that the residuals on the substrategies have zero skewness but some excess kurtosis we could generate the random s using a student's-t distribution.

and run 10^J trials. The actual returns resulted in an information ratio we will call IR_H^*. The simulated residual returns will form the basis of the 10^J random trials. Random trial j will yield an information ratio IR_{H_j}.

Step 1: The Setup

Use the actual data to calculate $\boldsymbol{\mu}, \mathbf{V}$, the benchmark return, $r_B(t)$, the annual variance of the benchmark return, σ_B^2, the betas of the substrategies as per Equation (6), the realized annual information ratio, IR_H^*, from Equation (4), the residual variance matrix **R**, from Equation (6), and its eigenvalue/eigenvector decomposition **E**, **D**, per Equation (7).

Step 2: The Trials

For each $j = 1:10^J$, and for each period t = 1:T, select an N vector of random residual returns $\varepsilon_j(t)$ using the process described in Equation (8). Calculate the returns for trial j and period t:

$$\mathbf{r}_j(t) = \boldsymbol{\beta} \cdot r_B(t) + \boldsymbol{\varepsilon}_j(t) \quad t = 1:T \tag{9}$$

The vector $\boldsymbol{\beta}$ and benchmark return $r_B(t)$ are from the original data. Only the residuals, $\varepsilon_j(t)$, are simulated.

Proceed as if Equation (9) were the original data. Find the resulting hindsight portfolio, H_j, for this trial using Equation (1) or (2), and calculate its realized information ratio, IR_{H_j}, using Equation (3).

Step 3: Evaluation

Find where the information ratio of the actual data, IR_H^*, ranks in the vector of 10^J simulated results, $IR_{H_j} : j = 1:10^J$. If x percent of the simulated results are larger than IR_H^* then we say there is an x percent probability of getting the result IR_H^* by chance.

This result is no different from the statistical F statistic, Equation (5), since the benchmark return and hence benchmark Sharpe ratio are the same in every trial. It has the benefit of a straightforward interpretation and allows for nonnormal residuals. This ad hoc test illustrates a more general point. Often statistical formalism serves to limit insight rather than enhance it.

Conclusion

The efficiency test described in this chapter provides an interesting approach to the perennial topic of market efficiency and the value of active management. This is a topic that has generated light and heat and sustained the employment of numerous numerate finance professors.

The GRS test we have described, along with the simulation-based alternative, are more direct than most, and they can be understood in terms of some basic investment notions such as Sharpe ratios and information ratios.

20

Are Benchmark Portfolios Efficient?[1]

Tests for the US, UK, Japan, Germany, and Australia

Are investment benchmarks efficient? Is it true, as often said, that although the US market is efficient there are ample opportunities in foreign markets? How can we talk about such questions in a systematic way and avoid being overwhelmed by recent evidence, authoritatively stated opinion, or marketing hype? In this chapter we try to give a partial answer to these questions with the use of a splendid invention from academia.

Gibbons, Ross, and Shanken (GRS) (1989) have come up with a statistical test to determine if a benchmark portfolio is efficient. The test is directed at the practical question: "Is there a possibility of outperforming this benchmark?" This is a question with immediate significance for the investment manager. It applies in any local context. We can use the test to determine the chances of a manager trying to beat a benchmark of Australian resource stocks, or the Singapore Straits Times Index, or the S&P 500.

We apply the GRS test to benchmarks in five equity markets: the United States, the United Kingdom, Australia, Japan, and Germany. The benchmarks are, respectively, the S&P 500, the FTA, the ALL-ORDS, the TOPIX, and the DAX. The results indicate that the first four of these were not efficient over the period in question.

1. This chapter originally appeared as "Are Benchmark Portfolios Efficient?" by Richard C. Grinold in the *Journal of Portfolio Management*, Fall 1992, 34–40. The author revised the original paper in October 2018. He thanks Jay Shanken for his guidance and help over the tight spots.

This should lift the spirits of the active manager. These results, and indeed all such results, however, should be considered an indication and not necessarily proof. Statistical tests carry their own baggage.

Statistical tests of efficiency involve a two-step process. In step 1 we abstract from reality by making assumptions. Nobody believes these assumptions. They are the admissions price for the test, and we hope they do only a small amount of damage. Typical assumptions, indeed the assumptions GRS use, are: (1) the process that generates the returns does not change with time, and (2) the returns are normally distributed.[2]

The first is needed to limit the problem to finding a fixed but hidden target rather than the harder problem of a moving and hidden target. The second assumption helps make sense out of the statistical tests. It is possible to get around the normality assumption and try to sort out the power of the statistical tests when the returns are not normal. The answer is inevitably that we need more observations in order to get the same level of assurance. This puts more strain on the first assumption because a longer period of observation makes the assumption of stationarity more tenuous.

Once the assumptions are made, we perform the tests and try to sort out the results. This can be difficult for two reasons. First, the conclusion may be affected by our initial assumptions. We are testing both our assumptions and the notion of benchmark efficiency.

A second, and less obvious, problem is in the statistician's notebook (if it indeed exists). Truth in packaging cries out for details on the number of tests run before the conclusions are presented. With today's computers, a fertile imagination, and knowledge of other tests, it is possible to produce spectacular results.

The Gibbons, Ross, and Shanken Test

The GRS test uses an old-fashioned, back-to-basics, Markowitz, mean-standard deviation notion of efficiency. The GRS test can be explained in a mean-standard deviation framework where excess return μ is plotted against risk σ. Excess return is return less the return on a risk-free investment over the same period. It is often called the risk premium.

We observe an investment universe with N assets over T periods. In our case, $N = 5$, and the periods are months.[3] The number of months ranges from $T = 67$ months for Germany to $T = 220$ months for the United States. GRS make the assumptions of stationarity and normality that we detail above.

The task is to see if the benchmark is efficient in terms of expectations. What makes this task so difficult is that we do not know the expected excess returns; we have to try to deduce them from observations. In this analysis, and in many others, it is crucial to distinguish between the ex ante world of expectations and the ex post world of realizations. Let's consider these in turn.

2. Actually, GRS require normality only for the residual component of returns, i.e., that component that is not correlated with the benchmark.

3. In the original article we used $N = 4$, since we did not count the benchmark. In this edited version we have made that adjustment. The conclusions are the same.

Expectations

We'll start with expected excess return for each asset and the predicted covariances in return between all pairs of assets, with both expectation and covariances expressed on an annual basis. With that information we can portray the investment opportunities open to us in mean-standard deviation space. This picture will look different depending on whether the benchmark portfolio is efficient or not.

In Exhibit 1 the benchmark is not efficient; in Exhibit 2 the benchmark is efficient.

The hyperbola in Exhibits 1 and 2 encloses all the fully invested (no cash) mean-standard deviation outcomes available to the investor. The risk-free asset, represented by *RF*, has a zero expected excess return and zero risk. The efficient frontier is a line from the origin (*RF*) tangent to the hyperbola. This represents all possible combinations of the risk-free asset and fully invested portfolios. The point *B* represents the expected excess return and standard deviation of the benchmark.

As a comparison with the benchmark, we selected a portfolio, call it *Q*, that has the same predicted risk as the benchmark and maximal expected excess returns. Thus, *Q* is on the efficient frontier directly above *B*.

Exhibit 1 is the active manager's view of the world—there is a beatable benchmark. If the active manager has special insights about the expected excess returns and covariances, the active manager can succeed. Skill can be rewarded.

EXHIBIT 1 Ex Ante Investment Choices: Benchmark Is Not Efficient

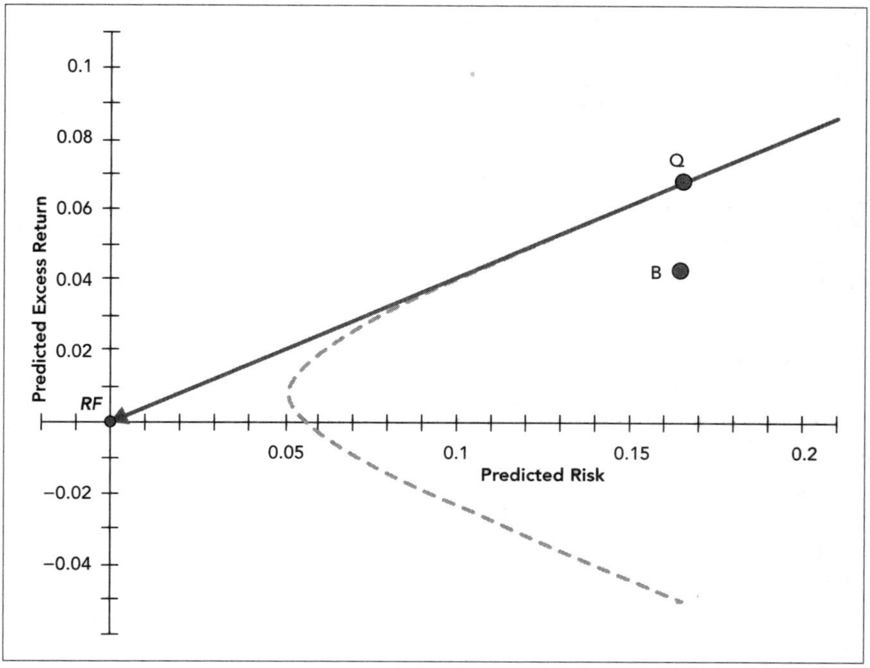

Exhibit 2 represents the passive manager's view of the world. The benchmark and Q coincide meaning the benchmark is, in terms of expectations, on the efficient frontier. This is the active manager's dread. With knowledge of the expected excess returns and covariances, active managers would need luck to outperform the benchmark.

EXHIBIT 2 Ex Ante Investment Choices: Benchmark Is Efficient

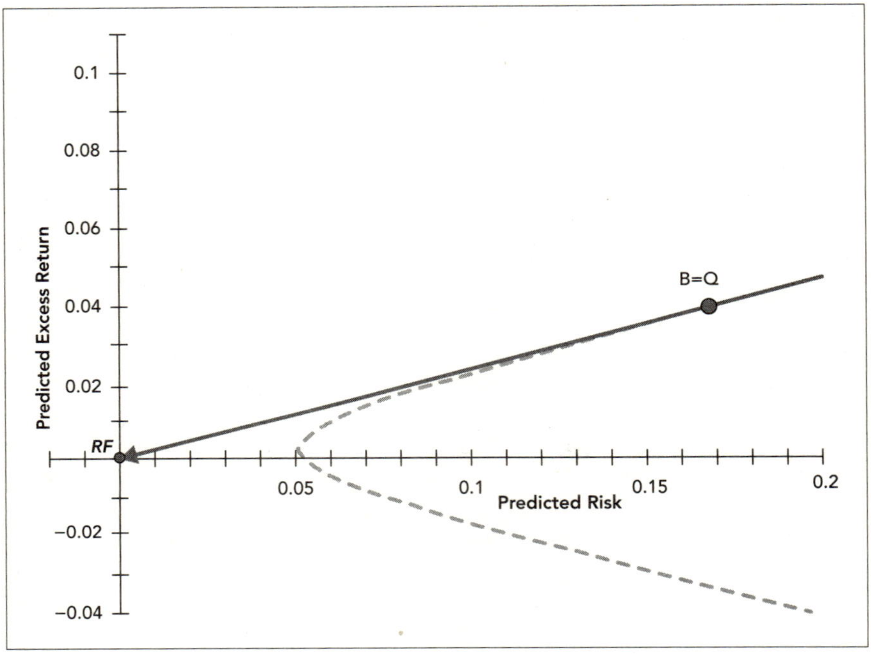

Note the difference. With an inefficient benchmark, insight into the expected excess returns and covariance gives us a positive chance at success. With an efficient benchmark active management is an unattractive proposition.

Realizations

The GRS test looks at realized returns to determine whether Exhibit 1 or Exhibit 2 represents the true state of affairs. GRS works with the realized returns rather than the expectations.

After we have observed the returns for *T* periods, we can draw an ex post efficient frontier. This will look similar to the ex ante frontiers drawn in Exhibits 1 and 2. The difference is that we can calculate, after the fact, the makeup of the most efficient portfolio over that period. Given the excess returns, $r_n(t)$, on the assets and the benchmark, we can calculate the realized excess returns and the realized covariances:

$$\begin{aligned} \mu_n \cdot \Delta t &\equiv \bar{r}_n = \frac{1}{T} \cdot \sum_{t=1:T} r_n(t) \\ V_{n,m} \cdot \Delta t &\equiv \left\{ \frac{1}{T} \cdot \sum_{t=1:T} \{r_n(t) - \bar{r}_n\} \cdot \{r_m(t) - \bar{r}_m\} \right\} \end{aligned} \tag{1}$$

Note that both μ_n and **V** are expressed in annual terms. We want to find a portfolio, call it portfolio H for *hindsight*, on the ex post efficient frontier. To do this we arbitrary picked a level of return, 12% per year, and calculated the portfolio with 12% annual realized return and minimum risk.[4]

$$\begin{aligned} &\text{Minimize } \sum_{n=1:N} \sum_{m=1:N} h_n \cdot V_{n,m} \cdot h_m \\ &\text{Subject to } \sum_{n=1:N} \mu_n \cdot h_n = 0.12 \end{aligned} \tag{2}$$

The h_n can be negative, and they are not required to sum to one. If $\sum_{n=1:N} h_n$ is less than one, then cash is held in the portfolio. If $\sum_{n=1:N} h_n$ is greater than one, then the excess is financed by borrowing.

Even if the benchmark portfolio is efficient in terms of expectations as in Exhibit 2, it will not be efficient in terms of the realizations; that is, the realized average returns will not equal the expected returns. There will be sample error and the maximization, Equation (2), will exploit that sample error.

The realized efficient set in Exhibit 3 is the line from RF through H. The realized performance of the benchmark is indicated by the point B.

The statistics help us distinguish the case where the benchmark is efficient (Exhibit 2) from the case where the benchmark is not efficient (Exhibit 1). The question is decided by asking if B is close enough to the line through RF and H.[5] The GRS test tells us if we are close enough.

Sharpe Ratios and Information Ratios

The point P in Exhibit 3, $[\mu_P, \sigma_P]$, gives the realized excess return and volatility of a generic portfolio P calculated using the realized excess returns and covariances from Equation (1).

The slope of the line from the origin RF through the point $[\mu_P, \sigma_P]$ is called the *Sharpe ratio* of portfolio P: $SR_P = \mu_P / \sigma_P$. In Exhibit 3, we show the Sharpe ratios for portfolios B, P, and H. The hindsight portfolio H, by construction, has the highest realized Sharpe ratio.

4. An alternative is to find the portfolio on the efficient frontier that has the same risk as the benchmark as we did with the ex ante frontier. It does not alter the results, but it produces better graphs. Unfortunately, that would require a great deal of recalculation.

5. Decided as much as statisticians decide anything. In fact, you get something like: there is a less than 5% chance of observing these results by chance.

The residual return of any portfolio is that component of return uncorrelated with the benchmark's return.[6] The *information ratio* for portfolio P, IR_P, is the ratio of the average residual return, α_P, to the residual risk, ω_P; $IR_P = \alpha_P / \omega_P$; see Equation (3) below. The information ratio is important in active management (see Grinold (1989), Grinold and Kahn (2000)).

The information ratio of the hindsight portfolio H is critical because the GRS test uses a statistic based on the Sharpe ratio of the benchmark, SR_B, and the information ratio of portfolio H, IR_H.[7]

EXHIBIT 3 Ex Post Investment Outcomes

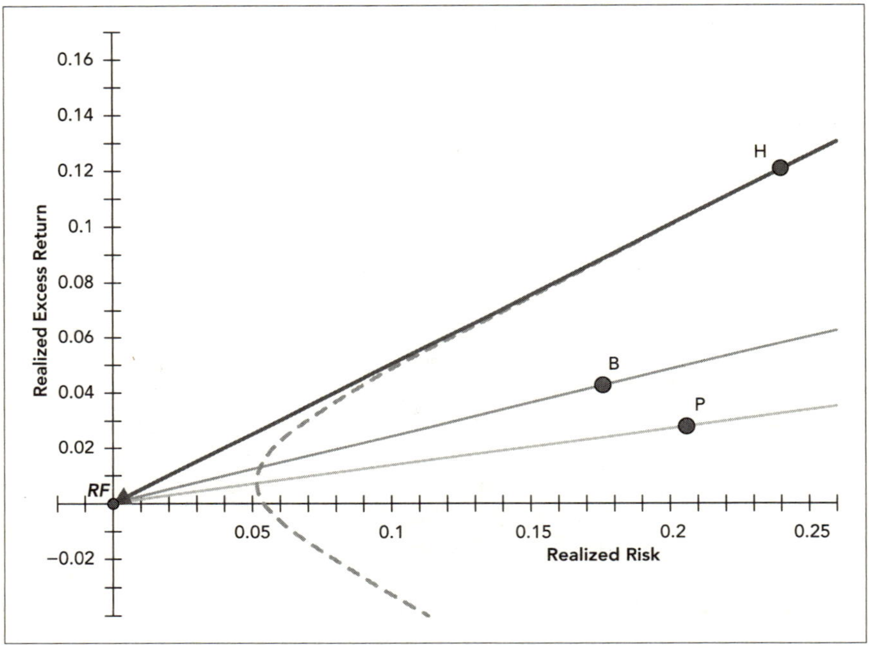

After we have calculated the excess returns on the assets and on hindsight portfolio H, we calculate the relevant properties using the following regression. For any portfolio P we have:

$$r_P(t) = a_P + \beta_P \cdot r_B(t) + \varepsilon_P(t) \quad t = 1:T$$

$$\alpha_P \equiv {}^{a_P}\!/_{\Delta t}, \qquad \omega_P \cdot \sqrt{\Delta t} \equiv \sqrt{\frac{1}{T} \cdot \sum_{t=1:T} \varepsilon_P^2(t)}, \quad IR_P \equiv {}^{\alpha_P}\!/_{\omega_P} \tag{3}$$

6. If $r_P(t)$ and $r_B(t)$ are the time series of excess returns on the portfolio P and benchmark B, respectively, and we do the regression $r_P(t) = \alpha_P + \beta_P \cdot r_B(t) + \varepsilon_P(t)$, then $\alpha_P + \varepsilon_P(t)$ is the residual return.

7. H has the highest information ratio. One can show that the information ratio of P is equal to the predicted correlation of return of P and H times the information ratio of H. This is a concept destined to become famous as the transfer coefficient when Clarke, de Silva, and Thorley (2002) spotted its central role as a metric for implementation efficiency.

In particular, for the ex post efficient H, Equation (3) gives us the information ratio IR_H.

The test statistic is:[8]

$$F = k \cdot \frac{IR_H^2 \cdot \Delta t}{1 + SR_B^2 \cdot \Delta t} \quad \text{where } k = \frac{T - N - 1}{N} \tag{4}$$

In our case, $\Delta t = 1/12$ for monthly returns and both SR_B and IR_H are expressed in terms of annual returns and risks.

Under the assumption that the benchmark is efficient, the statistic F will have the F distribution with degrees of freedom N and $T - N - 1$.

Defining the Investment Choices

The GRS test requires T time periods and N assets, where N must be less than $T - 1$. As the number of stocks in most benchmarks is large, and not many data are available, we must limit the ability of the investor to select among the assets. GRS give three examples using US data of how one might deal with this problem. They are:

1. Divide the assets into 12 sector portfolios. The benchmark is a capitalization-weighted portfolio of the CRSP assets.
2. Divide the assets into 10 portfolios ordered by capitalization. The benchmark is a capitalization-weighted portfolio of the CRSP assets.
3. Divide the assets into 10 portfolios ordered by historical (regression) beta. The benchmark B is an equal-weighted index of the CRSP assets.

Tilt Portfolios

We will take a different tack and use the benchmark plus four tilt portfolios as our assets. Tilt portfolios are also called factor portfolios or mimicking portfolios. The tilt portfolios are set up using the BARRA system and employ the factors or concepts: VOLATILITY, MOMENTUM, SIZE, and VALUE.[9] Each tilt portfolio represents a pure bet on a single factor because it neutralizes any incidental exposure to other factors.

For example, the VOLATILITY tilt portfolio matches the benchmark portfolio B on all industries and on all the risk factors (e.g., SIZE, MOMENTUM, and VALUE) of the BARRA model except it has an exposure to the

8. It turns out that the Sharpe ratio of H squared is equal to the Sharpe ratio of B squared plus the information ratio of H squared, see Equation (23) in the appendix to the GRS paper. This relationship is always true in terms of expectations; i.e., if we knew the expected excess returns and covariances this result will hold. It is also true in terms of realizations, except one has to be careful to use maximum likelihood estimates of the variance (no adjustment for degrees of freedom). The 12 in this formula comes from our stating the Sharpe ratio and information ratio in annual rather than monthly terms. The annual Sharpe ratio or information ratio is the monthly number multiplied by the square root of 12. We performed all tests with monthly data.

9. These concepts are defined in a slightly different way in each market, mostly due the type and timing of data availability.

volatility factor that is greater than the benchmark's exposure to the volatility factor. Even if stocks in the financial sector are more volatile than stocks in the industrial sector, the VOLATILITY tilt portfolio will not overemphasize the financials at the expense of the industrials. It will, instead, hold each sector at its benchmark weight and tend to hold the more volatile stocks within each sector.

The SIZE portfolio favors larger stocks at the expense of smaller stocks. Note that this allows us to take a position on smaller stocks. For example, a mix of 0.9 on the benchmark, 0.25 on the VALUE tilt, and minus 0.15 on the SIZE portfolio would be a mix that emphasizes smaller value stocks. In the same way, we can emphasize low-volatility stocks by holding a negative exposure for the VOLATILITY tilt portfolio.

The tilt portfolios are extremely effective in capturing a concept. The GRS size decile portfolios uses 10 assets to capture the notion of size, while the SIZE tilt portfolio captures that idea with one asset.

Using the tilt portfolios clears us of some charges of data mining.[10] These tilt portfolios were all designed before the GRS test was derived. The tilts were fashioned to explain as much volatility as possible with intelligible factors. We use the same factors in each market.

How Can We Interpret These Tests?

Before we are distracted by the numbers, we should adjust our expectations about what we may or may not learn from these tests. Our specification of the investment choices establishes a context; the test takes place within that context (see the two Dybvig and Ross articles (1985)). If the benchmark is inefficient *in that context*, an investment manager with knowledge of the expected excess returns on the available investment choices would have an opportunity to outperform the benchmark.

If the benchmark is efficient in our context, we cannot make the symmetric statement that the manager would not have a chance to outperform. We can make a weaker statement: any manager who limits the choices in the same way that we have limited ours, and who restricts the portfolio strategy to a constant mix of the choices, would be in a tight spot. A manager who has other investment choices has not been tested by this procedure.

For example, suppose we are using the investment choices allowed by the four tilt portfolios. A manager who makes sector bets is not challenged by the tests we have outlined because all our investment choices have an identical sector mix; that is, no matter how we combine the tilt funds we always get the same sector exposure as the benchmark. To test the sector manager, we would have to define the investment choices in terms of sector portfolios. Even this may not be enough.

10. Only the man from Mars is totally innocent. These factors were selected in the United States in the mid 1970s for their ability to explain risk. By the early 1980s, it became apparent, see Rosenberg et. al. (1985), that certain factors were associated with exceptional performance.

There is a more subtle point. We are allowing the manager to hold a portfolio that overweights some sectors and underweights others, but we are not allowing for sector rotation. Suppose the investment manager has a technical investment rule, such as overweight a sector that did well in the last quarter and poorly in the three quarters before that, and underweight a sector that did poorly in the last quarter and well in the three quarters before that.

We could not test that sector rotation strategy with a choice set that is based on holding the sectors in constant proportion (rebalancing) throughout. It may be that the expected excess returns on the sectors are consistent with benchmark efficiency, but the expected excess returns conditional on performance over the last four quarters are not consistent with benchmark efficiency (see Dybvig and Ross (1985)).

The Data

Exhibit 4 (see next page) shows the ex post frontier for the United States using data from January 1973 through April 1991; $T = 220$. Point B represents the S&P 500, point H the hindsight portfolio with maximum Sharpe ratio, and VOL, MOM, SZE, and VAL the four tilt portfolios. The hindsight portfolio H was calculated using Equation (2).

Although the tilt portfolios do not perform in a way that is drastically different from the benchmark, the ability to mix the four with the benchmark and the risk-free asset produces dramatic results.

The ex post efficient frontier shown in Exhibit 4 is based on the combinations that can be obtained with no restrictions on the mix of cash, the benchmark, and the four tilts. With no restrictions we can achieve an information ratio of 1.85. If we restrict the mix so that we do not allow cash (fully invested), and we keep the portfolio beta equal to one, then the information ratio drops to 1.67.

Experience indicates that implementation for a sizable institutional portfolio that includes restrictions on short sales, liquidity, and transaction costs would drop the information ratio for a strategy with about 3% residual risk to one-half or one-third of the unrestricted value. In our case that would be still leave a respectable information ratio of about 0.9 to 0.6.

The properties of the US portfolios and the portfolios in all the other countries are described in Exhibit 5. The risk and return numbers are in % per year. Several important points are worth noting:

- The Sharpe ratios average about 0.31.[11]
- The t-statistics indicate the significance of the alpha in a regression of the portfolio's excess return against the benchmark's excess return; see Equation (3).[12]

11. This average is for all months in the sample regardless of the country. Thus the United States with 220 months has more influence than Germany with only 67 months.

12. The t-statistics are calculated using the approximation of the information ratio times the square root of the number of years of data. That would be sqrt(220/12) = 4.28 for the United States.

EXHIBIT 4 US Results

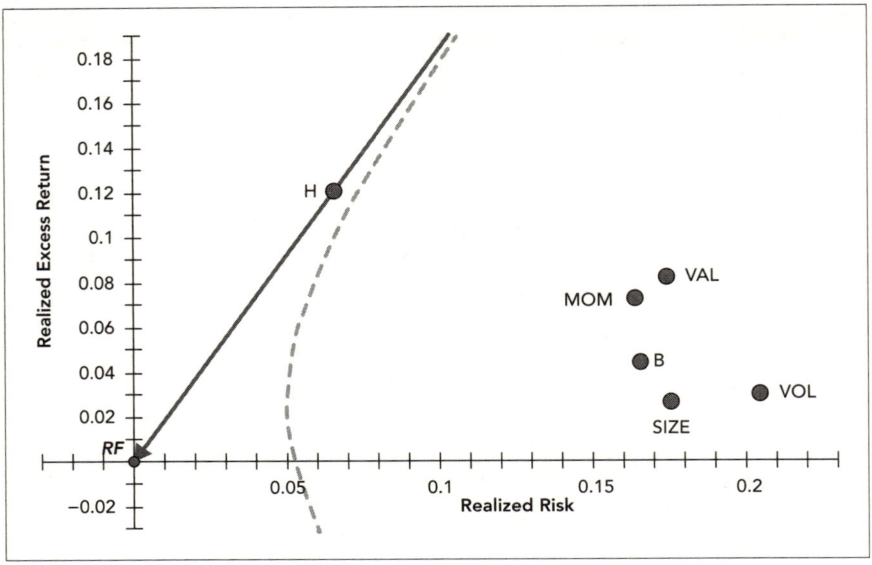

- The beta of the hindsight portfolios *H* are close to zero, averaging about 0.06. Portfolio *H* is the result of an unconstrained optimization and can be strange. In fact, for Germany and Japan, portfolio *H* has a net short position in *B* and the four tilts.
- VALUE does well in all five markets and has a significant t-statistic in four markets.
- SIZE, stressing small stocks, has been marginally good in the United States and Japan, and of no significant value elsewhere.
- MOMENTUM, going with the winners, has been a successful policy in the English-speaking countries, while the opposite is true in Germany and Japan.
- The t-statistics for portfolio *H* are very significant in four of the countries and significant in Germany. Portfolio *H*, however, was selected after the fact. The regression test doesn't correct for that bit of data mining. The GRS test does.

With the returns from Exhibit 5 in hand, we can proceed with the test.

EXHIBIT 5 Performance Results

PERIOD	PORTFOLIO	MU	SIGMA	SR	BETA	ALPHA	OMEGA	IR	T-STAT
Australia	B: ALL ORDS	5.71	23.42	0.24	1	0	0	N.A.	N.A.
1/82–8/91	Volatility	5.95	28.22	0.21	1.17	–0.77	6.25	–0.12	–0.37
T=116	Momentum	11.16	23.65	0.47	0.99	5.51	4.91	1.12	3.48
	Size	5.55	25.50	0.22	1.07	–0.58	4.36	–0.13	–0.40
	Value	9.58	23.42	0.41	0.99	3.93	3.49	1.13	3.51
	Port. H	12.00	7.43	1.62	0.05	11.73	7.34	1.60	4.97
Germany	B: DAX	3.46	23.53	0.15	1	0	0	N.A.	N.A.
1/85–1/91	Volatility	4.40	27.04	0.16	1.14	0.45	3.32	0.14	0.33
T=67	Momentum	0.30	22.37	0.01	0.94	–2.96	3.21	–0.92	–2.17
	Size	2.47	25.28	0.10	1.06	–1.20	3.90	–0.31	–0.73
	Value	4.91	23.68	0.21	0.99	1.48	3.95	0.37	0.87
	Port. H	12.00	11.12	1.08	0.06	11.78	11.09	1.07	2.53
Japan	B: TOPIX	6.96	17.19	0.40	1	0	0	N.A.	N.A.
4/78–2/91	Volatility	8.59	19.68	0.44	1.14	0.69	2.41	0.29	1.02
T=148	Momentum	3.86	17.20	0.22	0.98	–2.95	3.53	–0.84	–2.95
	Size	3.94	19.63	0.20	1.1	–3.74	5.07	–0.74	–2.60
	Value	9.72	17.38	0.56	1	2.76	2.61	1.06	3.72
	Port. H	12.00	7.10	1.69	0.1	11.31	6.89	1.64	5.76
UK	B: FTA	8.70	18.45	0.47	1	0	0	N.A.	N.A.
1/81–2/91	Volatility	8.67	20.27	0.43	1.1	–0.89	1.98	–0.45	–1.43
T = 122	Momentum	12.04	18.29	0.66	0.98	3.51	2.66	1.32	4.21
	Size	9.54	19.82	0.48	1.06	0.28	2.74	0.10	0.32
	Value	11.93	18.41	0.65	0.99	3.32	2.34	1.42	4.53
	Port. H	12.00	5.02	2.39	0.05	11.54	4.92	2.35	7.49
US	B: S&P 500	4.12	16.65	0.24	1	0	0	N.A.	N.A.
1/73–4/91	Volatility	2.92	20.48	0.14	1.21	–2.07	3.48	–0.59	–2.52
T=220	Momentum	7.07	16.41	0.43	0.95	3.13	3.96	0.78	3.34
	Size	2.58	17.58	0.14	1.04	–1.72	2.75	–0.62	–2.64
	Value	7.58	17.29	0.43	1.03	3.34	2.61	1.28	5.48
	Port. H	12.00	6.40	1.87	0.05	11.79	6.35	1.85	7.92

The Tests

Results of the tests are summarized in Exhibit 6. For each of the five countries, we show the data used to calculate the F statistic in Equation (4). The numerator (N) and denominator ($T - N - 1$) degrees of freedom are shown. The probability number shows the chance of such an outcome if we assume that the benchmark portfolio is ex ante efficient.

As one can see, benchmark efficiency is unlikely in four of the five countries and extremely unlikely in Japan, the United Kingdom, and the United States. We see that Germany is not significant at the 5% level.

EXHIBIT 6 Test Results

BENCHMARK	SR(B)	IR(H)	F-STAT	N	T-N-1	PROB*
AUS: ALL ORDS	0.24	1.60	6.00	5	110	0.0012
GER: DAX	0.15	1.07	1.52	5	61	0.4913
Japan: TOPIX	0.40	1.64	8.02	5	142	0.0001
UK: FTA	0.47	2.35	13.44	5	116	0.0000
USA: S&P 500	0.24	1.85	15.40	5	214	0.0000

* This is the probability that portfolio Q's performance is due to chance.

The caveats mentioned earlier about statistical tests should serve to moderate any glee or despair over these results. They indicate that tilt strategies have been effective over the periods in question. We may never know the extent that data mining, nonstationarity, nonnormality, or failing to account for transactions costs have influenced our results. It is possible to turn the econometrics up a notch or two to check for conditional heteroscedasticity (see Shanken (1990)).

Conclusions

We have tested the efficiency of investment benchmarks in five major markets. We find that the benchmarks are not ex ante efficient in four of the five cases. Value-based investing has been successful in all the markets.

These results should be viewed as indicative and not conclusive. The tests are based on assumptions of normality and stationarity and on our specification of the investment choices. We test strategies that tilted toward (or away from) four factors: VOLATILITY, MOMENTUM, SIZE, and VALUE. Our selection of the investment choices is motivated by prior knowledge that these factors are useful for characterizing asset returns, and any test of this sort leaves a rich mix of strategies untested.

References

Clarke, Roger, Harindra de Silva, and Steven Thorley. 2002. "Portfolio Constraints and the Fundamental Law of Active Management." *Financial Analysts Journal*, September/October.

Dybvig, P. H., and Stephen A. Ross. 1985. "The Analytics of Performance Measurement Using a Security Market Line." *Journal of Finance* 40 (2): 401–16.

Dybvig, P. H., and Stephen A. Ross. 1985. "Differential Information and Performance Measurement Using a Security Market Line." *Journal of Finance* 40 (2): 383–99.

Gibbons, M., S. A. Ross, and J. Shanken. 1989. "A Test for the Efficiency of a Given Portfolio." *Econometrica* 57 (September): 1121–52.

Grinold, Richard. 1989. "The Fundamental Law of Active Management." *Journal of Portfolio Management*, Spring, 30–37.

Grinold, Richard C., and Ronald N. Kahn. 2000. *Active Portfolio Management*. 2nd ed. New York: McGraw-Hill.

Shanken, J. 1990. "Inter-temporal Asset Pricing." *Journal of Econometrics* 45: 99–120.

Rosenberg, Barr, Kenneth Reid, and Ronald Lanstein. 1985. "Persuasive Evidence of Market Inefficiency." *Journal of Portfolio Management* 11 (3): 9–17.

SECTION 3.2

Expected Return: Smart Beta

21

Introduction to the Smart Beta Section

Smart beta is a challenging concept to explain at a cocktail party. It requires a few steps to explain the connection between a category of investment product and a positive adjective applied to a Greek letter. It's even a challenging concept in a cocktail party of investment professionals. You see, smart beta is more a new product category than a precisely defined investment concept.

The product most directly connected with the origin of smart beta as a contemporary product category is fundamental indexing, introduced by Research Affiliates in 2005.[1] They proposed their RAFI (Research Affiliates Fundamental Index) product as a new type of index, with weights determined by fundamental measures of company size (e.g., book value, sales, and cash flows) rather than by market capitalizations. Their simple, rules-based construction outperformed market capitalization-weighted indices in historical backtests. This approach to portfolio construction naturally, even if not explicitly, overweights value and small size factors relative to cap-weighting.[2] Soon other products joined RAFI in emphasizing—either explicitly or also via portfolio construction rules—a set of investment ideas long known and widely used over decades if not longer. In response to these developments, the London consulting firm Towers Watson coined the term *smart beta* in 2007.[3]

This section will include four articles on the topic of smart beta:

- "Who Should Buy Smart Beta?" by Ronald N. Kahn and Michael Lemmon

1. Arnott, Hsu, and Moore (2005).
2. Research Affiliates often emphasize that their fundamental indices add value in part through effective rebalancing, as market prices can be more volatile than their fundamental measures of company size. Value investing can generate similar rebalancing.
3. According to Debbie Carlson (2018).

- "Smart Beta: The Owner's Manual" by Ronald N. Kahn and Michael Lemmon
- "Smart Beta Illustrated" by Ronald N. Kahn and Michael Lemmon
- "The Asset Manager's Dilemma: How Smart Beta Is Disrupting the Investment Management Industry" by Ronald N. Kahn and Michael Lemmon

Through these articles, we will provide our definition of smart beta, describe where it fits in investor portfolios, and describe its role as a disruptive innovation. As an added bonus, after introducing the first article, we will provide an aside on quantitative equity strategies and the early origins of smart beta investing.

"Who Should Buy Smart Beta?"

We wrote this first paper for BlackRock clients who were trying to understand the concept of smart beta and its appeal to investors. The title is a riff off of the elegant Leland (1980) paper, "Who Should Buy Portfolio Insurance?" Enough time has passed since that paper and since investor interest in portfolio insurance that no reader ever commented on the title. Interestingly, even in 2014, it wasn't clear what name would finally stick to these products. We originally entitled our paper "Who Should Buy Strategic Beta?," however, we later dropped the attempt to label the category *strategic beta* and retitled the article.

Overall, this paper explained what smart beta strategies are, and why investors should consider them. One important element we emphasized concerned who is responsible for investment performance, as discussed below.

Smart beta products are active products with some of the advantages of index products.[4] They have transformed the active-passive landscape from an either/or classification to a continuum. They are active in that their goal is to outperform market benchmarks. Like index products, their construction is simple, transparent, and rules-based, which tends to lead to low fees and costs, and high (though still limited) capacity relative to traditional active strategies.

They attempt to enhance risk-adjusted returns through exposure to desirable specific characteristics, or *factors*. As of 2019, they are most popular in equities where they make use of five investment insights:

- Value stocks (as measured, e.g., by book-to-price or earnings-to-price ratios, or dividend yields) outperform growth stocks.
- Positive momentum stocks (as measured, e.g., by past 12-month returns) outperform negative momentum stocks.
- Small-cap stocks outperform large-cap stocks.

4. Smart beta products are typically long-only while "factor investing" refers to long-short versions. It's not clear that this naming convention will stick over time.

- High-quality stocks (as measured, e.g., by accruals-to-total-assets or gross profitability) outperform low-quality stocks.
- Low-volatility stocks outperform high-volatility stocks, especially on a risk-adjusted basis.

All these insights refer to investment performance on average over time. In each case, there is reason to believe that the outperformance will continue in the future. Each of these insights concerns a risk premium (value, size), a behavioral anomaly (value, momentum, quality), or a structural impediment (low volatility).

These ideas are all long known and widely used. The historical record for value investing goes back to the Dutch investment trusts of the late 1700s,[5] and the concept undoubtedly existed well before then. Even the low volatility effect—perhaps the least well known of these—was described in a paper by Black, Jensen, and Scholes (hardly obscure academics) in 1972.

Long-only smart beta products work by overweighting stocks with positive attributes according to these smart beta factors, and underweighting the corresponding stocks with negative attributes, according to a transparent risk-based approach. When we talk about smart beta products, this is what we mean. There are some smart beta products—like RAFI—defined instead by their portfolio construction approach: weighted by book value instead of market cap, equal-weighted, and so on. In most cases, those portfolio construction approaches lead to positive exposures to the five insights mentioned previously. We prefer to talk about smart beta directly in terms of exposures to these insights.

What about investment performance? Smart beta portfolio managers promise to deliver desired exposures via simple and transparent rules. But while portfolio characteristics are certain, portfolio returns are not. Like index investors, investors in smart beta—and not the fund managers—take on the responsibility for investment performance. The investors decide they want the smart beta factor exposures. The fund managers simply deliver the exposures.

Who should buy smart beta? Investors who believe that markets are inefficient along factor dimensions, and that they can identify factors that will deliver positive returns.

The Early Origins of Smart Beta

In some sense, there are two distinct origins of smart beta investing. There is the origin of smart beta as a contemporary product category, and there is the earlier origin of a set of products less often connected to smart beta but relying on most of the same ideas.

As already noted, the underlying smart beta investment ideas go back quite far, and investment products that sound very much like today's smart

5. Rouwenhorst (2016).

beta products started appearing in the mid-1980s under the name of quantitative equity strategies. To focus on an early example we know quite well, the US Factor Tilts and Timing product launched as a joint venture between Barra and Wells Fargo Investment Advisors in 1985. This product is now called the BlackRock US Alpha Tilts fund and is still running.

Exhibit 1 shows the cover of a report by Richard Grinold to the Wells Fargo Scientific Advisory Board the month after the fund launched:

EXHIBIT 1 Report on an Early Quantitative Equity Strategy

BARRA

FACTOR TILTS & TIMING STRATEGIES

presentation to

Wells Fargo Scientific Advisory Board

Richard Grinold

November 1985

The report described in detail Barra's E2 US equity risk model, including its industry and style factors, and discussed the evidence that some of those style factors exhibited significant outperformance (alpha).

Exhibit 2, from the same report, described the transparent, rules-based approach to portfolio formation.

In particular, the approach included forecasting exceptional returns for five factors. Three of the factors—yield, book/price, and earnings/price—are value measures. Success was Barra's name for momentum (past 12-month returns). Of the five equity factors used in smart beta products today, US Alpha Tilts used three of them in 1985.

From those origins in the mid-1980s, quantitative equity strategies grew fairly slowly until the early 2000s. These products, offered by a small group

EXHIBIT 2 Smart Beta/Factor Product Circa 1985

STEPS IN THE COMPUTATION OF THE OPTIMAL PORTFOLIO
1. CONCENTRATE ON FIVE FACTORS YIELD SIZE SUCCESS BOOK/PRICE EARNINGS/PRICE
2. EACH PERIOD PREDICT THE ALPHA FOR THE FIVE FACTORS. ALL OTHER FACTORS ASSUMED TO HAVE ZERO ALPHA.

of firms, initially appealed to a dedicated group of believers in this new approach. Over time, the strategies added additional ideas including quality. They also expanded from the United States to cover equity markets globally. After generally successfully navigating the tech boom of the late 1990s and its subsequent collapse, as well as the accounting scandals of the early 2000s, quantitative equity strategies grew rapidly up until 2007 and the beginnings of the financial crisis.

These strategies experienced their own particular crisis in early August 2007. By then an enormous amount of money—likely close to $2 trillion—had flown into these products. At that point, problems with subprime mortgages—products completely unrelated to quantitative equity strategies—were causing margin calls in levered products invested in those instruments. Rather than selling illiquid subprime mortgages at fire sale prices, investors who also held quantitative equity strategies sold them instead, because of their high liquidity. Unfortunately, this led to significant selling across many correlated products (they all followed mainly the same smart beta factors), leading to enormous price gyrations during the first week of August 2007. The price gyrations were quite surprising in that the overall market didn't move much. Within quantitative equity products, however, the overweight (or long) positions all declined and the underweight (or short) positions all rose. The negative returns over that week were far beyond what risk models had predicted, disappointing investors. Several quantitative equity hedge funds went under that week, even though many products that survived the week had recovered by the end of August. Nonetheless, investors realized that these funds weren't quite what they had thought. Over the next three years, the overall exposure of quantitative equity products in the market declined by about 75%.

The Bifurcation of Quantitative Equity Strategies

In the face of the dramatic loss of assets, not to mention the overall financial crisis, the teams offering quantitative equity products bifurcated into two separate groups. On the one side—where most teams ended up—were those who argued for staying the course. These factors—value, momentum, size, quality—had all had other drawdowns over the past several decades, and yet on average they had performed well. Furthermore, there were reasons to believe they would continue to perform well in the future. They were either risk premia, behavioral anomalies, or the result of a structural impediment. Stay the course.

On the other hand, some quantitative equity teams decided to reinvent themselves, to move away from the well-known factors and identify new sources of return. Speaking for the Systematic Active Equity team at BlackRock, our desire to reinvent ourselves was not about losing confidence in the well-known factors, but rather our desire to move away from a crowded, commoditized strategy.

One way to see this bifurcation is through the sources of return. The stay-the-course camp relied on risk premia, behavioral anomalies, and structural impediments to justify expected positive returns from well-known factors. Academically, we could call this the Ross camp, based on his arbitrage pricing theory.[6]

The reinvention camp eventually focused on identifying returns arising from informational inefficiencies. These only last as long as the market doesn't understand them, and so each eventually stops working. Teams in this camp rely on significant research and innovation to keep developing new ideas to replace old ones that have stopped working. Academically, we could call this the Grossman-Stiglitz camp, based on their theory of informationally inefficient markets.[7]

The stay-the-course, Ross camp of quantitative equity strategies has now merged into the smart beta camp started by RAFI. The low volatility effect is now a prominent fifth factor in many smart beta strategies. While the term only goes back to 2007, smart beta strategies began in the 1980s.

6. Ross (1976). We could also call this the Ross, Kahneman, and Tversky camp since behavioral anomalies, described in Kahneman and Tversky (1979), play a role in these strategies as well.
7. Grossman and Stiglitz (1980).

"Smart Beta: The Owner's Manual"

Smart beta products have captured the interest of investors. But where do they fit in their portfolios? The typical investor, who currently owns active and index products, should own active, index, and smart beta products. This paper introduces a framework that decomposes any strategy's return over time into a broad cap-weighted index return, the return to static exposures to smart beta factors, the return to timing smart beta factors, and the return above and beyond smart beta. Smart beta risk constitutes roughly one-third of the active risk of an average active equity manager, and roughly two-thirds of the active risk of an average fixed income manager. Diversifying across active managers increases the fraction in smart beta. Most investors will want all of these return sources in their portfolio, and this framework facilitates optimizing the blend.

"Smart Beta Illustrated"

This unpublished article works out an example of the approach described in "Smart Beta: The Owner's Manual."

Investors have become comfortable investing in active managers and index funds and are now interested in smart beta products. But how do these fit into their portfolios? We separate active returns into a smart beta component and a pure alpha component:

- Smart beta products can deliver smart beta more cost-effectively than can active managers.
- Only active managers can deliver pure alpha returns.

We apply this framework to a specific example. We start with three active managers and an index fund. Adding a smart beta product (funded from both the active and index positions) and rebalancing toward the active managers delivering mainly pure alpha increases expected return after fees and costs from 0.83% to 0.90% while keeping active risk constant at 1.35%.

While this is just one example, it illustrates how smart beta products expand the efficient frontier beyond that of just active and index products.

"The Asset Manager's Dilemma: How Smart Beta Is Disrupting the Investment Management Industry"

Smart beta products are a disruptive financial innovation with the potential to significantly affect the business of traditional active management. They provide an important component of active management via simple, transparent, rules-based portfolios delivered at lower fees. They are not an investment innovation—the ideas underlying smart beta factors have been known for decades or even much longer. They are a product innovation, carving out important components of successful active management and selling them more cheaply. Managers who are offering smart beta—whether knowingly or not—for active fees are in danger of being disrupted.

This development clarifies that what investors need from their active managers is pure alpha—returns beyond those from static exposures to smart beta factors. To effectively position themselves for this evolution in active management, asset managers need to understand the mix of smart beta and pure alpha in their products, as well as their comparative advantages relative to competitors in delivering these important components.

While this article explicitly discusses several reasons why smart beta products may fall short of disrupting investment management, it is a bit limited in its discussion of how a period of significant underperformance could impede the bifurcation of traditional active into smart beta and pure alpha. As discussed in more detail in Kahn (2018), the biggest problem for smart beta products would not be a long period of performance below expectations but rather a short period of very significant underperformance—like that which impacted quantitative equity products in August 2007, when they were effectively smart beta products.

References

Arnott, Robert D., Jason C. Hsu, and Philip Moore. 2005. "Fundamental Indexation." *Financial Analysts Journal* 61 (March/April): 83–99.

Black, Fischer, Michael C. Jensen, and Myron Scholes. 1972. "The Capital Asset Pricing Model: Some Empirical Tests." In *Studies in the Theory of Capital Markets*, edited by Michael C. Jensen, 249–65. New York: Praeger.

Carlson, Debbie. 2018. "Smart Beta Versus Factor Funds: What's the Difference?" etf.com. May 10. https://www.etf.com/sections/features-and-news/smart-beta-vs-factor-funds-whats-difference.

Kahn, Ronald N. 2018. *The Future of Investment Management.* CFA Institute Research Foundation.

Kahneman, Daniel, and Amos Tversky. 1979. "Prospect Theory: An Analysis of Decision Under Risk." *Econometrica* 47 (March): 263–91.

Leland, Hayne E. 1980. "Who Should Buy Portfolio Insurance?" *Journal of Finance* 35 (May): 581–94.

Grossman, Sanford J., and Joseph E. Stiglitz. 1980. "On the Impossibility of Informationally Efficient Markets." *American Economic Review* 70 (June): 393–408.

Ross, Stephen A. 1976. "The Arbitrage Theory of Capital Asset Pricing." *Journal of Economic Theory* 13: 341–60.

Rouwenhorst, Geert K. 2016. "Structural Finance and the Origins of Mutual Funds in 18th Century Netherlands." In *Financial Market History*, edited by David Chambers and Elroy Dimson. University of Cambridge Press, CFA Research Publication.

22

Who Should Buy Smart Beta?[1]

A New Strategy and Its Implications for Investors

It used to be easy to classify investment strategies. Active managers—representing the vast majority of all investors—picked stocks and/or bonds based on bottom-up or top-down views, and built portfolios barely influenced by any market index. Their goal was high returns with limited downside. Passive index fund managers, who only came into existence in the 1970s, carefully matched the holdings of specific cap-weighted market indices, with the goal of matching market index performance. Managers of these different types of strategies talked differently, made very different promises, and worked for different firms.

Over the past decade, however, this clear active–passive distinction has blurred. Now, smart beta occupies intermediate ground, with some of the portfolio construction characteristics of passive management but some of the goals of active management.

1. This originally appeared as a BlackRock client publication by Ronald N. Kahn and Michael Lemmon in May 2014. It was initially entitled "Who Should Buy Strategic Beta" and then subsequently distributed under the current name.

Smart Beta Defined

The Greek letter beta (β) first assumed special significance in finance with the development of the capital asset pricing model.[2] This model contains one factor: the market, which we typically represent as a broad cap-weighted index.[3] Every investor chooses how much of the market to hold based on his or her tolerance for risk. In aggregate, investors hold the market. It is hence the consensus portfolio. If some choose less than their fair share, others must choose more. Importantly, there exists a risk premium to induce investors to hold the market. In this model, expected returns are proportional to exposure to the market, a term Sharpe labeled *beta*.

About a decade later, the arbitrage pricing theory[4] posited a set of risk factors with associated risk premia. This model can contain many factors, and the *only* sources of expected returns are exposures (betas) to these factors.

The new strategies that we will call *smart beta* are descendants of these pioneering early efforts. These strategies involve exposures (betas) to one or more factors.

Are smart beta products active? Their combination of betas will not typically match the market's particular combination of betas. Hence smart beta funds take positions that differ from the market (the consensus portfolio). In this way, they are active strategies. But being different from the market is part of their interest to investors.[5]

Smart beta strategies use simple, rules-based, transparent approaches to building portfolios. In many cases, smart beta strategies fully replicate publicly available indices, albeit indices with more turnover than broad cap-weighted indices. In this way, their implementation is passive not active. This is another key source of their interest to investors.

Smart beta strategies sit between active and passive. They are active in not matching consensus holdings (the broad cap-weighted indices). They are passive in that they are simple, rules-based, transparent, and often fully replicate indices.

To survey the investment strategy landscape at a sufficiently fine detail to clearly distinguish active from smart beta from passive, we will distinguish these different approaches along several dimensions:

- Basic descriptions
- Fees and trading costs
- Capacity
- Return characteristics

2. Sharpe proposed this model in 1964. Treynor (1961), Lintner (1965), and Mossin (1966) were on roughly the same track in the same era.

3. Sharpe's theory defines the market extremely broadly, as the cap-weighted index of everything. But in practice, it focuses on broad cap-weighted indices of particular asset classes (e.g., US large-cap stocks).

4. Ross (1976).

5. Fixed income may offer a special case, where some smart beta products better capture the broad fixed income market than do the established indices. To the extent that smart beta is a better market portfolio, it is a passive strategy.

- Division of responsibilities between investor and manager
- Who should buy them

The first three dimensions are fairly basic and descriptive. The last three dimensions identify key investment issues that investors need to understand before choosing these strategies.

The new smart beta strategies offer some of the advantages of active strategies with some of the characteristics of passive strategies. These are active strategies in that their goal is to generate positive risk-adjusted returns, though they can fail in that goal. They resemble passive strategies in their rules-based portfolio construction and their low fees and costs and high capacity relative to active strategies.

Smart beta strategies use transparent rules to build portfolios with specific characteristics that are important for explaining security returns. We often refer to such characteristics—for example value or momentum or quality—as *factors*. Some smart beta products target specific exposures to those factors, such as a portfolio whose book-to-price ratio is a specific amount above the broad market average. Others build portfolios with less specific targeting, such weighting assets by book value instead of market value, but such approaches also generate factor exposures, albeit with a bit more time variation.

Note though that even if smart beta portfolio characteristics are fairly certain, factor returns are not. Investors in smart beta strategies, along with their consultants and advisors, must understand that they—and not the manager—assume responsibility for investment performance. Such investors should believe that markets are inefficient along particular factor dimensions, and that they can identify those attractive factors. Exhibit 1 shows where smart beta fits in the investment landscape.

EXHIBIT 1 Where Smart Beta Fits in the Investment Landscape

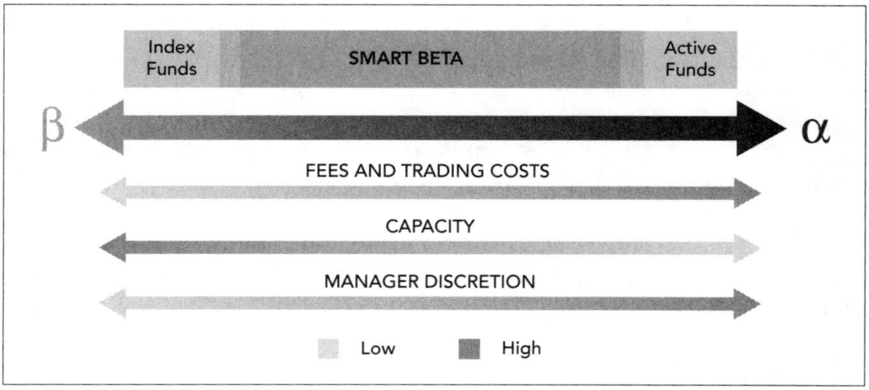

Passive, Active, and Smart Beta Strategies

Passive, Index Fund Strategies

Traditionally, index funds seek to replicate the performance of broad market cap-weighted indices. Examples of those market indices include the S&P 500, the MSCI ACWI global equity index, and the Barclays Aggregate US Bond Market Index.

Index funds seek to deliver benchmark returns as closely as possible through full replication (owning all the assets in the benchmark in precise proportion to index weight), or by owning a subset of the index assets at weights optimized to match the index return and risk characteristics as closely as possible. Index funds are now commonly used by both institutional and retail investors, accessed via mutual funds, ETFs, or institutional portfolios (separate accounts or comingled funds). With few exceptions, index funds are long-only funds.

Index funds offer a very high level of transparency. For fully replicating funds, if you know the index constituents, you know the fund holdings.

Active Strategies

Active strategies invest in assets specifically chosen by the manager based on the view that they will deliver superior returns, based on bottom-up or top-down analysis. Active management is a very broad category. It can include stock or bond picking: choosing individual securities based on bottom-up analysis. It can include timing strategies: timing the market, timing industries, or timing factors (e.g., the next three months will be good for value stocks). Tactical trades, such as buying stocks you expect to outperform if control of the US House of Representatives switches party in the next election, are also active strategies.

Active strategies are available as mutual funds, institutional portfolios (separate accounts and comingled funds), and hedge funds. There are currently a very small number of active ETFs. Active strategies can be long-only, long-short, and partial long-short (e.g., 130/30).

Transparency is low with active strategies. In fact, managers need to build up positions before revealing them to others, and more generally do not reveal strategy details so as to avoid others arbitraging the returns away. Low transparency is generally required for long-term successful active management. In the United States, mutual funds are required to report holdings quarterly, with a lag of up to 60 days.

Smart Beta

Smart beta takes well-known factors long used in active strategies and expresses them in passive form. In practice, this means choosing strategies that use prespecified rules to keep fairly constant exposures to factors with desirable long-term return characteristics that include positive expected return and, possibly, low volatility or low correlation with other sources of return. Examples of equity smart beta strategies include:

- Funds that systematically overweight value stocks or small stocks.
- Funds that systematically overweight high-dividend-paying stocks.
- Funds that systematically overweight momentum stocks (stocks that performed well over the past 12 months) or quality stocks (stocks with low accruals/assets or high gross profitability).
- Funds that systematically overweight low-beta, low-volatility stocks.

Of course, smart beta strategies can encompass asset classes beyond equities. For example, value and momentum strategies, which are well established in equities, have also performed well in bonds, currencies, and commodities.[6]

Also, some smart beta strategies are multiasset strategies. For example, there are smart beta strategies that seek to better allocate among the factors that underlie asset class risk premia—factors such as economic risk, inflation risk, real rate risk, credit risk, liquidity risk, or political risk.

Finally, there are some smart beta strategies, for example in fixed income, that seek to outperform existing indices by avoiding quirks of how those indices are constructed—such as by softening the hard cutoffs based on maturity or rating.

There are many ways to build portfolios to achieve the desired exposures, including explicit screens or more implicit weighting of stocks based on assets or sales but not market cap. The strategies may be varied, but smart beta portfolios have one thing in common: they are all rules-based. Portfolio holdings, weightings, and exposures are clearly delineated in a published methodology and can therefore be replicated in passive form.

Smart beta strategies specifically are not cap-weighted. By definition, active strategies try to outperform the market and hence hold positions that deviate from broad cap-weighted index portfolios. In that sense, smart beta strategies *are* active strategies. And like all active strategies, they can underperform their cap-weighted benchmark. However, they are a particular form of active strategy—with some of the characteristics of passive strategies—and so reasonably fall somewhere between active and passive.

Along these lines, one important aspect of smart beta strategies is that their underlying factors or characteristics have desirable expected risk-adjusted returns. And there is evidence that value, momentum, quality, and low-beta stocks have outperformed broad markets over long periods of time.[7] But not all rules-based portfolios clearly meet the desirable-expected-risk-adjusted-returns criterion. For example, ESG-screened index funds[8] are desirable more for moral or political reasons than for expected return

6. See Asness, Moskowitz, and Pedersen (2013).

7. Published research showing the historical outperformance of these factors includes:
- Value: Lakonishok, Shleifer, and Vishny (1994).
- Momentum: Jegadeesh and Titman (1993).
- Quality: Sloan (1996).
- Low Beta: Black, Jensen, and Scholes (1972), Black and Scholes (1974).

8. These funds typically screen out stocks based on environmental, social, and/or governance (ESG) criteria.

reasons. The key question for investors is always what will outperform going forward. It's not enough that certain factors have outperformed historically. There must be some reason they will outperform in the future.

Smart beta strategies are available as mutual funds, institutional portfolios (separate accounts and comingled funds), and ETFs. Unlike active strategies, which cause problems for the create-and-redeem feature of ETFs, the rules-based nature of smart beta fits well in the ETF format. Most smart beta products are long-only, though long-short implementations can offer more pure exposure to factors: that is, they can provide exposure to specific factors with all other factors hedged out. Some smart beta products provide prepackaged blends of factor exposures (for example, an equal blend of value, quality, and momentum), and others provide exposures to individual factors.

Smart beta strategies offer transparency approaching and often matching that of index funds. If the smart beta fund is tracking a publicly available index, there is complete transparency. Even for those strategies that follow a more proprietary methodology, the managers will typically explain the factors they are targeting.

Fees and Trading Costs

For indicative purposes, Exhibit 2 shows median fees and turnover levels for a universe of equity mutual funds available in the United States and included in the Simfund MF database as of March 31, 2014.[9] While we do not have reported data on transaction costs, we use turnover level as a proxy. We feel that transactions costs should roughly scale with turnover.

Our goal in Exhibit 2 is to demonstrate the differences in fees and costs between index funds, active funds, and smart beta funds. We chose to focus on mutual funds in the United States because they include many active, index, and smart beta products.

As Exhibit 2 illustrates, large-cap index funds exhibit very low median management fees and turnover levels. These are only slightly higher for small-cap and sector index funds. Turnover is very low for market-cap-weighted funds, as cap-weights naturally rebalance. Index turnover will rise with index adds and deletes.

For active funds, median management fees and turnover levels are high—certainly much higher than for index funds.

Median smart beta management fees are somewhere between those of index funds and those of active funds. According to Exhibit 2, median

9. Statistics on management fees and turnover levels come from BlackRock analysis of the Strategic Insights Simfund MF database. We analyzed a universe of active and index equity mutual funds available in the United States, excluding funds-of-funds, ETFs, and money market funds. Smart beta products include those labeled as index and those labeled as active. BlackRock provided the categorization of funds into the types listed in Exhibit 2. Note that Exhibit 2 includes management fees, while other media often report total expense ratios, which also include fund operating expenses beyond management fees.

turnover levels for smart beta products are closer to small-cap and sector index funds than active funds.

EXHIBIT 2 Median Mutual Fund Management Fees and Turnover Levels

FUND TYPE	MANAGEMENT FEES	TURNOVER
Large-cap Index Funds	0.10%	9%
Small-cap and Sector Index Funds	0.12%	17%
Smart Beta	0.50%	15%
Active Funds	0.80%	53%

Source: Simfund MF database, March 31, 2014.

Capacity

Everyone can invest in market-cap-weighted index funds. (This is sometimes called macro consistency.) The capacity is huge. The capacity of active strategies, on the other hand, is limited by the speed of the underlying ideas, trading costs, and competition from other managers who employ some of the same ideas.

Once again, smart beta strategies are in the middle. As Exhibit 2 shows, on average they have low turnover relative to active strategies. Therefore, they will tend to have higher capacity. Nevertheless, because they deviate away from market-cap weighting, their capacity is lower than passive strategies, and more complex implementations (such as long-short) may have even more significant capacity limitations.

Return Characteristics

One very important distinction between these various strategies is their associated return characteristics.

Index funds will closely match the return of the underlying index. Not only will the index fund very closely match the index return (especially for developed market large-cap indices), but these funds will be consistent above median performers, due to their low fees and trading costs.[10] As Sharpe famously observed in his "Arithmetic of Active Management," broad market cap-weighted indices capture the market, and index funds match the market return.[11] The average active manager must also hold the market, and hence match market returns before subtracting fees and costs. So broad market

10. According to Malkiel (1995) for the 10-year period from 1982 through 1991, after including all funds, even those that went out of business over that period, the average equity mutual fund underperformed by 1.83% per year. Even with round trip transactions costs conservatively estimated at 1%, based on the data in Exhibit 2, developed market large-cap index funds should not underperform by anything close to 1.83%. So they will be above median performers.
11. See Sharpe (1991).

index funds should outperform the average active manager and be consistent above median performers.

Active fund returns vary widely around benchmark returns. The average actively managed fund underperforms over time by about the average of fees and trading costs.[12] However, there is considerable variation around that average for individual funds. There is some evidence—though debated among academics—for persistence of investment performance.[13] But it is not large. So, for example, the probability that an active fund with above median performance (i.e., in the top 50% of funds) will continue to deliver above median performance in the next period might be above 50% (which is the random chance result), but at best it is 60%.[14] Identifying skilled managers is a key challenge for investors in active strategies.

While smart beta strategies may show top quartile performance according to backtests, nothing stops them from having bottom quartile performance over some period in the future. For example, a number of alternatively weighted indices that outperform cap-weighted benchmarks on average nevertheless exhibit underperformance over extended periods of time.[15]

Beyond strong historical performance, smart beta strategies usually rely on one of three ideas to motivate a belief in strong future performance. Some strategies maintain exposure to risk factors, sources of risk that should earn an associated return.[16] For example, value stocks or small-cap stocks are riskier, and investors in such stocks may be compensated for this risk. Other strategies depend on behavioral biases to generate superior performance. One argument for investing in quality, for example, is that investors fixate on company earnings rather than the components of earnings, even though those components have very different levels of persistence. Still other strategies, such as minimum volatility, rely on structural impediments. Minimum volatility strategies may outperform in the future for structural reasons; with limited available leverage, investors overpay for high-beta stocks in the search for excess return. Sometimes the arguments for strong future performance combine these ideas. Minimum volatility strategies may also outperform due to behavioral biases as when investors focus on glamour stocks over more boring low-beta stocks.

Of course arguments based on a premium for risk, behavioral biases, or structural impediments are just that: arguments. They are not guarantees. Smart beta investors should understand the exposures inherent in the selected strategy and have a belief that the selected factors will be rewarded going forward.

12. See Malkiel (1995).
13. Jones and Wermers (2011).
14. See Kahn and Rudd (1995).
15. See Clare, Motson, and Thomas (2013).
16. The arbitrage pricing theory by Ross (1976) states that risk factors, and only risk factors, are potential sources of expected returns. We can trace smart beta back to this paper, though smart beta factors now include factors beyond risk premia.

Division of Responsibilities Between Investor and Manager

To understand the division of responsibility, start with strategic asset allocation. Investors, along with their consultants and advisors, choose a strategic allocation to asset classes. The investors, along with those consultants and advisors, take responsibility for strategic asset allocation. This responsibility can involve considerable risk between the asset class allocation and the underlying liabilities.

Given the strategic asset allocation, the investors, along with consultants and advisors, then choose managers for those asset classes.

When investors choose an index fund to match part of the strategic asset allocation, the index fund manager is responsible for tracking the index. The investors, along with their consultants and advisors, take responsibility for the asset class index performance as part of their strategic asset allocation responsibilities.

When investors choose an active strategy, they are responsible for choosing the manager. The manager is responsible for investment performance relative to the asset class benchmark. Successful investing in active strategies depends on hiring the right manager.

By investing in a smart beta strategy, investors take on some of the responsibilities of an active manager. The manager of a smart beta product is responsible for providing the promised exposures (i.e., following the prespecified rules). Investment performance relative to the asset class benchmark is now the responsibility of the investors. Exhibit 3 illustrates these divisions of responsibility.

EXHIBIT 3 Divisions of Responsibility

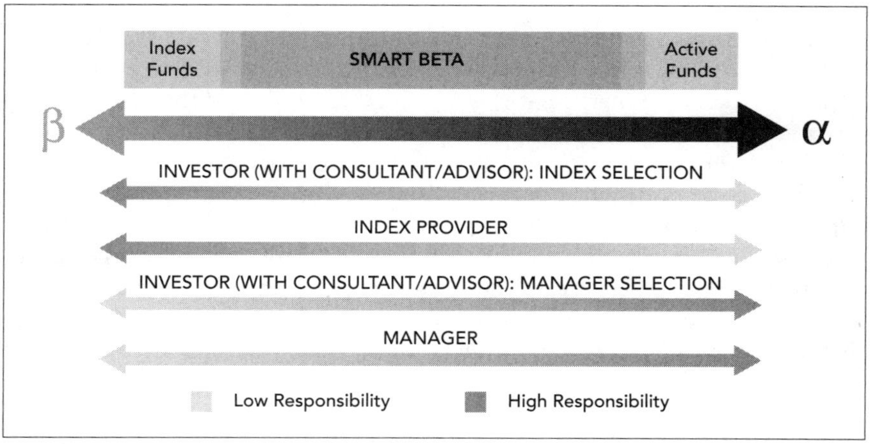

Who Should Buy These Strategies?

So what are the required underlying beliefs for an institutional or retail investor to rationally invest in each of these strategies? All investment strategies involve risk, and the specific amount that investors will allocate to these products will depend on their tolerance for risk.

Passive Index Funds

Investors should buy index funds if they believe particular markets are efficient. They should also buy index funds if they believe markets are inefficient, but they do not believe they can successfully identify skillful active managers or attractive factor exposures. Index funds offer the additional benefits of higher transparency, lower transactions costs, and lower management fees.

Active Strategies

Investors should buy active strategies if they believe markets are inefficient *and* they believe they can successfully identify skillful active managers. In evaluating the skill of the manager, investors should consider the extent to which static tilts to factors can explain the manager's performance, because smart beta strategies can replicate those tilts less expensively. For example, value, momentum, and size factors can explain a significant portion of mutual fund returns,[17] as well as hedge fund returns.[18] Truly skilled managers should be able to deliver returns in excess of those that can be obtained from static factor tilts.

Smart Beta

To buy smart beta products, investors should believe markets are inefficient *and* there exist factors with positive risk-adjusted returns (i.e., they should believe markets are inefficient in very specific ways), *and* they can identify those attractive factors.

Smart beta strategies can also appeal to investors who would normally invest in active strategies, but whose fund size is very large compared to the capacity of most active strategies.

As noted above, investors choose passive, active, or smart beta products to fit into an overall asset allocation. Smart beta products can fit into an existing asset allocation in at least three ways. First, these products can directly substitute for active products. In this case, a prepackaged blend of

17. See Carhart (1997).
18. See Hasanhodzic and Lo (2007).

factors should dominate combining individual factor products.[19] Second, these products can directly substitute for passive products. Once again, a prepackaged blend of factors should dominate combining individual factor products. Third, these products can also augment an existing combination of passive and active products, to hedge or enhance factor exposures arising through the active products. Here, individual factor products may dominate over prepackaged blends.

Summary

The current landscape of investment strategies is now a continuum, with passive index fund strategies at one end, active strategies at the other end, and smart beta in the middle. These smart beta strategies have gained wide recognition since around 2010.[20] They have some characteristics of active strategies in that they are not cap-weighted and they attempt to deliver positive risk-adjusted returns. They also have some characteristics of passive strategies, in that portfolios follow from prespecified rules. We have identified a number of key dimensions along which smart beta differs from passive and active. Investors considering all these strategy types should understand the key differences, especially the return characteristics, the division of responsibility between investor and manager, and the required set of rational beliefs to choose each type of strategy.

References

Asness, Clifford, Tobias Moskowitz, and Lasse Pedersen. 2013. "Value and Momentum Everywhere." *Journal of Finance* 68 (June): 929–85.

Black, Fischer, Michael C. Jensen, and Myron Scholes. 1965. "The Capital Asset Pricing Model: Some Empirical Tests." In *Studies in the Theory of Capital Markets*, edited by Michael C. Jensen. New York: Praeger.

Black, Fischer, and Myron Scholes. 1974. "From Theory to a New Financial Product." *Journal of Finance.*

Carhart, Mark M. 1997. "On Persistence in Mutual Fund Performance." *Journal of Finance* 52 (March): 57–82.

Clare, Andrew, Nick Motson, and Steve Thomas. 2013. "An Evaluation of Alternative Equity Indices. Part 1: Heuristic and Optimized Weighting Schemes." March. Cass Business School Consulting Paper. www.cassknowledge.com.

19. Prepackaged smart beta products have two related advantages over combining individual factor products. Because individual factors will have some offsetting positions, the prepackaged blend can save on transactions costs and lead to more efficient long-only implementations. Their primary disadvantage is that the factor weightings are fixed. The advantages are sufficiently large that they often trump any investor disagreement with the weighting of the factors in the prepackaged product. But, for example, they are not appropriate for investors who want exposure to only one factor.

20. According to the *Economist* (May 3, 2014), around $330 billion is now invested in smart beta funds.

Hasanhodzic, Jasmina, and Andrew W. Lo. 2007. "Can Hedge Fund Returns Be Replicated? The Linear Case." *Journal of Investment Management* 5 (2): 5–45.
Jegadeesh, Narasimhan, and Sheridan Titman. 1993. "Returns to Buying Winners and Selling Losers: Implications for Stock Market Efficiency." *Journal of Finance* 48 (1).
Jones, Robert C., and Russ Wermers. 2011. "Active Management in Mostly Efficient Markets." *Financial Analysts Journal*, November/December.
Kahn, Ronald N., and Andrew Rudd. 1995. "Does Historical Performance Predict Future Performance?" *Financial Analysts Journal.*
Lakonishok, Josef, Andrei Shleifer, and Robert W. Vishny. 1994. "Contrarian Investment, Extrapolation, and Risk." *Journal of Finance* 49 (5).
Lintner, John. 1965. "The Valuation of Risk Assets and the Selection of Risky Investments in Stock Portfolios and Capital Budgets." *Review of Economics and Statistics.*
Malkiel, Burton. 1995. "Returns from Investing in Equity Mutual Funds 1971 to 1991." *Journal of Finance.*
Mossin, Jan. 1966. "Equilibrium in a Capital Asset Market." *Econometrica.*
Ross, Stephen A. 1976. "The Arbitrage Theory of Capital Asset Pricing." *Journal of Economic Theory.*
Sharpe, William F. 1964. "Capital Asset Prices: A Theory of Market Equilibrium under Conditions of Risk." *Journal of Finance.*
Sharpe, William F. 1991. "The Arithmetic of Active Management." *Financial Analysts Journal* 47 (January/February): 7–9.
Sloan, Richard. 1996. "Do Stock Prices Fully Reflect Information in Accruals and Cash Flows About Future Earnings?" *Accounting Review.*
Treynor, Jack. 1961. "Toward a Theory of the Market Value of Risky Assets." Unpublished manuscript.

23

Smart Beta: The Owner's Manual[1]

Smart beta strategies offer some of the return advantages of active strategies with some of the implementation advantages of passive strategies. These are active strategies in that they attempt to enhance risk-adjusted returns through exposure to desirable characteristics, or *factors*. They have some of the benefits of passive strategies, in that portfolio construction is simple, rules-based, and transparent, which tends to lead to high capacity and low fees and costs, relative to traditional active strategies.

These strategies have generated considerable interest among investors, and their numbers are growing. But where do they fit in investors' portfolios? Most investors, who now invest in index and active products, will benefit by investing in index, active, and smart beta products. Including these new products will increase expected returns after costs and/or lower risk.[2]

So what are smart beta strategies? We can trace the origin of this contemporary product category back to fundamental indexing, introduced by Research Affiliates in 2005,[3] though quantitative equity strategies, which started in the mid-1980s, shared many of the same attributes. What all smart beta products have in common are fairly constant exposures to factors that have performed well on average historically, and which investors have reasons to believe will continue to add risk-adjusted returns.[4] Most product development to date has occurred in equities,[5] and these products typically provide exposure to some combination of value, momentum, size (with small

1. This chapter originally appeared as "Smart Beta: The Owner's Manual" by Ronald N. Kahn and Michael Lemmon in the *Journal of Portfolio Management*, Winter 2015.

2. Beyond their implications for investors, we believe they represent a disruptive innovation for active managers. We explore this more fully in Kahn and Lemmon (2014b), included as Chapter 25 in this book.

3. Arnott, Hsu, and Moore (2005).

4. For more details, see Kahn and Lemmon (2014a), included as Chapter 22 in this book.

5. There now exist some fixed-income smart beta products as well as multi-asset smart beta products.

caps outperforming large caps), quality, and volatility (with low-beta or low-volatility stocks outperforming high-beta or high-volatility stocks). All are equity factors that have outperformed equity markets (on average) over time, on a risk-adjusted basis. And there are reasons to believe that all will continue to outperform (on average over time) in the future. These factors may be driven by associated risk premia or result from a behavioral anomaly or market structural impediment. Of course, these reasons are not guarantees, and these equity factors have exhibited significant underperformance over specific three- to five-year periods historically.

A Framework for Understanding Strategy Returns and Risks

To help us analyze how to best use smart beta and how it fits in with passive indexing and active management, we rely on the following framework.

We can consider the return to any investment product over one month, for instance, as a combination of active returns and capitalization-weighted benchmark returns. We can further decompose the active returns into smart beta factor returns and active return above and beyond smart beta factors. Exhibit 1 illustrates this decomposition:

EXHIBIT 1 Decomposition of Single-Period Investment Return

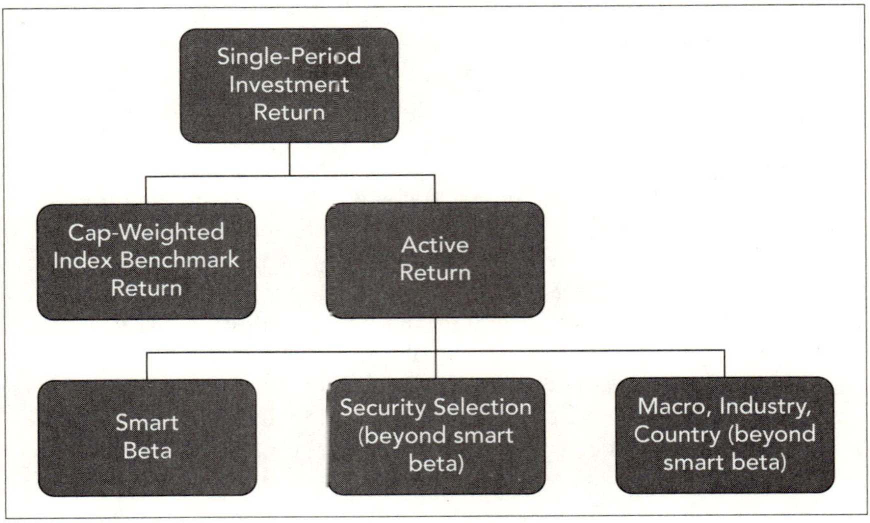

The active return consists of three components:

- A smart beta return (the return due to the fund's exposure to smart beta factors).

- A return based on security selection (beyond smart beta factors).[6]
- A return based on macro, industry, country, and asset class bets beyond smart beta factors.

This decomposition is very general. It can apply within any asset class. It can apply across asset classes if we consider smart beta factors that cut across asset classes.

Although this decomposition of each period's return is interesting, we are even more interested in decomposing investment strategy returns over time. If we aggregate this decomposition over time, we end up with the decomposition shown in Exhibit 2.

EXHIBIT 2 Decomposition of Investment Return over Time

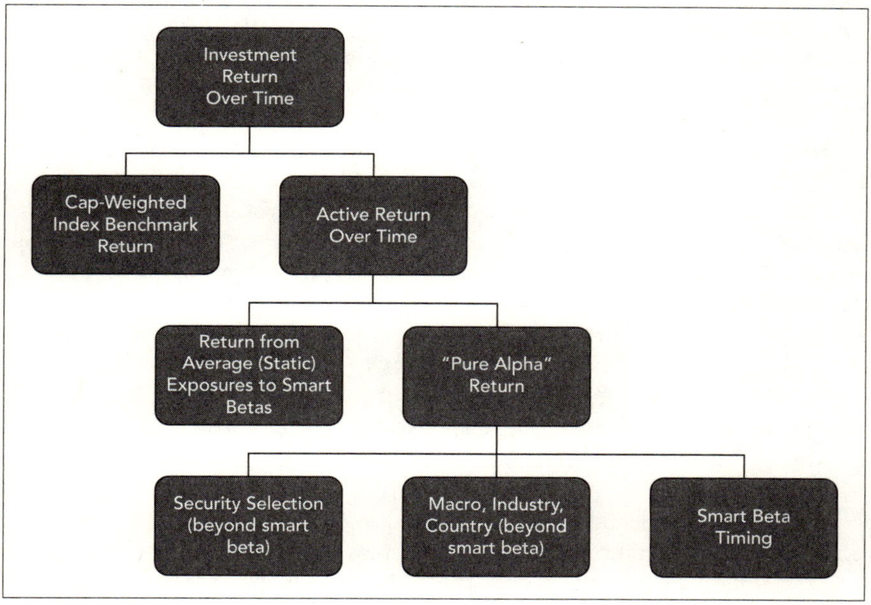

Over time, the active return for any investment product is the sum of an average smart beta term and *pure alpha* return. By this definition:

- The smart beta return arises from static (i.e., long-term average) exposures to smart beta factors.
- The pure alpha consists of three pieces:
  - The average security selection return (beyond smart beta factors)
  - The average macro, industry, and country returns (beyond smart beta factors)
  - The return due to smart beta timing

6. In equities, there are stock-picking managers who first screen on book-to-price ratios, for example, and then apply fundamental analysis to the stocks that pass that value screen. Their resulting active return and risk will contain both smart beta and security selection beyond smart beta, even if they think of themselves as pure stock pickers.

The smart beta timing piece is only nonzero if the smart beta exposures vary over time and is only positive if those exposures are higher when the smart beta factor return exceeds its expectation and lower when the smart beta factor return falls short of its expectation.

Here is one way to estimate the return decomposition in Exhibit 2 down to the pure alpha level. First, we can calculate the active return by simply subtracting the benchmark return from the product return. We can do this period by period over time. That's the easy part. How do we break the active return into the static smart beta piece and the pure alpha piece? One direct approach is to regress the time-series of active returns against time-series of the smart beta factor returns. We discuss this in the appendix to this chapter (Equation (A3) in particular). This will estimate coefficients that capture the average or static exposure of the active returns to each of the smart beta factors. The pure alpha return will be the residual from that regression.

The Exhibit 2 decomposition also updates and clarifies the goals of active management: to deliver active returns above and beyond that available via static exposures to smart beta factors. Those static exposures to smart beta factors are now available at low cost relative to traditional active products.

In fact, a decomposition of pricing is implicit in this decomposition of returns. We can buy the cap-weighted benchmark for the cost of indexing. We can buy static exposures to smart beta factors for the cost of smart beta products. And we can buy active management (beyond static exposures to smart beta factors) for the cost of active management.

Investors need their active managers to deliver the sources of return beyond those available via static exposures to smart beta factors. Active managers who cannot do that may lose out to these low-cost smart beta products. This is how smart beta represents a disruptive innovation for active management.

Although our decomposition has focused on returns, each return source also has its associated risk. Smart beta factors carry active risk relative to the cap-weighted benchmark, as does the active return above and beyond smart beta factors. The expected returns associated with these risks will lead us to consider smart beta and active products. The trade-off of those expected returns with the associated risks will determine specific product allocations.

We can quickly see how different investment products fit into this classification. Cap-weighted index funds take no smart beta or active risk. Smart beta products include exposures to one or more smart beta factors. These products take no active risk beyond smart beta factor risk. Active products generally can include exposures to smart beta, smart beta timing, and active returns beyond smart beta. Different specific, active products will involve different allocations between those sources of active return. (We may even want to use smart beta factors as part of a performance benchmark for active management, to separate the smart beta piece from the pure alpha piece as defined earlier.) As we adjust our mix of passive indexing, smart beta, and active, we adjust our expected return and risk from each component.

Where Does Smart Beta Fit in Investor Portfolios?

To illustrate in more detail how smart beta products can fit into investor portfolios, we focus on the typical investor who currently invests in both active and passive products. Since our framework is very general, the analysis can apply to equity investors considering equity smart beta, or fixed-income investors considering fixed-income smart beta, or multi-asset class investors considering multi-asset smart beta.

As we have seen, aggregate returns to the active holdings consist of three pieces:

- Returns from constant exposures to smart beta factors
- Returns that arise from manager timing of those factors
- Returns that arise from manager skill, above and beyond those factors

Understanding this decomposition allows the investor to diagnose issues and take appropriate actions. Because active managers can deliver all those components of return, it is useful to understand empirically the extent to which active managers focus on smart beta.

Exhibit 3 (see next page) shows a histogram of the fraction of active risk that can be explained by four smart beta factors (market, size, value, and momentum)[7] for the 138 global active-equity managers in the eVestment database with returns over the three-year period from April 2011 through March 2014. As seen in the exhibit, for an average manager, static exposures to these four smart beta factors explain about 35%—or about one-third—of their active risk budget.[8] For about 25% of these managers, smart beta contributes 20% or less of their active risk, and for about 35% of these managers, smart beta contributes 50% or more of their active risk. According to this analysis, many of these active managers are not focused on delivering what only active managers can deliver: returns beyond static exposures to smart beta factors.

This situation becomes more pronounced when an investor hires multiple managers, each of whom derives some returns from exposure to smart beta factors. As an example, consider an investor who hires four fundamental value managers, each with active risk of 5%, where each manager obtains 3% of their active risk from constant exposure to a value factor and 4% from stock-specific risk, which is uncorrelated across managers. The active risk for each manager is 5%, because $(5\%)^2 = (3\%)^2 + (4\%)^2$. At the manager level, 36% of their active variance comes from the value factor and 64% comes from stock-specific variance. This is because $36\% = (3\%)^2 / (5\%)^2$ and $64\% = (4\%)^2 / (5\%)^2$.

If the investor now allocates an equal dollar amount to each manager, the resulting aggregate portfolio will have an active risk of only 3.6%,

7. Although not technically a smart beta factor, we include the market factor because a number of funds deliver at least part of their active returns through static exposures to the cap-weighted benchmark.
8. To be technically specific, smart beta constitutes 35% of the active variance, on average.

EXHIBIT 3 138 Global Equity Investment Managers: 4/11–3/14, Four Smart Beta Factors (Market, Size, Value, and Momentum)

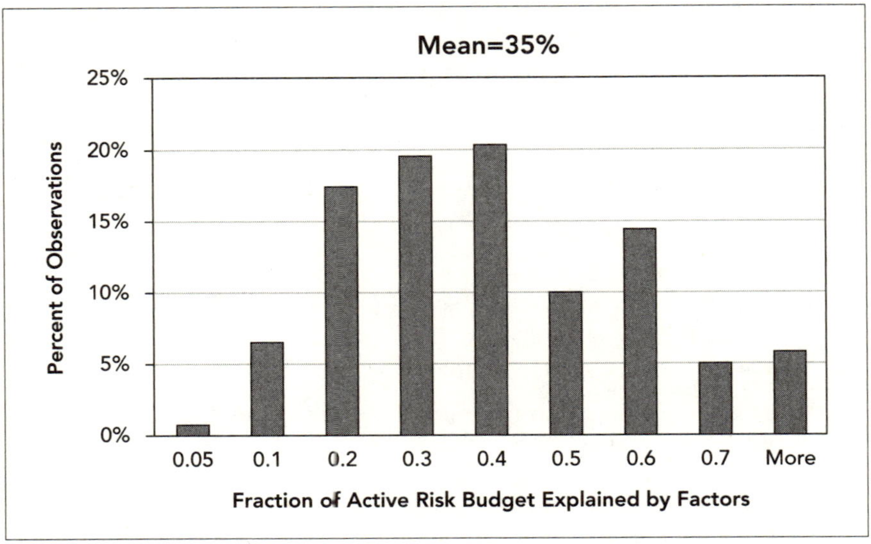

consisting of 3% risk from exposure to the value factor (risk which does not diversify across managers) and only 2% stock-specific risk (which does diversify across managers). So, at the aggregate level, 69% of the active variance comes from the value factor, and only 31% comes from stock-specific variance. In other words, each individual manager provides mainly stock-specific risk, but in aggregate they provide mainly factor risk.

This is a general problem for multimanager portfolios, and Chapter 30, "The Dangers of Diversification," discusses this in detail. Even if each individual manager takes mainly stock-specific risk, the aggregate portfolio can have a much higher fraction of active risk in smart beta factors. Exhibit 4 shows this very clearly. It uses the same database of global equity investment managers and looks at 1,000 simulations, each building an equal-weighted portfolio of 10 managers chosen at random.

Exhibit 4 displays the same histogram as Exhibit 3, but this time for these multimanager portfolios. Consistent with the previous numerical example, the histogram for the multimanager portfolios shifts to the right, indicating that smart beta factors explain a greater fraction of active risk in multimanager portfolios. For an average multimanager portfolio, static exposures to these smart beta factors explain about 43% of the active risk, versus about 35% for the average individual manager. In this multimanager analysis, smart beta factors contribute 20% or less of the active risk only about 10% of the time, and they contribute 50% or more of the active risk about 55% of the time. You can be happier with your active managers in isolation and less happy with them in aggregate. In fact, Exhibit 4 implies that many active investors should be at least somewhat disappointed by aggregate

EXHIBIT 4 1,000 Ten-Manager Portfolios: Chosen from 138 Global Equity Investment Managers: 4/11–3/14, Four Strategic Beta Factors (Market, Size, Value, and Momentum)

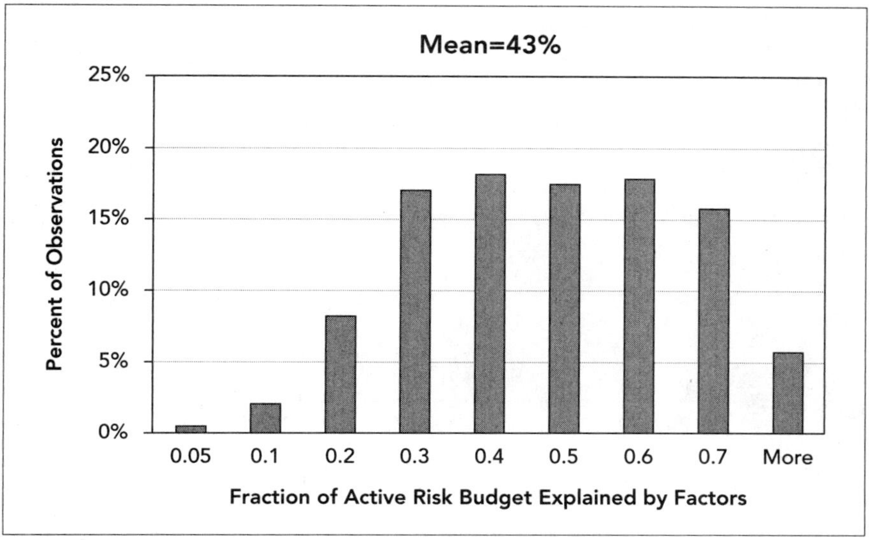

active performance, as on average they are overpaying for 43% of their aggregate active risk.[9] It's OK to buy smart beta from an active manager, as long as you are paying the smart beta price.

The issue of smart beta factor exposures being magnified in multimanager portfolios is even more dramatic in fixed income. Exhibit 5 (see next page) shows a histogram of the fraction of active risk explained by two smart beta factors (duration and credit) for the 121 US Core Plus fixed-income managers in the eVestment database with returns over the period April 2011 to March 2014.

As seen in the exhibit, on average 67% of active risk in these fixed-income strategies can be explained by smart beta factors. For about 38% of the funds, 90% or more of the active risk can be explained by smart beta factors. Compared to equities, fixed-income managers appear to derive an even greater proportion of their active risk from static exposures to smart beta factors.

Exhibit 6 (see next page) shows the same analysis for 1,000 randomly generated equal-weighted portfolios of 10 fixed-income managers drawn from the sample described previously.

9. The 43% figure is just indicative, based on our analysis of a specific group of international equity managers, over a particular period, using a particular set of smart beta factors. The actual amount will vary by investor.

EXHIBIT 5 **121 US Core Plus Fixed Income Investment Managers: 4/11–3/13, Two Strategic Beta Factors (Duration and Credit)**

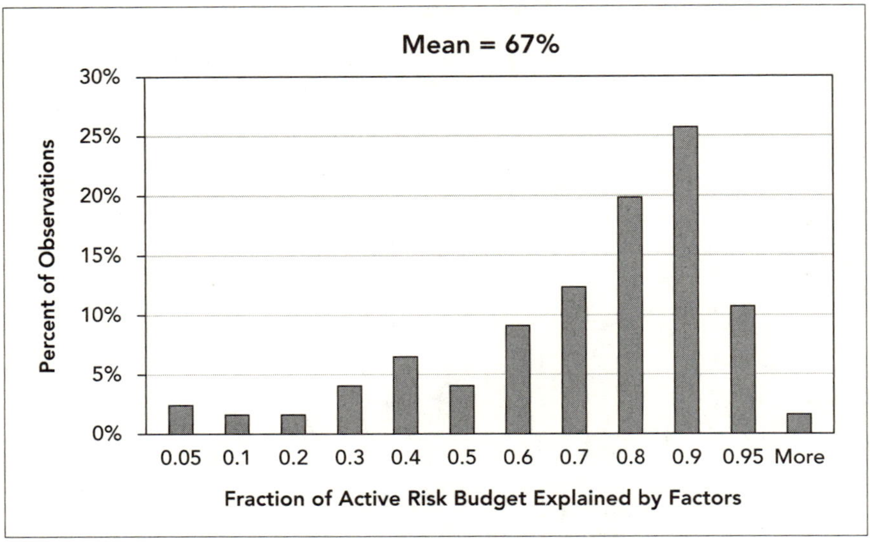

EXHIBIT 6 **1,000 Ten-Manager Portfolios, Chosen from 121 US Core Plus Fixed-Income Investment Managers: 4/11–3/13, Two Strategic Beta Factors (Duration and Credit)**

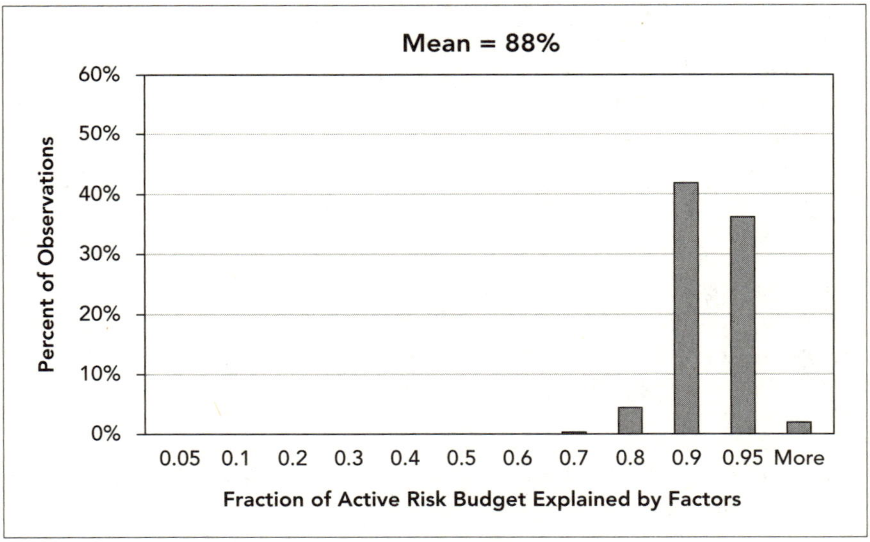

As seen in the exhibit, for more than 90% of the 10-manager fixed-income portfolios, two smart beta factors explain more than 90% of the active returns. In fixed income, investors in multimanager portfolios are overpaying for nearly all of their aggregate active risk.[10]

An Optimal Blend of Active, Smart Beta, and Index Products

Our typical investor owns both active and index products. Based on our empirical analysis, such an investor may be paying active fees for smart beta exposures, with the likelihood of that increasing with the number of active managers in the portfolio. There should be opportunities, then, to use low-cost smart beta products for smart beta exposures and use active managers for returns beyond smart beta.[11] Smart beta products should expand the after-cost efficient frontier provided by active and index products. Most investors should benefit then from investing in smart beta products in addition to their active and index products. To identify the best blend of active, smart beta, and index products, they need to understand their expected active returns and risks.

For the active management piece, our return decomposition will help them to identify managers who can consistently deliver pure alpha (and mainly pure alpha) and estimate their expected alpha and active risk going forward.

For the smart beta piece, we focus first on the factors, and later find products that can best deliver our desired blend of factors.[12] Similar to the process of identifying successful active managers, the smart beta investor should, among other things, consider the following:

- What are the underlying reasons to believe the factors will continue to deliver risk-adjusted returns?
- Has anything changed over time that could impact those underlying reasons?
- What are the expected returns after fees and costs?
- What are the volatilities and correlations among the smart beta factors?
- What levels and periods of drawdowns have they experienced historically?

The cap-weighted index fund piece is easiest. Its expected active return is zero, as is its active risk.

10. The 90% figure is just indicative, based on our analysis of a specific group of fixed-income managers, over a particular period, using a particular set of smart beta factors. The actual amount will vary by investor.

11. Alternatively, investors can buy the smart beta exposures from their active managers, so long as they pay the smart beta price.

12. Some investors can choose to manage this optimal blend themselves, either to take this task in-house or to avoid limiting themselves to existing products.

The last required piece is an understanding of the investor's tolerance for risk. What level of absolute and relative drawdowns over three- or five-year periods can the investor handle? Is this a long-term investor who can stomach large drawdowns if they lead to outperformance over the long term, or is this investor sensitive to annual performance?

Given the set of expected active returns, risks, and correlations, as well as the investor's risk aversion, we can identify an optimal blend of active products, smart beta factors, and index products.[13] Note that while this analysis of expected return and risk can sound daunting, it is no different than the type of analysis most investors conduct to support their strategic asset allocation. And consultants and managers can help with the analysis and in developing optimal blends.

At this point, investors must consider several practical issues as they look for products to deliver their desired blend of smart beta factors.

First, do they want a long-only implementation of smart beta factors, or are they open to long-short implementations? Long-only implementations deliver considerable market risk along with factor risk and thus may also affect the allocation to benchmark strategies in the investor's portfolio. Do their guidelines allow shorting? Is shorting allowed but limited and possibly more valuable when used for their investments in alternatives? The advantage of long-short implementations is that they better capture the true factor and so presumably have a higher ratio of return to risk.[14] The disadvantages include the additional costs of shorting, the additional complexity of implementation, the scarcity of long-short smart beta product offerings, and their lower capacity relative to long-only.

Capacity is another practical issue. Because capacity is perceived to be a bigger issue for active management than for smart beta, one effect of capacity considerations has been to move the largest investors from active management toward smart beta.[15] That said, there will be capacity constraints for all smart beta factors. For example, the smart beta size factor overweights small-cap stocks to capture their outperformance relative to large-cap stocks. But there is limited capacity available for investing in small-cap stocks. More generally, as the popularity of smart beta products grows, given that these products invest in the same few ideas, all of them will face capacity constraints. If you overpay for a compelling investment idea, it will not deliver the return you are expecting.

Another practical consideration is whether the investor wants a prepackaged blend of factors or wants to invest in the factors separately. Assuming the investor's optimal combination of smart beta factors invests in more than

13. The appendix shows how to set up the mathematical optimization problem. Chapter 24, "Smart Beta Illustrated," goes through an explicit example.
14. Grinold and Kahn (2000).
15. One example related to this case is the Norwegian Government Pension Fund Global (GPFG). This fund has been written about extensively elsewhere (Ang, et. al. (2009) and Chambers et. al. (2012)). The investment philosophy underpinning the GPFG is at: http://www.regjeringen.no/en/dep/fin/Selected-topics/the-government-pension-fund/government-pension-fund-global-gpfg/investment-strategy.html?id=696849.

one factor, the investor ideally wants a blended product.[16] However, available products may not offer exactly the investor's optimal combination. The investor will need to trade off a blend that doesn't perfectly match their optimal combination against some inherent advantages of blends that, beyond diversification, include offsetting trades (which can lower costs by lowering turnover) and offsetting positions (which can help avoid the long-only constraint in long-only products).

Finally, to manage the smart beta investments going forward, the investor must have the proper internal organization and governance structure to take on the responsibility for understanding and communicating investment performance to their stakeholders.

Navigating the Product Landscape

After investors have decided on a desired set of smart beta exposures, how do they navigate the wide variety of available product offerings to choose specific smart beta managers and investments? Here are a few guideposts to consider.

First, to the extent that they want to choose either an ETF product or a long-short product, there are advantages to choosing managers with experience with ETFs or with shorting securities, respectively. Both of these product types require skills beyond standard asset management, and so experience is important.

Second, investing in smart beta requires a belief that particular smart beta factors will provide risk-adjusted returns going forward. Given that, we recommend choosing smart beta managers who clearly explain their products' sources of return, and who can provide reasons why they might deliver superior risk-adjusted returns going forward. (Of course, the responsibility for smart beta investment performance remains with the investor.)

Third, investors should consider how smart beta products and managers have performed historically. Here, the question is less about the performance of the smart beta factors than about the manager's ability to deliver the promised exposure to the factors. When investors choose a passive index fund manager, they consider how closely the manager has tracked the index historically. We recommend the same approach here: how well has the manager delivered (or tracked) the promised smart beta factors?

Fourth, investors can decide whether to use smart beta factors provided by independent third parties or smart beta factors customized by particular managers. Do the benefits of a customized smart beta portfolio, which may more accurately capture the factor and avoid crowded trades if the third-party index becomes very popular, outweigh the benefits of an off-the-shelf product?

16. These individual smart beta factors are risky and tend to exhibit significant periods of underperformance, even if they outperform (on average) over time. Diversified mixes of smart beta factors can mitigate that behavior to some extent.

Fifth, how much do different smart beta products cost? Other things being equal, lower-cost products are more desirable. As investors consider costs, however, they should make sure they are comparing products that deliver the same smart beta exposures.

Finally, given that this is still a rapidly developing product area, investors should prefer the thought-leading managers in this space. Such managers may better keep their investors up-to-date on the latest thinking about smart beta.

Conclusions

Smart beta products have generated considerable interest among investors, given their combination of desirable features of active and passive products. The typical investor currently owns active and index products, and should own active, index, and smart beta products.

Investors currently receive static exposures to smart beta factors from their active managers. These exposures are increasingly available via low-cost smart beta products. For reasons of cost and transparency, investors should switch and gain their smart beta exposures via smart beta products.

Even if individual active managers take a minority of their active risk in static exposures to smart beta factors, in aggregate a portfolio of active products can deliver mainly smart beta risk, because these risks are correlated across managers. Hence, active managers need to focus as much as possible on delivering pure alpha (active returns beyond static exposures to smart beta factors) to their investors. This is what investors need, as they can only get pure alpha from active management.

The development of smart beta products should inspire all investors to review their current allocations to active and index products. A revamped allocation to active, index, and smart beta products could increase their expected returns (after costs) and/or lower their active risk, relative to their current allocations.

References

Ang, Andrew, W. N. Goetzmann, and S. M. Schaefer. 2009. "Evaluation of Active Management of the Norwegian Government Pension Fund—Global." Report to the Norwegian Ministry of Finance.

Arnott, Robert D., Jason C. Hsu, and Philip Moore. 2005. "Fundamental Indexation." *Financial Analysts Journal* 61 (March/April): 83–99.

Chambers, David, E. Dimson, and A. Ilmanen. 2012. "The Norway Model." *Journal of Portfolio Management*, Winter.

Grinold, Richard C., and R. N. Kahn. 2000. "The Efficiency Gains of Long-Short Investing." *Financial Analysts Journal*, September/October.

Kahn, Ronald N., and M. Lemmon. 2014a. "Who Should Buy Smart Beta: A New Strategy and Its Implications for Investors." BlackRock publication, May.

Kahn, Ronald N., and M. Lemmon. 2014b. "The Asset Manager's Dilemma: How Smart Beta is Disrupting the Investment Management Industry." BlackRock manuscript, September. Subsequently published in the *Financial Analysts Journal* 72(1), 2016.

CHAPTER 23
Smart Beta: The Owner's Manual

Appendix

This appendix will provide a few additional mathematical details concerning the optimization that can determine optimal allocations to active managers and smart beta products. We base this analysis on the standard mean-variance framework where the goal is to maximize the return per unit of risk of the investor's portfolio.

Return and Risk Forecasts

Smart Beta Factors

The smart beta factor returns are returns to long-short portfolios designed to capture the particular factor while trying to avoid exposure to other factors. For example, an equity portfolio long value stocks, short growth stocks, and with position sizes chosen to otherwise minimize risk could capture the value factor. We will later tie these back to actual product offerings, which may be long-only, and may include blends of factors.

To estimate the expected factor returns, $E\{f_i\}$, we will use historical performance, possibly shrunk toward our priors about future performance.

To simplify some notation later, we will define these expected returns as:

$$\mu_i \equiv E\{f_i\},$$
$$\boldsymbol{\mu} \equiv E\{\mathbf{f}\}. \tag{A1}$$

This also introduces useful vector notation, so that $\boldsymbol{\mu}$ is a column vector containing the set of expected returns.

We will also need the covariance matrix of these smart beta factor returns. We will denote this as:

$$F_{ij} \equiv Cov\{f_i, f_j\}. \tag{A2}$$

We can estimate these from historical data. (There is a long literature on how to do this, and we will not discuss that here.)

Active Managers

Let's assume we are considering N active managers, and we have histories of their returns: $r_n(t)$. First, let's decompose these active returns into returns due to static exposures to smart beta factors, and returns residual to those factors. To do this, we run the following time-series regression for each of the N managers, using their historical returns:

$$r_n(t) - r_B(t) \equiv \delta_n = \sum_{i=1}^{I} \overline{\beta}_{n,i} \cdot f_i(t) + \theta_n(t). \tag{A3}$$

While our discussion in the main text allowed for time-varying exposures to smart beta factors, this historical regression will estimate only average exposures over the entire historical analysis period.

The residual, $\theta_n(t)$, is the pure alpha piece. It will include any factor timing. It will also include the intercept from the regression. We will generally include the benchmark index return amongst the smart beta factors, so $\theta_n(t)$ will be residual to the benchmark and all other smart beta factors.[17]

Now we can forecast the expected pure alpha for each manager:

$$\alpha_n = E\{\theta_n\}. \tag{A4}$$

Regression (A3) provides the historical data to help us estimate these. Once again, we can shrink the historical average residual returns toward our priors about future performance.

Next, we need the covariance matrix of the residual returns:

$$\Omega_{nm} \equiv Cov\{\theta_n, \theta_m\}. \tag{A5}$$

We can estimate these using our historical time-series of residual returns. The variance terms, $Var\{\theta_n\}$, are the diagonal elements of the covariance matrix. These should be less than or equal to the active return variance, $Var\{\delta_n\}$, since we have stripped out the static smart beta components. To estimate the covariances of these residual returns, we could use the same historical estimation method. In some cases, we could also assume the correlations are zero, potentially useful if we have limited historical data. And we can combine these approaches, shrinking the historical estimates toward zero.

Cross-Correlations

The final risk components to estimate are the correlations between the smart beta factor returns and the active manager residual returns (θ_n). By virtue of Equation (A3), these should be zero.

17. We could set this up in alternative ways, for example by regressing the total return and not the active return against the smart beta factors. We use Equation (A3) because investors often focus on active returns. We can get to the same place either way.

Expected Return and Risk at the Manager Level

Based on our analysis above, the expected active return for each manager is:

$$E\{\delta_n\} = \bar{\boldsymbol{\beta}}_n^T \cdot \boldsymbol{\mu} + \alpha_n - fees\,\&\,costs_n . \tag{A6}$$

Equation (A6) shows that the expected active return for each manager results from both the managers' static exposures to smart beta factors and their expected pure alpha returns. Note that we explicitly account for fees and costs in Equation (A6). Fees and costs are an important component of the analysis, as we described in the main text. Smart beta products will generally deliver smart beta exposures more cheaply than will active managers. Hence, we need fees and costs as part of the analysis.

The covariance of any two active manager returns is:

$$V_{nm} = Cov\{\delta_n, \delta_m\} = \bar{\boldsymbol{\beta}}_n^T \cdot \mathbf{F} \cdot \bar{\boldsymbol{\beta}}_m + \Omega_{nm} . \tag{A7}$$

Smart Beta Products

While we have described a method for estimating expected active return and risk for active managers, we can apply exactly the same approach to smart beta products. Due to transactions costs and constraints (e.g., the long-only constraint), smart beta products will not exactly deliver the smart beta factor returns we have analyzed above. We can use the same regression analysis to identify average smart beta exposures. This approach will work for products that blend smart beta factors, as well as single factor products. There are advantages to products that blend smart beta factors, due to netting of positions that can lessen the impact of the long-only constraint and netting of trades that can lower costs. For those reasons, investors should generally look to hire one smart beta manager to run a blended factor fund rather than multiple smart beta managers running single factor products.

One difference analyzing smart beta products compared to active funds concerns the expected pure alpha returns. We will observe some historical pure alpha return (presumably not statistically significant), however our expectation for pure alpha going forward should be zero.

Exposures and Holdings

We will represent our capital allocations to active managers and smart beta products as $\{h_n\}$, or $\mathbf{h}$ in matrix notation. These are fractions of capital allocated to each manager. They are constrained:

$$h_n \geq 0. \tag{A8}$$

$$0 \leq \sum_{n=1}^{N} h_n \leq 1. \tag{A9}$$

We can't short any of the managers. And in aggregate, we are somewhere between zero allocation to active management and being fully allocated to active management. The remainder of the allocation will consist of an index fund with zero expected active return and zero active risk.

Here is the expected active return (δ_P) and the active risk (ω_P^2) at the overall portfolio level:

$$E\{\delta_P\} = \mathbf{h}^T \cdot E\{\boldsymbol{\delta}\}. \tag{A10}$$

$$\omega_P^2 = \mathbf{h}^T \cdot \mathbf{V} \cdot \mathbf{h}. \tag{A11}$$

Utility and Optimal Allocations

We will use a standard mean-variance utility function:

$$U = E\{\delta_P\} - \lambda \cdot \omega_P^2. \tag{A12}$$

where λ captures the investor's aversion to risk. This is a standard maximization calculation and leads to optimal holdings.[18] Once we know the holdings, we can calculate the expected active returns and active risks, and then other statistics like the smart beta exposures and the decomposition of expected active return and risk into smart beta and pure alpha components.

18. An alternative formulation of the optimization problem is to maximize the expected active return subject to the previously mentioned constraints as well as the constraint that the active risk equals a specific target number. This alternative formulation is useful, for example, in seeing how adding a new smart beta product can increase expected active return while keeping active risk constant.

24

Smart Beta Illustrated[1]

Investors have become comfortable building portfolios that combine active managers and index funds. They can analyze active manager styles, develop forecasts of active manager returns and risks, and construct optimal blends of different funds.

How do smart beta funds fit into this mix? These funds are active strategies with some of the advantages of index strategies.[2] To analyze expected return and risk in the new world of smart beta, we decompose active returns into two components:[3]

- Returns due to static exposures to smart beta factors
- Pure alpha returns, beyond those coming from static exposures to smart beta factors

The expected returns and risks for smart beta products depend on our analysis of smart beta factors and product exposures to those factors. The expected returns to active products now require decomposing their returns into those two components and then analyzing each component. This analysis will also facilitate understanding the correlations between all these products. Since fees are part of the story (we want to avoid paying active fees for smart beta exposures), we explicitly need to analyze expected returns after fees and costs.

This paper will describe a specific example: a global equity portfolio currently consisting of three active managers plus an index fund, considering an investment in smart beta. This example involves real data on smart beta factors and on three actual active managers (which we will not identify by

1. This article was originally written by Ronald N. Kahn and Michael Lemmon. It was not previously published.
2. Ronald N. Kahn and Michael Lemmon, "Who Should Buy Smart Beta? A New Strategy and Its Implications for Investors," BlackRock publication, May 2014. This is Chapter 22 in this book.
3. Ronald N. Kahn and Michael Lemmon, "Smart Beta: The Owner's Manual," *Journal of Portfolio Management*, Winter 2015, 76–83 (Chapter 23 in this book); and "Making Smart Decisions About Smart Beta," BlackRock publication, October 2014.

name but are included in the eVestment database).[4] We believe the approach presented here is a plausible way to forecast expected returns and risks from historical data, though it's not the only plausible approach. This is only an example. The results do depend on the fact that we use only three active managers (for simplicity of discussion, not because that's the typical number), and in fact all three have had strong performance (so underperformance plays no role in our portfolio rebalance). Our goal is to illustrate how to analyze where smart beta fits into an investment portfolio. We will exercise caution in extrapolating the results of this specific example to the general case.

Intuition

Before delving into the details, it's worth highlighting some intuition. We are interested in investing across a set of active products as efficiently as possible, so that we achieve the highest expected return net of costs for the active risk we are taking. Our index fund investment will help set the overall active risk level: once we find the best relative weights among the active managers, the balance between them and the index fund will set the overall active risk level.

- As to what determines the best weights across the active managers, we roughly allocate risk to managers in proportion to their information ratios (ratios of expected active return to active risk).[5] This is exactly true if the manager active returns are uncorrelated, though in

---

4. How did we choose the three example managers? In putting together this illustrative example, we wanted to be:

- somewhat realistic,
- loosely based on how investors diversify across active manager styles, and
- focused on the potential role of smart beta products in the case when the existing active managers are strong performers.

To help with the realism, we used data from real managers. In particular, we chose from among the 94 active global equity managers included in the eVestment database with returns over the five-year period from January 2010 through December 2014.

To loosely mirror investor behavior, we wanted to choose managers with different styles, such as value, growth, and eclectic. We can assess this by regressing the manager active returns against the smart beta factor returns. This will provide each manager's exposures to all the factors; however, we shouldn't expect managers to very neatly divide into style categories.

To limit ourselves to strongly performing managers, we only considered managers with above-median information ratios (before fees).

To be even more specific, to choose a value manager, we selected the above-median information ratio manager with the largest exposure to value. This manager also had high exposure to quality, and so we labeled this our "High-Quality Value" manager.

To choose a growth manager, we sorted the above-median information ratio managers by exposure to momentum, and we chose the manager with the second-highest exposure. This manager also had a high overall R^2 (so smart beta factors explain a relatively high fraction of the active return), and we labeled this manager our "Core" manager.

To choose an eclectic manager, we selected the above-median information ratio manager with the fifth smallest R^2, meaning a manager for whom the smart beta factors explained a very low fraction of the manager's active returns. Among those funds with the lowest R^2, the fund we chose had the highest information ratio.

5. Ronald N. Kahn, "What Plan Sponsors Need from their Active Equity Managers," Proceedings of the AIMR Conference on Equity Portfolio Construction, September 2002.

the general case we need to account for those correlations (which we will do in this example).

- As to product intuition, smart beta products can deliver smart beta exposures more cost-effectively than can active managers. And only active managers can deliver pure alpha returns. So adding a smart beta product should expand our opportunity set, and with smart beta exposures now available inexpensively, we should emphasize active managers delivering mainly pure alpha returns.
- As we work through the details, we expect that funding for the smart beta product can come from both the active managers and the index fund.

The Example

We will consider an institution that currently invests in global equities via three active managers plus an index fund. We will loosely describe the active managers as a high-quality value manager, a core manager (with relatively small positive exposures to several smart beta factors), and an eclectic manager (with relatively low and variable—both positive and negative—exposures to smart beta factors); we will shortly provide their detailed exposures to smart beta factors and pure alpha. All three managers are included in the eVestment database and have been strong historical performers (with information ratios over the five years ending in 2014 ranging from 0.65 to 1.1 before fees). Initially, as Exhibit 1 shows, the investor has 9% in the high-quality value fund, 27% in the core fund, 27% in the eclectic fund, and 37% in the index fund. We will first analyze the existing portfolio, and then see how a smart beta product can improve the mix.

EXHIBIT 1 Initial Holdings

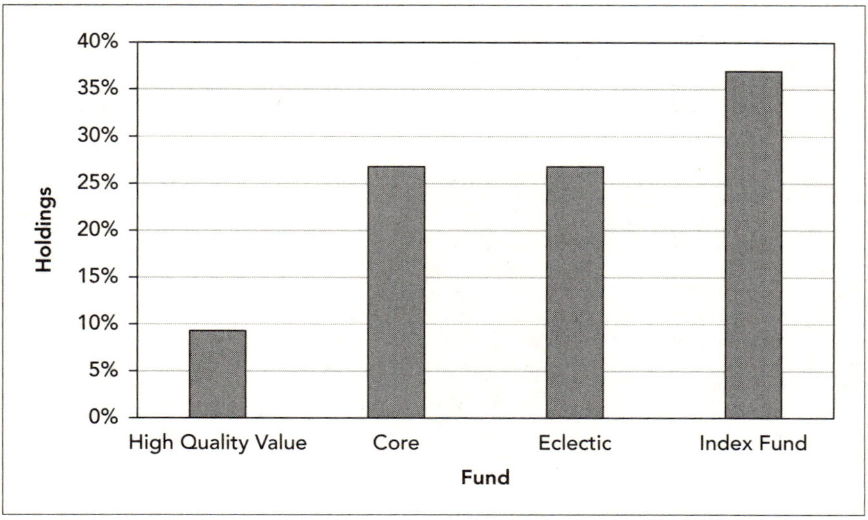

Global Equity Smart Beta

Smart beta factors play a central role in our framework, and we start here with them. We will focus on five well-known equity smart beta factors:

- Small size: outperformance of small stocks over large stocks
- Value: outperformance of high book-to-price or earnings-to-price stocks
- Quality: outperformance of high earnings quality or high profitability stocks
- Momentum: outperformance of stocks that have gone up over the prior 12 months
- Low risk: outperformance of low-volatility or low-beta stocks

Each of these factors has delivered attractive risk-adjusted returns on average over time, and there exist reasons to believe they will continue to deliver them in the future. Small size and value may be risk premia. Quality and momentum may be behavioral anomalies. And low risk may arise due to a structural impediment against leverage.

Let's look at the historical evidence. For each of these factors, we build a *characteristic portfolio*: an optimized long-short portfolio that bets on one factor while limiting exposures to other factors. These characteristic portfolios are not investable, in that they have long or short positions in every stock, and we construct them without regard for liquidity, borrowing availability, or transactions or borrowing costs. We use these portfolios to understand the return and risk characteristics of the factors. Investable factor portfolios, as we will see, will be imperfect implementations of these paper portfolios.

Exhibit 2 (see next page) shows the cumulative returns to these global factors over the 10-year period from January 2005 through December 2014, and Exhibit 3 (see next page) shows the historical returns, risks, and information ratios (ratios of return to risk) for these factors. For these specific factor returns, we measure size by market capitalization; value by a mix of book-to-price, earnings-to-price, and operating cash flow to enterprise value measures; quality by operating cashflow relative to total assets and change in net operating assets; momentum by 11-month returns 1-month lagged and analyst revisions; and risk by historical stock volatility.

EXHIBIT 2 Global Smart Beta Factors Cumulative Returns

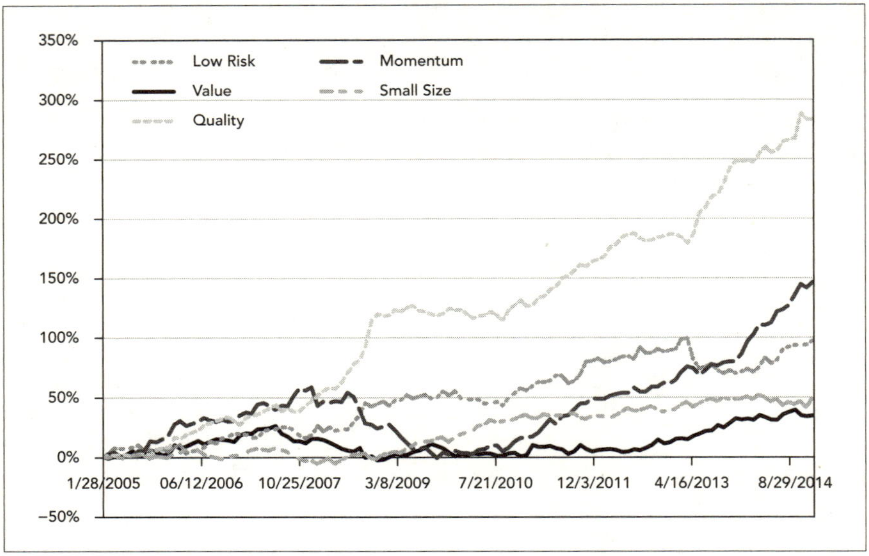

EXHIBIT 3 Global Smart Beta Factor Historical Performance (1/05–12/14)

	SMALL SIZE	VALUE	QUALITY	MOMENTUM	LOW RISK
Annual Mean	4.40%	3.60%	13.74%	9.76%	7.09%
Annual STD	6.64%	8.05%	7.47%	10.11%	9.33%
IR	0.66	0.45	1.84	0.97	0.76

Overall, performance over this historical period looks quite strong for all these factors, with information ratios between 0.45 for value and 1.84 for quality. Note also that all of the factors exhibit periods of drawdowns despite having positive performance on average over the full sample period.

Exhibit 4 shows the historical correlations between the factors.

EXHIBIT 4 Global Smart Beta Factor Historical Correlations (1/05–12/14)

	LOW RISK	VALUE	QUALITY	MOMENTUM	SMALL SIZE
Low Risk	1.00	−0.08	0.09	−0.03	0.05
Value	−0.08	1.00	0.00	0.13	0.03
Quality	0.09	0.00	1.00	−0.06	−0.02
Momentum	−0.03	0.13	−0.06	1.00	0.11
Small Size	0.05	0.03	−0.02	0.11	1.00

The correlations are fairly low, consistent with there being different return drivers for the various factors. The largest magnitude correlation is between value and momentum (0.13). But keep in mind that the standard error of a correlation estimated from 120 data points is about 0.09, so in fact none of these correlations are statistically significant.

How should we forecast the expected returns and risks of these factors? Here is our approach. To forecast risk, we will simply use the historical covariance matrix. There are many other possible approaches here, starting with exponential smoothing to overweight the more recent returns. We will stick to the historical covariance matrix for simplicity, and in recognition that forecasting the returns is the bigger challenge.

What about the expected returns? As Exhibit 3 showed, all these factors delivered exceptionally high information ratios over this historical period. For an active manager, an information ratio of 0.5 before fees would be top quartile.[6] So we expect over the long term that these factors should have information ratios of around 0.4 at best. So here is what we will do. As we show in Exhibit 5, we will forecast factor information ratios by shrinking the historical information ratios two-thirds of the way back toward 0.4. To be concrete, our forecast information ratio for low risk, for example, will be $0.52 = \left(\frac{2}{3}\right)0.40 + \left(\frac{1}{3}\right)0.76$.

EXHIBIT 5 Global Smart Beta Factor Forecasts

	HISTORICAL	SHRINK 2/3 TOWARD 0.4	EXPECTED RETURN
Low Risk	0.76	0.52	4.84%
Value	0.45	0.42	3.34%
Quality	1.84	0.88	6.54%
Momentum	0.97	0.59	5.93%
Small Size	0.66	0.49	0.65%

Exhibit 5 also shows how we use the factor risk levels to convert forecast information ratios into forecast active returns (by multiplying the shrunk *IR* by the historical risk of the factor).

The shrinkage of these historical information ratios toward 0.4 is somewhat ad hoc, but it has the general flavor of a Bayesian adjustment with 0.4 as our prior forecast of the information ratio. Our weight of two-thirds on the prior and only one-third on the historical number implies we have more confidence (i.e., a lower standard error of estimate) for the prior than the historical number, and roughly implies that our priors are based on twice as much historical data.

6. See Richard C. Grinold and Ronald N. Kahn, *Active Portfolio Management* (New York: McGraw-Hill, 2000), Chapter 5.

Active Managers

Now that we have analyzed the smart beta factors, we can use them to decompose the active manager returns into two components, and then forecast their expected returns and risks. To do this, we first regress the manager historical monthly active returns before fees against the factor returns to determine their static exposures to smart beta:

$$r_n(t) - r_B(t) = \sum_{j=Size,Value,...} X_{nj} \cdot f_j(t) + u_n(t) \tag{1}$$

Here $r_n(t)$ is the monthly return to fund n, $r_B(t)$ is the monthly return to the global equity cap-weighted benchmark (and so the left-hand side of Equation (1) is fund n's active return), the $\{f_j(t)\}$ are the monthly returns to the smart beta factors, X_{nj} is fund n's estimated static exposure to factor j, and $u_n(t)$ is fund n's pure alpha return in month t. Exhibit 6 displays the results, where our regression runs over the five-year period ending in December 2014. Instead of displaying the regression coefficients directly (the $\{X_{nj}\}$), for better interpretability, we display $X_{nj} \cdot \sigma_j$, where σ_j is the volatility of factor j. This directly shows us how much risk each manager is taking along each factor dimension. For example, we can see that our high-quality value manager takes over 1.5% active risk betting on quality. This is more intuitive than saying that this manager's exposure to the quality factor is, say, 1.2.

EXHIBIT 6 Active Manager Static Risk Exposures to Smart Beta (Historical Data: 1/10–12/14)

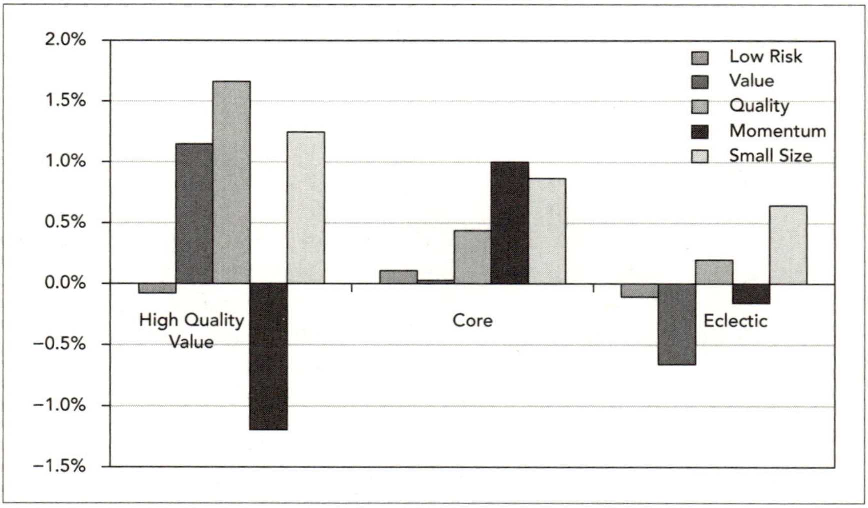

We can see that our manager labels are only approximate. Our high-quality value manager appears to also bet on small size and against momentum, in addition to betting on value and quality. Our core manager bets on momentum, with smaller bets on quality and small size. And our eclectic manager's largest smart beta bet is a small bet against value. The fact that all three managers have positive exposure to small size is largely the result of long-only portfolio construction, where small stocks have very small weights in the benchmark limiting the extent to which managers can underweight these stocks in the portfolio.

Now remember that we are so far only focusing on the smart beta exposures of these managers. We will come back to their pure alpha returns shortly. And also remember that we estimate these smart beta exposures via regression, and hence with estimation error. There are other ways to estimate these exposures, but they generally require holdings data on the funds.

Knowing each fund's exposure to the smart beta factors, combined with the already estimated expected returns to those factors, leads to estimates of manager expected returns from their static exposures to smart beta. What about the manager pure alpha returns?

First note that our regression analysis already separates manager returns into smart beta and pure alpha. So, we can calculate each manager's historical pure alpha returns, risks, and information ratios. To forecast these pure alpha returns, we assume the pure alpha risk will remain constant, and we shrink the historical pure alpha information ratios 50% back toward zero (which is the unconditional expected information ratio before fees across all managers, since active management is a zero-sum game at best[7]). This is close to the approach we used for the factors, but here our prior is 0.0 instead of 0.4, and we shrink by 50% instead of 67%. While these are plausible choices, they are certainly not the only choices. In this example, we have more confidence in the smart beta prior relative to historical performance than we do in the information ratio prior relative to historical performance. One could easily justify the opposite choice of higher confidence in the information ratio prior.

Exhibit 7 shows the results.

EXHIBIT 7 Manager Pure Alpha Forecasts

	IR		
MANAGERS	HISTORICAL	SHRINK 50%	ALPHA
High Quality Value	0.53	0.27	2.17%
Core	–0.11	–0.05	–0.11%
Eclectic	1.17	0.59	1.67%

You can see a bit more justification for the core and eclectic labels, as the core manager doesn't deliver much pure alpha and the eclectic manager delivers significant amounts of it.

7. See William F. Sharpe, "The Arithmetic of Active Management," *Financial Analysts Journal* 47 no. 1 (January/February 1991): 7–9; and Eugene F. Fama and Kenneth R. French, "Luck Versus Skill in the Cross Section of Mutual Fund Returns," *Journal of Finance* 65, no. 5 (October 2010).

What about the correlations of the managers' active returns? These will mainly depend on the managers' exposures to the factors, and the factor volatilities and correlations. We will assume for this analysis that the managers' pure alpha returns are uncorrelated. An alternative approach would be to use the historical correlations and perhaps shrink them toward zero. In this example, the correlations between these three managers are all less than 0.02 in magnitude.

Exhibit 8 shows the forecasts of active returns and active risks for the three active managers.

EXHIBIT 8 Active Manager Product Analysis and Forecasts

	SMART BETA		PURE ALPHA		PRODUCTS				
ACTIVE MANAGERS	E(RETURN)	RISK	E(RETURN)	RISK	MGMT FEE	E(R) – FEES	RISK	SB RISK %	*IR*
High Quality Value	1.79%	2.56%	2.17%	8.12%	0.70%	3.25%	8.52%	9.0%	0.38
Core	1.45%	1.44%	–0.11%	1.93%	0.55%	0.79%	2.41%	35.7%	0.33
Eclectic	0.06%	0.94%	1.67%	2.84%	0.56%	1.17%	2.99%	9.8%	0.39

Their expected smart beta returns come from their exposures to the smart beta factors and our expected factor returns. The expected pure alpha returns come from Exhibit 7. We have added the published management fees for the three products (based on $100 million separate accounts). Putting this all together, we can see that:

- The high-quality value manager delivers the highest expected return, but also takes about three times the active risk of the other managers. (That's why it has a smaller capital allocation in the initial portfolio.)
- The core manager has the lowest expected return after fees, the lowest active risk, and the highest percentage of smart beta risk. So, in part, this manager is delivering smart beta at active fees.
- The eclectic manager's expected return from smart beta is very small, and active risk is predominantly pure alpha. This manager is mainly delivering pure alpha return, and also has the highest information ratio of the three.
- We expect all three managers to deliver similar information ratios, though they differ in their mix of smart beta and pure alpha.

For comparison, the average historical fraction of smart beta risk is 26.3% for all 94 managers in our sample from the eVestment database of global equity managers over the period from January 2010 through December 2014. Two out of our three managers deliver below-average fractions of smart beta risk.

The Current Portfolio

As mentioned earlier, this institution currently invests 9% in the high-quality value manager, 27% in the core manager, 27% in the eclectic manager, and

37% in an index fund (with zero active risk). Using our analysis, we forecast a portfolio-level active risk of 1.35% with an expected active return of 0.83% net of fees.

It turns out that these holdings are optimal in that they lead to the highest expected active return net of fees from these four products for 1.35% active risk, assuming no leverage or shorting. *The only way we might achieve a higher expected return at 1.35% risk is through the addition of other products.*

The investor has taken full advantage of the available opportunities offered by these four products. This isn't always true. For example, it is common to see equal allocations to several active managers. In this case, that would lead to an expected return of 0.74% at 1.35% risk. (It would also lead to most of the active risk taken by the high-quality value manager, as that product's active risk level is much higher than the other two active products.)

As to smart beta risk, for this particular allocation to active managers, our analysis shows that 21% of the active variance is factor risk. In portfolios with more active managers, we would expect a higher fraction in smart beta factors. This is because smart beta exposures tend to be correlated across managers, while pure alpha risk tends to diversify across managers.[8]

Adding Smart Beta

Let's now add a low-cost smart beta product—designed to provide a blended exposure to factors—and see if it can improve our expected return at 1.35% risk.

The smart beta product we will analyze is long-only, and designed to deliver exposures to value, quality, momentum, low risk, and small size. The returns to this product, and hence our analyses of exposures, are based on realistic backtests that fully account for expected transactions costs.

Exhibit 9 (see next page) shows the product risk exposures to our factors, estimated by regressing monthly returns against the factor returns over the period January 2005 to December 2014, and then multiplying the regression coefficients times the factor volatilities. As you can see, the product does not deliver equal risk exposures to all these factors, in part due to the distortions of the long-only constraint. In fact, the largest smart beta bets are on momentum, and then quality. We also backtested an equitized long-short version of the product. Removing the long-only constraint leads to roughly equal risk exposures to value, quality, momentum, and low risk.

8. This is higher than the 13% weighted average of the underlying funds. As we expect due to correlations, the portfolio has a higher exposure to factor risk than do the underlying funds. See our articles, "Smart Beta: The Owner's Manual" (Chapter 23 in this book) or "Making Smart Decisions About Smart Beta" for empirical evidence on this point.

EXHIBIT 9 Smart Beta Product Exposure to Factors

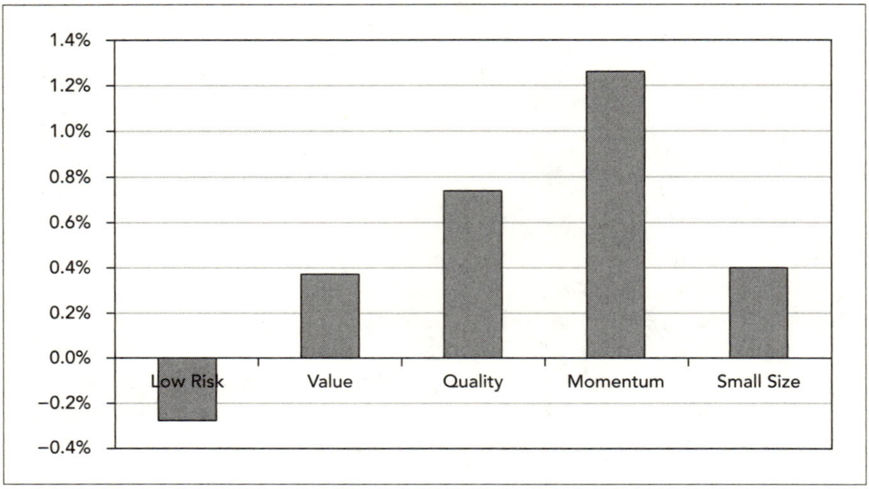

Exhibit 10 shows how these exposures, plus observed pure alpha volatility, translate into our forward view of the product.

EXHIBIT 10 Smart Beta Product Forecasts

	SMART BETA		PURE ALPHA		PRODUCTS				
ACTIVE MANAGERS	E(RETURN)	RISK	E(RETURN)	RISK	MGMT FEE	E(R) − FEES	RISK	SB RISK %	*IR*
Smart Beta: Long-Only	1.56%	1.59%	0.00%	2.19%	0.35%	1.21%	2.71%	34.6%	0.45

We forecast that the product will deliver zero pure alpha, though it takes pure alpha risk. (It can't track the uninvestable characteristic portfolio perfectly. As with our active managers, we use realized historical pure alpha risk as our forecast of pure alpha risk.) We assume a fee level of 0.35%, below that of the active products but above indexing.

Adding this new product and reoptimizing leads us to a new set of optimal holdings, as shown in Exhibit 11 (see next page). To be specific, after adding this new product, we found the holdings of all five products (with holdings constrained to be nonnegative) with the highest expected active return after fees, and with active risk constrained to be 1.35% (the same active risk before we added this new product).

EXHIBIT 11 Optimal Holdings: Before and After Smart Beta

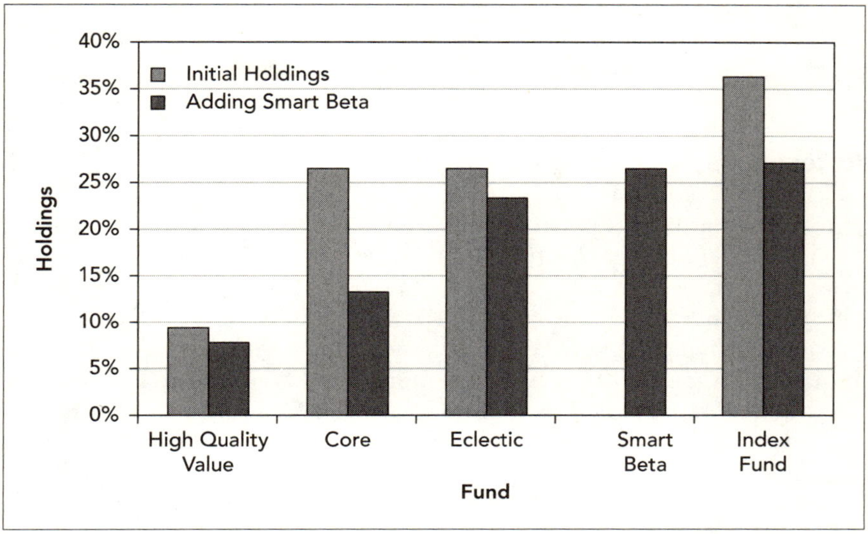

In adding smart beta, the aggregate allocation to active managers shrinks from 63% to 46%, and the index holdings shrink from 37% to 27%. The optimal smart beta holding is 27%. The new investment in smart beta is funded from both active and index holdings. Among active holdings, we mainly sell out of the core manager, who is delivering smart beta at active fees. The eclectic manager becomes the largest active manager holding once we add smart beta, as that manager mainly delivers pure alpha. The net result of these changes is to increase our expected active return from 0.83% to 0.90%. The smart beta share of active variance also increases from 21% to 26%. Overall, the addition of smart beta significantly expands the efficient frontier, leading to a meaningful improvement in expected return while keeping risk constant.

Conclusions

Our goal in this chapter has been to illustrate how to analyze and include smart beta products into a portfolio containing active and index products.

We started by using smart beta factors as a framework for understanding expected return and risk for all these products, and then seeing if current holdings were optimal among the four funds. We then added a long-only smart beta product designed to deliver a blend of exposures at relatively low cost. This addition expands the efficient frontier, leading to a higher expected return after costs while keeping risk constant. We also see that funding for smart beta products comes from both index and active products, and that in the presence of smart beta products, we tend to sell out of active products that mainly deliver smart beta at active fees and tend to favor products that mainly deliver positive pure alpha returns.

While differences in results will depend on case specifics, this example shows the opportunity offered by smart beta products.

References

Fama, Eugene F., and Kenneth R. French. 2010. "Luck Versus Skill in the Cross Section of Mutual Fund Returns." *Journal of Finance* 65 (October).

Grinold, Richard C., and Ronald N. Kahn. 2000. *Active Portfolio Management*, Chapter 5. New York: McGraw-Hill.

Ronald N. Kahn. 2002. "What Plan Sponsors Need from Their Active Equity Managers." *Proceedings of the AIMR Conference on Equity Portfolio Construction*, September.

Kahn, Ronald N., and Michael Lemmon. 2014a. "Who Should Buy Smart Beta? A New Strategy and Its Implications for Investors." BlackRock publication, May.

Kahn, Ronald N., and Michael Lemmon. 2014b. "Making Smart Decisions About Smart Beta." BlackRock publication, October.

Kahn, Ronald N., and Michael Lemmon. 2015. "Smart Beta: The Owner's Manual." *Journal of Portfolio Management*, Winter, 76–83.

Sharpe, William F. 1991. "The Arithmetic of Active Management." *Financial Analysts Journal* 47 (January/February): 7–9.

25

The Asset Manager's Dilemma[1]

How Smart Beta Is Disrupting the Investment Management Industry

Smart beta has attracted considerable investor interest. Numerous articles on the topic have appeared in popular magazines as well as academic forums. Many investment seminars now include sessions on smart beta. As of 2014, about $330 billion was invested in smart beta products; Towers Watson clients had doubled their allocation to smart beta over the prior year.[2]

Are smart beta strategies new? Are they just the latest fad in investment management? Or are they an innovation poised to significantly affect traditional investment management? According to one commentator, "Smart beta, done right, is a fund manager's worst enemy."[3] And only somewhat less ominously, an *Economist* article describes how the investment industry is being squeezed by both index funds and smart beta, predicting that only hedge funds and private equity will remain beyond the reach of those two categories.[4]

1. This chapter originally appeared as "The Asset Manager's Dilemma: How Smart Beta Is Disrupting the Investment Management Industry" by Ronald N. Kahn and Michael Lemmon in the *Financial Analysts Journal* 72, no. 1 (2016).
2. "Fund Management: Will Invest for Food" (2014).
3. Conway (2014).
4. "Fund Management: Will Invest for Food" (2014).

Innovation[5]

In Clayton Christensen's (1997) influential book *The Innovator's Dilemma*, he describes three types of innovation: revolutionary, sustaining, and disruptive. Revolutionary innovations are rare and result in products so improved that they simply replace the prior products, as the internal combustion engine replaced the horse in powering transportation. Sustaining innovations are common and improve existing products incrementally, often in response to client demands. A new version of Microsoft Word is a sustaining innovation. Disruptive innovations are somewhat rare and create new markets. They are responses not to client demands but, rather, to client needs, whether expressed or not. We believe that smart beta is a disruptive innovation with the potential to significantly affect the market for investment products, particularly traditional active products.

The ultimate goal of disruptive innovation in investment management is to deliver superior investment outcomes and meet investors' *needs* (as opposed to requests). In the case of smart beta, the investment outcome is higher returns and/or lower risk after fees and costs. The innovation is motivated by a vision of how clients ought to invest—even when they do not realize a change is needed. So, investors sometimes adopt these disruptive innovations only slowly. Disruptive innovations often do not come from focus groups or client interviews, because clients are not asking for these types of innovations (e.g., no one was demanding personal computers when they first came out). Rather, they result from understanding current practice and having a vision of how to advance that practice. For example, when indexing strategies were first developed, no client demand existed.[6] In fact, most of the disruptive innovations in asset management have arisen despite seemingly little, if any, appetite for them in the marketplace—in certain cases, in spite of explicit opposition to them.

Smart Beta

Smart beta strategies are active strategies with some of the characteristics of passive strategies. They use simple, rules-based, transparent approaches to building portfolios that deliver fairly static exposures (relative to capitalization-weighted benchmarks) to characteristics historically associated with excess risk-adjusted returns. They are active strategies because their goal is outperformance, they require periodic rebalancing in order to maintain the desired exposures, and like any active strategy, they can underperform their cap-weighted benchmark.

5. Much of this section comes from Grossman, Kahn, Mehta, and Briones (2010). Blake Grossman presented this material at the 2008 CFA Institute Annual Conference in Vancouver, Canada (May 11–14), available in *CFA Institute Conference Proceedings Quarterly* 25, no. 4 (December 2008): 14–23.
6. See, for example, Ancel (2012). It also took a surprisingly long time—decades even—for client demand to build up.

Smart beta strategies are not especially new,[7] though the product most directly connected with the origin of smart beta as a contemporary product category is fundamental indexing, introduced by Research Affiliates in 2005.[8] We can trace smart beta products conceptually to a 1976 paper on arbitrage pricing theory by Stephen Ross, who posited return premiums associated with various risk factors. Since then, researchers have documented positive risk-adjusted returns associated with factors beyond risk, including behavioral anomalies and structural impediments. The factors associated with these returns tend to be well known to investors. For example, in equities, the proposed factors include value, momentum, size, quality, and low volatility.[9] Of course, investors do not necessarily agree on how to define these factors, and different definitions and different products can exhibit dispersion of performance.[10] What is new about smart beta is not the underlying ideas. It is the simple and transparent packaging—carving out and lowering the cost of one significant component of active management.

In an earlier paper, "Smart Beta: The Owner's Manual," which is Chapter 23 in this book, we decomposed the expected return of any investment product into three components:[11]

- The return to a cap-weighted index benchmark.
- The active return from the product's static exposures to smart beta factors.
- The active return above and beyond static exposures to smart beta factors. (Sources here can include bottom-up security selection, top-down macro views, and the timing of smart beta factors.) We refer to this third component as *pure alpha*.

This decomposition of returns is also a decomposition of fees, which are low for cap-weighted index funds, intermediate for smart beta, and high for active strategies.

Smart Beta as a Disruptive Innovation

Smart beta strategies are a disruptive innovation with the potential to significantly affect the investment management industry, particularly traditional active management. The reason for this potential is that many traditional active managers deliver a significant fraction of their active returns via static exposures to smart beta factors while charging active fees.

7. Many of these ideas have played a role in quantitative active equity products since at least the 1980s. The early products, however, were neither simple nor rules-based, and they evolved over time, adding new ideas and dropping old ones. Except possibly in the 2005–07 period, prior to the financial crisis, they did not attract a significant fraction of investment assets. See Chapter 21 for more details.
8. Arnott, Hsu, and Moore (2005).
9. For an overview of factor-based investing, including evidence for the historical outperformance of these factors, see, for example, Ang (2014).
10. For example, should we define value on the basis of book-to-price, earnings-to-price, or some combination? The returns will vary with our choice.
11. Kahn and Lemmon (2015).

To illustrate the scope for disruption, we examined a sample of 79 global equity managers from the eVestment database. The managers we selected were benchmarked to either the MSCI World Index or the MSCI ACWI, reported fee data for a $50 million investment, and had a minimum of 36 monthly returns over the five years of January 2010 to December 2014.

Using the active returns for each fund, we ran time-series regressions on six smart beta factors computed from the Barra Global Equity Model (GEM3)—namely, the market, small size, value, quality, momentum, and low volatility.[12] The R^2 from these regressions is a measure of the fraction of managers' active return variance that can be explained by smart beta factors. As can be seen in the histogram in Exhibit 1, there is a large distribution in the R^2 across managers. For the average manager, static exposures to these smart beta factors explain about 33% of the active variance (i.e., the R^2 statistic from these time-series regressions averages 33%); for 24 of the 79 managers (i.e., 30% of the managers), smart beta factors explain more than 40% of the active variance.[13] So, active managers vary quite significantly in how much smart beta they deliver.

Although this analysis of specific funds over a particular period is hardly comprehensive, it clearly indicates that smart beta exposures are already a significant part of active management. What this finding means for investors in active products depends on how much smart beta they receive relative to the fees they pay. To explore this finding, we examined the relationship between the fees reported by these managers and the fraction of active risk that can be explained by smart beta factors. The median manager in our database charged a fee of 65 bps. We assumed that this amount was representative of the fees charged by active managers for alpha. In contrast, smart beta is now available at lower cost. Consider, for example, the two global equity multifactor smart beta exchange-traded funds (ETFs) currently trading in the United States. The iShares Enhanced International Large-Cap ETF (IEIL) has an expense ratio of 35 bps, and the iShares FactorSelect MSCI Global ETF (ACWF) has an expense ratio of 49 bps—implying an average expense of about 42 bps for pure smart beta exposures.

We do not wish to overemphasize this simplistic analysis of smart beta fees. The key point is that smart beta fees are significantly lower than active management fees. Successfully delivering pure alpha requires research capabilities and insights into a sometimes rapidly changing world. This component of active management should be—and is—more expensive than smart beta.

12. Specifically, the market factor is the world factor from Barra, small size is –1 times the Barra size factor, value is an equal-weighted combination of the Barra book-to-price and earnings yield factors, quality is an equal-weighted average of the Barra growth factor and –1 times the Barra leverage factor, momentum is the Barra momentum factor, and low volatility is –1 times the Barra residual volatility factor.

13. This situation generally becomes more pronounced when an investor hires several managers, each of whom derives some of his or her returns from exposure to smart beta factors. Even if each manager takes mainly stock-specific risk, the aggregate portfolio can have a much higher fraction of active risk in smart beta factors. See the Appendix to this chapter for a concise mathematical treatment of this issue.

EXHIBIT 1 Fraction of Managers' Active Variance (R^2) Explained by Six Smart Beta Factors, January 2010–December 2014

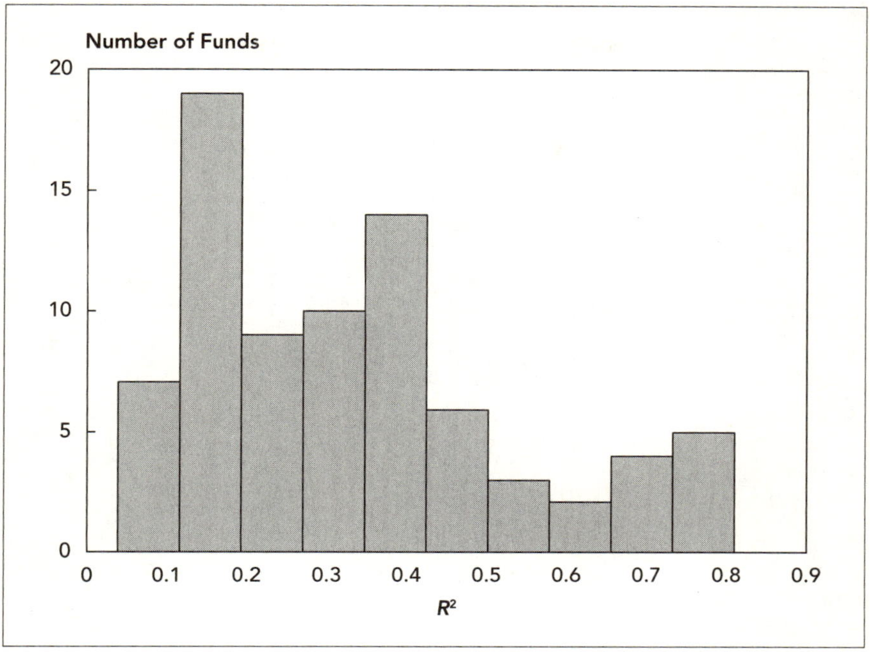

So, if an active global equity product delivers 100% pure alpha ($R^2 = 0$), its fee should be about 65 bps.[14] If it delivers 100% smart beta ($R^2 = 1$), its fee should be about 42 bps. For simplicity, we modeled predicted fees as a linear function of these R^2 statistics.[15] Exhibit 2 shows the predicted and actual fees for these products. The highlighted funds are roughly those that, in our opinion, are most likely to be disrupted by smart beta. These funds deliver a large portion of their active risk to investors in the form of static smart beta exposure while maintaining active fees. Interestingly, the funds near the far right-hand side, with a very high fraction of smart beta risk, appear to have fees more in line with their factor exposures. A closer examination of this set of funds shows that they are dominated by low-volatility and defensive funds (i.e., they are smart beta funds).

14. Given that the average R^2 statistic for these managers is 33%, in retrospect, it would have been better to assume a fee of 65 basis points for an R^2 of 33%. That would not impact any of our conclusions.

15. If we mix a 100% smart beta product with a 100% pure alpha product and both products have active risk ω^* (so the mix will have active risk less than or equal to ω^*), the predicted fees should decrease monotonically with R^2 and are close to linear except when we approach very close to $R^2 = 0$ and $R^2 = 1$.

EXHIBIT 2 Actual Fees and Predicted Fees vs. the Fraction of Managers' Active Variance (R^2) Explained by Six Smart Beta Factors, January 2010–December 2014

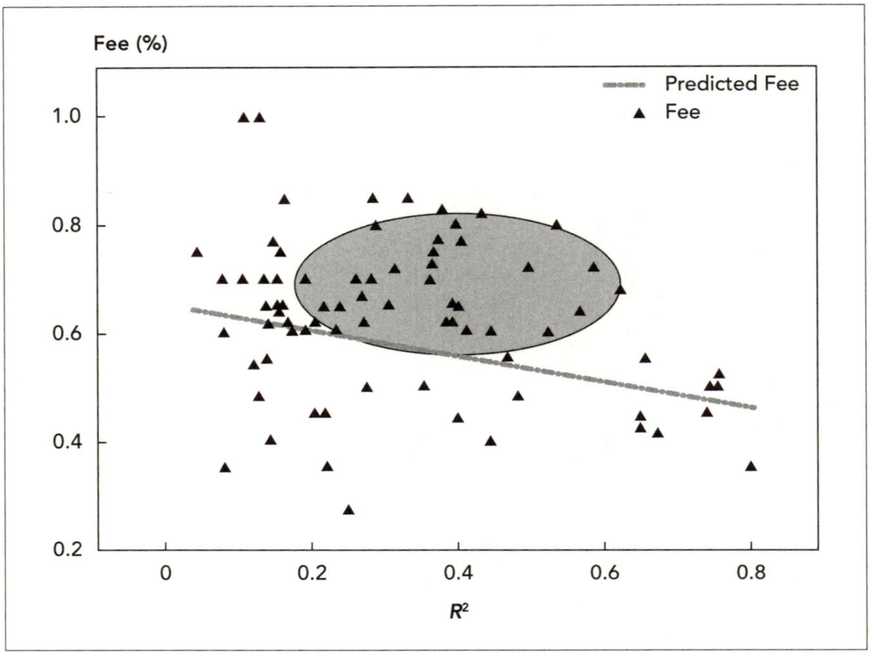

In this analysis—showing that smart beta is already an important part of active management and that some funds that deliver mainly smart beta may be significantly overpriced—we focused on equities. And in fact, most smart beta products today are equity smart beta products. But we expect to see more fixed-income and multi-asset smart beta products in the future, and they will have as much potential to disrupt those asset classes as what we now see in equities.

We have discussed several reasons—including reducing costs and sourcing valuable return components—why investors who use traditional active managers should shift partly to smart beta and partly to pure alpha managers who deliver returns beyond static exposures to factors.

But how do we know that smart beta will not go the way of portfolio insurance or other occasionally popular innovations in investing? We argue that smart beta is different from past innovations that typically encouraged investors to drop long-held constraints (e.g., on short selling) only to confront risks those constraints had protected against. Smart beta products take ideas already in use—albeit as components of their existing active strategies—and deliver them more cheaply and transparently. The innovation is about cost and packaging, not about doing something investors have never done before. Nevertheless, in spite of these motivating reasons, this disruptive transition may happen slowly or stall entirely, owing to at least three challenges.

First, there is at least some anecdotal evidence that investors may hear more about the benefits of smart beta than about the risks.[16] Smart beta factors have delivered positive risk-adjusted returns over time *on average*, but they have underperformed over various three- to five-year periods. There is a danger that negative smart beta investment performance will impede the evolution from traditional active to smart beta and pure alpha, especially if we enter a period of significant underperformance of many smart beta factors just as investor interest increases (Gennaioli, Shleifer, and Vishny (2012)). One potential source of underperformance is the capacity constraints of smart beta investing. Capacity is generally quite high, but the success of smart beta products, given their focus on just a few factors, may push up prices and lead investors to overpay.[17]

Even without significant underperformance, we could see a wide dispersion of returns for different definitions of smart beta (e.g., book-to-price versus earnings-to-price for value). This result could dampen enthusiasm among investors who do not understand that smart beta factors are not uniquely defined.

This issue is further magnified because smart beta products change the division of responsibility between investor and manager. An investor can fire an active manager who underperforms the cap-weighted benchmark over time. The investor is responsible for hiring the manager, and the manager is responsible for outperforming the benchmark. But an investor should not fire a smart beta manager who delivers the promised exposures if those exposures lead to underperformance. The investor, not the manager, is responsible for the choice of those exposures.[18]

Second, and partly driven by the change in the division of responsibility between investor and manager, the schism of traditional active management into two distinct product types will require a significant effort to educate investors. A large and growing body of academic and practitioner research on the various smart beta factors can help guide investors. This literature provides information on the various hypotheses underlying the drivers of smart beta factor returns and documents factor performance across time, geography, and asset classes.

Nevertheless, investors need additional knowledge to navigate this vast amount of information, and they need the technology to analyze their existing portfolio exposures and to build optimal combinations of index, smart

16. At an Aon Hewitt/Cass Business School conference in London on March 20, 2014, a poll of the approximately 65 attendees (mainly pension fund trustees) revealed that although all were interested in smart beta, 57% said they could tolerate only less than 10% underperformance over any three-year period. But the historical tests of many smart beta factors violate this condition.

17. For more on this point, see Arnott, Beck, and Kalesnik (2016). For more on what could go wrong with smart beta, see Kahn (2018), pp. 109–111.

18. Invariably the investor would hold the manager responsible for a particular choice of smart beta factor if it underperformed relative to other choices, even though the investor knew about that choice ex ante.

beta, and active products.[19] To the extent that most investors are not asking for this knowledge and technology, the education effort will require evangelism, not just technical papers. Of course, the current high level of discussion of this topic means that it is resonating with investors. So, education has already had an impact.

Third, the asset management business is fragmented and is represented by a multiplicity of voices. The evangelists for smart beta have some views in common but differ in many ways, including which factors are most appealing and how to build portfolios. The proliferation of smart beta products and indexes has confused investors, even if many of those products share similar smart beta exposures. And some traditional active managers will oppose this transformation out of self-interest.

Conclusion

We have argued that smart beta products—by carving out a significant component of active management and offering it more cheaply and more transparently—will disrupt the business of active management. In particular, we believe that active management will evolve into two separate product types: smart beta products with lower fees and pure alpha products with higher fees.

Because smart beta products are about delivering exposures at low cost, there should be advantages to scale. For pure alpha products, there should be advantages for managers with strong research capabilities and perhaps the portfolio-engineering skills to keep smart beta exposures low. Although some managers could offer both types of products, in general their keys to success are different. Thus, focusing on one product or the other should work better than trying to do both.

Some active managers already deliver mainly pure alpha. They are aligned for this evolution, though they may not yet understand the significance of smart beta products for their business. Smart beta managers are also aligned for this evolution, but there will be some bumps along the way, as we noted when discussing why the transition might happen slowly or even stall.

Most active managers deliver some combination of smart beta and pure alpha, possibly at fee levels inconsistent with their particular mix. These managers face dilemmas, depending on their mix versus their fees.

Consider the managers who deliver a mix of smart beta and pure alpha at fees roughly consistent with that mix. Although they could try to convince their clients that these products are fairly priced and worthy of consideration, they face the challenge of trying to do two different things well: they must compete with pure alpha managers on pure alpha and with smart beta

19. For example, a June 2015 search on Google Scholar for the term "momentum investing" showed over 11,000 hits since 2013.

managers on smart beta. By trying to do both, they will be at a disadvantage for both product types relative to the focused competition.

For these managers, the dilemma is to choose whether to go with smart beta or pure alpha. They can, of course, work to protect their current franchise and impede this transformation of traditional active management, but that course is risky if the transformation is inevitable, especially if it happens quickly (e.g., over the next three years). These managers should analyze their relative strengths and move toward offering either smart beta or pure alpha with appropriate fees.

The managers who offer a mix of smart beta and pure alpha at fees too high for the mix face more than a dilemma: They face extinction. As we can see in Exhibit 2, these are the managers who offer smart beta at active fees. It is only a matter of time before clients understand this situation. These managers need to understand that they are competing with smart beta providers who can deliver the same returns more cheaply and transparently. Their long-term survival will require them to lower fees and increase transparency.

Finally, here is a prescription for all active managers: You need to analyze the mix of smart beta and pure alpha in your products as well as the consistency of that mix with your product fees. You must also understand your comparative advantages in offering smart beta or pure alpha relative to competitors. Only after doing all that can you effectively position yourself for this evolution in active management.

References

Ancel, Kate. 2012. "The Origin of the First Index Fund." Working paper, University of Chicago Booth School of Business (28 March). http://research.chicagobooth.edu/fama-miller/docs/the-origin-of-the-first-index-fund.pdf.

Ang, Andrew. 2014. *Asset Management: A Systematic Approach to Factor Investing*. New York: Oxford University Press.

Arnott, Rob, Noah Beck, and Vitali Kalesnik. 2016. "To Win with 'Smart Beta' Ask If the Price Is Right." *Research Affiliates*, June.

Arnott, Robert D., Jason C. Hsu, and Philip Moore. 2005. "Fundamental Indexation." *Financial Analysts Journal* 61 (March/April): 83–99.

Christensen, Clayton M. 1997. *The Innovator's Dilemma*. New York: Harvard Business School Press.

Conway, Brendan. 2014. "Smart Beta, Done Right, Is a Fund Manager's Worst Enemy." *Focus on Funds* (blog), *Barron's* (20 May).

"Fund Management: Will Invest for Food." 2014. *Economist* (3 May).

Gennaioli, Nicola, Andrei Shleifer, and Robert Vishny. 2012. "Neglected Risks, Financial Innovation, and Financial Fragility." *Journal of Financial Economics* 104 (June): 452–68.

Grossman, Blake, Ronald N. Kahn, Manish Mehta, and Jon Briones. 2010. "Nurturing Innovation in an Asset Management Firm." Unpublished paper, Barclays Global Investors (July).

Kahn, Ronald N., and Michael Lemmon. 2015. "Smart Beta: The Owner's Manual." *Journal of Portfolio Management* 41 (Winter): 76–83.

Kahn, Ronald N. 2018. *The Future of Investment Management*. CFA Institute Research Foundation.

Ross, Stephen A. 1976. "The Arbitrage Theory of Capital Asset Pricing." *Journal of Economic Theory* 13 (December): 341–60.

CHAPTER 25

The Asset Manager's Dilemma

Appendix

Example of Multimanager Factor Risk

To understand why smart beta exposures increase in multimanager portfolios, consider an investor who hires four fundamental value managers, each with active risk of 5%, whereby the managers obtain 3% of their active risk from constant exposure to a value factor and 4% from stock-specific risk (which is uncorrelated across managers). So, the active risk for each manager is 5%, because $(5\%)^2 = (3\%)^2 + (4\%)^2$. At the manager level, 36% of the active variance comes from the value factor and 64% comes from stock-specific variance, because $36\% = (3\%)^2/(5\%)^2$ and $64\% = (4\%)^2/(5\%)^2$.

If the investor allocates an equal dollar amount to each manager, the resulting aggregate portfolio will have a tracking error of only 3.6%, consisting of 3% risk from exposure to the value factor (risk that does not diversify across managers) and only 2% stock-specific risk (which does diversify across managers, and $4\%/\sqrt{4} = 2\%$). So, $(3.6\%)^2 = (3\%)^2 + (2\%)^2$. At the aggregate level, 69% of the active variance comes from the value factor, and only 31% comes from stock-specific variance. In other words, although individual managers provide mainly stock-specific risk, in aggregate they provide mainly factor risk.

SECTION 3.3

Risk

26

Introduction to the Risk Section

This chapter introduces the following article:

- "Heat, Light, and Downside Risk" by Ronald N. Kahn and Daniel Stefek

We wrote this paper during one of the many debates that have arisen over the best definition of risk.[1] The chapter on risk in *Active Portfolio Management* states that risk is standard deviation. It was Harry Markowitz's definition of risk and worked well for our purposes (active management), where we needed a definition of risk:

- That was symmetric (to equally handle overweights and underweights)
- That we could aggregate from assets to portfolios
- That we could accurately forecast

The second and third criteria are quite restricting.

Consider our need to aggregate risk from assets to portfolios. For standard deviation, this requires a covariance matrix: not only the standard deviations of all the assets in the portfolio but also all the pairwise correlations. For a portfolio of 100 assets, we need 100 standard deviations and 4,950 correlations. For 1,000 assets, the required number of pairwise correlations rises to 499,500. The required number of correlations grows as the square of the number of assets, one important motivation for the development of risk models. Proposed measures of downside risk would require ever more estimates like co-skewness in addition to correlation, and so as a practical matter require simulations based on either historical sampling or simplified assumptions about the multivariate return distribution.

1. This paper appeared sufficiently long ago that the reference to the "Point/Counterpoint" sketches on *Saturday Night Live* may be lost on many readers. These sketches still live on YouTube.

This chapter mainly focused on the third criterion, forecastability. How well can we forecast these downside risk measures—especially once we take out the component of downside risk that follows from estimating variance and standard deviation and assuming a symmetric or normal distribution? The answer is not very well, at least for the assets and asset classes considered over that particular time period. We emphasize that this forecasting challenge applies to assets and not derivatives with asymmetric return distributions engineered into the contracts. If institutional investors cared about downside risk, they would purchase options. In aggregate, they do not. Based on revealed preference, the typical institutional investor doesn't care about asymmetric risk.

One nice feature of this paper—viewed with the perspective of 25 years—is the extensive discussion of preference-based and information-based strategies. Having worked almost entirely on information-based strategies over that period, it's useful to review these concepts and consider how to construct portfolios that combine both components. If we are considering both types of strategies together, as Leland noted, "optimal strategies, therefore, are preference dependent and no measure that depends on the distribution of portfolio returns alone will correctly rank all alternatives for all investors."[2] In *Active Portfolio Management*, we focused solely on information-based strategies, defined risk as standard deviation, used mean-variance utility, and showed that the information ratio—which depends only on the distribution of portfolio returns—correctly ranks all alternatives for all investors.

Following on Leland's comment that no one measure will correctly rank all alternatives, William Ziemba (2005) introduces a risk measure he calls *symmetric downside risk* for use in evaluating the performance of "great investors and speculators," including those who follow capital growth wagering ideas, also known as the Kelly criterion. Ziemba's risk measure looks like semivariance but is defined relative to zero rather than the mean return (and with a factor of two):

$$\textit{Symmetric downside risk} = \sigma_{DSR}$$

$$\sigma_{DSR}^2 = \left(\frac{2}{N-1}\right) \cdot \sum_{r_n<0} r_n^2$$

He then argues that the Sharpe ratio based on this measure of risk leads to a better ranking of great investors, especially Warren Buffett, who he argues follows a Kelly approach. As Ziemba notes at the end of his article, "My downside-risk Sharpe ratio measure is ad hoc, as all performance measures are, and adds to but does not close the debate on this subject."[3] In the context of this chapter, Ziemba does not address the question of whether we can forecast his downside risk measure.

There is another point worth mentioning regarding the distribution of portfolio returns. The chapter does not discuss this point. We typically model

2. Leland (1999), p. 32. Full reference included in the main chapter.
3. Ziemba (2005), p. 120.

returns using factor models, and so separate individual asset returns into a factor piece and an idiosyncratic piece. The idiosyncratic component of an asset's return is uncorrelated with the idiosyncratic component of any other asset's return, assuming we have correctly identified the factors. The idiosyncratic returns will have fat and possibly asymmetric tails. But in a diversified portfolio, much of that will diversify away. The idiosyncratic return at the portfolio level will be relatively well-behaved if the portfolio is sufficiently diversified. Much of the troublesome fat tails and negative skewness at the diversified portfolio level will come through the factor returns. In fact, the more diversified the portfolio, the more factor returns are the major source of tail risk. This is a key point in "The Dangers of Diversification," Chapter 30 in this book.

Since we wrote this paper, a whole approach to firmwide risk management has developed around the concept of value at risk (VAR), defined, for example, as the loss in dollars over a day associated with the fifth percentile of the daily return distribution.[4] With this definition, a VAR of $1 million means that there is a 5% chance of losing $1 million or more in a day. Financial firms and their regulators monitor this statistic closely. It impacts firm capital requirements. A financial firm such as a bank will typically have very many positions including many with option-like characteristics. They estimate VAR via simulations based on either historical sampling or simplified assumptions about the multivariate return distribution. The VAR approach typically involves asymmetries in a setting very different from active portfolio management.

After 25 years, this paper stands up reasonably well. Ron's group at BlackRock still successfully uses mean-variance optimization for portfolio construction.[5] The firm Vinva Investment Management, where Richard is a founding shareholder and advisory board member, is even named for $V^{-1} \cdot \alpha$. More generally, mean-variance optimization is widely used within the world of quantitative equity strategies.

"Mean-Variance and Scenario-Based Approaches to Portfolio Selection" by Richard Grinold (Chapter 32 in this book) addresses a somewhat related topic, as mean-downside risk approaches to portfolio selection would require scenario-based approaches. That published paper reaches somewhat similar conclusions, especially in the standard active management case involving an investment universe with hundreds or thousands of assets.

Reference (in addition to those in the chapter)

Ziemba, William T. 2005. "The Symmetric Downside-Risk Sharpe Ratio." *Journal of Portfolio Management* 32 (Fall): 108–22.

4. Looking at the first percentile and/or using a two-week period are also popular choices.

5. While we manage almost all our funds and all our assets using mean-variance optimization, we do run one fund as a "minimum conditional VAR" portfolio of Japanese equities using historical simulation to predict conditional VAR. Portfolio construction focuses not on active risk but total risk. Conditional VAR is closely related to VAR. It is the expected loss conditional on being in, for example, the bottom 5% of the return distribution. We found some evidence when we researched this fund that historical simulation could more accurately predict conditional VAR than using standard deviation and assuming a symmetric distribution.

27

Heat, Light, and Downside Risk[1]

A debate over downside risk has been raging furiously in some corners of the investment community. The Fall 1994 issue of the *Journal of Investing*, devoted to this topic, reminded us of nothing so much as the old "Point/Counterpoint" skit on *Saturday Night Live.*[2] While this topic has generated considerable heat, precious little light has been forthcoming.

One problem is that some debate participants have confounded several distinct ideas. The debate over downside risk concerns distributions and statistics, information, preferences, and performance analysis. To understand the debate, one must understand these separate ideas and their implications for downside risk. And another important idea has been lacking from the debate: forecastability. If downside risk cannot be forecast with any accuracy, its use in portfolio construction is highly questionable.

This paper is our attempt to shine light on the general topic of downside risk. Clearly mean-variance analysis does not suffice to analyze all investments. Given that, however, moving beyond mean-variance requires a clear understanding of the issues. Some current attempts at this are ad hoc and even incorrect. We will develop a consistent framework for understanding the debate (providing light) and seeing a solution.

1. This chapter is a previously unpublished white paper by Ronald N. Kahn and Daniel Stefek, produced in December 1996. The authors thank Hayne Leland for many conversations and significant contributions to this effort. We also thank Stan Beckers for keeping us focused on the practical issues. We take full responsibility for remaining lapses in theory and relevance.

2. The specific articles—Balzer (1994), Kaplan and Siegel (1994), Merriken (1994), Rom and Ferguson (1994a and 1994b), and Sortino and Price (1994)—are all listed in the References.

Information-Based and Preference-Based Strategies[3]

Let's begin with a worldview of investing. There exist two distinct types of investment strategies: information-based and preference-based. Information-based strategies attempt to identify mispriced assets and correctly time markets. Almost all active institutional money managers in the United States, equity and fixed income, claim to follow information-based strategies.

Preference-based strategies do not rely on superior information. Instead, they adjust the distribution of portfolio returns to suit the preferences of the individual investor. Some preference-based strategies are quite popular among institutional investors. For example, a constant-rebalance strategy to a 60/40 equity/fixed income mix is a preference-based strategy. Other preference-based strategies include dollar cost averaging, stop-loss orders, and portfolio insurance. Portfolio insurance attempts to provide downside protection to investors more averse than average to the risk of negative returns. Portfolio insurance is a preference-based strategy. It has nothing to do with finding mispriced assets or market timing. There is a fair price for the insurance policy. Some investors, based on their preferences, will pay this fair price to adjust their portfolio returns.

The "average investor," who holds the market portfolio and sets prices, does not invest in preference-based strategies. These appeal only to investors whose preferences set them distinctly apart from the average investor.

In general, investors can follow a combination of information and preference-based strategies. And because dynamic strategies can replicate option payoffs, investors can follow option-like preference-based strategies through appropriate dynamics, without actually owning options.

This worldview will inform how we approach portfolio construction and performance analysis. Portfolio construction must accommodate both information-based and preference-based strategies. Performance analysis must attempt to separate these two influences on returns and identify whether managers have added value through superior information. Performance analysis must not be gameable. Preference-based strategies should not generate the appearance of superior information on the part of the manager.

In the following sections, we will develop a more detailed theory of portfolio construction and performance analysis. We will describe how our worldview suggests an approach to these topics, and how it sheds light on the downside risk debate. We begin by reviewing what academics have to say on this topic. We will then look at the issue empirically: what do the data have to say? Then, after discussing current practice relevant to downside risk, we will end with recommendations.

3. See Leland (1984).

What Academics Have to Say

Academics usually begin with an idealized model realistic enough to capture the relevant issue while simplified to ignore the many real-world complications hopefully irrelevant to the issue. In the case of downside risk, this idealized model is the "Black-Scholes" world. In this world, the market return is lognormally distributed. All option prices obey the Black-Scholes theory. Taxes and transactions costs are all zero. Investors freely use leverage and short selling.

Brennan (1979) and He and Leland (1993) have shown that the average Black-Scholes investor must have a power utility function, that is, with utility proportional to end-of-period wealth, raised to a power. With power utility functions, investors not only like mean returns and avoid return variance, they like all odd moments of the return distribution including skewness and abhor all even moments of the distribution, not only variance but also kurtosis.

Now for a surprising result. The Black-Scholes world is inconsistent with standard CAPM/mean-variance theory. In particular, in this world, the market portfolio, with its lognormal return distribution, is not *mean-variance* efficient.

What do we mean by this? The market portfolio is not the portfolio with the maximum Sharpe ratio (annualized ratio of mean to standard deviation of excess return, with excess return defined relative to the risk-free return). For example, the market portfolio short a call option will have a higher Sharpe ratio than the market portfolio. But those two portfolios differ not only in their mean and variance, but also in their skewness, kurtosis, and other moments. And in the Black-Scholes world, efficiency depends on all those moments.

From another angle, given two portfolios with the same Sharpe ratio but different higher moments, a pure mean-variance investor will be indifferent between the two portfolios while, in general, the Black-Scholes investors will not be. When we properly account for all moments, the market portfolio is efficient in the Black-Scholes world.

Leland (1996) has developed a generalization of the CAPM/mean-variance framework that does properly account for all moments of the distribution. This new framework identifies the market portfolio as efficient. Beyond this, it can also identify the value added from information-based strategies and help separate information-driven and preference-driven returns.

So, the Black-Scholes world begins with fairly simple and familiar assumptions, demonstrates the breakdown of mean-variance analysis, and supports a consistent framework for analyzing efficiency. We do not claim that this model perfectly describes the real world. However, it provides a framework to inform how we should construct portfolios, and a benchmark for performance analysis, in a context where mean-variance analysis breaks down.

Portfolio Construction

Within the Black-Scholes world, Brennan and Solanki (1981) have shown that portfolio construction very neatly separates into a two-stage process.[4] We use standard mean-variance analysis to build an information-based portfolio. We then use leverage, options, or dynamic strategies built off this mean-variance efficient portfolio to implement any preference-based strategy. This second stage involves a more general utility function, trading off mean, variance, skewness, kurtosis, and other possible measures of downside risk. (See the appendix to this chapter for a discussion of distributions, statistics, and definitions of downside risk.)

While in principle we can implement portfolio construction in one stage, with no loss of utility, this two-stage approach can provide substantial insight and structure to the process, as we will see.

This two-step approach not only separates the information-based and preference-based strategies, it will also typically divide portfolio construction involving fundamental (i.e., not derivative) assets or asset classes from portfolio construction involving derivatives. For institutional investors who do not use derivatives or dynamic strategies, this implies that standard mean-variance analysis is appropriate. Those institutional investors using derivatives should first run mean-variance analysis on the underlying assets, and then overlay a derivative strategy to tailor the overall return pattern to their preferences.[5]

This two-step process is efficient because, in the Black-Scholes world, option prices depend on variance. So, for example, the cheapest way to insure an information-based strategy is to first build the information-based portfolio in a mean-variance efficient way. That will allow for the cheapest insurance policy on the strategy.

These ideas have been discussed first by Brennan and Solanki (1981), and more recently by Leland (1984). They also emphasize that the average investor, no matter what his preferences, must hold the market portfolio. For an investor to implement a preference-based strategy on top of the market portfolio, he must care about skewness and downside risk more than the average investor.

Performance Analysis

Performance analysis must separate out information-based returns from preference-based returns and measure how the manager has added value through superior information. Standard CAPM/mean-variance analysis is

4. Technically, Brennan and Solanki assume that the portfolios built in the first stage exhibit log returns which are normally distributed. This is not an unreasonable assumption for diversified portfolios rebalanced on a monthly basis.

5. A potential exception concerns managers who invest in misvalued derivatives. For the Brennan and Solanki result to hold, portfolios built in the first stage must have lognormally distributed returns. Options are characterized by non-lognormal return patterns. Over the short (e.g., daily) holding periods typical of such strategies, this assumption may reasonably hold. If not, then investors in such strategies must account for information and preferences in one optimization.

not up to this task. The market portfolio in the Black-Scholes world does not look mean-variance efficient. And certain purely preference-based strategies appear to add value. For example, the covered call strategy, holding the market and selling call options on it, will have a higher Sharpe ratio than the market. Similarly, a portfolio insurance strategy will have a lower Sharpe ratio than the market. But these simple preference-based strategies have no more information content than the market index. Furthermore, the Sharpe ratio implies a ranking of these strategies inconsistent with certain preferences. Some investors prefer the covered call strategy. Some investors prefer the portfolio insurance strategy. The average investor prefers the indexation strategy. In general, according to Leland, "optimal strategies, therefore, are preference dependent and no measure that depends on the distribution of portfolio returns alone will correctly rank all alternatives for all investors."[6]

However, Leland has generalized the CAPM to separate information-based and preference-based returns in the Black-Scholes world. The CAPM states that:

$$E\{r_P\} = \beta_P \cdot E\{r_M\} \tag{1}$$

where r_P = excess portfolio return
r_M = excess market return

and

$$\beta_P \equiv \frac{Cov\{r_P, r_M\}}{Var\{r_M\}} \tag{2}$$

The portfolio alpha is then:

$$\alpha_P = r_P - \beta_P \cdot r_M \tag{3}$$

and the CAPM expected alpha is zero. Significant positive alphas denote manager outperformance.

Leland's generalization of the CAPM states that:

$$E\{r_P\} = B_P \cdot E\{r_M\} \tag{4}$$

with:

$$B_P \equiv \frac{Cov\left\{r_P, -(1+r_M)^{-b}\right\}}{Cov\left\{r_M, -(1+r_M)^{-b}\right\}} \tag{5}$$

and:

$$b \equiv \frac{\ln\left(E\{1+r_M\}\right) - \ln\left(1+i_f\right)}{Var\{\ln(1+r_M)\}} \tag{6}$$

The generalization of alpha is A:

$$A_P = r_P - B_P \cdot r_M \tag{7}$$

and its expectation is zero.

6. Leland (1999), p. 32.

In this framework, all pure preference-based strategies built off the market will have coefficient A equal to 0. This coefficient A measures the manager's information-based value added. A generalization of the information ratio, the annualized ratio of A to its standard deviation, should remain the focus of most interest to institutional active managers (see Grinold and Kahn (2000)), since information-based strategies still use standard mean-variance analysis.

The formula for Leland's coefficient B looks somewhat similar to the standard CAPM beta formula, yet any departure from financial bedrock is still disturbing. Our empirical analysis, however, shows that for US equities, the coefficients are almost identical to asset betas. Only for options and non-lognormal distributions do the B coefficients differ significantly from betas. This implies that standard CAPM/mean-variance performance analysis is still appropriate for most institutional portfolios. And, this new approach provides the correction for option-based or dynamic strategies.

The Academic View

What does this academic analysis tell us about the current debate concerning downside risk and portfolio construction? Many advocates of downside risk propose portfolio construction as a one-step process, trading off mean returns against some measure of downside risk. This approach combines into one step both information-based and preference-based strategies, at the very least losing the insight that accompanies that distinction. When we examine the data, we will find a bigger problem as well.

Leland's analysis of performance sheds considerable light on the downside risk debate concerning performance analysis. No proposed ratio of portfolio return to downside risk, in fact no measure dependent solely on the distribution of the portfolio's return, will solve the performance analysis problem. For example, sorting portfolios according to their "Sortino ratio," the ratio of mean to one particular definition of downside risk, will not match the preferences of all investors. And it will say nothing about which managers have added value through superior information. Historical downside risk contributes nothing to performance analysis.

What the Data Have to Say

The academic view just discussed focused on how to think about information and preference-based strategies and their utility functions, portfolio construction, and performance analysis. In that analysis, they start by assuming we know the relevant distributions of returns, including all its moments. We now investigate that assumption. If our knowledge of the return distribution is limited, at some point even if downside risk aversion correctly captures our utility, mean-variance portfolio construction may lead to preferable portfolios. What do the data say about that?

In standard mean-variance portfolio construction, we assume considerable uncertainty in our forecast means combined with reasonable accuracy in our forecast variances. Simply put, we do a good job forecasting variance. The starting assumption for mean-downside risk portfolio construction is that we do a good job forecasting downside risk. At a very minimum, to advocate downside risk over variance implies the ability to forecast differences between downside risk and variance.

But let's look at the empirical evidence. In particular, how well can we forecast downside risk for fundamental asset and asset class returns. We will not look here at forecasting downside risk for options. If we can forecast just the variances of these fundamental assets, then we can do a reasonable job forecasting downside risk for their associated options, because the asymmetries in option returns are built into their definition, rather than their underlying asset return distribution.

Forecastability

Accurate forecasting of any quantity requires that some aspect of that quantity remain constant over time. Historical risk will be a good predictor of future risk if risk remains relatively constant over time. If risk isn't perfectly constant over time, consistent relationships between risk and other variables can improve our forecasts. If risk shows no persistence at all over time, we will have considerable difficulty forecasting it.

We have conducted a simple study to see whether risk persists over time. We have looked at monthly excess returns[7] for:

- 578 World Markets Model (WMM) assets,[8]
- 290 domestic equity mutual funds,
- 185 domestic bond mutual funds,
- 1,160 individual US equities included in BARRA's HICAP universe.

We have also looked at monthly residual returns for those same individual US equities.[9] In each case we look at two consecutive five-year periods: January 1986 through December 1990 and January 1991 through December 1995 for the mutual funds; and September 1986 through August 1991 and September 1991 through August 1996 for the WMM assets and individual equity returns. In this chapter, we will investigate whether three risk measures persist over time: standard deviation, variance, and semivariance. For completeness, we will also investigate the persistence of skewness and kurtosis. In the appendix, we will investigate some additional risk measures: target semivariance and shortfall probability.

7. We look at monthly returns because these roughly correspond to a typical institutional investor horizon, and also provide sufficient observations for accurate statistics. These results may depend on the horizon. Particularly as we move to shorter horizons, i.e., daily, we expect larger deviations from normal or lognormal returns.

8. These are the assets covered by Barra's World Markets Model.

9. We define residual returns as residuals to the regression of excess returns against BARRA HICAP index excess returns.

Note that our test looks at the long-term persistence of various risk measures. An alternative approach we did not pursue was to use daily data and examine shorter-term persistence. We know that over shorter horizons, ARCH and GARCH techniques[10] can improve the forecasting of variance. There may be approaches that would work for downside risk measures, but we have not tested them here.

If we observe T returns, we estimate the mean, μ, and variance, σ^2, of those returns as:

$$\mu = \frac{1}{T} \cdot \sum_{t=1}^{T} r_t$$
$$\sigma^2 = \frac{1}{T-1} \cdot \sum_{t=1}^{T} (r_t - \mu)^2 \tag{8}$$

Given Equation (8), we estimate the semivariance as:

$$SV = \frac{1}{T-1} \cdot \sum_{r_t < \mu} (r_t - \mu)^2 \tag{9}$$

If returns are normally distributed, or even just symmetrically distributed about the mean, then the semivariance should be half the variance. Target semivariance is similar to Equation (9), though the sum is only over returns that fall below the target and the deviation (the squared term) compares the return to the target not the mean. We provide continuous definitions of all of these statistics in the appendix.

Because semivariance is interesting for how it differs from just half the variance (i.e., what it says about return asymmetries), we will also investigate the persistence of *abnormal semivariance* (ASV), which we define as:

$$ASV \equiv SV - \frac{\sigma^2}{2} \tag{10}$$

The abnormal measure looks at the true additional information contained in this downside risk measure, not just what we could extrapolate from the mean and variance.

Our test of persistence is simple. We calculate each risk measure in each period, and then regress risk in period 2 against risk in period 1:

$$risk_n(2) = a + b \cdot risk_n(1) + \varepsilon_n \tag{11}$$

Evidence of persistence will be high R^2 statistics for the regression and significant positive t-statistics for our estimate of b.

Before examining the results in Exhibit 1, we have added one final wrinkle to the analysis. Some of these statistics are very sensitive to outliers. This can be a problem. For example, the probability of return less than an extreme negative value will depend on very few observations. But it is also exactly the outliers that some of these statistics attempt to characterize. Hence, we have calculated these statistics two ways. First, we have analyzed

10. Engle (1982) for the original reference, or Bollerslev, Chou, and Kroner (1992) for a review.

screened data: deleting October 1987 entirely, and deleting every monthly asset return in excess of 50% in magnitude, and every monthly asset class or fund return in excess of 17% in magnitude. But second, we have also analyzed the unscreened data. We present all these results in Exhibit 1, with the second line for each statistic corresponding to the unscreened dataset.

One issue we haven't addressed in this analysis is survivorship bias. Given that we are analyzing 10 years of data—two 5-year periods—the assets or funds with very significant downside risk are less likely to survive than those that avoid such drawdowns. One implication of survivorship bias is that we could end up with fewer observations involving large drawdowns and hence less statistical confidence on its persistence.

EXHIBIT 1 Persistence of Standard Deviation, Variance, and Semivariance

RISK MEASURE	STATISTIC	WMM ASSETS	EQUITY FUND	BOND FUND	EQUITY EXCESS	EQUITY RESIDUAL	AVERAGE
Standard Deviation	*b*	0.78	0.89	0.61	0.82	0.82	0.78
		0.57	0.81	0.56	0.37	0.37	0.54
	t(b)	54.87	41.00	15.34	41.86	43.13	39.24
		31.80	34.16	15.05	14.00	14.18	21.84
	R2	0.84	0.85	0.56	0.61	0.62	0.70
		0.64	0.80	0.55	0.14	0.15	0.46
Variance	*b*	0.63	0.77	0.45	0.75	0.80	0.68
		0.14	0.65	0.38	0.03	0.03	0.25
	t(b)	37.07	43.86	13.53	37.74	38.52	34.14
		9.94	33.67	12.86	1.48	1.48	11.89
	R2	0.71	0.87	0.50	0.56	0.57	0.64
		0.14	0.80	0.47	0.00	0.00	0.28
Semi-Variance	*b*	0.61	0.80	0.45	0.73	0.78	0.67
		0.40	0.54	0.33	0.43	0.44	0.43
	t(b)	38.80	34.53	11.34	35.86	36.16	31.34
		23.74	22.90	10.31	15.23	14.60	17.36
	R2	0.73	0.80	0.41	0.53	0.53	0.60
		0.49	0.64	0.36	0.17	0.16	0.36
Abnormal Semi-Variance	*b*	0.24	0.26	0.24	0.23	0.28	0.25
		0.00	0.15	0.11	0.01	0.01	0.06
	t(b)	6.35	9.44	4.00	8.32	9.74	7.57
		0.27	6.98	2.81	0.38	0.33	2.15
	R2	0.07	0.23	0.08	0.06	0.08	0.10
		0.00	0.14	0.04	0.00	0.00	0.04

RISK MEASURE	STATISTIC	WMM ASSETS	EQUITY FUND	BOND FUND	EQUITY EXCESS	EQUITY RESIDUAL	AVERAGE
Skewness	*b*	0.22	0.33	0.38	0.08	0.06	0.21
		0.03	0.11	0.34	0.17	0.13	0.16
	t(b)	4.66	4.81	5.46	2.51	2.08	3.90
		0.76	2.85	4.95	6.17	4.58	3.86
	R2	0.04	0.07	0.14	0.00	0.00	0.05
		0.00	0.02	0.11	0.03	0.02	0.04
Kurtosis	*b*	0.12	0.47	0.18	0.06	0.05	0.18
		0.08	0.05	0.17	0.13	0.14	0.11
	t(b)	2.22	6.60	3.01	2.03	1.80	3.13
		1.61	2.14	2.97	4.56	5.35	3.33
	R2	0.01	0.13	0.04	0.00	0.00	0.04
		0.00	0.01	0.04	0.02	0.02	0.02

(Assets and periods described in the text.)

We observe several interesting results in Exhibit 1. First, standard deviation and variance exhibit very high persistence. We see very high R^2 statistics and very highly significant *t*-statistics. They are significant in absolute terms. They are also, on average, higher than the persistence results for the other measures. For standard deviation, the R^2 statistic across these asset types averages 0.70, while for variance it averages 0.64.

Second, semivariance also exhibits high persistence, though not on average as much persistence as standard deviation and variance. However, when we measure this downside risk statistic relative to a naive expectation based on mean and standard deviation, this persistence disappears. The R^2 statistic drops from an average of 0.60 to an average of 0.10.

The average *t*-statistic also drops, though it remains significant on average. This combination of significant *t*-statistic and low R^2 statistic implies that there is some significant (i.e., nonzero) connection between abnormal semivariance in different periods, but that connection explains very little of the cross-sectional variation in the measure. To understand this, Exhibits 2, 3, and 4 display the scatterplots for equity mutual fund standard deviation, variance, and abnormal target semivariance (with the target set for –10% annualized—see the appendix for more details). We would prefer to show the scatterplot for abnormal semivariance than abnormal target semivariance, but so many years after we ran this analysis, we no longer have the underlying data.

EXHIBIT 2 Equity Mutual Fund Standard Deviation

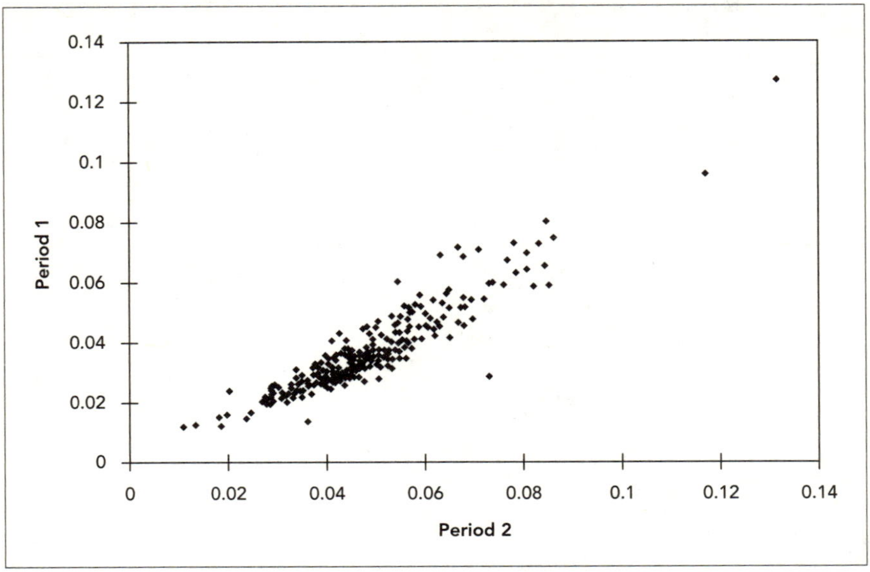

EXHIBIT 3 Equity Mutual Fund Variance

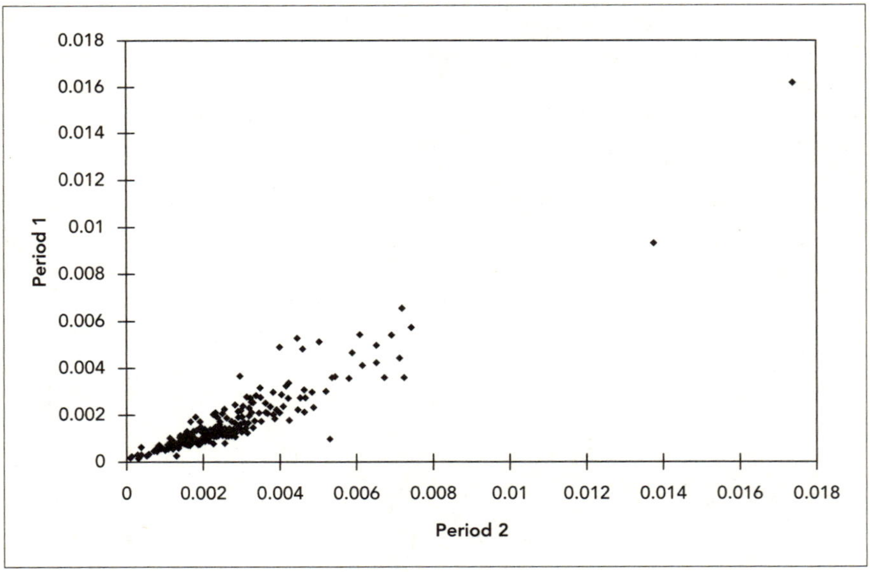

EXHIBIT 4 Equity Mutual Fund Abnormal Target Semivariance

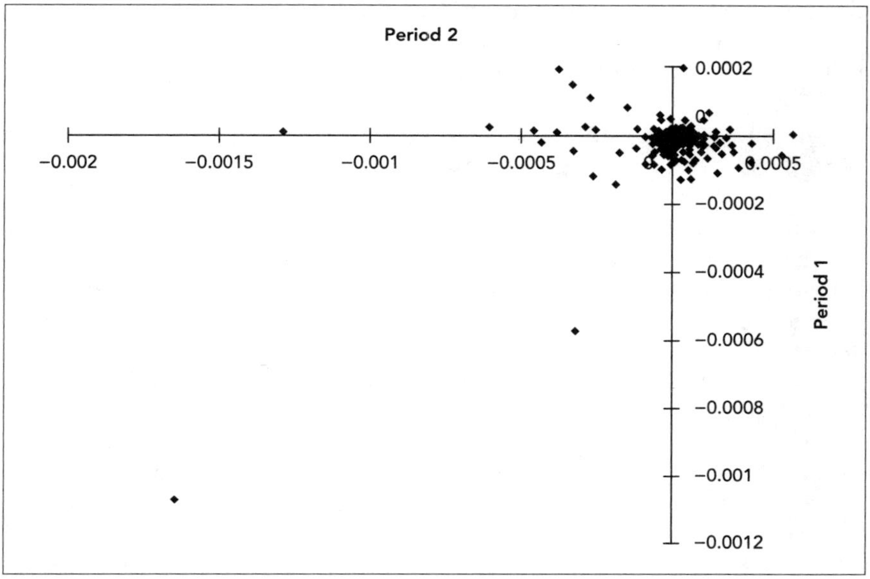

The R^2 for these are 0.85, 0.87, and 0.22, respectively, with t-statistics of 41.00, 43.86, and 9.01, respectively. As you can see, while abnormal target semivariance exhibits significant t-statistics, the forecastability looks extremely low. In fact, deleting the obvious three outliers from Exhibit 4 lowers the R^2 to 0.02 and the t-statistic to a negative number: –2.44. Those three outliers—Lexington Strategic Investments, United Services Gold Shares, and American Heritage—all use high leverage to invest in South African gold stocks or very illiquid securities like restricted stock. It doesn't require the mathematical machinery of downside risk to determine whether these are appropriate investments.

Third, our analysis shows very little persistence for skewness and kurtosis. This result is completely consistent with the decline in persistence of the downside risk measures when we compare them to normal expectations. The abnormal component of the downside risk measure is connected to the higher moments of the distribution, and skewness and kurtosis in particular. We see little persistence of abnormal downside risk because skewness and kurtosis show little persistence. The observed persistence in downside risk mainly arises from the persistence of variance.

Fourth, for almost every risk measure, we see a marked drop in persistence when we move from screened to unscreened data.[11] These data argue in favor of screening data before forecasting risk.

11. On closer inspection, we found that about 30 observations out of 150,000, and none in October 1987, caused this marked reduction in persistence. After screening observations with monthly returns in excess of 400%, we observed an R^2 of 0.52 for the persistence of equity excess return standard deviation, compared to the R^2 of 0.14 obtained with the unscreened data. The R^2 for the other measures similarly increase.

Overall, Exhibit 1 shows that the standard risk measures—standard deviation and variance—are much more forecastable than semivariance, skewness, or kurtosis. Almost all apparent persistence of downside risk traces back to persistence of variance. In the light of these results, we conclude that downside risk is inappropriate for the construction of portfolios.

Actually, the situation is worse than these statistics convey. Forecasting portfolio risk requires not only the risk of each asset potentially in the portfolio, but also relationships between asset movements (correlation, coskewness, etc.). In fact, the bulk of the required numbers concern these comovements, not the risks of the individual assets. Many years of effort have led to powerful modeling techniques for forecasting correlations. No similar techniques exist for forecasting higher order comovements. This is a major reason why accurately forecasting portfolio downside risk is so difficult.

Forecasting downside risk is problematic for assets or asset classes, but it is possible for investments with structural asymmetries, such as options or dynamic strategies like portfolio insurance. These investments have asymmetries that persist over time because the asymmetries do not rely on asymmetries of asset returns, but on the payout patterns built into the investments.

In fact, options and dynamic strategies can exhibit very large deviations from symmetry and normality that do persist over time. Fortunately, this is consistent with our two-step approach to portfolio construction. Use mean-variance analysis to build an information-based portfolio of fundamental assets. Then use a more complete utility function to overlay any derivatives or dynamic strategy to match investor preferences.

Current Practice

Many people, including a large fraction of institutional investors, essentially follow the academic and empirical advice. They implement information-based strategies using standard mean-variance analysis. Some embellish this with a preference-based strategy implemented in a second stage as a dynamic strategy.

There also exists a large group of investors who visibly stray from the academic prescription by buying individual options, not simply one option on an overall mean-variance efficient portfolio. Is this suboptimal behavior? No. Most typically, institutional investors buy individual options to circumvent constraints on leverage and short selling, or to improve liquidity. Options provide inherent leverage. Put options provide a mechanism for betting against assets without officially short selling. Options on foreign market indices provide exposure with relatively little loss of liquidity.

In all these typical cases, investors purchase options to implement bets on the fundamental assets, not to implement a preference-based strategy. The nonlinear option payout is not the primary concern. On paper, these investors would prefer the two-stage academic approach, but constraints preclude that implementation. It is also true that options on mean-variance efficient portfolios other than standard market benchmarks are not readily traded, leading to additional costs for investors who demand such bespoke products.

One standard practice where investors use individual options to implement preference-based strategies involves currencies. Most international investors, no matter what their domicile, are very averse to currency losses, even if they have a view on currencies. The answer is to use options. Investors pay a bit extra for this, but then receive downside currency protection. Such investments combine information and preference-based strategies.

For all these institutional investors who buy options, two-stage portfolio construction may still apply. In stage 1, they could implement an information-based strategy based on fundamental assets using mean-variance optimization, while ignoring institutional constraints. Stage 2 could then add options to implement preferences, circumvent constraints, and manage liquidity.

Beyond the institutional investors already discussed, there exist a small group who use downside risk to determine (typically) optimal asset allocation weights based on information and preferences. Academics would argue for a two-stage approach. The data imply that it's ineffective to implement such preference-based strategies using fundamental (as opposed to derivative) assets.

Conclusions and Recommendations

The raging debate over downside risk has generated much more heat than light so far. Unfortunately, many participants in this debate have confused the several distinct issues involved.

In this paper, we have started by distinguishing information-based from preference-based strategies. In general, a portfolio may include both. We have then described a model, the Black-Scholes world, in which to analyze the relevant issues concerning downside risk.

We find that portfolio construction is a two-step process. Step one implements the information-based strategy in a standard mean-variance optimization. Step two overlays a preference-based strategy consistent with the investor's preferences.

Our goal in performance analysis is to measure what the manager has added through superior information. A generalization of the CAPM alpha, proposed by Leland, can measure this value added. In many cases, this simply reduces to the CAPM alpha, but in the presence of preference-based strategies it can distinguish preference-based from information-based returns.

We distinguish our practical recommendations for institutional investors based on whether they typically invest in options. If they do not, then the standard mean-variance theory still provides the appropriate framework for portfolio construction. The Leland approach is appropriate for performance analysis, though if they do not use dynamic strategies, this reduces to a standard CAPM analysis. For these investors who avoid options, portfolio construction with downside risk and some currently advocated approaches to downside risk and performance analysis (e.g., the "Sortino ratio") are generally misguided.

Investors who do purchase options should implement strategies in a one-stage optimization combining information and preferences. They should limit their forecasts of asymmetries to only the options and dynamic strategies. Alternatively, they may be able to utilize the two-stage approach, relaxing institutional constraints and using only fundamental assets in the information-based stage 1, and adding options in stage 2 to implement preferences and to cover institutional constraints and liquidity issues. For performance, these investors need the Leland approach.

References

Balzer, Leslie A. 1994. "Measuring Investment Risk: A Review." *Journal of Investing* 3 (Fall): 47–58.

Bollerslev, Tim, Ray Y. Chou, and Kenneth F. Kroner. 1992. "ARCH Modeling in Finance." *Journal of Econometrics* 52: 5–59.

Brennan, M., and R. Solanki. 1981. "Optimal Portfolio Insurance." *Journal of Financial and Quantitative Analysis* 16: 279–300.

Brennan, M. 1979. "The Pricing of Contingent Claims in Discrete Time Models." *Journal of Finance* 34: 53–68.

Engle, Robert F. 1982. "Autoregressive Conditional Heteroscedasticity with Estimate of the Variance of United Kingdom Inflation." *Econometrica* 50 (July): 987–1007.

Grinold, Richard C., and Ronald N. Kahn. 2000. *Active Portfolio Management.* 2nd ed. New York: McGraw-Hill.

He, H., and H. Leland. 1993. "On Equilibrium Asset Price Processes." *Review of Financial Studies* 6: 593–617.

Kaplan, Paul D., and Laurence B. Siegel. 1994. "Portfolio Theory Is Alive and Well." *Journal of Investing* 3 (Fall): 18–23.

Leland, Hayne. 1984. "Optimal Investment Strategies and Path Independence." Berkeley Program in Finance Presentation, September 17.

Leland, Hayne. 1995. "Derivatives Performance Analysis." BARRA Equity Research Seminar, Pebble Beach, CA, June.

Leland, Hayne E. 1999. "Beyond Mean-Variance: Performance Measurement in a Nonsymmetrical World." *Financial Analysts Journal* 55 (January/February 1999), as corrected April 2001, 27–36. This paper appeared earlier as "Beyond Mean-Variance: Performance Measurement of Portfolios Using Options or Dynamic Strategies." University of California, Berkeley Program in Finance working paper, 1996.

Merriken, Harry E. 1994. "Analytical Approaches to Limit Downside Risk: Semivariance and the Need for Liquidity." *Journal of Investing* 3 (Fall) 65–72.

Rom, Brian M., and Kathleen W. Ferguson. 1994a. "Post-Modern Portfolio Theory Comes of Age." *Journal of Investing* 3 (Fall): 11–17.

Rom, Brian M., and Kathleen W. Ferguson. 1994b. "Portfolio Theory Is Alive and Well: A Response." *Journal of Investing* 3 (Fall): 24–44.
Sortino, F., and R. Vandermeer. 1991. "Downside Risk." *Journal of Portfolio Management* 17: 27–32.
Sortino, Frank A., and Lee N. Price. 1994. "Performance Measurement in a Downside Risk Framework." *Journal of Investing* 3 (Fall): 59–64.

CHAPTER 27

Heat, Light, and Downside Risk

Appendix

This appendix first discusses distributions, statistics, and downside risk, including results on the ratio of downside risk to upside risk in our returns data. It then applies the same analysis of the forecastability of downside risk measures as the main chapter, here applied to two additional measures of downside risk: target semivariance and shortfall probability.

Distributions, Statistics, and Downside Risk

All discussions of risk begin with the probability distribution of possible returns. This distribution describes the probability that the return will be between 1% and 1.01%, the probability of returns between 1.01% and 1.02%, etc. For example, Exhibit Al displays the realized distribution of monthly returns for the Fidelity Magellan Fund, based on its performance from January 1973 to September 1994. According to this distribution, for example, 26% of the Magellan Fund monthly returns fell between 2.5% and 7.5%.

The distribution of returns describes probabilities of all possible outcomes. It can answer all questions about returns, probabilities, and risk. It can be a forecast, or a summary of realized returns. It can apply to daily or monthly returns, total returns, or active returns relative to a benchmark. Assets, portfolios, and dynamic strategies all have return distributions.

There are a set of statistics that capture the characteristics of the distribution. These include the mean, standard deviation, skewness, and kurtosis. Denoting $\rho(r)dr$ as the probability that the return r lies in the range from r to $r + dr$; and μ, σ, s, and k as the mean, standard deviation, skewness, and kurtosis, respectively, then:

$$\mu = E\{r\} = \int_{-\infty}^{\infty} r \cdot \rho(r) \cdot dr \tag{A1}$$

$$\sigma^2 = E\left\{(r - \mu)^2\right\} \tag{A2}$$

EXHIBIT A1 **Magellan Fund January 1973–September 1994**

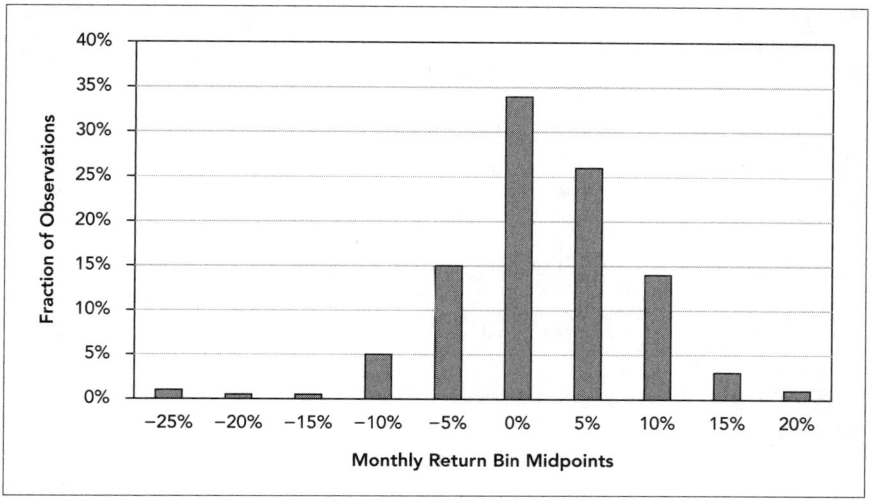

$$s = E\left\{\left(\frac{r-\mu}{\sigma}\right)^3\right\} \tag{A3}$$

$$k = E\left\{\left(\frac{r-\mu}{\sigma}\right)^4\right\} - 3 \tag{A4}$$

The standard deviation measures the spread of the distribution about its mean. Investors commonly refer to the standard deviation as the volatility. The variance is the square of the standard deviation. Some people refer to the kurtosis described in Equation (A4) as the excess kurtosis due to the subtraction of 3 in the definition. According to Equation (A4), the kurtosis of the normal distribution is zero.

For the Magellan Fund, the realized monthly standard deviation over this period was 6.3% and the mean was 1.6%. If these returns were normally distributed, then two thirds of the monthly returns would have fallen within 6.3% of the mean, in the band between −4.7% and 7.9%. In fact, 73% of the Magellan Fund returns were in that band, reasonably close to the normal distribution result. The Magellan Fund's annual mean and standard deviation were 19.2% and 21.8%, respectively. Roughly two-thirds of the fund's annual returns were in a band from −2.6% to 41%.

As the standard deviation decreases, the band within which most returns will fall narrows. The standard deviation measures the uncertainty of the return. Standard deviation was Harry Markowitz's definition of risk, and it has been the standard in the institutional investment community ever since. It is a very well-understood and unambiguous statistic.

Critics of the standard deviation point out that it measures the possibility of returns both above and below the mean. Most investors would define risk based on small or negative returns (though short sellers have the opposite view). This has generated the downside risk debate: is a statistic that focuses only on undesirable returns a better definition of risk?

Discussions of such downside risk statistics usually begin with semivariance. Semivariance is defined in analogy to variance, based on deviations from the mean, but using only returns below the mean. In the main chapter, we described how to estimate the semivariance from an observed set of returns. Here we provide the continuous definition:

$$SV = \int_{-\infty}^{\mu} (r - \mu)^2 \cdot \rho(r) \cdot dr \tag{A5}$$

If the returns are symmetric, that is, the return is equally likely to be x percent above or x percent below the mean ($\rho(\mu + x) = \rho(\mu - x)$), then the semivariance is just exactly one-half the variance. Authors differ in defining downside risk. One approach defines downside risk as the square root of the semivariance, in analogy to the relation between standard deviation and variance. Other authors define downside risk relative to target semivariance, a generalization of semivariance measured relative to a target return r_0 rather than the mean μ.

The Magellan Fund had a realized semivariance of 21.6, which was 55% of its variance of 39.5. According to Exhibit A1, the distribution extended slightly farther to the left (negative returns) than to the right (positive returns), and so the semivariance was slightly more than half the variance.

Beyond just a single mutual fund example, we have looked at the relation between semivariance and variance for a large set of fundamental asset and asset class returns.

Given the definition of semivariance in Equation (A5), which is a measure of downside risk, we can equivalently define an upside risk as:

$$\begin{gathered} Upside\ SV = \int_{\mu}^{\infty} (r - \mu)^2 \cdot \rho(r) \cdot dr \\ Variance = SV + Upside\ SV \end{gathered} \tag{A6}$$

As you can see, the semivariance plus the upside semivariance add up to the variance. If returns are symmetrically distributed, then semivariance equals upside semivariance equals half the variance. We can measure the level of asymmetry in the return distribution through the ratio of semivariance to upside semivariance.

With that in mind, we have looked at excess returns for the 578 assets in BARRA's World Markets Model, 290 domestic equity mutual funds, and 185 domestic bond mutual funds; as well as excess and residual returns for 1,160 individual US equities included in BARRA's HICAP universe. In each case, we look at two consecutive five-year periods: January 1986 through

December 1990 and January 1991 through December 1995 for the mutual funds; and September 1986 through August 1991 and September 1991 through August 1996 for the asset class and individual equity returns. We have looked at this relationship using both screened and unscreened data. To screen these data, we deleted October 1987 entirely, and deleted every monthly asset return in excess of 50% in magnitude, and every monthly asset class or fund return in excess of 17% in magnitude.

Exhibit A2 displays the results, with screened results listed above unscreened results.

EXHIBIT A2 **Ratio of Semivariance to Upside Semivariance**

PERIOD	WMM ASSETS	EQUITY FUND	BOND FUND	EQUITY EXCESS	EQUITY RESIDUAL
Period 1	1.00	1.04	1.13	1.00	0.85
	1.13	1.50	1.13	1.00	0.85
Period 2	0.96	1.00	1.17	0.89	0.89
	0.96	1.00	1.17	0.89	0.89

If > 1, downside risk dominates upside risk.
If <1, upside risk dominates downside risk.

Perhaps the most interesting observation about Exhibit A2 is that across many different asset types, semivariance and upside semivariance are roughly balanced. We can see the impact of October 1987 in the difference between the screened and unscreened results in Period 1.

Downside risk answers the critics of standard deviation by focusing entirely on the undesirable returns. However, to the extent that investment returns are reasonably symmetric, most definitions of downside risk are simply proportional to standard deviation or variance and so contain no additional information. For the asset classes and individual assets investigated above, on average the semivariance lies fairly close to half the variance.

One class of assets whose returns are not symmetric is options. While the return distributions for the underlying assets may be nearly symmetric, the option payouts engineer asymmetries into the option returns. And since dynamic strategies can replicate option payouts, these strategies too exhibit asymmetric return distributions.

Testing Forecastability of Additional Measures of Downside Risk

The main text of this chapter investigated the forecastability—in particular the persistence—of standard deviation, variance, and semivariance. Here we provide results for some additional measures of downside risk: target semivariance, *TSV*, and shortfall probability, *SP*.

We define the target semivariance in analogy to the semivariance (Equation (A5)) but with the target return replacing the mean return:

$$TSV = \int_{-\infty}^{t} (r-t)^2 \cdot \rho(r) \cdot dr \tag{A7}$$

The shortfall probability is just the fraction of the return distribution that falls below the target:

$$SP = \int_{-\infty}^{t} \rho(r) \cdot dr \tag{A8}$$

For these tests, we have used an annual return target of –10% for the target in our target semivariance analysis and our shortfall probability.[12] Similar to our analysis of semivariance, when we examined abnormal semivariance, here too we investigated the persistence of *abnormal* measures, by relating these statistics to expected quantities assuming normal distributions. We define abnormal target semivariance, *ATSV*, as the measured target semivariance, minus the target semivariance expected, given the mean and standard deviation, and assuming a normal distribution. Denoting mean as μ, standard deviation as σ, and target as t:

$$ATSV = TSV - \frac{1}{\sqrt{2\pi\sigma^2}} \int_{-\infty}^{t} Exp\left\{-\left(\frac{1}{2}\right)\cdot\left(\frac{r-\mu}{\sigma}\right)^2\right\}\cdot(r-t)^2 \cdot dr \tag{A9}$$

In Equation (A9), we subtract from the target semivariance the result assuming returns are normally distributed. Integrating this normal distribution integral, we can reduce this somewhat to:

$$\begin{aligned} ATSV = TSV &- \left[\sigma^2 + (\mu - t)^2\right]\cdot \mathrm{N}\left\{-\left(\frac{\mu - t}{\sigma}\right)\right\} \\ &+ \left[\frac{\sigma\cdot(\mu - t)}{\sqrt{2\pi}}\right]\cdot Exp\left\{-\left(\frac{1}{2}\right)\cdot\left(\frac{\mu - t}{\sigma}\right)^2\right\} \end{aligned} \tag{A10}$$

where $N\{\cdot\}$ denotes the cumulative normal distribution function.

Similarly, we will define abnormal downside probability as the measured downside probability minus the downside probability expected, given the mean and standard deviation, and assuming a normal distribution:

$$ASP = SP - \mathrm{N}\left\{\frac{t-\mu}{\sigma}\right\}. \tag{A11}$$

Exhibit A3 provides the results of our persistence analysis of target semivariance and shortfall probability along with their abnormal versions. We use exactly the same assets, time periods, screening criteria, and test setup as used in the main text.

12. Since we analyze monthly data, we use a monthly target of –2.89% = –10% / Sqrt(12).

EXHIBIT A3 Persistence of Target Semivariance and Shortfall Probability

RISK MEASURE	STATISTIC	WMM ASSETS	EQUITY FUND	BOND FUND	EQUITY EXCESS	EQUITY RESIDUAL	AVERAGE
Target Semivariance	*b*	0.43	0.80	0.27	0.62	0.66	0.56
		0.31	0.37	0.09	0.52	0.56	0.37
	t(b)	23.66	30.00	5.11	25.30	25.05	21.82
		13.72	15.19	3.85	20.70	19.91	14.67
	R2	0.50	0.76	0.12	0.36	0.36	0.42
		0.25	0.44	0.07	0.27	0.26	0.26
Abnormal Target Semivariance	*b*	0.24	0.23	0.61	0.25	0.30	0.33
		0.00	0.08	0.10	0.01	0.01	0.04
	t(b)	7.18	9.01	6.00	9.23	10.45	8.37
		−0.06	4.84	3.23	0.45	0.40	1.77
	R2	0.08	0.22	0.16	0.07	0.09	0.12
		0.00	0.07	0.05	0.00	0.00	0.02
Shortfall Probability	*b*	0.87	0.90	0.36	0.48	0.45	0.61
		0.85	0.92	0.35	0.48	0.46	0.61
	t(b)	42.14	18.90	9.39	16.36	16.23	20.60
		43.84	18.90	9.39	16.31	17.05	21.10
	R2	0.76	0.55	0.32	0.19	0.19	0.40
		0.77	0.55	0.32	0.19	0.20	0.41
Abnormal Shortfall Probability	*b*	0.02	0.04	0.12	0.13	0.07	0.08
		0.00	0.00	0.12	0.12	0.11	0.07
	t(b)	0.41	0.63	1.97	4.57	2.22	1.96
		−0.08	0.02	2.34	4.38	3.54	2.04
	R2	0.00	0.00	0.02	0.02	0.00	0.01
		0.00	0.00	0.02	0.02	0.01	0.00

Target semivariance and shortfall probability exhibit significant persistence; however, when we measure these downside risk statistics relative to a naive expectation based on mean, standard deviation, and the normal distribution, this persistence disappears. For target semivariance, the R^2 statistics drop from an average of 0.42 to an average of 0.12. For shortfall probability, the R^2 statistics drop from an average of 0.40 to an average of 0.01.

We also see a drop in persistence as we move from screened to unscreened data, especially for target semivariance and abnormal target semivariance. Shortfall probability is less sensitive to outliers, perhaps intuitive as the measure itself doesn't include the magnitude of the return. It is just a count of the number of observed returns falling below a target.

Overall, these results for target semivariance and shortfall probability are in line with the results for semivariance discussed in the main chapter.

SECTION 3.4

Portfolio Construction

28

Introduction to the Portfolio Construction Section

This introduction covers the next five chapters in the book, which are based on the following articles:

- "Optimal Gearing" by Ronald N. Kahn, Seanna Johnson, and Dean Petrich
- "The Dangers of Diversification" by Gerald Garvey, Ronald N. Kahn, and Raffaele Savi
- "The Surprisingly Small Impact of Asset Growth on Expected Alpha" by Ronald N. Kahn and J. Scott Shaffer
- "Mean-Variance and Scenario-Based Approaches to Portfolio Selection" by Richard C. Grinold
- "Five Myths About Fees" by Ronald N. Kahn, Matthew H. Scanlan, and Laurence B. Siegel

The "Five Myths About Fees" paper won the 2007 Bernstein Fabozzi/Jacobs Levy Award for the best article appearing in volume 32 of the *Journal of Portfolio Management*.

"Optimal Gearing"

We wrote this paper to document a subtlety of long-short portfolio construction. We can characterize long-short portfolios by their risk level ($\mathbf{h}^T \cdot \mathbf{V} \cdot \mathbf{h}$) and their leverage or *gearing* ($G = \frac{1}{2}\sum_n |h_n|$). It is well understood that as we scale risk up and down in the absence of constraints and costs, the expected alpha scales up and down with risk so as to keep the expected information ratio constant. What is less understood, though fairly obvious once you think about it, is that constraining gearing impacts that relationship. Put another way, as we scale risk up and down, gearing scales up and down as well. To increase risk by a factor of two, we double all our long positions and double all our short positions. But that doubles gearing as well. That natural connection between risk and gearing means that if we fix gearing, there is one risk level that will maximize our information ratio, and vice versa.

This chapter goes into some detail clarifying that point and describing what happens if we increase or decrease risk relative to the optimal risk for fixed gearing. It also describes how to identify long-short portfolios with too much or too little gearing relative to the risk level.

This article had the misfortune of appearing in the summer of 2007 right when the *Quant Crisis* of early August was happening. Between that and the broader financial crisis starting in 2008, interest in leverage dropped substantially. Title aside, though, this article describes a mathematical truth worth understanding about long-short portfolio construction, rather than promoting the use of leverage.

"The Dangers of Diversification"

This chapter describes a very different portfolio construction challenge—overdiversification across managers and products—based on our experience managing a multistrategy hedge fund through the Quant Crisis of August 2007.

To understand the challenge, we model each investment product as a combination of generic and orthogonal ideas. The generic ideas mainly include things we now call smart beta—well-known risk premia, behavioral anomalies, and structural impediments long associated with positive expected returns. These are sources of correlations across managers and products. Orthogonal ideas are return drivers unique to individual managers and uncorrelated across managers and products.

The generic ideas can appear to be relatively uncorrelated across products. This was our view of, for example, value factors in the United States, Europe, and Japan. Prior to August 2007, value factors in these three regions were not correlated. Furthermore, there isn't any fundamental reason to believe they should be correlated across regions. However, they are all popular strategies. That leads to correlations across managers and products driven by common investors. Those manager and product correlations, less visible in the return data, can become extremely dangerous during sharp drawdowns. In August 2007, the subprime mortgage crisis led to a search for liquidity and the simultaneous selling of many of these factors. In that extreme environment, factor volatilities and correlations spiked.

This chapter goes into mathematical and empirical detail on the challenges of diversifying across managers. The classic mean-variance approach to managing multiple manager portfolios faces at least three challenges. First, and most important, it concentrates risk in generic ideas correlated across managers. This can lead to unexpected tail risk. Second, it provides a temptation to overlever the resulting portfolio, which often appears to have very low risk but high information ratio. Third, it typically combines underlying funds managed for stand-alone performance rather than performance of the portfolio, often leading to overdiversification. We analyze these three challenges and propose solutions. Unfortunately, the solutions aren't easy to achieve. The key lesson is to emphasize orthogonal ideas and keep correlations with other managers as low as possible.

"The Surprisingly Small Impact of Asset Growth on Expected Alpha"

We wrote this paper in our effort to understand the capacity of an investment strategy. We start by observing that every investment product has an expected or promised active return for investors, and then define capacity as the maximum amount of assets we can manage and still deliver that expected active return.

We present a framework for analyzing capacity, particularly useful for understanding its driving forces and improving intuition. We show that with optimal (transaction cost-aware) portfolio management, expected alpha net of costs decays very slowly with increasing asset levels. We cannot estimate capacity very precisely due to its sensitivity to other parameters. Fortunately, large errors in estimated capacity lead to only small errors in expected alpha net of costs. On the other hand, suboptimal portfolio management (building portfolios without regard to costs) leads to substantially lower capacity. This framework does ignore some market details, leading it to overestimate capacity. Because such details can ultimately limit capacity, we advocate managing asset growth and regularly comparing size with available capacity.

Investors can monitor capacity, though negative returns do not signify capacity problems, and increasing costs usually signify suboptimal portfolio management. Managers can increase capacity by increasing their intrinsic information ratio (by increasing skill and/or breadth) and by lowering transactions costs (e.g., through better approaches to trading).

In retrospect, this paper missed something—not in the analysis but in its interpretation. Consistent with its title, the paper found high capacity for many strategies. That is true. However, all managers running similar (correlated) strategies effectively share that capacity. Our analysis estimates the aggregate capacity, not that of any one manager. This greatly increases the challenge of managing capacity. Any one manager can close the particular fund they manage, but not the correlated funds run by other managers. Similar to the difficult-to-achieve conclusion in "The Dangers of Diversification," it is best to avoid correlations with other managers.

"Mean-Variance and Scenario-Based Approaches to Portfolio Selection"

Mean-variance optimization using quadratic programming has been an important portfolio management tool for quantitative mangers since the early Markowitz and Sharpe results. Quadratic programming survived the journey from theory to practice because it is adaptable to the agency nature of most institutional investment management, where the institution, a pension fund, endowment, etc., assumes responsibility for the risk and return of a benchmark and the asset manager assumes responsibility for any difference in performance. Quadratic programming can be adapted to this split in responsibility.

Quadratic programming has shortcomings. It is blind to higher moments such as skewness and kurtosis. It also does not score well as a utility for wealth of the utility maximizing investor who is often the protagonist in financial economists' articles. For those reasons and the less defensible notion that more complicated is always better there is a temptation to go beyond mean-variance and quadratic programming and use return scenarios and expected utility maximization.

This chapter examines the use of utility maximization based on return scenarios. It was originally titled "The Sorcerer's Apprentice" after Goethe's tale of a novice who experiments with his boss's magic before he knows how to control it. Matters quickly get out of hand. The scenario-based (expected utility maximization) approach to portfolio optimization presents similar opportunities for misadventure. The paper shows how to avoid the danger. Alas, as with all sorcery, when we strip away the mask, we see there is less there than one would initially suppose. The conventional mean-variance approach gives comparable answers with less bother and peril.

Although the article is not very encouraging about the use of scenario-based optimization, it does present some positive results. The scenario-utility maximization has appeal for a plan sponsor doing a strategic asset allocation. Using the reverse-engineering technique, you can answer questions such as, how much would expected returns have to change to justify a move of strategic asset allocation from A to B?

The paper also outlines a method for generating return scenarios that is not dependent on replaying history. From a database of returns on N assets for T periods, the procedure can generate T^N scenarios rather than T. With minor modification the simulation idea can be used with a factor model of returns and can be used to simulate future returns on any portfolio regardless of its provenance.

Finally, the paper's analysis is based on a useful insight. If you start with a model portfolio that is optimal when you have no special information, then the first order conditions of the optimization define a valuation model, in the Arrow-Debreu sense, that can be used to value any combination of the returns on those assets.

The article draws a distinction between financial economics on one hand and investment engineering on the other. Ideas and techniques tend to flow from financial economics to investment engineering, but they are often used for reasons and in ways that were unintended. This article shows how you can adapt the financial economic notion of an expected utility maximizing investor to the investment engineering problem of building portfolios that depart from benchmark positions when research suggests an opportunity to realize some gain in return.

The chapter is a toned-down version of the 1999 article where we set out to show that a quadratic approximation of the expected utility would give similar results. On rereading, this appears to offer more heat than light, so we moved the section on approximation to an appendix and tightened up the argument somewhat.

Since the publication of the 1999 article the discussion has, as discussions will, continued. In the winter 2011 issue of the *Journal of Portfolio Management*, Mark Kritzman, in an invited editorial titled "The Graceful Aging of Mean-Variance Optimization," laid to rest some of the more extravagant criticism of mean-variance.[1]

It should be clear that this is not an either/or, zero-sum discussion. In some cases, both mean-variance and expected utility maximization may be perfectly acceptable approaches. Bill Sharpe makes this clear in his 2007 article "Expected Utility Asset Allocation."[2] That article covers much of the same territory as the coming chapter and concludes that expected utility maximization is worth a look in the context of a board setting the fund's strategic asset allocation.

"Five Myths About Fees"

Fees succinctly capture the economic relationship between investors and managers, and investors receive performance after fees. One measure of the central importance of fees is that they exist in different forms—fixed fees and incentive fees—with additional bells and whistles like high water marks. Furthermore, of the three dimensions of investing—return, risk, and cost—investors have direct control only over cost. Fees are a major component of costs.

In this chapter, we use those three dimensions of investing to analyze five myths about fees. Three of these myths directly concern appropriate fee magnitude and structure: fixed versus incentive, and the value of high water marks. Two additional myths concern fees in particular contexts. Do hedge funds deserve their high fees, and can investors always separate alpha from beta, and pay appropriately for each? We should flag one particular issue that has changed since we wrote the article. We have noted in the chapter that the trend of increasing hedge fund fees we observed in 2006 has

1. Mark Kritzman, "The Graceful Aging of Mean-Variance Optimization," *Journal of Portfolio Management* 37, , no. 2 (2011): 3–5.
2. W. F. Sharpe, "Expected Utility Asset Allocation," *Financial Analysts Journal* 63, no. 5 (2007): 18–30.

reversed over the decade that followed, in part in reaction to the issues we identify in that section.

Investors generally pay insufficient attention to fees. Yet fees should not be their overriding concern. High-fee products are worthwhile if they deliver sufficiently high returns and low risk. Some high-return products have fees that make them poor investments. Investors must analyze fees in this overall context of return, risk, and cost.

29

Optimal Gearing[1]

Not All Long-Short Portfolios Are Efficient

With the developments in quantitative finance over the past 50 years, investors have increasingly understood the importance of engineering portfolios to effectively represent their views. Markowitz (1959) began this process in the 1950s by specifying a clear mathematical approach to trading off expected return and risk. Sharpe (1963), Treynor and Black (1973), Rosenberg (1976), and others advanced the process by focused active investors on how to build portfolios to beat specific performance benchmarks.

More recent work by Grinold and Kahn (2000a) and Clarke, de Silva, and Thorley (2002) has proposed specific measures of implemental efficiency—especially the transfer coefficient—to capture precisely how well portfolios represent underlying views. This work has improved our understanding of how constraints and costs impact portfolios.

One particular application has been an analysis of the impact of the long-only constraint, quantifying the advantages of long-short investing. Clarke, de Silva, and Sapra (2004) have further analyzed the advantages of partial long-short investing.

Most investors today understand that long-short portfolios reflect manager views more accurately than do long-only portfolios. But is that the end of the story? Do all long-short portfolios exhibit similar efficiencies? Or do even long-short portfolio managers face choices that can significantly impact their efficiency?

This article will describe another important dimension—gearing—along which to consider implementation efficiency. Consider an equity market neutral portfolio manager designing a $100 million product to deliver the

1. This chapter originally appeared as "Optimal Gearing" by Seanna Johnson, Ronald N. Kahn, and Dean Petrich in the *Journal of Portfolio Management*, Summer 2007, 10–18. Seanna Kim was known as Seanna Johnson at the time we published this article.

maximum possible expected alpha at 10% risk. She can invest $100 million in a 10% risk portfolio. Or she can use $100 million to collateralize a $300 million portfolio run at 3.3% risk. Or she can choose among a continuum of possible combinations of active risk and leverage.

As we will show, portfolio efficiency and the expected alpha of the portfolio vary in surprising, interesting, and important ways along that continuum. There is an optimal level of gearing to maximize efficiency, but, conversely, a poor choice of gearing can make a poor long-short implementation even less efficient than long-only.

We introduce the method using a simple model and embellishments. We provide both a rule of thumb to judge whether a portfolio is overgeared or undergeared and an analysis of an actual portfolio facing exactly this issue.

Simple Model

We first find the optimal relationship between gearing and risk in a very simple model, using the general framework of Grinold and Kahn (2000b). Later, we generalize this model to investigate the efficiency loss due to incompatible gearing and risk levels.

We start with an investment universe consisting of N stocks, with uncorrelated residual returns, $\{\theta_n\}$, and identical residual risk levels, ω_0. We assume individual stock expected residual returns have the form:

$$E\{\theta_n\} \equiv \alpha_n = IC \cdot \omega_0 \cdot z_n, \tag{1}$$

with the same information coefficient, IC, for each stock. The terms $\{z_n\}$ are independent, normally distributed random variables with mean 0 and standard deviation 1.

Combining Equation (1) with the active management utility function:

$$\begin{aligned} U &= \mathbf{h}^T \cdot \boldsymbol{\alpha} - \lambda \mathbf{h}^T \cdot \mathbf{VR} \cdot \mathbf{h} \\ &\Rightarrow \sum_{n=1}^{N} h_n \cdot \alpha_n - \lambda h_n^2 \cdot \omega_0^2 \end{aligned} \tag{2}$$

where $\mathbf{h}$ represents portfolio holdings and $\mathbf{VR}$ is the covariance matrix of residual returns, leads to optimal holdings:

$$h_n^* = \frac{\alpha_n}{2\lambda\omega_0^2} \Rightarrow \left(\frac{IC}{2\lambda}\right) \cdot \left(\frac{z_n}{\omega_0}\right). \tag{3}$$

Using Equation (3), we can calculate the portfolio alpha and residual risk as:

$$\begin{aligned} \alpha^* &= \left(\frac{IC^2}{2\lambda}\right) \cdot \sum_{n=1}^{N} z_n^2 \\ \omega^* &= \left(\frac{IC}{2\lambda}\right) \cdot \sqrt{\sum_{n=1}^{N} z_n^2}\,. \end{aligned} \tag{4}$$

Now where does gearing enter here? Gearing depends upon the sum of long and short positions. A market neutral portfolio that is 100% long, 100% short, with 100% deposited in a collateral account has a gearing of one according to our definition (Equation (5), below). For example, a $100 million market neutral portfolio would have $100 million long, $100 million short, and $100 million deposited in a collateral account. In this example, we are ignoring real-world market frictions like margin on the short positions.

While this will be our definition for this paper—and it is a common definition—others define this as a gearing of two. With our view, we define portfolio *gearing* as:

$$G \equiv \frac{1}{2}\sum_{n=1}^{N}|h_n|. \tag{5}$$

According to Equation (5), a portfolio 100% long and 100% short has a gearing of one. Also, as a function of the active positions, h_n, we can impact gearing in two distinct ways. First, we can impact gearing through leverage. A portfolio that is 300% long and 300% short will immediately have three times the gearing of a portfolio that is 100% long and 100% short with proportionally all the same positions (i.e., the ratio of h_n to h_m for all n and m is the same in each portfolio). But second, we can also adjust gearing by varying the ratios of the position sizes, once again the ratio of h_n to h_m for all n and m. The first approach doesn't impact the transfer coefficient. The second approach does.

In our simple model, the portfolio gearing is related to the z-scores by:

$$G^* = \frac{1}{2}\left(\frac{\omega^*}{\omega_0\sqrt{N}}\right)\cdot\sum_{n=1}^{N}|z_n|. \tag{6}$$

If N is reasonably high, we can replace the sums in Equations (4) and (6) by their expectations. Using $E\{z^2\}=1$ and $E\{|z|\}=\sqrt{\frac{2}{\pi}}$, we find:

$$\begin{aligned}\alpha^* &= \frac{IC^2\cdot N}{2\lambda}\\ \omega^* &= \frac{IC\cdot\sqrt{N}}{2\lambda}\\ G^* &= \frac{IC\cdot N}{\sqrt{8\pi}\lambda\omega_0}\end{aligned} \tag{7}$$

A critical point is that there is only a single degree of freedom in Equation (7); if the investor fixes the risk aversion, that in turn fixes *all three* of the expected alpha, risk, and gearing. If the investor fixed the expected alpha instead, that determines the risk aversion, risk, and gearing. Attempting to specify any two of these independently runs the risk of pushing the portfolio away from the optimal relations among the expected alpha, risk, and gearing, with negative consequences for the *IR*.

In practice, typically investors fix the risk level. Eliminating the risk aversion in favor of the risk, we find a relation between risk and gearing at optimality:

$$G^* = \left(\frac{\omega^*}{\omega_0}\right) \cdot \sqrt{\frac{N}{2\pi}} \tag{8}$$

What can we learn from Equation (8)? First, at a high level, it relates the optimal gearing to the ratio of target portfolio residual risk, ω^*, to $\frac{\omega_0}{\sqrt{N}}$, the residual risk of an equal-weighted portfolio of N stocks, each with residual risk, ω_0. The higher that ratio, the higher the optimal gearing.

Consider an example. Our investment universe comprises 250 stocks, each with 25% residual volatility, and we build an optimal portfolio with 5% risk. According to Equation (8), that portfolio has a natural gearing of 1.26. That is, a completely unconstrained portfolio would naturally end up with gearing of 1.26. We can also use Equation (8) to show that a gearing of one portfolio ($G = 1$) has a natural volatility of 3.96%.

Now let's consider two different situations mentioned earlier. What if our portfolio manager builds a 10% risk portfolio with a gearing of one? Forcing the gearing to be exactly one, that is, imposing a gearing constraint, leads to a suboptimal portfolio. The natural ungeared portfolio has 3.96% risk. To increase that to 10%, while keeping gearing fixed, requires dropping assets to reach that higher risk level. At the extreme, the portfolio could end up with only one stock long and one stock short. In these undergeared portfolios, we are giving up on diversification, and on our information ratio, in order to reach a target risk level.

The second situation involved building a 3.3% risk portfolio and gearing it three times. In other words, they first build a gearing of one portfolio with 3.3% risk (an overgeared portfolio) and then use additional leverage to achieve a risk level of 10%.[2] That involves overgearing. They would have been better off building a gearing of one portfolio with 3.96% risk and then using a bit less leverage to achieve a risk of 10%. Our 3.3% portfolio will need to ignore some alpha information to reach that artificially low risk level. At the extreme, we will build equally weighted long and short portfolios (given that each stock has identical and independent residual risks). This solution, forcing the gearing of three, also leads to suboptimal portfolios.

The Simple Model Extended: Gearing Penalties

Of course, in the real world, portfolios may not have an optimal trade-off between risk and gearing. Suboptimal gearing has a cost.

2. As we will see below, if the natural risk of a gearing one portfolio is 3.96%, the lowest risk we can achieve while keeping gearing at one is 3.16%. That portfolio has equal long positions on all the positive alpha names and equal short positions on all the negative alpha names. A 3.3% risk portfolio with gearing of one is achievable but near the lower limit of risk.

To analyze its impact, we can extend the simple model's utility function, Equation (2), to include a penalty for gearing. To do this, we will separately account for long positions, l_n, and short positions, s_n, defining l_n and s_n as nonnegative. In this simple model with uncorrelated residual returns, no transactions costs, and symmetric alphas, a positive alpha will on average result in $s_n = 0$ and a negative alpha will on average result in $l_n = 0$. In what follows we will enforce that explicitly.

Our extended utility function is:

$$\begin{aligned} U \Rightarrow & \sum_{n=1}^{N} \alpha_n \cdot (l_n - s_n) - \lambda \cdot (l_n - s_n)^2 \cdot \omega_0^2 \\ & - IC \cdot \omega_0 \cdot \phi \cdot \sum_{n=1}^{N} l_n - IC \cdot \omega_0 \cdot \phi \cdot \sum_{n=1}^{N} s_n \\ & - \sum_{n=1}^{N} \eta_n^l \cdot l_n - \sum_{n=1}^{N} \eta_n^s \cdot s_n \end{aligned} \tag{9}$$

The first two terms in Equation (9) represent the alpha and risk as before. Remember that, depending on the sign of the alpha, we know that for any particular asset either l_n or s_n is zero. The (new) third and fourth terms penalize or encourage gearing, depending on whether ϕ, the gearing penalty, is positive or negative.[3] We multiply these terms by $IC \cdot \omega_0$ to ease the notational burden later. As a beneficial side effect, this also gives the gearing penalty a natural scale; for instance, $\phi = 1$ creates a gearing penalty equal to a one-standard-deviation alpha. The last two terms—asset specific holdings penalties—provide degrees of freedom necessary to satisfy the basic conditions that long and short holdings are nonnegative.

Note that the gearing penalty doesn't force our solution to a specific gearing. The penalty approach can do this on average, but different samples of alphas lead to different gearing levels that vary around an average.

Our game plan is to solve for the optimal holdings and see how our alpha, risk, gearing, and information ratio change as we vary the gearing penalty. We present the results here; further details of the calculations are in Appendix A.

For the portfolio alpha, α_P, we find:

$$\frac{\alpha_P}{\alpha^*} = \sqrt{\frac{2}{\pi}} \cdot \left[I_2(\phi_+) - \phi \cdot I_1(\phi_+) \right] \tag{10}$$

where:

$$I_n(x) \equiv \int_x^{\infty} \exp\left\{ \frac{-y^2}{2} \right\} y^n \, dy, \tag{11}$$

3. The astute reader will note that when ϕ is negative, we are adding a convex function to something we are maximizing. This is a recipe for trouble as the normal first-order conditions no longer guarantee optimality. We will also see (e.g., Exhibit 2) that for fixed risk that we cannot increase gearing beyond its natural level by more than about 25%. That maximum gearing occurs in our example when all the long positions are equal and all the short positions are equal.

and:

$$\phi_+ \equiv \begin{cases} 0 & \phi < 0 \\ \phi & \phi \geq 0 \end{cases} \tag{12}$$

The quantity α^* is defined in Equation (7), and is the alpha of the gearing-unconstrained ($\phi = 0$) portfolio.

Similarly, we can estimate portfolio risk, ω_P, and gearing as:

$$\frac{\omega_P}{\omega^*} = \left(\frac{2}{\pi}\right)^{1/4} \sqrt{I_2(\phi_+) - 2\phi I_1(\phi_+) + \phi^2 I_0(\phi_+)} \tag{13}$$

$$\frac{G}{G^*} = I_1(\phi_+) - \phi I_0(\phi_+) \tag{14}$$

where, again, we computed ω^* and G^* in Equation (7).

The intrinsic information ratio (IR) follows from the fundamental law of active management (Grinold (1989)), and is:

$$IR_{int} = \frac{\alpha^*}{\omega^*} = IC \cdot \sqrt{N} \tag{15}$$

The implemented information ratio is simply the ratio of the alpha and risk estimates. From these, we can calculate the transfer coefficient, TC, as the ratio of implemented information ratio to intrinsic information ratio:

$$\begin{aligned} TC &= \frac{\left(\alpha_P / \omega_P\right)}{\left(\alpha^* / \omega^*\right)} = \frac{IR}{IC \cdot \sqrt{N}} \\ &= \left(\frac{2}{\pi}\right)^{1/4} \left[\frac{I_2(\phi_+) - \phi I_1(\phi_+)}{\sqrt{I_2(\phi_+) - 2\phi I_1(\phi_+) + \phi^2 I_0(\phi_+)}}\right] \end{aligned} \tag{16}$$

Notice that, unlike the IR, the transfer coefficient is independent of N. With a gearing penalty of zero, the optimization naturally chooses the optimal gearing, and the transfer coefficient is 1.

Exhibit 1 shows the transfer coefficient at a fixed gearing, and Exhibit 2 shows the transfer coefficient at a fixed risk.

Characteristics of Undergeared Versus Overgeared Portfolios

Interestingly, undergeared and overgeared portfolios are quite different, and this leads to an asymmetry in the transfer coefficient for deviations away from optimal gearing. In fact, undergeared and overgeared portfolios are so different that it is possible to distinguish between severely undergeared and overgeared portfolios with only a glance at the portfolio holdings.

Exhibit 1 shows how the transfer coefficient varies as a function of risk, with the portfolio held at fixed gearing throughout. This graph is derived from Equations (13), (14), and (16) by eliminating the gearing penalty ϕ in terms of the gearing level and the risk aversion λ in terms of the risk level.

EXHIBIT 1 Transfer Coefficient at Fixed Gearing

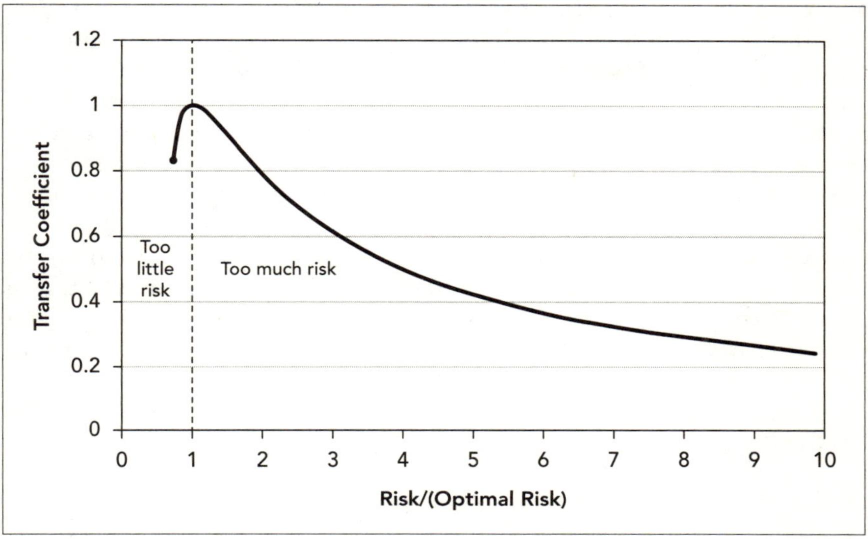

In the original portfolio manager example, we used Equation (8) to show that if the manager is constrained to $G = 1$, the ideal risk level is 3.96%. In Exhibit 1, the horizontal axis is measured in multiples of the idea risk, and for a multiple of 1, the transfer coefficient is at its maximum of 1. In this simple model, changes in the target gearing G would change the optimal risk level but not the shape of Exhibit 1.

At the right-hand side of Exhibit 1, the portfolio bears too much risk for the given level of gearing. To increase the risk, more and more portfolio weight is concentrated in high-alpha names, and assets with low alphas are forced out of the portfolio entirely (thereby discarding all the information in those alphas). In the limiting case, we end up with a single name on the long side and a single name on the short side. This may be fine from an alpha perspective, but it is devasting from a risk perspective, and the huge increase in risk causes the transfer coefficient to drop toward zero in our simple model. More plausibly, a portfolio with three times the ideas risk level has a transfer coefficient of only about 0.6, the same ballpark as an otherwise unconstrained long-only implementation.

Another perspective is that these high-risk, concentrated portfolios are undergeared, a point we return to below. A key characteristic of an undergeared portfolio is the collection of assets at exactly zero weight; this characteristic persists even in more realistic optimizations that include bounds, transaction costs, and so on.

At the left-hand side of Exhibit 1, the portfolio experiences too little risk for the level of gearing. The transfer coefficient drops off more quickly, but it proves impossible to reduce the risk beyond a certain point, and at that point the transfer coefficient is still over 80% of the maximum. The lower bound on the risk is a consequence of Hölder's inequality, which relates the risk level and the gearing level (see Appendix B). As we force the portfolio to lower and lower risk levels, it overdiversifies by taking substantial positions even in assets with low alphas. In the limiting case, the portfolio consists of two equal-weighted portfolios: all the assets with positive alphas are held with equal weight on the long side, and all the assets with negative alphas are held with equal weight on the short side. The portfolio ignores all but the sign of the alpha, but because there is still information in the sign alone, the *IR* approaches a positive constant as the portfolio approaches the minimum risk.[4]

Again, another perspective is that these low-risk portfolios are overgeared, and, given the earlier interpretation, it's clear that an identifying characteristic of an overgeared portfolio is the absence of assets in a region around zero weight, and again, this characteristic persists even in more realistic optimizations.

Exhibit 2 displays the transfer coefficient as a function of gearing, for fixed risk.

EXHIBIT 2 Transfer Coefficient at Fixed Risk

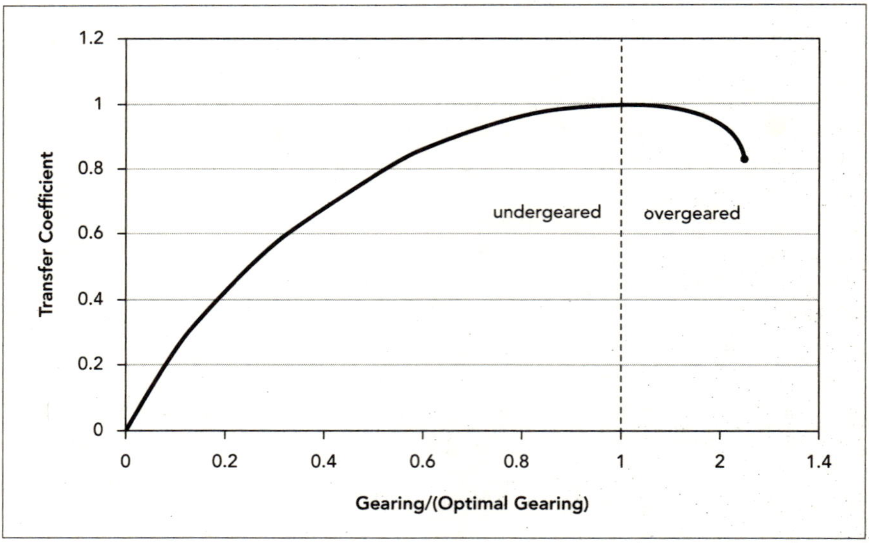

On the right, the portfolios are overgeared, and tend to have equal-weighted long and short sides, with no assets near zero weight. On the left, the portfolios are undergeared, and tend to have a collection of assets at exactly zero weight. The transfer coefficient drops off more rapidly for

4. The equal weighting follows from our assumption that all assets have equal risk and are uncorrelated. More generally, overgearing should, in the limit, lead to long and short portfolios built to minimize risk.

overgeared portfolios, but is bounded below, while severe undergearing can reduce the transfer coefficient all the way to zero.

To summarize the differences, undergeared portfolios tend to show an abnormally large number of holdings at exactly zero weight; overgeared portfolios tend to show an abnormal absence of assets in an entire region around zero weight; and perfectly geared portfolios show a smooth distribution of portfolio weights. In our simple model with no transactions costs and normally distributed alphas, the portfolio weights (Equation (3)) are normally distributed when the portfolio is optimally geared.

For completeness, Exhibit 3 shows the efficient frontier for three different levels of gearing, as well as the gearing unconstrained line.

EXHIBIT 3 Efficient Frontiers

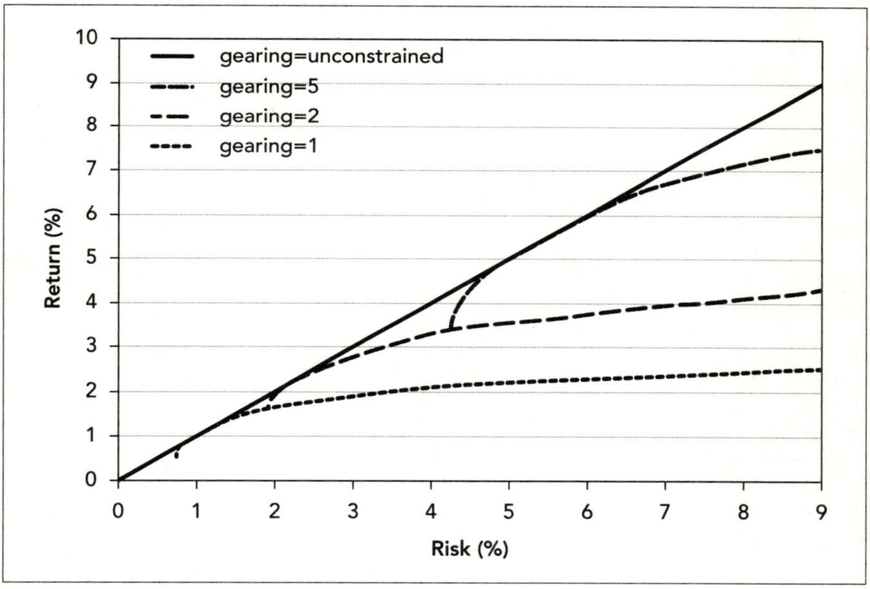

The form of the efficient frontiers follows from the analysis so far. There is a point of highest *IR*, where the gearing, expected risk, and expected return are all compatible. To the left of that point, the portfolio is overgeared, and the efficient frontier terminates at the maximally overgeared portfolio—in this case, an equal-weighted portfolio. To the right of the point of maximum *IR*, the portfolios are undergeared. Although our simple model shows no upper bound on the risk, in principle at the far right the efficient frontier also terminates, at the risk and return characteristics of the maximum alpha asset.

Exhibit 3 also clarifies that the scenarios we are considering here aren't simply movements along the capital market line. The capital market line is straight precisely because gearing varies with risk as we move along it. If we fix the gearing, the efficient frontier curves as shown in Exhibit 3.

Empirical Analysis

We now want to verify aspects of the prior analysis under more realistic conditions. We can show how gearing affects implemented information ratios by generating random alphas and building optimal market neutral portfolios at different risk and gearing levels. For this case, we ignore all constraints other than the gearing constraint, and ignore transactions costs, but include a realistic covariance between assets.

Exhibit 4 shows the subsequent active efficient frontiers based on the expected risk and return. In spite of widely differing underlying parameters, the behavior displayed in Exhibit 4 very closely matches the pattern in Exhibit 3.

EXHIBIT 4 Efficient Frontiers—No Other Constraints

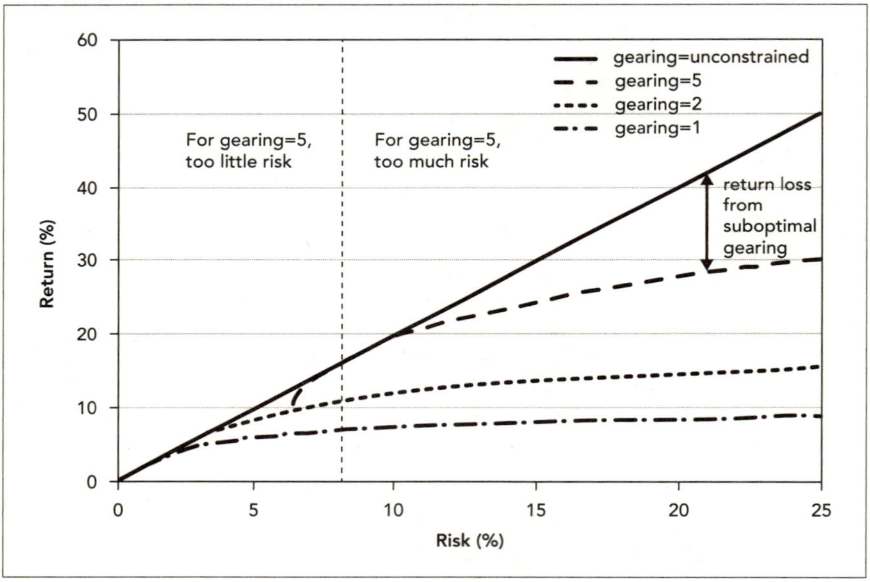

The distance between the straight line and the curved frontier is the loss in *IR* from the gearing constraint, and, as we saw before, this can be very high. To achieve levels of risk beyond the optimal point, the portfolio reduces diversification and concentrates in few names. At risk levels below optimal, the portfolio overdiversifies, ignoring information available in the alphas to lower risk.

Exhibit 5 shows the results of more realistic analysis, including alpha, risk, transaction costs, asset-level bounds, and in three of the four cases a gearing constraint.

EXHIBIT 5 In Practice Efficient Frontiers

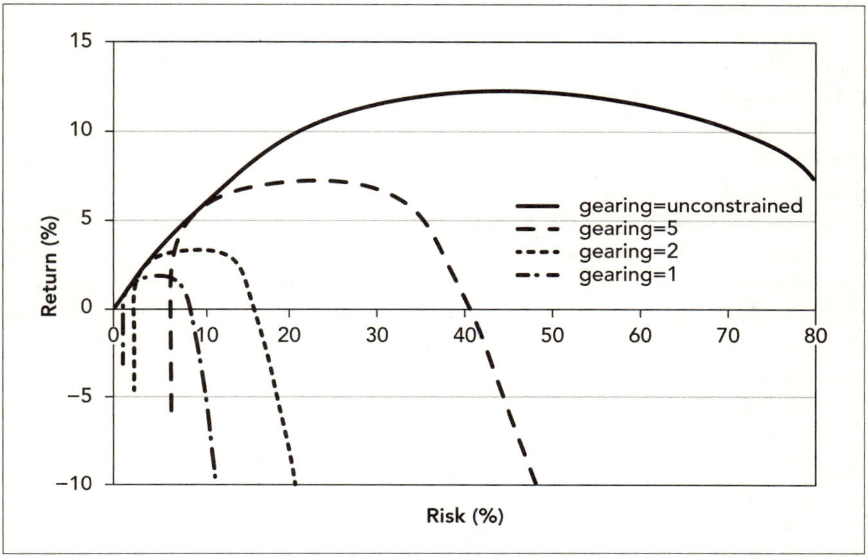

The graph is again based on expected alpha and risk, and the risk is allowed to go to extremely high levels only to indicate that even the gearing unconstrained curve dips down for high enough risk levels.

A crucial difference between Exhibits 4 and 5 is that in Exhibit 5 the gearing-constrained portfolios have negative expected returns for some risk levels. This is due entirely to expected transaction costs, indicating that the cost of suboptimal gearing is potentially much higher for portfolios that bear significant transaction costs.

In Exhibit 5 the gearing-unconstrained curve has the highest return for any value of the risk, because the portfolio is allowed to naturally find the level of gearing compatible with the risk. The other curves have a shape similar to those generated by our extended model but have somewhat different behavior at very low and very high risk.

In our simplified model, without transaction costs, the minimum-risk portfolio at a fixed gearing is an equal-weighted portfolio. The minimum-risk portfolios in Exhibit 5 are very similar to those in our simple model, but when the portfolios are subject to transaction costs, it is costly for assets to flip from the long side to the short side or vice versa. The net result is that for minimum-risk portfolios and the level of transaction costs we have chosen, the transaction costs overcome the alpha, leading to a negative expected *IR*. In the middle of each fixed-gearing curve, there is a more normal balance between alpha, risk, transaction costs, and gearing, resulting in *IR*s that are positive, but still lower than the gearing-unconstrained *IR*. As before, at a fixed gearing there is a single optimal risk level, or, at a fixed risk there is a single optimal gearing level. Finally, to the far right in Exhibit 5, at very high risk levels the performance drops precipitously again as excessive transaction costs are incurred in order to reach the risk target.

Other Real-World Issues

Empirical analysis inevitably identifies other practical issues important for determining optimal gearing. For instance, optimal gearing will vary over time. From Equation (8), we know that gearing depends on the risk target, the asset risk levels, and number of the assets in the opportunity set. As asset risk levels change, to keep portfolio risk constant and the transfer coefficient high requires changing gearing in a compatible way. As volume patterns change, or funds grow, even N can change as less liquid names move out of the investment universe.

Our models so far have assumed stock borrowing is free, which doesn't hold in the real world. If analysis implies that we should increase gearing, for example, and run a portfolio at lower risk, we must also account for the higher stock borrowing costs that will entail.

Finally, the regulatory environment may limit the allowed values for the gearing, even to the point of eliminating the point of highest IR. In particular, if regulations force the portfolios to be undergeared (as opposed to overgeared), the resulting transfer coefficients can potentially be as low as the transfer coefficients of long-only portfolios.

Conclusions

In constructing investment products, managers may set risk targets according to client preferences, and meet those risk targets by altering the asset mix suboptimally. In products that use leverage, managers typically set gearing independent of choice of risk. Yet, as we have shown, risk and gearing incompatibility has a surprisingly large cost. The efficiency loss is asymmetric; undergearing is ultimately more costly than overgearing. Overgeared portfolios are identified by their equal weighting of assets, with no assets near absolute weight of zero; undergeared portfolios are identified by an abnormal collection of assets at exactly zero weight.

While this analysis has focused on the costs of ignoring the connection between risk and gearing in market neutral portfolios, it is but an example of a more general issue beyond market neutral—compatibly setting portfolio risk, gearing, and shorting when we can freely specify all three.

References

Clark, Roger, Harindra de Silva, and Steven Sapra. 2004. "Toward More Information-Efficient Portfolios." *Journal of Portfolio Management*, Fall, 54–62.

Clark, Roger, Harindra de Silva, and Stephen Thorley. 2002. "Portfolio Constraints and the Fundamental Law of Active Management." *Financial Analysts Journal* 58 (September/October): 48–66.

Grinold, Richard C. 1989. "The Fundamental Law of Active Management." *Journal of Portfolio Management* 15 (3): 30–37.

Grinold, Richard C., and Ronald N. Kahn. 2000a. *Active Portfolio Management*. 2nd ed. New York: McGraw-Hill.

Grinold, Richard C., and Ronald N. Kahn. 2000b. "The Efficiency Gains of Long-Short Investing." *Financial Analysts Journal* 56 (November/December).

Markowitz, H. M. 1959. *Portfolio Selection: Efficient Diversification of Investment*. Cowles Foundation Monograph 16. New Haven, CT: Yale University Press.

Rosenberg, Barr. 1976. "Security Appraisal and Unsystematic Risk in Institutional Investment." *Proceedings of the Seminar on the Analysis of Security Prices*, 171–237. Chicago: University of Chicago Press.

Sharpe, William F. 1963. "A Simplified Model for Portfolio Analysis." *Management Science* 9 (January): 277–93.

Treynor, Jack, and Fischer Black. 1973. "How to Use Security Analysis to Improve Portfolio Selection." *Journal of Business* 46 (1): 68–86.

CHAPTER 29

Optimal Gearing

Appendix A

Portfolios Subject to Gearing Penalties

Maximizing utility leads to the holdings:

$$l_n = \frac{1}{2\lambda\omega_0^2}\left(\alpha_n - IC \cdot \omega_0 \cdot \phi - \eta_n^l\right)$$

$$s_n = \frac{1}{2\lambda\omega_0^2}\left(-\alpha_n - IC \cdot \omega_0 \cdot \phi - \eta_n^s\right) \tag{A1}$$

where we choose η_n^l and η_n^s to enforce $l_n \geq 0$ and $s_n \geq 0$. For instance, if $(\alpha_n - IC \cdot \omega_0 \cdot \phi) \leq 0$ for a positive alpha, we set η_n^l to exactly $(\alpha_n - IC \cdot \omega_0 \cdot \phi)$ to pin the asset at $l_n = 0$. If $(\alpha_n - IC \cdot \omega_0 \cdot \phi) \geq 0$ for a positive alpha, we need not enforce $l_n \geq 0$ explicitly and can set η_n^l to zero.

Given the optimal portfolio, Equation (A1), we can calculate its characteristics—alpha, residual risk, and gearing—and how they vary as we change the risk aversion and the gearing penalty.

While we must separately analyze the cases of positive and negative penalties, ϕ, for gearing, we can summarize the results with single formulas. To calculate the expected portfolio alpha, we estimate the expected average contribution per stock (active position times stock alpha), and multiply by the number of stocks.

Three integrals arise in the calculations below. They are all of this type described in Equation (11) in the main text. Some of these integrals can be done explicitly. A few particular values of use are: $I_0(0) = I_2(0) = \sqrt{\frac{\pi}{2}}$ and $I_1(0) = 1$.

We will calculate the portfolio risk in detail, starting with the simpler $\phi \le 0$ case. The short and long sides give the same contribution, so we only need to calculate one. The expected variance of an asset on the long side is:

$$\begin{aligned}
\omega_0^2 E\left[l_i^2\right] &= \omega_0^2 \int_0^\infty P(\alpha)\, l^2 \, d\alpha \\
&= \omega_0^2 \int_0^\infty \frac{1}{\sqrt{2\pi IC^2\omega_0^2}} \exp\left\{\frac{-\alpha^2}{2IC^2\omega_0^2}\right\}\left(\frac{1}{2\lambda\omega_0^2}\right)^2 (\alpha - IC\cdot\omega_0\cdot\varphi)^2 \, d\alpha \\
&= \frac{IC^2}{4\lambda^2\sqrt{2\pi}} \int_0^\infty \exp\left\{\frac{-x^2}{2}\right\}(x-\varphi)^2 \, dx \\
&= \frac{IC^2}{4\lambda^2\sqrt{2\pi}}\left[I_2(0) - 2\varphi I_1(0) + \varphi^2 I_0(0)\right]
\end{aligned} \tag{A2}$$

When $\phi \ge 0$, the gearing penalty forces the long side assets toward zero, and if the alpha is low enough the gearing penalty will force the asset out of the portfolio entirely. Then:

$$\begin{aligned}
\omega_0^2 E\left[l_i^2\right] &= \omega_0^2 \int_0^\infty P(\alpha)\, l^2 \, d\alpha \\
&= \omega_0^2 \int_0^\infty \frac{1}{\sqrt{2\pi IC^2\omega_0^2}} \exp\left\{\frac{-\alpha^2}{2IC^2\omega_0^2}\right\}\left(\frac{1}{2\lambda\omega_0^2}\right)^2 (\alpha - IC\cdot\omega_0\cdot\phi)_+^2 \, d\alpha \\
&= \frac{IC^2}{4\lambda^2\sqrt{2\pi}} \int_\phi^\infty \exp\left\{\frac{-x^2}{2}\right\}(x-\phi)^2 \, dx \\
&= \frac{IC^2}{4\lambda^2\sqrt{2\pi}}\left[I_2(\phi) - 2\phi I_1(\phi) + \phi I_0(\phi)\right]
\end{aligned} \tag{A3}$$

$$\omega_0^2 E\left[l_i^2\right] = \frac{IC^2}{4\lambda^2\sqrt{2\pi}}\left[I_2(\phi_+) - 2\phi I_1(\phi_+) + \phi^2 I_0(\phi_+)\right] \tag{A4}$$

Recalling that both the long and short sides contribute to the risk, the total portfolio risk is:

$$\frac{\omega_P}{\omega^*} = \left(\frac{2}{\pi}\right)^{1/4} \sqrt{I_2(\phi_+) - 2\phi I_1(\phi_+) + \phi^2 I_0(\phi_+)} \tag{A5}$$

in terms of the $\phi = 0$ risk level, $\omega^* = \dfrac{IC\sqrt{N}}{2\lambda}$.

The expected gearing and alpha calculations are very similar to the expected variance calculation, and so are omitted. The formula for the gearing is:

$$\frac{G}{G^*} = I_1(\phi_+) - \phi I_0(\phi_+) \tag{A6}$$

in terms of the $\phi = 0$ gearing, $G^* = \frac{N \cdot IC}{2\lambda\omega_0\sqrt{2\pi}}$. The formula for the alpha is:

$$\frac{\alpha_P}{\alpha^*} = \sqrt{\frac{2}{\pi}}\left[I_2(\phi_+) - \phi I_1(\phi_+)\right] \tag{A7}$$

in terms of the $\phi = 0$ alpha, $\alpha^* = \frac{N \cdot IC^2}{2\lambda}$.

Appendix B

Hölder's Inequality and the Upper Bound on Gearing

Hölder's inequality is:

$$\sum_{i=1}^{N}|x_i y_i| \le \left(\sum_{i=1}^{N}|x_i|^p\right)^{\frac{1}{p}}\left(\sum_{i=1}^{N}|y_i|^q\right)^{\frac{1}{q}} \tag{B1}$$

where $\frac{1}{p}+\frac{1}{q}=1$.

Plugging $p = q = 2$, $x_i = \frac{1}{\omega_i}$, and $y_i = \omega_i h_i$ into Hölder's inequality yields:

$$\sum_{i=1}^{N}|h_i| \le \sqrt{\sum_{i=1}^{N}\frac{1}{\omega_i^2}}\sqrt{\sum_{i=1}^{N}\omega_i^2 h_i^2},$$

or:

$$G \le \frac{\sqrt{N}}{2}\frac{\omega^*}{\bar{\omega}} \tag{B2}$$

where ω_i is the specific risk of asset i, ω^* is the portfolio specific risk, and $\bar{\omega}$ is a typical asset risk, defined by $\bar{\omega} \equiv \left(\frac{1}{N}\sum_i {}^{1}\!/_{\omega_i^2}\right)^{-1/2}$.

Combining the upper bound with the calculation of optimal gearing in our simple model shows that the ratio of the maximum gearing to the optimal gearing satisfies:

$$\frac{G_{\max}}{G^*} = \sqrt{\frac{\pi}{2}} \approx 1.25. \tag{B3}$$

This ratio is a pure number, independent of the risk level, *IC*, and so on. Notice that the maximum gearing produced by our extended simple model satisfies this relationship.

Finally, note that similar bounds can be found by applying the Cauchy-Schwarz inequality, which is obviously related to Hölder's inequality.

30

The Dangers of Diversification[1]

Managing Multiple Manager Portfolios

Investors have long built diversified portfolios to meet their return objectives. They diversify across asset classes and across managers. Unfortunately, the promise of diversification doesn't always materialize, especially in the case of diversifying across managers. Ex ante, multiple manager portfolios look like they have high information ratios and low risk. Ex post, and especially during crisis periods, those portfolios experience poor performance with risk much higher than expected. Multiple manager portfolios act to concentrate risk into generic ideas that are a significant source of that high risk and poor performance.

This chapter will attempt to provide new insight into this age-old problem. Our goal is to clearly analyze the challenges of diversifying across managers. But as you will see, although we will propose some solutions, these are not easy to achieve. We have found no magic bullets.

Our insight into this issue developed because our training in quantitative investing confronted our experience managing a multistrategy hedge fund through the 2007–2008 financial crisis. We hope to bring the best of theory and practice to this issue. For concreteness, we will specifically focus on the challenges of running a multistrategy fund. In this case, we not only control the allocation across the funds, we control the underlying funds. This is

1. This chapter originally appeared as "The Dangers of Diversification: Managing Multiple Manager Portfolios" by Gerald Garvey, Ronald N. Kahn, and Raffaele Savi in the *Journal of Portfolio Management*, Winter 2017, 13–23. The authors thank Jan Speth for data analysis and Sharon Hill for useful comments as the discussant for this paper at a *Journal of Investment Management* conference. This chapter reflects the opinions of the authors and not necessarily those of their employer.

better than the challenge faced by most investors, who can adjust allocations but not the individual funds.

Managing multiple managers or multiple funds is a central issue facing pension funds, endowments, foundations, funds of funds, managers of multistrategy funds, and consultants. In fact, it's a central issue for all investors trading off expected return against risk. And there is a standard approach for addressing this issue. If we understand the expected return to each manager or fund, as well as their variances and covariances, we can build an optimal combination of managers or funds just as we build optimal combinations of individual securities. This idea goes back at least to Barr Rosenberg in the 1970s, if not earlier. Peter Bernstein reports the following in *Capital Ideas* (2005):

> Rosenberg could see no reason why Markowitz's ideas about individual stocks would not apply equally well to a stable of individual portfolio managers. Managers should be willing to take on more risk, to have the courage of their convictions—just as long as the client employed a diversified group of managers.
>
> When I reminded Rosenberg that MULMAN[2] had changed the world, he replied with typical understatement, "That's interesting. Well, I don't know. It did improve the dialog between the more thoughtful clients and their managers."

But in fact there are at least three problems with the solutions that come out of this analysis. First, and arguably most important, is the problem of *generic risk concentration.* Multistrategy portfolios concentrate generic ideas and diversify away orthogonal ideas. Many investors have not sufficiently appreciated this problem.

Imagine that each underlying fund's return results from a combination of generic and orthogonal ideas. Generic ideas are well known and used, typically applicable across regions, and sometimes highly correlated across managers (think "smart beta").[3] So generic equity ideas include value, momentum, size, quality, and the low-beta anomaly. Orthogonal ideas are not widely known or used, not always usable in every region because of data availability, unique to individual managers, and uncorrelated across managers. During the financial crisis, generic factor correlations spiked, as did generic factor risk. This was a dominant source of multistrategy risk, and a plausible mechanism underlying tail risk for such funds. Furthermore, generic factor risk and correlations across such factors often increase significantly during crises (and not just the 2007–2008 financial crisis), whereas nonfactor risks generally do not.

Beyond the problem of multistrategy portfolios' concentration of generic risk, these portfolios face two other problems: *the temptation to leverage* and *the tendency to forget the big picture.* The temptation to leverage arises because the multistrategy fund has very low forecast risk according to this

2. This refers to the Barra product for optimizing a set of multiple managers.
3. For more on smart beta, see Kahn and Lemmon (2015), for example. This is Chapter 23 in this book.

analysis.[4] The ex ante multistrategy information ratio is quite high. But we can't eat ex ante information ratios. In principal, we can use leverage to boost risk while keeping the information ratio roughly unchanged, but since the financial crisis, investors are uncomfortable with much leverage, which is also harder to acquire. The phrase "forgetting the big picture" aptly describes how we tend to run the underlying funds as if they are stand-alone funds rather than components of a multistrategy fund. But a central tenet of modern finance is that we need to focus on the portfolio, not its separate constituents.

Concentrating Generic Risk

Let's examine all these problems in more detail, starting with generic risk concentration. To start, consider the following simple model. Assume every underlying fund relies on a combination of orthogonal and generic insights, and so every underlying fund's risk budget is invested partly in orthogonal insights and partly in generic insights. How does the fraction of the multistrategy fund's risk budget invested in generic insights compare to that same fraction for the underlying funds?

Exhibit 1 shows the analysis in the simple case where we assume generic insights are 100% correlated across funds and orthogonal insights are completely uncorrelated across funds. (The assumption that generic insights are 100% correlated is extreme, and we will next analyze the empirical evidence.) Exhibit 1 shows that the multistrategy fund structure concentrates risk into generic insights—the more funds, the more concentration.

Now let's consider some empirical evidence. We will focus on the four generic insights contained in the Fama–French (1992) and Carhart (1997) models: market beta, size, value, and momentum. And we will analyze the 862 active US large-cap long-only funds in the eVestment database with monthly returns from January 2011 through December 2013. Regressing each fund's active returns against the Fama–French–Carhart factors, one factor at a time, the R^2 statistic provides the fraction of the active variance attributable to each factor.[5] We assign a sign to this result based on the sign of the regression coefficient. For example, a growth fund may have a negative exposure to value, and so we give the R^2 statistic a negative sign.

To see the impact of the multistrategy fund structure, we will simulate multistrategy portfolios by equal weighting five funds chosen at random. We generate 1,000 such simulated multistrategy portfolios and compare the fraction of multistrategy fund risk in a factor to the average fraction of the five underlying funds. Exhibit 2 shows the results for our four factors, including regression lines through the 1,000 point scatterplots.

4. The risk forecast is too low. It assumes a "normal" environment without accounting for the probability of a crisis and much higher factor correlations.

5. We are running four separate univariate regressions instead of one multivariate regression, so we can analyze each factor separately. But in this case, because the factors are relatively uncorrelated, overall risk allocated to the factors shouldn't differ too much from just adding the individual R^2.

EXHIBIT 1 Fraction of Multistrategy Risk Budget in Generic Ideas

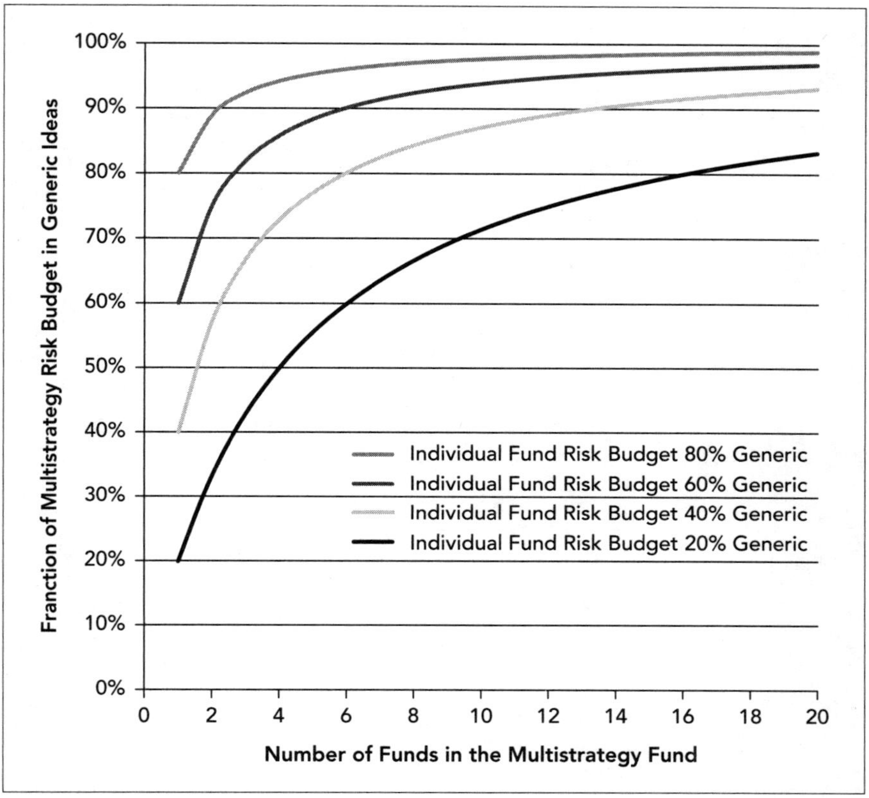

Overall, the results are in line with the theory. The five-fund portfolios have more of their risk budgets in these generic ideas than do the underlying funds. According to the linear fit, the increase ranges from a low of 1.3 for value to a high of 2.1 for size. So, for example, an average five-fund portfolio will have 2.1 times as much of its risk (variance) in size as do the underlying funds on average. Size may exhibit the largest effect because most long-only funds overweight small stocks. Value may exhibit the smallest effect because there are many growth funds to counterbalance the value funds. But for each factor analyzed, as expected, the five-fund portfolios increase the concentration in generic factor risk.

To understand the importance of generic factor risk in the context of a multistrategy fund, let's consider a numerical example based upon real-world experience going through the financial crisis. We consider a multistrategy fund that equally weights five underlying long-short funds, each run at 5% risk. The multistrategy fund will add leverage to achieve 10% overall risk.

EXHIBIT 2 Factor Risk for Multifund Portfolios Versus Underlying Funds

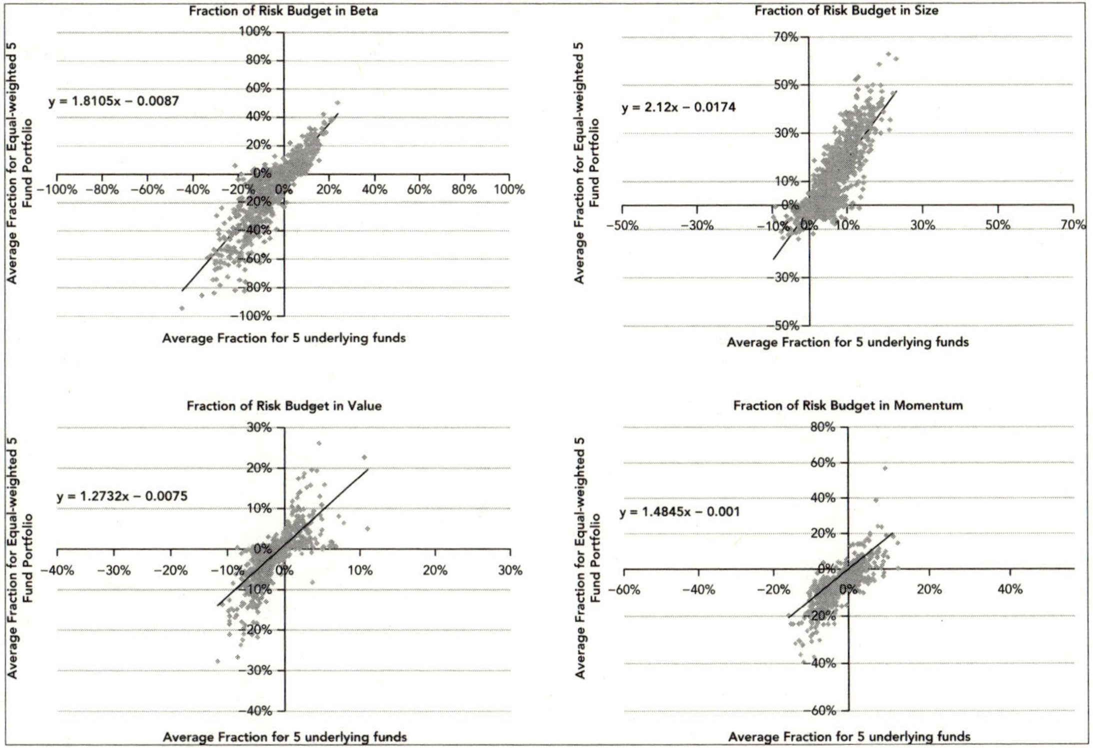

Source: eVestment, BlackRock

Each fund contains both generic and orthogonal insights, and so the return, r_n, to underlying fund n consists of a generic piece, g_n, and an orthogonal piece, o_n:

$$r_n = g_n + o_n. \tag{1}$$

For example, the underlying funds could invest in different regions (North America, Europe, Asia) and combine exposure to value (e.g., book-to-price) with exposures to orthogonal insights in each region.

Each fund's risk is hence:

$$\sigma_n^2 = \sigma_g^2 + \sigma_o^2. \tag{2}$$

In this simple model, we assume that each underlying fund takes the same amount of generic and orthogonal risk (so there is no subscript n for σ_g and σ_o), and each fund therefore has the same overall risk level and risk budget allocation between generic and orthogonal risk. In particular, the fraction of the risk budget invested in generic insights is:

$$fr_g \equiv \frac{\sigma_g^2}{\sigma_g^2 + \sigma_o^2}. \tag{3}$$

For concreteness, we will assume that when constructing the multistrategy fund (in the precrisis period), each fund is 40% generic and 60% orthogonal (i.e., $fr_g = 40\%$), and that the generic returns are 10% correlated:

$$Corr\{g_n, g_m\} = 0.1, \quad n \neq m. \tag{4}$$

Based on these assumptions, plus the previous assumption that each fund takes 5% risk, we find that:

$$\sigma_g = 3.2\% \tag{5}$$

$$\sigma_o = 3.9\% \tag{6}$$

$$Corr\{r_n, r_m\} = 0.04, \quad n \neq m. \tag{7}$$

This leads to an unlevered multistrategy fund risk of 2.4%, and hence the need for leverage of 4.15 to achieve the 10% risk level.[6] Also, though each underlying fund has 40% of its risk budget in generic ideas, at the multistrategy level, 48% of the risk budget is in generic ideas.

So far, so good. But during the financial crisis, and especially during the quant crisis of early August 2007, we saw generic factor risk increase significantly and saw correlations across generic factors spike. Using roughly the numbers we observed for the value factor across regions,[7] let's assume that

6. The unlevered fund would be 100% long and 100% short, while the levered fund would be 415% long and 415% short.

7. The exact number depends significantly on the specific definition of value, as well as the measurement period during the financial crisis. We will discuss some empirical evidence in the next section.

generic risk increases by a factor of 3.5, from 3.2% to 11.1%, and that correlations across generic factors increase by a factor of 5.0, from 0.1 to 0.5:

$$\sigma_g : \quad 3.2\% \Rightarrow 11.1\%$$

$$Corr\{g_n, g_m\} \quad n \neq m: \quad 0.1 \Rightarrow 0.5. \tag{8}$$

The orthogonal risks remain unchanged.

What then happens to our underlying funds and to the multistrategy fund? The underlying funds go from 5% risk to 11.8% risk, increasing by a factor of 2.4. Each underlying fund goes from 40% generic risk to 89% generic risk. And the correlations across the funds jump from 0.04 to 0.45. At the multistrategy level, risk goes from 10% to 36%, increasing therefore by a factor of 3.6. And the multistrategy fund goes from 48% generic risk to 96% generic risk. So the multistrategy fund risk increases much more than the underlying fund risk, because not only do the underlying fund risks increase, but the correlations between the funds also increase. And almost all of the multistrategy fund risk is generic risk.

Generic Factor Risks and Correlations

The quant crisis of early August 2007 inspired some of the numbers in our example, but spikes in volatilities and correlations occur more often than just that one very extreme event. Let's look at the evidence for this, focusing on the value and momentum factors in three Barra models: USE3 for US equities, EUE3 for European equities, and JPE3 for Japanese equities.

Let's first look at how volatilities spike, focusing here on factor volatilities estimated using daily factor returns with a 23-day half-life over the period from December 31, 1996, through June 10, 2016. For these six factors, we have daily estimated volatilities for almost 10 years. We calculate the average of these six volatilities every day, rank them, and identify the dates corresponding to the 50th percentile, the 95th percentile, and the 99th percentile. Exhibit 3 shows the six volatilities on each of those dates.

EXHIBIT 3 Selected Factor Volatilities Across Regions

	VALUE			MOMENTUM		
PERCENTILE	USE3	EUE3	JPE3	USE3	EUE3	JPE3
50	1.32%	1.72%	1.62%	2.80%	2.45%	2.98%
95	2.93%	2.55%	2.30%	7.59%	4.72%	5.43%
99	3.84%	3.39%	4.02%	13.55%	7.44%	7.60%

Sources: MSCI, BlackRock

Exhibit 3 shows that value and momentum volatilities tend to spike together (remember that each row corresponds to a particular set of dates). We can also see that momentum is a more volatile factor than value.

In our example, we assumed that generic factor risk was initially 3.2%, roughly consistent with the numbers in Exhibit 3. We also assumed that volatility jumped to 11.1%, higher than most of the numbers in Exhibit 3. However, the example was inspired by factor behavior during the quant crisis of early August 2007, which played out over just a few days, and Exhibit 3 uses volatilities estimated with 23-day half-lives—that is, longer periods.

What about correlations across these factors? Let's look at correlations between USE3, EUE3, and JPE3 factor returns conditional on the returns to USE3 factors. In other words, what happens to cross-regional factor correlations when US factor returns are particularly negative? Exhibit 4 displays these correlations of five-day returns (with overlapping periods) from December 31, 1994, through June 10, 2016.

EXHIBIT 4 Conditional Factor Correlations Across Regions

	VALUE CORRELATIONS		MOMENTUM CORRELATIONS	
USE3 FACTOR RETURN PERCENTILE	USE3–EUE3	USE3–JPE3	USE3–EUE3	USE3–JPE3
5	0.45	0.15	0.74	0.47
50	−0.02	0.09	0.35	−0.03

Sources: MSCI, BlackRock

According to Exhibit 4, when US value significantly underperforms, the correlation with European value jumps from a median of about zero to 0.45, and the correlation with Japan value moves somewhat less, from a median of 0.09 to 0.15. The increases in correlations across regions jumps even more in the case of momentum. In periods when US momentum significantly underperforms, the correlation with European momentum jumps from a median of 0.35 to 0.74, and the correlation with Japanese momentum jumps from a median near zero to 0.47. These increases in correlations are roughly consistent with our previous example, in which we assumed generic factor correlations jumped from 0.1 to 0.5.

Finally, let's look at data on total versus specific risk distributions. Is it true that in crises, total risks increase more than residual risks? Exhibit 5 shows the distributions of average stock total and specific risk for US, European, and Japanese stocks in the MSCI ACWI index for dates from December 31, 1996, through June 10, 2016. Specific returns are residual to the Barra factors for the region; all returns are in local currency. We estimate risk (volatility) over time using a 23-day half-life, and for every date we average total and specific risk across stocks.

EXHIBIT 5 Distributions of Total and Specific Risk

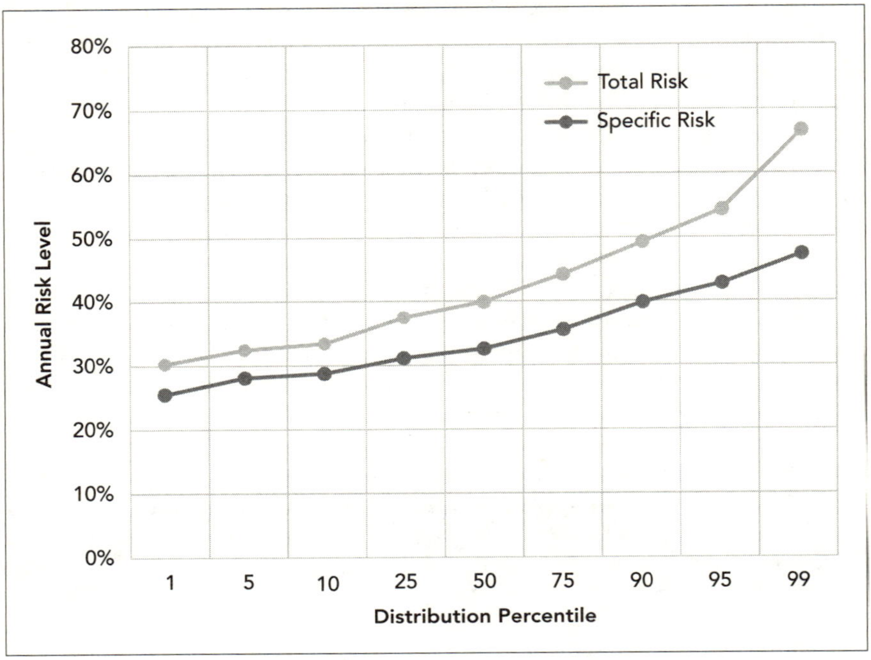

Sources: MSCI, BlackRock

As you can see, total risk and specific risk both vary over time, but total risk varies more than specific risk, and has bigger outliers at the high end of the range.

The Temptation to Leverage and the Tendency to Forget the Big Picture

Beyond concentrating generic risk, we discussed two additional problems faced by multistrategy funds. The temptation to leverage arises because the multistrategy risk level is too low. It appears that we have created a product with very low risk and a very high information ratio (because the risks diversify across funds while the returns still add up), but these high information ratios, combined with very low risk, lead to underwhelming expected returns.

Finance theory going back at least to Tobin (1958) tells us to then use leverage to achieve our desired level of risk, with limited impact on our information ratio. But is leverage the answer in this case? We have already discussed how correlations and risks can increase dramatically during crises. We can quickly find ourselves overlevered, leading to too much risk. Also, leverage will increase the challenge of managing funds through such periods.

Since the financial crisis, most investors have had a limited appetite for risk. Leverage does not seem to be the answer to this problem.

Forgetting the big picture is somewhat more subtle. Portfolio managers tend to manage each underlying fund in the multistrategy fund as if it is a stand-alone fund, in particular, with a level of diversification appropriate for a stand-alone fund. But, in fact, investors cannot access those underlying funds. They aren't available stand-alone. Investors can only access the multistrategy fund, which can then appear overdiversified, with thousands of positions long and short.

If the multistrategy fund focused solely on US equities and the underlying funds had specialists investing in particular sectors, we might expect each sector portfolio to be fairly risky. This is because the opportunities for diversification are more limited, with only the multistrategy portfolio achieving an attractive level of risk. In fact, that setup might be one that avoids the issues discussed in this paper. But if the underlying funds invest in different regions (e.g., North America, Europe, Asia) or in different managers investing broadly in the same region, then each fund can achieve significant diversification.

This problem of potential overdiversification relates to the temptation of leverage, in that it's all about the risk level of the underlying funds and the multistrategy fund. It does not address the concentration of generic risk problem. We discuss potential solutions to both problems in the next section.

Potential Solutions

As we have seen, multistrategy funds face a number of challenges, from risk concentrated in generic ideas to unlevered risk that appears too low. The potential solutions—which are not necessarily easy to implement—must involve focusing underlying fund risk on orthogonal ideas and increasing that risk without leverage. We can't provide recipes for identifying and implementing orthogonal ideas, though we can point out that there exist business motivations beyond the investment motivations for avoiding generic ideas. Smart beta products are increasingly popular, and they offer exposure to these generic ideas at very low fees. Active managers will have business challenges offering generic ideas at active management fees.[8]

So let's focus on the other part of the solution: increasing underlying fund risk without leverage. This must involve concentrating these underlying funds to benefit the multistrategy fund, even if somewhat suboptimal at the underlying fund level. To understand this, we need to understand these questions:

- How does concentration impact fund risk?
- How does concentration impact the fund's information ratio?

8. For a more detailed discussion of this issue, see Kahn and Lemmon (2016), "The Asset Manager's Dilemma." This is Chapter 25 in this book.

To understand the impact of concentration on the fund's information ratio, we will focus in particular on the fund's *transfer coefficient*—the ratio of the concentrated fund's ex ante information ratio relative to the ex ante information ratio of the ideal portfolio before concentration. It is also the correlation of returns between those two portfolios, which we will use in its calculation.

Concentration and Its Impacts

We start with forecast residual returns—alphas—of the form:[9]

$$\alpha_n = IC \cdot \omega_n \cdot z_n, \tag{9}$$

where IC is the information coefficient (the correlation of forecast and realized residual returns), ω_n is the residual risk for stock n, and z_n is a score with mean zero and standard deviation one. For simplicity, we assume the information coefficient is the same for all stocks in our investment universe. We build optimal portfolios, **h**, by maximizing the active utility:

$$U = \mathbf{h}^T \cdot \boldsymbol{\alpha} - \lambda \mathbf{h}^T \cdot \mathbf{V} \cdot \mathbf{h}, \tag{10}$$

where **V** is the residual covariance matrix and λ measures investor risk aversion. Assuming that residual returns are uncorrelated, and with identical residual risk ω_0 (both assumptions important only for deriving an analytic result), we find optimal holdings:

$$h_n^* = \left(\frac{IC}{2\lambda}\right) \cdot \left(\frac{z_n}{\omega_0}\right). \tag{11}$$

Note, though, that the holdings in Equation (11) correspond to an unlevered portfolio (100% long, 100% short) only for a particular choice of λ. To set leverage equal to one, assuming normally distributed scores, we rescale these holdings so that:[10]

$$h_n^* \Rightarrow \frac{\sqrt{2\pi}}{N} \cdot z_n. \tag{12}$$

This leads to portfolio risk of:

$$\omega_P^2 = \left(\frac{2\pi\omega_0^2}{N^2}\right) \cdot \sum_{n=1}^{N} z_n^2. \tag{13}$$

Each asset's contribution to the variance of the optimal portfolio is:

$$Contribution_n = \left(\frac{2\pi\omega_0^2}{N^2}\right) \cdot z_n^2. \tag{14}$$

9. See Grinold (1994) or Grinold and Kahn (2000).

10. To derive Equation (12), we use the result that the average absolute value of a normally distributed random variable with a mean of zero and a standard deviation of 1 is $\sqrt{\frac{2}{\pi}}$. See the Appendix to this chapter for a derivation of this result and several others.

Equation (14) allows us to rank stocks by their contribution to risk. Given that the scores, $\{z_n\}$, have a mean of zero and a standard deviation of one, many of the optimal holdings contribute little to risk. The best way to concentrate the portfolio is to eliminate positions that contribute the least to risk. For example, we could eliminate all stock positions with $|z_n| \le z^*$ and then rescale the portfolio:

$$h_n^*(concentrated) = \begin{Bmatrix} c \cdot z_n & |z_n| > z^* \\ 0 & otherwise \end{Bmatrix}, \tag{15}$$

where we choose c to keep leverage at 1.0.

As we do this, what happens to the transfer coefficient? This is the correlation of returns to the ideal portfolio (Equation (12)) and the concentrated portfolio (Equation (15)). Exhibit 6 displays this theoretical result based on a number of simplifying assumptions,[11] along with empirical results for four signals used by our investment team.

EXHIBIT 6 Transfer Coefficient as a Function of Stocks Eliminated

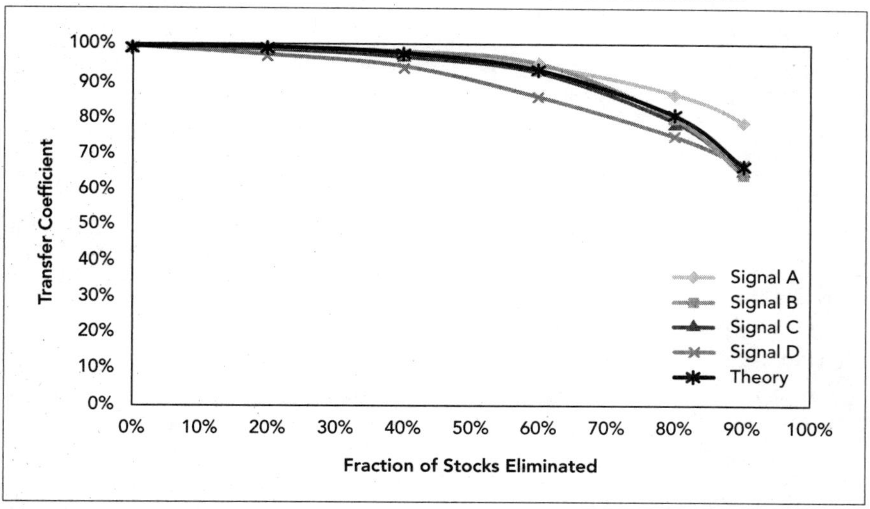

Source: BlackRock

According to Exhibit 6, the empirical results match the theory fairly well. Interestingly, we can eliminate at least 60% of the positions before having much of any impact on the transfer coefficient. In Signal A, the scores have fatter tails than a normal distribution, so we can eliminate relatively more positions before impacting the transfer coefficient, and in Signal D, the scores are more uniformly distributed than a normal distribution, so we can eliminate relatively fewer before impacting the transfer coefficient.

What about the impact of concentration on portfolio risk? Here, as we eliminate positions, we want to rescale the remaining positions so they still

11. See the appendix.

have leverage equal to one. Exhibit 7 shows the results, once again for the theory as well as the empirical result for the four signals.

EXHIBIT 7 Increase in Risk as We Eliminate Positions

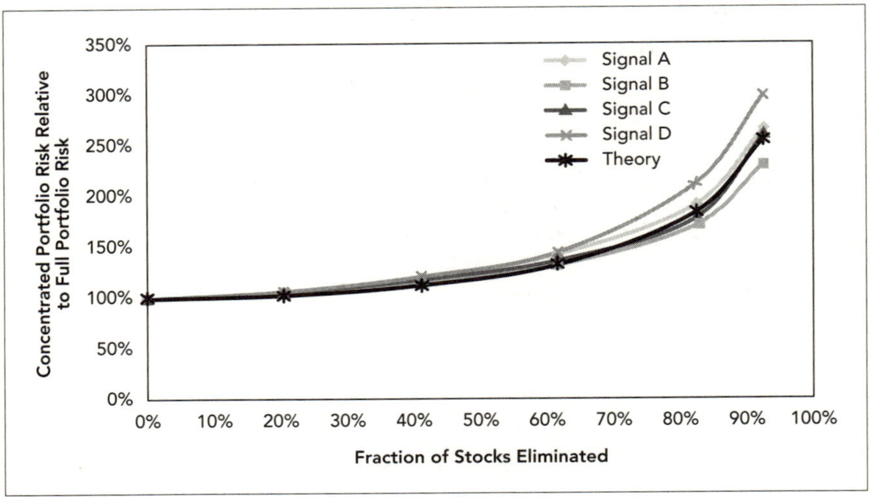

Source: BlackRock

Once again, we see that the theory fits the data reasonably well. We also see the other side of our observation that we can eliminate at least 60% of the positions without impacting the transfer coefficient. We don't impact risk very much either. Clearly, to increase risk via concentration, we must eliminate 75% to 90% of the positions.

We can put these results together in Exhibit 8 and observe the impact on the transfer coefficient as a function of the risk increase.

Thus, doubling the risk by concentrating the portfolio will drop the transfer coefficient to about 0.75, and tripling the risk through concentrating the portfolio will drop the transfer coefficient to about 0.6.

We still need to address one final point concerning how increasing risk through concentration impacts the transfer coefficient. We have focused here on the transfer coefficient of the underlying funds in our multistrategy fund. But in the end, we care about the transfer coefficient of the multistrategy fund. How does that depend on the transfer coefficients of the underlying funds. Assuming that each underlying fund has the same transfer coefficient, and that the multistrategy fund is an equal-weighted combination of the underlying funds, and leaving all the details to the technical appendix to this chapter, we find the result displayed in Exhibit 9.

Exhibit 9 displays the relationship between the multistrategy transfer coefficient and that of the underlying funds, for several levels of correlation between the ideal underlying portfolios. Note that the multistrategy transfer coefficient exceeds that of the underlying funds, so long as the correlation between the ideal underlying funds exceeds zero. Thus, correlations across the funds boost the multistrategy transfer coefficient—an intuitive result.

EXHIBIT 8 Transfer Coefficient as Function of Risk Increase

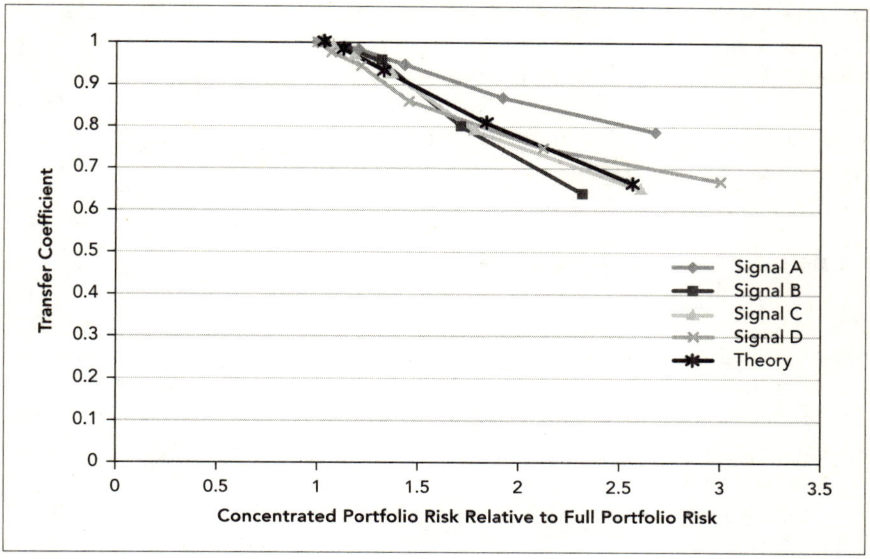

Source: BlackRock

EXHIBIT 9 Multistrategy Transfer Coefficient

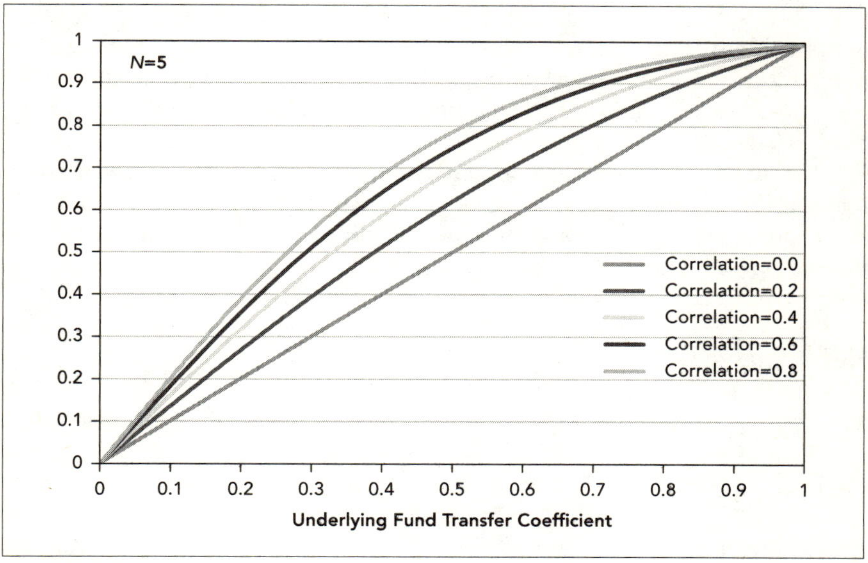

Source: BlackRock

However, an insidious aspect of this relationship is that the multistrategy transfer coefficient will go up in bad states of the world where correlations increase—precisely where we would prefer the transfer coefficient to be lower. Of course, what we would really prefer in bad states of the world are better forecasts, not worse implementation. Also note that the maximum possible boost in transfer coefficient occurs when the underlying fund transfer coefficients are about 0.5.

Concluding Observations

We have discussed a number of challenges with running a multistrategy fund, as well as some potential solutions to those challenges. For managers of multistrategy funds, these solutions are straightforward if not easy. The underlying funds should either focus substantially on orthogonal ideas, avoiding generic "smart beta" ideas, or offer the smart beta ideas for slightly more than passive investing fees. And those underlying funds need to use concentration to increase risk to attractive levels at the multistrategy level. These two efforts can help mitigate multistrategy risk spikes during crises.

As mentioned at the beginning of this paper, these challenges can impact all investors who allocate across multiple funds. Unfortunately, this involves choosing among the funds offered. Investors have very little ability to change those funds, but they can at least understand the attractiveness of funds that focus on delivering orthogonal insights. To the extent they invest in smart beta factors, they may want to manage these in a separate portfolio. Investors should also prefer higher active-risk funds, though manager incentives tend to keep active risk levels low.[12]

Finally, it is interesting to observe these systematic challenges in a problem most investors thought solved decades ago. In a world of varying risks and correlations, and limits to leverage, the old solution breaks down, requiring the considerations presented here.

References

Bernstein, Peter L. 2005. *Capital Ideas: The Improbable Origins of Modern Wall Street*. Hoboken, NJ: John Wiley & Sons.

Carhart, Mark M. 1997. "On Persistence in Mutual Fund Performance." *Journal of Finance* 52 (1): 57–82.

Fama, Eugene F., and Kenneth R. French. 1992. "The Cross-Section of Expected Stock Returns." *Journal of Finance* 47 (2): 427–65.

Grinold, Richard C. 1994. "Alpha Equals IC Times Volatility Times Score, or Real Alphas Don't Get Eaten." *Journal of Portfolio Management* 20 (4): 9–16.

12. Barr Rosenberg makes this point in the quote presented earlier in this chapter from Bernstein (2005). Richard Roll (1992) also makes this point.

Grinold, Richard C., and Ronald N. Kahn. 2000. *Active Portfolio Management*. New York: McGraw-Hill.
Kahn, Ronald N., and Michael Lemmon. 2015. "Smart Beta: The Owner's Manual." *Journal of Portfolio Management* 41 (Winter): 76–83.
Kahn, Ronald N., and Michael Lemmon. 2016. "The Asset Manager's Dilemma: How Smart Beta Is Disrupting the Investment Management Industry." *Financial Analysts Journal* 72 (January/February): 15–20.
Roll, Richard. 1992. "A Mean/Variance Analysis of Tracking Error." *Journal of Portfolio Management* 18 (Summer): 13–22.
Tobin, James. 1958. "Liquidity Preference as Behavior Towards Risk." *Review of Economic Studies* 25: 65–86.

Appendix

Scaled Holdings and the Multistrategy Transfer Coefficient

This appendix provides additional mathematical details behind two of our calculations: the correct portfolio scaling to build an unlevered long-short portfolio and the analysis of the transfer coefficient of a multistrategy fund.

Scaling Holdings for an Unlevered Portfolio

As in the main text, we assume residual returns are uncorrelated, all residual risks are an identical ω_0, we construct portfolios to maximize the mean-variance utility shown in Equation (10), and our forecast residual returns have the form shown in Equation (9): $\alpha_n = IC \cdot \omega_0 \cdot z_n$. Equation (11) in the main text provides the optimal holdings as:

$$h_n^* = \left(\frac{IC}{2\lambda}\right) \cdot \left(\frac{z_n}{\omega_0}\right) \tag{A1}$$

Note that the risk aversion parameter, λ, provides the overall scale.

We will define leverage or gearing as:

$$G \equiv \frac{1}{2}\sum_{n=1}^{N}|h_n|. \tag{A2}$$

With this definition, a portfolio that is 100% long and 100% short is unlevered, with a gearing of 1.[13]

13. Some people define leverage without the factor of ½ in Equation (A2).

We can now calculate the gearing associated with the holdings in Equation (A1):

$$G = \frac{1}{2}\left(\frac{IC}{2\lambda\omega_0}\right)\cdot\sum_{n=1}^{N}|z_n| = \left(\frac{IC \cdot N}{4\lambda\omega_0}\right)\cdot\left(\frac{1}{N}\right)\cdot\sum_{n=1}^{N}|z_n|$$

$$\Rightarrow \left(\frac{IC \cdot N}{4\lambda\omega_0}\right)\cdot E\{|z|\} \tag{A3}$$

Remember that the z_n each have a mean of zero and a standard deviation of 1. We replace the last part of the first line in Equation (A3) with the expected value of a random variable with a mean of zero and a standard deviation of 1. Equation (A3) includes an estimate of this expected value over our N observations.

To make further progress, we must make the additional assumption that the variables z_n are normally distributed. Then we can calculate this expected value:

$$E\{|z|\} = \frac{1}{\sqrt{2\pi}}\cdot\int_{-\infty}^{\infty}|z|\cdot e^{-\left(\frac{z^2}{2}\right)}\cdot dz$$

$$= \sqrt{\frac{2}{\pi}}\cdot\int_{0}^{\infty} z\cdot e^{-\left(\frac{z^2}{2}\right)}\cdot dz \tag{A4}$$

In Equation (A4), we are using the probability density of the normal distribution and then realizing that the integrand is symmetric about zero and so we can just double the result of the integral from 0 to ∞.

The indirect integral associated with Equation (A4) is easy to solve and the direct integral then gives an answer of 1:

$$\int z\cdot e^{-\left(\frac{z^2}{2}\right)}\cdot dz = -e^{-\left(\frac{z^2}{2}\right)}$$

$$\int_{0}^{\infty} z\cdot e^{-\left(\frac{z^2}{2}\right)}\cdot dz \Rightarrow 1 \tag{A5}$$

We can substitute Equation (A5) into Equation (A4) to find that:

$$E\{|z|\} = \sqrt{\frac{2}{\pi}}. \tag{A6}$$

The standard deviation of z is 1 and the expected value of its absolute value is about 0.8.

Substituting this result into Equation (A3) tells us that the gearing of the portfolio holdings is:

$$G = \left(\frac{IC \cdot N}{4\lambda\omega_0} \right) \cdot \sqrt{\frac{2}{\pi}} \tag{A7}$$

To achieve a gearing of 1 will require us to set the risk aversion λ equal to:

$$\lambda \Rightarrow \frac{IC \cdot N}{\omega_0 \cdot \sqrt{8\pi}} \tag{A8}$$

If we substitute this into the Equation (A1), we find:

$$h_n^* = \frac{\sqrt{2\pi}}{N} \cdot z_n \tag{A9}$$

This is Equation (12) in the main text.

The Transfer Coefficient of a Multistrategy Fund

What is the connection between the transfer coefficient of a multistrategy fund and the transfer coefficients of the underlying funds? Here is an analysis.

We start with N underlying funds. Each fund has return r_n and volatility σ_n. Each of these funds has a corresponding optimal paper portfolio with return q_n and volatility σq_n. In fact, we can model the portfolio return as:

$$r_n(t) = a_n \cdot q_n(t) + \varepsilon_n(t). \tag{A10}$$

Our concentrated portfolio return is a combination of optimal paper portfolio return and random noise. According to Equation (A10):

$$\sigma_n^2 = a_n^2 \cdot \sigma q_n^2 + \sigma\varepsilon_n^2. \tag{A11}$$

In our case of concentrating the optimal portfolio to increase risk:

$$\sigma_n > \sigma q_n. \tag{A12}$$

The transfer coefficient for fund n is:

$$TC_n \equiv Corr\{r_n, q_n\} = \frac{Cov\{r_n, q_n\}}{\sigma_n \cdot \sigma q_n} = \frac{a_n \cdot \sigma q_n}{\sigma_n}. \tag{A13}$$

Correlations

We start by defining the correlations between optimal paper portfolios as:

$$\rho_{mn} \equiv Corr\{q_n, q_m\} = \frac{Cov\{q_n, q_m\}}{\sigma q_m \cdot \sigma q_n} \tag{A14}$$

Key Assumptions

1. Each underlying fund has the same *TC*: $TC_n = TC$. Similarly, each fund has the same volatility and same relationship to its optimal paper portfolio: $\sigma_n = \sigma$, $\sigma q_n = \sigma q$, $\sigma\varepsilon_n = \sigma\varepsilon$, $a_n = a$.
2. The pairwise correlations between the optimal paper portfolios, ρ_{mn}, is identical across pairs: $\rho_{mn} = \rho$.
3. The multistrategy fund is an equal-weighted combination of the underlying funds.

$$r_{MS} = \left(\frac{1}{N}\right) \cdot \sum_{n=1}^{N} r_n. \tag{A15}$$

The multistrategy optimal paper portfolio is similarly:

$$q_{MS} = \left(\frac{1}{N}\right) \cdot \sum_{n=1}^{N} q_n. \tag{A16}$$

Correlations Across Funds

Now that we know the correlations between optimal paper portfolios, we can calculate the correlations between funds:

$$\rho'_{mn} \equiv Corr\{r_m, r_n\} = \frac{Cov\{r_m, r_n\}}{\sigma_m \cdot \sigma_n} = \frac{a^2 \cdot \sigma q^2 \cdot \rho_{mn}}{\sigma^2}. \tag{A17}$$

In Equation (A17), we have used some of the above assumptions to eliminate the dependence on *m* and *n*. Since the pairwise correlations between the optimal paper portfolios are all identical, we can see from Equation (A17) that the pairwise correlations between the funds are also all identical. Using that, and Equation (A13):

$$\rho' = TC^2 \cdot \rho. \tag{A18}$$

We can see from Equation (A18) that the pairwise fund correlation is less than the pairwise optimal paper portfolio correlation (except if $TC = 1$, in which case $\rho' = \rho$). We expect that result. It is a secondary reason why we are using concentration, and so it is reassuring to see it.

It will also be useful to calculate the covariance between fund *n* and optimal paper portfolio *m*, for $n \neq m$:

$$Cov\{r_n, q_m\} = a \cdot Cov\{q_n, q_m\} = a \cdot \sigma q^2 \cdot \rho, \quad n \neq m \tag{A19}$$

If $n = m$, we have Equation (A19) with $\rho \Rightarrow 1$.

Using Equation (A13), we can rewrite this as:

$$Cov\{r_n, q_m\} = TC \cdot \sigma \cdot \sigma q \cdot \rho, \quad n \neq m \tag{A20}$$

Multistrategy Transfer Coefficient

We can now calculate the transfer coefficient for the multistrategy fund:

$$TC_{MS} = \frac{Cov\{r_{MS}, q_{MS}\}}{\sigma_{MS} \cdot \sigma q_{MS}}. \tag{A21}$$

Let's tackle the components of Equation (A21) separately. We start with the covariance term:

$$Cov\left\{\left(\frac{1}{N}\right)\cdot\sum_{n=1}^{N} r_n, \left(\frac{1}{N}\right)\cdot\sum_{n=1}^{N} q_n\right\} = \left(\frac{1}{N^2}\right)\cdot\left[\sum_{n=1}^{N} Cov\{r_n, q_n\} + \sum_{n=1}^{N}\sum_{m\neq n} Cov\{r_n, q_m\}\right] \tag{A22}$$

$$= \left(\frac{1}{N^2}\right)\cdot\left[\begin{array}{l} N\cdot TC\cdot\sigma\cdot\sigma q \\ +N\cdot(N-1)\cdot TC\cdot\sigma\cdot\sigma q\cdot\rho \end{array}\right]$$

We can simplify this to:

$$Cov\{r_{MS}, q_{MS}\} = \left(\frac{TC\cdot\sigma\cdot\sigma q}{N}\right)\cdot\left[1+(N-1)\cdot\rho\right]. \tag{A23}$$

Now we need the risk estimates for the multistrategy fund and the optimal multistrategy paper portfolio. In each case, these are equal-weighted combinations of funds with identical pairwise correlations. And we know the answer in that case:[14]

$$\sigma_{MS} = \sigma\cdot\sqrt{\frac{1+\rho'\cdot(N-1)}{N}}. \tag{A24}$$

$$\sigma q_{MS} = \sigma q\cdot\sqrt{\frac{1+\rho\cdot(N-1)}{N}}. \tag{A25}$$

So substituting Equations (A23), (A24), and (A25) into Equation (A21), we find:

$$TC_{MS} \Rightarrow TC\cdot\sqrt{\frac{1+(N-1)\cdot\rho}{1+(N-1)\cdot\rho'}} \tag{A26}$$

$$= TC\cdot\sqrt{\frac{1+(N-1)\cdot\rho}{1+(N-1)\cdot\rho\cdot TC^2}}.$$

Exhibit 9 in the main text displays the multistrategy transfer coefficient as a function of the underlying fund transfer coefficient, for the case of $N = 5$, and for various different (optimal paper portfolio) correlation levels.[15]

14. See, for example, Equation (3.4) in Grinold and Kahn (2000). (See references in the main chapter.)

15. It might be more natural to analyze this as a function of fund correlations and not optimal paper portfolio correlations. And it would be easy to rewrite Equation in terms of ρ' instead of ρ. But because $\rho' = TC^2\cdot\rho$, for a fixed ρ', there is a minimum allowable TC below which $\rho > 1$. So, we have used optimal paper portfolio correlations in Exhibit 9.

A few observations:

- We can see that the multistrategy transfer coefficient exceeds the transfer coefficient at the fund level, as long as the correlation between funds exceeds zero. That implies that fund correlations help boost the transfer coefficient.
- An insidious aspect of the connection between correlations and increased *TC* is that correlations increase in bad states of the world. The multistrategy *TC* is higher in those states—exactly where we would prefer the *TC* to be lower (though as noted in the main text, we would really prefer our forecasts to be better in those states).
- Interestingly, for fund transfer coefficients around 0.5, the multistrategy boost is the largest. The maximum boost ranges from about 0.1 to about 0.25 as move from 0.2 to 0.8.
- We can also see from Equation (A26) that in the limit of very many funds, the multistrategy transfer coefficient will approach 1, independent of the transfer coefficient of the underlying funds. Of course, for investment reasons explored elsewhere, the limit of very many funds isn't very appealing.

31

The Surprisingly Small Impact of Asset Growth on Expected Alpha[1]

Warning: Optimal Portfolio Management Required

On August 27, 1997, Fidelity Investments announced it was closing its flagship Magellan Fund to new investors. The fund had underperformed the S&P 500 Index in 1994, 1995, and 1996 and was underperforming year-to-date in 1997. During that same period, assets had nearly doubled, growing from just under $32 billion to over $60 billion.

According to *European Business News* (1997) at the time, "The move represents a bid . . . to quash criticism that the fund had grown too big to be managed effectively. Some say [portfolio manager Jeffrey] Vinik's 30% shift into cash and bonds in 1996 was a direct result of the fund's extreme size and the manager's difficulty finding places to invest. Under the fund's new manager, the fund is again fully invested, but some critics say it now more closely resembles an index fund."

In somewhat conflicting observations, commentators also noted both that this move would have little impact on Magellan's asset growth, given the fund's substantial inflows from existing clients, and that this could increase Fidelity's profits if it led (through slower inflows) to better investment

1. This chapter originally appeared as "The Surprisingly Small Impact of Asset Growth on Expected Alpha" by Ronald N. Kahn and J. Scott Shaffer in the *Journal of Portfolio Management*, Fall 2005, 49–60. The authors thank Ernest Chow, Scott Clifford, Charles Lee, Richard Grinold, Dean Petrich, and Kathleen Taylor for many helpful ideas and suggestions, and Peter Landin for the title.

returns, because fees would rise substantially if the fund outperformed the S&P 500.

Was the Magellan Fund out of capacity in August 1997? Did its growth in assets lead to its underperformance? More generally, what is capacity, and how do we determine it?

Managers, sponsors, and consultants all have an interest in understanding capacity. Managers have the means to analyze and monitor capacity in considerable detail. Sponsors and consultants can't achieve that same level of detail but can monitor products for warning signs of capacity issues.

This chapter proposes a framework for characterizing capacity, and then applies it to an example product. We discuss how products should adjust as assets grow, provide some guidelines for monitoring capacity, and suggest ways to possibly increase capacity. While this framework proves quite useful, we also consider its important real-world shortcomings, which can lead it to overestimate capacity. Ultimately, those real-world details can limit capacity.

Framework

We have encountered many approaches to analyzing capacity. At one end, there are ad hoc pronouncements (e.g., capacity is 1% of market size) or general observations (e.g., "Almost every active equity manager we have come across that has gone past 2% of market cap has underperformed over the period since then."[2]) While these have the benefit of concreteness—and few products exceed such limits—they surely can't apply to everything from high-turnover statistical arbitrage to Warren Buffett's very long investment horizon.

At the other end of the spectrum, we have also seen much more detailed analyses, typically applied in backtests. Researchers look at the simulated historical performance of an investment product as they vary its assets under management. The performance tends to degrade with increasing assets, because trading costs increase. Either the fund spends more on trading, or it is less able to implement good ideas (or both).

This approach requires forecasts of trading costs that depend on trade size (i.e., trading 100,000 shares costs more in percentage terms than trading 100 shares). But this approach depends too heavily on historical performance. If an idea performed extremely well over a particular period (perhaps before more investors started using the same idea), studies based only on that period may erroneously indicate extremely high capacity.

The academic finance literature has addressed this issue with regard to market anomalies. First, can investors exploit these anomalies after costs? Second, are costs the reason why such anomalies still remain? Early researchers looked only at explicit costs (commissions and spreads), and so could address only whether investors could exploit these anomalies at

2. Private communication with William Muysken, Global Head of Research, Mercer Investment Consulting.

all. More recent work has included market impact, which allows the estimation of capacity for these anomalies. All these academic studies mainly build simplistic portfolios—long the top decile and short the bottom decile, with stocks equal or capitalization-weighted within deciles—without regard to costs.

Academic efforts include Korajczyk and Sadka (2004) and Chen, Stanzl, and Watanabe (2002). Korajczyk and Sadka (2004) look at the returns to momentum investing after trading costs and observe the asset levels at which such after-cost returns drop to zero. Chen, Stanzl, and Watanabe (2002) similarly examine size, book-to-market, and momentum strategies in the presence of trading costs. Korajczyk and Sadka take the additional step of analyzing a third portfolio construction approach, with positions dependent on market cap *and* volume, but even they do not adjust position sizes or turnover as assets increase.

Perold and Salomon (1991) provide perhaps the earliest analysis. They define capacity according to maximizing total dollars of alpha. They then estimate capacity top-down using simple assumptions of average alpha, linear market impact, and a 100-position portfolio with 100% annual turnover. They work with reasonable estimates of these quantities and do not forecast alphas or transactions costs for specific stocks.

Our approach provides detailed results, as well as sensitivity analysis, without depending too much on historical performance. It explicitly optimizes portfolio construction and trading for the asset level involved.

This approach analyzes capacity using expected active returns net of costs. In simple terms, how many of our ideas can we implement in the portfolio to deliver returns to investors? For any given asset level, we forecast the expected active return we can implement in steady state, given trading costs. We then subtract the expected costs and compare that forecast active return net of costs to the performance our clients expect.

We have applied this approach to a wide range of products—from low-risk long-only to high-risk long-short—and believe it has broad applicability. Because of the detailed input requirements, this analysis is only available to managers analyzing their own products, but the general results and intuition can also help sponsors and consultants.

Alpha Net of Costs

Following the approach of Grinold and Kahn (2000a), we assume we are given a performance benchmark. (For a long-short product, the benchmark may be cash.) We define active return, θ, as the difference between the return to our portfolio and the return to the benchmark:[3]

$$\begin{aligned}\theta &= r_P - r_B \\ &= (\mathbf{h}_P - \mathbf{h}_B)^T \cdot \mathbf{r}\end{aligned} \tag{1}$$

3. We will ignore the distinction between active and residual returns in this analysis, or, equivalently, assume that the portfolio has $\beta = 1$.

where **h** refers to the holdings in the portfolio or benchmark.

The active return fluctuates. We define alpha, α, as the expected active return, and omega, ω, as the active risk (i.e., the standard deviation of the active return):

$$\begin{aligned} \alpha &= E\{\theta\} \\ \omega &= StDev\{\theta\} \end{aligned} \tag{2}$$

We forecast active returns and risks for individual assets and portfolios.

Finally, we define the *information ratio* as the ratio of forecast active return to active risk:

$$IR = \frac{\alpha}{\omega} \tag{3}$$

The model for alpha net of cost is:

$$\alpha_{net} = \alpha_{gross} - \tau \cdot tc(A, \tau) \tag{4}$$

where τ measures the annual turnover, tc measures average trading costs, and A measures the asset level. The term $\tau \cdot tc$ measures the annual trading costs at the fund level. For example, if trades cost 1% on average, and the fund experiences 50% annual turnover, trading costs the fund 0.50% per year.

We expect average trading costs to depend on asset level and turnover. As the dollar volume of trading increases, we expect trading costs to increase. We model the ex ante gross alpha as:

$$\alpha_{gross} = IR_{int} \cdot \omega \cdot e(\tau) \tag{5}$$

The gross alpha we implement depends on three quantities: the intrinsic information ratio, IR_{int}, the active risk level, ω, and our efficiency of implementation, e.[4]

The intrinsic information ratio is the ratio of expected active return to active risk we could achieve in the absence of all constraints and costs. It depends only on our asset-level alphas, and the asset-by-asset covariance matrix, **V**:[5]

$$IR_{int}^2 = \boldsymbol{\alpha}^T \cdot \mathbf{V}^{-1} \cdot \boldsymbol{\alpha} \tag{6}$$

The efficiency measures how much of that intrinsic information ratio makes it into the portfolio, after constraints and costs. Given the actual portfolio, $\mathbf{h}_P$, which reflects the impact of constraints and costs, we can forecast its alpha, α_P, (based on its holdings, and our asset-level alphas) and its risk, ω_P:

$$\alpha_P = \mathbf{h}_P^T \cdot \boldsymbol{\alpha} \tag{7}$$

$$\omega_P^2 = (\mathbf{h}_P - \mathbf{h}_B)^T \cdot \mathbf{V} \cdot (\mathbf{h}_P - \mathbf{h}_B) \tag{8}$$

4. This concept appears in Grinold and Kahn (2000a), pp. 433–36; Grinold and Kahn (2000b); and as the transfer coefficient in Clarke, de Silva, and Thorley (2002).

5. For a derivation of this relationship, see Grinold and Kahn (2000a), pp. 135–37.

We define efficiency as:

$$IR_P \equiv \frac{\alpha_P}{\omega_P} = e(\tau) \cdot IR_{int} \tag{9}$$

The maximum efficiency is 100%. We expect efficiency to increase with turnover, up to a maximum set by constraints. At very high turnover, we overcome efficiency drag due to costs. Of course, after costs, very high turnover will be suboptimal.

So overall, we define alpha net of costs as:

$$\alpha_{net} = IR_{int} \cdot \omega \cdot e(\tau) - \tau \cdot tc(A, \tau) \tag{10}$$

How do we estimate this quantity? We can freely specify the intrinsic information ratio, IR_{int}, depending on our assessment of the power of our investment ideas looking forward. The value we achieved historically will influence this forward view, but we can forecast this quantity even without a track record.

The active risk level is typically a specified characteristic of the product.

The greater challenges are to estimate efficiency, turnover, and average transactions costs. Here we will rely on backtests, but we will not use simulated investment returns. Rather, we use only the efficiency, turnover, and cost estimates.

We approach this by first estimating efficiency and average transactions costs as functions of asset levels and turnover. We can then choose the turnover level that maximizes alpha net of costs, Equation (10). A maximum exists because, as we will demonstrate, efficiency initially rises faster than costs, but then costs catch up.

Here is one straightforward approach. We run a series of backtests over, for example, three years of monthly data. For each backtest, we choose an asset level. We also scale our transactions costs. As we scale costs down, turnover rises. Note that we are scaling the costs as a means of varying turnover. For most of these runs, costs are artificially too large or too small. But our only goal here is to estimate efficiency as a function of turnover. We will later correctly account for transactions costs.

Using Equation (9), we can estimate efficiency every month. We can calculate the average efficiency and average turnover monthly for the last two years of each backtest. We ignore the first year in an attempt to estimate steady-state quantities. (We start each backtest from the benchmark.)

We can also estimate the average trading costs incurred by the portfolio over those final two years of each backtest. Here we use the actual, not scaled, transactions costs.

Note that this approach optimizes expected alpha net of costs. Expected performance can fall significantly below this level when managers run portfolios suboptimally, in particular by ignoring the impact of asset levels. We will see this explicitly, as part of the example.

Expected Performance

To complete our analysis of capacity, we must compare alpha net of costs with the expected performance level, which we denote as $\bar{\alpha}$. We define capacity, A_{max}, as the asset level such that:

$$\alpha_{net} = IR_{int} \cdot \omega \cdot e(\tau) - \tau \cdot tc(A_{max}, \tau) = \bar{\alpha} \tag{11}$$

We have defined capacity such that our alpha net of costs meets the performance expectations of the product.

Note that this does not mean that actual performance will always meet or exceed expectations. Our actual performance will fluctuate from year to year with a mean of α and a standard deviation of ω. At capacity, assuming a symmetrical distribution of active returns, we should expect to beat expectations exactly half the time. Hence, as we discuss later, poor performance alone is not a good indicator of capacity problems.

We also treat the expected performance, $\bar{\alpha}$, as known and clearly agreed upon ex ante by investors and managers. This is not always the case.

Example

To better understand this approach, consider as an example a large-cap US equity product. We assume the product operates at 5.0% active risk (a typical domestic equity mutual fund level), and that investors expect 1.4% average active returns before fees.

The product has an intrinsic information ratio of 1.2, so in the absence of *any* constraints or costs, this product could deliver 6% active return on average. But this is a long-only fund that faces transactions costs. We need to specify its efficiency as a function of turnover. In our experience analyzing the capacity of varied products, we have used:

$$e(\tau) = e_{max} \cdot \left[1 - Exp\left\{-\left(\frac{\tau}{\tau^*}\right)^{\gamma}\right\}\right] \tag{12}$$

to capture this functional dependence. This form includes a maximum efficiency, e_{max}, and shows rapid increase in efficiency for $\tau << \tau^*$ and slow increase in efficiency for $\tau >> \tau^*$.

The exponent γ in Equation (12) arises because of the distribution of alpha horizons in our investment universe. If all our forecasts have the same horizon, then we can model efficiency as a simpler exponential function with $\gamma = 1$. If some forecasts have shorter horizons than others, the more typical case, we observe $\gamma < 1$.

In our work on product capacity, we have often found it useful to fit functional forms to our backtest results on efficiency and average costs, and then analyze capacity based on these fitted results. This is a convenience, not a requirement.

The maximum efficiency of a long-only product decreases with increasing active risk.[6] For this example, we assume $e_{max} = 50\%$.

The parameters τ^* and γ depend on the speed of our alpha information. With very slow-moving information, low turnover can achieve most of the possible efficiency. For this example, we choose $\tau^* = 60\%$ and $\gamma = 0.5$, leading to the results graphed in Exhibit 1.

EXHIBIT 1 Efficiency

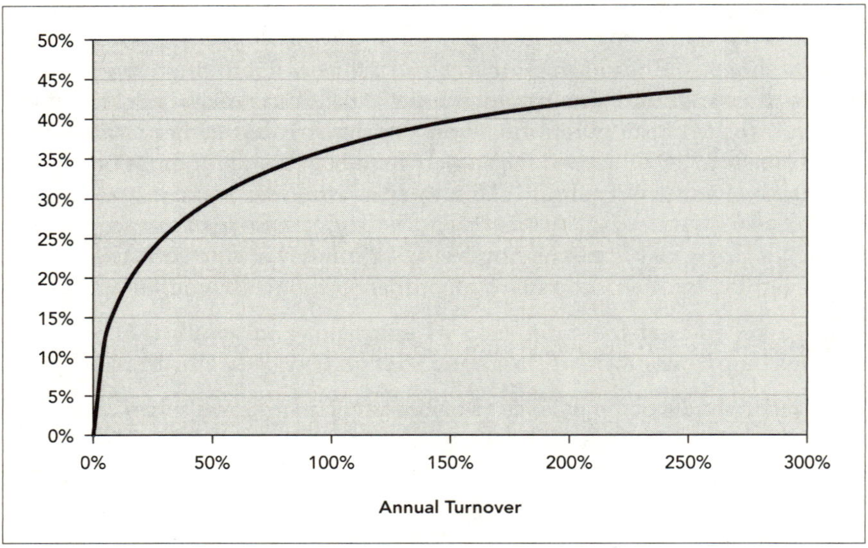

For average costs, we assume:

$$tc(A, \tau) = a + b \cdot \sqrt{A \cdot \tau} \tag{13}$$

Average trading costs include a constant term to capture average spread and commissions, plus a term that increases with dollars traded per year. The square root dependency is characteristic of many models of market impact.[7]

For this example, we assume $a = 15$ basis points, and $b = 20$ basis points per $\sqrt{\$billion / year}$. This leads to the average cost function displayed in Exhibit 2. So, if we were managing $10 billion, and had 100% turnover per year, our average trading cost would be about 80 basis points; if we turned over 200% per year, our average costs would exceed 1%.

6. Grinold and Kahn (2000b). Higher levels of active risk require larger overweights and underweights, which run into the long-only constraint more often.

7. See, for example, Grinold and Kahn (2000a), pp. 450–54. The *BARRA Market Impact Model Handbook* (1997), p. 85, also provides quantitative evidence for this dependency.

EXHIBIT 2 **Average Costs (A = $10 Billion)**

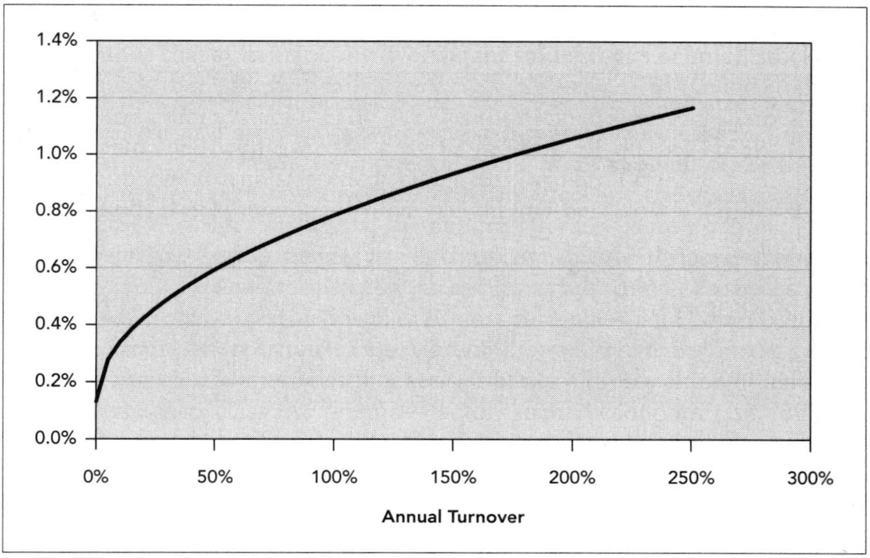

We now have everything we need to analyze capacity. For any given asset level, we choose the turnover level that maximizes Equation (10), the alpha delivered to clients. Using Equations (12) and (13), plus our assumed parameters, Exhibit 3 displays the result.

EXHIBIT 3 **Optimal Turnover**

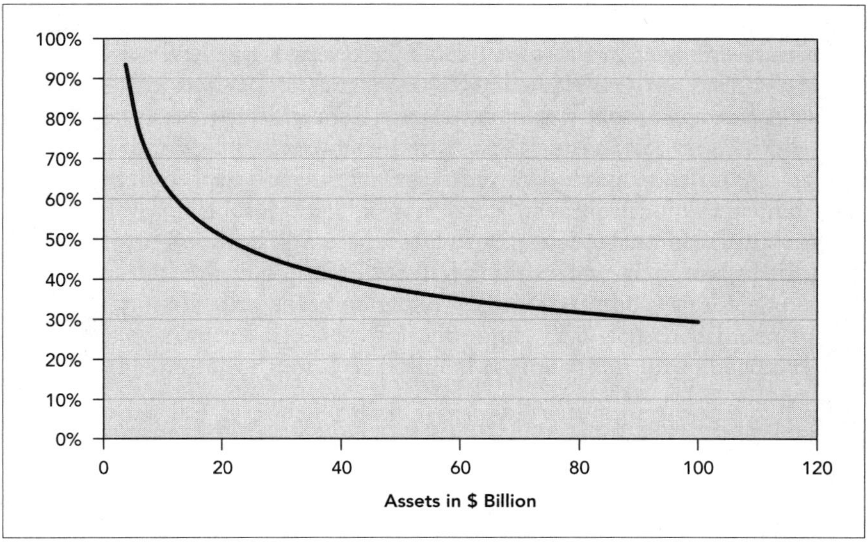

Not surprisingly, turnover falls as assets grow. At $10 billion in assets, the fund exhibits 62% turnover. This drops to 50% turnover as assets double to $20 billion.

Now that we have solved for the optimal turnover for each asset level, Exhibit 4 displays alpha before costs, the costs, and the alpha net of costs, as functions of asset level. We see several behaviors we have found quite characteristic of capacity studies. These include:

- Alpha net of costs decays slowly with increasing assets, especially for larger asset levels.
- Costs change relatively little as assets increase. Evidently, turnover declines to almost exactly offset the increase in average costs per trade as assets grow. This implies that managing capacity requires more than just monitoring costs.
- Performance erodes because alpha before costs erodes.

EXHIBIT 4 Forecast Alpha as a Function of Asset Level

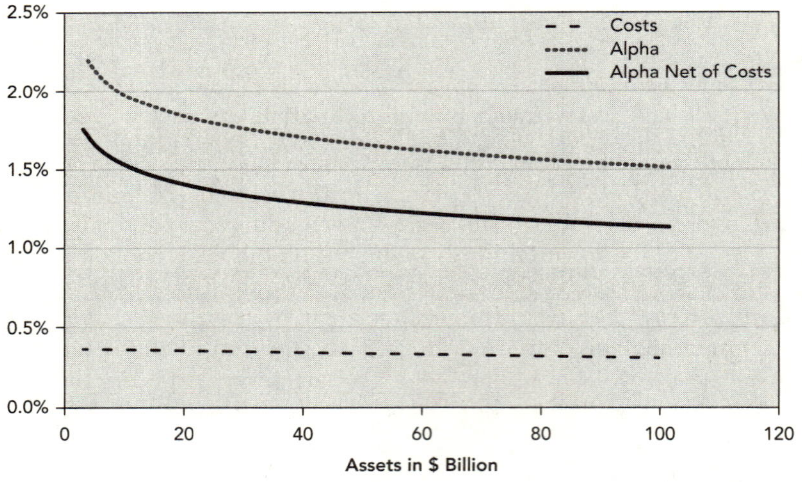

Given this behavior for alpha net of costs, what can we say about the capacity of this product? Remember that investors expect on average 1.4% alpha over time. In Exhibit 4, the alpha net of costs line crosses 1.4% at $20 billion. This is the capacity of the product.

As a practical matter, if current assets were, say, $2 billion, we would not use this analysis to assume we could add an additional $18 billion without worry. Instead, we typically use this analysis to judge whether we can increase asset levels by, for example, 20%, after which we would repeat the analysis.

Suboptimal Portfolio Management

Before analyzing the sensitivity of our results to various parameter choices, let's examine a more fundamental issue, the impact of ignoring asset level implications in portfolio management. What would happen to alpha net of costs if our example manager kept turnover constant as assets increased?[8]

For concreteness, we assume the manager turns over about 75% per year, the optimal turnover at $5 billion. For lower asset levels, 75% turnover is too low. For higher asset levels, it's too high. Exhibit 5 shows the resulting alpha net of costs compared with the optimal behavior result.

EXHIBIT 5 The Impact of Suboptimal Portfolio Management

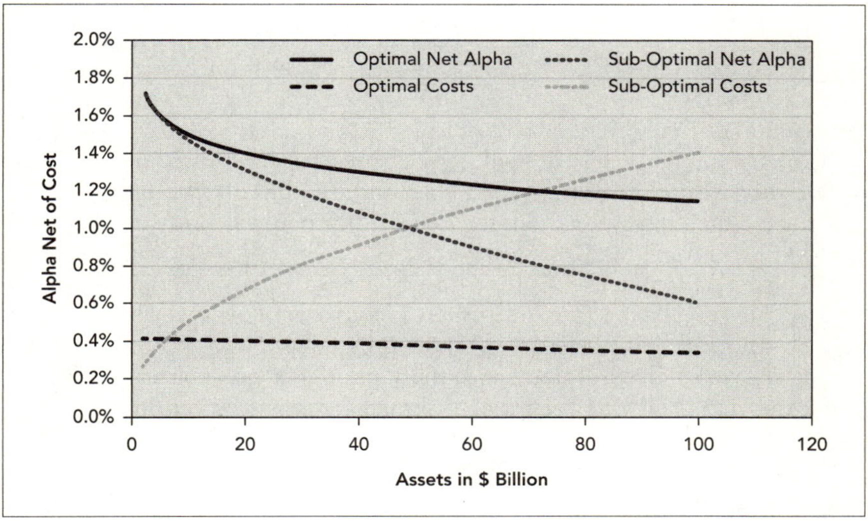

In this particular example, suboptimal portfolio management reduces capacity from $20 billion to $15 billion, a 25% reduction. More important, as assets exceed capacity, net alpha drops quickly, especially compared with the optimal case.

Exhibit 5 also shows the cause: steadily rising costs compared with the optimal case. For example, at $50 billion, optimal portfolio management can still deliver an expected 1.26% alpha net of costs. This falls to 0.99% for suboptimal portfolio management. To put it another way, at that asset level, suboptimal portfolio management leaves $135 million per year in expected alpha on the table just through a poor investment process.

8. This describes not only many investment managers, but also all academic studies in this area.

Sensitivity Analysis

To provide context for understanding this capacity estimate of \$20 billion, we find it useful to examine some additional sensitivity analysis. In particular, we analyze the sensitivity to our input IR_{int} and to the forecast costs.

Let's start with sensitivity to IR_{int}. In addition to our analysis assuming an IR_{int} of 1.2, we also analyzed raising and lowering that by 0.2. Exhibit 6 displays the alpha net of costs in all three cases, plus the estimated costs in each case.

EXHIBIT 6 Sensitivity to *IR*

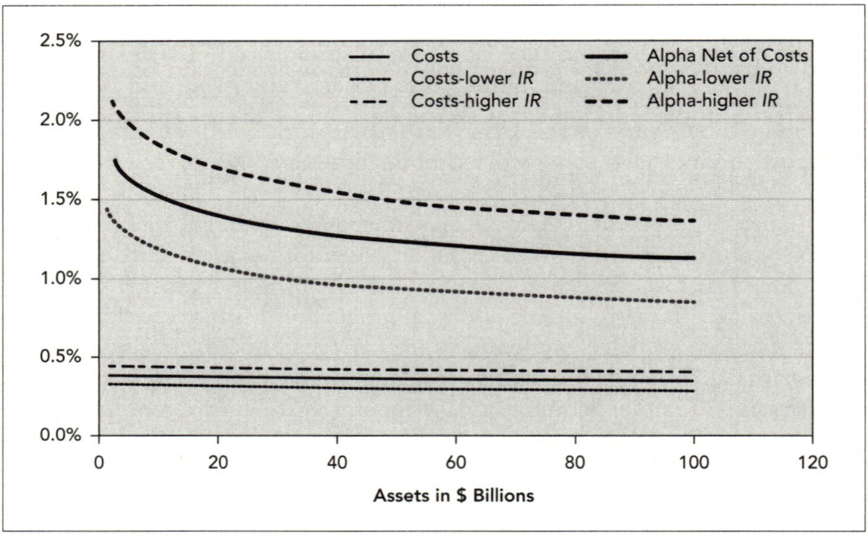

Not surprisingly, alpha net of costs increases with IR_{int}. In the absence of costs, we would expect an increase of 0.2 in *IR* to increase alpha by 1%, given the 5% active risk. As we can see in Exhibit 6, the alpha net of costs increases by only about 0.25%, due to the effect of constraints and transactions costs. We also operate at a higher cost level as IR_{int} increases. For an *IR* increase of 0.2, our costs increase by about 0.07%.

Capacity is extremely sensitive to IR_{int}. Increasing IR_{int} by 17%, to 1.4, increases capacity by a factor of five, to \$100 billion. Lowering IR_{int} by 17%, to 1.0, cuts capacity by a factor of 10, to \$2 billion

We can similarly analyze cases to estimate capacity sensitivity to transactions costs. Exhibit 7 shows the results of additional analyses, where we have simply scaled overall transactions costs, Equation (13), up or down by 20%. Effectively, we have analyzed a = 18 basis points and b = 24 basis points per $\sqrt{\$billion\,/\,year}$, and a = 12 basis points, and b = 16 basis points per $\sqrt{\$billion\,/\,year}$.

EXHIBIT 7 Sensitivity to Trading Costs

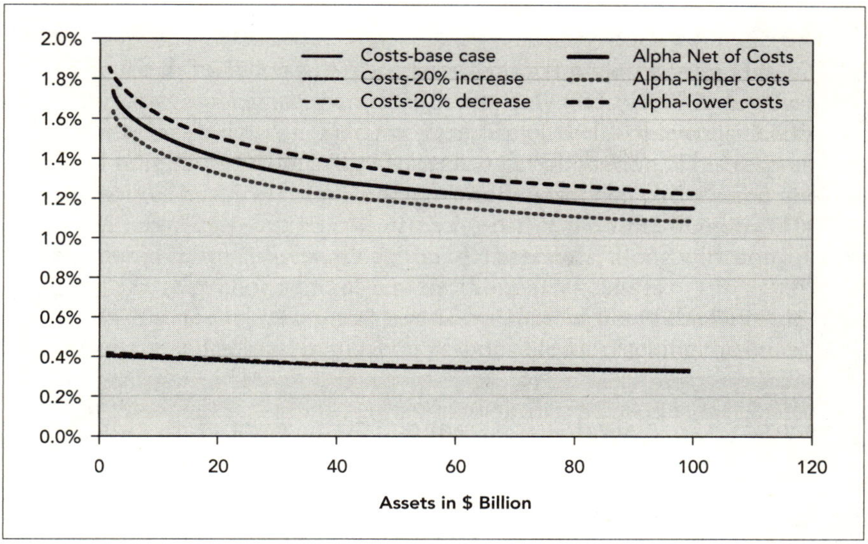

According to Exhibit 7, raising costs by 20% lowers capacity by 35%, to $13 billion. Lowering costs by 20% raises capacity by 75%, to $35 billion.

Our sensitivity analysis highlights a very important point: we cannot estimate capacity with much precision. While we previously estimated capacity as $20 billion, we should more accurately state that the capacity probably lies somewhere in the range between, for example, $10 billion and $50 billion.

But while capacity is extremely sensitive to IR_{int} and transactions costs, alpha net of costs is much less sensitive. For example, what if the "true" IR_{int} is 1.2, but we overestimate it to be 1.4, and set capacity to $100 billion? We would not be able to deliver 1.4% alpha on average over time. But, in fact, we could deliver 1.15% alpha on average over time.

Exhibit 8 shows the situation. Our overestimate of capacity leads to an average alpha that falls short of expectations by 0.25% per year. That is a surprisingly small shortfall for overestimating capacity by a factor of five. For example, it would increase our probability of delivering a negative active return over a one-year period from 39% to 41%: hardly noticeable over any period of reasonable interest.

Exhibits 9 and 10 summarize the situation.

EXHIBIT 8 **Active Return Distribution**

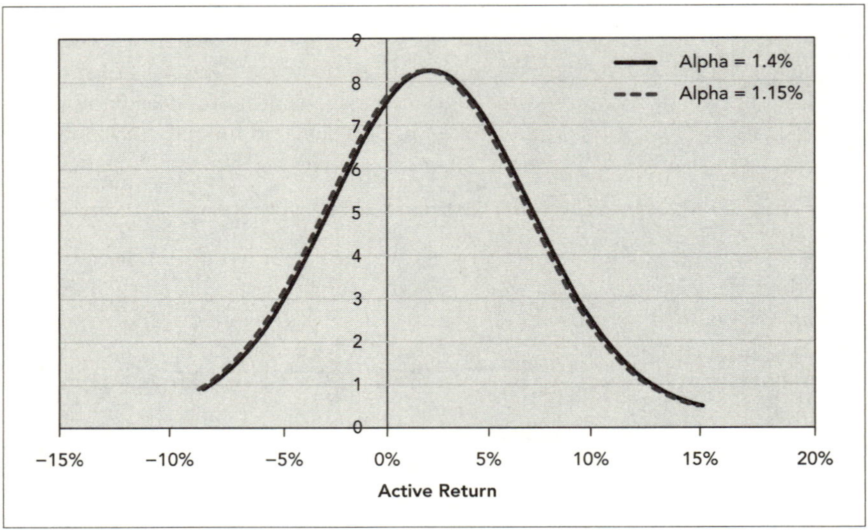

EXHIBIT 9 **Capacity Sensitivity**

		CAPACITY IN $ BILLION		
		IR=1.0	IR=1.2	IR=1.4
cost scaling	1.2	1	13	68
	1.0	2	20	100
	0.8	4	35	170

EXHIBIT 10 **Expected Alpha Sensitivity**

		ALPHA, A=$30 BILLION		
		IR=1.0	IR=1.2	IR=1.4
cost multiplier	1.2	1.00%	1.27%	1.55%
	1.0	1.06%	1.34%	1.63%
	0.8	1.13%	1.43%	1.73%

And, of course, the extreme sensitivity of capacity relates directly to the relative insensitivity of alpha net of costs. Because alpha changes so slowly with assets, moving the curve up or down small amounts will move capacity by large amounts. Fortunately, it appears that errors in capacity do not lead to substantial errors in deliverable alpha over time.

We should note that our analysis of sensitivity does depend on our choice of expected performance. If expected performance was, for example, 1.65% (a target set where alpha net of costs declines more steeply with assets), we would observe somewhat lower sensitivity (and a correspondingly more precise capacity estimate).

This analysis of the sensitivity of estimated capacity and alpha net of costs tells us two things. First, we cannot estimate capacity very accurately. Second, inaccurate estimates do not lead to dramatic performance problems.

Shortcomings of the Approach

We have presented a reasoned and clear approach for analyzing capacity and applied it to a particular example. Even so, this analysis falls short in several areas, which we can categorize by impact on our fundamental result: Equation (10).

First, our models of trading costs break down as trading volumes approach significant fractions of average daily volume. At these high levels, some trades are not completed, regardless of price. More generally, this approach requires analysis of trading volumes far beyond one's typical experience. These shortcomings will lead us to underestimate costs in general, and hence overestimate capacity, according to Equation (10).

In analyzing long-short capacity, we cannot accurately anticipate problems with locating stocks to borrow as assets increase. We also cannot easily account for other market constraints such as poison pills, which become important at high asset levels. These important market and regulatory issues will reduce our efficiency. And perhaps more important, the analysis ignores the impact of competitors following similar investment strategies. That can reduce our intrinsic information ratio by arbitraging away some of our ideas.[9]

This methodology also falls short in assuming we can always reach the target risk level. At very high asset levels, we may find this impossible. The trading costs are too high to build up and maintain the active positions consistent with target risk.

Reducing our efficiency, intrinsic information ratio, or risk level will lower the first term on the right-hand side of Equation (10), implying that we overestimate capacity if we ignore these effects.

One way to see an overall shortcoming here is by realizing that our slow decay of alpha net of costs implies that dollars of alpha (i.e., $A \cdot \alpha$) keep increasing with asset level. If this is true, the Perold and Salomon (1991) methodology would thus imply infinite capacity. At extreme asset levels, however, we must reach a maximum of dollars of alpha. This maximum will depend on the number of available stocks, and on institutional and trading constraints.

Our avoidance of these real-world issues can lead to overestimates of capacity. In fact, these real-world issues ultimately limit capacity, given that this framework implies capacity is typically very high, assuming optimal portfolio management. To mitigate this problem, we typically use capacity

9. With the benefit of hindsight, a better way to understand this is to see that all the investors who follow similar investment strategies effectively share the capacity. In our example, we estimated a capacity of $20 billion. If other managers were following a correlated strategy, they would effectively share that capacity.

analysis to investigate only whether we can increase asset levels by, for example, 20%. This helps avoid extrapolating far beyond our experience. We then manage asset growth and regularly analyze where we are relative to available capacity as assets increase.

The analysis also assumes optimal portfolio construction, given alphas, risks, costs, and constraints. As we have seen, poor portfolio construction can artificially limit capacity. Consider, for example, the technique of buying one's top 50 stocks and equal-weighting them. Such an approach ignores any impact of asset levels. The approach will have significantly lower capacity than a product with similar alpha views but the ability to increase the number of stocks if the trade-off between lower alpha before costs (in going beyond the top 50 stocks) and lower costs (reducing impact by trading across more stocks) makes that worthwhile. This will also lead to overestimates of capacity for suboptimally managed products.

Monitoring Capacity

We have mostly described how managers should analyze their own products. Now we describe how to monitor capacity, including using some aspects accessible to sponsors and consultants.

Monitoring returns is not the same as monitoring capacity. Asset levels significantly above capacity can erode alpha net of costs, but shouldn't actually generate negative returns, except through suboptimal portfolio management. The Magellan Fund's negative performance cited above cannot, by itself, tell us if it was out of capacity in August 1997.

We have seen that alpha net of costs typically decays quite slowly with increasing assets, and that in optimal approaches, trading costs remain quite constant over a large range of asset levels. Hence, monitoring realized transactions costs at the portfolio level will not flag the problem. (It will, however, identify managers who invest suboptimally.)

The most recognizable characteristic of this issue is the decay in alpha before costs as asset levels increase—so managers should monitor this quantity.

We can observe another characteristic by examining the product's risk budget. The product aims for a target active risk level. At low asset levels, it distributes that risk mainly based on alpha and risk considerations. As assets and costs increase, the product uses more of its risk budget in the most liquid stocks. This can cause problems if alphas are higher for less liquid stocks—a not atypical situation.

To monitor capacity, we should also monitor the risk allocation within the product. Sponsors and consultants should monitor, in particular, the fraction of active risk allocated to the most liquid stocks in the investment universe.

Finally, we have noted that costs remain fairly constant as assets increase. This occurs because turnover declines, and the fund spreads out trades over more stocks, as assets increase. Sponsors and consultants should expect to see these behaviors in optimally run portfolios as assets grow. And they should grow concerned if they do not observe lower turnover and an increasing number of stock positions as product assets grow.

Increasing Capacity

This analysis also points to at least two general approaches to increasing capacity. Capacity is very sensitive to intrinsic information ratios and transactions costs. Small improvements in those quantities will have bigger impacts on capacity. As Grinold (1989) shows, we can improve the intrinsic information ratio through increased skill (information coefficient) and/or increased breadth (number of independent bets per year). Research on new and better investment ideas can increase capacity.

The sensitivity to transactions costs motivates research and development of trading strategies and approaches designed to lower costs.

Conclusions

Capacity is an important concern for managers, sponsors, and consultants. We have prescribed a framework for analyzing capacity and observed several surprising behaviors:

- Alpha net of costs decays slowly with growing asset levels.
- Capacity is quite sensitive to the assumed intrinsic information ratio and costs.
- For this reason, we cannot precisely estimate capacity. Inaccuracies in such estimates have limited impact on alpha net of costs.
- Suboptimal portfolio management substantially lowers capacity.
- We can monitor capacity, although negative returns do not signify capacity problems and increasing costs usually signify suboptimal portfolio management.
- Managers can increase capacity by increasing their intrinsic information ratio and/or lowering their costs.

References

BARRA Market Impact Model Handbook. 1997. Berkeley, CA: BARRA.

Chen, Zhiwu, Werner Stanzl, and Masahiro Watanabe. 2002. "Price Impact Costs and the Limit of Arbitrage." Working paper, Yale University, February 26.

Clarke, Roger, Harindra de Silva, and Steven Thorley. 2002. "Portfolio Constraints and the Fundamental Law of Active Management." *Financial Analysts Journal* 58 (September/October): 48–66.

European Business News. 1997. August 28. http://www.hri.org/news/europe/ebn/1997/97-08-28.ebn.html#15.

Grinold, Richard C. 1989. "The Fundamental Law of Active Management." *Journal of Portfolio Management* 15 (3): 30–37.

Grinold, Richard C., and Ronald N. Kahn. 2000a. *Active Portfolio Management*. 2nd ed. New York: McGraw Hill.

Grinold, Richard C., and Ronald N. Kahn. 2000b. "The Efficiency Gains of Long-Short Investing." *Financial Analysts Journal* 56 (November/December): 40–53.

Korajczyk, Robert A., and Ronnie Sadka. 2004. "Are Momentum Profits Robust to Trading Costs?" *Journal of Finance* 59 (June): 1039–1082.

Perold, André F., and Robert S. Salomon Jr. 1991. "The Right Amount of Assets Under Management." *Financial Analysts Journal* 47 (May/June): 31–39.

32

Mean-Variance and Scenario-Based Approaches to Portfolio Selection[1]

As in The Sorcerer's Apprentice—Matters Can Get Quickly out of Hand

I. Introduction

There are two approaches to the single-period portfolio optimization problem: mean-variance[2] and scenario-based optimization.[3] The scenario approach is also known as returns-based expected utility optimization. Mean-variance has dominated in the investment management profession, while expected utility is highly regarded in the academy. There is interest among professionals in moving beyond mean and variance to capture skewness and other higher moments of portfolio returns.[4]

We compare and contrast the two approaches. The original conclusion of this article was that the risks of moving from mean-variance portfolio selection to a returns-based procedure are large and the benefits are small. As we detail the dangers one encounters in the use of returns-based optimization, we'll also show how to avoid them. However, even if we skirt all the pitfalls, there is little to show for it. We get similar answers with more fuss.

1. A previous version of this chapter appeared as "Mean-Variance and Scenario-Based Approaches to Portfolio Selection" by Richard C. Grinold in the *Journal of Portfolio Management*, Winter 1999, 10–22.
2. Markowitz (1988), Sharpe (1970), Rudd and Rosenberg (1979).
3. Arrow (1970), Samuelson (1969), Merton (1990), Hakansson (1970).
4. The Fall 1994 issue of the *Journal of Investing*, vol. 3, no. 3, is devoted to this topic.

Our conclusion 19 years after publication is not that harsh. If there are a large number of assets, the asset population changes from period to period, and performance is measured relative to a benchmark, then there is a very strong case for the mean-variance approach. If there are a few assets, the asset population is stable, and performance is measured in total return, then an expected utility return-based optimization becomes attractive if it is executed in a thoughtful manner.

Expected utility maximization has great appeal. It deals with the entire distribution of outcomes and therefore allows for more general objectives. It is indispensable in portfolio management problems where options or other distribution-altering assets can enter the mix.

At the same time returns-based optimization has several major challenges:

- The entire distribution of outcomes must be specified. By some means, one must create a set of outcomes that is rich enough to realistically replicate the entire sample space. The specification of returns has to incorporate what we want to retain from the past and what we anticipate in the future.
- A realistic objective must be specified. The portfolio manager should understand all the implications in this selection. The selection of an objective is a de facto selection of a valuation model. This is a major concern when options are a part of the portfolio strategy.
- For better or for worse, most professional investment management is explicitly or implicitly linked to performance comparisons with benchmarks.[5] The value added by investment managers is measured by active return, the difference between the portfolio's return and the benchmark's return. This arrangement leads to a disjoint view of risk. The risk of the benchmark's return and the active risk caused by a manager's portfolio holdings deviating from the benchmark's holdings are viewed differently. Managers are focused on active risk as the price paid in their attempt to produce a superior return. The returns-based expected utility approach should address this real concern.

The chapter covers a technical subject with as few equations and as little jargon as possible. In a deeper sense this is not a technical subject. It concerns the use of a tool to solve an investment problem and, above all, making sure that the portfolio manager, unlike the sorcerer's apprentice mentioned in the introduction to this section, is in control of the process.

We start with the essentials of the mean-variance and returns-based models. One of the hurdles we face in applying the returns-based procedure is specifying the sample of returns. This presents a challenge and an opportunity. In particular, one challenge is specifying an unconditional expected excess return. This specification adds a fail-safe feature to the optimization

5. Benchmarks are crucial in the world of institutional investing. In much of the United States there are explicit benchmarks. Outside of the United States and in the mutual funds industry there are peer group rankings that effectively serve as benchmarks.

(grounds it in reality). The specification of the unconditional expected excess returns requires a nonlinear version of the "grapes from wine" or reverse engineering stratagem.

With the unconditional expected returns specified, we indicate how investment research in the form of forecasts of exceptional return can be employed in a manner that produces sensible portfolios. Toward the close we indicate how options or cash can be added to the mix.

We are not going to cover several related topics: determining how many points are enough in the return distribution, models of semivariance, importance sampling,[6] or predicting kurtosis and skewness.[7] We have ignored transactions costs although it should be apparent how they could be added to the analysis.

II. Mean-Variance Portfolio Selection

Mean-variance optimization asks us to select a portfolio P with holdings $\mathbf{p} = \{p_n\}_{n=1,N}$ of N assets in order to maximize:

$$\{\mu + \alpha\}' \cdot \mathbf{p} - \frac{\gamma}{2} \cdot \mathbf{p}' \cdot \mathbf{V} \cdot \mathbf{p}. \tag{P1}$$

The optimization is subject to constraints that the portfolio holdings *sum to one* and lie in a set of permissible portfolios C;[8] that is, we want $\mathbf{p} \in C$ and $\mathbf{e}' \cdot \mathbf{p} = \sum_{n=1:N} p_n = 1$.

The terms in Equation (P1) are:

- γ is a coefficient of risk aversion.
- $\mathbf{V}$ is an N by N covariance matrix for asset returns.
- μ is an N vector of *unconditional* expected excess returns. In this case excess means in excess of the return on a risk-free investment.
- $\{\mu + \alpha\}$ is an N vector of *conditional* expected excess returns. The alpha, α, is the information that separates the unconditional and conditional expectations.
- $\mathbf{e}$ is a summation vector; a vector of ones.

The mean-variance approach has been successful because of its flexibility, robustness, and an ability to address concerns of great importance to portfolio managers. For many problems, accurate covariance estimates, $\mathbf{V}$, are available either internally or through a vendor of risk models. The availability of $\mathbf{V}$ allows portfolio managers to concentrate on α, the crucial source of value added.[9]

6. See Dantzig and Infanger (1993).
7. See Kahn and Stefek (1996) on "Heat, Light, and Downside Risk." This is Chapter 27 in this book.
8. C is compact and convex.
9. See Chopra and Ziemba (1993).

When there is no information, that is, when $\boldsymbol{\alpha} = 0$, then we should make sure that the optimization will land us in a safe place. This safe place is usually a benchmark or model portfolio such as the S&P 500, TOPIX, FTSE, All Ords, etc. To illustrate this fail-safe approach, consider a portfolio M with positions described by an N element vector $\mathbf{m}$. M can stand for model portfolio or market portfolio according to your tastes. If the model portfolio satisfies the constraints, a reasonable assumption, that $\mathbf{m} \in \mathrm{C}$ and $\mathbf{e}' \cdot \mathbf{m} = 1$, then we can use:

$$\boldsymbol{\mu} = \gamma \cdot \mathbf{V} \cdot \mathbf{m}. \tag{1}$$

to define $\boldsymbol{\mu}$. This reverse engineering procedure is called "grapes from wine."[10] Notice that multiplying Equation (1) through by the model holdings $\mathbf{m}$ yields:

$$\mu_M = \gamma \cdot \sigma_M^2, \tag{2}$$

where $\mu_M = \boldsymbol{\mu}' \cdot \mathbf{m}$ and $\sigma_M^2 = \mathbf{m}' \cdot \mathbf{V} \cdot \mathbf{m}$. Equation (2) relates the unconditional expected excess return on the model portfolio to the risk aversion and the variance of the model portfolio. That ratio, μ_M / σ_M, is called a Sharpe ratio, SR. In the example we follow throughout this chapter, $\mu_M = 5.5\%$ and $\sigma_M = 15.56\%$. Thus, we have $SR = 5.5/15.56 = 0.353$ and by Equation (2) we can infer the risk aversion parameter must be $\gamma = SR/\sigma_M = 0.353/.1556 = 2.27$.

The reader can verify that:

$$SR = \sqrt{\boldsymbol{\mu}' \cdot \mathbf{V}^{-1} \cdot \boldsymbol{\mu}}. \tag{3}$$

Deviations of the portfolio holdings $\mathbf{h}$ from the model/benchmark holdings $\mathbf{m}$ are the positions the investment manager takes in order to add value. Taking these active positions causes additional risk. That *active risk* is defined for portfolio P as:

$$\omega_P = \sqrt{\{\mathbf{p} - \mathbf{m}\}' \cdot \mathbf{V} \cdot \{\mathbf{p} - \mathbf{m}\}}. \tag{4}$$

The lure enticing the manager to take active risk is the information $\boldsymbol{\alpha}$. The strength of the alpha is captured by the information ratio, the amount of active return we expect to squeeze out of these alphas per unit of active risk.[11] The information ratio depends on the alphas. It is defined as:

$$IR(\boldsymbol{\alpha}) = \sqrt{\boldsymbol{\alpha}' \cdot \mathbf{V}^{-1} \cdot \boldsymbol{\alpha}}. \tag{5}$$

Note the similarity of (3) and (5). The larger the information ratio, the more active risk we will be willing to take. If portfolio $\mathbf{p}$ is *optimal* for (P1), then its predicted active risk (Equation (4)) is approximately given by:

$$\omega_P \approx \frac{IR(\boldsymbol{\alpha})}{\gamma}. \tag{6}$$

10. Grapes from wine is a useful and general technique. See Grinold (1996), "Domestic Grapes from Imported Wine," for an application to currency markets.
11. See Grinold and Kahn ([1995] 2000), Chapter 4.

The approximation is very close if there are few constraints or if $IR(\alpha)$ is small, say, less than 0.1. For the risk aversion in the example cited above, $\gamma = 2.27$, and a very low information ratio of 0.1, then Equation (6) translates to an active risk of approximately 4.40%.

Investment managers tend to believe that their information is very valuable, for example an information ratio close to 1.0, meaning an ability to add nearly 1.0% in extra return per 1.0% of active risk. With that type of information, we should, according to Equation (6), be willing to have an active risk of 44%. However, in practice the active risk of managers ranges from 2% up to 10% with a median around 6%. If we presume that our information is good enough to add 1.0% per 1.0% of active risk and we are willing to take on 6% active risk, then (6) tells us that a risk aversion of 16.67 would be required. This risk aversion is more than seven times greater than the risk aversion we inferred with Equation (3) using the benchmark's risk and expected excess return.

What to do? There is a disconnect caused by the two risks, model and active, and by the two measures of investment potential: 5.5% return for 15.5% risk in the model portfolio and a presumed 6.0% active return for 6.0% active risk with the information. To circumvent this problem, many mangers address the active risk versus active return issue directly by maximizing a modified version of (P1) that is defined in terms of first differences:

$$\alpha' \cdot \mathbf{p} - \frac{\lambda}{2} \cdot \{\mathbf{p} - \mathbf{m}\}' \cdot \mathbf{V} \cdot \{\mathbf{p} - \mathbf{m}\} \qquad \text{(P2)}$$

subject to $\mathbf{p} \in C$ and $\mathbf{e}' \cdot \mathbf{p} = 1$.

Problem (P2) makes the active risk versus active return trade-off explicitly with a penalty for active variance, λ, that is large enough to balance the investment manager's estimate of their prowess, that is, a high $IR(\alpha)$, against their fear of deviating too far from the model portfolio, a low ω_p. Note that the unconditional expected excess returns, μ, play no direct role in (P2).[12]

Notice also that problem (P2) is, through equation (1), equivalent to:

$$\left\{\mu + \frac{\gamma}{\lambda} \cdot \alpha\right\}' \cdot \mathbf{p} - \frac{\gamma}{2} \cdot \mathbf{p}' \cdot \mathbf{V} \cdot \mathbf{p} \qquad \text{(P3)}$$

subject to $\mathbf{p} \in C$ and $\mathbf{e}' \cdot \mathbf{p} = 1$.

In sum, problem (P1) is the financial economics approach and (P2) the investment engineering approach. If we maintain that distinction, we can avoid confusion. That's why it is helpful to refer to γ in (P1) as risk aversion, a term with some economic meaning, while calling λ in (P2) a penalty for active variance to highlight its role as one of the dials on the portfolio engineer's console.

The hybrid problem, (P3), combines the form of (P1) with the motivation of (P2). It shows how we can adapt the expected utility approach and make it suitable for investment engineering.

12. In a parallel to the Sharpe ratio, we have a position $\mathbf{q}$ defined by $\alpha = \lambda \cdot \mathbf{V} \cdot \mathbf{q}$ such that $IR(\alpha) = \lambda \cdot \sqrt{\mathbf{q}' \cdot \mathbf{V} \cdot \mathbf{q}}$.

III. Expected Utility

The utility model has antecedents in the economic literature on individual decision making under certainty and uncertainty. This may not be extremely relevant for the case of an institutional investment manager who is acting as an agent that is one and more often more steps away from the owner of the funds. In the case of endowments and defined benefit plans it is difficult to identify the ultimate beneficiary.

Nevertheless, the utility approach has theoretical roots, and it allows us to deal with the entire distribution of outcomes and thus capture asymmetry between positive and negative performance.

As before there are N assets, and we now stipulate that there are S possible outcomes. Outcome s occurs with probability π_s, and when outcome s occurs the assets have total returns $\mathbf{r}_s = \{r_{s,n}\}_{n=1,N}$. The return on asset n is a random variable denoted $\tilde{r}_n = \{r_{s,n}\}_{s=1,S}$. The return on portfolio P in outcome s is simply:

$$\mathbf{r}_s' \cdot \mathbf{p} = \sum_{n=1,N} r_{s,n} \cdot p_n = r_{s,P} \,. \tag{7}$$

The associated random return for portfolio P is $\tilde{r}_P = \{r_{s,P}\}_{s=1,S}$.

The expected utility problem is to maximize:

$$\sum_{s=1,S} \pi_s \cdot U\left[\mathbf{r}_s' \cdot \mathbf{p}\right] \quad \text{subject to } \mathbf{p} \in \mathrm{C} \text{ and } \mathbf{e}' \cdot \mathbf{p} = 1. \tag{P4}$$

The utility function, $U[r]$, is strictly increasing, $\dot{U}[r] > 0$, and strictly concave, $\ddot{U}[r] < 0$.

A class of functions that is frequently used is the power utility:

$$U[r] = \left\{ \begin{array}{c} \dfrac{r^{1-\gamma}}{1-\gamma} \text{ for } \gamma > 0, \gamma \neq 1 \\ \ln(r) \text{ for } \gamma = 1 \end{array} \right\}, \tag{8}$$

$$\text{where } \dot{U}[r] = \frac{1}{r^{\gamma}} > 0 \quad \text{and } \ddot{U}[r] = \frac{-\gamma}{r^{\gamma+1}} < 0.$$

The parameter gamma plays the same role here as the risk aversion in (P1) and (P3).

The key to making a quadratic approximation to the expected utility maximization problem is a second-order expansion of the expected utility. If r_P, r_M are the total returns on some portfolio P and the benchmark/model portfolio M then:

$$U[r_P] - U[r_M] \approx \dot{U}[r_M] \cdot (r_P - r_M) + \frac{1}{2} \cdot \ddot{U}[r_M] \cdot (r_P - r_M)^2. \tag{9}$$

If we go through some algebraic and financial economic manipulations, then maximizing the expected value of the right-hand side of (9) becomes a quadratic program. That development was covered in the original article. In this chapter we have moved that tangential discussion to the Appendix and improved it.

IV. The Returns

In order to solve the utility maximization problem (P4) we have to specify the returns. This presents a challenge and an opportunity. It represents considerably more work than a mean-variance optimizer would normally face. The mean-variance user builds or rents a covariance matrix **V** and concentrates on the alphas.

The (P4) user could be lazy and use a sample of historical returns. That is unwise. A portfolio optimization program is a tool for generating portfolios. Like any tool it comes with certain cautions and needs calibration so it will serve its purpose.

Here is a more proactive guideline for generating the returns and calibrating the optimization tool. Our primary goal is retaining control over the first two moments. Control over the second moment is advisable since options and other market data will generally give us a better forecast of future volatility than past returns alone. It will become apparent in following sections why we want to control the first moment to make sure the scenario-based expected utility optimization selects a reasonable portfolio in the absence of special information.

The model for returns with no conditional information is general and straightforward. We assume that with probability π_s the total return on asset n is:

$$r_{n,s} = r_F + \mu_n \cdot \Delta t + \sigma_n \cdot z_{n,s} \cdot \sqrt{\Delta t}. \tag{10}$$

The terms in (10) are:

- r_F is the total return[13] on a risk-free investment over the period $[0, \Delta t]$.
- μ_n is the annual expected excess return on the nth asset.
- σ_n is the annual volatility of asset n.
- $z_{n,s}$ is the distribution's random component capturing the higher moments.

We construct the returns so that $\sum_s \pi_s \cdot z_{n,s} = 0$ and $\sum_s \pi_s \cdot \{z_{n,s}\}^2 = 1.0$.

This does not mean that the assets are normally distributed or uncorrelated. It does mean that we have separated the first moments, r_F, μ_n, and volatility, σ_n, from the correlations and higher moments that are determined by the $z_{n,s}$.

The structure, Equation (10), is compatible with a model driven by a history of returns. If the scenarios are indexed $s = 1{:}S$ with $s = 1$ the earliest and $s = S$ the most recent, we may want to tilt the selection in favor of more recent events by setting $\pi_{S-j} = \phi^j \cdot \pi_S$ for some $0 < \phi < 1$.

To generate the returns, Equation (10), from historical returns simply take the history of asset n's excess returns, subtract the mean, and divide by the standard deviation to get the $\{z_{n,s}\}$. Then you can use an estimate of future volatility, σ_n, the current rates of interest, i_F, and, as we see in the next

13. By total return, we mean 1 plus the risk-free rate of return over the period.

section, a set of unconditional expected excess returns, μ_n, to harmonize with our larger goal of producing sensible portfolios.

Example

The small example used in this paper is for illustration only. It is large enough to be interesting but small enough that it can be examined in detail. There are four equity asset classes: continental European equity (eur), Japanese equity (jpn), United Kingdom equity (ukd) and United States equity (usa). The comparison benchmark (bmk) is 20% in Europe, 30% in Japan, 10% in the United Kingdom, and 40% in the United States. The returns are based on monthly historical returns from January 1978 through December of 1995. Exhibit 1 contains summary statistics. Note the prevalence of negative skewness and positive excess kurtosis; both these descriptors would be zero in the pure normal case. The volatilities (sigma) for the four asset classes are based on forecasts; the volatility for the benchmark is calculated based on the inputs and correlations extant in the data.

EXHIBIT 1 Statistical Summary of Returns Used in the Examples

	EUR	JPN	UKD	USA	BMK
Volatility (input)	19.0%	22.5%	21.0%	18.0%	15.59%
Skewness	–1.06	–0.1	–0.88	–0.64	–1.09
Kurtosis	5.07	1.71	3.35	3.44	4.81
Correlation: EUR	1.00	0.44	0.68	0.61	0.81
Correlation: JPN		1.00	0.34	0.30	0.73
Correlation: UKD			1.00	0.65	0.75
Correlation: USA				1.00	0.83

The appendix includes a description of a multiple factor approach to generating return scenarios.

V. Unconditional Expected Excess Returns

In this section, we demonstrate how to choose the expected excess return for each asset in a manner that will ensure that the benchmark/model portfolio M is optimal in the absence of any special information.

To get this done we need three minor assumptions concerning the benchmark portfolio that are used in this section and the next:

A.1 The model/benchmark portfolio M is ***interior*** to the set C.
A.2 Portfolio M has holdings that sum to one; $\mathbf{e}' \cdot \mathbf{m} = 1$.
A.3 The unconditional expected excess return on the portfolio M, μ_M, is known.

Assumption A.1 means that portfolio M satisfies all of the constraints that define the set C with some room to spare. Assumption A.2 indicates that portfolio M is fully invested.

By Assumption A.3, the model portfolio returns are completely specified, see Equation (11) below. We could replace Assumption A.3 with an equivalent assumption that the Sharpe ratio of portfolio M is known, since we know the predicted risk, σ_M, of portfolio M and $\mu = \sigma_M \cdot SR$. The returns on portfolio M for each scenario are completely known.

$$r_{s,M} = r_F + \mu_M \cdot \Delta t + \left\{ \sum_{n=1:N} m_n \cdot \sigma_n \cdot z_{s,n} \right\} \cdot \sqrt{\Delta t}. \tag{11}$$

We will *select* the unconditional expected excess returns $\boldsymbol{\mu} = \{\mu_n\}_{n=1:N}$ so that portfolio M is optimal when $\boldsymbol{\alpha} = \mathbf{0}$. By Assumption A.1, we only need to impose the constraint $\mathbf{e}' \cdot \mathbf{m} = 1$ since portfolio M is not hard up against any of the other constraints.

The first-order conditions for expected utility optimization with the added constraint $\mathbf{e}' \cdot \mathbf{p} = 1$ are:

$$\sum_{s=1,S} \pi_s \cdot \dot{U}\left[r_{s,M}\right] \cdot r_{s,n} = \kappa; \quad n = 1, N. \tag{12}$$

In Equation (12), κ is the Lagrange multiplier associated with the full investment constraint. If we multiply the Equations (12) by m_n and sum, we get:

$$\sum_{s=1,S} \pi_s \cdot \dot{U}\left[r_{s,M}\right] \cdot r_{s,M} = \kappa. \tag{13}$$

Equation (13) determines κ since $\tilde{r}_M$ is completely described by Equation (11). We can use Equation (12) and κ to determine μ_n for each n.

That's the easy way to calculate the unconditional expected excess returns. We'll do it the hard way that requires a detour that is interesting and will be useful in later sections. We use a modified set of probabilities that are called the risk-neutral probabilities in some studies of option pricing.

Define new probabilities for the outcomes by:

$$\pi_s^* = \pi_s \cdot \dot{U}\left[r_{s,M}\right] \Big/ \sum_{\upsilon=1,S} \pi_\upsilon \cdot \dot{U}\left[r_{\upsilon,M}\right] = \pi_s \cdot \dot{U}\left[r_{s,M}\right] \Big/ E\left\langle \dot{U}\left[\tilde{r}_M\right] \right\rangle. \tag{14}$$

With these new probabilities and for *any* random variable $\tilde{x} = \{x_s\}_{s=1,S}$, we can define expectation as:

$$E^*\left\langle \tilde{x} \right\rangle = \sum_{s=1,S} \pi_s^* \cdot x_s, \text{ and } E\left\langle \dot{U}\left[\tilde{r}_M\right] \cdot \tilde{x} \right\rangle = E\left\langle \dot{U}\left[\tilde{r}_M\right] \right\rangle \cdot E^*\left\langle \tilde{x} \right\rangle. \tag{15}$$

This implies:

$$E\left\langle \dot{U}\left[\tilde{r}_M\right] \cdot \left(r_P - r_M\right) \right\rangle = E\left\langle \dot{U}\left[\tilde{r}_M\right] \right\rangle \cdot E^*\left\langle r_P - r_M \right\rangle. \tag{16}$$

Note that $\dot{U}[r_M]$ decreases as r_M increases. Hence the modified probabilities make bad outcomes more likely and good outcomes less likely where bad and good are determined by the performance of the model portfolio.

If we equate Equations (12) and (13) for any n and divide by $E\langle \dot{U}[\tilde{r}_M] \rangle$ we get:

$$E^*\langle \tilde{r}_n \rangle = E^*\langle \tilde{r}_M \rangle; \quad n = 1, 2, \ldots, N. \tag{17}$$

This relationship is enough to determine the unconditional expected excess returns:

$$\mu_n \cdot \Delta t = \mu_M \cdot \Delta t + \sum_{\ell=1:N} \{m_\ell \cdot \sigma_\ell \cdot E^*\langle \tilde{z}_\ell \rangle\} \cdot \sqrt{\Delta t} - \sigma_n \cdot E^*\langle \tilde{z}_n \rangle \cdot \sqrt{\Delta t} \tag{18}$$

for each asset.

Exhibit 2 shows the unconditional expected excess returns in our example in six cases: the mean variance case with risk aversion 2.25, and for five cases of Equation (18) with gamma equal to 0.10, 1.50, 2.25, 3.00, and 10.00. In all cases μ_M is 5.50%.

EXHIBIT 2 Unconditional Expected Excess Returns in Several Cases

EXPECTED EXCESS RETURN	EUR	JPN	UKD	USA
Mean-Var, gamma=2.25	5.46%	5.78%	5.56%	5.28%
Scenario, gamma=2.25	5.67%	5.59%	5.79%	5.27%
Scenario, gamma=0.1	5.501	5.510%	5.505%	5.491%
Scenario, gamma=1.5	5.56%	5.60%	5.63%	5.36%
Scenario, gamma=2.25	5.67%	5.59%	5.79%	5.27%
Scenario, gamma=3	5.75%	5.56%	5.90%	5.23%
Scenario, gamma=10	10.21%	0.88%	10.97%	5.24%

There are three things of note in Exhibit 2:

- The analogous cases, quadratic lambda = 2.25 and power gamma = 2.25 yield similar but not identical results.
- When the gamma is 0.10, that is, there is low risk aversion, then small differences in expected excess return explain large differences in the model portfolio's holdings. Similarly, when the gamma is 10.0 then huge differences in expected excess return are needed to explain the model portfolio's holdings.
- We get reasonable answers over a broad range of inputs, gamma from 1.5 to 3.0.

VI. Response to Special Information

In Section V, we showed how to set the expected returns to be consistent with the optimality of a model portfolio in the absence of special information. In this section we will show how to adapt special information for the optimization (P4) in order to get portfolios that have something close to a target level of active risk. Recall from Section II that there can be a disconnect between the risk aversion that is consistent with our assumed Sharpe ratio, in our case 0.353, and the penalty for active variance, about 20, needed to produce a portfolio with a reasonable level of active risk. Also recall that problem (P3) handled that challenge by rescaling the alphas. We will follow the same route here and scale the alphas to make sure the optimization behaves as desired.

The information is contained in a vector of asset alphas, denoted $\boldsymbol{\alpha}$. When there is information, we write the modified return as:

$$\tilde{\mathbf{r}} + \delta \cdot \boldsymbol{\alpha}. \tag{19}$$

In Equation (19):

- $\tilde{\mathbf{r}}$ are the scenario returns generated by the process described in Sections IV and V.
- $\boldsymbol{\alpha}$ is an N element vector of exceptional return forecasts.
- $\delta \geq 0$ is a parameter that indicates our intention to explore incremental additions of alpha to the return mix.

Since it is best to take on one challenge at a time, we will assume:

A.4 The alphas are benchmark neutral; i.e., the model portfolio has a zero alpha; $\alpha_M = \boldsymbol{\alpha}' \cdot \mathbf{m} = 0$.

Note we can always write the returns as $\tilde{\mathbf{r}} + \left\{\frac{\Delta\mu_M}{\mu_M}\right\} \cdot \boldsymbol{\mu} + \delta \cdot \boldsymbol{\alpha}$ where the alphas are model neutral, as per assumption A.4, and $\Delta\mu_M$ is positive or negative indicating some forecast of positive or negative exceptional return for the model portfolio. In Section VII, we'll look at the effect of a forecast that changes the expected excess return on portfolio M. For this section we'll assume $\Delta\mu_M = 0$.

As a result of our work in Section V, the model portfolio M is optimal when $\delta = 0$. The idea is to increase delta until we get a portfolio with a desired level of active risk. After we have found a value for δ that we are comfortable with, we will be solving:

$$\sum_{s=1,S} \pi_s \cdot U\left[\{\mathbf{r}_s + \delta \cdot \boldsymbol{\alpha}\}' \cdot \mathbf{p}\right] \tag{P5}$$

subject to $\mathbf{p} \in C$ and $\mathbf{e}' \cdot \mathbf{p} = 1$.

Exhibit 3 is an example of alphas where the scale parameter turned out to be $\delta = 0.082$.

EXHIBIT 3 Original Alphas and the Scaled-Back Alphas

	EUR	JPN	UKD	USA
Annual Alpha	−4.00%	6.00%	6.00%	−4.00%
Scaled Annual Alpha	−0.33%	0.49%	0.49%	−0.33%

We have demonstrated how the expected utility/returns-based approach to producing portfolios can be tamed so it:

- Yields the model portfolio as optimal in the absence of special information,
- Can incorporate current volatility forecasts,
- Allows for the parametric introduction of special information (alpha) and thus the choice of a portfolio with a desirable level of active risk.

This is sufficient to protect against the more dangerous uses where an analyst tosses historical data into an optimizer and generates the output.

Does the scenario/expected utility approach produce better portfolios than the more traditional mean-variance approach? In one sense, any portfolio that is optimal for an expected utility maximization is also optimal for some mean-variance optimization and vice versa. The set of possible outcomes are the same. But in the ex post realized returns sense all portfolios are not equal. If portfolio P_1 with positions $\mathbf{p}_1$ does very well relative to the model portfolio, $\mathbf{m}$, then portfolio P_2 with positions $\mathbf{p}_2 = (2 \cdot \mathbf{m}) - \mathbf{p}_1$, will do poorly. This suggests trying to answer this question by doing backtests, although that generally introduces more randomness than insight. It is often just the sophisticated way to flip a coin.

The choice of technique seems to be specific to the application. In large portfolios of 1,000 or so stocks, it seems mean-variance has clear advantage. In the case of asset allocation or an active global macro fund then it is less clear.

The second part of the appendix discusses a quadratic approximation to problem (P5).

VII. Cash

In Section V, we showed how to set unconditional expected excess returns so our model/benchmark portfolio is optimal in the absence of special information. Section VI proposed scaling the special information and parametrically searching for a desired level of active risk. In this section, we consider what happens if we allow the riskless asset, also known as cash, as part of the overall mix. Cash has total return r_F with certainty. The way we deal with cash will depend on the context, which we will specify in Assumption A.5.

A.5 The benchmark holds no cash. We are not allowed to short cash, that is, no leverage. In ordinary circumstances we aspire to be fully invested, that is, hold no cash.

In our example, we will try make "ordinary circumstances" more explicit by specifying that we expect that the cash position will exceed 40% only once in five years.

This section shows how we can make the optimization and forecasting process consistent with the aspirations contained in assumption A.5.

We will test the sensitivity of the expected utility model and cash holdings under our base case values of μ_M equal to 5.5% and a power utility with a risk aversion γ equal to 2.25. The easiest approach for calibration is to consider a two-asset optimization where one can either hold the model portfolio or cash. We will initially consider allowing both long and short cash positions. Let h be the fraction of the investment in the model portfolio M with a corresponding $1-h$ invested in cash. To make things simple we are considering a period of one year.

The optimal level of h is determined by maximizing:

$$\sum_{s=1,S} \pi_s \cdot U\left[r_F + h \cdot \{\Delta\mu_M + r_{s,M} - r_F\}\right] \tag{20}$$

where r_F is the total return to cash over the period.

The results are shown in Exhibit 4 that plots $\Delta\mu_M$ on the x-axis and the optimal amount of cash held, $1-h$, on the y-axis.

EXHIBIT 4 Case with μ_M Equal to 5.5% and Risk Aversion γ Equal to 2.25

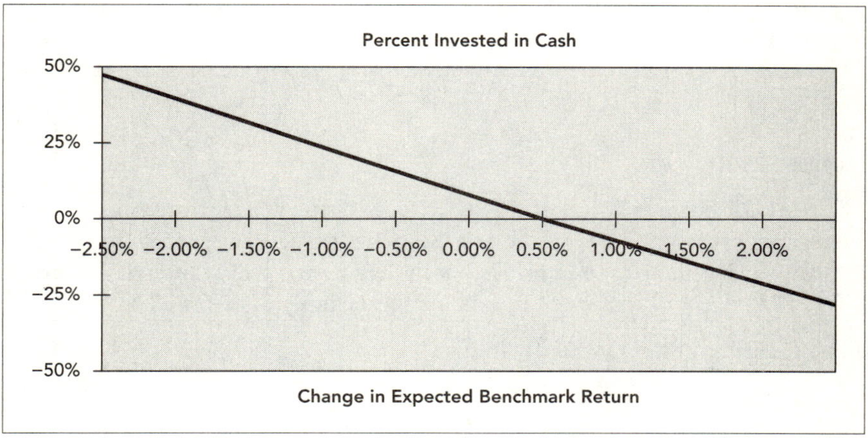

This is not what we wanted. When $\Delta\mu_M$ equals 0.00, the base case, we hold 10% cash.[14]

There are two parameters that we can manipulate to escape this uncomfortable position; either increase μ_M or decrease the risk aversion γ. A second try at Equation (20) does a little of both: increase μ_M from 5.5% to 6.00%

14. A quick look at the first-order conditions for (P4) indicates that cash will not enter the optimal mix as long as $r_F < E^*\langle\tilde{r}_M\rangle$. For our example with $\mu_M = 5.5\%$ this will be the case if $\gamma \leq 2.06675$. When $\mu_M = 6.03\%$, we get no cash for $\gamma \leq 2.25$.

and decrease γ from 2.25 to 2.00. With these new parameters we get a more satisfactory result (Exhibit 5).

EXHIBIT 5 Case with μ_M Equal to 6.0% and Risk Aversion γ Equal to 2.00

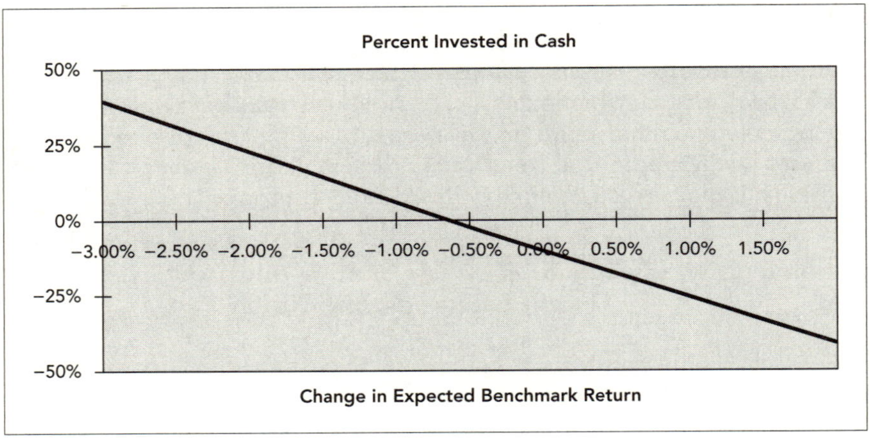

In this altered configuration, we would require a forecast of $\Delta\mu_M$ equal to –0.60% before cash would enter the portfolio while –3.00% value of $\Delta\mu_M$ implies a 40% cash holding.

The process that generates $\Delta\mu_M$ (see Grinold (1994)) can be expressed as:

$$\Delta\mu_M = IC \cdot \sigma_M \cdot \chi, \tag{21}$$

where:

- IC is the correlation of the forecast with the realized return.
- σ_M is the volatility of the benchmark return.
- χ is a standardized variable with mean zero and standard deviation 1.0. We will think of the χ as being normally distributed.

The line in Exhibit 5 is roughly linear:

$$1 - h \approx -17.8 \cdot \Delta\mu_M - 0.125 \tag{22}$$

We start with $\sigma_M = 15.6\%$ and a desire to have $\Delta\mu_M \leq -3.00\%$ be a once in five-year event. A score of $\chi = -2.12$ corresponds to one month in 60, so an IC of 0.09 is consistent with our desires.[15]

$$\Delta\mu_M = 0.09 \cdot 0.156 \cdot \{-2.12\} = -0.0298. \tag{23}$$

A more useful relationship is the link between the cash position and the score. With the IC = 0.09 and volatility 15.6% we have roughly:

$$1 - h = -0.25 \cdot (\chi + 0.5) \tag{24}$$

15. We are using annual data. With monthly data we would have a volatility of 4.49% = 0.1555/sqrt(12) and an IC of 0.026 = 0.09/sqrt(12).

With Equation (24), we can use the assumption of χ being normally distributed with mean zero and standard deviation one to explore the response of the cash position to our forecast. For example, what is the probability there is cash in the portfolio? For this to happen the right side of Equation (24) has to be positive, so we need χ less than -0.5, which for normal (0,1) happens about 31% of the time.

By proceeding in this manner, the investment engineer can pretune the portfolio-generating process so the cash position reflects a reasonable response to the research leading to the forecast $\Delta\mu_M$.

VIII. Options

We take a broad view and define an option as any instrument whose value is determined by the returns. In outcome s with returns $\mathbf{r}_s$ the option has value $c_s = f(\mathbf{r}_s)$; where $\tilde{c} = \{c_s\}_{s=1,S}$ is the associated random variable. A typical example is a call on the value of one of the assets with a strike value κ: for example, $c_s = Max\left[0, r_{n,s} - \kappa\right]$. A less typical example is the best performing asset: $c_s = Max_{n=1,N}\left[r_{n,s}\right]$. If the option has an expiration date, say, one year, that is beyond the end of the period, say, one month, then we can use an appropriate option valuation formula to calculate its value at the end of the month.

The analysis that follows is conditional on our assumed motivation for using options:

A.6 Options are used to provide a better opportunity to take advantage of the alphas we judge to exist for the underlying assets. In particular, we *are not* trying to take advantage of some incorrect pricing of the options themselves.

If we did feel that we had some insight that allowed us to value options more accurately than the market, then the single-period optimization used in this paper is not adequate. A multiperiod approach that allows for replicating strategies would be more appropriate.

In addition, we assume:

A.7 The benchmark holds no options.[16]

One of the difficulties with options and optimization is that the method used to value the options may be out of synch with the preferences as expressed by the model portfolio and the objective function. For that reason, we will value the option using the rules laid out in Section V. In our internal

16. This assumption is made to simplify the analysis. It would be possible to allow options in the benchmark, but the scheme suggested in Section V to find unconditional expected excess returns and used below to value the options would involve an iterative process for finding the option's value.

market we can set an initial value, c_0 on the option. According to Equation (17), we must have:

$$E^*\left\langle \tilde{c}\big/ c_0 \right\rangle = E^*\langle \tilde{r}_M\rangle, \text{ so } c_0 = E^*\langle \tilde{c}\rangle \big/ E^*\langle \tilde{r}_M\rangle. \tag{25}$$

It is important to note that c_0 is not the market price. It is the price that makes holding options unattractive vis-à-vis holding the benchmark.

When scaled alphas are included, we find:

$$c_s + \Delta c_s = f\left(\mathbf{r}_s + \delta \cdot \boldsymbol{\alpha}\right). \tag{26}$$

We add the option to the mix of assets; it becomes asset $N + 1$. The details on the option's returns are:

$$r_{N+1,s} = \frac{c_s + \Delta c_s}{c_0}. \tag{27}$$

As an example, take a one-month call on the Japanese equity market. The strike is the risk-free rate. If we take a Black–Scholes approach this option is worth \$2.81. The valuation formula (25) gives a value of \$2.37. At \$2.37 with no alphas, the option would not be part of the mix. At \$2.81 and no alphas, we would want to write the options.

In Exhibit 6, we look at the active positions in three cases. In the first case, we use the alphas from Section VI, Exhibit 3 with parameters $\mu_M = 0.055$ and $\gamma = 2.25$. In the second optimization we have introduced the option on Japanese equity as a possible asset. As one can see, we certainly didn't jump at this opportunity. There is a very small desire to write some of those call options and to increase the Japanese holdings so slightly it is lost in the round off. In contrast to this nonevent, consider what happens in the third case in Exhibit 6 where we ignore the assumption A.6 and use an external valuation for the option. Then our optimization will sense a near arbitrage opportunity and will write options and increase the holdings of Japanese equity up to 100% (a 70% active position). With no upper limits on the holdings the optimal portfolio would be zero in Europe, the US, and UK with 105.71% in Japan and writing options equal in value to 5.71% of the portfolio.

EXHIBIT 6 How the Addition of an Option Affects the Mix Whether It Is Fairly Valued or Not

ACTIVE POSITIONS	EUR	JPN	UKD	USA	OPTION
optimal: no options	–14.59%	7.00%	17.79%	–10.20%	0.00%
optimal: with an option	–14.59%	7.00%	17.79%	–10.20%	–0.01%
misvalued option, no alphas	–20.00%	70.00%	–6.03%	–38.45%	–5.52%

Thus, we glean two points:

- When options can be part of the mix and their valuation is consistent with the valuation of the other assets as per Equation (25), then there is very little motivation to use options as part of the optimal mix. This observation is based on more than one example and is driven by the idea that the optimization will pursue the alpha directly through the assets and not indirectly through the option. This is even true if we fashion an option that seems perfect to exploit the alphas. In the context of our example, this is an option that pays the maximum of zero or the average return on the high-alpha Japan and UK minus the average return on the low alpha Europe and USA. The valuation of this option with no alphas is $1.52 and with the alphas included it is $1.55. However, we still do not find this option attractive. The reason is that the optimization can do something like replicate this option on roughly the same terms.

- When we do not follow assumption A.6, there is an inconsistency between the option's valuation and the internal valuation implicit in our selection of a model portfolio and utility function. In that case the optimization will perceive a near arbitrage opportunity whether it was our intention to present one or not.

The presence of options allows us to radically change the skewness and excess kurtosis of the distribution of outcomes.[17] In Exhibit 7 we display the moments and active risk of the return distributions.

EXHIBIT 7 Changing the Return Distribution with an Option

	EXPECTED EXCESS RETURN	STANDARD DEVIATION	SKEWNESS	EXCESS KURTOSIS	ACTIVE RISK
Benchmark	5.50%	15.56%	–1.09	4.81	N.A.
Optimal: no options	5.77%	16.09%	–0.96	4.06	3.03%
Optimal: with an option	5.75%	16.04%	–0.98	4.08	3.01%
Misvalued option, no alphas	11.41%	15.48%	–1.64	2.94	20.36%
Benchmark, no crash	5.50%	15.20%	–0.44	1.44	N.A.

As we can see, the benchmark portfolio and the optimal portfolios with and without options have similar distributions of outcomes as captured by mean, standard deviation, skewness, and kurtosis. It is interesting to see how, with the incorrectly valued option, one opts for more negative skewness in return for a significantly higher expected excess return.

The distribution of asset returns in our example is generated from historical returns from 1978 through 1995 and therefore has the return of October 1987 in the mix. The final row shows the significant impact of dropping that one month in 216 months. More than half of the skewness and kurtosis for the benchmark are due to that one data point.

17. A random variable is standardized by subtracting its mean and dividing by its standard deviation. The skewness is the third moment of the standardized random variable and the kurtosis is the fourth moment. Excess kurtosis is kurtosis minus 3. The normal has zero skewness and zero excess kurtosis.

IX. Summary

We have shown how the expected utility approach to a single-period portfolio optimization problem can be adapted to:

- Produce unconditional expected returns consistent with a benchmark
- React to special information, aka alpha, so that portfolios will have a reasonable level of active risk
- Employ cash in a manner consistent with our investment objectives
- Allow options as part of the asset mix

The expected utility approach can be reasonable for relatively small asset allocation or global macro situations if it, like any tool, is used with care.

References

Arrow, K. J. 1970. *Essays in the Theory of Risk Bearing.* Amsterdam: North-Holland.

Brennan, M., and H. Solanki. 1981. "Optimal Portfolio Insurance." *Journal of Financial and Quantitative Analysis* 16 (3): 279–300.

Chopra, V. K., and W. T. Ziemba. 1993. "The Effect of Errors in Means, Variances and Covariances on Optimal Portfolio Choice." *Journal of Portfolio Management*, Winter, 6–11.

Cox, J. C., and H. E. Leland. 1982. "On Dynamic Investment Strategies." *Proceedings of the Seminar on the Analysis of Security Prices*, 139–73. CRSP, Graduate School of Business University of Chicago.

Dantzig, G. B., and G. Infanger. 1993. "Multi-Stage Stochastic Linear Programs for Portfolio Optimization." *Annals of Operations Research*, 59–76.

Grinold, R. C., and R. N. Kahn. (1995) 2000. *Active Portfolio Management: Quantitative Theory and Applications.* Chicago: Probus Press, with 2nd ed., New York: McGraw-Hill.

Grinold, R. C. 1994. "Alpha Is Volatility Times IC Times Score." *Journal of Portfolio Management*, Summer, 9–16.

Grinold, R. C. 1996. "Domestic Grapes from Imported Wine." *Journal of Portfolio Management*, Special Fischer Black Issue, December, 29–40.

Hakansson, N. H. 1970. "Optimal Investment and Consumption Strategies Under Risk for a Class of Utility Functions. *Econometrica* 38 (5): 587–607.

Kahn, R. N., and D. Stefek. 1996. "Heat, Light and Downside Risk." BARRA, December.

Kallberg, J. G., and W. T. Ziemba. 1982. "Comparison of Alternative Utility Functions in Portfolio Selection Problems." *Management Science* 29 (11): 1257–76.

Leland, H. E. 1980. "Who Should Buy Portfolio Insurance." *Journal of Finance* 35 (May): 581–94.

Markowitz, H. M. 1988. *Mean Variance Analysis in Portfolio Choice and Capital Markets.* Oxford: Basil Blackwell.
Merton, R. C. 1990. *Continuous Time Finance.* Oxford: Blackwell.
Rudd, A., and B. Rosenberg. 1979. "Realistic Portfolio Optimization." *TIMS Studies in Management Science: Portfolio Theory*, #11, 21–46. Amsterdam: North Holland Press.
Rudd, A. 1987. "Business Risk and Investment Risk." *Investment Management Review*, November-December, 19–27.
Samuelson, P. A. 1969. "Lifetime Portfolio Selection by Dynamic Stochastic Programming." *Review of Economic Studies* 51 (August): 239–46.
Sharpe, W. F. 1970. *Portfolio Theory and Capital Markets.* New York: McGraw Hill.

CHAPTER 32

Mean-Variance and Scenario-Based Approaches to Portfolio Selection

Appendix

This appendix contains two sections. The first describes a method for generating scenarios using a multiple factor model for risk. The second section describes a quadratic approximation to the expected utility optimization.

Generating Scenarios with a Multiple Factor Risk Model

There are N assets and K factors. At time t, the N by N forecast of covariance is:

$$\begin{aligned} &\mathbf{V}(t) = \mathbf{X}(t) \cdot \mathbf{F}(t) \cdot \mathbf{X}'(t) + \boldsymbol{\Delta}(t) \\ &\mathbf{X}(t) \text{ is an } N \text{ by } K \text{ matrix of factor exposures} \\ &\mathbf{F}(t) \text{ is a } K \text{ by } K \text{ factor covariance matrix} \\ &\boldsymbol{\Delta}(t) \text{ is an } N \text{ by } N \text{ diagonal matrix of specific variance} \end{aligned} \tag{A1}$$

This structure is useful for the prediction of risk and also for the attribution of return. At the end of period t, we use a regression to split the asset return into factor and specific return components.

$$\begin{aligned} &\boldsymbol{\theta}(t) = \mathbf{X}(t) \cdot \hat{\mathbf{f}}(t) + \hat{\mathbf{u}}(t) \\ &\boldsymbol{\theta}(t) \text{ are the excess returns on the } N \text{ assets, } t \text{ to } t+\Delta t \\ &\hat{\mathbf{f}}(t) \text{ are the } K \text{ attributed factor returns} \\ &\hat{\mathbf{u}}(t) \text{ are the specific (residual) returns on the } N \text{ assets} \end{aligned} \tag{A2}$$

Let $\{\mathbf{f}(t)\}_{t=1,T}$ be the series of estimated factor returns with any average removed, and similarly for $\{\mathbf{u}(t)\}_{t=1,T}$, the specific returns with any average removed.

The positive definite symmetric matrix $\mathbf{F}(t)$ can be represented by its eigenvalue and eigenvector decomposition.

$$\begin{aligned}&\mathbf{F}(t)=\mathbf{Q}(t)\cdot\mathbf{D}(t)\cdot\mathbf{D}(t)\cdot\mathbf{Q}'(t)\\&\text{where }\mathbf{D}(t)\text{ is a positive diagonal matrix}\\&\mathbf{Q}(t)\cdot\mathbf{Q}'(t)=\mathbf{I},\ \textit{i.e.}\ \mathbf{Q}^{-1}(t)=\mathbf{Q}'(t)\end{aligned}\tag{A3}$$

With this split we can find a vector of standardized principal component returns at each date.

$$\begin{aligned}&\mathbf{g}(t)=\mathbf{D}^{-1}(t)\cdot\mathbf{Q}'(t)\cdot\mathbf{f}(t)\text{ which implies}\\&\mathrm{E}\langle\mathbf{g}(t)\rangle=0\text{ and }\mathrm{E}\langle\mathbf{g}(t)\cdot\mathbf{g}'(t)\rangle=\mathbf{I}\end{aligned}\tag{A4}$$

The factors are numbered in their ability to explain variance, so that $D_{1,1}(t)\geq D_{2,2}(t)\geq\ldots D_{K,K}(t)$.

This history of standardized principal component returns, $\{g_k(t)\}_{k=1,K}^{t=1,T}$ is one component of the scenario generation system. The second component comes from the history of specific returns.

It is somewhat easier for the uncorrelated specific returns. From the realized return $u_n(t)$ and its predicted volatility[18] $\delta_n(t)$ we define standardized specific returns:

$$\begin{aligned}&v_n(t)=\frac{u_n(t)}{\delta_n(t)}\text{ for }n=1:N\text{ and }t=1:T\\&E\langle v_n(t)\rangle=0,\ E\langle v_n^2(t)\rangle=1\end{aligned}\tag{A5}$$

This gives us a collection of $N\cdot T$ standardized specific returns.

At this point we could and probably should go one step further and construct a model, a cumulative distribution function, for, say, the first three principal components so we won't be hostage to the sample history along the most important dimensions. Doing this requires a high level of skill in statistics and economics, along with a great deal of good sense. The attempt would take us too far afield, so we will just presume that this has been done.

Armed with the history from times 1 to T we are at time $T + 1$ and want to generate scenarios. We have current factor exposures along with the factor covariance matrix and specific return risk predictions: $\mathbf{X}(T+1),\mathbf{F}(T+1),\delta_n(T+1)$.

We can do the eigenvector and eigenvalue decomposition of $\mathbf{F}(T+1)$:

$$\begin{aligned}&\mathbf{F}(T+1)=\mathbf{Q}(T+1)\cdot\mathbf{D}(T+1)\cdot\mathbf{D}(T+1)\cdot\mathbf{Q}'(T+1)\\&\mathbf{D}(T+1)\text{ is a positive diagonal matrix}\\&\mathbf{Q}(T+1)\cdot\mathbf{Q}'(T+1)=\mathbf{I},\ \textit{i.e.}\ \mathbf{Q}^{-1}(T+1)=\mathbf{Q}'(T+1)\end{aligned}\tag{A6}$$

18. Do not confuse the specific volatility $\delta_n(t)$ prediction with the delta used in the main body of the text that is used to adjust the alpha forecasts to lead to desirable levels of active risk.

With this background work completed we can churn out sample returns. For one sample s:

1. For each $k = 1, 2, \ldots, K$ randomly choose a t from 1 to T and let $g_{k,s} = g_k(t)$. Call the resulting vector $\mathbf{g}_s$.
2. Use the vector $\mathbf{g}_s$ to define the factor returns using:

$$\mathbf{f}_s = \mathbf{Q}(T+1) \cdot \mathbf{D}(T+1) \cdot \mathbf{g} \tag{A7}$$

3. For each n, randomly select an m from 1 to N and a t from 1 to T, then let $u_{n,s} = \delta_n(T+1) \cdot \upsilon_m(t)$. Call the resulting N element vector $\mathbf{u}_s$.
4. The random component of returns is given by:

$$\mathbf{X}(T+1) \cdot \mathbf{f}_s + \mathbf{u}_s \tag{A8}$$

We next take the S components generated by the process described above and for each asset remove the sample mean and divide by the sample standard deviation. This produces the $z_{n,s}$ variables that we assumed were available in the main text.

The factor structure can be exploited in the prediction of exceptional return. In other words, some of the attributes in the matrix $\mathbf{X}(T+1)$ may be useful in the generation of alphas. The way we have separated scenario generation from return prediction allows us to deal with any predictive capabilities of the factor model separately.

The Approximating Quadratic Program

Problem (P5) is:

$$\begin{aligned} &\text{Maximize} \sum_{s=1:S} \pi_s \cdot U[\mathbf{r}_s' \cdot \mathbf{p} + \delta \cdot \boldsymbol{\alpha}' \cdot \mathbf{p}] \\ &\text{subject to} \sum_{n=1:N} p_n = 1, \quad \mathbf{p} \in \mathrm{C} \end{aligned} \tag{P5}$$

We assume that the alphas of the model portfolio M are zero. We will make a second-order expansion of the utility function around the returns of the model portfolio:

$$U[r_M + \Delta r] - U[r_M] \approx \dot{U}[r_M] \cdot \Delta r + \frac{1}{2} \cdot \ddot{U}[r_M] \cdot \Delta r^2 \tag{A9}$$

Our goal is to maximize the expected value of the right-hand side of Equation (A9) subject to the constraints in (P5).

In the text we used the risk neutral probabilities π_s^* to generate the expected excess returns. We will use them again and yet another set of modified probabilities π_s^{**} defined as:

$$\begin{aligned}\pi_s^* &= \frac{\pi_s \cdot \dot{U}\left[r_{M,s}\right]}{E\left\langle \dot{U}\left[\tilde{r}_M\right]\right\rangle} \Rightarrow E\left\langle \dot{U}\left[\tilde{r}_M\right]\cdot \tilde{X}\right\rangle = E\left\langle \dot{U}\left[\tilde{r}_M\right]\right\rangle \cdot E^*\left\langle \tilde{X}\right\rangle \\ \pi_s^{**} &= \frac{-\pi_s \cdot \ddot{U}\left[r_{M,s}\right]}{E\left\langle -\ddot{U}\left[\tilde{r}_M\right]\right\rangle} \Rightarrow E\left\langle \ddot{U}\left[\tilde{r}_M\right]\cdot \tilde{X}\right\rangle = E\left\langle \ddot{U}\left[\tilde{r}_M\right]\right\rangle \cdot E^{**}\left\langle \tilde{X}\right\rangle\end{aligned} \tag{A10}$$

The expected value of the right side of Equation (A9) is therefore:

$$\begin{aligned}&E\left\langle \dot{U}\left[\tilde{r}_M\right]\cdot \Delta\tilde{r}\right\rangle - \frac{1}{2}\cdot E\left\langle -\ddot{U}\left[\tilde{r}_M\right]\cdot \Delta\tilde{r}^2\right\rangle = \\ &E\left\langle \dot{U}\left[\tilde{r}_M\right]\right\rangle \cdot E^*\left\langle \Delta\tilde{r}\right\rangle - \frac{1}{2}\cdot E\left\langle -\ddot{U}\left[\tilde{r}_M\right]\right\rangle \cdot E^{**}\left\langle \Delta\tilde{r}^2\right\rangle\end{aligned} \tag{A11}$$

From the second equation in (A10) we can deduce that:

$$\begin{aligned}E\left\langle -\ddot{U}\left[\tilde{r}_M\right]\right\rangle &= E\left\langle \dot{U}\left[\tilde{r}_M\right]\cdot \left\{\frac{-\ddot{U}\left[\tilde{r}_M\right]}{\dot{U}\left[\tilde{r}_M\right]}\right\}\right\rangle \\ &= E\left\langle \dot{U}\left[\tilde{r}_M\right]\right\rangle \cdot E^*\left\langle \left\{\frac{-\ddot{U}\left[\tilde{r}_M\right]}{\dot{U}\left[\tilde{r}_M\right]}\right\}\right\rangle\end{aligned} \tag{A12}$$

If we define a random *aversion* function as:

$$\begin{aligned}&a\left(\tilde{r}_M\right) \equiv \frac{-\ddot{U}\left[\tilde{r}_M\right]}{\dot{U}\left[\tilde{r}_M\right]} \quad \text{then} \\ &E\left\langle -\ddot{U}\left[\tilde{r}_M\right]\right\rangle = E\left\langle \dot{U}\left[\tilde{r}_M\right]\right\rangle \cdot E^*\left\langle a\left(\tilde{r}_M\right)\right\rangle.\end{aligned} \tag{A13}$$

If we are using a power utility:

$$a\left(r_{M,s}\right) = \frac{\gamma}{r_{M,s}}. \tag{A14}$$

With Equation (A13) and division of Equation (A11) by $E\left\langle \dot{U}\left[\tilde{r}_M\right]\right\rangle > 0$ we have the quadratic optimization problem of finding a portfolio P, with positions $\mathbf{p}$ in order to:

$$\begin{aligned}&\text{Maximize } E^*\left\langle \Delta\tilde{r}_P\right\rangle - \frac{E\left\langle a\left(\tilde{r}_M\right)\right\rangle}{2}\cdot E^{**}\left\langle \Delta\tilde{r}_P^2\right\rangle \\ &\text{where} \quad \Delta r_{P,s} \equiv \left\{\mathbf{r}_s + \delta\cdot\boldsymbol{\alpha}\right\}'\cdot\left\{\mathbf{p}-\mathbf{m}\right\} \\ &\text{and} \quad \mathbf{e}'\cdot\mathbf{p} = 1, \quad \mathbf{p}\in C\end{aligned} \tag{P6}$$

In (P6) both the model M and portfolio P are fully invested so we can take advantage of $E^*\left\langle \tilde{r}\right\rangle = \phi\cdot\mathbf{e}$ to write:

$$E^*\left\langle \Delta\tilde{r}_P\right\rangle = \delta\cdot\boldsymbol{\alpha}'\cdot\left\{\mathbf{p}-\mathbf{m}\right\}. \tag{A15}$$

The second moment term simplifies as well.

$$E^{**}\left\langle \{\tilde{\mathbf{r}}+\delta\cdot\boldsymbol{\alpha}\}\cdot\{\tilde{\mathbf{r}}+\delta\cdot\boldsymbol{\alpha}\}'\right\rangle = \\ E^{**}\left\langle \tilde{\mathbf{r}}\cdot\tilde{\mathbf{r}}'\right\rangle + 2\cdot\delta\cdot E^{**}\langle\tilde{\mathbf{r}}\rangle\cdot\boldsymbol{\alpha}' + \delta^2\cdot\boldsymbol{\alpha}\cdot\boldsymbol{\alpha}' \tag{A16}$$

EXERCISE In the special case of a power utility, Equation (A14), show that M, the model portfolio, is optimal for (P6) in the special case where $\delta = 0$ (or $\alpha = 0$).

33

Five Myths About Fees[1]

The Truth Behind Analyzing Fees, in the Context of Investment Goals

Of the three dimensions of investment management—return, risk, and cost—investors have direct control only over cost. Cost includes transaction costs and investment management fees. We focus here on fees.

While return, risk, and even transaction costs have been widely studied, fees are poorly understood and there is little literature on them. Yet they are critically important. The present value of fees in a long-term investment relationship represents the transfer of a significant fraction of the investor's capital to the manager. Moreover, the incentives provided by the fee structure have a strong influence on the manager's strategy, particularly on the fund's volatility, the mix of alpha and beta bets, and the fund's size.

Investment management fees are a timely topic because of three trends in the investment landscape:

- Investors increasingly look to separate alpha from beta.
- The cost of beta has dropped to very low levels.

1. This chapter originally appeared as "Five Myths About Fees" by Ronald N. Kahn, Matthew H. Scanlan, and Laurence B. Siegel in the *Journal of Portfolio Management*, Spring 2006, 56–64. It won the 2007 Bernstein Fabozzi/Jacobs Levy Award for the best article in the *Journal of Portfolio Management* that year (technically in Volume 32 of the journal).

- An explosion of new alpha providers, including hedge funds, private equity firms, and even otherwise traditional managers, utilize unconventional fee structures.

Notably, the movement that focuses on separating alpha from beta also places strong emphasis on paying active fees only for the alpha portion of any investment, and looking closely at costs.[2] Very briefly, the literature says that:

- Investors can obtain beta at very low cost through index funds, exchange-traded funds (ETFs), futures, and swaps. Thus beta is one of life's great bargains, if you believe that the market payoff for beta risk will be attractive.
- Alpha is scarce (because active management is a zero-sum game), difficult to find, and very valuable. It is expensive and should be.
- The beta and alpha decisions are separate. An investor can build a portfolio of alpha sources from any mix of asset classes, then add or subtract beta exposures as desired.

Our perspective in this chapter is that of the client, but we must also understand the manager's perspective. Fee negotiation is a game; sometimes client and manager interests are aligned and sometimes they are opposed. To understand the game, we must identify the motivations faced by all the players.

The investor's goal is to maximize expected returns subject to a risk budget constraint. For most investors, this involves maximizing expected alpha after fees. This isn't easy.

It's difficult enough to maximize expected alpha *before* fees. Managers deliver alpha with great uncertainty. It takes time to distinguish winners from losers, or (among winners) to distinguish the truly skillful from the merely lucky. And even time can never eliminate all such ambiguity. Yet investors must rise to this challenge to rationally allocate risk to active managers.

Incentive fees make the challenge of estimating expected alpha after fees even tougher. These fees both depend on performance and can influence the underlying strategy. And clients must often decide whether their expected alpha after fees is higher with an incentive fee, or the more traditional fixed or *ad valorem* fee.

Our goal is to provide some guideposts for clients seeking to maximize expected alpha after fees. Toward that end, we'll identify, and correct, a number of popular myths regarding fees. Along the way, we'll describe key elements of the fee negotiation game, and determine conditions under which the client should prefer fixed or incentive fees.

Let's start with a list of popular myths about fees. We will address the issues raised by each myth to analyze the truth behind them.

- Myth 1: Fees should be as low as possible.

2. See, for example, Kneafsey (2003), Leibowitz and Bova (2005), Thomas (2005), or Waring and Siegel (2003).

- Myth 2: Incentive fees are always better than fixed fees.
- Myth 3: High water marks always help investors.
- Myth 4: Hedge funds are where the alpha is. They deserve their high fees.
- Myth 5: You can always separate alpha from beta and pay appropriate fees for each.

Let's examine these one at a time.

Myth 1. Fees Should Be as Low as Possible

This baseline myth makes sense. Most people understand that they should pay the lowest possible price for a given good. *For a given good* is the tricky part, however.

We've already noted that index fund fees are very low. They range as low as 0.01% for very large accounts managed to track highly liquid indices, and cap out around 0.20%, except in a few difficult-to-trade asset classes. Swaps, futures contracts, exchange-traded funds, and other ways of achieving beta exposure are also relative bargains. (We quote fees in this article as annual rates charged as a percentage of assets.)

Compared to index fees, typical fees for active management seem toweringly high. And, the zero-sum nature of active management means that on average clients waste these fees. It is difficult to put a number on typical active management fees as the products vary so widely, but on average for equities, these are roughly 0.50% for traditional long-only investments, and 1.35% for retail accounts.[3]

Alternative investments, such as hedge funds and private equity funds, charge annual fixed fees of 1% to 2% of assets under management, *plus* an incentive fee equal to 20% or more of performance above some benchmark.

To provide additional perspective, consider the fee as a transfer of capital to the manager over the course of a somewhat typical 10-year holding period.[4] A 0.10% fee on a retail index fund transfers about 1% of capital, while the 0.50% and 1.35% active institutional and retail fees transfer 5% and 13.5% of capital. Since clients pay fees with certainty for the expectation of uncertain alpha, these are significant sacrifices to make in the hope of alpha.

Goetzmann, Ingersoll, and Ross (2003) use an option pricing model to estimate the value of hedge fund management contracts. Using reasonable inputs, including estimates of the rate at which investors exit the fund and thus stop paying management fees, they find a contract is worth 10% to 20%, and even as much as 33%, of the amount invested. A permanent

3. The institutional average comes from the eVestment Alliance 2005 Fee Study, and an institutional product review for the third quarter of 2005 from the firm Casey, Quirk and Associates. The retail numbers are based on third-quarter 2005 data for domestic stock mutual funds (excluding institutional share classes) in the Morningstar Principia database.

4. We base the 10-year holding period on research by the firm Casey, Quirk and Associates showing that plan sponsors typically turn over 10% of their investment manager pool per year.

allocation to a portfolio of hedge funds involves quite a large transfer of capital from the investor to the population of managers.

So active fees are much higher than index fees and involve significant transfers of capital to managers. This would seem to imply that investors should try to minimize their fees by hiring index managers and the lowest-cost active managers. But institutional and retail investors each hire active managers for upward of 70% of their assets. Does this make sense?

As Waring, et. al. (2000) have discussed, hiring active managers makes sense only under two conditions. One, the investor believes that successful active management is possible, that is, that there exist managers who will produce alpha on average in the future. Second, the investor must be able to identify those—presumably rare—skilled managers.

Any investor satisfying those conditions should rationally aim to maximize expected alpha after fees, not just to minimize fees. Achieving this objective means sharing the alpha with the manager. For any given level of expected alpha, the investor should try to minimize the fee. But in equilibrium, the investor must share a substantial fraction of the alpha with the manager, because alpha is rare and valuable.

So what is the right level of active management fees? The market provides one answer, in the market prices described above. For example, according to the market, 0.50% is about the right price for a traditional long-only active equity product.

But the market may not be right and is certainly wrong on average. What about a more fundamental approach to determining the right fee level? Let's start by considering the utility offered by different managers. We will measure investor utility as:

$$U = \alpha - \lambda \cdot \omega^2, \tag{1}$$

where Equation (1) includes alpha net of fees, the investor's risk aversion, λ, and active risk, ω. Risk-averse investor utility falls short of the net alpha due to the penalty for risk. If two managers provide the same gross alpha, but different risk levels, the lower-risk manager provides higher utility to the investor.

Equation (1) has two implications. First, manager fees should fall significantly not only below gross alpha, but also below gross utility. Second, in the case of two managers with identical gross alpha, investors should be willing to pay higher fees to the lower-risk manager. Note that the lower-risk manager has the higher information ratio (IR), where:

$$IR \equiv \frac{\alpha}{\omega}. \tag{2}$$

Ennis (2005) explores similar territory, trying to identify plausible ranges of fees, working from the impact of fees on the likelihood of achieving positive alpha after fees. Exhibit 1 captures the spirit of his approach and results, which closely agree with the utility analysis.

EXHIBIT 1 Probability of Positive Net Alpha (Given Expected Before-Fee Alpha of 4.2%)

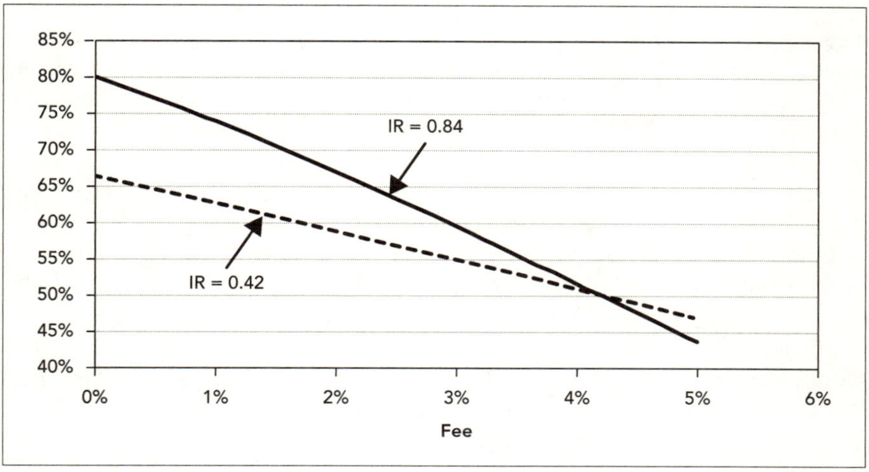

Take, as an example, a manager (Manager 1) who takes active risk of 5%, and whom the investor expects to deliver 4.2% alpha before fees. Assuming normal distributions, the investor expects this manager to deliver positive alpha before fees with 80% probability. But as fees rise, this probability of positive after-fee alpha falls dramatically. Note that a 50% probability of positive alpha corresponds to zero expected alpha—the annual active return is as likely to be positive as negative.

One obvious lesson from Exhibit 1: Fees must remain significantly below the expected alpha. But Exhibit 1 includes a more subtle lesson as well. Consider Manager 2, with the same expected alpha before fees, but with higher active risk (10%) and hence lower information ratio. Exhibit 1 implies that investors would pay higher fees to the more consistent (higher *IR*) manager. This agrees with our analysis based on utility.

Beyond this analysis of utility and probability of outperformance, more consistent managers have an additional advantage: investors have higher confidence in their skill.

So what is the truth about keeping fees as low as possible? Our fundamental analysis has shown that investors should be willing to pay higher fees to managers with certain characteristics, especially the ability to consistently deliver strong alpha and high information ratios. Ascertaining those characteristics is very challenging. Still, what matters is not the fee level, but the manager's ability to deliver utility after fees.

Myth 2. Incentive Fees Are Always Better Than Fixed Fees

Incentive fees have many advantages over fixed fees, but they have disadvantages as well. The better choice will depend on circumstances. For example, we will construct a simple model showing that as investors become more able to choose skillful managers, their preference moves from incentive to fixed fees.

But first, let's describe how incentive fees work, and the advantages and disadvantages of both fixed and incentive fees. The simplest incentive fees include a base fee plus a percentage of the return above some performance benchmark. More complicated structures add caps, high water marks, and other features to the calculation of the sharing amount. When managers offer investors the choice of either a fixed or an incentive fee, the base fee should lie below the fixed fee, and the *expected* total incentive fee (base plus expected performance share) should exceed the fixed fee alternative. A fixed (certain) fee should equate to a higher but uncertain fee.

With that basic structure in mind, let's discuss the pros and cons of each fee structure. The pros and cons of fixed fees mainly arise because they pay a fixed amount for variable performance. The certainty associated with fixed fees benefits both clients and managers. The disconnect between fees and performance raises several issues, some benefiting clients, some benefiting managers.

The certainty of fixed fees allows clients to accurately budget for these costs and provide managers with low-volatility revenue. This in turn facilitates investment in the manager's business—additional research, product improvements—of benefit to managers and clients.

The disconnect between fixed fees and variable performance raises two main issues. First, the fee in a given year or over time may be too high or too low. This can advantage the manager at the expense of the client, or vice versa, at least in the short run. In the longer run, paying the wrong fee causes problems for both manager and client. If the fee is too high for the alpha delivered, a manager may benefit for a while, until the client terminates the manager. Exacerbating the damage, this situation sometimes leads clients to keep poorly performing managers too long, in the hopes of earning back the fee. If the fee is too low, the client benefits until the manager neglects the product, underresources it, fires the client, or gathers too much in additional assets.

This brings up the second issue arising out of the disconnect between fees and performance, in particular the interaction of fees with the different interests of clients and managers. Clients want high returns. Managers want high profits. With fixed fees, the manager maximizes profits through extensive asset gathering, even if asset gathering dilutes performance.

All active strategies have capacity limits. As assets grow, trading costs rise, and the manager has increasing difficulty implementing insights in the portfolio. Expected returns fall (see, for example, Kahn and Shaffer (2005), which is Chapter 31 in this book). Capacity constraints create conflicts of interest between the client and the manager.

So what about incentive fees? They address the structural problem of fixed fees by directly connecting pay and performance. This seems like an unambiguous improvement except that performance can arise out of skill or luck, and this raises a different issue.

But first, incentive fees do address the two issues concerning fixed fees. By connecting fees to performance, they avoid years where fees and performance are out of balance. And incentive fees also help align the different interests of clients and managers. They motivate managers to deliver strong performance, and to avoid raising assets to the detriment of performance. They even motivate the key investment professionals to focus on investing, not asset gathering. Managers and clients can both prosper from these aspects of incentive fees.

Incentive fees even have some related side benefits. Paying only for performance can facilitate investing with unorthodox or more risky managers. It can also lead to better pools of managers, by eliminating the temptation to stick with poorly performing managers to try to earn back the fees already paid.

On the negative side, the volatility associated with performance fees causes problems for clients and managers, for the same reasons that the certainty of fixed fees creates benefits. Clients can't budget as easily for incentive fee costs. Managers face volatile revenue streams.

The new issue raised by incentive fees follows from the observation that managers receive the same fee whether performance comes from skill or luck. And, given that incentive fees have option-like character (especially in their payment for positive performance without a symmetric penalty for negative performance), they become more valuable with increasing volatility of alpha. Managers can therefore increase incentive fee value by adjusting the investment strategy. This is not in the interest of the client.

Beyond the temptation to increase volatility, incentive fees offer more general gaming opportunities. As Black (1976) noted:

> When things go badly, some people react by doubling their bets. They increase their exposure to risk in hopes of recouping their losses . . . [W]hen things go well they may reduce their exposure to risk so they can't lose what they have won. It's a very common gambling strategy and it's a very common philosophy of life.

Unfortunately, while incentive fees create this temptation for managers, the resulting behavior does not correspond to how clients want their money managed. Note that the various embellishments to incentive fees—high water marks, longer measurement periods—do not eliminate these issues.

So each type of fee has advantages and disadvantages. And either can be a reasonable way to compensate a manager. So why might a particular client prefer one over the other? In part, this will depend on how a client weighs the particular advantages and disadvantages we have discussed. Beyond that, preferences will depend on the ability to pick skillful managers.

Assume that of the population of active managers, 20% are skillful enough to deliver an alpha of 1.5% per year before fees. The remaining 80% cannot beat their benchmark and thus deliver an alpha of –0.20% before fees.[5] The assumption that 20% of managers are skillful is more favorable than the most optimistic persistence-of-performance studies would imply (see, for example, Grinold and Kahn 2000, p. 566).

We will further specify that there exist only two possible fee schedules: a flat 0.30% fee, or an incentive fee of 0.20% plus 20% of the positive alpha. With the incentive fee, skillful managers receive $0.20\% + 20\% \times 1.50\% = 0.50\%$ on average, while unskillful managers receive 0.20%.

A client with no ability to identify skillful managers has a 20% chance of success, since skillful managers make up 20% of all managers. Before fees, the client's expected alpha is:

$$E\{\alpha\} = 20\% \cdot (1.50\%) + 80\% \cdot (-0.20\%) \Rightarrow 0.14\%. \tag{3}$$

With fixed fees, the client loses 0.16% on active management. What about using incentive fees? The expected incentive fee in this case is:

$$E\{fee\} = 20\% \cdot (0.50\%) + 80\% \cdot (.20\%) \Rightarrow 0.26\%. \tag{4}$$

So, with incentive fees, the client loses 0.12% on active management. While neither case looks attractive—and active management should not look attractive to investors with no ability to pick managers—the incentive fee looks better than the fixed fee.

With perfect skill in picking active managers, on the other hand, the client will prefer fixed fees. For skillful managers, the fixed fees are 0.30%, while the incentive fees average 0.50%.

Between these extremes, there exists a point of indifference between the two types of fee schedules. Exhibit 2 shows how this point depends in this example on the investor's skill in picking managers.

Exhibit 2 identifies three important regions, depending on skill in hiring managers. Below a 29% probability of success, investors should not pursue active management. The expected alpha after fees is negative. Between a 29% and a 34% probability of hiring skilled managers, investors should prefer incentive fees to fixed fees in this model. Above a 34% probability, investors prefer fixed fees.

For comparison with required skill in other areas of active management, we can convert this to a required *information coefficient*, or *IC*. The *IC*, the correlation of forecast and realized returns, measures active management skill. With no skill, $IC = 0$; with perfect skill, $IC = 1$. Skillful stock pickers exhibit *IC*s around 0.05 to 0.10. For skillful asset allocation managers, or

5. For those worried about active management as a zero-sum game, we can assume the skillful managers have somewhat smaller asset size, so that the size-weighted alpha is zero. We will ignore this issue for the purpose of this simple model.

EXHIBIT 2 Indifference Analysis Between Fixed and Incentive Fee

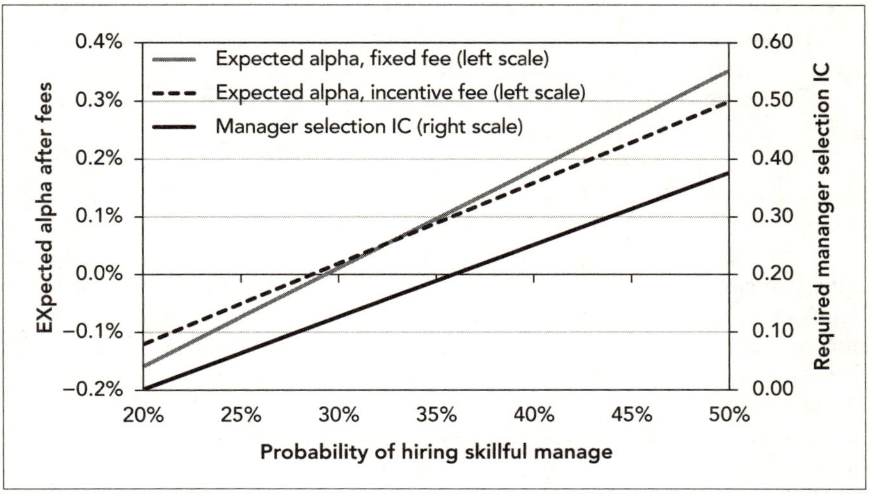

market timers, these range from 0.10 to 0.20 at best. In our simple model, investors require an *IC* of 0.11 to achieve positive alpha net of costs, and an *IC* of 0.18 to prefer fixed to incentive fees.

The specific ranges change as we change model assumptions. In general, as the fixed fees increase, investors increasingly prefer incentive fees. As manager skill increases, investors increasingly prefer fixed fees.

Myth 3. High Water Marks Always Help Investors

To make incentive fees more palatable to investors, many firms offer high water mark provisions. Such a provision calculates the incentive fee based on the highest previously achieved net asset value (NAV). This prevents an investor from paying twice for the same performance. Suppose that a fund experiences the returns shown in Exhibit 3, and that the incentive share is 20%.

EXHIBIT 3 Incentive Fee Calculations

			DOLLAR RETURN SUBJECT TO INCENTIVE FEE	
YEAR	NAV	% RETURN	STANDARD	HIGH-WATER
0	$10			
1	$20	100%	$10	$10
2	$15	–25%	$0	$0
3	$30	100%	$15	$10

Without a high water mark, the incentive fee is $2 in year 1 and $3 in year 3, for a total of $5. With the high water mark provision, the manager collects no fee on the increase in value from $15 back to the old high of $20. The fee in year 3 is only $2, for a total fee of $4.

What could be fairer? With the high water mark, the investor avoids paying twice for the travel from $15 to $20.

In fact, high water marks do help investors in that they lower the overall fee for a given pattern of investment returns. Unfortunately, they also introduce perverse incentives that can alter future return patterns.

Consider the predicament of the manager in our example after year 2. Any gain smaller than $5 produces no incentive fee. This increases the manager's motivation to take additional risk, whether the investor wants to or not. Specifically, the manager may favor bets that add at least $5 to NAV, preferring larger but less probable returns to the smaller but steadier returns preferred by clients.

If the probability of returning to the high water mark within a reasonable time is too low, the manager may close the fund and start up a new fund, with a new high water mark. The investor, then, also faces a new high water mark, with a new manager. The investor thus pays twice for the same travel, although by different managers.

So high water marks help investors only when the decline in NAV does not incite the manager to increase risk or to close the fund. This may correspond to a narrow range of outcomes. We would caution investors to monitor the behavior of managers with high water marks carefully when they are losing money.

Myth 4. Hedge Funds Are Where the Alpha Is. They Deserve Their High Fees.

Let's start with the evidence that many investors believe hedge funds are high-alpha, and then consider the more complex truth behind this myth.

Institutional investors, pension plans in particular, are today in desperate need of alpha. At the peak of the technology stock bubble, most plans were fully funded or even overfunded, and the search for alpha was a fun but not strictly necessary part of the job. But equity markets and interest rates have dropped since then, and most plans are now significantly underfunded. Along with increased contributions, they need alpha to deliver on promises to beneficiaries. The demand for alpha has never been higher.

Consistent with this demand for alpha, as Exhibit 4 shows, we have seen large asset flows into hedge funds. Since hedge funds offer pure alpha returns for the most part, assets flowing into hedge funds are almost entirely assets in search of alpha.

EXHIBIT 4 The Size of the Hedge Fund Universe, 1990–2005

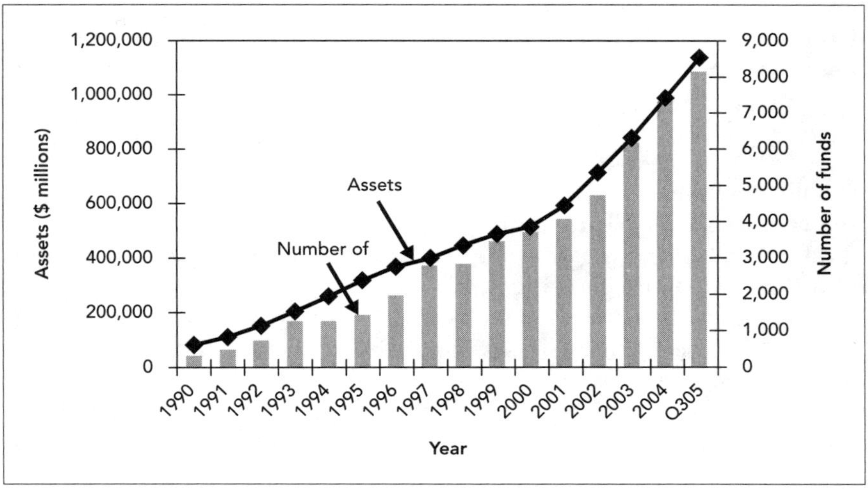

Exhibit 4 also shows a large increase in the number of hedge funds. This provides a reasonable proxy for the flow of investment managers into the hedge fund arena.

Finally, in 2006 we wrote:

> We seem to have seen a significant rise in average hedge fund fees. Ten years ago, almost all hedge funds charged 1% of assets, plus 20% of performance above a benchmark. Now many hedge funds charge 2% of assets, and/or incentive shares above 20%. Almost no funds charge less than 1% of assets, or 20% incentive shares. And, over these past ten years, we have also seen the growth in hedge funds of funds, with fund of fund fees layered on top of the hedge fund fees. We can't exactly quantify the average fee paid per dollar invested in hedge funds today, but with many investors paying significantly more, and basically none paying less, average fees have clearly grown over the past ten years.[6]

We have observed strong and increasing demand for alpha, confronting its limited supply. In response, prices and supply have increased. Unfortunately, the increase in supply is an increase in the supply of hedge fund managers offering alpha, not necessarily any increase in actual alpha.

So, what is the truth here? First, are hedge funds where the alpha is? Structurally, hedge funds offer two distinct advantages over more traditional

6. Not to get too far ahead of ourselves, but from the perspective of 2019—a decade after the financial crisis—the trends in hedge fund management fees have changed. From 2007 to 2016, average hedge fund management fees have dropped from 1.66% to 1.51%, according to a report from Preqin (2017). Furthermore, ever since 2014, fewer new hedge fund launches charge a 2% management fee than charge a 1.5% to 1.99% management fee. As many of the issues discussed in Myth 4 played out, hedge fund fees have been dropping.

investments. They avoid constraints, like the long-only constraint, that can hinder investment performance. And they have the flexibility to invest in many nontraditional assets, from private equity to distressed debt to derivatives. Clarke, de Silva, and Thorley (2002) modify the fundamental law of active management (Grinold 1989) to say:

$$IR = IC \cdot \sqrt{BR} \cdot TR. \tag{5}$$

The information ratio of an investment product depends on the information coefficient (a measure of manager skill), the Breadth, *BR*, (a measure of opportunity), and the Transfer Coefficient, *TR*, (a measure of how efficiently the manager's ideas impact the portfolio). Structurally, hedge funds can offer higher breadth (through the availability of more assets) and higher transfer coefficients (through lack of portfolio constraints) than more traditional products.

Beyond structure, what about talent? Exhibit 4 demonstrated the flow of managers into hedge funds. That's not surprising. Beyond just responding to the increasing demand for alpha, in which environment would you rather work?

- A large and traditional firm owned by someone else, where you spend considerable time marketing and asset gathering, you manage other people's money versus a benchmark, and you charge 0.50% and 0%.
- Your own business, where you spend most of your time on investing, you manage most of your liquid net worth alongside your investors, you ignore benchmarks, and you charge 2% and 20%.[7]

Of course, hedge funds are not all wine and roses for managers. They fail much more quickly than institutional funds, because (like most entrepreneurial efforts) they are usually undercapitalized and forced to take risks that more established managers can avoid. And the perceived need to invest one's own money in the fund makes running a hedge fund even riskier.[8]

Still, there is no question that hedge funds have attracted many investment managers, including many leaving traditional investment firms.

While the structural advantages clearly exist, and many investment managers have moved from traditional firms to hedge funds, beware the idea that hedge funds are where all the alpha is. First, Sharpe's (1991) arithmetic of active management shows that aggregate alpha must be zero. The increase in the number of hedge funds can't alter that. Aggregate alpha was zero 10 years ago, and it's still zero today. Second, the many advantages of hedge funds listed above appeal to both skilled and unskilled managers. Both have flowed into hedge funds. Unfortunately, it isn't easy to tell these two groups apart.

---

7. Thanks to Elizabeth Hilpman of Barlow Partners for this example. She originally presented this in "Hedge Fund Management," a speech at the AIMR Financial Analysts Seminar, Evanston, Illinois, July 26, 2001.

8. Brown, Goetzmann, and Ibbotson (1999) estimate an annual attrition rate of 20% per year for existing funds, with a presumably higher rate for new funds.

Third, traditional investment firms—particularly those focused on institutional clients like pension plans—have not stood still as demand for alpha, and hedge funds, has grown. Most now offer products with the same structural advantages as hedge funds, plus the transparency and institutional quality long demanded by these clients. They have recognized the work environment advantages of hedge funds, and at least started to address the issues most important for attracting and retaining key investment staff. Institutional clients are desirable clients, due to their size, sophistication, and typically longer commitment to products. As long as traditional firms can retain their institutional clients, they should also be able to and attract retain key investment staff.

Finally, at least so far, traditional firms are the main sources for lower turnover strategies designed specifically for the institutional investor need for alpha in bulk.

So hedge funds are not where all the alpha is. They haven't created any alpha in aggregate, and there are many good reasons for investors to continue to use more traditional investment firms. But at the same time, there are many talented hedge fund managers. Do they always deserve their high fees?

The simple answer is no. No manager is great independent of his or her fees. At some price, a manager is just not worth it. This was at least part of the motivation behind some Harvard alumni vowing in 2004 to stop donating to the university while it paid its employees as much as $30 million for alpha delivered. A hedge fund decision should always include an analysis of the impact of manager fees on the net performance delivered to clients. This is always part of hiring traditional managers and should be part of hiring hedge fund managers as well.

Myth 5. You Can Always Separate Alpha from Beta and Pay Appropriate Fees for Each

As we have seen, fees for alpha dramatically outpace fees for beta. You should never pay alpha fees for beta performance. Separating alpha from beta makes this rule completely transparent.

In some cases, investors already do purchase separated alpha and beta. Many products—including index funds, ETFs, futures, and swaps—offer low-cost, cleanly separated beta. A few products, including pure market neutral equity funds (beta = 0) offer appropriately priced pure alpha. Beyond long-short, an active, long-only equity manager who carefully adheres to style, capitalization, industry, and factor neutrality delivers an essentially pure alpha active return.

But most active products today deliver a combination of alpha and beta. Furthermore, there exist challenges to cleanly separating the two in many such products. Some managers deliver beta that does not correspond to any readily available index. Some managers deliver alpha through timing of beta exposures.

Consider, for example, a sector rotation manager. When does a position represent beta, and when does it represent alpha? Many international managers underweighted Japan for all of the 1990s. Was that a tactical position, or just their choice of beta?

A different problem arises in some asset classes like real estate or private equity, where there are no pure beta instruments to facilitate indexing, benchmarking, or hedging.

Mixed (alpha and beta) products pose a danger for investors of paying alpha fees for beta performance. Consider a long-biased equity hedge fund with an average beta of 0.6. In a given year, the equity market rises 16% above the risk-free return, and the hedge fund delivers 11% above risk-free. A standard 1% and 20% fee arrangement would lead to a fee of 3.2%. But we might expect that fund to return 9.6% above risk-free just due to the average beta. That would imply a true alpha of only 1.4%, and a more appropriate fee of 1.28%. Investors in such a product should understand its sources of return, and at a minimum try to pay, on average, alpha fees only for alpha performance.

So you can't always separate alpha from beta. This doesn't mean you will necessarily overpay for such products. It does mean you must carefully analyze what proportions of alpha and beta the product delivers, and appropriately pay for the combination.

Conclusions

We show in Myth 5 that while some investment products offer pure alpha or pure beta, most active products offer a combination not easily separately into those pieces. So, an investor who cares about fees above all else, and who thus only wants to purchase alpha and beta separately, could do so. In fact, some institutional funds do invest completely in beta, and in principal at least, others could invest only in beta products plus equity market neutral funds.

But for most investors, restricting investments to only separated alpha and beta products is too limiting. There are many talented managers whose insights only appear in mixed alpha and beta products. Whole asset classes with distinct beta, like real estate and private equity, are available almost exclusively as mixed products. The opportunity costs are simply too high to ignore such products.

Our goal has been to focus attention on the importance of fees. Too often, investors consider fees only after already deciding on an investment product. That's too late.

At the same time, fees should not be the overriding single concern. For example, don't invest only in perfectly separated alpha and beta products just because of the fee transparency.

In the end, we return to the three dimensions of active management: return, risk, and cost. High-fee products are worthwhile if they deliver sufficiently high returns and low risk. Some high-return products have fees that make them poor investments. Investors must analyze fees in this overall context to manage their portfolio appropriately.

References

Black, Fischer. 1976. "Why and How Does an Investor Diversify?" *Fischer Black on Markets* 1 (5): 6. Quoted in Perry Mehrling, *Fischer Black and the Revolutionary Idea of Finance*, Hoboken, NJ: John Wiley & Sons, 2005, 217.

Brown, Stephen, William N. Goetzmann, and Roger G. Ibbotson. 1999. "Offshore Hedge Funds: Survival and Performance, 1989–1995." *Journal of Business*, January, 91–118.

Clarke, Roger, Harindra de Silva, and Steven Thorley. 2002. "Portfolio Constraints and the Fundamental Law of Active Management." *Financial Analysts Journal*, September/October, 48–66.

Ennis, Richard M. 2005. "Are Active Management Fees Too High?" *Financial Analysts Journal* 61 (September/October): 44–51.

Goetzmann, William N., Jonathan Ingersoll, and Stephen A. Ross. 2003. "High-Water Marks and Hedge Fund Management Contracts." *Journal of Finance*, August.

Grinold, Richard C., and Ronald N. Kahn. 2000. *Active Portfolio Management*. 2nd ed. New York: McGraw-Hill.

Grinold, Richard C. 1989. "The Fundamental Law of Active Management." *Journal of Portfolio Management* 15 (Spring): 30–37.

Kahn, Ronald N., and J. Scott Shaffer. 2005. "The Surprisingly Small Impact of Asset Growth on Expected Alpha." *Journal of Portfolio Management* 32 (Fall): 49–60.

Kneafsey, Kevin. 2003. "Solving the Investor's Problem." *Investment Insights*, August. Barclays Global Investors, San Francisco.

Leibowitz, Martin L., and Anthony Bova. 2005. "Allocation Betas." *Financial Analysts Journal*, July/August.

Preqin Ltd. 2017. "Hedge Fund Fees: Investor Views and Fund Manager Reaction." *Preqin Hedge Fund Spotlight*, March, 7–9.

Sharpe, William F. 1991. "The Arithmetic of Active Management." *Financial Analysts Journal*, January/February.

Thomas, Lee R, III. 2005. "Engineering an Alpha Engine." *Journal of Investing*, Winter, 23–32.

Waring, Barton, Duane Whitney, John Pirone, and Charles Castille. 2000. "Optimizing Manager Structure and Budgeting Manager Risk." *Journal of Portfolio Management* 26 (Spring).

Waring, M. Barton, and Laurence B. Siegel. 2003. "The Dimensions of Active Management." *Journal of Portfolio Management*, Spring, 35–51.

SECTION 4

Extras

34

Introduction to the Extras Section

The three chapters in this section cover topics that may be of interest to the readers of this book, though they are less focused on solving a particular technical challenge of active portfolio management. They include some discussion of career paths and of the general success of our approach to portfolio management. They are less technical than the rest of the book.

"Presentations upon Receiving the James R. Vertin Award"

The authors were the 2013 winners of the CFA Institute's James R. Vertin Award. According to the CFA website, the award "is presented periodically to recognize individuals who have produced a body of research notable for its relevance and enduring value to investment professionals.[1] It is appropriate to include our remarks upon winning this award in this book, as the work the award recognized included *Active Portfolio Management* plus the many articles we have included in this book.

We received this award at a ceremony in Toronto on June 3, 2013, where we gave the presentations contained in Chapter 35. Richard describes his path through academic finance and into active management. Ron talks about the evolution of investing from art to science.

1. https://www.cfainstitute.org/en/research/foundation/vertin-award.

"What Investors Can Learn from a *Very* Alternative Market"

In the spring of 2003, Ron was driving to work when he heard an interview with Michael Lewis. Lewis was discussing his new book, *Moneyball: The Art of Winning an Unfair Game*, a description of how Billy Beane, the Oakland A's general manager, exploited inefficiencies in the management of baseball to produce teams that won far more games than their collective salaries would imply. He immediately thought, "This isn't a baseball book, it's an investment book."

That initial thought led to:

- A careful read of *Moneyball*.
- Billy Beane speaking at some Barclays Global Investors events for our senior executives and clients.
- An essay in the *Financial Analysts Journal*, "What Investors Can Learn from a *Very* Alternative Market" along with a similar version, "The Science of Winning," which appeared in Barclays Global Investors *Investment Insights* publication. Both essays compare the success of scientific analysis and behavioral finance in baseball to investing.

The release of the movie *Moneyball*, eight years after the book came out, provided an opportunity to review the essay and distribute it to BlackRock clients. In the intervening years, BlackRock had purchased Barclays Global Investors.

So how did the concepts in *Moneyball* hold up in the years between the book publication and the movie release? Baseball has become more efficient along the dimensions by which Billy Beane exploited the sport in 2002. Many teams have adopted the ideas originally described by Bill James (the baseball writer and statistician who developed the sabermetrics framework) and ignored by almost everyone in professional baseball, with the exception of Billy Beane. The Boston Red Sox failed to hire Billy Beane but then hired Theo Epstein as general manager to implement the same program. They also hired Bill James as advisor. The Red Sox' combination of money and scientific analysis finally broke the Curse of the Bambino, leading to a World Series win in 2004, and further wins in 2007, 2013, and 2018.

As for Billy Beane, he won the playoff of ideas, if not the actual baseball playoffs. The story in baseball played out like many investment opportunities. Someone discovers and exploits an anomaly, until others catch wind of it and join in, ultimately arbitraging away the opportunity.

How has the essay held up since it was published in 2003? The essay makes two key points regarding investing—that behavioral finance has helped explain known anomalies rather than lead to new investment ideas and that rigorous scientific analysis underpins investment success.

On the first point, behavioral finance has become more prevalent in active management, if not more predictive. A key question all active managers ask is why their investment ideas should work. Why do the opportunities exist? Why does the market get some things wrong? Eight years ago, behavioral finance already helped explain why opportunities existed: value investing works because investors (incorrectly) extrapolate from recent experience. Momentum investing works because investors tend to hold on to losers and sell winners, slowing the diffusion of information into prices. But we knew about value and momentum well before behavioral finance became popular.

What behavioral finance wasn't doing back then was identifying new investment opportunities based on understanding behavior (as Billy Beane had done in baseball).

That is still the case. Academics publish ever more behavioral finance papers, but they still aren't identifying exploitable investment opportunities following directly from irrational investor behavior.

As to rigorous scientific analysis, surprisingly there have been attacks on its applicability to investing, at least as practiced by quantitative investors. The quant crisis of August 2007, and the three to four years of subsequent underperformance by quant equity managers, brought into question all the components of quantitative investing. But as I described in "Quantitative Equity Investing: Out-of-Style?," the problem with quant managers was too much money invested in the same opportunities, not rigorous scientific analysis.[2] How could that go out of style? Since Ron wrote that essay, we have seen quant managers come back, after the exit of those excess funds, and as they have used scientific analysis to identify new ideas.

Moneyball the movie is surprisingly good. It came out eight years after the book appeared, turning a story about statistics and ideas into gripping entertainment. And even if Billy Beane has yet to win the World Series, his ideas have changed the game. This chapter discusses behavioral finance and rigorous scientific analysis. These ideas haven't come to dominate investing over the past eight years. But rigorous scientific analysis in particular is only likely to grow in importance to investment success.

"UCLA Master of Financial Engineering Commencement Address"

Ron gave the commencement address for the 2014 graduates of UCLA's Master of Financial Engineering (MFE) program on December 19, 2014. The talk discussed his career path, attempted to provide some career advice for graduates, and spoke about the opportunities for MFE students in active management that smart beta and big data are creating.

Reference

Kahn, Ronald N. 2010. "Quantitative Equity Investing: Out of Style?" *Journal of Portfolio Management* 36 (Winter): 5–6.

2. Kahn (2010).

35

Presentations upon Receiving the James R. Vertin Award[1]

Richard Grinold

Rather than give a technical talk, I'll take a personal approach and describe how I got here and some interesting things that happened along the way. The early part is not very interesting or unusual: born, grew up, went to school, college, worked for a year, Navy for three and a half years, then graduate school. The first surprise came after graduate school, when I stayed on as a professor. This was not the plan. I thought I would get a "real" job, but something—inertia, a lack of imagination, a dearth of interesting alternatives—left me in school. After a year marking time as a postdoc, I found myself teaching management science at the University of California Berkeley's Business School; this was unexplored territory.

After I had spent four years at Berkeley, an opportunity came up to teach a finance course. I had never taken a finance course, so I accepted. In our more enlightened times, this move might have been classified as "experimenting on students without their consent." I'm not sure about the students, but I, at least, survived the experiment, and a few years later, I was allowed to teach a seminar in finance. I chose pension fund finance as the topic because I knew nothing about it. Students and professor would learn together. For a text, I selected a monograph I had not read called *The Financial Reality of*

1. We presented these remarks in an awards ceremony in Toronto on June 3, 2013. They then appeared in the *Research Foundation Year in Review 2013*.

Pension Funding Under ERISA by the then-editor of the *Financial Analysts Journal* (*FAJ*), Jack Treynor.[2] I was pleasantly surprised and found the book to contain an agreeable blend of analytical insight and common sense. After I realized Treynor was also masquerading as Walter Bagehot in the pages of the *FAJ*, I started looking for more of Treynor's insights and became a regular *FAJ* reader.

Never underestimate serendipity. I was fortunate in that the fates had placed my office next to that of Barr Rosenberg. In the late 1970s, Barr asked me to consult for what was then a strange new firm called BARRA. Work at BARRA showed me many of the actual challenges faced by investment managers. Among the greatest of these challenges was the torment in preparing for and taking the CFA exam. Every June, BARRA would hold a research seminar at Pebble Beach, California. The conference started on a Sunday and usually on the day following the CFA exams. The survivors of these Level I, II, or III exams became the social engine of the conference and did some serious unwinding.

It was also at BARRA that I met Ronald Kahn. Ron is that rare spirit who is both extremely intelligent and unpretentious. I'm not sure how Ron found us, but we were fortunate. I do recall our first interview, in 1987, which went something like this:

> RCG: So, you studied physics at Princeton and Harvard . . . and your thesis?
>
> RNK: The early universe.
>
> RCG: Ahh . . . How early?
>
> RNK: The first 10 seconds.
>
> RCG: That is early! And what are you doing now?
>
> RNK: Studying the extinction of the dinosaurs.
>
> RCG: Ah, that's a 13-billion-year-less-10-second jump. Shouldn't be difficult to shuffle forward a mere 65 million years and get in touch with the post–Black Monday equity market.

Of course, we hired him, and it was a brilliant decision.

Work in the financial industry required a set of skills that were complementary to the skills required in academe. I was fortunate to have spent enough time in school to learn a few things but not enough time to get indoctrinated. I knew what the Kool-Aid looked like, but I had not sipped from the cup. Although economics and finance use mathematics and statistics in the same way as the physical sciences use them, the purpose in the social sciences is to maintain the logic of an argument, to get from *A* to *B* safely and prevent sloppy thinking. This doesn't mean the results at *B* are useful; it just means that the steps from *A* to *B* are valid.

---

2. With coauthors Patrick J. Regan and William W. Priest.

Nevertheless, the precision of the argument lends an aura of truth to the result, an effect that is unwarranted and often misleading. After all, finance and economics are *social* sciences. Results are guidelines; they will be, at best, sort of true most of the time. In the investment world, one hears such comments as "It was a bad year for value stocks." As one wag has pointed out, you don't hear scientists saying, "It was a bad year for gravity."

Consider the capital asset pricing model (CAPM): The vital takeaway of the CAPM for the would-be active manager is not that markets are efficient, full stop, but that the burden of proof lies heavily on anyone who has a scheme to outperform the markets. In particular, one should be suspicious of elaborate arguments in which hypotheses are compounded and results smack of wheels within wheels. I tend to like simple, even crude models that provide a first-order relationship between important variables.

Eventually, I found myself in the world of active portfolio management. I was lucky enough to work for James Vertin's old firm, Wells Fargo Nikko Investment Advisors, which eventually morphed into Barclays Global Investors (BGI).

BGI was a wonderful place. It was crammed full of interesting and intelligent people who were motivated by two modest goals: to be the very best in the business and to revolutionize the investment management industry. They were and they did.

I thank you for this award and for the ongoing efforts of the Research Foundation of CFA Institute.

Ronald Kahn

"Evolving into the Science of Investing"

Let me start by thanking the Research Foundation of the CFA Institute for awarding Richard Grinold and me the James R. Vertin Award. It is a great honor. I also want to thank Richard Grinold—mentor, manager, colleague, and coauthor—for taking a chance back in 1987 and hiring a physics PhD with no knowledge of finance. What an adventure this has been.

Richard Grinold and I started our book, *Active Portfolio Management*, by stating:

> The art of investing is evolving into the science of investing. This evolution has been happening slowly and will continue for some time . . . New generations of increasingly scientific investment managers will rely more on analysis, process, and structure than on intuition, advice, and whim.

So how has this evolution into the science of investing been going? How much progress have we made? My perspective on this is different in 2013 than it was in 2006.

To investigate this question, let's start by reviewing some of the prior research on the adoption of new (noninvestment) technology. Individuals and institutions adopt new technology based on cost/benefit analysis under uncertainty and with limited information. The decision is often less about whether or not to adopt a new technology than about whether to adopt it now or later.

The speed of adoption depends on the details of that cost/benefit analysis and how it changes over time. If we focus on organizations either creating new technology or deciding to use new technology, the cost analysis includes the costs of either developing or acquiring and implementing the technology. Part of the costs will cover education and training, especially if the skill level required for the new technology is high. The benefit analysis will cover the added value of the new technology. This can vary over time, due to network effects. Many technologies, e.g., fax machines or e-mail, become more valuable as they are more widely used.

Generically, new technology adoption typically follows S-shaped curves of adoption over time. Initially we see a small number of early adopters. Then, successful technologies experience a more rapid growth in adoption. Finally, adoption saturates as the set of potential adopters dwindles.

Exhibit 1 shows these adoption curves for selected consumer products:[3]

EXHIBIT 1 Diffusion Rates in the US for Selected Consumer Products

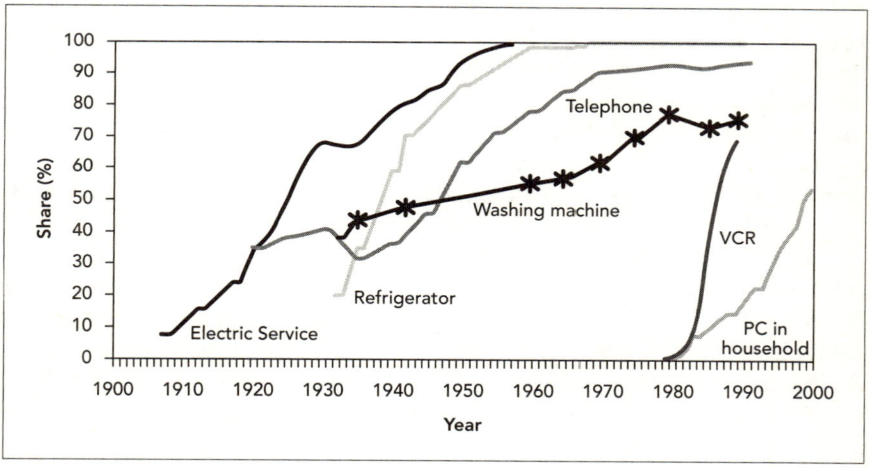

Bronwyn Hall and Beethika Khan

We can see that refrigerators and VCRs experienced very rapid adoptions in the US, while washing machines and electric service were adopted more slowly. We can also see that eventually the entire US adopted electric service and refrigerators, while perhaps 25% of the population has not adopted washing machines. Presumably most of these people use washing machines at Laundromats.

This is all well and good, but let's look at examples in the world of investing. We will consider three particular cases: equity indexing, equity risk

3. Source: Hall and Khan (2003).

modeling, and quantitative active equity strategies. All of these fall under the general rubric of scientific investing. In each case, we will consider adoption in the context of this model of technology adoption.

Equity Indexing

The idea for equity indexing goes back to 1964, when Sharpe developed the CAPM.[4] In 1974, Black and Scholes published a paper describing initial attempts to build such a product:

> The modern theory of finance suggests that most investors should put part or all of their money into a "market portfolio" . . . Attempts to create a fund based on these principles and to make it available to a large number of investors have uncovered some important problems. Legal costs due to government regulations, the costs of managing a fund, and especially the costs of selling it are all much higher than one might expect. *Despite these problems, efforts to create such funds seem destined for eventual success.* [italics added][5]

Well, Black and Scholes were certainly correct in their forecast that index funds would eventually succeed. But the costs of developing indexing were high, as they describe above. The level of financial modeling skill required in developing these products was quite high relative to standards at that time. Education was a particular challenge, especially educating potential investors on the advantages of being average! The benefits only become clear after significant education. In the case of indexing, there was no particular network effect. The benefits of indexing exist for the first adopter and do not particularly increase with the number of adopters.

Remarkably, the Wells Fargo Investment Advisors equity index product, the first index fund, was unprofitable for its first 13 years. Today indexing is a huge and profitable business. As an interesting aside for this occasion, James R. Vertin played a central role in Wells Fargo's pioneering efforts to develop index funds.

As to maximum adoption, we expect equity indexing to saturate at less than 100%. In spite of the many benefits of indexing, we do not expect 100% of all assets to be indexed. If that did happen, it would threaten price discovery.

What has been the history of adoption of equity indexing? Exhibit 2 shows US Institutional Equity Indexed Assets Under Management (AUM) levels from the early 1970s through 2007.

4. Sharpe (1964). Treynor (1961), Lintner (1965), and Mossin (1966) were on roughly the same track in the same era.

5. Black and Scholes (1974).

EXHIBIT 2 US Institutional Indexed Equity Assets Under Management in $ Billion

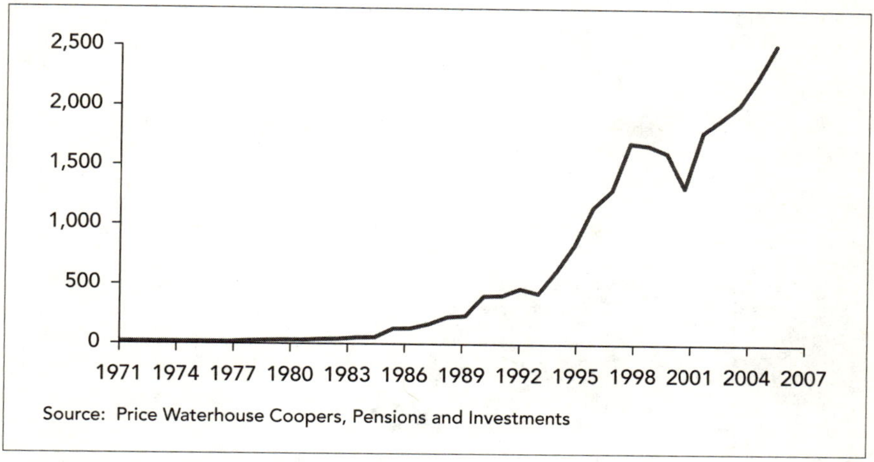

Price Waterhouse Coopers, Pensions and Investments

From 1971 through 1983, total AUM was less than $15 billion. Total AUM crossed $1 trillion in 1997. While Exhibit 2 doesn't display the typical S-curve shape, based on the time required to cross $1 trillion we argue that adoption of equity indexing required about 25 years.

Equity Risk Modeling

The ideas underlying equity risk modeling go back to Markowitz, Sharpe, and Rosenberg.[6] By the mid-1970s, Barra equity risk models were commercially available. Interestingly, the National Science Foundation funded their initial development. As with indexing, risk models required a high level of financial modeling skill—both to develop and to use—compared to the standards at that time. As to the benefits of risk modeling, they become quite obvious after big losses due to poor risk management. There has been a network effect associated with risk models, at least in some applications. For example, Barra model output became a standard requirement to receive quotes for trading baskets of stocks.

Risk models were not immediately adopted upon their initial development. Barr Rosenberg appeared on the cover of *Institutional Investor* magazine in 1978 under the heading, "Who is Barr Rosenberg, and what the hell is he talking about?" The illustration (see Exhibit 3) showed Rosenberg in the lotus position, seated on a prayer rug, with flowers in his hair, and with a group of much smaller money managers in suits bowing down to him.

6. Markowitz (1959), Sharpe (1963), Rosenberg (1974).

EXHIBIT 3 Barr Rosenberg on Cover of *Institutional Investor* Magazine, 1978

Institutional Investor magazine, 1978

Charitably we can call that the age of early adopters for equity risk models.

While I don't have a graph of the growth of assets managed using risk models, I suspect the vast majority of assets are now in products managed in part by using risk model analysis. Risk modeling should saturate at near 100%, as every investor benefits from understanding the risks in their portfolio. So like equity indexing, adoption has taken about 25 years.

Quantitative Equity Investing

Quantitative equity investing applies rigorous and systematic analysis (i.e., the scientific method) to develop return forecasts. It views investing as a mathematical optimization problem, trading off expected return against risk and cost. Quantitative equity strategies are designed to maximize consistency of positive returns, i.e., the *information ratio* (ratio of active return to risk). This is a philosophy of investing, not a specific strategy like investing based on book-to-price ratios or price momentum.

Quantitative equity strategies began in the late 1970s and early 1980s, as some financial economists began identifying persistent mispricings, and applying quantitative approaches to forecasting equity returns.

Quantitative equity strategies are costly to develop and continually improve. And success requires continuous improvement, as ideas stop working as markets understand them. (There are no beneficial network effects in active management, only detrimental network effects.) Quantitative equity strategies require high levels of financial modeling skill, and, critically, a nose for great investment ideas. They also involve significant costs to educate clients as to their benefits. As with all active strategies, signal-to-noise ratios are low. Convincing clients to adopt these strategies requires education and time.

With all that as background, the history of adoption of these strategies has been quite mixed, as Exhibit 4 demonstrates.

EXHIBIT 4 Indicative Quant AUM (in $Billion) from 13F Filings

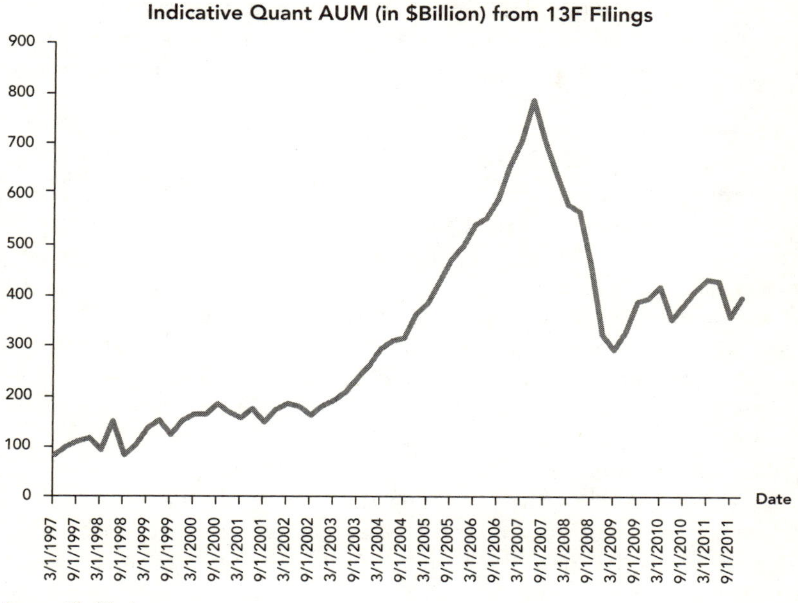

Source: BlackRock

BlackRock

Exhibit 4 shows indicative levels of assets invested in quantitative equity strategies, based on 13F filings of firms exclusively following quantitative equity strategies. This is an underestimate of the true AUM levels invested in these strategies as it ignores firms that offer wider ranges of investment styles. But we believe it is indicative of the pattern of investing in these strategies.

Quantitative equity strategies began in the late 1970s and early 1980s, but Exhibit 4 starts in 1997. As you can see, quantitative equity strategies experienced a large growth spurt from 2003 through the middle of 2007, after which they declined very quickly. This is a pattern we would not expect to see with indexing or risk modeling but can see with active investing. By 2007, too much money had flowed into these strategies. The subprime mortgage crisis required many investors to raise capital to meet margin requirements. Rather than sell illiquid subprime mortgages, many of them withdrew funds from the much more liquid quantitative equity strategies. Unfortunately, most quantitative equity managers followed similar strategies and hence held correlated positions. This led to very volatile performance in

August 2007, followed by more leisurely paced withdrawals over the following two years. We estimate that, as of 2013, quantitative equity investments are down by 75% from their peak in mid-2007.

Continued Evolving into the Science of Investing

If I were giving this talk in 2006, the evolution into the science of investing would look very positive. Equity indexing was already widespread, as were equity risk models. And quantitative equity strategies had experienced significant growth. The perspective from 2013 isn't quite as rosy, given the significant drop in quantitative equity strategies.

There are some reasons to be pessimistic about this evolution. During the financial crisis, a senior investment professional (not a scientific investor) commented to me, "Don't these quant things blow up every five years or so?" This sophisticated professional had lumped together quantitative equity strategies, portfolio insurance, long-term capital, mortgage derivatives—basically every investment idea over the past 25 years that involved college-level math. The education effort still has far to go.

Another investor, a pioneering academic turned investment professional, told me, "We were lucky to have lived during the golden age of financial innovation. But now it's over." So even some scientific investors are pessimistic about this evolution into the science of investing.

But I am optimistic that the evolution will continue, for three reasons.

First, the world has already changed. Indexing is very well established, as are equity risk models. And if too many assets had flowed into quantitative equity strategies, not all have left. Asset levels have stabilized and even started to grow again. The optimal saturation point is somewhere between current levels and the highs of 2007. We should never have expected that the adoption of quantitative equity strategies would come close to the adoption of indexing. Beyond these strategies, investments in many different asset classes are increasingly managed in part with scientific ideas.

Second, clients are in critical need of innovation and improvements in asset management. Unfortunately, the world is full of examples of underfunded pension plans and poorly managed investments.

Third, the scientific method has won out in most fields of human endeavor. Why should investing be different? I have to believe that rigor and analysis are on the right side of history. The Research Foundation and the CFA Institute believe that as well.

Thank you.

References

Black, Fischer, and Myron S. Scholes. 1974. "From Theory to a New Financial Product." *Journal of Finance* 29 (2): 399–412.

Clarke, Roger, Harindra de Silva, and Steven Thorley. 2002. "Portfolio Constraints and the Fundamental Law of Active Management." *Financial Analysts Journal* 58 (September/October): 48–66.

Grinold, Richard C., and Ronald N. Kahn. 2000. *Active Portfolio Management.* 2nd ed. New York: McGraw-Hill.

Grinold, Richard C., and Ronald N. Kahn. 2011. "Breadth, Skill, and Time." *Journal of Portfolio Management* 38 (Fall): 18–28.

Grinold, Richard C., and Ronald N. Kahn. 2014. "James R. Vertin Award." *Research Foundation Year in Review 2013*. CFA Institute Research Foundation, 63–73.

Grinold, Richard C. 2007. "Dynamic Portfolio Analysis." *Journal of Portfolio Management* 34 (Fall): 12–26.

Hall, Bronwyn, and Beethika Khan. 2003. "Adoption of New Technology." In *New Economy Handbook*, edited by Derek C. Jones. Academic Press.

Lintner, John. 1965. "The Valuation of Risky Assets and the Selection of Risky Investments in Stock Portfolios and Capital Budgets." *Review of Economics and Statistics* 47 (February): 13–37.

Markowitz, H. 1959. *Portfolio Selection: Efficient Diversification of Investment.* Cowles Foundation Monograph 16. New Haven, CT: Yale University Press.

Mossin, Jan. 1966. "Equilibrium in a Capital Asset Market." *Econometrica* 34 (October): 768–83.

Rosenberg, B. 1974. "Extra-Market Components of Covariance in Security Markets." *Journal of Financial and Quantitative Analysis*, March, 263–74.

Sharpe, William F. 1963. "A Simplified Model for Portfolio Analysis." *Management Science* 9 (January): 277–93.

Sharpe, William F. 1964. "Capital Asset Prices: A Theory of Market Equilibrium Under Conditions of Risk." *Journal of Finance* 19 (September): 425–42.

Sharpe, William F. 1991. "The Arithmetic of Active Management." *Financial Analysts Journal* 47 (January/February): 7–9.

Treynor, J. L. 1961. "Toward a Theory of the Market Value of Risky Assets." Unpublished manuscript.

Treynor, Jack. 2007. *Treynor on Institutional Investing.* Hoboken, NJ: John Wiley & Sons.

36

What Investors Can Learn from a *Very* Alternative Market[1]

Traditional finance assumes that investors are rational—or, if they are not rational, at least that their departures from rationality are random and arbitrary and should wash out on average. But psychologists have demonstrated that investors are irrational in systematic and predictable ways. Understanding these irrationalities—now cataloged by behavioral finance researchers—may lead to exploitable inefficiencies.

Perhaps not surprisingly, psychologists have identified a long list of consistent human foibles. They can be explained by plausible evolutionary arguments. David Hirshleifer, an Ohio State University professor of finance, has described several categories of these effects on our behavior: problems in social interaction, heuristic simplification, and self-deception.[2] Social interaction effects include conforming, following the crowd, and herding. Heuristic simplification arises when "limited attention, memory, and processing capabilities force a focus on subsets of available information." Such effects include generalizing from personal experience and extrapolating from recent events. Self-deception includes biased self-attribution—attributing positive outcomes to our skill and negative outcomes to bad luck. Self-deception results in overconfidence.

1. This chapter originally appeared as "What Investors Can Learn from a *Very* Alternative Market" by Ronald N. Kahn in the *Financial Analysts Journal*, September/October 2004, 17–20. It also appeared as "The Science of Winning: Lessons on Behavioral Finance from a Very Alternative Market" by Ronald N. Kahn in *Investment Insights* from Barclays Global Investors 6, no. 6 (September 2003), re-released from BlackRock (14, no. 5, October 2011).

2. Hirshleifer discussed this topic in a presentation to the American Finance Association annual meeting in New Orleans, Louisiana, January 2001. See Hirshleifer (2001).

Successful active management requires both the existence of market inefficiencies and the analytical skills to find and exploit them. But successful active management tends to eliminate market anomalies over time, as more active managers learn about them. From the perspective of an active manager, the promise of behavioral finance is that an understanding of behavior will lead to new exploitable inefficiencies. Behavioral finance has not yet delivered on that promise. It has helped explain known market anomalies, but it has not led to the discovery of new ones.

Putting a positive spin on this situation, Richard Thaler, a professor of behavioral science and economics, principal at Fuller & Thaler Asset Management, and 2017 Nobel Prize winner in economics has asserted:

> While behaviorists think that it is theoretically possible to beat the market . . . individual investors do not have the time or training to do that on their own.

So, behavioral finance does propose new investment ideas, but only skilled professionals can discern and apply them.

In a more measured assessment, Princeton professor and Vanguard Group board member Burton Malkiel said:

> There are lots of good lessons to be taken from behavioral finance . . . But what it doesn't do is provide any kind of clear road map for cool sharp-penciled professionals to beat the market.[3]

In addition to these two professors, finance academics in general are debating the practical value of behavioral finance (for example, see Rubinstein 2001). So, to date, the practical, ex ante usefulness of behavioral finance for active managers in the financial markets is arguable.

But a market does exist whose participants are characterized by:

- social interactions that lead to follow-the-crowd behavior,
- heuristic simplification, including generalizing personal experience and extrapolating from recent events, and
- self-deception and overconfidence.

Indeed, these characteristics are pronounced in this market. The professional "investor" who first understood them realized that they should lead to significant, exploitable, and previously unrecognized anomalies, which he did, in fact, subsequently exploit. This market is professional baseball. The professional is Billy Beane, the general manager of the Oakland Athletics.

In a wonderful book, *Moneyball: The Art of Winning an Unfair Game*, Michael Lewis (2003) describes the following fascinating investment scenario. How does one of the poorest teams in baseball consistently outperform much wealthier teams, when the prevailing belief is that money buys baseball success?[4]

---

3. Thaler and Malkiel were both quoted in Olin (2003).

4. In fact, in a report published in July 2000, the Commissioner's Blue Ribbon Panel on Baseball Economics concluded that "*Large and growing revenue disparities exist* and are causing problems of chronic competitive imbalance" (Levin, Mitchell, Volcker, and Will 2000, 1).

The answer lies in behavioral finance and in a rigorous and scientific approach to investing. Human irrationalities affect both investing and baseball. As John Henry, hedge fund manager and Boston Red Sox owner, put it:

> People in both fields operate with beliefs and biases. To the extent you can eliminate both and replace them with data, you gain a clear advantage. (Lewis 2003, 90–91)

Baseball is an interesting example of an inefficient investment market. It is inefficient because of the behavior of market participants. But over the past 25 years, observers *outside* the baseball mainstream have developed and applied rigorous scientific analyses to identify these irrational behaviors. Bill James was the pioneer in this endeavor, in a field now known as *sabermetrics* (for the Society for American Baseball Research). He was soon joined by a number of trained statisticians and scientists attracted by a love of the game and an interest in applying their training to understand it better. (This pattern is much like what happened in the investment business, which has long attracted scientists—"quants"—eager to analyze markets scientifically.) Beane was the first baseball insider to pay attention to these results, realize they led to market inefficiencies, and apply that understanding to running a team.

The irrational behaviors in baseball were connected with what was important to winning games. Follow-the-crowd behavior dominated thinking about baseball, especially among professionals. At one point, Beane's assistant, Harvard-trained statistician Paul DePodesta, showed (through quantitative modeling) that:

> [a]n extra point of on-base percentage was worth three times an extra point of slugging percentage . . . In major league baseball, Paul's argument was practically heresy . . . Billy Beane thought heresy was good: heresy meant opportunity. A player's ability to get on base—especially when he got on base in unspectacular ways—tended to be dramatically underpriced in relation to other abilities. (Lewis 2003, 128–29)

Quantitative analysis identified the misunderstanding. Beane connected it to a market inefficiency.

Heuristic simplification includes generalizing personal experience and extrapolating from recent events. Baseball is rife with such behavior, from former players extrapolating from their own experience to managers being overly influenced by recent performance. For example, one ploy Beane used was to acquire players right after apparently career-threatening injuries. Not only were these injuries often not career threatening, but their recent nature had further impaired the seller's judgment.

Adding to these baseball prejudices were the rampant effects of overconfidence. People were constantly fooled by what they thought they observed. For example, baseball hitting is possibly the most difficult standard task in all of professional sports: The most skilled participants succeed only one-third of the time. But, although baseball professionals insist that they can observe the difference between hitters, James has pointed out:

> One absolutely cannot tell, by watching, the difference between a 0.300 hitter and a 0.275 hitter. The difference is one hit every two weeks. (Lewis 2003, 68)

Another effect of overconfidence was the strong tendency of baseball scouts to judge players on appearance rather than statistics. The book includes several examples of players available at bargain rates simply because scouts identified them as "bad body," in spite of the players' impressive performance statistics.

We can see parallels between financial markets and the very alternative market of baseball. Participants in both markets exhibit systematic irrational behavior. This behavior leads to market anomalies. As more participants understand and exploit the anomalies, the anomalies tend to diminish. (Other general managers are increasingly wary of trading with Beane.)[5]

But there is one distinct difference in how these ideas have played out in financial markets and baseball. In contrast to players in the financial markets, who discovered the anomalies before the theory, Beane understood the irrational behavior first, through sabermetrics, and this understanding then led him to the market anomalies. In fact, Beane was almost uniquely qualified to understand and implement these ideas. He was a high school superstar and the dream of every baseball scout because he excelled along every dimension they monitored (running, throwing, fielding, hitting, hitting with power). The scouts convinced him to skip college and go directly to professional ball. There, he foundered for many years. He lacked important skills that the scouts could not easily measure (basically, he choked much of the time). He was a personal failure of the scouting system. As a result, he was open to heretical ideas in running a team. And as an insider—a former player turned general manager—he could also act on heretical ideas.

His exploitation of market anomalies rivaled that of any investor. Not only did he find bargains, but he used his understanding of baseball anomalies to turn cheap players into expensive players, whom he then sold:

> You could take a slightly above average pitcher and drop him into the closer's role, let him accumulate some gaudy number of saves, and then sell him off. You could, in essence, buy a stock, pump it up with false publicity, and sell it off for much more than you'd paid for it. Billy Beane had already done it twice, and assumed he could do so over and over again. (Lewis 2003, 125)

The baseball market and investing are analogous but not the same. Baseball market participants appear to incorrectly understand what produces runs and wins games. Hence, they improperly price baseball player

5. Beane showed no concern, however, that the Lewis book would jeopardize his edge. Beane believes the behavioral irrationalities are so ingrained they will never disappear.

characteristics. The investment analogy would be that investors do not understand what produces earnings, so they incorrectly price stock characteristics.[6] If we use the wrong characteristics and other participants use better characteristics, we will, on average, lose in trading with them. This effect is particularly true when market prices closely track earnings. Over time, the forces for market efficiency eliminate participants with the wrong approach. Uncertainty delays this result, but a lucky streak can last only so many trades.

Other marked differences are visible between the challenges faced by investors and those faced by baseball general managers. In investing, thousands of different stocks trade every minute, which helps the market eliminate biased approaches to forecasting.[7] The forces imposing efficiency in baseball operate much more slowly—because of the relatively few players, games, teams, and trades, as well as baseball's protected marketplace. Investors must analyze vastly more data in many markets. The baseball market is relatively small. Furthermore, predicting baseball success is fundamentally much easier than predicting investment success. For example, top baseball players and teams can succeed year after year, whereas the winning stocks of one year can dramatically underperform the next. Still, we may at some point see a fairly sudden (for baseball) correction in that market.

Because investment markets can often impose efficiency (or at least eliminate large inefficiencies) quickly, we would expect fewer biases in investing for behavioral finance to identify and help exploit than in baseball. But the challenges are clear: Does systematic and irrational behavior lead most market participants to identify wrong characteristics for forecasting future earnings? And can behavioral finance identify and exploit such a situation ex ante?

We have experienced bubbles, but behavioral finance did not stand out in exploiting them. We also know of anomalies, such as the return to value investing, that may arise because of irrational behavior in the forecasting of future earnings—but they also may arise as a premium for higher risk. For the most unambiguous validation, behavioral finance researchers must predict and exploit new anomalies ex ante.[8]

Despite its shortcomings, behavioral finance has succeeded in clearly identifying problems with the concept of the rational "economic man." Moreover, its successes in explaining known anomalies demand the attention of investors and warrant further research.

Finally, although irrational behavior provides opportunities in baseball, clear, rational analysis of market data—science—identified those opportunities. And if exploiting the large behavioral anomalies in baseball required

6. In neither case are we talking about certainties. Baseball and investing are not exact sciences. Even if we know the characteristics to help us forecast future earnings, we cannot forecast those earnings exactly.
7. The technology bubble of the late 1990s demonstrates that markets may not quickly eliminate biased approaches to forecasting. Technology stock prices during that time depended mainly on earnings expected far in the future. Biases in forecasts of such distant earnings do not show up quickly, even with huge trading volumes.
8. Naturally, given the economics involved, we may never hear of the successful ex ante predictions of behavioral finance.

rigorous scientific analysis, imagine how much more important such analysis is for investment management, where anomalies are more subtle and fleeting.

Scientific analysis has, of course, another important advantage. It can identify *opportunities* whether they arise from irrational behavior, from institutional constraints, or as compensation for risk—even if they are true temporary anomalies.[9]

The clearest lesson for us from baseball is exactly this importance of rigorous scientific analysis to successful investing.

References

Hirshleifer, David. 2001. "Investor Psychology and Asset Pricing." *Journal of Finance* 56 (August): 1533–98.

Levin, Richard C., George J. Mitchell, Paul A. Volcker, and George F. Will. 2000. *The Report of the Independent Members of the Commissioner's Blue Ribbon Panel on Baseball Economics*. mlb.com/mlb/downloads/blue_ribbon.pdf.

Lewis, Michael. 2003. *Moneyball*. New York: W.W. Norton.

Lowenstein, Roger. 2001. *When Genius Failed: The Rise and Fall of Long-Term Capital Management*. New York: Random House.

Olin, Dirk. 2003. "Prospect Theory." *New York Times Magazine*, June 2003, 8–33.

Rubinstein, Mark. 2001. "Rational Markets: Yes or No? The Affirmative Case." *Financial Analysts Journal* 57 (May/June): 15–29.

9. Of course, the practitioners of scientific analysis face the same behavioral challenges as any other investors, as was shown by the apparent overconfidence of the leaders of Long-Term Capital Management. (The story of LTCM has been told and analyzed in numerous papers; for an example, see Lowenstein 2001.)

37

UCLA Master of Financial Engineering Commencement Address[1]

I have always had an appreciation for Master of Financial Engineering programs. Part of that comes from my role and experience hiring MFE graduates: smart, well-trained professionals who produce right from Day 1 and steadily increase their contributions and responsibilities. That's the rational, analytical appreciation. My emotional, intuitive appreciation comes from the fact that MFE programs didn't exist when I switched from physics to finance in 1987. I know exactly the size hole that MFE programs have filled in the career paths of scientists and engineers looking to enter finance.

I'd like to convey to you a sense of that hole, to help you appreciate your program. I'd also like to describe a few career lessons I've learned that could be useful as you start your financial engineering careers. And, I'd like to apply some of those lessons to the current situation in quantitative equity investment management, which will offer some interesting career opportunities over the next few years.

Looking back, I can describe my career as a continuous linear path. But as I lived it, it was not continuous or linear, but rather involved a number of jump discontinuities. In college, I switched from engineering to physics, which I found incredibly interesting. Physics focuses on understanding the world at a very detailed level, which appealed to me. In graduate school, I switched from experimental physics to theoretical physics, once again drawn by passion for particular topics. But in the mid-1980s, now a postdoctoral

1. Ronald N. Kahn presented this talk at the commencement ceremony for the graduates of UCLA's Master of Financial Engineering program on December 19, 2014. This talk covered some of the themes in the chapters on smart beta and on the dangers of diversification.

fellow in physics at UC Berkeley, I found myself facing relatively few physics opportunities, looking for alternatives, and discovering finance. I knew very little about the field, mainly that it involved quantitative analysis and data, but that was enough to make it a promising direction.

So how did one switch from physics to finance in the era before MFE programs? Did one look for jobs via open position postings, or using a headhunter, or reaching out to alumni contacts? Yes. The odds of any particular contact or interview leading to a job were so low that success required maximizing the number of those contacts. (I assumed, perhaps charitably, that any negative outcomes were uncorrelated events.) I applied for openings listed in the newspaper. (In those long-ago days, companies advertised openings in newspapers.) I worked with a headhunter who sent me on several trips, at my own expense, back to New York for interviews. And I used alumni networks to identify possible job openings.

Based on the suggestion of an interviewer on one of those New York trips, I also read the Black–Scholes option pricing paper to give myself some technical introduction to finance. This is obviously quite inferior to classes in "Stochastic Calculus," "Derivatives," and "Empirical Methods in Finance," but it was all I had.

Then I got lucky. Let me tell you something from my long career in investment management: *never turn down luck*. An alumni contact suggested I talk to Barra, an investment technology firm based in Berkeley that builds risk models and associated software for asset managers and asset owners. (It's now part of MSCI.) This firm was founded by finance professors and offered an academic environment not only familiar to a theoretical physicist, but even more important—the perfect environment in which to learn finance. Remember: I didn't know anything about finance.

Now in case you think Barra welcomed a physicist with open arms, they weren't at all sure this experiment would work out. As Richard Grinold, then a Berkeley finance professor and director of research at Barra, put it when he offered me a job, "We are going to pay you by the hour, so it will be easier to say goodbye." It's funny to remember that comment now, because Richard and I are closely linked in the eyes of many investment professionals, based on our book, and our many papers, and our many years working together, including on this book. Richard also said he was teaching a graduate seminar at Berkeley, and that I should sit in on it. My most formal training was reading selected finance papers in that seminar.

In my early days at Barra, my knowledge of finance was basically an inch wide and a mile deep. I worked on a project analyzing embedded options in bonds, an important issue in the 1980s. I knew the Cox, Ingersoll, Ross model backwards and forwards. But I knew little else. It was dangerous to put me in front of clients. It took a few years of work experience to build out my finance understanding.

So that's the source of my emotional, intuitive appreciation of MFE programs. The hallmarks of the MFE program—a broad training in finance, and the established path and network offered by a recognized degree—were things I didn't have.

I went on to have quite a successful career at Barra. One thing that contributed to my success was something my PhD advisor in physics had told me years earlier. He said that when you are an undergraduate, your professors teach you. When you are a PhD student, you teach your professors. A job isn't graduate school, but still, I strove to teach my manager (Richard Grinold in those early days) something new at least once a month. Since I knew so little about finance, it was more about numerical methods or programming. But over time, it was more about finance.

Another thing that helped was recognizing that finance is not physics. I remember another physicist in finance once saying, during a year when value investing had underperformed, "in my previous career, no one ever said it had been a bad year for gravity."

In 1998, after 11 years at Barra, I made a significant career change. I had been director of research there for more than seven years, and I was considering an offer from Barclays Global Investors (BGI) to switch into asset management: thus switching from helping others manage investments to managing investments myself. One thing that drew me to asset management was the critical importance of research and innovation in its success. I've always been a researcher at heart.

I had a long conversation with Blake Grossman, who was chief investment officer of BGI at that time. Blake listed several possible opportunities at the firm. The international equity team was good, but Blake felt they could be better. There was an opportunity to build out a very low active risk product to compete against index funds. And there was an opportunity with the Japanese equity team. By this time the Japanese equity market was in year eight of a prolonged slump. And, at that point, BGI's quantitative active equity products had strongly underperformed the falling Japanese equity market over the prior one and a half years. So Japanese equities were down strongly, and BGI's Japanese equity products were down even more.

The international equity opportunity was one in which it would be hard to distinguish myself, since it was already a good team, just not a great team. I didn't know anything about very low active risk strategies. I could learn, but certainly had no demonstrated ability. The Japanese opportunity sounded by far the most interesting. I had spent considerable time in Japan while at Barra, and had in fact studied the particular market dislocations that had affected a number of Barra clients over the prior one and a half years. Some further talks with the BGI Japanese equity team led me to believe that they didn't know how to fix the problems and were hoping someone would come to the rescue. A discredited asset class, poor performance, no one internally stepping up to help. What a perfect opportunity!

Today you are facing the challenge of starting your careers as financial engineers. As you progress, look for the opportunities that arise out of failings and disruptions. I'll speak specifically about three developments that make this a great time for financial engineers to enter active equity management. (I'm an active equity manager, and that's the world I know best.) Some of these developments apply to other areas of finance as well. And looking for opportunities out of failings and disruptions works well across every field.

The first development is a disruptive innovation called smart beta. It's an unusual disruptive innovation in that while it's clearly disruptive for active investment management, it's not much of an innovation, at least in 2014.

So what is smart beta? The name refers to factors—like value, small size, momentum, quality, and low volatility—associated with positive risk-adjusted returns over time. The historical evidence shows that these have all been good investment themes, and there are reasons in each case to believe they will continue to outperform on average over time in the future. Some of these are risk premia: small stocks and low-price stocks are riskier, and hence we might expect higher returns over time. Some of these are behavioral biases: for example, investors don't always recognize low-quality stocks because they don't separate earnings into cash flow from operations and accruals, even though these have differing levels of persistence. Those behavioral mistakes create investment opportunities. And some may arise from structural impediments. High-volatility stocks may be overpriced in part due to the lack of available leverage, causing investors to overpay for high-volatility stocks in their search for higher returns. This is another investment opportunity.

These smart beta ideas for equity investors have been around for quite a while. Ben Graham wrote about value investing in the 1930s, though the factor modeling approach is more recent, going back to the 1970s. All of these specific ideas have been know for at least 20 years if not more.

One way to measure the prevalence of these ideas is to examine the fraction of active returns (returns relative to a benchmark) these factors explain. For a broad universe of institutional global equity managers—fundamental managers and quantitative managers—over the past three years, we find that one-third of their active risk is in smart beta on average, with some managers almost 90% in smart beta. These ideas are not only widely known, they are widely used! And as I would expect UCLA MFE graduates to know, if you invest in several such funds, as is typical for larger investors, the overall fraction of active risk in smart beta will be even higher, because these factors are correlated across managers while the rest of the active returns are uncorrelated.

So where is the disruption? And why are investors talking about smart beta now? Over the past several years, there has been a general dissatisfaction with active management combined with a growing interest in passive management—namely index funds and exchange-traded funds (ETFs). Investors are finally listening to what finance professors have been saying for years: that the average active manager will underperform by roughly the combination of fees and costs, 1% to 2% per year for domestic equity mutual funds. And ETFs, at the same time, have made buying index funds extremely easy and flexible.

Smart beta provides the appeals of index funds and ETFs—simplicity, transparency, low cost—and the excess return appeal of active management. And here's the disruption for active managers: much of what we are providing in aggregate is now available significantly more cheaply. This will threaten most active managers. You can't be a successful active manager going forward if all you are providing is smart beta for active fees.

So that's one reason active equity management is a particularly interesting career opportunity currently. MFE graduates have the skills to work on smart beta products. But there is a second opportunity based on what successful active management will require in the future, given these new products. Active management is no longer about delivering smart beta. It's about delivering pure alpha—active returns beyond smart beta.

How do we pick stocks without using value, size, momentum, quality, or low volatility? One way is to somehow process publicly available stock-specific information faster than the market. And here, the second key development can help: big data.

Active management is all about data. How do we identify things the market has yet to figure out? Data. (And what are UCLA MFE's well-trained to work with? Data.) We are living in the Data Decade. There is vastly more data available than ever before. Of course, it's messy data. Much of it is text. It also includes search data, social media data, smartphone data, and so on. It isn't organized into EXCEL spreadsheets.

Big data has the potential to significantly impact active management. We can access information we always knew was important, but now we can access it more effectively than before. We always paid attention to analysts' estimates of future earnings. But that was just two or three numbers per stock: the expected earnings over the next couple of fiscal years, and maybe the analyst's recommendation. Now we can read and understand analysts' written comments about those same stocks. At BlackRock, we receive 5,000 analyst reports every day. No human being can read that many reports per day and assess them consistently. Our computers can do that. They aren't as good as humans at reading any one report, though they keep getting better. Their advantage is in processing so much data. A different example: MIT's Billion Prices Project now estimates country-level inflation daily, rather than wait for the delayed monthly estimates, by web-scraping prices posted online. Information eagerly awaited once a month is now available every day. And, for some countries, these daily estimates are much more accurate than the official government numbers.

We can also access information that was never previously available, like what employees think about their company. A few years ago, Netflix ran into trouble when they changed their pricing policies as they tried to shift from mailing DVDs to streaming content. The stock price plunged and employee sentiment dropped. By tapping into social media, we could see when employee sentiment turned around. The stock price then followed. We now follow employee sentiment at many companies via social media postings.

The travails of the Spanish economy through the financial crisis are well known. When we saw Spanish consumers increase their online searches for cars, washing machines, and other big-ticket items, that was an early sign that the economy and the Spanish equity market were turning around.

All of this big data information helps us predict stock returns, and isn't smart beta. Furthermore, we have long been working in a world of low signal-to-noise ratios and limited data. Of necessity, we have relied on structural models. Big data offers the potential to move beyond such models, to let the data speak more clearly.

Now picking stocks by processing information faster than the market is a game that requires constant innovation through research. The edge we have in any particular signal doesn't last long—the market figures these things out. Hopefully they will work for a year or so. We need to constantly identify new ideas. This is a full employment opportunity for good quantitative researchers.

Smart beta, big data—these may dramatically reshape active management over the next few years, and MFEs have just the right training to take advantage of these. (That said, the MFE program crams quite a lot into one year. You may still need special training in big data and machine learning techniques, and I encourage you to consider that.) Big data will also impact other areas of finance and offer opportunities there as well.

The final disruption I'll mention has been the many ethical failings of Financial Services, at a minimum through the financial crisis. This industry can provide fantastic careers—interesting problems, talented colleagues, the opportunity to help millions of individuals secure their financial futures, all while being well paid. But the industry has fallen short, and we can see many examples of financial products that help the creator much more than the client.

We have all seen those polls of most and least trusted professions. Nurses are at the very top and congressmen and car salespeople at the very bottom. Well actually senators are viewed slightly more positively than members of the House of Representatives, and right in between them: stockbrokers. (These polls aren't extremely specific on careers, and for better or worse, stockbrokers represent all of us in the public's mind.)

We all want to work in a profession we can be proud of, and that our families can be proud of. We can more effectively help our clients if they trust us. And we can better weather the storms that volatile financial markets will toss us if our clients trust us.

Of course we need to earn that trust. Every one of us needs to live up to the highest ethical standards to raise the standard of this industry. As just one example, when developing a new product, ask whether most of the expected benefit accrues to the client. If not, don't offer it. Many years ago, I worked on a white-labeled product to be sold by another firm. We had long negotiations about the product fees. We demanded that the fees be sufficiently low that clients could earn a reasonable expected return after fees. It makes no sense to build products that don't help clients. The long-term career opportunity is the path of high ethical standards.

So as you start your careers, look for the failings and disruptions that lead to opportunities. In active equity management, these include smart beta, big data, and an industry that has had some ethical challenges. Across finance more generally, big data is likely to have an impact, especially on MFE careers, and all of us need to live up to high ethical standards.

Before ending, I have to make a final comment looking back on my switch from physics into finance, and my subsequent career. I switched careers because I didn't see interesting opportunities in physics. I was frankly pushed more than pulled. Finance offered a steady career, the ability to support my family, and even the possibility of fame. But after switching, I discovered that finance offered all the things I thought were only available in physics: very smart colleagues, fascinating problems, and the opportunity to help millions of people. It is a terrific career, and I wish you all the best in finding those opportunities. Congratulations to all of you, and to your families.

SECTION 5

Conclusion

38

Advances in Active Portfolio Management Conclusions

In *Advances in Active Portfolio Management*, we have tried to organize and present several important strands of research that mainly appeared after our prior book, *Active Portfolio Management*. We have recapped insights and ideas from that book, provided several advances in the framework and approach mainly around dynamic portfolio management and portfolio analysis, and then used the framework to address several specific issues concerning expected returns, risk, and portfolio construction.

In addition to the convenience of pulling together this material in one book, we have enhanced the material through detailed introductions and edits to more fully reflect our understanding of all these topics as of 2019. We have included several chapters of material never before in print. The set of "Extras" at the end can provide some additional perspective for our readers.

While we have organized the book around advances to the framework and applications of the framework, one emerging theme that cuts across these sections is *optimal portfolio design*. Of course, quantitative insights into portfolio design go back at least to the fundamental law of active management. As we note in Chapter 4, "every manager needs some winning combination of skill, breadth, and efficiency." That's product design at its most basic.

Building on that, the section on dynamic portfolio management contributes insights into the trade-off between information turnover and trading costs and the impact on the after-cost information ratio (ACIR). Chapter 20, "Are Benchmark Portfolios Efficient?" adds one perspective on where the active opportunities are greatest, arguably product design at a very high level. The smart beta chapters provide more specific guidance on product design, in particular the desirability of separating smart beta from pure alpha given their very different fee levels.

Finally, the portfolio construction section furnishes several insights into optimal product design. Chapter 29 on "Optimal Gearing" discusses how we must coordinate risk level and gearing for optimal implementation. Chapter 30 on "The Dangers of Diversification" describes, among other things, how we can overdiversify multistrategy funds with surprisingly negative consequences in bad market states. After that, Chapter 33 on "Five Myths About Fees" presents insights into structuring fees, a basic component of product design.

In the rest of this concluding chapter, we want to review the track record of quantitative investing—relevant given our previous book's role in providing the framework and education for much of the field and this book's goal of advancing and applying the framework for quantitative active management—and then briefly look forward from here.

The Track Record of Quantitative Investing

Our previous book, *Active Portfolio Management*, provided a framework for quantitative investment strategies. It organized a set of ideas, some of them previously known, into a coherent process for active management.

When the first edition appeared in 1995, quantitative investing was a fairly small endeavor. We discussed several aspects of this in our Vertin Award presentations (Chapter 35), though not in the context of 1995 in particular.

Index funds, examples of quantitative non-active management, were much smaller in 1995 than they are today. According to Exhibit 2 in Chapter 35, indexed US institutional equity assets under management were about $500 billion in 1995. By 2018, these had risen to $3.5 trillion (close to 8% annual growth over 23 years).[1] Retail-focused equity index mutual funds rose even faster over this period, from about $55 billion in 1995 to $4 trillion in 2015, almost 24% annual growth over 20 years.[2] Without quibbling over exact definitions of index funds, this space has clearly grown enormously since 1995.

Chapter 35 also discusses the growth and impact of equity risk models since their initial development in the 1970s. We didn't provide detailed data on risk model usage over time, but asserted that by 2013, "the vast majority of assets are now in products managed in part by using risk model analysis."[3] Both of us worked at Barra on risk modeling in the 1980s and 1990s and witnessed the substantial growth in adoption of risk models over that period. By 1995, equity risk models in particular were quite widely used.

1. Wynne (2018)
2. Udland (2016)
3. This book, Chapter 35.

The story of quantitative equity investing is a bit more checkered, and this is the area most directly tied to *Active Portfolio Management.* Of course, we don't measure the success of that book—or more generally our framework and approach to active management—by quantitative equity assets under management. Those depend in part on having a rigorous framework and approach but depend even more on having compelling investment ideas: *superior information.* Our books have focused exclusively on that first component—the framework and approach.

Figure 4 in Chapter 35 shows a dramatic increase in quantitative equity assets under management from the 1990s through to 2007, followed by a very significant fall. As we have discussed elsewhere in this book, the Quant Crisis of early August 2007 occurred because there was too much money invested in similar quantitative equity strategies.[4] When the subprime mortgage crisis caused some investors to need to raise capital quickly, instead of selling illiquid subprime mortgages, they sold liquid quantitative equity strategies. (Several prop trading desks and multistrategy hedge funds held positions in both strategies.) Coordinated and significant selling caused huge losses in these funds even as the overall markets appeared quiescent. For a typical quantitative equity hedge fund, almost every long position declined, and every short position increased—remarkably unlikely according to risk model predictions. Most of those losses reversed by the end of August 2007, but not before many leveraged hedge funds went out of business. Many quantitative equity investors also lost faith in their understanding of how these funds worked, and sold their stakes over the subsequent two to three years, shrinking aggregate exposure by about 75%.

The book *Active Portfolio Management* didn't single-handedly cause the large run-up in quantitative equity assets, though it certainly democratized the framework and approach and helped inform many new entrants into the field. Several other books covering similar territory appeared after *Active Portfolio Management* but only after the dramatic increase in quantitative equity assets had begun, and in some cases only after those assets had fallen significantly.[5] While not a particularly good measure of the impact of that book, the growth in quantitative equity assets does testify to some extent to the book's impact on the field.

Remember, though, that that book ends with an anecdote from Jack Treynor about how you can't make money in active management by investing in broadly agreed upon ideas.[6] In that book and in this book, our focus is on a rigorous and systematic approach to investing *given* superior information. Neither book offers specific investment ideas for the reasons Jack Treynor mentioned.

4. See Chapter 21 ("Introduction to the Smart Beta Section"), Chapter 28 ("Introduction to the Portfolio Construction Section"), Chapter 30 ("The Dangers of Diversification"), Chapter 31 ("The Surprisingly Small Impact of Asset Growth on Expected Alpha"), and Chapter 35 ("Presentations upon Receiving the 2013 James R. Vertin Award").

5. See, for example, Litterman, et al (2003), Chincarini and Kim (2006), Qian, Hua, and Sorensen (2007), and Zhou and Jain (2014).

6. Grinold and Kahn (2000), 580.

Relatedly, we have been asked on occasion, "Why do quant strategies blow up every few years?" The questioners are asking about periods when a number of strategies labeled as quantitative all seem to decline simultaneously (as in early August 2007). Nonquantitative strategies blow up all the time, often as one-off explosions. Not always, though. We saw a rash of subprime mortgage–related blowups during the financial crisis among products that were not quantitative. Fundamental investors can also invest in correlated ideas at times.

Now there is nothing in our framework and approach that should lead to correlated blowups. But it is true that quantitative strategies are easy to scale, and quantitative investors have often investigated the same underlying databases in search of superior information. So, the opportunity to overinvest in quantitative strategies is there.

How do quantitative equity strategies look post the financial crisis? The first thing to note is that this group essentially bifurcated after the 2007 Quant Crisis. Many quantitative equity investors argued for "staying the course," pointing out, for example, that value investing has performed well over the past 100 years even though there were drawdowns over that period. We now call that course *smart beta*. Other investors, including us, decided to focus instead on pure alpha strategies mainly uncorrelated with other quantitative investors.

We have seen significant growth in the smart beta category over recent years. According to FTSE Russell (2018), smart beta assets grew from $280 billion in 2012 to $999 billion at the end of 2017. These were strategies that suffered during the Quant Crisis of August 2007 and that could happen again.

It is harder to track quantitative strategies focused on pure alpha. Anecdotally, at least, we see growing interest in strategies based on big data and machine learning. These generally fall into that category. While these strategies could also suffer correlated drawdowns, the range of databases and investment ideas is, in principle, far more broad. These strategies will experience drawdowns—as do all active strategies at times—but they are less likely to suffer correlated drawdowns.

Beyond using quantitative equity assets as an imperfect measure of the success of our framework and approach, another track record metric is the general level of interest in the field as measured by organizations, conferences, and journals now devoted to quantitative investing. Well before *Active Portfolio Management* appeared, we already had:

- Society of Quantitative Analysts (founded 1965)
- Q-Group (the Institute for Quantitative Research in Finance, founded 1966)
- Barra Research Seminars (started 1976)
- Quantec, later London Quant Group (started 1986)
- Inquire UK (started 1988)
- Inquire Europe (started 1990)

These are just the more notable organizations and conferences from our perspective. All of these organizations and conferences still exist (Barra was purchased by MSCI, and the Quantec conference morphed into the London Quant Group), and most are thriving. The Berkeley Program in Finance Conference was also prominent and popular around this time though the conference series ended in 2001.

Closer to the publication of *Active Portfolio Management*, we saw additional organizations and conferences appearing:

- International Association for Quantitative Finance (founded in 1992 and awarding the "Financial Engineer of the Year" award since 1993)
- Chicago Quantitative Alliance (founded 1993)

Much more recently, the *Journal of Investment Management* appeared in 2003 and started running conferences in 2006.

Most of these conferences continue to be popular and have generally grown in attendance over time since the 1990s.

As far as journals go, the *Financial Analysts Journal*, where some of our chapters first appeared, began in 1945 and covers a range of topics broader than just quantitative finance. The *Journal of Portfolio Management*, where most of our chapters first appeared, began in 1974. They have been joined in recent years by:

- *Journal of Fixed Income* (1991)
- *Journal of Investing* (1992)
- *Journal of Investment Management* (2003)
- *Journal of Financial Data Science* (2019)

among others.

By this very different measure of the track record of quantitative investing, interest in the field appears healthy and robust.

In Conclusion

The principles of quantitative active management are centered on the analysis of return, risk, and cost. These principles were developed and described in *Active Portfolio Management.*

In *Advances in Active Portfolio Management*, we have restated those principles in a more contemporary idiom and presented significant advances in the area of product design, portfolio analytics, and dynamic portfolio management.

The framework continues to evolve. We now have access to vast new sources of data. The age of big data has arrived. This profusion of data is accompanied by—indeed made possible by—dramatic increases in computing power. Machine learning and other advanced techniques are available. The quantitative active manager who can use these powerful tools wisely will prevail in the difficult challenge of active portfolio management.

References

Chincarini, Ludwig B., and Daehwan Kim. 2006. *Quantitative Equity Portfolio Management.* NY: McGraw-Hill.

FTSE Russell. 2018. "Five-Year Trends and Outlook for Smart Beta." *FTSE Russell Insights*, June.

Grinold, Richard C., and Ronald N. Kahn. 2000. *Active Portfolio Management.* 2nd ed. NY: McGraw-Hill.

Litterman, Bob, and the Quantitative Resources Group at Goldman Sachs Asset Management. 2003. *Modern Investment Management: An Equilibrium Approach.* Hoboken, NJ: John Wiley & Sons.

Qian, Edward E., Ronald H. Hua, and Eric H. Sorensen. 2007. *Quantitative Equity Portfolio Management: Modern Techniques and Applications.* Boca Raton, FL: Chapman and Hall/CRC Financial Mathematics Series.

Udland, Myles. 2016. "The Incredible Rise of the $4 Trillion Equity Index Fund Business in 1 Chart." *Business Insider*, January 4. businessinsider.com/index-fund-assets-under-management-2016-1.

Wynne, Trilbe. 2018. "Passive Investing Continues to Captivate Global Audience." *Pensions & Investments Special Report: Index Managers*, October 15. pionline.com/article/20181015/PRINT/181019928.

Zhou, Xinfeng, and Sameer Jain. 2014. *Active Equity Management.* Xinfeng Zhou publisher.

Index

Page numbers followed by e indicate an exhibit on the corresponding page.

B

E

F

G

H

I

M

N

Q

R

S

T

About the Authors

RICHARD C. GRINOLD

Richard Grinold is a Founding Director and a member of the Advisory Council of Vinva Investment Management of Sydney, Australia. He was the Global Director of Research at Barclays Global Investors from 1994 to 2009. The group was responsible for active investment strategies of 350 billion US dollars invested in equity, fixed income, and global macro asset allocation strategies. Prior to that he was Director of Research and later President of BARRA, a leading global investment technology company.

Richard spent the years 1969–1988 on the faculty of the School of Business Administration at the University of California, Berkeley. He was a Research Fellow at Harvard in 1968–69, and a Fellow at CORE in Louvain Belgium in 1974. He also served as a visiting professor at HEC near Paris in 1979–1980, and at the Harvard Business School in 1983–1984.

He has published more than fifty papers in academic and professional journals, including "The Fundamental Law of Active Management" and "Dynamic Portfolio Analysis."He twice received the Bernstein Fabozzi/Jacobs Levy Award for outstanding papers, "Attribution" and "The Description of Portfolios," and in 2008 was awarded the Bernstein Fabozzi/Jacobs Levy Award for best paper, "Dynamic Portfolio Analysis." In 2013 he and Ronald Kahn received the James R. Vertin Award of the CFA Institute.

Richard received his Ph.D. in Operations Research from U.C. Berkeley in 1968. He studied physics at Tufts University and helped to wire up the Harvard-MIT Cambridge Electron Accelerator. Other milestones include serving as the navigator of the USS Gainard DD-706 and ten years of selling programs at Harvard Stadium that led to his being the cover boy for the precursor of *Harvard Magazine* in November, 1953.

RONALD N. KAHN

Ronald Kahn is a Managing Director and the Global Head of Systematic Equity Research at BlackRock in San Francisco. Prior to BlackRock's acquisition of Barclays Global Investors (BGI), he was Global Head of Equity Research at BGI. He is responsible for the research underpinning BlackRock's Systematic Active Equity products.

Previous roles at BGI include Global Head of Equity Research, Head of Active Equities in the US, and Director of Research for Japanese Equities.

Ronald Kahn is a well-known expert on portfolio management, risk modeling, and quantitative investing. He was Director of Research at Barra for many years and ran the Barra Research Seminars. He has published numerous articles on investment management and is the author (with Richard Grinold) of the influential book, *Active Portfolio Management: Quantitative Theory and Applications*. Richard and Ron are the 2013 winners of James R. Vertin award, presented periodically by the CFA Institute to recognize individuals who have produced a body of research notable for its relevance and enduring value to investment professionals. Ron is a 2007 winner of the Bernstein Fabozzi/Jacobs Levy Award for best article in the *Journal of Portfolio Management*. He is on the editorial advisory boards of the *Journal of Portfolio Management* and the *Journal of Investment Consulting*. The 2007 book *How I Became a Quant* includes Ron's essay describing his transition from physics to finance.

In 2016, he presented the Thys Visser Memorial Lecture Series at Stellenbosch University. This is a "biannual lecture series by leading international scholars." These talks became the basis for his book *The Future of Investment Management*, which the Research Foundation of the CFA Institute published in 2018.

Since 2005, he has taught the equities half of the course "International Equity and Currency Markets" in UC Berkeley's Master of Financial Engineering Program.

He joined Barra in 1987 and became Director of Research in 1991. He joined Barclays Global Investors in 1998.

He received an A.B. in Physics, *summa cum laude*, from Princeton University in 1978. He received a Ph.D. in Physics from Harvard University in 1985 for his work on computer simulations of the very early universe. In his spare time, he runs a lavender farm in Sonoma, California.